COMPUTER ORGANIZATION

McGraw-Hill Series in Computer Science

Brown and Vranesic: *Fundamentals of Digital Logic with VHDL Design*
De Micheli: *Synthesis and Optimization of Digital Circuits*
Forouzan: *Data Communications and Networking*
Forouzan: *TCP/IP Protocol Suite*
Hamacher, Vranesic, and Zaky: *Computer Organization*
Hayes: *Computer Architecture and Organization*
Hwang: *Advanced Computer Architecture: Parallelism, Scalability, Programmability*
Hwang: *Scalable Parallel Computing: Technology, Architecture, Programming*
Jain, Kasturi, and Schnuck: *Introduction To Machine Vision*
Krishna and Shin: *Real-Time Systems*
Leon Garcia: *Communication Networks: Fundamental Concepts and Key Architectures*
Marcovitz: *Introduction to Logic Design*
Patt and Patel: *Introduction to Computing Systems: From Bits and Gates to C and Beyond*
Rosen: *Discrete Mathematics and its Applications*
Russell: *Telecommunications Protocols*

COMPUTER ORGANIZATION

FIFTH EDITION

Carl Hamacher
Queen's University

Zvonko Vranesic
University of Toronto

Safwat Zaky
University of Toronto

Boston   Burr Ridge, IL   Dubuque, IA   Madison, WI   New York   San Francisco   St. Louis
Bangkok   Bogotá   Caracas   Kuala Lumpur   Lisbon   London   Madrid   Mexico City
Milan   Montreal   New Delhi   Santiago   Seoul   Singapore   Sydney   Taipei   Toronto

McGraw-Hill Higher Education

A Division of The McGraw-Hill Companies

COMPUTER ORGANIZATION, FIFTH EDITION

Published by McGraw-Hill, a business unit of The McGraw-Hill Companies, Inc., 1221 Avenue of the Americas, New York, NY 10020. Copyright © 2002, 1996, 1990, 1984, 1978 by The McGraw-Hill Companies, Inc. All rights reserved. No part of this publication may be reproduced or distributed in any form or by any means, or stored in a database or retrieval system, without the prior written consent of The McGraw-Hill Companies, Inc., including, but not limited to, in any network or other electronic storage or transmission, or broadcast for distance learning.

Some ancillaries, including electronic and print components, may not be available to customers outside the United States.

This book is printed on acid-free paper.

International   1 2 3 4 5 6 7 8 9 0 DOC/DOC 0 9 8 7 6 5 4 3 2 1
Domestic   2 3 4 5 6 7 8 9 0 DOC/DOC 0 9 8 7 6 5 4 3 2

ISBN 0–07–232086–9
ISBN 0–07–112218–4 (ISE)

General manager: *Thomas E. Casson*
Publisher: *Elizabeth A. Jones*
Sponsoring editor: *Catherine Fields Shultz*
Senior developmental editor: *Kelley Butcher*
Executive marketing manager: *John Wannemacher*
Project manager: *Christine Walker*
Senior production supervisor: *Laura Fuller*
Coordinator of freelance design: *Rick D. Noel*
Cover designer: *Cynthia Crampton*
Cover image: *Computer illustration "Fall in High Park" by Eli I. Vranesic*
Senior supplement producer: *Audrey A. Reiter*
Media technology senior producer: *Phillip Meek*
Compositor: *Interactive Composition Corporation*
Typeface: *10.5/12 Times Roman*
Printer: *R. R. Donnelley & Sons Company/Crawfordsville, IN*

Library of Congress Cataloging-in-Publication Data

Hamacher, Carl.
    Computer organization / Carl Hamacher, Zvonko Vranesic, Safwat Zaky. — 5th ed.
        p.   cm.
    ISBN 0–07–232086–9
    1. Computer organization. I. Vranesic, Zvonko. II. Zaky, Safwat. III. Title.

QA76.9.C643 .H36   2002
004.2′2—dc21   2001030712
                                                             CIP

INTERNATIONAL EDITION ISBN 0–07–112218–4
Copyright © 2002. Exclusive rights by The McGraw-Hill Companies, Inc., for manufacture and export. This book cannot be re-exported from the country to which it is sold by McGraw-Hill. The International Edition is not available in North America.

www.mhhe.com

ABOUT THE AUTHORS

Carl Hamacher received his B.A.Sc. degree in engineering physics from the University of Waterloo, Canada, an M.Sc. degree in electrical engineering from Queen's University, Kingston, Canada, and a Ph.D. degree in electrical engineering from Syracuse University, New York. From 1968 to 1990 he was at the University of Toronto, where he was a Professor in the Departments of Electrical Engineering and Computer Science. He served as director of the Computer Systems Research Institute during 1984 to 1988, and as chairman of the Division of Engineering Science during 1988 to 1990. Since January 1991 he has been a Professor of Electrical and Computer Engineering at Queen's University. He served as the dean of the Faculty of Applied Science from 1991 to 1996. During 1978 to 1979, he was a visiting scientist at the IBM Research Laboratory in San Jose, California. In 1986, he was a research visitor at the Laboratory for Circuits and Systems associated with the University of Grenoble in France. In 1996 to 1997, he was a visiting professor in the Computer Science Department at the University of California at Riverside and in the LIP6 Laboratory of the University of Paris VI, France.

His research interests are in multiprocessors and multicomputers, focusing on their interconnection networks.

Zvonko Vranesic received his B.A.Sc., M.A.Sc., and Ph.D. degrees, in electrical engineering from the University of Toronto. From 1963 to 1965 he worked as a design engineer with the Northern Electric Co., Ltd. in Bramalea, Ontario. In 1968, he joined the University of Toronto, where he is now a Professor in the Department of Electrical and Computer Engineering and the Department of Computer Science. During 1978 to 1979, he was a senior visitor at the University of Cambridge, England, and during 1984 to 1985 he was at the University of Paris VI, France. In 2000 to 2001, he was a principal software engineer at Altera Corporation in Toronto. From 1995 to 2000, he served as chair of the Division of Engineering Science at the University of Toronto.

His current research interests include computer architecture, field-programmable VLSI technology, and multiple-valued logic systems. He is a coauthor of three other books: *Fundamentals of Digital Logic with VHDL Design, Microcomputer Structures,* and *Field-Programmable Gate Arrays.* In 1990, he received the Wighton Fellowship for "innovative and distinctive contributions to undergraduate laboratory instruction."

Safwat Zaky received his B.Sc. degree in electrical engineering and B.Sc. in mathematics, both from Cairo University, Egypt, and his M.A.Sc. and Ph.D. degrees in electrical engineering from the University of Toronto. From 1969 to 1972 he was with Bell Northern Research, Bramalea, Ontario, where he worked on applications of electro-optics and magnetics in mass storage and telephone switching. In 1973, he joined the University of Toronto, where he is now a Professor in the Department of Electrical and Computer Engineering and the Department of Computer Science. Presently, he serves as chair of the Department of Electrical and Computer Engineering. From 1980 to 1981, he was a senior visitor at the Computer Laboratory, University of Cambridge, England.

His research interests are in the areas of computer architecture, reliability of digital circuits, and electromagnetic compatibility. He is a coauthor of the book *Microcomputer Structures* and is a recipient of the IEEE Third Millennium Medal.

To Liz, Anne, and Shirley

CONTENTS

Chapter 3

ARM, MOTOROLA, AND INTEL INSTRUCTION SETS   103

Chapter 4

INPUT/OUTPUT ORGANIZATION   203

APPENDIX D: INTEL IA-32 INSTRUCTION SET 769

APPENDIX E: CHARACTER CODES AND NUMBER CONVERSION 789

INDEX 795

PREFACE

This book is intended for use in a first-level course on computer organization in electrical engineering, computer engineering, and computer science curricula. The book is self-contained, assuming only that the reader has a basic knowledge of computer programming in a high-level language. Many students who study computer organization will have had an introductory course on digital logic circuits. Therefore, this subject is not covered in the main body of the book. However, we have provided an extensive appendix on logic circuits for those students who need it.

The book reflects our experience in teaching computer organization to three distinct groups of undergraduates: electrical and computer engineering undergraduates, computer science specialists, and engineering science undergraduates. We have always approached the teaching of courses in this area from a practical point of view. Thus, a key consideration in shaping the contents of the book has been to illustrate the principles of computer organization using examples drawn from commercially available computers. Our main examples are based on the following processors: ARM, Motorola 680X0, Intel Pentium, and Sun UltraSPARC.

It is important to recognize that digital system design is not a straightforward process of applying optimal design algorithms. Many design decisions are based largely on heuristic judgment and experience. They involve cost/performance and hardware/software tradeoffs over a range of alternatives. It is our goal to convey these notions to the reader.

We have endeavored to provide sufficient details to encourage the student to dig beyond the surface when dealing with ideas that seem to be intuitively obvious. We believe that this is best accomplished by giving real examples that are adequately documented. Block diagrams are a powerful means of describing organizational features of a computer. However, they can easily lead to an oversimplified view of the problems involved. Hence, they must be accompanied by the details of implementation alternatives.

The book is aimed at a one-semester course in engineering or computer science programs. It is suitable for both hardware- and software-oriented students. Even though the emphasis is on hardware, we have addressed a number of software issues, including basic aspects of compilers and operating systems related to instruction execution performance, coordination of parallel operations at the system level, and real-time applications. An understanding of hardware/software interaction and tradeoffs is necessary for computer specialists.

THE SCOPE OF THE BOOK

We now review the topics covered in sequence, chapter by chapter. The first eight chapters cover the basic principles of computer organization, operation, and performance.

The remaining four chapters deal with embedded systems, peripheral devices, processor family evolution patterns, and large computer systems.

Chapter 1 provides an overview of computer hardware and software and informally introduces terms that are dealt with in more depth in the remainder of the book. This chapter discusses the basic functional units and the ways they are interconnected to form a complete computer system. The role of system software is introduced and basic aspects of performance evaluation are discussed. A brief treatment of the history of computer development is also provided.

Chapter 2 gives a methodical treatment of machine instructions, addressing techniques, and instruction sequencing. Basic aspects of 2's-complement arithmetic are introduced to facilitate the discussion of the generation of effective addresses. Program examples at the machine instruction level, expressed in a generic assembly language, are used to discuss loops, subroutines, simple input-output programming, sorting, and linked list operations.

Chapter 3 illustrates implementation of the concepts introduced in Chapter 2 on three commercial processors — ARM, 68000, and Pentium. The ARM processor illustrates the RISC design style, the 68000 has an easy-to-teach CISC design, while the Pentium represents the most successful commercial design that combines the elements of both the CISC and RISC styles. The material is organized into three independent and complete parts. Each part includes all of the examples from Chapter 2 implemented in the context of the specific processor. It is sufficient to cover only one of the three parts to provide the continuity needed to follow the rest of the book. If laboratory experiments using one of the three processors are associated with the course, the relevant part of Chapter 3 can be covered in parallel with Chapter 2.

Input-output organization is developed in Chapter 4. The basics of I/O data transfer synchronization are presented, and a series of increasingly complex I/O structures are explained. Interrupts and direct-memory access methods are described in detail, including a discussion of the role of software interrupts in operating systems. Bus protocols and standards are also presented, with the PCI, SCSI, and USB standards being used as representative commercial examples.

Semiconductor memories, including SDRAM, Rambus, and Flash memory implementations, are discussed in Chapter 5. Caches and multiple-module memory systems are explained as ways for increasing main memory bandwidth. Caches are discussed in some detail, including performance modeling. Virtual-memory systems, memory management, and rapid address translation techniques are also presented. Magnetic and optical disks are discussed as components in the memory hierarchy.

Chapter 6 treats the arithmetic unit of a computer. Logic design for fixed-point add, subtract, multiply, and divide hardware, operating on 2's-complement numbers, is described. Lookahead adders and high-speed multipliers are explained, including descriptions of the Booth multiplier recoding and carry-save addition techniques. Floating-point number representation and operations, in the context of the IEEE Standard, are presented.

Chapter 7 begins with a register-transfer-level treatment of the implementation of instruction fetching and execution in a processor. This is followed by a discussion of processor implementation by both hardwired and microprogrammed control.

Chapter 8 provides a detailed coverage of the use of pipelining and multiple function units in the design of high-performance processors. The role of the compiler and the relationship between pipelined execution and instruction set design are explored. Superscalar processors are discussed, and the Sun Microsystems UltraSPARC II processor organization is used to illustrate the concepts.

Today there are many more processors in use in embedded systems than in general-purpose computers. This increasingly important subject, where a single chip integrates the processing, I/O, and timer functionality needed in a wide range of low-cost applications, is treated in Chapter 9. System integration issues, interconnections, and real-time software are discussed.

Chapter 10 presents peripheral devices and computer interconnections. Typical input/output devices are described and hardware needed to support computer graphics applications is introduced. Commonly used communication links, such as DSL, are discussed.

The evolution of the ARM, Motorola, and Intel processor families is discussed in Chapter 11. This chapter highlights the design changes that led to higher performance. The PowerPC, SPARC, Alpha, and Intel IA-64 families are also discussed.

Chapter 12 extends the discussion of computer organization to large systems that use many processors operating in parallel. Interconnection networks for multiprocessors are described, and an introduction to cache coherence controls is presented. Shared-memory and message-passing schemes are discussed.

CHANGES IN THE FIFTH EDITION

Major changes in content and organization have been made in preparing the fifth edition of this book. They include the following:

- Chapter 2 of the fourth edition has been split into two chapters — Chapters 2 and 3 — in the fifth edition. An expanded treatment of basic issues, explained using generic instructions, is presented in Chapter 2. More programming examples for typical tasks, both numeric and non-numeric, are provided. Chapter 3 uses the instruction sets of ARM, 68000, and Pentium processors to show how the basic concepts of instruction set design have been implemented in both the RISC and CISC design styles.

- The discussion of the role of pipelining and multiple functional units in processor design has been extended significantly. The UltraSPARC architecture is used to provide specific examples of performance-enhancing design features.

- A new chapter on embedded-processor systems has been added. A generic design of a typical system is used as the basis for detailed discussion of example applications.

In addition to these main changes, many recent technology and design advances have been added to a number of chapters.

WHAT CAN BE COVERED IN A ONE-SEMESTER COURSE

This book is suitable for use at the university or college level as a text for a one-semester course in computer organization. It is intended for use in the first course on computer organization that the students will take.

There is more than enough material in the book for a one-semester course. The core material is given in Chapters 1 through 8. For students who have not had a course in logic circuits, the basic material in Appendix A should be studied at the beginning of the course and certainly prior to covering Chapter 4.

Chapters 9 through 12 contain a variety of useful material that the instructor may choose from if time permits. Particularly suitable are the discussion of embedded systems in Chapter 9 and the description of hardware found in most personal computers given in Chapter 10.

ACKNOWLEDGMENTS

We wish to express our thanks to many people who have helped during the preparation of this fifth edition. Gail Burgess and Kelly Chan helped with the technical preparation of the manuscript. Alex Grbic, Frank Hsu and Robert Lu provided valuable help with a number of programming examples. Our colleagues Tarek Abdelrahman, Stephen Brown, Paul Chow, Glenn Gulak and Jonathan Rose offered constructive comments. We are particularly grateful to Stephen and Tarek for their help with important details. The reviewers, Gojko Babic of The Ohio State University, Nathaniel Davis of Virginia Polytechnic Institute and State University, Jose Fortes of Purdue University, John Greiner of Rice University, Sung Hu of San Francisco State University, Ali Hurson of Pennsylvania State University, Lizy Kurian John of University of Texas at Austin, Stefan Leue of Albert Ludwigs Universitat in Freiburg, Fabrizio Lombardi of Northeastern University, Wayne Loucks of University of Waterloo, Prasant Mohapatra of Iowa State University, Daniel Tabak of George Mason University, and John Valois of Rensselaer Polytechnic Institute gave us many excellent suggestions and provided constructive criticism. We want to thank Eli Vranesic for permission to use his painting "Fall in High Park" on the front cover; he created it using the computer as a paint brush. Finally, we truly appreciate the support of our editor, Catherine Fields Shultz, and her McGraw-Hill associates: Kelley Butcher, Michelle Flomenhoft, Kalah Graham, Betsy Jones, Rick Noel, Heather Sabo, and Christine Walker.

Carl Hamacher
Zvonko Vranesic
Safwat Zaky

1

BASIC STRUCTURE OF COMPUTERS

CHAPTER OBJECTIVES

In this chapter you will be introduced to:

- The basic structure of a computer
- Machine instructions and their execution
- System software that enables the preparation and execution of programs
- Performance issues in computer systems
- The history of computer development

This book is about computer organization. It describes the function and design of the various units of digital computers that store and process information. It also deals with the units of the computer that receive information from external sources and send computed results to external destinations. Most of the material in this book is devoted to *computer hardware* and *computer architecture*. Computer hardware consists of electronic circuits, displays, magnetic and optical storage media, electromechanical equipment, and communication facilities. Computer architecture encompasses the specification of an instruction set and the hardware units that implement the instructions.

Many aspects of programming and software components in computer systems are also discussed in this book. It is important to consider both hardware and software aspects of the design of various computer components in order to achieve a good understanding of computer systems.

This chapter introduces a number of hardware and software concepts, presents some common terminology, and gives a broad overview of the fundamental aspects of the subject. More detailed discussions follow in subsequent chapters.

1.1 COMPUTER TYPES

Let us first define the term *digital computer,* or simply *computer*. In the simplest terms, a contemporary computer is a fast electronic calculating machine that accepts digitized input information, processes it according to a list of internally stored instructions, and produces the resulting output information. The list of instructions is called a computer *program,* and the internal storage is called computer *memory.*

Many types of computers exist that differ widely in size, cost, computational power, and intended use. The most common computer is the *personal computer,* which has found wide use in homes, schools, and business offices. It is the most common form of *desktop computers*. Desktop computers have processing and storage units, visual display and audio output units, and a keyboard that can all be located easily on a home or office desk. The storage media include hard disks, CD-ROMs, and diskettes. Portable *notebook computers* are a compact version of the personal computer with all of these components packaged into a single unit the size of a thin briefcase. *Workstations* with high-resolution graphics input/output capability, although still retaining the dimensions of desktop computers, have significantly more computational power than personal computers. Workstations are often used in engineering applications, especially for interactive design work.

Beyond workstations, a range of large and very powerful computer systems exist that are called *enterprise systems* and *servers* at the low end of the range, and *supercomputers* at the high end. Enterprise systems, or *mainframes,* are used for business data processing in medium to large corporations that require much more computing power and storage capacity than workstations can provide. Servers contain sizable database storage units and are capable of handling large volumes of requests to access the data. In many cases, servers are widely accessible to the education, business, and personal user communities. The requests and responses are usually transported over Internet communication facilities. Indeed, the Internet and its associated servers have become a dominant worldwide source of all types of information. The Internet communication facilities consist of a complex structure of high-speed fiber-optic backbone links interconnected with broadcast cable and telephone connections to schools, businesses, and homes.

Supercomputers are used for the large-scale numerical calculations required in applications such as weather forecasting and aircraft design and simulation. In enterprise systems, servers, and supercomputers, the functional units, including multiple processors, may consist of a number of separate and often large units.

1.2 FUNCTIONAL UNITS

A computer consists of five functionally independent main parts: input, memory, arithmetic and logic, output, and control units, as shown in Figure 1.1. The input unit accepts coded information from human operators, from electromechanical devices such as keyboards, or from other computers over digital communication lines. The information received is either stored in the computer's memory for later reference or immediately used by the arithmetic and logic circuitry to perform the desired operations. The processing steps are determined by a program stored in the memory. Finally, the results are sent back to the outside world through the output unit. All of these actions are coordinated by the control unit. Figure 1.1 does not show the connections among the functional units. These connections, which can be made in several ways, are discussed throughout this book. We refer to the arithmetic and logic circuits, in conjunction with the main control circuits, as the *processor,* and input and output equipment is often collectively referred to as the *input-output* (I/O) unit.

We now take a closer look at the information handled by a computer. It is convenient to categorize this information as either instructions or data. *Instructions,* or *machine instructions,* are explicit commands that

- Govern the transfer of information within a computer as well as between the computer and its I/O devices
- Specify the arithmetic and logic operations to be performed

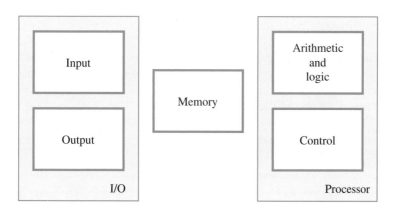

Figure 1.1 Basic functional units of a computer.

A list of instructions that performs a task is called a *program.* Usually the program is stored in the memory. The processor then fetches the instructions that make up the program from the memory, one after another, and performs the desired operations. The computer is completely controlled by the *stored program,* except for possible external interruption by an operator or by I/O devices connected to the machine.

Data are numbers and encoded characters that are used as operands by the instructions. The term data, however, is often used to mean any digital information. Within this definition of data, an entire program (that is, a list of instructions) may be considered as data if it is to be processed by another program. An example of this is the task of *compiling* a high-level language *source program* into a list of machine instructions constituting a machine language program, called the *object program.* The source program is the input data to the *compiler* program which translates the source program into a machine language program.

Information handled by a computer must be encoded in a suitable format. Most present-day hardware employs digital circuits that have only two stable states, ON and OFF (see Appendix A). Each number, character, or instruction is encoded as a string of binary digits called *bits,* each having one of two possible values, 0 or 1. Numbers are usually represented in positional binary notation, as discussed in detail in Chapters 2 and 6. Occasionally, the *binary-coded decimal* (BCD) format is employed, in which each decimal digit is encoded by four bits.

Alphanumeric characters are also expressed in terms of binary codes. Several coding schemes have been developed. Two of the most widely used schemes are ASCII (American Standard Code for Information Interchange), in which each character is represented as a 7-bit code, and EBCDIC (Extended Binary-Coded Decimal Interchange Code), in which eight bits are used to denote a character. A more detailed description of binary notation and coding schemes is given in Appendix E.

1.2.1 INPUT UNIT

Computers accept coded information through input units, which read the data. The most well-known input device is the keyboard. Whenever a key is pressed, the corresponding letter or digit is automatically translated into its corresponding binary code and transmitted over a cable to either the memory or the processor.

Many other kinds of input devices are available, including joysticks, trackballs, and mouses. These are often used as graphic input devices in conjunction with displays. Microphones can be used to capture audio input which is then sampled and converted into digital codes for storage and processing. Detailed discussion of input devices and their operation is found in Chapter 10.

1.2.2 MEMORY UNIT

The function of the memory unit is to store programs and data. There are two classes of storage, called primary and secondary.

Primary storage is a fast memory that operates at electronic speeds. Programs must be stored in the memory while they are being executed. The memory contains a large number of semiconductor storage cells, each capable of storing one bit of information. These cells are rarely read or written as individual cells but instead are processed in groups of fixed size called *words*. The memory is organized so that the contents of one word, containing n bits, can be stored or retrieved in one basic operation.

To provide easy access to any word in the memory, a distinct *address* is associated with each word location. Addresses are numbers that identify successive locations. A given word is accessed by specifying its address and issuing a control command that starts the storage or retrieval process.

The number of bits in each word is often referred to as the *word length* of the computer. Typical word lengths range from 16 to 64 bits. The capacity of the memory is one factor that characterizes the size of a computer. Small machines typically have only a few tens of millions of words, whereas medium and large machines normally have many tens or hundreds of millions of words. Data are usually processed within a machine in units of words, multiples of words, or parts of words. When the memory is accessed, usually only one word of data is read or written.

Programs must reside in the memory during execution. Instructions and data can be written into the memory or read out under the control of the processor. It is essential to be able to access any word location in the memory as quickly as possible. Memory in which any location can be reached in a short and fixed amount of time after specifying its address is called *random-access memory* (RAM). The time required to access one word is called the *memory access time*. This time is fixed, independent of the location of the word being accessed. It typically ranges from a few nanoseconds (ns) to about 100 ns for modern RAM units. The memory of a computer is normally implemented as a *memory hierarchy* of three or four levels of semiconductor RAM units with different speeds and sizes. The small, fast, RAM units are called *caches*. They are tightly coupled with the processor and are often contained on the same integrated circuit chip to achieve high performance. The largest and slowest unit is referred to as the *main memory*. We will give a brief description of how information is accessed in the memory hierarchy later in the chapter. Chapter 5 discusses the operational and performance aspects of the computer memory in detail.

Although primary storage is essential, it tends to be expensive. Thus additional, cheaper, *secondary storage* is used when large amounts of data and many programs have to be stored, particularly for information that is accessed infrequently. A wide selection of secondary storage devices is available, including *magnetic disks* and *tapes* and *optical disks* (CD-ROMs). These devices are also described in Chapter 5.

1.2.3 ARITHMETIC AND LOGIC UNIT

Most computer operations are executed in the *arithmetic and logic unit* (ALU) of the processor. Consider a typical example: Suppose two numbers located in the memory are to be added. They are brought into the processor, and the actual addition is carried out by the ALU. The sum may then be stored in the memory or retained in the processor for immediate use.

Any other arithmetic or logic operation, for example, multiplication, division, or comparison of numbers, is initiated by bringing the required operands into the processor, where the operation is performed by the ALU. When operands are brought into the processor, they are stored in high-speed storage elements called *registers*. Each register can store one word of data. Access times to registers are somewhat faster than access times to the fastest cache unit in the memory hierarchy.

The control and the arithmetic and logic units are many times faster than other devices connected to a computer system. This enables a single processor to control a number of external devices such as keyboards, displays, magnetic and optical disks, sensors, and mechanical controllers.

1.2.4 OUTPUT UNIT

The output unit is the counterpart of the input unit. Its function is to send processed results to the outside world. The most familiar example of such a device is a *printer*. Printers employ mechanical impact heads, ink jet streams, or photocopying techniques, as in laser printers, to perform the printing. It is possible to produce printers capable of printing as many as 10,000 lines per minute. This is a tremendous speed for a mechanical device but is still very slow compared to the electronic speed of a processor unit.

Some units, such as graphic displays, provide both an output function and an input function. The dual role of such units is the reason for using the single name I/O unit in many cases.

1.2.5 CONTROL UNIT

The memory, arithmetic and logic, and input and output units store and process information and perform input and output operations. The operation of these units must be coordinated in some way. This is the task of the control unit. The control unit is effectively the nerve center that sends control signals to other units and senses their states.

I/O transfers, consisting of input and output operations, are controlled by the instructions of I/O programs that identify the devices involved and the information to be transferred. However, the actual *timing signals* that govern the transfers are generated by the control circuits. Timing signals are signals that determine when a given action is to take place. Data transfers between the processor and the memory are also controlled by the control unit through timing signals. It is reasonable to think of a control unit as a well-defined, physically separate unit that interacts with other parts of the machine. In practice, however, this is seldom the case. Much of the control circuitry is physically distributed throughout the machine. A large set of control lines (wires) carries the signals used for timing and synchronization of events in all units.

The operation of a computer can be summarized as follows:

* The computer accepts information in the form of programs and data through an input unit and stores it in the memory.

- Information stored in the memory is fetched, under program control, into an arithmetic and logic unit, where it is processed.

- Processed information leaves the computer through an output unit.

- All activities inside the machine are directed by the control unit.

1.3 BASIC OPERATIONAL CONCEPTS

In Section 1.2, we stated that the activity in a computer is governed by instructions. To perform a given task, an appropriate program consisting of a list of instructions is stored in the memory. Individual instructions are brought from the memory into the processor, which executes the specified operations. Data to be used as operands are also stored in the memory. A typical instruction may be

Add   LOCA,R0

This instruction adds the operand at memory location LOCA to the operand in a register in the processor, R0, and places the sum into register R0. The original contents of location LOCA are preserved, whereas those of R0 are overwritten. This instruction requires the performance of several steps. First, the instruction is fetched from the memory into the processor. Next, the operand at LOCA is fetched and added to the contents of R0. Finally, the resulting sum is stored in register R0.

The preceding Add instruction combines a memory access operation with an ALU operation. In many modern computers, these two types of operations are performed by separate instructions for performance reasons that are explained in Chapter 8. The effect of the above instruction can be realized by the two-instruction sequence

Load   LOCA,R1
Add   R1,R0

The first of these instructions transfers the contents of memory location LOCA into processor register R1, and the second instruction adds the contents of registers R1 and R0 and places the sum into R0. Note that this destroys the former contents of register R1 as well as those of R0, whereas the original contents of memory location LOCA are preserved.

Transfers between the memory and the processor are started by sending the address of the memory location to be accessed to the memory unit and issuing the appropriate control signals. The data are then transferred to or from the memory.

Figure 1.2 shows how the memory and the processor can be connected. It also shows a few essential operational details of the processor that have not been discussed yet. The interconnection pattern for these components is not shown explicitly since here we discuss only their functional characteristics. Chapter 7 describes the details of the interconnection as part of processor design.

In addition to the ALU and the control circuitry, the processor contains a number of registers used for several different purposes. The *instruction register* (IR) holds the instruction that is currently being executed. Its output is available to the control circuits,

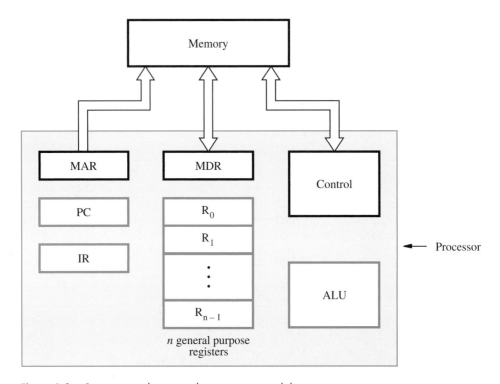

Figure 1.2   Connections between the processor and the memory.

which generate the timing signals that control the various processing elements involved in executing the instruction. The *program counter* (PC) is another specialized register. It keeps track of the execution of a program. It contains the memory address of the next instruction to be fetched and executed. During the execution of an instruction, the contents of the PC are updated to correspond to the address of the next instruction to be executed. It is customary to say that the PC *points* to the next instruction that is to be fetched from the memory. Besides the IR and PC, Figure 1.2 shows *n general-purpose registers,* R_0 through R_{n-1}. Their roles are explained in Chapter 2.

Finally, two registers facilitate communication with the memory. These are the *memory address register* (MAR) and the *memory data register* (MDR). The MAR holds the address of the location to be accessed. The MDR contains the data to be written into or read out of the addressed location.

Let us now consider some typical operating steps. Programs reside in the memory and usually get there through the input unit. Execution of the program starts when the PC is set to point to the first instruction of the program. The contents of the PC are transferred to the MAR and a Read control signal is sent to the memory. After the time required to access the memory elapses, the addressed word (in this case, the first instruction of the program) is read out of the memory and loaded into the MDR. Next, the contents of the MDR are transferred to the IR. At this point, the instruction is ready to be decoded and executed.

If the instruction involves an operation to be performed by the ALU, it is necessary to obtain the required operands. If an operand resides in the memory (it could also be in a general-purpose register in the processor), it has to be fetched by sending its address to the MAR and initiating a Read cycle. When the operand has been read from the memory into the MDR, it is transferred from the MDR to the ALU. After one or more operands are fetched in this way, the ALU can perform the desired operation. If the result of this operation is to be stored in the memory, then the result is sent to the MDR. The address of the location where the result is to be stored is sent to the MAR, and a Write cycle is initiated. At some point during the execution of the current instruction, the contents of the PC are incremented so that the PC points to the next instruction to be executed. Thus, as soon as the execution of the current instruction is completed, a new instruction fetch may be started.

In addition to transferring data between the memory and the processor, the computer accepts data from input devices and sends data to output devices. Thus, some machine instructions with the ability to handle I/O transfers are provided.

Normal execution of programs may be preempted if some device requires urgent servicing. For example, a monitoring device in a computer-controlled industrial process may detect a dangerous condition. In order to deal with the situation immediately, the normal execution of the current program must be interrupted. To do this, the device raises an *interrupt* signal. An interrupt is a request from an I/O device for service by the processor. The processor provides the requested service by executing an appropriate *interrupt-service routine.* Because such diversions may alter the internal state of the processor, its state must be saved in memory locations before servicing the interrupt. Normally, the contents of the PC, the general registers, and some control information are stored in memory. When the interrupt-service routine is completed, the state of the processor is restored so that the interrupted program may continue.

The processor unit shown in Figure 1.2 is usually implemented on a single Very Large Scale Integrated (VLSI) chip, with at least one of the cache units of the memory hierarchy contained on the same chip.

1.4 Bus Structures

So far, we have discussed the functions of individual parts of a computer. To form an operational system, these parts must be connected in some organized way. There are many ways of doing this. We consider the simplest and most common of these here.

To achieve a reasonable speed of operation, a computer must be organized so that all its units can handle one full word of data at a given time. When a word of data is transferred between units, all its bits are transferred in parallel, that is, the bits are transferred simultaneously over many wires, or lines, one bit per line. A group of lines that serves as a connecting path for several devices is called a *bus.* In addition to the lines that carry the data, the bus must have lines for address and control purposes.

The simplest way to interconnect functional units is to use a *single bus,* as shown in Figure 1.3. All units are connected to this bus. Because the bus can be used for only one transfer at a time, only two units can actively use the bus at any given time. Bus

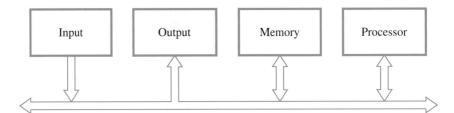

Figure 1.3 Single-bus structure.

control lines are used to arbitrate multiple requests for use of the bus. The main virtue of the single-bus structure is its low cost and its flexibility for attaching peripheral devices. Systems that contain multiple buses achieve more concurrency in operations by allowing two or more transfers to be carried out at the same time. This leads to better performance but at an increased cost.

The devices connected to a bus vary widely in their speed of operation. Some electromechanical devices, such as keyboards and printers, are relatively slow. Others, like magnetic or optical disks, are considerably faster. Memory and processor units operate at electronic speeds, making them the fastest parts of a computer. Because all these devices must communicate with each other over a bus, an efficient transfer mechanism that is not constrained by the slow devices and that can be used to smooth out the differences in timing among processors, memories, and external devices is necessary.

A common approach is to include *buffer registers* with the devices to hold the information during transfers. To illustrate this technique, consider the transfer of an encoded character from a processor to a character printer. The processor sends the character over the bus to the printer buffer. Since the buffer is an electronic register, this transfer requires relatively little time. Once the buffer is loaded, the printer can start printing without further intervention by the processor. The bus and the processor are no longer needed and can be released for other activity. The printer continues printing the character in its buffer and is not available for further transfers until this process is completed. Thus, buffer registers smooth out timing differences among processors, memories, and I/O devices. They prevent a high-speed processor from being locked to a slow I/O device during a sequence of data transfers. This allows the processor to switch rapidly from one device to another, interweaving its processing activity with data transfers involving several I/O devices.

1.5 SOFTWARE

In order for a user to enter and run an application program, the computer must already contain some system software in its memory. *System software* is a collection of programs that are executed as needed to perform functions such as

- Receiving and interpreting user commands
- Entering and editing application programs and storing them as files in secondary storage devices

- Managing the storage and retrieval of files in secondary storage devices
- Running standard application programs such as word processors, spreadsheets, or games, with data supplied by the user
- Controlling I/O units to receive input information and produce output results
- Translating programs from source form prepared by the user into object form consisting of machine instructions
- Linking and running user-written application programs with existing standard library routines, such as numerical computation packages

System software is thus responsible for the coordination of all activities in a computing system. The purpose of this section is to introduce some basic aspects of system software.

Application programs are usually written in a high-level programming language, such as C, C++, Java, or Fortran, in which the programmer specifies mathematical or text-processing operations. These operations are described in a format that is independent of the particular computer used to execute the program. A programmer using a high-level language need not know the details of machine program instructions. A system software program called a *compiler* translates the high-level language program into a suitable machine language program containing instructions such as the Add and Load instructions discussed in Section 1.3.

Another important system program that all programmers use is a *text editor*. It is used for entering and editing application programs. The user of this program interactively executes commands that allow statements of a source program entered at a keyboard to be accumulated in a *file*. A file is simply a sequence of alphanumeric characters or binary data that is stored in memory or in secondary storage. A file can be referred to by a name chosen by the user.

We do not pursue the details of compilers, editors, or file systems in this book, but let us take a closer look at a key system software component called the *operating system* (OS). This is a large program, or actually a collection of routines, that is used to control the sharing of and interaction among various computer units as they execute application programs. The OS routines perform the tasks required to assign computer resources to individual application programs. These tasks include assigning memory and magnetic disk space to program and data files, moving data between memory and disk units, and handling I/O operations.

In order to understand the basics of operating systems, let us consider a system with one processor, one disk, and one printer. First we discuss the steps involved in running one application program. Once we have explained these steps, we can understand how the operating system manages the execution of more than one application program at the same time. Assume that the application program has been compiled from a high-level language form into a machine language form and stored on the disk. The first step is to transfer this file into the memory. When the transfer is complete, execution of the program is started. Assume that part of the program's task involves reading a data file from the disk into the memory, performing some computation on the data, and printing the results. When execution of the program reaches the point where the data file is needed, the program requests the operating system to transfer the data file from the

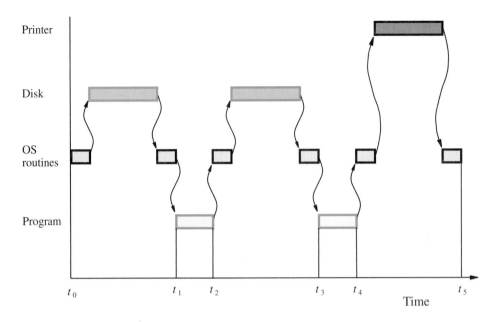

Figure 1.4 User program and OS routine sharing of the processor.

disk to the memory. The OS performs this task and passes execution control back to the application program, which then proceeds to perform the required computation. When the computation is completed and the results are ready to be printed, the application program again sends a request to the operating system. An OS routine is then executed to cause the printer to print the results.

We have seen how execution control passes back and forth between the application program and the OS routines. A convenient way to illustrate this sharing of the processor execution time is by a time-line diagram, such as that shown in Figure 1.4. During the time period t_0 to t_1, an OS routine initiates loading the application program from disk to memory, waits until the transfer is completed, and then passes execution control to the application program. A similar pattern of activity occurs during period t_2 to t_3 and period t_4 to t_5, when the operating system transfers the data file from the disk and prints the results. At t_5, the operating system may load and execute another application program.

Now, let us point out a way that computer resources can be used more efficiently if several application programs are to be processed. Notice that the disk and the processor are idle during most of the time period t_4 to t_5. The operating system can load the next program to be executed into the memory from the disk while the printer is operating. Similarly, during t_0 to t_1, the operating system can arrange to print the previous program's results while the current program is being loaded from the disk. Thus, the operating system manages the concurrent execution of several application programs to make the best possible use of computer resources. This pattern of concurrent execution is called *multiprogramming* or *multitasking*.

1.6 PERFORMANCE

The most important measure of the performance of a computer is how quickly it can execute programs. The speed with which a computer executes programs is affected by the design of its hardware and its machine language instructions. Because programs are usually written in a high-level language, performance is also affected by the compiler that translates programs into machine language. For best performance, it is necessary to design the compiler, the machine instruction set, and the hardware in a coordinated way. We do not describe the details of compiler design in this book. We concentrate on the design of instruction sets and hardware.

In Section 1.5, we described how the operating system overlaps processing, disk transfers, and printing for several programs to make the best possible use of the resources available. The total time required to execute the program in Figure 1.4 is $t_5 - t_0$. This *elapsed time* is a measure of the performance of the entire computer system. It is affected by the speed of the processor, the disk, and the printer. To discuss the performance of the processor, we should consider only the periods during which the processor is active. These are the periods labeled Program and OS routines in Figure 1.4. We will refer to the sum of these periods as the *processor time* needed to execute the program. In what follows, we will identify some of the key parameters that affect the processor time and point out the chapters in which the relevant issues are discussed. We encourage the readers to keep this broad overview of performance in mind as they study the material presented in subsequent chapters.

Just as the elapsed time for the execution of a program depends on all units in a computer system, the processor time depends on the hardware involved in the execution of individual machine instructions. This hardware comprises the processor and the memory, which are usually connected by a bus, as shown in Figure 1.3. The pertinent parts of this figure are repeated in Figure 1.5, including the cache memory as part of the processor unit. Let us examine the flow of program instructions and data between the memory and the processor. At the start of execution, all program instructions and the required data are stored in the main memory. As execution proceeds, instructions are fetched one by one over the bus into the processor, and a copy is placed in the cache. When the execution of an instruction calls for data located in the main memory, the data are

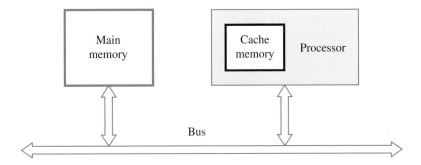

Figure 1.5 The processor cache.

fetched and a copy is placed in the cache. Later, if the same instruction or data item is needed a second time, it is read directly from the cache.

The processor and a relatively small cache memory can be fabricated on a single integrated circuit chip. The internal speed of performing the basic steps of instruction processing on such chips is very high and is considerably faster than the speed at which instructions and data can be fetched from the main memory. A program will be executed faster if the movement of instructions and data between the main memory and the processor is minimized, which is achieved by using the cache. For example, suppose a number of instructions are executed repeatedly over a short period of time, as happens in a program loop. If these instructions are available in the cache, they can be fetched quickly during the period of repeated use. The same applies to data that are used repeatedly. Design, operation, and performance issues for the main memory and the cache are discussed in Chapter 5.

1.6.1 PROCESSOR CLOCK

Processor circuits are controlled by a timing signal called a *clock*. The clock defines regular time intervals, called *clock cycles*. To execute a machine instruction, the processor divides the action to be performed into a sequence of basic steps, such that each step can be completed in one clock cycle. The length P of one clock cycle is an important parameter that affects processor performance. Its inverse is the clock rate, $R = 1/P$, which is measured in cycles per second. Processors used in today's personal computers and workstations have clock rates that range from a few hundred million to over a billion cycles per second. In standard electrical engineering terminology, the term "cycles per second" is called *hertz* (Hz). The term "million" is denoted by the prefix *Mega* (M), and "billion" is denoted by the prefix *Giga* (G). Hence, 500 million cycles per second is usually abbreviated to 500 Megahertz (MHz), and 1250 million cycles per second is abbreviated to 1.25 Gigahertz (GHz). The corresponding clock periods are 2 and 0.8 nanoseconds (ns), respectively.

1.6.2 BASIC PERFORMANCE EQUATION

We now focus our attention on the processor time component of the total elapsed time. Let T be the processor time required to execute a program that has been prepared in some high-level language. The compiler generates a machine language object program that corresponds to the source program. Assume that complete execution of the program requires the execution of N machine language instructions. The number N is the actual number of instruction executions, and is not necessarily equal to the number of machine instructions in the object program. Some instructions may be executed more than once, which is the case for instructions inside a program loop. Others may not be executed at all, depending on the input data used. Suppose that the average number of basic steps needed to execute one machine instruction is S, where each basic step is completed in one clock cycle. If the clock rate is R cycles per second, the program execution time is given by

$$T = \frac{N \times S}{R} \qquad\qquad [1.1]$$

This is often referred to as the *basic performance equation*.

The performance parameter T for an application program is much more important to the user than the individual values of the parameters N, S, or R. To achieve high performance, the computer designer must seek ways to reduce the value of T, which means reducing N and S, and increasing R. The value of N is reduced if the source program is compiled into fewer machine instructions. The value of S is reduced if instructions have a smaller number of basic steps to perform or if the execution of instructions is overlapped. Using a higher-frequency clock increases the value or R, which means that the time required to complete a basic execution step is reduced.

We must emphasize that N, S, and R are not independent parameters; changing one may affect another. Introducing a new feature in the design of a processor will lead to improved performance only if the overall result is to reduce the value of T. A processor advertised as having a 900-MHz clock does not necessarily provide better performance than a 700-MHz processor because it may have a different value of S.

1.6.3   PIPELINING AND SUPERSCALAR OPERATION

In the discussion above, we assumed that instructions are executed one after another. Hence, the value of S is the total number of basic steps, or clock cycles, required to execute an instruction. A substantial improvement in performance can be achieved by overlapping the execution of successive instructions, using a technique called *pipelining*. Consider the instruction

Add   R1,R2,R3

which adds the contents of registers R1 and R2, and places the sum into R3. The contents of R1 and R2 are first transferred to the inputs of the ALU. After the add operation is performed, the sum is transferred to R3. The processor can read the next instruction from the memory while the addition operation is being performed. Then, if that instruction also uses the ALU, its operands can be transferred to the ALU inputs at the same time that the result of the Add instruction is being transferred to R3. In the ideal case, if all instructions are overlapped to the maximum degree possible, execution proceeds at the rate of one instruction completed in each clock cycle. Individual instructions still require several clock cycles to complete. But, for the purpose of computing T, the effective value of S is 1.

Pipelining is discussed in detail in Chapter 8. As we will see, the ideal value $S = 1$ cannot be attained in practice for a variety of reasons. However, pipelining increases the rate of executing instructions significantly and causes the effective value of S to approach 1.

A higher degree of concurrency can be achieved if multiple instruction pipelines are implemented in the processor. This means that multiple functional units are used, creating parallel paths through which different instructions can be executed in parallel. With such an arrangement, it becomes possible to start the execution of several instructions in every clock cycle. This mode of operation is called *superscalar execution.* If it can be sustained for a long time during program execution, the effective value of S can be reduced to less than one. Of course, parallel execution must preserve the logical correctness of programs, that is, the results produced must be the same as those produced by serial execution of program instructions. Many of today's high-performance processors are designed to operate in this manner.

1.6.4   CLOCK RATE

There are two possibilities for increasing the clock rate, R. First, improving the *integrated-circuit* (IC) technology makes logic circuits faster, which reduces the time needed to complete a basic step. This allows the clock period, P, to be reduced and the clock rate, R, to be increased. Second, reducing the amount of processing done in one basic step also makes it possible to reduce the clock period, P. However, if the actions that have to be performed by an instruction remain the same, the number of basic steps needed may increase.

Increases in the value of R that are entirely caused by improvements in IC technology affect all aspects of the processor's operation equally with the exception of the time it takes to access the main memory. In the presence of a cache, the percentage of accesses to the main memory is small. Hence, much of the performance gain expected from the use of faster technology can be realized. The value of T will be reduced by the same factor as R is increased because S and N are not affected. The impact on performance of changing the way in which instructions are divided into basic steps is more difficult to assess. This issue is discussed in Chapter 8.

1.6.5   INSTRUCTION SET: CISC AND RISC

Simple instructions require a small number of basic steps to execute. Complex instructions involve a large number of steps. For a processor that has only simple instructions, a large number of instructions may be needed to perform a given programming task. This could lead to a large value for N and a small value for S. On the other hand, if individual instructions perform more complex operations, fewer instructions will be needed, leading to a lower value of N and a larger value of S. It is not obvious if one choice is better than the other.

A key consideration in comparing the two choices is the use of pipelining. We pointed out earlier that the effective value of S in a pipelined processor is close to 1 even though the number of basic steps per instruction may be considerably larger. This seems to imply that complex instructions combined with pipelining would achieve the best performance. However, it is much easier to implement efficient pipelining in processors with simple instruction sets. The suitability of the instruction set for pipelined execution is an important and often deciding consideration.

The design of the instruction set of a processor and the options available are discussed in Chapter 2. The relative merits of processors with simple instructions and processors with more complex instructions have been studied a great deal [1]. The former are called *Reduced Instruction Set Computers* (RISC), and the latter are referred to as *Complex Instruction Set Computers* (CISC). We give examples of RISC and CISC processors in Chapters 3 and 11, and discuss their merits. Although we use the terms RISC and CISC in order to be compatible with contemporary descriptions, we caution the reader not to assume that they correspond to clearly defined classes of processors. A given processor design is a result of many trade-offs. The terms RISC and CISC refer to design principles and techniques, which we discuss in several places in the book.

1.6.6 COMPILER

A compiler translates a high-level language program into a sequence of machine instructions. To reduce N, we need to have a suitable machine instruction set and a compiler that makes good use of it. An *optimizing compiler* takes advantage of various features of the target processor to reduce the product $N \times S$, which is the total number of clock cycles needed to execute a program. We will see in Chapter 8 that the number of cycles is dependent not only on the choice of instructions, but also on the order in which they appear in the program. The compiler may rearrange program instructions to achieve better performance. Of course, such changes must not affect the result of the computation.

Superficially, a compiler appears as a separate entity from the processor with which it is used and may even be available from a different vendor. However, a high-quality compiler must be closely linked to the processor architecture. The compiler and the processor are often designed at the same time, with much interaction between the designers to achieve best results. The ultimate objective is to reduce the total number of clock cycles needed to perform a required programming task.

1.6.7 PERFORMANCE MEASUREMENT

It is important to be able to assess the performance of a computer. Computer designers use performance estimates to evaluate the effectiveness of new features. Manufacturers use performance indicators in the marketing process. Buyers use such data to choose among many available computer models.

The previous discussion suggests that the only parameter that properly describes the performance of a computer is the execution time, T, for the programs of interest. Despite the conceptual simplicity of Equation 1.1, computing the value of T is not simple. Moreover, parameters such as the clock speed and various architectural features are not reliable indicators of the expected performance.

For these reasons, the computer community adopted the idea of measuring computer performance using benchmark programs. To make comparisons possible, standardized programs must be used. The performance measure is the time it takes a computer to execute a given benchmark. Initially, some attempts were made to create artificial programs that could be used as standard benchmarks. But, synthetic programs do not properly predict performance obtained when real application programs are run.

The accepted practice today is to use an agreed-upon selection of real application programs to evaluate performance. A nonprofit organization called System Performance Evaluation Corporation (SPEC) selects and publishes representative application programs for different application domains, together with test results for many commercially available computers. For general-purpose computers, a suite of benchmark programs was selected in 1989. It was modified somewhat and published in 1995 and again in 2000.

The programs selected range from game playing, compiler, and database applications to numerically intensive programs in astrophysics and quantum chemistry. In each case, the program is compiled for the computer under test, and the running time on a real computer is measured. (Simulation is not allowed.) The same program is also compiled and run on one computer selected as a reference. For SPEC95, the reference is the SUN SPARCstation 10/40. For SPEC2000, the reference computer is an Ultra-SPARC10 workstation with a 300-MHz UltraSPARC-IIi processor. The SPEC rating is computed as follows

$$\text{SPEC rating} = \frac{\text{Running time on the reference computer}}{\text{Running time on the computer under test}}$$

Thus a SPEC rating of 50 means that the computer under test is 50 times as fast as the UltraSPARC10 for this particular benchmark. The test is repeated for all the programs in the SPEC suite, and the geometric mean of the results is computed. Let SPEC_i be the rating for program i in the suite. The overall SPEC rating for the computer is given by

$$\text{SPEC rating} = \left(\prod_{i=1}^{n} \text{SPEC}_i \right)^{\frac{1}{n}}$$

where n is the number of programs in the suite.

Because the actual execution time is measured, the SPEC rating is a measure of the combined effect of all factors affecting performance, including the compiler, the operating system, the processor, and the memory of the computer being tested. Details about the SPEC benchmark programs and results of the tests conducted can be found on the SPEC web page [2].

1.7 MULTIPROCESSORS AND MULTICOMPUTERS

So far, we have considered computers with one processor. Large computer systems may contain a number of processor units, in which case they are called *multiprocessor* systems. These systems either execute a number of different application tasks in parallel, or they execute subtasks of a single large task in parallel. All processors usually have access to all of the memory in such systems, and the term *shared-memory multiprocessor* systems is often used to make this clear. The high performance of these systems comes with much increased complexity and cost. In addition to multiple processors and memory units, cost is increased because of the need for more complex interconnection networks.

In contrast to multiprocessor systems, it is also possible to use an interconnected group of complete computers to achieve high total computational power. The computers normally have access only to their own memory units. When the tasks they are executing need to communicate data, they do so by exchanging *messages* over a communication network. This property distinguishes them from shared-memory multiprocessors, leading to the name *message-passing multicomputers.*

Shared-memory multiprocessors and message-passing multicomputers, along with the interconnection networks used in such systems, are described in Chapter 12.

1.8   HISTORICAL PERSPECTIVE

Computers as we know them today have been developed over the past 60 years. A long, slow evolution of mechanical calculating devices preceded the development of computers. Many sources describe this history. Hayes [3], for example, gives an excellent account of computer history, including dates, inventors, designers, research organizations, and manufacturers. Here, we briefly sketch the history of computer development.

In the 300 years before the mid-1900s, a series of increasingly complex mechanical devices, constructed from gear wheels, levers, and pulleys, were used to perform the basic operations of addition, subtraction, multiplication, and division. Holes on punched cards were mechanically sensed and used to control the automatic sequencing of a list of calculations and essentially provide a programming capability. These devices enabled the computation of complete mathematical tables of logarithms and trigonometric functions as approximated by polynomials. Output results were punched on cards or printed on paper. Electromechanical relay devices, such as those used in early telephone switching systems, provided the means for performing logic functions in computers built during World War II. At the same time, the first electronic computer was designed and built at the University of Pennsylvania, based on vacuum tube technology that was in use in radios and military radar equipment. Vacuum tubes were used to perform logic operations and to store data. This technology began the modern era of electronic digital computers.

Development of the technologies used to fabricate the processors, memories, and I/O units of computers has been divided into four generations: the first generation, 1945 to 1955; the second generation, 1955 to 1965; the third generation, 1965 to 1975; and the fourth generation, 1975 to the present.

1.8.1   THE FIRST GENERATION

The key concept of a stored program was introduced by John von Neumann. Programs and their data were located in the same memory, as they are today. Assembly language was used to prepare programs and was translated into machine language for execution.

Basic arithmetic operations were performed in a few milliseconds using vacuum tube technology to implement logic functions. This provided a 100- to 1000-fold increase in speed relative to the earlier mechanical and relay-based electromechanical technology. Mercury delay-line memory was used at first, and I/O functions were performed by devices similar to typewriters. Magnetic core memories and magnetic tape storage devices were also developed.

1.8.2 THE SECOND GENERATION

The transistor was invented at AT&T Bell Laboratories in the late 1940s and quickly replaced the vacuum tube. This basic technology shift marked the start of the second generation. Magnetic core memories and magnetic drum storage devices were more widely used in the second generation. High-level languages, such as Fortran, were developed, making the preparation of application programs much easier. System programs called compilers were developed to translate these high-level language programs into a corresponding assembly language program, which was then translated into executable machine language form. Separate I/O processors were developed that could operate in parallel with the central processor that executed programs, thus improving overall performance. IBM became a major computer manufacturer during this time.

1.8.3 THE THIRD GENERATION

The ability to fabricate many transistors on a single silicon chip, called integrated-circuit technology, enabled lower-cost and faster processors and memory elements to be built. Integrated-circuit memories began to replace magnetic core memories. This technological development marked the beginning of the third generation. Other developments included the introduction of microprogramming, parallelism, and pipelining. Operating system software allowed efficient sharing of a computer system by several user programs. Cache and virtual memories were developed. Cache memory makes the main memory appear faster than it really is, and virtual memory makes it appear larger. System 360 mainframe computers from IBM and the line of PDP minicomputers from Digital Equipment Corporation were dominant commercial products of the third generation.

1.8.4 THE FOURTH GENERATION

In the early 1970s, integrated-circuit fabrication techniques had evolved to the point where complete processors and large sections of the main memory of small computers could be implemented on single chips. Tens of thousands of transistors could be placed on a single chip, and the name *Very Large Scale Integration* (VLSI) was coined to describe this technology. VLSI technology allowed a complete processor to be fabricated on a single chip; this became known as a microprocessor. Companies such as Intel, National Semiconductor, Motorola, Texas Instruments, and Advanced Micro Devices, were the driving forces of this technology.

Organizational concepts such as concurrency, pipelining, caches, and virtual memories evolved to produce the high-performance computing systems of today as the fourth generation matured. Portable notebook computers, desktop personal computers and workstations, interconnected by local area networks, wide area networks, and the Internet, have become the dominant mode of computing. Centralized computing on mainframes is now used primarily for business applications in large companies.

1.8.5   BEYOND THE FOURTH GENERATION

Generation numbers beyond four have been used occasionally to describe some computer systems that have a dominant organizational or application-driven feature. In recent years, there has been a tendency to use such features rather than a generation number to describe these evolving systems. Computers featuring artificial intelligence, massively parallel machines, and extensively distributed systems are examples of current trends. Perhaps most importantly, the growth of the computer industry is fueled by increasingly powerful and affordable desktop computers and widespread use of the vast information resources on the Internet.

1.8.6   EVOLUTION OF PERFORMANCE

The shift from mechanical and electromechanical devices to the first electronic devices based on vacuum tubes caused a 100- to 1000-fold speed increase, from seconds to milliseconds. The replacement of tubes by transistors led to another 1000-fold increase in speed, when basic operations could be performed in microseconds. Increased density in the fabrication of integrated circuits has led to current microprocessor chips that perform basic operations in a nanosecond or less, achieving a further 1000-fold increase in speed. In addition to developments in technology, there have been many innovations in the architecture of computers, such as the use of caches and pipelining, which have had a significant impact on computer performance.

1.9   CONCLUDING REMARKS

This chapter considered many aspects of computer structures and operation. Much of the terminology needed to deal with the subject was introduced, and an overview of some important design concepts was presented. The subsequent chapters will provide complete explanations of these terms and concepts, and will place the various parts of this chapter into proper perspective.

PROBLEMS

1.1 List the steps needed to execute the machine instruction

$$\text{Add} \quad \text{LOCA,R0}$$

in terms of transfers between the components shown in Figure 1.2 and some simple control commands. Assume that the instruction itself is stored in the memory at location INSTR and that this address is initially in register PC. The first two steps might be expressed as

- Transfer the contents of register PC to register MAR.
- Issue a Read command to the memory, and then wait until it has transferred the requested word into register MDR.

Remember to include the steps needed to update the contents of PC from INSTR to INSTR+1 so that the next instruction can be fetched.

1.2 Repeat Problem 1.1 for the machine instruction

$$\text{Add} \quad \text{R1,R2,R3}$$

which was discussed in Section 1.6.3.

1.3 (*a*) Give a short sequence of machine instructions for the task: "Add the contents of memory location A to those of location B, and place the answer in location C." Instructions

$$\text{Load} \quad \text{LOC,R}_i$$

and

$$\text{Store} \quad \text{R}_i,\text{LOC}$$

are the only instructions available to transfer data between the memory and general-purpose register R_i. Add instructions were described in Sections 1.3 and 1.6.3. Do not destroy the contents of either location A or B.

(*b*) Suppose that Move and Add instructions are available with the format

$$\text{Move/Add} \quad \text{Location1,Location2}$$

These instructions move or add a copy of the operand at the first location to the second location, overwriting the original operand at the second location. Location*i* can be in either the memory or the processor register set. Is it possible to use fewer instructions to accomplish the task in Part *a*? If yes, give the sequence.

1.4 (*a*) Section 1.5 discusses how the input and output steps of a collection of programs such as the one shown in Figure 1.4 could be overlapped to reduce the total time needed to execute them. Let each of the six OS routine execution intervals be 1 unit of time, with each disk operation requiring 3 units, printing requiring 3 units, and each program execution interval requiring 2 units of time. Compute the ratio of best overlapped time to nonoverlapped time for a long sequence of programs. Ignore start-up and ending transients.

(*b*) Section 1.5 indicated that program computation can be overlapped with either input or output operations or both. Ignoring the relatively short time needed for OS routines, what is the ratio of best overlapped time to nonoverlapped time for completing the execution of a collection of programs, where each program has about equal balance among input, compute, and output activities?

1.5 (*a*) Program execution time, T, as defined in Section 1.6.2, is to be examined for a certain high-level language program. The program can be run on a RISC or a CISC computer. Both computers use pipelined instruction execution, but pipelining in the RISC machine is more effective than in the CISC machine. Specifically, the effective value of S in the T expression for the RISC machine is 1.2, but it is only 1.5 for the CISC machine. Both machines have the same clock rate, R. What is the largest allowable value for N, the number of instructions executed on the CISC machine, expressed as a percentage of the N value for the RISC machine, if time for execution on the CISC machine is to be no longer than that on the RISC machine?

(*b*) Repeat Part *a* if the clock rate, R, for the RISC machine is 15 percent higher than that for the CISC machine.

1.6 (*a*) A processor cache, as shown in Figure 1.5, is discussed in Section 1.6. Suppose that execution time for a program is directly proportional to instruction access time and that access to an instruction in the cache is 20 times faster than access to an instruction in the main memory. Assume that a requested instruction is found in the cache with probability 0.96, and also assume that if an instruction is not found in the cache, it must first be fetched from the main memory to the cache and then fetched from the cache to be executed. Compute the ratio of program execution time without the cache to program execution time with the cache. This ratio is usually defined as the speedup factor resulting from the presence of the cache.

(*b*) If the size of the cache is doubled, assume that the probability of not finding a requested instruction there is cut in half. Repeat Part *a* for a doubled cache size.

REFERENCES

1. D.A. Patterson and J.L. Hennessy, *Computer Organization and Design — The Hardware/Software Interface,* 2nd ed., Morgan Kaufmann, San Mateo, Calif., 1998.

2. System Performance Evaluation Corporation web page: www.spec.org.

3. J.P. Hayes, *Computer Architecture and Organization,* 3rd ed., McGraw-Hill, New York, 1998.

2

MACHINE INSTRUCTIONS AND PROGRAMS

CHAPTER OBJECTIVES

In this chapter you will learn about:

- Machine instructions and program execution, including branching and subroutine call and return operations
- Number representation and addition/subtraction in the 2's-complement system
- Addressing methods for accessing register and memory operands
- Assembly language for representing machine instructions, data, and programs
- Program-controlled Input/Output operations
- Operations on stack, queue, list, linked-list, and array data structures

This chapter considers the way programs are executed in a computer from the machine instruction set viewpoint. Chapter 1 introduced the general concept that both program instructions and data operands are stored in the memory. In this chapter, we study the ways in which sequences of instructions are brought from the memory into the processor and executed to perform a given task. The addressing methods commonly used for accessing operands in memory locations and processor registers are presented.

The emphasis here is on basic concepts. We use a generic style to describe machine instructions and operand addressing methods that are typical of those found in commercial processors. A sufficient number of instructions and addressing methods are introduced to enable us to present complete, realistic programs for simple tasks. These generic programs are specified at the assembly language level. In assembly language, machine instructions and operand addressing information are represented by symbolic names. A complete instruction set is often referred to as the *instruction set architecture* (ISA) of a processor. In addition to specifying instructions, an ISA also specifies the addressing methods used for accessing data operands and the processor registers available for use by the instructions. For the discussion of basic concepts in this chapter, it is not necessary to define a complete instruction set, and we will not attempt to do so. Instead, we will present enough examples to illustrate the capabilities needed.

Chapter 3 presents ISAs for three commercial processors produced by the ARM, Motorola, and Intel companies. This chapter's generic programs are presented in Chapter 3 in each of those three instruction sets, providing the reader with examples from real machines.

The vast majority of programs are written in high-level languages such as C, C++, Java, or Fortran. The main purpose of using assembly language programming in this book is to describe how computers operate. To execute a high-level language program on a processor, the program must first be translated into the assembly language of that processor. The assembly language is a readable representation of the machine language for the processor. The relationship between high-level language and machine language features is a key consideration in computer design. We will discuss this issue a number of times.

All computers deal with numbers. They have instructions that perform basic arithmetic operations on data operands. Also, during the process of executing the machine instructions of a program, it is necessary to perform arithmetic operations to generate the numbers that represent addresses for accessing operand locations in the memory. To understand how these tasks are accomplished, the reader must know how numbers are represented in a computer and how they are manipulated in addition and subtraction operations. Therefore, in the first section of this chapter, we will introduce this topic. A detailed discussion of logic circuits that implement computer arithmetic is given in Chapter 6.

In addition to numeric data, computers deal with characters and character strings in order to process textual information. Here, in the first section, we also describe how characters are represented in the computer.

2.1 NUMBERS, ARITHMETIC OPERATIONS, AND CHARACTERS

Computers are built using logic circuits that operate on information represented by two-valued electrical signals (see Appendix A). We label the two values as 0 and 1; and we define the amount of information represented by such a signal as a *bit* of information, where bit stands for *binary digit*. The most natural way to represent a number in a computer system is by a string of bits, called a binary number. A text character can also be represented by a string of bits called a character code.

    We will first describe binary number representations and arithmetic operations on these numbers, and then describe character representations.

2.1.1 NUMBER REPRESENTATION

Consider an n-bit vector

$$B = b_{n-1} \ldots b_1 b_0$$

where $b_i = 0$ or 1 for $0 \le i \le n - 1$. This vector can represent unsigned integer values V in the range 0 to $2^n - 1$, where

$$V(B) = b_{n-1} \times 2^{n-1} + \cdots + b_1 \times 2^1 + b_0 \times 2^0$$

We obviously need to represent both positive and negative numbers. Three systems are used for representing such numbers:

- Sign-and-magnitude
- 1's-complement
- 2's-complement

In all three systems, the leftmost bit is 0 for positive numbers and 1 for negative numbers. Figure 2.1 illustrates all three representations using 4-bit numbers. Positive values have identical representations in all systems, but negative values have different representations. In the *sign-and-magnitude* system, negative values are represented by changing the most significant bit (b_3 in Figure 2.1) from 0 to 1 in the B vector of the corresponding positive value. For example, $+5$ is represented by 0101, and -5 is represented by 1101. In *1's-complement* representation, negative values are obtained by complementing each bit of the corresponding positive number. Thus, the representation for -3 is obtained by complementing each bit in the vector 0011 to yield 1100. Clearly, the same operation, bit complementing, is done in converting a negative number to the corresponding positive value. Converting either way is referred to as forming the 1's-complement of a given number. The operation of forming the 1's-complement of a given number is equivalent to subtracting that number from $2^n - 1$, that is, from 1111 in the case of the 4-bit numbers in Figure 2.1. Finally, in the *2's-complement* system, forming the 2's-complement of a number is done by subtracting that number from 2^n.

B	Values represented		
$b_3b_2b_1b_0$	Sign and magnitude	1's complement	2's complement
0 1 1 1	+ 7	+ 7	+ 7
0 1 1 0	+ 6	+ 6	+ 6
0 1 0 1	+ 5	+ 5	+ 5
0 1 0 0	+ 4	+ 4	+ 4
0 0 1 1	+ 3	+ 3	+ 3
0 0 1 0	+ 2	+ 2	+ 2
0 0 0 1	+ 1	+ 1	+ 1
0 0 0 0	+ 0	+ 0	+ 0
1 0 0 0	− 0	− 7	− 8
1 0 0 1	− 1	− 6	− 7
1 0 1 0	− 2	− 5	− 6
1 0 1 1	− 3	− 4	− 5
1 1 0 0	− 4	− 3	− 4
1 1 0 1	− 5	− 2	− 3
1 1 1 0	− 6	− 1	− 2
1 1 1 1	− 7	− 0	− 1

Figure 2.1   Binary, signed-integer representations.

Hence, the 2's-complement of a number is obtained by adding 1 to the 1's-complement of that number.

Note that there are distinct representations for +0 and −0 in both the sign-and-magnitude and 1's-complement systems, but the 2's-complement system has only one representation for 0. For 4-bit numbers, the value −8 is representable in the 2's-complement system but not in the other systems. The sign-and-magnitude system seems the most natural, because we deal with sign-and-magnitude decimal values in manual computations. The 1's-complement system is easily related to this system, but the 2's-complement system seems unnatural. However, we will show in Section 2.1.3 that the 2's-complement system yields the most efficient way to carry out addition and subtraction operations. It is the one most often used in computers.

2.1.2   ADDITION OF POSITIVE NUMBERS

Consider adding two 1-bit numbers. The results are shown in Figure 2.2. Note that the sum of 1 and 1 requires the 2-bit vector 10 to represent the value 2. We say that the *sum* is 0 and the *carry-out* is 1. In order to add multiple-bit numbers, we use a method analogous to that used for manual computation with decimal numbers. We add bit pairs starting from the low-order (right) end of the bit vectors, propagating carries toward the high-order (left) end.

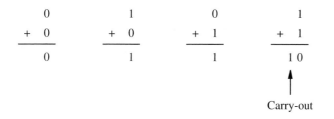

Figure 2.2   Addition of 1-bit numbers.

2.1.3 ADDITION AND SUBTRACTION OF SIGNED NUMBERS

We introduced three systems for representing positive and negative numbers, or, simply, signed numbers. These systems differ only in the way they represent negative values. Their relative merits from the standpoint of ease of performing arithmetic operations can be summarized as follows: The sign-and-magnitude system is the simplest representation, but it is also the most awkward for addition and subtraction operations. The 1's-complement method is somewhat better. The 2's-complement system is the most efficient method for performing addition and subtraction operations.

To understand 2's-complement arithmetic, consider addition modulo N (written as mod N). A helpful graphical device for the description of addition mod N of positive integers is a circle with the N values, 0 through $N - 1$, marked along its perimeter, as shown in Figure 2.3a. Consider the case $N = 16$. The operation $(7 + 4)$ mod 16 yields the value 11. To perform this operation graphically, locate 7 on the circle and then move 4 units in the clockwise direction to arrive at the answer 11. Similarly, $(9 + 14)$ mod $16 = 7$; this is modeled on the circle by locating 9 and moving 14 units in the clockwise direction to arrive at the answer 7. This graphical technique works for the computation of $(a + b)$ mod 16 for any positive numbers a and b, that is, to perform addition, locate a and move b units in the clockwise direction to arrive at $(a + b)$ mod 16.

Now consider a different interpretation of the mod 16 circle. Let the values 0 through 15 be represented by the 4-bit binary vectors $0000, 0001, \ldots, 1111$, according to the binary number system. Then reinterpret these binary vectors to represent the signed numbers from -8 through $+7$ in the 2's-complement method (see Figure 2.1), as shown in Figure 2.3b.

Let us apply the mod 16 addition technique to the simple example of adding $+7$ to -3. The 2's-complement representation for these numbers is 0111 and 1101, respectively. To add these numbers, locate 0111 on the circle in Figure 2.3b. Then move 1101 (13) steps in the clockwise direction to arrive at 0100, which yields the correct answer of $+4$. If we perform this addition by adding bit pairs from right to left, we obtain

$$
\begin{array}{r}
0\,1\,1\,1 \\
+\,1\,1\,0\,1 \\
\hline
1\ 0\,1\,0\,0 \\
\end{array}
$$
↑
Carry-out

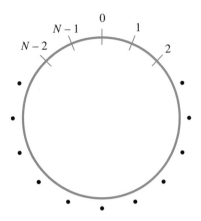

(a) Circle representation of integers mod N

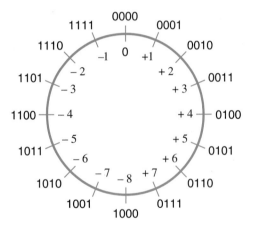

(b) Mod 16 system for 2's-complement numbers

Figure 2.3   Modular number systems and the 2's-complement system.

Note that if we ignore the carry-out from the fourth bit position in this addition, we obtain the correct answer. In fact, this is always the case. Ignoring this carry-out is a natural result of using mod N arithmetic. As we move around the circle in Figure 2.3*b*, the value next to 1111 would normally be 10000. Instead, we go back to the value 0000.

We now state the rules governing the addition and subtraction of n-bit signed numbers using the 2's-complement representation system.

1. To *add* two numbers, add their n-bit representations, ignoring the carry-out signal from the *most significant bit* (MSB) position. The sum will be the algebraically correct value in the 2's-complement representation as long as the answer is in the range -2^{n-1} through $+2^{n-1} - 1$.

2. To *subtract* two numbers X and Y, that is, to perform $X - Y$, form the 2's-complement of Y and then add it to X, as in rule 1. Again, the result will be the algebraically correct value in the 2's-complement representation system if the answer is in the range -2^{n-1} through $+2^{n-1} - 1$.

Figure 2.4 shows some examples of addition and subtraction. In all these 4-bit examples, the answers fall into the representable range of -8 through $+7$. When answers do not fall within the representable range, we say that arithmetic overflow has occurred. The next section discusses such situations. The four addition operations (*a*) through (*d*) in Figure 2.4 follow rule 1, and the six subtraction operations (*e*) through (*j*) follow rule 2. The subtraction operation requires the subtrahend (the bottom value) to be

(a)
```
   0 0 1 0    (+2)
 + 0 0 1 1    (+3)
 ─────────
   0 1 0 1    (+5)
```

(b)
```
   0 1 0 0    (+4)
 + 1 0 1 0    (-6)
 ─────────
   1 1 1 0    (-2)
```

(c)
```
   1 0 1 1    (-5)
 + 1 1 1 0    (-2)
 ─────────
   1 0 0 1    (-7)
```

(d)
```
   0 1 1 1    (+7)
 + 1 1 0 1    (-3)
 ─────────
   0 1 0 0    (+4)
```

(e)
```
   1 1 0 1    (-3)            1 1 0 1
 - 1 0 0 1    (-7)    ⟹    + 0 1 1 1
 ─────────                 ─────────
                             0 1 0 0    (+4)
```

(f)
```
   0 0 1 0    (+2)            0 0 1 0
 - 0 1 0 0    (+4)    ⟹    + 1 1 0 0
 ─────────                 ─────────
                             1 1 1 0    (-2)
```

(g)
```
   0 1 1 0    (+6)            0 1 1 0
 - 0 0 1 1    (+3)    ⟹    + 1 1 0 1
 ─────────                 ─────────
                             0 0 1 1    (+3)
```

(h)
```
   1 0 0 1    (-7)            1 0 0 1
 - 1 0 1 1    (-5)    ⟹    + 0 1 0 1
 ─────────                 ─────────
                             1 1 1 0    (-2)
```

(i)
```
   1 0 0 1    (-7)            1 0 0 1
 - 0 0 0 1    (+1)    ⟹    + 1 1 1 1
 ─────────                 ─────────
                             1 0 0 0    (-8)
```

(j)
```
   0 0 1 0    (+2)            0 0 1 0
 - 1 1 0 1    (-3)    ⟹    + 0 0 1 1
 ─────────                 ─────────
                             0 1 0 1    (+5)
```

Figure 2.4 2's-complement add and subtract operations.

2's-complemented. This operation is done in exactly the same manner for both positive and negative numbers.

We often need to represent a number in the 2's-complement system by using a number of bits that is larger than some given size. For a positive number, this is achieved by adding 0s to the left. For a negative number, the leftmost bit, which is the sign bit, is a 1, and a longer number with the same value is obtained by replicating the sign bit to the left as many times as desired. To see why this is correct, examine the mod 16 circle of Figure 2.3b. Compare it to larger circles for the mod 32 or mod 64 cases. The representations for values -1, -2, etc., would be exactly the same, with 1s added to the left. In summary, to represent a signed number in 2's-complement form using a larger number of bits, repeat the sign bit as many times as needed to the left. This operation is called *sign extension*.

The simplicity of either adding or subtracting signed numbers in 2's-complement representation is the reason why this number representation is used in modern computers. It might seem that the 1's-complement representation would be just as good as the 2's-complement system. However, although complementation is easy, the result obtained after an addition operation is not always correct. The carry-out, c_n, cannot be ignored. If $c_n = 0$, the result obtained is correct. If $c_n = 1$, then a 1 must be added to the result to make it correct. The need for this correction cycle, which is conditional on the carry-out from the add operation, means that addition and subtraction cannot be implemented as conveniently in the 1's-complement system as in the 2's-complement system.

2.1.4 OVERFLOW IN INTEGER ARITHMETIC

In the 2's-complement number representation system, n bits can represent values in the range -2^{n-1} to $+2^{n-1} - 1$. For example, using four bits, the range of numbers that can be represented is -8 through $+7$, as shown in Figure 2.1. When the result of an arithmetic operation is outside the representable range, an *arithmetic overflow* has occurred.

When adding unsigned numbers, the carry-out, c_n, from the most significant bit position serves as the overflow indicator. However, this does not work for adding signed numbers. For example, when using 4-bit signed numbers, if we try to add the numbers $+7$ and $+4$, the output sum vector, S, is 1011, which is the code for -5, an incorrect result. The carry-out signal from the MSB position is 0. Similarly, if we try to add -4 and -6, we get $S = 0110 = +6$, another incorrect result, and in this case, the carry-out signal is 1. Thus, overflow may occur if both summands have the same sign. Clearly, the addition of numbers with different signs cannot cause overflow. This leads to the following conclusions:

1. Overflow can occur only when adding two numbers that have the same sign.

2. The carry-out signal from the sign-bit position is not a sufficient indicator of overflow when adding signed numbers.

A simple way to detect overflow is to examine the signs of the two summands X and Y and the sign of the result. When both operands X and Y have the same sign, an overflow occurs when the sign of S is not the same as the signs of X and Y.

2.1.5 CHARACTERS

In addition to numbers, computers must be able to handle nonnumeric text information consisting of characters. Characters can be letters of the alphabet, decimal digits, punctuation marks, and so on. They are represented by codes that are usually eight bits long. One of the most widely used such codes is the American Standards Committee on Information Interchange (ASCII) code described in Appendix E.

2.2 MEMORY LOCATIONS AND ADDRESSES

Number and character operands, as well as instructions, are stored in the memory of a computer. We will now consider how the memory is organized. The memory consists of many millions of storage *cells,* each of which can store a bit of information having the value 0 or 1. Because a single bit represents a very small amount of information, bits are seldom handled individually. The usual approach is to deal with them in groups of fixed size. For this purpose, the memory is organized so that a group of n bits can be stored or retrieved in a single, basic operation. Each group of n bits is referred to as a *word* of information, and n is called the *word length*. The memory of a computer can be schematically represented as a collection of words as shown in Figure 2.5.

Modern computers have word lengths that typically range from 16 to 64 bits. If the word length of a computer is 32 bits, a single word can store a 32-bit 2's-complement number or four ASCII characters, each occupying 8 bits, as shown in Figure 2.6. A unit of 8 bits is called a *byte*. Machine instructions may require one or more words for their representation. We will discuss how machine instructions are encoded into memory words in a later section after we have described instructions at the assembly language level.

Accessing the memory to store or retrieve a single item of information, either a word or a byte, requires distinct names or *addresses* for each item location. It is customary to use numbers from 0 through $2^k - 1$, for some suitable value of k, as the addresses of successive locations in the memory. The 2^k addresses constitute the *address space* of the computer, and the memory can have up to 2^k addressable locations. For example, a 24-bit address generates an address space of 2^{24} (16,777,216) locations. This number is usually written as 16M (16 mega), where 1M is the number 2^{20} (1,048,576). A 32-bit address creates an address space of 2^{32} or 4G (4 giga) locations, where 1G is 2^{30}. Other notational conventions that are commonly used are K (kilo) for the number 2^{10} (1,024), and T (tera) for the number 2^{40}.

2.2.1 BYTE ADDRESSABILITY

We now have three basic information quantities to deal with: the bit, byte, and word. A byte is always 8 bits, but the word length typically ranges from 16 to 64 bits. It is impractical to assign distinct addresses to individual bit locations in the memory. The most practical assignment is to have successive addresses refer to successive byte

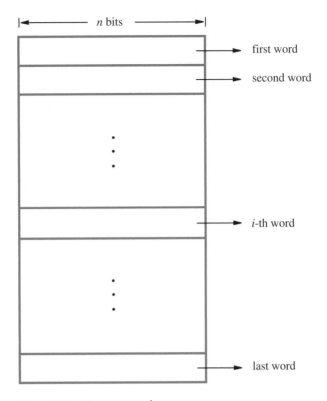

Figure 2.5   Memory words.

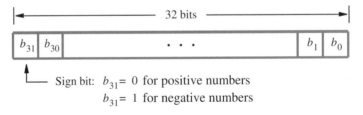

(a) A signed integer

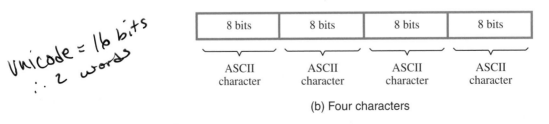

(b) Four characters

Figure 2.6· Examples of encoded information in a 32-bit word.

Unicode = 16 bits
∴ 2 words

locations in the memory. This is the assignment used in most modern computers, and is the one we will normally use in this book. The term *byte-addressable memory* is used for this assignment. Byte locations have addresses 0, 1, 2, ... Thus, if the word length of the machine is 32 bits, successive words are located at addresses 0, 4, 8, . . . , with each word consisting of four bytes.

2.2.2 BIG-ENDIAN AND LITTLE-ENDIAN ASSIGNMENTS

There are two ways that byte addresses can be assigned across words, as shown in Figure 2.7. The name *big-endian* is used when lower byte addresses are used for the more significant bytes (the leftmost bytes) of the word. The name *little-endian* is used for the opposite ordering, where the lower byte addresses are used for the less significant bytes (the rightmost bytes) of the word. The words "more significant" and "less significant" are used in relation to the weights (powers of 2) assigned to bits when the word represents a number, as described in Section 2.1.1. Both little-endian and big-endian assignments are used in commercial machines. In both cases, byte addresses 0, 4, 8, . . . , are taken as the addresses of successive words in the memory and are the addresses used when specifying memory read and write operations for words.

In addition to specifying the address ordering of bytes within a word, it is also necessary to specify the labeling of bits within a byte or a word. The most common convention, and the one we will use in this book, is shown in Figure 2.6*a*. It is the

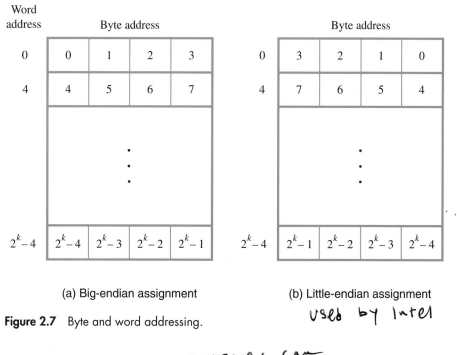

(a) Big-endian assignment   (b) Little-endian assignment

Figure 2.7 Byte and word addressing.

most natural ordering for the encoding of numerical data. The same ordering is also used for labeling bits within a byte, that is, b_7, b_6, . . . , b_0, from left to right. There are computers, however, that use the reverse ordering.

2.2.3 WORD ALIGNMENT

In the case of a 32-bit word length, natural word boundaries occur at addresses 0, 4, 8, . . . , as shown in Figure 2.7. We say that the word locations have *aligned* addresses. In general, words are said to be aligned in memory if they begin at a byte address that is a multiple of the number of bytes in a word. For practical reasons associated with manipulating binary-coded addresses, the number of bytes in a word is a power of 2. Hence, if the word length is 16 (2 bytes), aligned words begin at byte addresses 0, 2, 4, . . . , and for a word length of 64 (2^3 bytes), aligned words begin at byte addresses 0, 8, 16, ...

There is no fundamental reason why words cannot begin at an arbitrary byte address. In that case, words are said to have *unaligned* addresses. While the most common case is to use aligned addresses, some computers allow the use of unaligned word addresses.

2.2.4 ACCESSING NUMBERS, CHARACTERS, AND CHARACTER STRINGS

A number usually occupies one word. It can be accessed in the memory by specifying its word address. Similarly, individual characters can be accessed by their byte address.

In many applications, it is necessary to handle character strings of variable length. The beginning of the string is indicated by giving the address of the byte containing its first character. Successive byte locations contain successive characters of the string. There are two ways to indicate the length of the string. A special control character with the meaning "end of string" can be used as the last character in the string, or a separate memory word location or processor register can contain a number indicating the length of the string in bytes.

2.3 MEMORY OPERATIONS

Both program instructions and data operands are stored in the memory. To execute an instruction, the processor control circuits must cause the word (or words) containing the instruction to be transferred from the memory to the processor. Operands and results must also be moved between the memory and the processor. Thus, two basic operations involving the memory are needed, namely, *Load* (or *Read* or *Fetch*) and *Store* (or *Write*).

The Load operation transfers a copy of the contents of a specific memory location to the processor. The memory contents remain unchanged. To start a Load operation, the processor sends the address of the desired location to the memory and requests that its contents be read. The memory reads the data stored at that address and sends them to the processor.

The Store operation transfers an item of information from the processor to a specific memory location, destroying the former contents of that location. The processor sends the address of the desired location to the memory, together with the data to be written into that location.

An information item of either one word or one byte can be transferred between the processor and the memory in a single operation. As described in Chapter 1, the processor contains a small number of registers, each capable of holding a word. These registers are either the source or the destination of a transfer to or from the memory. When a byte is transferred, it is usually located in the low-order (rightmost) byte position of the register.

The details of the hardware implementation of these operations are treated in Chapters 5 and 7. In this chapter, we are taking the ISA viewpoint, so we concentrate on the logical handling of instructions and operands. Specific hardware components, such as processor registers, are discussed only to the extent necessary to understand the execution of machine instructions and programs.

2.4 INSTRUCTIONS AND INSTRUCTION SEQUENCING

The tasks carried out by a computer program consist of a sequence of small steps, such as adding two numbers, testing for a particular condition, reading a character from the keyboard, or sending a character to be displayed on a display screen. A computer must have instructions capable of performing four types of operations:

- Data transfers between the memory and the processor registers
- Arithmetic and logic operations on data
- Program sequencing and control
- I/O transfers

We begin by discussing the first two types of instructions. To facilitate the discussion, we need some notation which we present first.

2.4.1 REGISTER TRANSFER NOTATION

We need to describe the transfer of information from one location in the computer to another. Possible locations that may be involved in such transfers are memory locations, processor registers, or registers in the I/O subsystem. Most of the time, we identify a location by a symbolic name standing for its hardware binary address. For example, names for the addresses of memory locations may be LOC, PLACE, A, VAR2; processor register names may be R0, R5; and I/O register names may be DATAIN, OUTSTATUS, and so on. The contents of a location are denoted by placing square brackets around the name of the location. Thus, the expression

$$R1 \leftarrow [LOC]$$

means that the contents of memory location LOC are transferred into processor register R1.

As another example, consider the operation that adds the contents of registers R1 and R2, and then places their sum into register R3. This action is indicated as

$$R3 \leftarrow [R1] + [R2]$$

This type of notation is known as *Register Transfer Notation* (RTN). Note that the right-hand side of an RTN expression always denotes a value, and the left-hand side is the name of a location where the value is to be placed, overwriting the old contents of that location.

2.4.2 ASSEMBLY LANGUAGE NOTATION

We need another type of notation to represent machine instructions and programs. For this, we use an *assembly language* format. For example, an instruction that causes the transfer described above, from memory location LOC to processor register R1, is specified by the statement

Move   LOC,R1

The contents of LOC are unchanged by the execution of this instruction, but the old contents of register R1 are overwritten.

The second example of adding two numbers contained in processor registers R1 and R2 and placing their sum in R3 can be specified by the assembly language statement

Add   R1,R2,R3

2.4.3 BASIC INSTRUCTION TYPES

The operation of adding two numbers is a fundamental capability in any computer. The statement

$$C = A + B$$

in a high-level language program is a command to the computer to add the current values of the two variables called A and B, and to assign the sum to a third variable, C. When the program containing this statement is compiled, the three variables, A, B, and C, are assigned to distinct locations in the memory. We will use the variable names to refer to the corresponding memory location addresses. The contents of these locations represent the values of the three variables. Hence, the above high-level language statement requires the action

$$C \leftarrow [A] + [B]$$

to take place in the computer. To carry out this action, the contents of memory locations A and B are fetched from the memory and transferred into the processor where their sum is computed. This result is then sent back to the memory and stored in location C.

Let us first assume that this action is to be accomplished by a single machine instruction. Furthermore, assume that this instruction contains the memory addresses of the three operands — A, B, and C. This *three-address* instruction can be represented symbolically as

$$\text{Add} \quad \text{A,B,C}$$

Operands A and B are called the *source* operands, C is called the *destination* operand, and Add is the operation to be performed on the operands. A general instruction of this type has the format

$$\text{Operation} \quad \text{Source1,Source2,Destination}$$

If k bits are needed to specify the memory address of each operand, the encoded form of the above instruction must contain $3k$ bits for addressing purposes in addition to the bits needed to denote the Add operation. For a modern processor with a 32-bit address space, a 3-address instruction is too large to fit in one word for a reasonable word length. Thus, a format that allows multiple words to be used for a single instruction would be needed to represent an instruction of this type.

An alternative approach is to use a sequence of simpler instructions to perform the same task, with each instruction having only one or two operands. Suppose that *two-address* instructions of the form

$$\text{Operation} \quad \text{Source,Destination}$$

are available. An Add instruction of this type is

$$\text{Add} \quad \text{A,B}$$

which performs the operation $B \leftarrow [A] + [B]$. When the sum is calculated, the result is sent to the memory and stored in location B, replacing the original contents of this location. This means that operand B is both a source and a destination.

A single two-address instruction cannot be used to solve our original problem, which is to add the contents of locations A and B, without destroying either of them, and to place the sum in location C. The problem can be solved by using another two-address instruction that copies the contents of one memory location into another. Such an instruction is

$$\text{Move} \quad \text{B,C}$$

which performs the operation $C \leftarrow [B]$, leaving the contents of location B unchanged. The word "Move" is a misnomer here; it should be "Copy." However, this instruction name is deeply entrenched in computer nomenclature. The operation $C \leftarrow [A] + [B]$

can now be performed by the two-instruction sequence

$$\text{Move} \quad \text{B,C}$$
$$\text{Add} \quad \text{A,C}$$

In all the instructions given above, the source operands are specified first, followed by the destination. This order is used in the assembly language expressions for machine instructions in many computers. But there are also many computers in which the order of the source and destination operands is reversed. We will see examples of both orderings in Chapter 3. It is unfortunate that no single convention has been adopted by all manufacturers. In fact, even for a particular computer, its assembly language may use a different order for different instructions. In this chapter, we will continue to give the source operands first.

We have defined three- and two-address instructions. But, even two-address instructions will not normally fit into one word for usual word lengths and address sizes. Another possibility is to have machine instructions that specify only one memory operand. When a second operand is needed, as in the case of an Add instruction, it is understood implicitly to be in a unique location. A processor register, usually called the *accumulator,* may be used for this purpose. Thus, the *one-address* instruction

$$\text{Add} \quad \text{A}$$

means the following: Add the contents of memory location A to the contents of the accumulator register and place the sum back into the accumulator. Let us also introduce the one-address instructions

$$\text{Load} \quad \text{A}$$

and

$$\text{Store} \quad \text{A}$$

The Load instruction copies the contents of memory location A into the accumulator, and the Store instruction copies the contents of the accumulator into memory location A. Using only one-address instructions, the operation $C \leftarrow [A] + [B]$ can be performed by executing the sequence of instructions

$$\text{Load} \quad \text{A}$$
$$\text{Add} \quad \text{B}$$
$$\text{Store} \quad \text{C}$$

Note that the operand specified in the instruction may be a source or a destination, depending on the instruction. In the Load instruction, address A specifies the source operand, and the destination location, the accumulator, is implied. On the other hand, C denotes the destination location in the Store instruction, whereas the source, the accumulator, is implied.

Some early computers were designed around a single accumulator structure. Most modern computers have a number of general-purpose processor registers — typically 8 to 32, and even considerably more in some cases. Access to data in these registers is much faster than to data stored in memory locations because the registers are inside the processor. Because the number of registers is relatively small, only a few bits are needed to specify which register takes part in an operation. For example, for 32 registers, only 5 bits are needed. This is much less than the number of bits needed to give the address of a location in the memory. Because the use of registers allows faster processing and results in shorter instructions, registers are used to store data temporarily in the processor during processing.

Let R*i* represent a general-purpose register. The instructions

$$\text{Load} \quad \text{A,R}i$$

$$\text{Store} \quad \text{R}i\text{,A}$$

and

$$\text{Add} \quad \text{A,R}i$$

are generalizations of the Load, Store, and Add instructions for the single-accumulator case, in which register R*i* performs the function of the accumulator. Even in these cases, when only one memory address is directly specified in an instruction, the instruction may not fit into one word.

When a processor has several general-purpose registers, many instructions involve only operands that are in the registers. In fact, in many modern processors, computations can be performed directly only on data held in processor registers. Instructions such as

$$\text{Add} \quad \text{R}i\text{,R}j$$

or

$$\text{Add} \quad \text{R}i\text{,R}j\text{,R}k$$

are of this type. In both of these instructions, the source operands are the contents of registers R*i* and R*j*. In the first instruction, R*j* also serves as the destination register, whereas in the second instruction, a third register, R*k*, is used as the destination. Such instructions, where only register names are contained in the instruction, will normally fit into one word.

It is often necessary to transfer data between different locations. This is achieved with the instruction

$$\text{Move} \quad \text{Source,Destination}$$

which places a copy of the contents of Source into Destination. When data are moved to or from a processor register, the Move instruction can be used rather than the Load or Store instructions because the order of the source and destination operands determines which operation is intended. Thus,

$$\text{Move} \quad \text{A,R}i$$

is the same as

$$\text{Load} \quad \text{A,R}i$$

and

$$\text{Move} \quad \text{R}i\text{,A}$$

is the same as

Store   Ri,A

In this chapter, we will use Move instead of Load or Store.

In processors where arithmetic operations are allowed only on operands that are in processor registers, the C = A + B task can be performed by the instruction sequence

Move   A,Ri

Move   B,Rj

Add   Ri,Rj

Move   Rj,C

In processors where one operand may be in the memory but the other must be in a register, an instruction sequence for the required task would be

Move   A,Ri

Add   B,Ri

Move   Ri,C

The speed with which a given task is carried out depends on the time it takes to transfer instructions from memory into the processor and to access the operands referenced by these instructions. Transfers that involve the memory are much slower than transfers within the processor. Hence, a substantial increase in speed is achieved when several operations are performed in succession on data in processor registers without the need to copy data to or from the memory. When machine language programs are generated by compilers from high-level languages, it is important to minimize the frequency with which data is moved back and forth between the memory and processor registers.

We have discussed three-, two-, and one-address instructions. It is also possible to use instructions in which the locations of all operands are defined implicitly. Such instructions are found in machines that store operands in a structure called a *pushdown stack*. In this case, the instructions are called *zero-address* instructions. The concept of a pushdown stack is introduced in Section 2.8, and a computer that uses this approach is discussed in Chapter 11.

2.4.4 INSTRUCTION EXECUTION AND STRAIGHT-LINE SEQUENCING

In the preceding discussion of instruction formats, we used the task C ← [A] + [B] for illustration. Figure 2.8 shows a possible program segment for this task as it appears in the memory of a computer. We have assumed that the computer allows one memory operand per instruction and has a number of processor registers. We assume that the word length is 32 bits and the memory is byte addressable. The three instructions of the program are in successive word locations, starting at location i. Since each instruction is 4 bytes long, the second and third instructions start at addresses $i + 4$ and $i + 8$. For simplicity, we also assume that a full memory address can be directly specified in a single-word instruction, although this is not usually possible for address space sizes and word lengths of current processors.

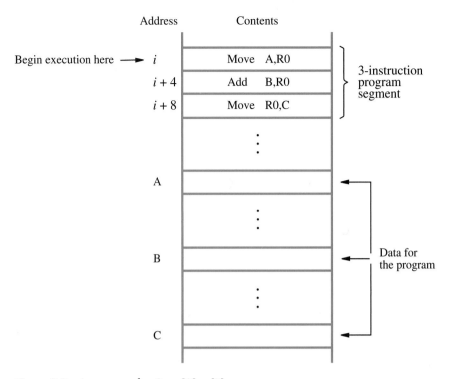

Figure 2.8 A program for C ← [A] + [B].

Let us consider how this program is executed. The processor contains a register called the *program counter* (PC), which holds the address of the instruction to be executed next. To begin executing a program, the address of its first instruction (*i* in our example) must be placed into the PC. Then, the processor control circuits use the information in the PC to fetch and execute instructions, one at a time, in the order of increasing addresses. This is called *straight-line sequencing*. During the execution of each instruction, the PC is incremented by 4 to point to the next instruction. Thus, after the Move instruction at location *i* + 8 is executed, the PC contains the value *i* + 12, which is the address of the first instruction of the next program segment.

Executing a given instruction is a two-phase procedure. In the first phase, called *instruction fetch*, the instruction is fetched from the memory location whose address is in the PC. This instruction is placed in the *instruction register* (IR) in the processor. At the start of the second phase, called *instruction execute*, the instruction in IR is examined to determine which operation is to be performed. The specified operation is then performed by the processor. This often involves fetching operands from the memory or from processor registers, performing an arithmetic or logic operation, and storing the result in the destination location. At some point during this two-phase procedure, the contents of the PC are advanced to point to the next instruction. When the execute phase of an instruction is completed, the PC contains the address of the next instruction, and a new instruction fetch phase can begin. In most processors, the execute phase itself is divided into a small number of distinct phases corresponding to fetching operands, performing the operation, and storing the result.

2.4.5 BRANCHING

Consider the task of adding a list of n numbers. The program outlined in Figure 2.9 is a generalization of the program in Figure 2.8. The addresses of the memory locations containing the n numbers are symbolically given as NUM1, NUM2, ..., NUMn, and a separate Add instruction is used to add each number to the contents of register R0. After all the numbers have been added, the result is placed in memory location SUM.

Instead of using a long list of Add instructions, it is possible to place a single Add instruction in a program loop, as shown in Figure 2.10. The loop is a straight-line sequence of instructions executed as many times as needed. It starts at location LOOP and ends at the instruction Branch>0. During each pass through this loop, the address of

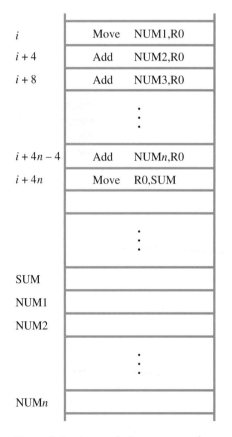

Figure 2.9 A straight-line program for adding n numbers.

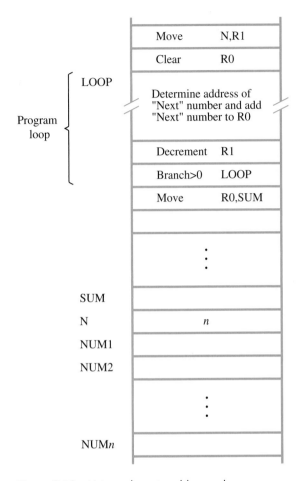

Figure 2.10 Using a loop to add *n* numbers.

the next list entry is determined, and that entry is fetched and added to R0. The address of an operand can be specified in various ways, as will be described in Section 2.5. For now, we concentrate on how to create and control a program loop.

Assume that the number of entries in the list, *n*, is stored in memory location N, as shown. Register R1 is used as a counter to determine the number of times the loop is executed. Hence, the contents of location N are loaded into register R1 at the beginning of the program. Then, within the body of the loop, the instruction

Decrement   R1

reduces the contents of R1 by 1 each time through the loop. (A similar type of operation is performed by an Increment instruction, which adds 1 to its operand.) Execution of the loop is repeated as long as the result of the decrement operation is greater than zero.

We now introduce *branch* instructions. This type of instruction loads a new value into the program counter. As a result, the processor fetches and executes the instruction at this new address, called the *branch target,* instead of the instruction at the location that follows the branch instruction in sequential address order. A *conditional branch* instruction causes a branch only if a specified condition is satisfied. If the condition is not satisfied, the PC is incremented in the normal way, and the next instruction in sequential address order is fetched and executed.

In the program in Figure 2.10, the instruction

$$\text{Branch}>0 \quad \text{LOOP}$$

(branch if greater than 0) is a conditional branch instruction that causes a branch to location LOOP if the result of the immediately preceding instruction, which is the decremented value in register R1, is greater than zero. This means that the loop is repeated as long as there are entries in the list that are yet to be added to R0. At the end of the nth pass through the loop, the Decrement instruction produces a value of zero, and, hence, branching does not occur. Instead, the Move instruction is fetched and executed. It moves the final result from R0 into memory location SUM.

The capability to test conditions and subsequently choose one of a set of alternative ways to continue computation has many more applications than just loop control. Such a capability is found in the instruction sets of all computers and is fundamental to the programming of most nontrivial tasks.

2.4.6 CONDITION CODES

The processor keeps track of information about the results of various operations for use by subsequent conditional branch instructions. This is accomplished by recording the required information in individual bits, often called *condition code flags*. These flags are usually grouped together in a special processor register called the *condition code register* or *status register*. Individual condition code flags are set to 1 or cleared to 0, depending on the outcome of the operation performed.

Four commonly used flags are

N (negative)   Set to 1 if the result is negative; otherwise, cleared to 0

Z (zero)   Set to 1 if the result is 0; otherwise, cleared to 0

V (overflow)   Set to 1 if arithmetic overflow occurs; otherwise, cleared to 0

C (carry)   Set to 1 if a carry-out results from the operation; otherwise, cleared to 0

The N and Z flags indicate whether the result of an arithmetic or logic operation is negative or zero. The N and Z flags may also be affected by instructions that transfer data, such as Move, Load, or Store. This makes it possible for a later conditional branch instruction to cause a branch based on the sign and value of the operand that was moved. Some computers also provide a special Test instruction that examines a value in a register or in the memory and sets or clears the N and Z flags accordingly.

The V flag indicates whether overflow has taken place. As explained in Section 2.1.4, overflow occurs when the result of an arithmetic operation is outside the range of values that can be represented by the number of bits available for the operands. The processor sets the V flag to allow the programmer to test whether overflow has occurred and branch to an appropriate routine that corrects the problem. Instructions such as BranchIfOverflow are provided for this purpose. Also, as we will see in Chapter 4, a program interrupt may occur automatically as a result of the V bit being set, and the operating system will resolve what to do.

The C flag is set to 1 if a carry occurs from the most significant bit position during an arithmetic operation. This flag makes it possible to perform arithmetic operations on operands that are longer than the word length of the processor. Such operations are used in multiple-precision arithmetic, which is discussed in Chapter 6.

The instruction Branch>0, discussed in Section 2.4.5, is an example of a branch instruction that tests one or more of the condition flags. It causes a branch if the value tested is neither negative nor equal to zero. That is, the branch is taken if neither N nor Z is 1. Many other conditional branch instructions are provided to enable a variety of conditions to be tested. The conditions are given as logic expressions involving the condition code flags.

In some computers, the condition code flags are affected automatically by instructions that perform arithmetic or logic operations. However, this is not always the case. A number of computers have two versions of an Add instruction, for example. One version, Add, does not affect the flags, but a second version, AddSetCC, does. This provides the programmer — and the compiler — with more flexibility when preparing programs for pipelined execution, as we will discuss in Chapter 8.

2.4.7 GENERATING MEMORY ADDRESSES

Let us return to Figure 2.10. The purpose of the instruction block at LOOP is to add a different number from the list during each pass through the loop. Hence, the Add instruction in that block must refer to a different address during each pass. How are the addresses to be specified? The memory operand address cannot be given directly in a single Add instruction in the loop. Otherwise, it would need to be modified on each pass through the loop. As one possibility, suppose that a processor register, Ri, is used to hold the memory address of an operand. If it is initially loaded with the address NUM1 before the loop is entered and is then incremented by 4 on each pass through the loop, it can provide the needed capability.

This situation, and many others like it, give rise to the need for flexible ways to specify the address of an operand. The instruction set of a computer typically provides a number of such methods, called *addressing modes*. While the details differ from one computer to another, the underlying concepts are the same. We will discuss these in the next section.

2.5 ADDRESSING MODES

We have now seen some simple examples of assembly language programs. In general, a program operates on data that reside in the computer's memory. These data can be organized in a variety of ways. If we want to keep track of students' names, we can write them in a list. If we want to associate information with each name, for example to record telephone numbers or marks in various courses, we may organize this information in the form of a table. Programmers use organizations called *data structures* to represent the data used in computations. These include lists, linked lists, arrays, queues, and so on.

Programs are normally written in a high-level language, which enables the programmer to use constants, local and global variables, pointers, and arrays. When translating a high-level language program into assembly language, the compiler must be able to implement these constructs using the facilities provided in the instruction set of the computer in which the program will be run. The different ways in which the location of an operand is specified in an instruction are referred to as *addressing modes*. In this section we present the most important addressing modes found in modern processors. A summary is provided in Table 2.1.

Table 2.1   Generic addressing modes

Name	Assembler syntax	Addressing function
Immediate	#Value	Operand = Value
Register	Ri	EA = Ri
Absolute (Direct)	LOC	EA = LOC
Indirect	(Ri) (LOC)	EA = [Ri] EA = [LOC]
Index	X(Ri)	EA = [Ri] + X
Base with index	(Ri,Rj)	EA = [Ri] + [Rj]
Base with index and offset	X(Ri,Rj)	EA = [Ri] + [Rj] + X
Relative	X(PC)	EA = [PC] + X
Autoincrement	(Ri)+	EA = [Ri]; Increment Ri
Autodecrement	−(Ri)	Decrement Ri; EA = [Ri]

( ) indicates pointers

EA = effective address
Value = a signed number

2.5.1 IMPLEMENTATION OF VARIABLES AND CONSTANTS

Variables and constants are the simplest data types and are found in almost every computer program. In assembly language, a variable is represented by allocating a register or a memory location to hold its value. Thus, the value can be changed as needed using appropriate instructions.

The programs in Section 2.4 used only two addressing modes to access variables. We accessed an operand by specifying the name of the register or the address of the memory location where the operand is located. The precise definitions of these two modes are:

Register mode — The operand is the contents of a processor register; the name (address) of the register is given in the instruction.

Absolute mode — The operand is in a memory location; the address of this location is given explicitly in the instruction. (In some assembly languages, this mode is called *Direct*.)

The instruction

$$\text{Move} \quad \text{LOC,R2}$$

uses these two modes. Processor registers are used as temporary storage locations where the data in a register are accessed using the Register mode. The Absolute mode can represent global variables in a program. A declaration such as

$$\text{Integer A, B;}$$

in a high-level language program will cause the compiler to allocate a memory location to each of the variables A and B. Whenever they are referenced later in the program, the compiler can generate assembly language instructions that use the Absolute mode to access these variables.

Next, let us consider the representation of constants. Address and data constants can be represented in assembly language using the Immediate mode.

Immediate mode — The operand is given explicitly in the instruction.

For example, the instruction

$$\text{Move} \quad 200_{immediate}, \text{R0}$$

places the value 200 in register R0. Clearly, the Immediate mode is only used to specify the value of a source operand. Using a subscript to denote the Immediate mode is not appropriate in assembly languages. A common convention is to use the sharp sign (#) in front of the value to indicate that this value is to be used as an immediate operand. Hence, we write the instruction above in the form

$$\text{Move} \quad \text{\#200,R0}$$

Constant values are used frequently in high-level language programs. For example, the statement

$$A = B + 6$$

contains the constant 6. Assuming that A and B have been declared earlier as variables and may be accessed using the Absolute mode, this statement may be compiled as follows:

$$\text{Move}\quad \text{B,R1}$$
$$\text{Add}\quad \text{\#6,R1}$$
$$\text{Move}\quad \text{R1,A}$$

Constants are also used in assembly language to increment a counter, test for some bit pattern, and so on.

2.5.2 INDIRECTION AND POINTERS

In the addressing modes that follow, the instruction does not give the operand or its address explicitly. Instead, it provides information from which the memory address of the operand can be determined. We refer to this address as the *effective address* (EA) of the operand.

> *Indirect mode* — The effective address of the operand is the contents of a register or memory location whose address appears in the instruction.

We denote indirection by placing the name of the register or the memory address given in the instruction in parentheses as illustrated in Figure 2.11 and Table 2.1.

To execute the Add instruction in Figure 2.11*a*, the processor uses the value B, which is in register R1, as the effective address of the operand. It requests a read operation from the memory to read the contents of location B. The value read is the desired operand, which the processor adds to the contents of register R0. Indirect addressing through a memory location is also possible as shown in Figure 2.11*b*. In this case, the processor first reads the contents of memory location A, then requests a

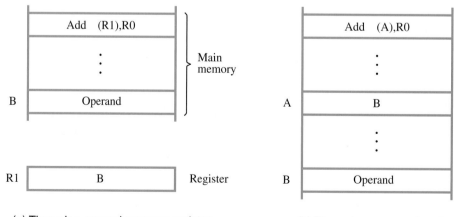

(a) Through a general-purpose register   (b) Through a memory location

Figure 2.11   Indirect addressing.

Address	Contents		
	Move	N,R1	Initialization
	Move	#NUM1,R2	
	Clear	R0	
LOOP	Add	(R2),R0	
	Add	#4,R2	
	Decrement	R1	
	Branch>0	LOOP	
	Move	R0,SUM	

Figure 2.12 Use of indirect addressing in the program of Figure 2.10.

second read operation using the value B as an address to obtain the operand.

The register or memory location that contains the address of an operand is called a *pointer*. Indirection and the use of pointers are important and powerful concepts in programming. Consider the analogy of a treasure hunt: In the instructions for the hunt you may be told to go to a house at a given address. Instead of finding the treasure there, you find a note that gives you another address where you will find the treasure. By changing the note, the location of the treasure can be changed, but the instructions for the hunt remain the same. Changing the note is equivalent to changing the contents of a pointer in a computer program. For example, by changing the contents of register R1 or location A in Figure 2.11, the same Add instruction fetches different operands to add to register R0.

Let us now return to the program in Figure 2.10 for adding a list of numbers. Indirect addressing can be used to access successive numbers in the list, resulting in the program shown in Figure 2.12. Register R2 is used as a pointer to the numbers in the list, and the operands are accessed indirectly through R2. The initialization section of the program loads the counter value *n* from memory location N into R1 and uses the Immediate addressing mode to place the address value NUM1, which is the address of the first number in the list, into R2. Then it clears R0 to 0. The first two instructions in the loop in Figure 2.12 implement the unspecified instruction block starting at LOOP in Figure 2.10. The first time through the loop, the instruction

$$\text{Add} \quad \text{(R2),R0}$$

fetches the operand at location NUM1 and adds it to R0. The second Add instruction adds 4 to the contents of the pointer R2, so that it will contain the address value NUM2 when the above instruction is executed in the second pass through the loop.

Consider the C-language statement

$$A = {}^*B;$$

where B is a pointer variable. This statement may be compiled into

$$\text{Move} \quad \text{B,R1}$$
$$\text{Move} \quad \text{(R1),A}$$

Using indirect addressing through memory, the same action can be achieved with

Move   (B),A

Despite its apparent simplicity, indirect addressing through memory has proven to be of limited usefulness as an addressing mode, and it is seldom found in modern computers. We will see in Chapter 8 that an instruction that involves accessing the memory twice to get an operand is not well suited to pipelined execution.

Indirect addressing through registers is used extensively. The program in Figure 2.12 shows the flexibility it provides. Also, when absolute addressing is not available, indirect addressing through registers makes it possible to access global variables by first loading the operand's address in a register.

2.5.3 INDEXING AND ARRAYS

The next addressing mode we discuss provides a different kind of flexibility for accessing operands. It is useful in dealing with lists and arrays.

> *Index mode* — The effective address of the operand is generated by adding a constant value to the contents of a register.

The register used may be either a special register provided for this purpose, or, more commonly, it may be any one of a set of general-purpose registers in the processor. In either case, it is referred to as an *index register*. We indicate the Index mode symbolically as

$$X(Ri)$$

where X denotes the constant value contained in the instruction and Ri is the name of the register involved. The effective address of the operand is given by

$$EA = X + [Ri]$$

The contents of the index register are not changed in the process of generating the effective address.

In an assembly language program, the constant X may be given either as an explicit number or as a symbolic name representing a numerical value. The way in which a symbolic name is associated with a specific numerical value will be discussed in Section 2.6. When the instruction is translated into machine code, the constant X is given as a part of the instruction and is usually represented by fewer bits than the word length of the computer. Since X is a signed integer, it must be sign-extended (see Section 2.1.3) to the register length before being added to the contents of the register.

Figure 2.13 illustrates two ways of using the Index mode. In Figure 2.13*a*, the index register, R1, contains the address of a memory location, and the value X defines an *offset* (also called a *displacement*) from this address to the location where the operand is found. An alternative use is illustrated in Figure 2.13*b*. Here, the constant X corresponds to a memory address, and the contents of the index register define the offset to the operand. In either case, the effective address is the sum of two values; one is given explicitly in the instruction, and the other is stored in a register.

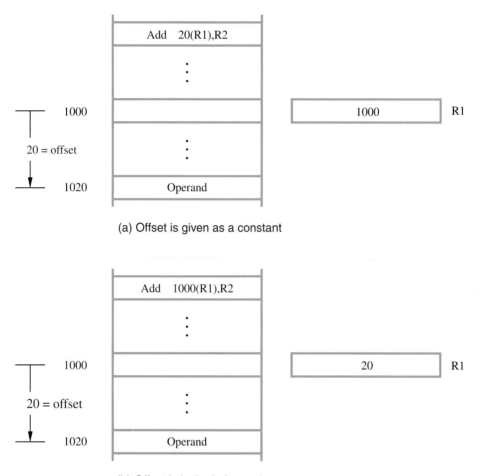

(a) Offset is given as a constant

(b) Offset is in the index register

Figure 2.13   Indexed addressing.

To see the usefulness of indexed addressing, consider a simple example involving a list of test scores for students taking a given course. Assume that the list of scores, beginning at location LIST, is structured as shown in Figure 2.14. A four-word memory block comprises a record that stores the relevant information for each student. Each record consists of the student's identification number (ID), followed by the scores the student earned on three tests. There are n students in the class, and the value n is stored in location N immediately in front of the list. The addresses given in the figure for the student IDs and test scores assume that the memory is byte addressable and that the word length is 32 bits.

We should note that the list in Figure 2.14 represents a two-dimensional array having n rows and four columns. Each row contains the entries for one student, and the columns give the IDs and test scores.

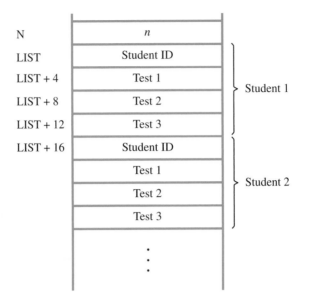

Figure 2.14   A list of students' marks.

Suppose that we wish to compute the sum of all scores obtained on each of the tests and store these three sums in memory locations SUM1, SUM2, and SUM3. A possible program for this task is given in Figure 2.15. In the body of the loop, the program uses the Index addressing mode in the manner depicted in Figure 2.13a to access each of the three scores in a student's record. Register R0 is used as the index register. Before the loop is entered, R0 is set to point to the ID location of the first student record; thus, it contains the address LIST.

On the first pass through the loop, test scores of the first student are added to the running sums held in registers R1, R2, and R3, which are initially cleared to 0. These scores are accessed using the Index addressing modes 4(R0), 8(R0), and 12(R0). The index register R0 is then incremented by 16 to point to the ID location of the second student. Register R4, initialized to contain the value n, is decremented by 1 at the end of each pass through the loop. When the contents of R4 reach 0, all student records have been accessed, and the loop terminates. Until then, the conditional branch instruction transfers control back to the start of the loop to process the next record. The last three instructions transfer the accumulated sums from registers R1, R2, and R3, into memory locations SUM1, SUM2, and SUM3, respectively.

It should be emphasized that the contents of the index register, R0, are not changed when it is used in the Index addressing mode to access the scores. The contents of R0 are changed only by the last Add instruction in the loop, to move from one student record to the next.

In general, the Index mode facilitates access to an operand whose location is defined relative to a reference point within the data structure in which the operand appears. In the example just given, the ID locations of successive student records are the reference points, and the test scores are the operands accessed by the Index addressing mode.

	Move	#LIST,R0
	Clear	R1
	Clear	R2
	Clear	R3
	Move	N,R4
LOOP	Add	4(R0),R1
	Add	8(R0),R2
	Add	12(R0),R3
	Add	#16,R0
	Decrement	R4
	Branch>0	LOOP
	Move	R1,SUM1
	Move	R2,SUM2
	Move	R3,SUM3

Figure 2.15 Indexed addressing used in accessing test scores in the list in Figure 2.14.

We have introduced the most basic form of indexed addressing. Several variations of this basic form provide for very efficient access to memory operands in practical programming situations. For example, a second register may be used to contain the offset X, in which case we can write the Index mode as

$$(Ri,Rj)$$

The effective address is the sum of the contents of registers Ri and Rj. The second register is usually called the *base* register. This form of indexed addressing provides more flexibility in accessing operands, because both components of the effective address can be changed.

As an example of where this flexibility may be useful, consider again the student record data structure shown in Figure 2.14. In the program in Figure 2.15, we used different index values in the three Add instructions at the beginning of the loop to access different test scores. Suppose each record contains a large number of items, many more than the three test scores of that example. In this case, we would need the ability to replace the three Add instructions with one instruction inside a second (nested) loop. Just as the successive starting locations of the records (the reference points) are maintained in the pointer register R0, offsets to the individual items relative to the contents of R0 could be maintained in another register. The contents of that register would be incremented in successive passes through the inner loop. (See Problem 2.9.)

Yet another version of the Index mode uses two registers plus a constant, which can be denoted as

$$X(Ri,Rj)$$

In this case, the effective address is the sum of the constant X and the contents of registers Ri and Rj. This added flexibility is useful in accessing multiple components inside each item in a record, where the beginning of an item is specified by the (Ri,Rj) part of the addressing mode. In other words, this mode implements a three-dimensional array.

2.5.4 RELATIVE ADDRESSING

We have defined the Index mode using general-purpose processor registers. A useful version of this mode is obtained if the program counter, PC, is used instead of a general-purpose register. Then, X(PC) can be used to address a memory location that is X bytes away from the location presently pointed to by the program counter. Since the addressed location is identified "relative" to the program counter, which always identifies the current execution point in a program, the name Relative mode is associated with this type of addressing.

> *Relative mode* — The effective address is determined by the Index mode using the program counter in place of the general-purpose register Ri.

This mode can be used to access data operands. But, its most common use is to specify the target address in branch instructions. An instruction such as

$$\text{Branch}>0 \quad \text{LOOP}$$

causes program execution to go to the branch target location identified by the name LOOP if the branch condition is satisfied. This location can be computed by specifying it as an offset from the current value of the program counter. Since the branch target may be either before or after the branch instruction, the offset is given as a signed number.

Recall that during the execution of an instruction, the processor increments the PC to point to the next instruction. Most computers use this updated value in computing the effective address in the Relative mode. For example, suppose that the Relative mode is used to generate the branch target address LOOP in the Branch instruction of the program in Figure 2.12. Assume that the four instructions of the loop body, starting at LOOP, are located at memory locations 1000, 1004, 1008, and 1012. Hence, the updated contents of the PC at the time the branch target address is generated will be 1016. To branch to location LOOP (1000), the offset value needed is X = −16.

Assembly languages allow branch instructions to be written using labels to denote the branch target as shown in Figure 2.12. When the assembler program processes such an instruction, it computes the required offset value, −16 in this case, and generates the corresponding machine instruction using the addressing mode −16(PC).

2.5.5 ADDITIONAL MODES

So far we have discussed the five basic addressing modes — Immediate, Register, Absolute (Direct), Indirect, and Index — found in most computers. We have given a number of common versions of the Index mode, not all of which may be found in any one computer. Although these modes suffice for general computation, many computers provide additional modes intended to aid certain programming tasks. The two modes described next are useful for accessing data items in successive locations in the memory.

Autoincrement mode — The effective address of the operand is the contents of a register specified in the instruction. After accessing the operand, the contents of this register are automatically incremented to point to the next item in a list.

We denote the Autoincrement mode by putting the specified register in parentheses, to show that the contents of the register are used as the effective address, followed by a plus sign to indicate that these contents are to be incremented after the operand is accessed. Thus, the Autoincrement mode is written as

$$(Ri)+$$

Implicitly, the increment amount is 1 when the mode is given in this form. But in a byte addressable memory, this mode would only be useful in accessing successive bytes of some list. To access successive words in a byte-addressable memory with a 32-bit word length, the increment must be 4. Computers that have the Autoincrement mode automatically increment the contents of the register by a value that corresponds to the size of the accessed operand. Thus, the increment is 1 for byte-sized operands, 2 for 16-bit operands, and 4 for 32-bit operands. Since the size of the operand is usually specified as part of the operation code of an instruction, it is sufficient to indicate the Autoincrement mode as $(Ri)+$.

If the Autoincrement mode is available, it can be used in the first Add instruction in Figure 2.12 and the second Add instruction can be eliminated. The modified program is shown in Figure 2.16.

As a companion for the Autoincrement mode, another useful mode accesses the items of a list in the reverse order:

Autodecrement mode — The contents of a register specified in the instruction are first automatically decremented and are then used as the effective address of the operand.

We denote the Autodecrement mode by putting the specified register in parentheses, preceded by a minus sign to indicate that the contents of the register are to be decremented before being used as the effective address. Thus, we write

$$-(Ri)$$

	Move	N,R1	⎫
	Move	#NUM1,R2	⎬ Initialization
	Clear	R0	⎭
LOOP	Add	(R2)+,R0	
	Decrement	R1	
	Branch>0	LOOP	
	Move	R0,SUM	

Figure 2.16 The Autoincrement addressing mode used in the program of Figure 2.12.

In this mode, operands are accessed in descending address order. The reader may wonder why the address is decremented before it is used in the Autodecrement mode and incremented after it is used in the Autoincrement mode. The main reason for this is given in Section 2.8, where we show how these two modes can be used together to implement an important data structure called a stack.

The actions performed by the Autoincrement and Autodecrement addressing modes can obviously be achieved by using two instructions, one to access the operand and the other to increment or decrement the register that contains the operand address. Combining the two operations in one instruction reduces the number of instructions needed to perform the desired task. However, we will show in Chapter 8 that it is not always advantageous to combine two operations in a single instruction.

2.6 ASSEMBLY LANGUAGE

Machine instructions are represented by patterns of 0s and 1s. Such patterns are awkward to deal with when discussing or preparing programs. Therefore, we use symbolic names to represent the patterns. So far, we have used normal words, such as Move, Add, Increment, and Branch, for the instruction operations to represent the corresponding binary code patterns. When writing programs for a specific computer, such words are normally replaced by acronyms called *mnemonics,* such as MOV, ADD, INC, and BR. Similarly, we use the notation R3 to refer to register 3, and LOC to refer to a memory location. A complete set of such symbolic names and rules for their use constitute a programming language, generally referred to as an *assembly language*. The set of rules for using the mnemonics in the specification of complete instructions and programs is called the *syntax* of the language.

Programs written in an assembly language can be automatically translated into a sequence of machine instructions by a program called an *assembler*. The assembler program is one of a collection of utility programs that are a part of the system software. The assembler, like any other program, is stored as a sequence of machine instructions in the memory of the computer. A user program is usually entered into the computer through a keyboard and stored either in the memory or on a magnetic disk. At this point, the user program is simply a set of lines of alphanumeric characters. When the assembler program is executed, it reads the user program, analyzes it, and then generates the desired machine language program. The latter contains patterns of 0s and 1s specifying instructions that will be executed by the computer. The user program in its original alphanumeric text format is called a *source program,* and the assembled machine language program is called an *object program*. We will discuss how the assembler program works in Section 2.6.2. First, we present a few aspects of the assembly language itself.

The assembly language for a given computer may or may not be case sensitive, that is, it may or may not distinguish between capital and lower case letters. We will use capital letters to denote all names and labels in our examples in order to improve the readability of the text. For example, we will write a Move instruction as

MOVE   R0,SUM

The mnemonic MOVE represents the binary pattern, or *OP code,* for the operation performed by the instruction. The assembler translates this mnemonic into the binary OP code that the computer understands.

The OP-code mnemonic is followed by at least one blank space character. Then the information that specifies the operands is given. In our example, the source operand is in register R0. This information is followed by the specification of the destination operand, separated from the source operand by a comma, with no intervening blanks. The destination operand is in the memory location that has its binary address represented by the name SUM.

Since there are several possible addressing modes for specifying operand locations, the assembly language must indicate which mode is being used. For example, a numerical value or a name used by itself, such as SUM in the preceding instruction, may be used to denote the Absolute mode. The sharp sign usually denotes an immediate operand. Thus, the instruction

$$\text{ADD} \quad \text{\#5,R3}$$

adds the number 5 to the contents of register R3 and puts the result back into register R3. The sharp sign is not the only way to denote the Immediate addressing mode. In some assembly languages, the intended addressing mode is indicated in the OP-code mnemonic. In this case, a given instruction has different OP-code mnemonics for different addressing modes. For example, the previous Add instruction may be written as

$$\text{ADDI} \quad \text{5,R3}$$

The suffix I in the mnemonic ADDI states that the source operand is given in the Immediate addressing mode.

Indirect addressing is usually specified by putting parentheses around the name or symbol denoting the pointer to the operand. For example, if the number 5 is to be placed in a memory location whose address is held in register R2, the desired action can be specified as

$$\text{MOVE} \quad \text{\#5,(R2)}$$

or perhaps

$$\text{MOVEI} \quad \text{5,(R2)}$$

2.6.1 ASSEMBLER DIRECTIVES

In addition to providing a mechanism for representing instructions in a program, the assembly language allows the programmer to specify other information needed to translate the source program into the object program. We have already mentioned that we need to assign numerical values to any names used in a program. Suppose that the name SUM is used to represent the value 200. This fact may be conveyed to the assembler program through a statement such as

$$\text{SUM} \quad \text{EQU} \quad \text{200}$$

This statement does not denote an instruction that will be executed when the object program is run; in fact, it will not even appear in the object program. It simply informs the assembler that the name SUM should be replaced by the value 200 wherever it appears in the program. Such statements, called *assembler directives* (or *commands*), are used by the assembler while it translates a source program into an object program.

To illustrate the use of assembly language further, let us reconsider the program in Figure 2.12. In order to run this program on a computer, it is necessary to write its source code in the required assembly language, specifying all the information needed to generate the corresponding object program. Suppose that each instruction and each data item occupies one word of memory. This is an oversimplification, but it helps keep the example straightforward. Also assume that the memory is byte addressable and that the word length is 32 bits. Suppose also that the object program is to be loaded in the main memory as shown in Figure 2.17. The figure shows the memory addresses where

	100	Move	N,R1
	104	Move	#NUM1,R2
	108	Clear	R0
LOOP	112	Add	(R2),R0
	116	Add	#4,R2
	120	Decrement	R1
	124	Branch>0	LOOP
	128	Move	R0,SUM
	132		
		⋮	
SUM	200		
N	204	100	
NUM1	208		
NUM2	212		
		⋮	
NUM*n*	604		

Figure 2.17 Memory arrangement for the program in Figure 2.12.

the machine instructions and the required data items are to be found after the program is loaded for execution. If the assembler is to produce an object program according to this arrangement, it has to know

- How to interpret the names
- Where to place the instructions in the memory
- Where to place the data operands in the memory

To provide this information, the source program may be written as shown in Figure 2.18. The program begins with assembler directives. We have already discussed the Equate directive, EQU, which informs the assembler about the value of SUM. The second assembler directive, ORIGIN, tells the assembler program where in the memory to place the data block that follows. In this case, the location specified has the address 204. Since this location is to be loaded with the value 100 (which is the number of entries in the list), a DATAWORD directive is used to inform the assembler of this requirement. It states that the data value 100 is to be placed in the memory word at address 204.

Any statement that results in instructions or data being placed in a memory location may be given a memory address label. The label is assigned a value equal to the address

	Memory address label	Operation	Addressing or data information
Assembler directives	SUM	EQU	200
		ORIGIN	204
	N	DATAWORD	100
	NUM1	RESERVE	400
		ORIGIN	100
Statements that	START	MOVE	N,R1
generate		MOVE	#NUM1,R2
machine		CLR	R0
instructions	LOOP	ADD	(R2),R0
		ADD	#4,R2
		DEC	R1
		BGTZ	LOOP
		MOVE	R0,SUM
Assembler directives		RETURN	
		END	START

Figure 2.18   Assembly language representation for the program in Figure 2.17.

BGTZ Branch 7 0

of that location. Because the DATAWORD statement is given the label N, the name N is assigned the value 204. Whenever N is encountered in the rest of the program, it will be replaced with this value. Using N as a label in this manner is equivalent to using the assembler directive

N   EQU   204

The RESERVE directive declares that a memory block of 400 bytes is to be reserved for data, and that the name NUM1 is to be associated with address 208. This directive does not cause any data to be loaded in these locations. Data may be loaded in the memory using an input procedure, as we will explain later in this chapter.

The second ORIGIN directive specifies that the instructions of the object program are to be loaded in the memory starting at address 100. It is followed by the source program instructions written with the appropriate mnemonics and syntax. The last statement in the source program is the assembler directive END, which tells the assembler that this is the end of the source program text. The END directive includes the label START, which is the address of the location at which execution of the program is to begin.

We have explained all statements in Figure 2.18 except RETURN. This is an assembler directive that identifies the point at which execution of the program should be terminated. It causes the assembler to insert an appropriate machine instruction that returns control to the operating system of the computer.

Most assembly languages require statements in a source program to be written in the form

Label   Operation   Operand(s)   Comment

These four *fields* are separated by an appropriate delimiter, typically one or more blank characters. The Label is an optional name associated with the memory address where the machine language instruction produced from the statement will be loaded. Labels may also be associated with addresses of data items. In Figure 2.18 there are five labels: SUM, N, NUM1, START, and LOOP.

The Operation field contains the OP-code mnemonic of the desired instruction or assembler directive. The Operand field contains addressing information for accessing one or more operands, depending on the type of instruction. The Comment field is ignored by the assembler program. It is used for documentation purposes to make the program easier to understand.

We have introduced only the very basic characteristics of assembly languages. These languages differ in detail and complexity from one computer to another.

2.6.2 ASSEMBLY AND EXECUTION OF PROGRAMS

A source program written in an assembly language must be assembled into a machine language object program before it can be executed. This is done by the assembler program, which replaces all symbols denoting operations and addressing modes with the binary codes used in machine instructions, and replaces all names and labels with their actual values.

The assembler assigns addresses to instructions and data blocks, starting at the address given in the ORIGIN assembler directives. It also inserts constants that may be given in DATAWORD commands and reserves memory space as requested by RESERVE commands.

A key part of the assembly process is determining the values that replace the names. In some cases, where the value of a name is specified by an EQU directive, this is a straightforward task. In other cases, where a name is defined in the Label field of a given instruction, the value represented by the name is determined by the location of this instruction in the assembled object program. Hence, the assembler must keep track of addresses as it generates the machine code for successive instructions. For example, the names START and LOOP will be assigned the values 100 and 112, respectively.

In some cases, the assembler does not directly replace a name representing an address with the actual value of this address. For example, in a branch instruction, the name that specifies the location to which a branch is to be made (the branch target) is not replaced by the actual address. A branch instruction is usually implemented in machine code by specifying the branch target using the Relative addressing mode, as explained in Section 2.5. The assembler computes the *branch offset,* which is the distance to the target, and puts it into the machine instruction.

As the assembler scans through a source program, it keeps track of all names and the numerical values that correspond to them in a *symbol table*. Thus, when a name appears a second time, it is replaced with its value from the table. A problem arises when a name appears as an operand before it is given a value. For example, this happens if a forward branch is required. The assembler will not be able to determine the branch target, because the name referred to has not yet been recorded in the symbol table. A simple solution to this problem is to have the assembler scan through the source program twice. During the first pass, it creates a complete symbol table. At the end of this pass, all names will have been assigned numerical values. The assembler then goes through the source program a second time and substitutes values for all names from the symbol table. Such an assembler is called a *two-pass assembler*.

The assembler stores the object program on a magnetic disk. The object program must be loaded into the memory of the computer before it is executed. For this to happen, another utility program called a *loader* must already be in the memory. Executing the loader performs a sequence of input operations needed to transfer the machine language program from the disk into a specified place in the memory. The loader must know the length of the program and the address in the memory where it will be stored. The assembler usually places this information in a header preceding the object code. Having loaded the object code, the loader starts execution of the object program by branching to the first instruction to be executed. Recall that the address of this instruction has been included in the assembly language program as the operand of the END assembler directive. The assembler includes this address in the header that precedes the object code on the disk.

[handwritten margin note: also "linker" hooks your program to existing useful programs]

When the object program begins executing, it proceeds to completion unless there are logical errors in the program. The user must be able to find errors easily. The assembler can detect and report syntax errors. To help the user find other programming errors, the system software usually includes a *debugger* program. This program enables the user to stop execution of the object program at some points of interest and to examine the contents of various processor registers and memory locations. We consider program debugging in more detail in Chapter 4.

2.6.3 NUMBER NOTATION

When dealing with numerical values, it is often convenient to use the familiar decimal notation. Of course, these values are stored in the computer as binary numbers. In some situations, it is more convenient to specify the binary patterns directly. Most assemblers allow numerical values to be specified in different ways, using conventions that are defined by the assembly language syntax. Consider, for example, the number 93, which is represented by the 8-bit binary number 01011101. If this value is to be used as an immediate operand, it can be given as a decimal number, as in the instruction

$$\text{ADD} \quad \#93,\text{R1}$$

or as a binary number identified by a prefix symbol such as a percent sign, as in

$$\text{ADD} \quad \#\%01011101,\text{R1}$$

Binary numbers can be written more compactly as *hexadecimal,* or *hex,* numbers, in which four bits are represented by a single hex digit. The hex notation is a direct extension of the BCD code given in Appendix E. The first ten patterns 0000, 0001, . . . , 1001, are represented by the digits 0, 1, . . . , 9, as in BCD. The remaining six 4-bit patterns, 1010, 1011, . . . , 1111, are represented by the letters A, B, . . . , F. In hexadecimal representation, the decimal value 93 becomes 5D. In assembly language, a hex representation is often identified by a dollar sign prefix. Thus, we would write

$$\text{ADD} \quad \#\$5D,\text{R1}$$

2.7 BASIC INPUT/OUTPUT OPERATIONS

Previous sections in this chapter described machine instructions and addressing modes. We have assumed that the data on which these instructions operate are already stored in the memory. We now examine the means by which data are transferred between the memory of a computer and the outside world. Input/Output (I/O) operations are essential, and the way they are performed can have a significant effect on the performance of the computer. This subject is discussed in detail in Chapter 4. Here, we introduce a few basic ideas.

Consider a task that reads in character input from a keyboard and produces character output on a display screen. A simple way of performing such I/O tasks is to use a method known as *program-controlled I/O*. The rate of data transfer from the keyboard to a computer is limited by the typing speed of the user, which is unlikely to exceed a few characters per second. The rate of output transfers from the computer to the display is much higher. It is determined by the rate at which characters can be transmitted over the link between the computer and the display device, typically several thousand characters per second. However, this is still much slower than the speed of a processor that can

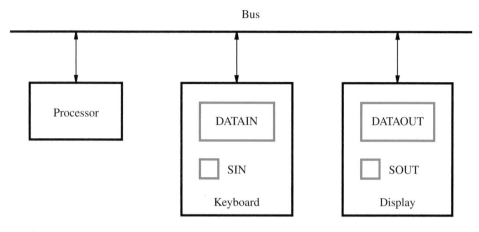

Figure 2.19 Bus connection for processor, keyboard, and display.

execute many millions of instructions per second. The difference in speed between the processor and I/O devices creates the need for mechanisms to synchronize the transfer of data between them.

A solution to this problem is as follows: On output, the processor sends the first character and then waits for a signal from the display that the character has been received. It then sends the second character, and so on. Input is sent from the keyboard in a similar way; the processor waits for a signal indicating that a character key has been struck and that its code is available in some buffer register associated with the keyboard. Then the processor proceeds to read that code.

The keyboard and the display are separate devices as shown in Figure 2.19. The action of striking a key on the keyboard does not automatically cause the corresponding character to be displayed on the screen. One block of instructions in the I/O program transfers the character into the processor, and another associated block of instructions causes the character to be displayed.

Consider the problem of moving a character code from the keyboard to the processor. Striking a key stores the corresponding character code in an 8-bit buffer register associated with the keyboard. Let us call this register DATAIN, as shown in Figure 2.19. To inform the processor that a valid character is in DATAIN, a status control flag, SIN, is set to 1. A program monitors SIN, and when SIN is set to 1, the processor reads the contents of DATAIN. When the character is transferred to the processor, SIN is automatically cleared to 0. If a second character is entered at the keyboard, SIN is again set to 1 and the process repeats.

An analogous process takes place when characters are transferred from the processor to the display. A buffer register, DATAOUT, and a status control flag, SOUT, are used for this transfer. When SOUT equals 1, the display is ready to receive a character. Under program control, the processor monitors SOUT, and when SOUT is set to 1, the processor transfers a character code to DATAOUT. The transfer of a character to DATAOUT clears SOUT to 0; when the display device is ready to receive a second character, SOUT is again set to 1. The buffer registers DATAIN and DATAOUT and the status flags SIN and SOUT are part of circuitry commonly known as a *device interface*. The circuitry for each device is connected to the processor via a bus, as indicated in Figure 2.19.

In order to perform I/O transfers, we need machine instructions that can check the state of the status flags and transfer data between the processor and the I/O device. These instructions are similar in format to those used for moving data between the processor and the memory. For example, the processor can monitor the keyboard status flag SIN and transfer a character from DATAIN to register R1 by the following sequence of operations:

READWAIT   Branch to READWAIT if SIN = 0

Input from DATAIN to R1

The Branch operation is usually implemented by two machine instructions. The first instruction tests the status flag and the second performs the branch. Although the details vary from computer to computer, the main idea is that the processor monitors the status flag by executing a short *wait loop* and proceeds to transfer the input data when SIN is set to 1 as a result of a key being struck. The Input operation resets SIN to 0.

An analogous sequence of operations is used for transferring output to the display. An example is

WRITEWAIT   Branch to WRITEWAIT if SOUT = 0

Output from R1 to DATAOUT

Again, the Branch operation is normally implemented by two machine instructions. The wait loop is executed repeatedly until the status flag SOUT is set to 1 by the display when it is free to receive a character. The Output operation transfers a character from R1 to DATAOUT to be displayed, and it clears SOUT to 0.

We assume that the initial state of SIN is 0 and the initial state of SOUT is 1. This initialization is normally performed by the device control circuits when the devices are placed under computer control before program execution begins.

Until now, we have assumed that the addresses issued by the processor to access instructions and operands always refer to memory locations. Many computers use an arrangement called *memory-mapped I/O* in which some memory address values are used to refer to peripheral device buffer registers, such as DATAIN and DATAOUT. Thus, no special instructions are needed to access the contents of these registers; data can be transferred between these registers and the processor using instructions that we have already discussed, such as Move, Load, or Store. For example, the contents of the keyboard character buffer DATAIN can be transferred to register R1 in the processor by the instruction

MoveByte   DATAIN,R1

Similarly, the contents of register R1 can be transferred to DATAOUT by the instruction

MoveByte   R1,DATAOUT

The status flags SIN and SOUT are automatically cleared when the buffer registers DATAIN and DATAOUT are referenced, respectively. The MoveByte operation code signifies that the operand size is a byte, to distinguish it from the operation code

Move that has been used for word operands. We have established that the two data buffers in Figure 2.19 may be addressed as if they were two memory locations. It is possible to deal with the status flags SIN and SOUT in the same way, by assigning them distinct addresses. However, it is more common to include SIN and SOUT in *device status* registers, one for each of the two devices. Let us assume that bit b_3 in registers INSTATUS and OUTSTATUS corresponds to SIN and SOUT, respectively. The read operation just described may now be implemented by the machine instruction sequence

```
READWAIT   Testbit     #3,INSTATUS
           Branch=0    READWAIT
           MoveByte    DATAIN,R1
```

The write operation may be implemented as

```
WRITEWAIT   Testbit     #3,OUTSTATUS
            Branch=0    WRITEWAIT
            MoveByte    R1,DATAOUT
```

The Testbit instruction tests the state of one bit in the destination location, where the bit position to be tested is indicated by the first operand. If the bit tested is equal to 0, then the condition of the branch instruction is true, and a branch is made to the beginning of the wait loop. When the device is ready, that is, when the bit tested becomes equal to 1, the data are read from the input buffer or written into the output buffer.

The program shown in Figure 2.20 uses these two operations to read a line of characters typed at a keyboard and send them out to a display device. As the characters are read in, one by one, they are stored in a data area in the memory and then echoed

	Move	#LOC,R0	Initialize pointer register R0 to point to the address of the first location in memory where the characters are to be stored.
READ	TestBit	#3,INSTATUS	Wait for a character to be entered in the keyboard buffer DATAIN.
	Branch=0	READ	
	MoveByte	DATAIN,(R0)	Transfer the character from DATAIN into the memory (this clears SIN to 0).
ECHO	TestBit	#3,OUTSTATUS	Wait for the display to become ready.
	Branch=0	ECHO	
	MoveByte	(R0),DATAOUT	Move the character just read to the display buffer register (this clears SOUT to 0).
	Compare	#CR,(R0)+	Check if the character just read is CR (carriage return). If it is not CR, then
	Branch≠0	READ	branch back and read another character. Also, increment the pointer to store the next character.

Figure 2.20   A program that reads a line of characters and displays it.

back out to the display. The program finishes when the carriage return character, CR, is read, stored, and sent to the display. The address of the first byte location of the memory data area where the line is to be stored is LOC. Register R0 is used to point to this area, and it is initially loaded with the address LOC by the first instruction in the program. R0 is incremented for each character read and displayed by the Autoincrement addressing mode used in the Compare instruction.

Program-controlled I/O requires continuous involvement of the processor in the I/O activities. Almost all of the execution time for the program in Figure 2.20 is accounted for in the two wait loops, while the processor waits for a character to be struck or for the display to become available. It is desirable to avoid wasting processor execution time in this situation. Other I/O techniques, based on the use of interrupts, may be used to improve the utilization of the processor. Such techniques will be discussed in Chapter 4.

2.8 STACKS AND QUEUES

A computer program often needs to perform a particular subtask using the familiar subroutine structure. In order to organize the control and information linkage between the main program and the subroutine, a data structure called a stack is used. This section will describe stacks, as well as a closely related data structure called a queue.

Data operated on by a program can be organized in a variety of ways. We have already encountered data structured as lists. Now, we consider an important data structure known as a stack. A *stack* is a list of data elements, usually words or bytes, with the accessing restriction that elements can be added or removed at one end of the list only. This end is called the top of the stack, and the other end is called the bottom. The structure is sometimes referred to as a *pushdown* stack. Imagine a pile of trays in a cafeteria; customers pick up new trays from the top of the pile, and clean trays are added to the pile by placing them onto the top of the pile. Another descriptive phrase, *last-in–first-out* (LIFO) stack, is also used to describe this type of storage mechanism; the last data item placed on the stack is the first one removed when retrieval begins. The terms *push* and *pop* are used to describe placing a new item on the stack and removing the top item from the stack, respectively.

Data stored in the memory of a computer can be organized as a stack, with successive elements occupying successive memory locations. Assume that the first element is placed in location BOTTOM, and when new elements are pushed onto the stack, they are placed in successively lower address locations. We use a stack that grows in the direction of decreasing memory addresses in our discussion, because this is a common practice.

Figure 2.21 shows a stack of word data items in the memory of a computer. It contains numerical values, with 43 at the bottom and −28 at the top. A processor register is used to keep track of the address of the element of the stack that is at the top at any given time. This register is called the *stack pointer* (SP). It could be one of the general-purpose registers or a register dedicated to this function. If we assume a

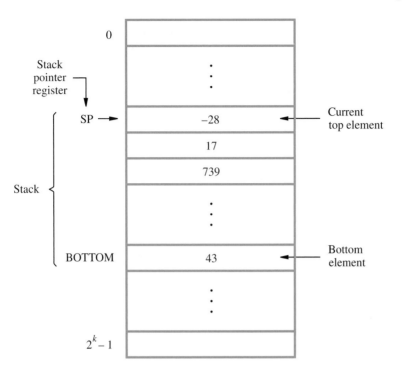

Figure 2.21 A stack of words in the memory.

byte-addressable memory with a 32-bit word length, the push operation can be implemented as

$$\text{Subtract} \quad \#4,\text{SP}$$
$$\text{Move} \quad \text{NEWITEM,(SP)}$$

where the Subtract instruction subtracts the source operand 4 from the destination operand contained in SP and places the result in SP. These two instructions move the word from location NEWITEM onto the top of the stack, decrementing the stack pointer by 4 before the move. The pop operation can be implemented as

$$\text{Move} \quad \text{(SP),ITEM}$$
$$\text{Add} \quad \#4,\text{SP}$$

These two instructions move the top value from the stack into location ITEM and then increment the stack pointer by 4 so that it points to the new top element. Figure 2.22 shows the effect of each of these operations on the stack in Figure 2.21.

   If the processor has the Autoincrement and Autodecrement addressing modes, then the push operation can be performed by the single instruction

$$\text{Move} \quad \text{NEWITEM,}-\text{(SP)}$$

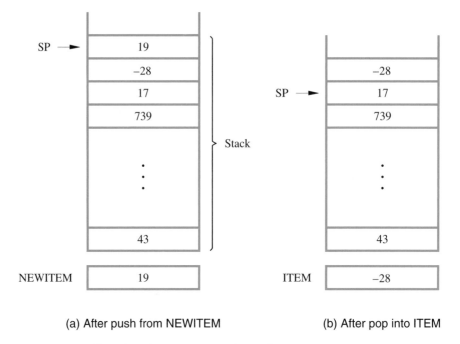

(a) After push from NEWITEM   (b) After pop into ITEM

Figure 2.22   Effect of stack operations on the stack in Figure 2.21.

and the pop operation can be performed by

Move   (SP)+,ITEM

When a stack is used in a program, it is usually allocated a fixed amount of space in the memory. In this case, we must avoid pushing an item onto the stack when the stack has reached its maximum size. Also, we must avoid attempting to pop an item off an empty stack, which could result from a programming error. Suppose that a stack runs from location 2000 (BOTTOM) down no further than location 1500. The stack pointer is loaded initially with the address value 2004. Recall that SP is decremented by 4 before new data are stored on the stack. Hence, an initial value of 2004 means that the first item pushed onto the stack will be at location 2000. To prevent either pushing an item on a full stack or popping an item off an empty stack, the single-instruction push and pop operations can be replaced by the instruction sequences shown in Figure 2.23.

The Compare instruction

Compare   src,dst

performs the operation

$$[dst] - [src]$$

and sets the condition code flags according to the result. It does not change the value of either operand.

SAFEPOP	Compare	#2000,SP	Check to see if the stack pointer contains
	Branch>0	EMPTYERROR	an address value greater than 2000. If it
			does, the stack is empty. Branch to the
			routine EMPTYERROR for appropriate
			action.
	Move	(SP)+,ITEM	Otherwise, pop the top of the stack into
			memory location ITEM.

(a) Routine for a safe pop operation

SAFEPUSH	Compare	#1500,SP	Check to see if the stack pointer
	Branch≤0	FULLERROR	contains an address value equal
			to or less than 1500. If it does, the
			stack is full. Branch to the routine
			FULLERROR for appropriate action.
	Move	NEWITEM,−(SP)	Otherwise, push the element in memory
			location NEWITEM onto the stack.

(b) Routine for a safe push operation

Figure 2.23 Checking for empty and full errors in pop and push operations.

Another useful data structure that is similar to the stack is called a *queue*. Data are stored in and retrieved from a queue on a first-in–first-out (FIFO) basis. Thus, if we assume that the queue grows in the direction of increasing addresses in the memory, which is a common practice, new data are added at the back (high-address end) and retrieved from the front (low-address end) of the queue.

There are two important differences between how a stack and a queue are implemented. One end of the stack is fixed (the bottom), while the other end rises and falls as data are pushed and popped. A single pointer is needed to point to the top of the stack at any given time. On the other hand, both ends of a queue move to higher addresses as data are added at the back and removed from the front. So two pointers are needed to keep track of the two ends of the queue.

Another difference between a stack and a queue is that, without further control, a queue would continuously move through the memory of a computer in the direction of higher addresses. One way to limit the queue to a fixed region in memory is to use a *circular buffer*. Let us assume that memory addresses from BEGINNING to END are assigned to the queue. The first entry in the queue is entered into location

BEGINNING, and successive entries are appended to the queue by entering them at successively higher addresses. By the time the back of the queue reaches END, space will have been created at the beginning if some items have been removed from the queue. Hence, the back pointer is reset to the value BEGINNING and the process continues. As in the case of a stack, care must be taken to detect when the region assigned to the data structure is either completely full or completely empty (see Problems 2.18 and 2.19).

2.9 SUBROUTINES

In a given program, it is often necessary to perform a particular subtask many times on different data values. Such a subtask is usually called a *subroutine*. For example, a subroutine may evaluate the *sine* function or sort a list of values into increasing or decreasing order.

It is possible to include the block of instructions that constitute a subroutine at every place where it is needed in the program. However, to save space, only one copy of the instructions that constitute the subroutine is placed in the memory, and any program that requires the use of the subroutine simply branches to its starting location. When a program branches to a subroutine we say that it is *calling* the subroutine. The instruction that performs this branch operation is named a Call instruction.

After a subroutine has been executed, the calling program must resume execution, continuing immediately after the instruction that called the subroutine. The subroutine is said to *return* to the program that called it by executing a Return instruction. Since the subroutine may be called from different places in a calling program, provision must be made for returning to the appropriate location. The location where the calling program resumes execution is the location pointed to by the updated PC while the Call instruction is being executed. Hence, the contents of the PC must be saved by the Call instruction to enable correct return to the calling program.

The way in which a computer makes it possible to call and return from subroutines is referred to as its *subroutine linkage* method. The simplest subroutine linkage method is to save the return address in a specific location, which may be a register dedicated to this function. Such a register is called the *link register*. When the subroutine completes its task, the Return instruction returns to the calling program by branching indirectly through the link register.

The Call instruction is just a special branch instruction that performs the following operations:

- Store the contents of the PC in the link register
- Branch to the target address specified by the instruction

The Return instruction is a special branch instruction that performs the operation:

- Branch to the address contained in the link register

Figure 2.24 illustrates this procedure.

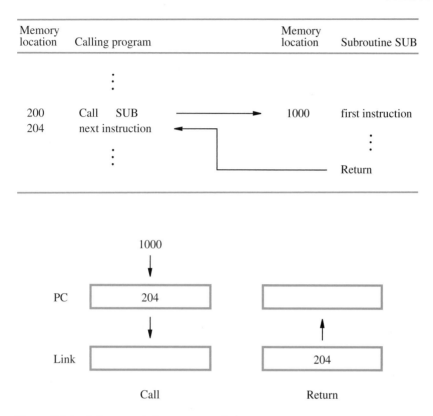

Figure 2.24 Subroutine linkage using a link register.

2.9.1 Subroutine Nesting and the Processor Stack

A common programming practice, called *subroutine nesting,* is to have one subroutine call another. In this case, the return address of the second call is also stored in the link register, destroying its previous contents. Hence, it is essential to save the contents of the link register in some other location before calling another subroutine. Otherwise, the return address of the first subroutine will be lost.

Subroutine nesting can be carried out to any depth. Eventually, the last subroutine called completes its computations and returns to the subroutine that called it. The return address needed for this first return is the last one generated in the nested call sequence. That is, return addresses are generated and used in a last-in–first-out order. This suggests that the return addresses associated with subroutine calls should be pushed onto a stack. Many processors do this automatically as one of the operations performed by the Call instruction. A particular register is designated as the stack pointer, SP, to be used in this operation. The stack pointer points to a stack called the *processor stack*. The Call instruction pushes the contents of the PC onto the processor stack and loads the subroutine address into the PC. The Return instruction pops the return address from the processor stack into the PC.

2.9.2 PARAMETER PASSING

When calling a subroutine, a program must provide to the subroutine the parameters, that is, the operands or their addresses, to be used in the computation. Later, the subroutine returns other parameters, in this case, the results of the computation. This exchange of information between a calling program and a subroutine is referred to as *parameter passing*. Parameter passing may be accomplished in several ways. The parameters may be placed in registers or in memory locations, where they can be accessed by the subroutine. Alternatively, the parameters may be placed on the processor stack used for saving the return address.

Passing parameters through processor registers is straightforward and efficient. Figure 2.25 shows how the program in Figure 2.16 for adding a list of numbers can be implemented as a subroutine, with the parameters passed through registers. The size of the list, n, contained in memory location N, and the address, NUM1, of the first number, are passed through registers R1 and R2. The sum computed by the subroutine is passed back to the calling program through register R0. The first four instructions in Figure 2.25 constitute the relevant part of the calling program. The first two instructions load n and NUM1 into R1 and R2. The Call instruction branches to the subroutine starting at location LISTADD. This instruction also pushes the return address onto the processor stack. The subroutine computes the sum and places it in R0. After the return operation is performed by the subroutine, the sum is stored in memory location SUM by the calling program.

Calling program

Move	N,R1	R1 serves as a counter.
Move	#NUM1,R2	R2 points to the list.
Call	LISTADD	Call subroutine.
Move	R0,SUM	Save result.

$\vdots$

Subroutine

LISTADD	Clear	R0	Initialize sum to 0.
LOOP	Add	(R2)+,R0	Add entry from list.
	Decrement	R1	
	Branch>0	LOOP	
	Return		Return to calling program.

Figure 2.25 Program of Figure 2.16 written as a subroutine; parameters passed through registers.

If many parameters are involved, there may not be enough general-purpose registers available for passing them to the subroutine. Using a stack, on the other hand, is highly flexible; a stack can handle a large number of parameters. The following example illustrates this approach. Figure 2.26a shows the program of Figure 2.16 rewritten as a subroutine, LISTADD, which can be called by any other program to add a list of numbers. The parameters passed to this subroutine are the address of the first number in the list and the number of entries. The subroutine performs the addition and returns the computed sum. The parameters are pushed onto the processor stack pointed to by register SP. Assume that before the subroutine is called, the top of the stack is at level 1 in Figure 2.26b. The calling program pushes the address NUM1 and the value n onto the stack and calls subroutine LISTADD. The Call instruction also pushes the return address onto the stack. The top of the stack is now at level 2.

The subroutine uses three registers. Since these registers may contain valid data that belong to the calling program, their contents should be saved by pushing them onto the stack. We have used a single instruction, MoveMultiple, to store the contents of registers R0 through R2 on the stack. Many processors have such instructions. The top of the stack is now at level 3. The subroutine accesses the parameters n and NUM1 from the stack using indexed addressing. Note that it does not change the stack pointer because valid data items are still at the top of the stack. The value n is loaded into R1 as the initial value of the count, and the address NUM1 is loaded into R2, which is used as a pointer to scan the list entries. At the end of the computation, register R0 contains the sum. Before the subroutine returns to the calling program, the contents of R0 are placed on the stack, replacing the parameter NUM1, which is no longer needed. Then the contents of the three registers used by the subroutine are restored from the stack. Now the top item on the stack is the return address at level 2. After the subroutine returns, the calling program stores the result in location SUM and lowers the top of the stack to its original level by incrementing the SP by 8.

Parameter Passing by Value and by Reference

Note the nature of the two parameters, NUM1 and n, passed to the subroutines in Figures 2.25 and 2.26. The purpose of the subroutines is to add a list of numbers. Instead of passing the actual list entries, the calling program passes the address of the first number in the list. This technique is called *passing by reference*. The second parameter is *passed by value,* that is, the actual number of entries, n, is passed to the subroutine.

2.9.3 THE STACK FRAME

Now, observe how space is used in the stack in the example in Figure 2.26. During execution of the subroutine, six locations at the top of the stack contain entries that are needed by the subroutine. These locations constitute a private work space for the subroutine, created at the time the subroutine is entered and freed up when the subroutine returns control to the calling program. Such space is called a *stack frame*. If the subroutine requires more space for local memory variables, they can also be allocated on the stack.

Assume top of stack is at level 1 below.

	Move	#NUM1,−(SP)	Push parameters onto stack.
	Move	N,−(SP)	
	Call	LISTADD	Call subroutine
			(top of stack at level 2).
	Move	4(SP),SUM	Save result.
	Add	#8,SP	Restore top of stack
			(top of stack at level 1).

⋮

LISTADD	MoveMultiple	R0−R2,−(SP)	Save registers
			(top of stack at level 3).
	Move	16(SP),R1	Initialize counter to n.
	Move	20(SP),R2	Initialize pointer to the list.
	Clear	R0	Initialize sum to 0.
LOOP	Add	(R2)+,R0	Add entry from list.
	Decrement	R1	
	Branch>0	LOOP	
	Move	R0,20(SP)	Put result on the stack.
	MoveMultiple	(SP)+,R0−R2	Restore registers.
	Return		Return to calling program.

(a) Calling program and subroutine

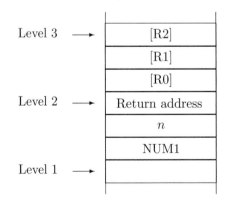

(b) Top of stack at various times

Figure 2.26   Program of Figure 2.16 written as a subroutine; parameters passed on the stack.

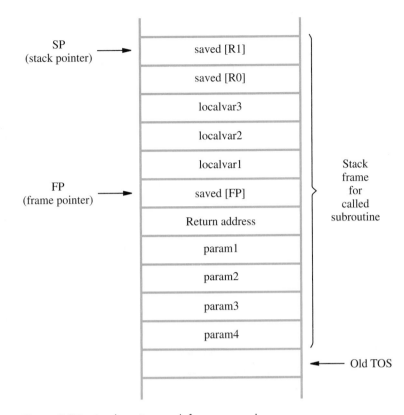

Figure 2.27 A subroutine stack frame example.

Figure 2.27 shows an example of a commonly used layout for information in a stack frame. In addition to the stack pointer SP, it is useful to have another pointer register, called the *frame pointer* (FP), for convenient access to the parameters passed to the subroutine and to the local memory variables used by the subroutine. These local variables are only used within the subroutine, so it is appropriate to allocate space for them in the stack frame associated with the subroutine. In the figure, we assume that four parameters are passed to the subroutine, three local variables are used within the subroutine, and registers R0 and R1 need to be saved because they will also be used within the subroutine.

With the FP register pointing to the location just above the stored return address, as shown in Figure 2.27, we can easily access the parameters and the local variables by using the Index addressing mode. The parameters can be accessed by using addresses 8(FP), 12(FP), ... The local variables can be accessed by using addresses −4(FP), −8(FP), ... The contents of FP remain fixed throughout the execution of the subroutine, unlike the stack pointer SP, which must always point to the current top element in the stack.

Now let us discuss how the pointers SP and FP are manipulated as the stack frame is built, used, and dismantled for a particular invocation of the subroutine. We begin by assuming that SP points to the old top-of-stack (TOS) element in Figure 2.27. Before the subroutine is called, the calling program pushes the four parameters onto the stack. The Call instruction is then executed, resulting in the return address being pushed onto the stack. Now, SP points to this return address, and the first instruction of the subroutine is about to be executed. This is the point at which the frame pointer FP is set to contain the proper memory address. Since FP is usually a general-purpose register, it may contain information of use to the calling program. Therefore, its contents are saved by pushing them onto the stack. Since the SP now points to this position, its contents are copied into FP.

Thus, the first two instructions executed in the subroutine are

$$\text{Move} \quad \text{FP,} -(\text{SP})$$

$$\text{Move} \quad \text{SP,FP}$$

After these instructions are executed, both SP and FP point to the saved FP contents. Space for the three local variables is now allocated on the stack by executing the instruction

$$\text{Subtract} \quad \#12,\text{SP}$$

Finally, the contents of processor registers R0 and R1 are saved by pushing them onto the stack. At this point, the stack frame has been set up as shown in the figure.

The subroutine now executes its task. When the task is completed, the subroutine pops the saved values of R1 and R0 back into those registers, removes the local variables from the stack frame by executing the instruction

$$\text{Add} \quad \#12,\text{SP}$$

and pops the saved old value of FP back into FP. At this point, SP points to the return address, so the Return instruction can be executed, transferring control back to the calling program.

The calling program is responsible for removing the parameters from the stack frame, some of which may be results passed back by the subroutine. The stack pointer now points to the old TOS, and we are back to where we started.

Stack Frames for Nested Subroutines

The stack is the proper data structure for holding return addresses when subroutines are nested. It should be clear that the complete stack frames for nested subroutines build up on the processor stack as they are called. In this regard, note that the saved contents of FP in the current frame at the top of the stack are the frame pointer contents for the stack frame of the subroutine that called the current subroutine.

An example of a main program calling a first subroutine SUB1, which then calls a second subroutine SUB2, is shown in Figure 2.28. The stack frames corresponding to these two nested subroutines are shown in Figure 2.29. All parameters involved in this example are passed on the stack. The figure only shows the flow of control and data among the three programs. The actual computations are not shown.

The flow of execution is as follows. The main program pushes the two parameters param2 and param1 onto the stack in that order and then calls SUB1. This first subroutine is responsible for computing a single answer and passing it back to the main program on the stack. During the course of its computations, SUB1 calls the second subroutine,

Memory location		Instructions	Comments

Main program

		⋮	
2000	Move	PARAM2,−(SP)	Place parameters on stack.
2004	Move	PARAM1,−(SP)	
2008	Call	SUB1	
2012	Move	(SP),RESULT	Store result.
2016	Add	#8,SP	Restore stack level.
2020	next instruction		
		⋮	

First subroutine

2100	SUB1	Move	FP,−(SP)	Save frame pointer register.
2104		Move	SP,FP	Load the frame pointer.
2108		MoveMultiple	R0−R3,−(SP)	Save registers.
2112		Move	8(FP),R0	Get first parameter.
		Move	12(FP),R1	Get second parameter.
			⋮	
		Move	PARAM3,−(SP)	Place a parameter on stack.
2160		Call	SUB2	
2164		Move	(SP)+,R2	Pop SUB2 result into R2.
			⋮	
		Move	R3,8(FP)	Place answer on stack.
		MoveMultiple	(SP)+,R0−R3	Restore registers.
		Move	(SP)+,FP	Restore frame pointer register.
		Return		Return to Main program.

Second subroutine

3000	SUB2	Move	FP,−(SP)	Save frame pointer register.
		Move	SP,FP	Load the frame pointer.
		MoveMultiple	R0−R1,−(SP)	Save registers R0 and R1.
		Move	8(FP),R0	Get the parameter.
			⋮	
		Move	R1,8(FP)	Place SUB2 result on stack.
		MoveMultiple	(SP)+,R0−R1	Restore registers R0 and R1.
		Move	(SP)+,FP	Restore frame pointer register.
		Return		Return to Subroutine 1.

Figure 2.28   Nested subroutines.

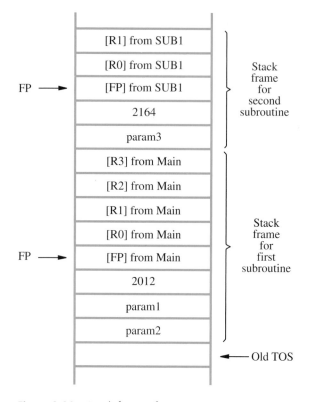

Figure 2.29 Stack frames for Figure 2.28.

SUB2, in order to perform some subtask. SUB1 passes a single parameter param3 to SUB2 and gets a result passed back to it. After SUB2 executes its Return instruction, this result is stored in register R2 by SUB1. SUB1 then continues its computations and eventually passes the required answer back to the main program on the stack. When SUB1 executes its return to the main program, the main program stores this answer in memory location RESULT and continues with its computations at "next instruction."

The comments in Figure 2.28 provide the details of how this flow of execution is managed. The first actions performed by each subroutine are to set the frame pointer, after saving its previous contents on the stack, and to save any other registers required. SUB1 uses four registers, R0 to R3, and SUB2 uses two registers, R0 and R1. These registers and the frame pointer are restored just before the returns are executed.

The Index addressing mode involving the frame pointer register FP is used to load parameters from the stack and place answers back on the stack. The byte offsets used in these operations are always 8, 12, . . . , as discussed for the general stack frame in Figure 2.27. Finally, note that the calling routines are responsible for removing parameters from the stack. This is done by the Add instruction in the main program, and by the Move instruction at location 2164 in SUB1.

2.10 ADDITIONAL INSTRUCTIONS

So far, we have introduced the following instructions: Move, Load, Store, Clear, Add, Subtract, Increment, Decrement, Branch, Testbit, Compare, Call, and Return. These 13 instructions, along with the addressing modes in Table 2.1, have allowed us to write routines to illustrate machine instruction sequencing, including branching and the subroutine structure. We also illustrated the basic memory-mapped I/O operations.

Even this small set of instructions has a number of redundancies. The Load and Store instructions can be replaced by Move, and the Increment and Decrement instructions can be replaced by Add and Subtract, respectively. Also, Clear can be replaced by a Move instruction containing an immediate operand of zero. Therefore, only 8 instructions would have been sufficient for our purposes. But, it is not unusual to have some redundancy in practical machine instruction sets. Certain simple operations can usually be accomplished in a number of different ways. Some alternatives may be more efficient than others. In this section we introduce a few more important instructions that are found in most instruction sets.

2.10.1 LOGIC INSTRUCTIONS

Logic operations such as AND, OR, and NOT, applied to individual bits, are the basic building blocks of digital circuits, as described in Appendix A. It is also useful to be able to perform logic operations in software, which is done using instructions that apply these operations to all bits of a word or byte independently and in parallel. For example, the instruction

$$\text{Not} \quad \text{dst}$$

complements all bits contained in the destination operand, changing 0s to 1s, and 1s to 0s. In Section 2.1.1, we saw that adding 1 to the 1's-complement of a signed positive number forms the negative version in 2's-complement representation. For example, in Figure 2.1, +3 (0011) is converted to −3 (1101) by adding 1 to the 1's-complement of 0011. If 3 is contained in register R0, the instructions

$$\text{Not} \quad \text{R0}$$
$$\text{Add} \quad \text{\#1,R0}$$

achieve the conversion. Many computers have a single instruction

$$\text{Negate} \quad \text{R0}$$

that accomplishes the same thing.

Now consider an application for the logic instruction And, which performs the bitwise AND operation on the source and destination operands. Suppose that four ASCII characters are contained in the 32-bit register R0. In some task, we wish to determine if the leftmost character is Z. If it is, a conditional branch to YES is to be made. From Appendix E, we find that the ASCII code for Z is 01011010, which is expressed in hexadecimal notation as 5A. The three-instruction sequence

And   #$FF000000,R0
Compare   #$5A000000,R0
Branch=0   YES

implements the desired action. The And instruction clears all bits in the rightmost three character positions of R0 to zero, leaving the leftmost character unchanged. This is the result of using an immediate source operand that has eight 1s at its left end, and 0s in the 24 bits to the right. The Compare instruction compares the remaining character at the left end of R0 with the binary representation for the character Z. The Branch instruction causes a branch to YES if there is a match.

The And instruction is often used in practical programming tasks where all bits of an operand except for some specified field are to be cleared to 0. In our example, the leftmost eight bits of R0 constitute the specified field.

2.10.2 SHIFT AND ROTATE INSTRUCTIONS

There are many applications that require the bits of an operand to be shifted right or left some specified number of bit positions. The details of how the shifts are performed depend on whether the operand is a signed number or some more general binary-coded information. For general operands, we use a logical shift. For a number, we use an arithmetic shift, which preserves the sign of the number.

Logical Shifts

Two logical shift instructions are needed, one for shifting left (LShiftL) and another for shifting right (LShiftR). These instructions shift an operand over a number of bit positions specified in a count operand contained in the instruction. The general form of a logical left shift instruction is

LShiftL   count,dst

The count operand may be given as an immediate operand, or it may be contained in a processor register. To complete the description of the left shift operation, we need to specify the bit values brought into the vacated positions at the right end of the destination operand, and to determine what happens to the bits shifted out of the left end. Vacated positions are filled with zeros, and the bits shifted out are passed through the Carry flag, C, and then dropped. Involving the C flag in shifts is useful in performing arithmetic operations on large numbers that occupy more than one word. Figure 2.30a shows an example of shifting the contents of register R0 left by two bit positions. The logical shift right instruction, LShiftR, works in the same manner except that it shifts to the right. Figure 2.30b illustrates this operation.

Digit-Packing Example

Consider the following short task that illustrates the use of both shift operations and logic operations. Suppose that two decimal digits represented in ASCII code are located

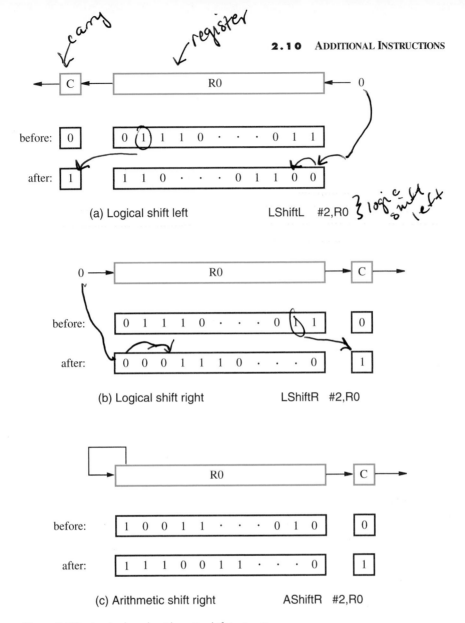

carry

register

C ← RO ← 0

before: 0 | 0 (1) 1 1 0 · · · 0 1 1

after: 1 | 1 1 0 · · · 0 1 1 0 0

(a) Logical shift left   LShiftL #2,RO *{ logic shift left }*

0 → RO → C →

before: 0 1 1 1 0 · · · 0 1 1 | 0

after: 0 0 0 1 1 1 0 · · · 0 | 1

(b) Logical shift right   LShiftR #2,RO

RO → C →

before: 1 0 0 1 1 · · · 0 1 0 | 0

after: 1 1 1 0 0 1 1 · · · 0 | 1

(c) Arithmetic shift right   AShiftR #2,RO

Figure 2.30 Logical and arithmetic shift instructions.

in memory at byte locations LOC and LOC + 1. We wish to represent each of these digits in the 4-bit BCD code and store both of them in a single byte location PACKED. The result is said to be in *packed-BCD* format. Tables E.1 and E.2 in Appendix E show that the rightmost four bits of the ASCII code for a decimal digit correspond to the BCD code for the digit. Hence, the required task is to extract the low-order four bits in LOC and LOC + 1 and concatenate them into the single byte at PACKED.

The instruction sequence shown in Figure 2.31 accomplishes the task using register RO as a pointer to the ASCII characters in memory, and using registers R1 and R2 to

Move	#LOC,R0	R0 points to data.
MoveByte	(R0)+,R1	Load first byte into R1.
LShiftL	#4,R1	Shift left by 4 bit positions.
MoveByte	(R0),R2	Load second byte into R2.
And	#$F,R2	Eliminate high-order bits.
Or	R1,R2	Concatenate the BCD digits.
MoveByte	R2,PACKED	Store the result.

Figure 2.31   A routine that packs two BCD digits.

develop the BCD digit codes. When a MoveByte instruction transfers a byte between memory and a 32-bit processor register, we assume that the byte is located in the rightmost eight bit positions of the register. The And instruction is used to mask out all but the four rightmost bits in R2. Note that the immediate source operand is written as $F, which, interpreted as a 32-bit pattern, has 28 zeros in the most-significant bit positions.

Arithmetic Shifts

A study of the 2's-complement binary number representation in Figure 2.1 reveals that shifting a number one bit position to the left is equivalent to multiplying it by 2; and shifting it to the right is equivalent to dividing it by 2. Of course, overflow might occur on shifting left, and the remainder is lost in shifting right. Another important observation is that on a right shift the sign bit must be repeated as the fill-in bit for the vacated position. This requirement on right shifting distinguishes arithmetic shifts from logical shifts in which the fill-in bit is always 0. Otherwise, the two types of shifts are very similar. An example of an arithmetic right shift, AShiftR, is shown in Figure 2.30c. The arithmetic left shift is exactly the same as the logical left shift.

Rotate Operations

In the shift operations, the bits shifted out of the operand are lost, except for the last bit shifted out which is retained in the Carry flag C. To preserve all bits, a set of rotate instructions can be used. They move the bits that are shifted out of one end of the operand back into the other end. Two versions of both the left and right rotate instructions are usually provided. In one version, the bits of the operand are simply rotated. In the other version, the rotation includes the C flag. Figure 2.32 shows the left and right rotate operations with and without the C flag being included in the rotation. Note that when the C flag is not included in the rotation, it still retains the last bit shifted out of the end of the register. The mnemonics RotateL, RotateLC, RotateR, and RotateRC, denote the instructions that perform the rotate operations. The main use for Rotate instructions is in algorithms for performing arithmetic operations other than addition and subtraction, which we will encounter in Chapter 6.

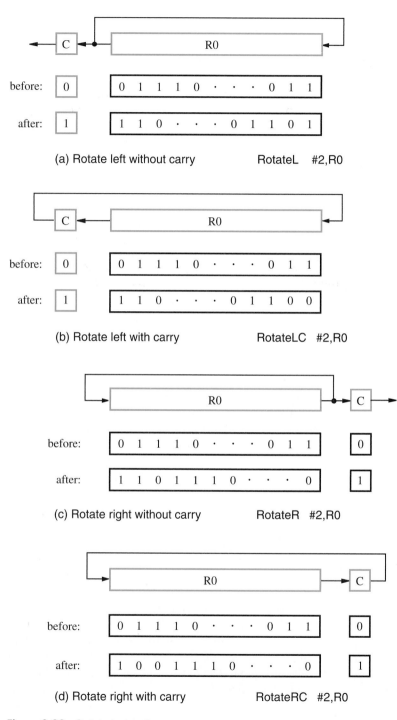

(a) Rotate left without carry   RotateL   #2,R0

(b) Rotate left with carry   RotateLC   #2,R0

(c) Rotate right without carry   RotateR   #2,R0

(d) Rotate right with carry   RotateRC   #2,R0

Figure 2.32 Rotate instructions.

2.10.3 MULTIPLICATION AND DIVISION

Two signed integers can be multiplied or divided by machine instructions with the same format as we saw earlier for an Add instruction. The instruction

$$\text{Multiply} \quad Ri, Rj$$

performs the operation

$$Rj \leftarrow [Ri] \times [Rj]$$

The product of two n-bit numbers can be as large as $2n$ bits. Therefore, the answer will not necessarily fit into register Rj. A number of instruction sets have a Multiply instruction that computes the low-order n bits of the product and places it in register Rj, as indicated. This is sufficient if it is known that all products in some particular application task will fit into n bits. To accommodate the general $2n$-bit product case, some processors produce the product in two registers, usually adjacent registers Rj and $R(j+1)$, with the high-order half being placed in register $R(j+1)$.

　　Although it is less common, some instruction sets provide a signed integer Divide instruction

$$\text{Divide} \quad Ri, Rj$$

which performs the operation

$$Rj \leftarrow [Rj]/[Ri]$$

placing the quotient in Rj. The remainder may be placed in $R(j+1)$, or it may be lost.

　　Computers that do not have Multiply and Divide instructions can perform these and other arithmetic operations by using sequences of more basic instructions such as Add, Subtract, Shift, and Rotate. This will become more apparent when we describe the implementation of arithmetic operations in Chapter 6.

2.11 EXAMPLE PROGRAMS

In this section we present three examples that further illustrate the use of machine instructions. The examples are representative of numeric (vector processing) and non-numeric (sorting and linked-list manipulation) applications.

2.11.1 VECTOR DOT PRODUCT PROGRAM

The first example is a numerical application that is an extension of the loop program of Figure 2.16 for adding numbers. In calculations that involve vectors and matrices, it is often necessary to compute the dot product of two vectors. Let A and B be two vectors of length n. Their dot product is defined as

$$\text{Dot Product} = \sum_{i=0}^{n-1} A(i) \times B(i)$$

	Move	#AVEC,R1	R1 points to vector A.
	Move	#BVEC,R2	R2 points to vector B.
	Move	N,R3	R3 serves as a counter.
	Clear	R0	R0 accumulates the dot product.
LOOP	Move	(R1)+,R4	Compute the product of
	Multiply	(R2)+,R4	next components.
	Add	R4,R0	Add to previous sum.
	Decrement	R3	Decrement the counter.
	Branch>0	LOOP	Loop again if not done.
	Move	R0,DOTPROD	Store dot product in memory.

Figure 2.33 A program for computing the dot product of two vectors.

Figure 2.33 shows a program for computing the dot product and storing it in memory location DOTPROD. The first elements of each vector, A(0) and B(0), are stored at memory locations AVEC and BVEC, with the remaining elements in the following word locations.

The task of accumulating a sum of products occurs in many signal-processing applications. In this case, one of the vectors consists of the most recent n signal samples in a continuing time sequence of inputs to a signal-processing unit. The other vector is a set of n weights. The n signal samples are multiplied by the weights, and the sum of these products constitutes an output signal sample.

Some computer instruction sets combine the operation of the Multiply and Add instructions used in the program in Figure 2.33 into a single MultiplyAccumulate instruction. We will see an example of this in the ARM processor in Chapter 3.

2.11.2 BYTE-SORTING PROGRAM

Consider a program for sorting a list of bytes stored in memory into ascending alphabetic order. Assume that the list consists of n bytes, not necessarily distinct, and that each byte contains the ASCII code for a character from the set of letters A through Z. In the ASCII code, presented in Appendix E, the letters A, B, ..., Z, are represented by 7-bit patterns that have increasing values when interpreted as binary numbers. When an ASCII character is stored in a byte location, it is customary to set the most-significant bit position to 0. Using this code, we can sort a list of characters alphabetically by sorting their codes in increasing numerical order, considering them as positive numbers.

Let the list be stored in memory locations LIST through LIST $+ n - 1$, and let n be a 32-bit value stored at address N. The sorting is to be done in place, that is, the sorted list is to occupy the same memory locations as the original list.

We sort the list using a straight-selection sort algorithm. First, the largest number is found and placed at the end of the list in location LIST $+ n - 1$. Then the largest

```
for   (j = n−1; j > 0; j = j − 1)
      { for ( k = j−1; k >= 0; k = k − 1 )
            { if   (LIST[k] > LIST[j])
                  {  TEMP = LIST[k];
                        LIST[k] = LIST[j];
                        LIST[j] = TEMP;
                  }
            }
      }
```

(a) C-language program for sorting

	Move	#LIST,R0	Load LIST into base register R0.
	Move	N,R1	Initialize outer loop index
	Subtract	#1,R1	register R1 to $j = n − 1$.
OUTER	Move	R1,R2	Initialize inner loop index
	Subtract	#1,R1	register R2 to $k = j− 1$.
	MoveByte	(R0,R1),R3	Load LIST(j) into R3, which holds
			current maximum in sublist.
INNER	CompareByte	R3,(R0,R2)	If LIST(k) ≤ [R3],
	Branch≤0	NEXT	do not exchange.
	MoveByte	(R0,R2),R4	Otherwise, exchange LIST(k)
	MoveByte	R3,(R0,R2)	with LIST(j) and load
	MoveByte	R4,(R0,R1)	new maximum into R3.
	MoveByte	R4,R3	Register R4 serves as TEMP.
NEXT	Decrement	R2	Decrement index registers R2 and
	Branch≥0	INNER	R1, which also serve as
	Decrement	R1	as loop counters, and branch
	Branch>0	OUTER	back if loops not finished.

(b) Assembly language program for sorting

Figure 2.34   A byte-sorting program using straight-selection sort.

number in the remaining sublist of $n − 1$ numbers is placed at the end of the sublist in location LIST + $n − 2$. The procedure is repeated until the list is sorted. A C-language program for this sorting algorithm is shown in Figure 2.34*a*, where the list is treated as a one-dimensional array LIST(0) through LIST($n − 1$). For each sublist LIST(j) through LIST(0), the number in LIST(j) is compared with each of the other numbers in the sublist. Whenever a larger number is found in the sublist, it is interchanged with the number in LIST(j).

The C-language program traverses the list backwards. This order of traversal simplifies loop termination in the machine language version of the program because the loop is exited when an index is decremented to 0.

An assembly language program that implements the sorting algorithm is given in Figure 2.34b. The comments in the program explain the use of various registers. The current maximum value is kept in register R3 while a sublist is being scanned. If a larger value is found, it is exchanged with the value in R3 and the new largest value is stored in LIST(j).

Control flow is handled differently in the two programs for purposes of efficiency in the assembly language program. Using the *if-then* control statement in the C-language program causes the three-line *then* clause to exchange LIST(k) and LIST(j) if LIST(k) > LIST(j). In the assembly language program, a branch is taken around the four-instruction exchange code if LIST(k) $\leq$ LIST(j).

If the machine instruction set allows a move operation from one memory location directly to another memory location, then the four-instruction exchange code in the inner loop in Figure 2.34b can be replaced by the three-instruction sequence

```
MoveByte    (R0,R2),(R0,R1)
MoveByte    R3,(R0,R2)
MoveByte    (R0,R1),R3
```

As we will see in Chapter 3, the 68000 processor has this capability.

Finally, we note that the program in Figure 2.34b works correctly only if the list has at least two elements because the check for loop termination is done at the end of each loop. Hence, there is at least one pass through the loop, regardless of the value of n.

2.11.3 LINKED LISTS

Many nonnumeric application programs require that an ordered list of information items be represented and stored in memory in such a way that it is easy to add items to the list or to delete items from the list at any position while maintaining the desired order of items. This is a more general situation than found in the stack and queue data structures, discussed in Section 2.8, where items can only be added or deleted at the ends. Consider the following example. The course list of student test scores that we used in Section 2.5 to illustrate the Index addressing mode contains the unique student ID number in the first word of each four-word student record shown in Figure 2.14. Suppose we try to maintain this list of records in consecutive memory locations in some contiguous block of memory in increasing order of student ID numbers. This would facilitate printing and posting the list of test scores ordered by ID number. After the list is built, if a student withdraws from the course an empty record slot is created. It is then necessary to jump over the empty slot when going through the records to add up test scores or to print a listing. A more awkward situation arises after the initial construction of the list if another student registers in the course. To keep the list ordered, all records, starting from the one with the first ID number larger than the new ID would need to be moved to higher address locations to create a four-word space for the new record. Similarly,

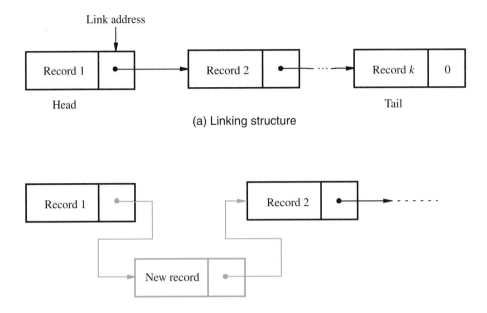

(a) Linking structure

(b) Inserting a new record between Record 1 and Record 2

Figure 2.35   Linked-list data structure.

to handle the previously mentioned withdrawal of a student, the resulting empty slot could be removed by moving all records after the empty slot to lower address locations, closing the gap.

A data structure called a *linked list* can be used to avoid both of these problems. Each record still occupies a consecutive four-word block in the memory, but successive records in the order do not necessarily occupy consecutive blocks in the memory address space. To enable connecting the blocks together to form the ordered list, each record contains an address value in a one-word *link* field that specifies the location of the next record in order. Hence the name linked list is used to describe this data structure. A schematic representation for a linked list is shown in Figure 2.35*a*. The first record in the list is called the *head,* and the last record is called the *tail.*

To insert a new record between record i and record $i + 1$, the link address in record i is copied into the link field in the new record and then the address of the new record is written into the link field of record i. This operation is shown schematically in Figure 2.35*b*. To delete record i, the address in its link field is copied into the link field of record $i - 1$.

Figure 2.36 shows an example of the student test score records linked together in memory, ordered by increasing ID numbers. Each record is now five words long. The first word, defined as the *key* field, contains the student ID number. The second word contains the link field, and the last three words are the data field that contains the three test scores. Assuming 32-bit words, a 2000-byte area of memory, starting at word address 1000, is allocated to contain the five-word records, 20 bytes per record, for up to 100 students. As students register for the course, they are assigned one of

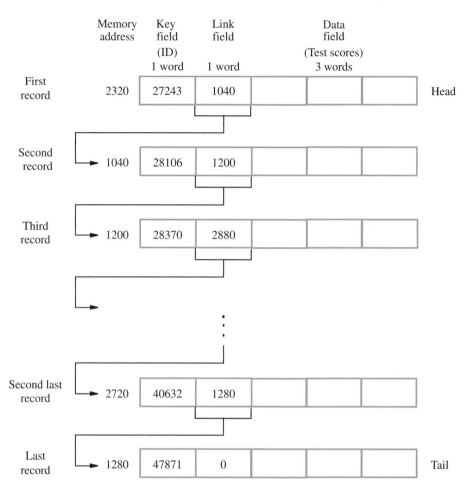

Figure 2.36 A list of student test scores organized as a linked list in memory.

the available five-word record blocks in memory. It may be convenient to do this in block address order 1000, 1020, 1040, ..., 2980, but that is not necessary. There is no particular relationship between student IDs and the order in which students register for the course. Therefore, the locations of the record blocks, ordered by student ID, will be scattered in some unpredictable way across the assigned memory area from block address 1000 to block address 2980.

The record with the current lowest ID number is at the head of the list, and the record with current highest ID number is in the tail position. A convenient way to access the list is to store the memory address of the head, in this case 2320, in a processor register called the *head pointer*. The address 1040 in the link field of the first record specifies the location of the second record. The link field of the second record contains the address 1200 of the third record, and so on. The link field of the last record is set to zero to denote that it is the tail entry in the list. If the list is empty, the head pointer contains zero.

Insertion of a New Record

Let us now give the steps needed to add a new record to the list shown in Figure 2.36. Suppose that the ID number of the new record is 28241, and the next available free record block is at address 2960. Trace forward from the head record until the first record with a larger ID is found. This is the record at memory location 1200, containing the ID 28370. Now insert the address link 1200 into the link field of the new record, and then insert the address of the new record, 2960, into the link field of the previous record at location 1040, overwriting the old value of 1200. Now, the new record has been inserted as the third record in the updated list, between the second and third records of the old list.

A subroutine for performing the insertion operation is shown in Figure 2.37. It is composed of three sections to handle the following three possible cases: the current list is empty, the new record becomes the new head of a nonempty list, or the new record is inserted in the list somewhere after the current head. The last case includes the possibility that the new record becomes the tail.

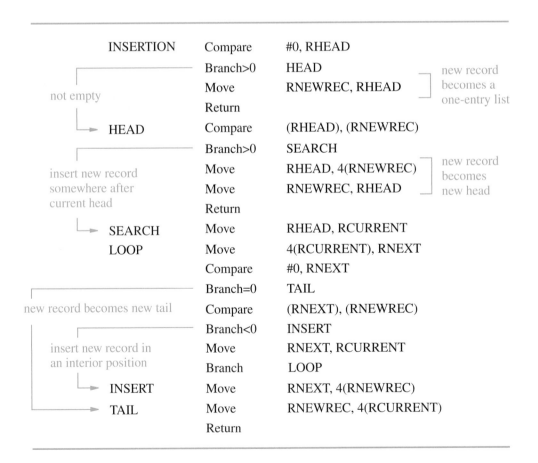

Figure 2.37 A subroutine for inserting a new record into a linked list.

Consider now how the subroutine handles the three possible cases. A number of processor registers are used in the subroutine. Instead of the usual names R0, R1, R2, and so on, we use more descriptive names to aid understanding. RHEAD is the head pointer, and RNEWREC contains the address of the new record. The two registers RCURRENT and RNEXT contain the addresses of the current record and the next record as the list is scanned to find the correct position for inserting the new record. The link field of the new record is initially set to zero. If it becomes the new tail, no further changes to this field are necessary.

The first Compare/Branch pair of instructions checks whether or not the list is empty. If it is empty (RHEAD contains 0), the new record becomes a one-entry list by moving its address into RHEAD, followed by a Return instruction; otherwise, the second Compare/Branch pair checks whether or not the new record becomes the new head. If it does, the two Move instructions make the necessary changes to the link field of the new record and the contents of RHEAD, and a Return is executed. If the new record does not become the new head, the last half of the subroutine determines the position in the list where the new record is to be inserted. It is then inserted at the correct interior position by the last two Move instructions, or it is made the new tail by the last Move instruction. We have omitted saving and restoring registers in this subroutine to improve readability and understanding of the insertion operation.

Deletion of a Record

The deletion of an existing record from a linked list is an easier operation than the insertion of a new record. We simply go forward through the list until we find the ID of the record that is to be deleted. The necessary link field adjustments are then made.

Figure 2.38 shows a subroutine that implements the deletion operation. We assume that a register RIDNUM contains the ID of the record to be deleted. Registers RHEAD, RCURRENT, and RNEXT, play the same roles as in the insertion subroutine. The first Compare/Branch pair of instructions checks whether or not the record to be deleted is the head. If it is, the record is deleted by moving the link field address of the head record into RHEAD. Note that if the head is the only record in the list, then its link field contains zero, signifying that it is also the tail. So moving this zero into RHEAD properly signifies the empty list condition. If the head record is not the record to be deleted, then a branch is made to SEARCH. Now, registers RCURRENT and RNEXT are used to search forward from the head until the desired record is found. When the desired record is found by the second Compare/Branch pair, a branch is made to DELETE. The record, pointed to by RNEXT, is removed by transferring its link field to the link field of the previous record, pointed to by RCURRENT. The last two Move instructions accomplish this transfer through the register RTEMP. If a memory-to-memory Move instruction is available, then the single instruction

$$\text{Move} \quad 4(\text{RNEXT}),4(\text{RCURRENT})$$

can replace these two Move instructions.

Error Conditions

The insertion and deletion subroutines in Figures 2.37 and 2.38 do not take into account the possibility of two error conditions. The insertion subroutine makes the

	DELETION	Compare	(RHEAD), RIDNUM
		Branch>0	SEARCH
		Move	4(RHEAD), RHEAD
not the head record		Return	
	SEARCH	Move	RHEAD, RCURRENT
	LOOP	Move	4(RCURRENT), RNEXT
		Compare	(RNEXT), RIDNUM
		Branch=0	DELETE
		Move	RNEXT, RCURRENT
		Branch	LOOP
	DELETE	Move	4(RNEXT), RTEMP
		Move	RTEMP, 4(RCURRENT)
		Return	

Figure 2.38   A subroutine for deleting a record from a linked list.

assumption that there is no record in the list with the new ID, and the deletion subroutine assumes that there is a record with the ID to be deleted. Modifying the subroutines to account for these error possibilities is considered in problems 2.23 and 2.24.

2.12   ENCODING OF MACHINE INSTRUCTIONS

We have introduced a variety of useful instructions and addressing modes. These instructions specify the actions that must be performed by the processor circuitry to carry out the desired tasks. We have often referred to them as machine instructions. Actually, the form in which we have presented the instructions is indicative of the forms used in assembly languages, except that we tried to avoid using acronyms for the various operations, which are awkward to memorize and are likely to be specific to a particular commercial processor. To be executed in a processor, an instruction must be encoded in a compact binary pattern. Such encoded instructions are properly referred to as *machine instructions*. The instructions that use symbolic names and acronyms are called *assembly language instructions,* which are converted into the machine instructions using the assembler program as explained in Section 2.6.

In the previous sections, we made a simplifying assumption that all instructions are one word in length. Since we usually refer to 32-bit words, our assumption implies that this length is adequate to represent the necessary information. Let us now consider the validity of this assumption.

We have seen instructions that perform operations such as add, subtract, move, shift, rotate, and branch. These instructions may use operands of different sizes, such as 32-bit and 8-bit numbers or 8-bit ASCII-encoded characters. The type of operation that is to be performed and the type of operands used may be specified using an encoded binary pattern referred to as the *OP code* for the given instruction. Suppose that 8 bits are allocated for this purpose, giving 256 possibilities for specifying different instructions. This leaves 24 bits to specify the rest of the required information.

Let us examine some typical cases. The instruction

Add   R1,R2

has to specify the registers R1 and R2, in addition to the OP code. If the processor has 16 registers, then four bits are needed to identify each register. Additional bits are needed to indicate that the Register addressing mode is used for each operand.

The instruction

Move   24(R0),R5

requires 16 bits to denote the OP code and the two registers, and some bits to express that the source operand uses the Index addressing mode and that the index value is 24. Suppose that three bits are used to specify an addressing mode in Table 2.1. Then six bits have to be available for this purpose, denoting the chosen addressing modes of the source and destination operands. Hence, there are 10 bits left to give the index value. If these 10 bits suffice to express an adequate range of signed numbers for indexing purposes, then the instruction fits into our 32-bit word.

The shift instruction

LshiftR   #2,R0

and the move instruction

Move   #$3A,R1

have to indicate the immediate values 2 and $3A, respectively, in addition to the 18 bits used to specify the OP code, the addressing modes, and the register. This limits the size of the immediate operand to what is expressible in 14 bits.

Consider next the branch instruction

Branch>0   LOOP

Again, 8 bits are used for the OP code, leaving 24 bits to specify the branch offset. Since the offset is a 2's-complement number, the branch target address must be within 2^{23} bytes of the location of the branch instruction. To branch to an instruction outside this range, a different addressing mode has to be used, such as Absolute or Register Indirect. Branch instructions that use these modes are usually called Jump instructions.

In all these examples, the instructions can be encoded in a 32-bit word. Figure 2.39a depicts a possible format. There is an 8-bit OP-code field and two 7-bit fields for specifying the source and destination operands. The 7-bit field identifies the addressing mode and the register involved (if any). The "Other info" field allows us to specify the additional information that may be needed, such as an index value or an immediate operand.

But, what happens if we want to specify a memory operand using the Absolute addressing mode? The instruction

Move   R2,LOC

8	7	7	10
OP code	Source	Dest	Other info

(a) One-word instruction

OP code	Source	Dest	Other info
Memory address/Immediate operand			

(b) Two-word instruction

OP code	Ri	Rj	Rk	Other info

(c) Three-operand instruction

Figure 2.39   Encoding instructions into 32-bit words.

requires 18 bits to denote the OP code, the addressing modes, and the register. This leaves 14 bits to express the address that corresponds to LOC, which is clearly insufficient. If we want to be able to give a complete 32-bit address in the instruction, then the only solution is to include a second word as a part of this instruction, in which case the additional word can contain the required memory address. A suitable format is shown in Figure 2.39b. The first word may be the same as in part a of the figure. The second is a full memory address. This format can also accommodate instructions such as

And   #$FF000000,R2

in which case the second word gives a full 32-bit immediate operand.

If we want to allow an instruction in which two operands can be specified using the Absolute addressing mode, for example

Move   LOC1,LOC2

then it becomes necessary to use two additional words for the 32-bit addresses of the operands.

This approach results in instructions of variable length, dependent on the number of operands and the type of addressing modes used. Using multiple words, we can implement quite complex instructions, closely resembling operations in high-level programming languages. The term *complex instruction set computer* (CISC) has been used to refer to processors that use instruction sets of this type.

There exists a radically different alternative to this approach. If we insist that all instructions must fit into a single 32-bit word, it is not possible to provide a 32-bit address or a 32-bit immediate operand within the instruction. But, it is still possible to define a highly functional instruction set, which makes extensive use of the processor registers. Thus, we can have

Add   R1,R2

but not

Add   LOC,R2

Instead of the latter instruction, we can use

Add   (R3),R2

provided that we load the address LOC into register R3 before the instruction is executed. In this case, register R3 is being used as a pointer to the desired memory location.

This raises the issue of how to load a 32-bit address into a register that serves as a pointer to memory locations. One possibility is to direct the assembler to place the desired address in a word location in a data area close to the program. Then the Relative addressing mode can be used to load the address. This assumes that the index field contained in the Load instruction is large enough to reach the location containing the desired address. Another possibility is to use logical and shift instructions to construct the desired 32-bit address by giving it in parts that are small enough to be specifiable using the Immediate addressing mode. This issue is considered in more detail for the ARM processor in Chapter 3. All ARM instructions are encoded into a single 32-bit word.

The restriction that an instruction must occupy only one word has led to a style of computers that have become known as *reduced instruction set computers* (RISC). The RISC approach introduced other restrictions, such as that all manipulation of data must be done on operands that are already in processor registers. This restriction means that the above addition would need a two-instruction sequence

Move   (R3),R1
Add   R1,R2

If the Add instruction only has to specify the two registers, it will need just a portion of a 32-bit word. So, we may provide a more powerful instruction that uses three operands

Add   R1,R2,R3

which performs the operation

$$R3 \leftarrow [R1] + [R2]$$

A possible format for such an instruction is shown in Figure 2.39*c*. Of course, the processor has to be able to deal with such three-operand instructions. In an instruction set where all arithmetic and logical operations use only register operands, the only memory references are made to load/store the operands into/from the processor registers.

RISC-type instruction sets typically have fewer and less complex instructions than CISC-type sets. We will discuss the relative merits of RISC and CISC approaches in Chapter 8, which deals with the details of processor design.

2.13 CONCLUDING REMARKS

This chapter introduced the representation and execution of instructions and programs at the assembly and machine level as seen by the programmer. The discussion emphasized the basic principles of addressing techniques and instruction sequencing. The programming examples illustrated the basic types of operations implemented by the instruction set of any modern computer. Several addressing modes were introduced, including the important concepts of pointers and indexed addressing. Basic I/O operations were discussed, showing how characters are transferred between the processor and keyboard and display devices. The subroutine concept and the instructions needed to implement it were also discussed. Subroutine linkage methods provided an example of the application of the stack data structure. The way in which machine instructions manipulate other data structures was also explained. Queues, arrays, and linked lists were considered. We described two different approaches to the design of machine instruction sets — the CISC and RISC approaches. The execution-time performance of these two design styles will be further developed in Chapter 8.

PROBLEMS

2.1 Represent the decimal values 5, -2, 14, -10, 26, -19, 51, and -43, as signed, 7-bit numbers in the following binary formats:

    (*a*) Sign-and-magnitude

    (*b*) 1's-complement

    (*c*) 2's-complement

(See Appendix E for decimal-to-binary integer conversion.)

2.2 (*a*) Convert the following pairs of decimal numbers to 5-bit, signed, 2's-complement, binary numbers and add them. State whether or not overflow occurs in each case.

    (*a*) 5 and 10

    (*b*) 7 and 13

    (*c*) -14 and 11

    (*d*) -5 and 7

    (*e*) -3 and -8

    (*f*) -10 and -13

(*b*) Repeat Part *a* for the subtract operation, where the second number of each pair is to be subtracted from the first number. State whether or not overflow occurs in each case.

2.3 Given a binary pattern in some memory location, is it possible to tell whether this pattern represents a machine instruction or a number?

2.4 A memory byte location contains the pattern 00101100. What does this pattern represent when interpreted as a binary number? What does it represent as an ASCII code?

2.5 Consider a computer that has a byte-addressable memory organized in 32-bit words according to the big-endian scheme. A program reads ASCII characters entered at a keyboard and stores them in successive byte locations, starting at location 1000. Show the contents of the two memory words at locations 1000 and 1004 after the name "Johnson" has been entered.

2.6 Repeat Problem 2.5 for the little-endian scheme.

2.7 A program reads ASCII characters representing the digits of a decimal number as they are entered at a keyboard and stores the characters in successive memory bytes. Examine the ASCII code in Appendix E and indicate what operation is needed to convert each character into an equivalent binary number.

2.8 Write a program that can evaluate the expression

$$A \times B + C \times D$$

in a single-accumulator processor. Assume that the processor has Load, Store, Multiply, and Add instructions, and that all values fit in the accumulator.

2.9 The list of student marks shown in Figure 2.14 is changed to contain j test scores for each student. Assume that there are n students. Write an assembly language program for computing the sums of the scores on each test and store these sums in the memory word locations at addresses SUM, SUM + 4, SUM + 8, ... The number of tests, j, is larger than the number of registers in the processor, so the type of program shown in Figure 2.15 for the 3-test case cannot be used. Use two nested loops, as suggested in Section 2.5.3. The inner loop should accumulate the sum for a particular test, and the outer loop should run over the number of tests, j. Assume that j is stored in memory location J, placed ahead of location N.

2.10 (*a*) Rewrite the dot product program in Figure 2.33 for an instruction set in which the arithmetic and logic operations can only be applied to operands in processor registers. The two instructions Load and Store are used to transfer operands between registers and the memory.

   (*b*) Calculate the values of the constants k_1 and k_2 in the expression $k_1 + k_2 n$, which represents the number of memory accesses required to execute your program for Part *a*, including instruction word fetches. Assume that each instruction occupies a single word.

2.11 Repeat Problem 2.10 for a computer with two-address instructions, which can perform operations such as

$$A \leftarrow [A] + [B]$$

where A and B can be either memory locations or processor registers. Which computer requires fewer memory accesses? (Chapter 8 on pipelining gives a different perspective on the answer to this question.)

2.12 "Having a large number of processor registers makes it possible to reduce the number of memory accesses needed to perform complex tasks." Devise a simple computational task to show the validity of this statement for a processor that has four registers compared to another that has only two registers.

2.13 Registers R1 and R2 of a computer contain the decimal values 1200 and 4600. What is the effective address of the memory operand in each of the following instructions?

(*a*)	Load	20(R1),R5
(*b*)	Move	#3000,R5
(*c*)	Store	R5,30(R1,R2)
(*d*)	Add	−(R2),R5
(*e*)	Subtract	(R1)+,R5

2.14 Assume that the list of student test scores shown in Figure 2.14 is stored in the memory as a linked list as shown in Figure 2.36. Write an assembly language program that accomplishes the same thing as the program in Figure 2.15. The head record is stored at memory location 1000.

2.15 Consider an array of numbers $A(i,j)$, where $i = 0$ through $n - 1$ is the row index, and $j = 0$ through $m - 1$ is the column index. The array is stored in the memory of a computer one row after another, with elements of each row occupying m successive word locations. Assume that the memory is byte-addressable and that the word length is 32 bits. Write a subroutine for adding column x to column y, element by element, leaving the sum elements in column y. The indices x and y are passed to the subroutine in registers R1 and R2. The parameters n and m are passed to the subroutine in registers R3 and R4, and the address of element $A(0,0)$ is passed in register R0. Any of the addressing modes in Table 2.1 can be used. At most, one operand of an instruction can be in the memory.

2.16 Both of the following statements cause the value 300 to be stored in location 1000, but at different times.

$$\text{ORIGIN} \qquad 1000$$
$$\text{DATAWORD} \quad 300$$

and

$$\text{Move} \quad \#300, 1000$$

Explain the difference.

2.17 Register R5 is used in a program to point to the top of a stack. Write a sequence of instructions using the Index, Autoincrement, and Autodecrement addressing modes to perform each of the following tasks:

(*a*) Pop the top two items off the stack, add them, and then push the result onto the stack.

(b) Copy the fifth item from the top into register R3.

(c) Remove the top ten items from the stack.

2.18 A FIFO queue of bytes is to be implemented in the memory, occupying a fixed region of k bytes. You need two pointers, an IN pointer and an OUT pointer. The IN pointer keeps track of the location where the next byte is to be appended to the queue, and the OUT pointer keeps track of the location containing the next byte to be removed from the queue.

(a) As data items are added to the queue, they are added at successively higher addresses until the end of the memory region is reached. What happens next, when a new item is to be added to the queue?

(b) Choose a suitable definition for the IN and OUT pointers, indicating what they point to in the data structure. Use a simple diagram to illustrate your answer.

(c) Show that if the state of the queue is described only by the two pointers, the situations when the queue is completely full and completely empty are indistinguishable.

(d) What condition would you add to solve the problem in part c?

(e) Propose a procedure for manipulating the two pointers IN and OUT to append and remove items from the queue.

2.19 Consider the queue structure described in Problem 2.18. Write APPEND and REMOVE routines that transfer data between a processor register and the queue. Be careful to inspect and update the state of the queue and the pointers each time an operation is attempted and performed.

2.20 Consider the following possibilities for saving the return address of a subroutine:

(a) In a processor register

(b) In a memory location associated with the call, so that a different location is used when the subroutine is called from different places

(c) On a stack

Which of these possibilities supports subroutine nesting and which supports subroutine recursion (that is, a subroutine that calls itself)?

2.21 The subroutine call instruction of a computer saves the return address in a processor register called the link register, RL. What would you do to allow subroutine nesting? Would your scheme allow the subroutine to call itself?

2.22 Assume you want to organize subroutine calls on a computer as follows: When routine Main wishes to call subroutine SUB1, it calls an intermediate routine, CALLSUB, and passes to it the address of SUB1 as a parameter in register R1. CALLSUB saves the return address on a stack, making sure that the upper limit of the stack is not exceeded. Then it branches to SUB1. To return to the calling program, subroutine SUB1 calls another intermediate routine, RETRN. This routine checks that the stack is not empty and then uses the top element to return to the original calling program.

Write routines CALLSUB and RETRN, assuming that the subroutine call instruction saves the return address in a link register, RL. The upper and lower limits of the stack are recorded in memory locations UPPERLIMIT and LOWERLIMIT, respectively.

2.23   The linked-list insertion subroutine in Figure 2.37 does not check if the ID of the new record matches that of a record already in the list. What happens in the execution of the subroutine if this is the case? Modify the subroutine to return the address of the matching record in register ERROR if this occurs or return a zero if the insertion is successful.

2.24   The linked-list deletion subroutine in Figure 2.38 assumes that a record with the ID contained in register RIDNUM is in the list. What happens in the execution of the subroutine if there is no record with this ID? Modify the subroutine to return a zero in RIDNUM if deletion is successful or leave RIDNUM unchanged if the record is not in the list.

ARM, MOTOROLA, AND INTEL INSTRUCTION SETS

CHAPTER OBJECTIVES

In this chapter, which has three independent parts, you will learn about the following instruction set architectures:

- ARM (Part I)
- Motorola 68000 (Part II)
- Intel IA-32 Pentium (Part III)

The basic ideas of instruction sets, addressing modes, and instruction execution were introduced in Chapter 2. Assembly language representation for machine instructions and programs was used to present a number of program examples. In this chapter, we study how these basic ideas have been implemented in ARM, Motorola 68000, and Intel IA-32 ISAs. The ARM instruction set exemplifies RISC design, and the 68000 and IA-32 instruction sets illustrate the CISC design style. The three parts of this chapter, one for each instruction set, are independent complete units. The generic programs presented in Chapter 2 are coded in each of the three instruction sets. It is important to have a good understanding of the full discussion of basic ideas and programs in Chapter 2 because the corresponding discussions here are more brief. Appendices B, C, and D give concise summaries of the three ISAs, and contain more detail than is provided here in Chapter 3.

PART I
THE ARM EXAMPLE

Advanced RISC Machines (ARM) Limited has designed a family of microprocessors, and it licenses the designs to other companies for chip fabrication and use in computer products and embedded systems. The ARM company is relatively new, having evolved out of the Acorn Computers company that developed processor designs in the early 1980s. The main use for ARM microprocessors is in low-power and low-cost embedded applications such as mobile telephones, communication modems, automotive engine management systems, and hand-held digital assistants [1]. The book by Furber [2] contains a wealth of information on ARM design and implementation; the Clements text [3] uses ARM as a major example, and the book by van Someren and Atack [4] describes assembly language programming for ARM. Detailed information is also available at the ARM web site [5]. All ARM processors share the same basic machine instruction set. The version used here is the one implemented by the ARM7 processor. Later versions added features that are not relevant for the level of discussion in this chapter. In Chapter 11, we describe some of the added features in these later versions of the architecture. The programs from Chapter 2 are presented here in the ARM assembly language in order to illustrate various aspects of the ARM architecture.

3.1 REGISTERS, MEMORY ACCESS, AND DATA TRANSFER

In the ARM architecture, memory is byte addressable, using 32-bit addresses, and the processor registers are 32 bits long. Two operand lengths are used in moving data between the memory and the processor registers: bytes (8 bits) and words (32 bits). Word addresses must be aligned, that is, they must be a multiple of 4. Both little-endian and big-endian memory addressing is supported. (See Section 2.2.2.) The choice is determined by an external input control line to the processor. When a byte is loaded from memory into a processor register or stored from a register into the memory, it is always located in the low-order byte position of the register.

Memory is accessed only by Load and Store instructions. All arithmetic and logic instructions operate only on data in processor registers. This arrangement is a basic feature of RISC architectures. Its implications for simplicity of processor design and performance will be examined in Chapter 8.

3.1.1 REGISTER STRUCTURE

The processor registers used by application programs are shown in Figure 3.1. There are sixteen 32-bit registers labeled R0 through R15, which consist of fifteen general purpose registers (R0 through R14) and the Program Counter (PC) register, R15. The general purpose registers can hold either memory addresses or data operands. The Current Program Status Register (CPSR), or simply the Status register, holds the condition code flags (N, Z, C, V), interrupt disable flags, and processor mode bits. The information represented by the condition code flags is described in Section 2.4.6. The use of processor mode bits and interrupt disable bits will be described in conjunction with input/output operations and interrupts in Chapter 4. Here, we will assume that the processor is in User mode and is executing an application program.

There are 15 additional general-purpose registers called the *banked* registers. They are duplicates of some of the R0 to R14 registers. They are used when the processor switches into Supervisor or Interrupt modes of operation. Saved copies of the Status register are also available in these nonUser modes. These banked registers and Status register copies will also be discussed in Chapter 4.

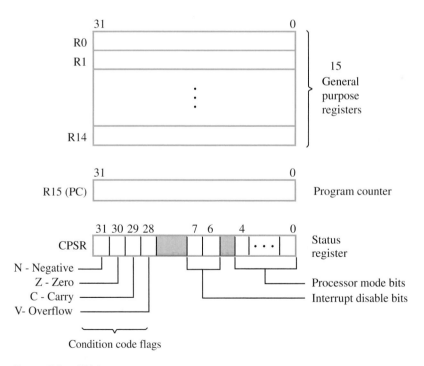

Figure 3.1   ARM register structure.

31	28	27	20	19	16	15	12	11	4	3	0
Condition		OP code		Rn		Rd		Other info		Rm	

Figure 3.2   ARM instruction format.

3.1.2   MEMORY ACCESS INSTRUCTIONS AND ADDRESSING MODES

Each instruction in the ARM architecture is encoded into a 32-bit word in a reasonably uniform way, typical of RISC designs. Access to memory is provided only by Load and Store instructions. The basic encoding format for these instructions, as well as for the Move, Arithmetic, and Logic instructions is shown in Figure 3.2. More detail is given in Appendix B. An instruction specifies a conditional execution code (Condition), the OP code, two or three registers (Rn, Rd, and Rm), and some other information. If register Rm is not needed, the "Other info" field extends to bit b_0. In a Load instruction, the operand is transferred from the memory into the general-purpose register named in the 4-bit Rd field. In a Store instruction, the operand is transferred from Rd into the memory. If the operand is a byte, it is always located in the low-order byte position of the register, and in a Load instruction, the high-order 24 bits of the register are filled with zeros.

Conditional Execution of Instructions

A distinctive and somewhat unusual feature of ARM processors is that all instructions are conditionally executed, depending on a condition specified in the instruction. The instruction is executed only if the current state of the processor condition code flags satisfies the condition specified in bits b_{31-28} of the instruction. Otherwise, the processor proceeds to the next instruction. One of the conditions is used to indicate that the instruction is always executed. The usefulness of conditional execution will be seen in the examples in Section 3.7. For now, we will ignore this feature and assume that the condition field of the instruction contains the "always executed" code.

Memory Addressing Modes

The basic method for addressing memory operands is to generate the effective address, EA, of the operand by adding a signed offset to the contents of a base register Rn, which is specified in the instruction as shown in Figure 3.2. The magnitude of the offset is either an immediate value, contained in the low-order 12 bits of the instruction, or it is the contents of a third register, Rm, named by the low-order four bits, b_{3-0}. The sign (direction) of the offset is contained in the OP-code field.

For example, the Load instruction

$$\text{LDR} \quad Rd,[Rn,\#\text{offset}]$$

specifies the offset (expressed as a signed number) in the immediate mode and performs the operation

$$Rd \leftarrow [[Rn] + \text{offset}]$$

Note that the destination register, Rd, is listed first. This is opposite to the order used in Chapter 2. The instruction

$$\text{LDR} \quad \text{R}d,[\text{R}n,\text{R}m]$$

performs the operation

$$\text{R}d \leftarrow [[\text{R}n]+[\text{R}m]]$$

Since the contents of Rm are the magnitude of the offset, Rm must be preceded by a minus sign if a negative offset is desired. In Chapter 2, these two addressing modes were defined as the Index and Base with index modes, respectively. An offset of zero does not have to be specified explicitly. Hence, the instruction

$$\text{LDR} \quad \text{R}d,[\text{R}n]$$

performs the operation

$$\text{R}d \leftarrow [[\text{R}n]]$$

using the addressing mode that was defined as the Indirect mode in Chapter 2.

The OP-code mnemonic LDR specifies that a 32-bit word is loaded from the memory into a register. A byte operand can be loaded into the low-order byte position of a register by using the mnemonic LDRB. The higher order bits are filled with zeros.

Store instructions have the mnemonics STR and STRB. For example, the instruction

$$\text{STR} \quad \text{R}d,[\text{R}n]$$

performs the operation

$$[\text{R}n] \leftarrow [\text{R}d]$$

transferring a word operand into the memory. The STRB instruction transfers the byte contained in the low-order end of Rd.

ARM documents refer to all of these modes, and others that we will describe shortly, as indexed addressing modes. The form that we have used in these first examples is called the Pre-indexed addressing mode because the effective address of the operand is generated by adding the offset to the contents of the base register Rn. The contents of register Rn are not changed. Addressing modes that are similar to the Autodecrement and Autoincrement modes that were discussed in Chapter 2 are also provided. They are called Pre-indexed with writeback and Post-indexed, respectively.

Definitions of all three modes are given as:

Pre-indexed mode — The effective address of the operand is the sum of the contents of the base register Rn and an offset value.

Pre-indexed with writeback mode — The effective address of the operand is generated in the same way as in the Pre-indexed mode, and then the effective address is written back into Rn.

Post-indexed mode — The effective address of the operand is the contents of Rn. The offset is then added to this address and the result is written back into Rn.

Table 3.1 specifies the assembly language syntax for these addressing modes, and

Table 3.1   ARM indexed addressing modes

Name	Assembler syntax	Addressing function
With immediate offset:		
Pre-indexed	[Rn, #offset]	EA = [Rn] + offset
Pre-indexed with writeback	[Rn, #offset]!	EA = [Rn] + offset; Rn ← [Rn] + offset
Post-indexed	[Rn], #offset	EA = [Rn]; Rn ← [Rn] + offset
With offset magnitude in Rm:		
Pre-indexed	[Rn, ± Rm, shift]	EA = [Rn] ± [Rm] shifted
Pre-indexed with writeback	[Rn, ± Rm, shift]!	EA = [Rn] ± [Rm] shifted; Rn ← [Rn] ± [Rm] shifted
Post-indexed	[Rn], ± Rm, shift	EA = [Rn]; Rn ← [Rn] ± [Rm] shifted
Relative (Pre-indexed with immediate offset)	Location	EA = Location = [PC] + offset

EA = effective address
offset = a signed number contained in the instruction
shift = direction #integer
      where direction is LSL for left shift or LSR for right shift, and
      integer is a 5-bit unsigned number specifying the shift amount
±Rm = the offset magnitude in register Rm can be added to or subtracted from the contents
      of base register Rn

gives expressions for the calculation of the effective address, EA, and the writeback operations. The exclamation mark signifies writeback in the Pre-indexed addressing mode. The Post-indexed mode always involves writeback, so the exclamation mark is not needed. Note that pre- and post-indexing are distinguished by the way the square brackets are used. When only the base register is enclosed in square brackets, its contents are used as the effective address. The offset is added to the register contents after the operand is accessed. In other words, post-indexing is specified. This is a generalized form of the Autoincrement addressing mode described in Section 2.5. When both the base register and the offset are placed inside the square brackets, the sum is used as the effective address of the operand, that is, pre-indexing is used. If writeback is to be performed, it must be indicated by the exclamation mark (!). Pre-indexing with writeback is a generalization of the Autodecrement addressing mode discussed in Section 2.5.

In all three addressing modes, the offset may be given as an immediate value in the range ±4095. Alternatively, the magnitude of the offset may be specified as the contents of the third register, Rm, with the sign (direction) of the offset specified by a ± prefix on the register name. For example, the instruction

$$\text{LDR} \quad \text{R0,[R1,−R2]!}$$

performs the operation

$$R0 \leftarrow [[R1] - [R2]]$$

The effective address of the operand, $[R1] - [R2]$, is then loaded into R1 because writeback is specified by the exclamation mark.

When the offset is given in a register, it may be scaled by a power of 2 by shifting to the right or to the left. This is indicated in the assembly language by placing the shift direction, LSL for left shift or LSR for right shift, and the shift amount, after the register name Rm, as shown in Table 3.1. The amount of the shift is specified by an immediate value in the range 0 to 31. For example, the contents of R2 in the example above may be multiplied by 16 before being used as an offset as follows:

$$LDR \quad R0,[R1,-R2,LSL \ \#4]!$$

This instruction will perform the operation

$$R0 \leftarrow [[R1] - 16 \times [R2]]$$

and will then load the effective address into R1.

The Program Counter, PC, may be used as the Base register Rn. In this case, the Relative addressing mode, as described in Section 2.5, is implemented. The assembler determines the immediate offset as the signed distance between the address of the operand and the contents of the updated PC. When the effective address is calculated at instruction execution time, the contents of the PC will have been updated to the address two words (8 bytes) forward from the instruction containing the Relative addressing mode. The reason for this is related to pipelined execution of instructions, which will be discussed in Chapter 8.

An example of the Relative mode is shown in Figure 3.3a. The address of the operand, given symbolically as ITEM in the instruction, is 1060. There is no Absolute addressing mode available in the ARM architecture. Therefore, when the address of an operand is given in this way in the assembly language, the assembler always uses the Relative addressing mode. This is implemented by the Pre-indexed mode with an immediate offset, using PC as the base register. As shown in the figure, the offset calculated by the assembler is 52 because the updated PC will contain 1008 when the offset is added to it during program execution, and the effective address to be generated is $1060 = 1008 + 52$. The operand must be within the range of 4095 bytes forward or backward from the updated PC. If the operand address given in the instruction is outside this range, an error is indicated by the assembler and a different addressing mode must be used to access the operand.

Figure 3.3b shows an example of the Pre-indexed mode with the offset contained in register R6 and the base value contained in R5. The Store instruction (STR) stores the contents of R3 into memory word location 1200.

The examples shown in Figure 3.4 illustrate the usefulness of the writeback feature in the Post-indexed and Pre-indexed addressing modes. Figure 3.4a shows the first three numbers of a list of 25 numbers that are spaced 25 words apart, starting at memory address 1000. They comprise the first row of a 25×25 matrix of numbers stored in column order. The first number of the first row of the matrix is stored in word location 1000. The numbers at addresses 1100, 1200, . . . , 3400 are successive numbers of the

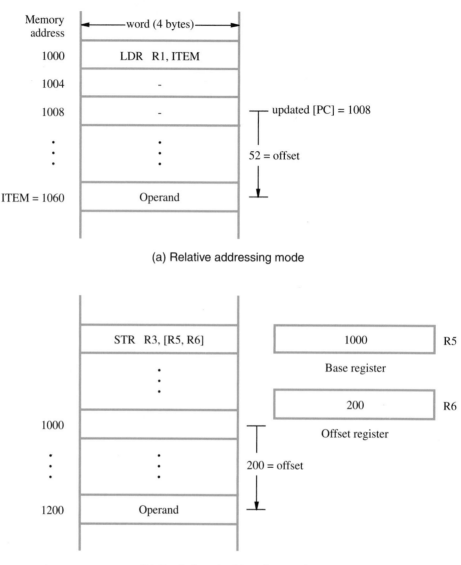

(a) Relative addressing mode

(b) Pre-indexed addressing mode

Figure 3.3 Examples of ARM memory addressing modes.

first row. The 25 memory locations 1000, 1004, 1008, . . . , 1096 contain the first column of the matrix.

Successive numbers in the first row of the matrix can be accessed conveniently using the Post-indexed addressing mode with writeback, with the offset contained in a register. Suppose that R2 is used as the base register and that it contains the initial address value 1000. Register R10 is used to hold the offset, and it is loaded with the

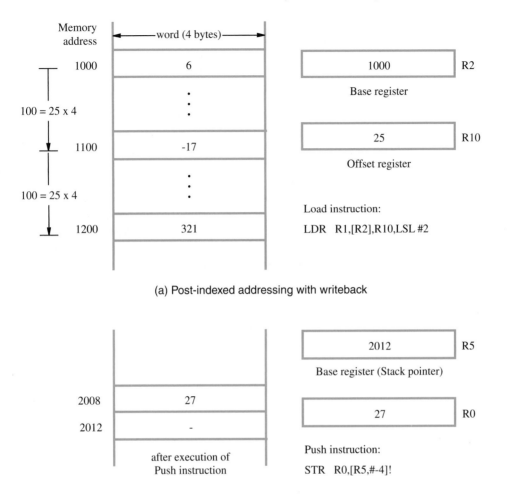

(a) Post-indexed addressing with writeback

(b) Pre-indexed addressing with writeback

Figure 3.4   ARM memory addressing modes involving writeback.

value 25. The instruction

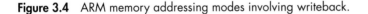

LDR   R1,[R2],R10,LSL #2

can then be used in a program loop that loads register R1 with successive elements of the first row of the matrix on successive passes through the loop. Let us examine how this works, step by step. The first time that the Load instruction is executed, the effective address is [R2] = 1000. Therefore, the number 6, at this address, is loaded into R1. Then, the writeback operation changes the contents of R2 from 1000 to 1100 so that it points to the second number, −17. It does this by shifting the contents, 25, of the offset register R10 left by two bit positions and then adding them to the contents of R2. The contents of R10 are not changed in this process. The left shift is equivalent to multiplying 25 by 4, generating the required offset 100. After this offset is added to the contents of R2, the new address 1100 is written back into R2. When the Load instruction is executed on the second pass through the loop, the second number, -17, is loaded into R1. The third number, 321, is loaded into R1 on the third pass, and so on.

This example involved adding the shifted contents of the offset register to the contents of the base register. As indicated in Table 3.1, the shifted offset can also be subtracted from the contents of the base register. Any shift distance in the range 0 through 31 can be selected, and either right or left shifting can be specified.

Figure 3.4*b* shows an example of pushing the contents, 27, of register R0 onto a stack. Register R5 is used as the stack pointer. Initially, it contains the address 2012 of the current TOS (top-of-stack) element. The Pre-indexed addressing mode with writeback, using an immediate offset, can be used to perform the Push operation with the instruction

$$\text{STR} \quad \text{R0,[R5,\#}-4]!$$

The immediate offset -4 is added to the contents, 2012, of R5 and written back into R5. This new TOS location, 2008, is used as the effective address for the Store operation. The contents, 27, of register R0 are stored at location 2008.

Load/Store Multiple Operands

In addition to the Load and Store instructions for single operands, there are two instructions for loading and storing multiple operands. They are called Block transfer instructions. Any subset of the general purpose registers can be loaded or stored. Only word operands are allowed, and the OP codes used are LDM (Load Multiple) and STM (Store Multiple). The memory operands must be in successive word locations. All of the forms of pre- and post-indexing with and without writeback are available. They operate on a Base register Rn specified in the instruction. The offset magnitude is always 4 in these instructions so it does not have to be specified explicitly in the instruction. The list of registers must appear in increasing order in the assembly language expression for the instruction. As an example, assume that register R10 is the Base register and that it contains the value 1000 initially. Then, the instruction

$$\text{LDMIA} \quad \text{R10!,\{R0,R1,R6,R7\}}$$

transfers the words from locations 1000, 1004, 1008, and 1012 into registers R0, R1, R6, and R7, leaving the address value 1016 in R10 after the last transfer. The suffix IA in the OP code indicates "Increment After," corresponding to post-indexing. We will discuss the Load/Store Multiple instructions further in Section 3.6 in conjunction with implementing subroutines, where they are used to save and restore registers on a stack in an efficient way.

3.1.3 REGISTER MOVE INSTRUCTIONS

It is often necessary to copy the contents of one register into another register or to load an immediate value into a register. The Move instruction

$$\text{MOV} \quad Rd, Rm$$

uses the format shown in Figure 3.2 to copy the contents of register Rm into register Rd. An immediate operand in the low-order 8 bits of the instruction can also be loaded into register Rd by the Move instruction. For example,

$$\text{MOV} \quad R0, \#76$$

places the immediate value 76 into register R0. In both forms of the Move instruction, the source operand can be shifted before being placed in the destination register.

3.2 ARITHMETIC AND LOGIC INSTRUCTIONS

The ARM instruction set has a number of instructions for arithmetic and logic operations on operands that are either contained in the general-purpose registers or given as immediate operands in the instruction itself. Memory operands are not allowed for these instructions. There are instructions for different forms of addition and subtraction, and there are two instructions for multiplication. There are instructions for the AND, OR, NOT, XOR, and Bit-Clear logic operations. Instructions such as Compare are provided to set condition code flags based on the results from arithmetic or logic operations on two operands. They do not store the actual results in a register. The format for most of these instructions is shown in Figure 3.2.

3.2.1 ARITHMETIC INSTRUCTIONS

The basic assembly language expression for arithmetic instructions is

$$\text{OPcode} \quad Rd, Rn, Rm$$

where the operation specified by the OP code is performed using the operands in general-purpose registers Rn and Rm. The result is placed in register Rd. For example, the instruction

$$\text{ADD} \quad R0, R2, R4$$

performs the operation

$$R0 \leftarrow [R2] + [R4]$$

and the instruction

$$\text{SUB} \quad R0, R6, R5$$

performs the operation

$$R0 \leftarrow [R6] - [R5]$$

Instead of being contained in register Rm, the second operand can be given in the Immediate mode. Thus,

ADD   R0,R3,#17

performs the operation

$$R0 \leftarrow [R3] + 17$$

The immediate value is contained in the 8-bit field in bits b_{7-0} of the instruction.

The second operand can be shifted or rotated before being used in the operation. When a shift or rotation is required, it is specified last in the assembly language expression for the instruction. The instruction

ADD   R0,R1,R5,LSL #4

operates as follows: The second operand, which is contained in register R5, is shifted left 4 bit positions (equivalent to [R5] × 16), and it is then added to the contents of register R1; the sum is placed in register R0.

Two versions of a Multiply instruction are provided. The first version multiplies the contents of two registers and places the low-order 32-bits of the product in a third register. The high-order bits of the product, if there are any, are discarded. For example, the instruction

MUL   R0,R1,R2

performs the operation

$$R0 \leftarrow [R1] \times [R2]$$

The second version specifies a fourth register whose contents are added to the product before storing the result in the destination register. Hence, the instruction

MLA   R0,R1,R2,R3

performs the operation

$$R0 \leftarrow [R1] \times [R2] + [R3]$$

This is called a Multiply-Accumulate operation. It is often used in numerical algorithms for digital signal processing. We will see an example of this type of application in Section 3.7. The fourth register is encoded in the Other information field of Figure 3.2. There are no provisions made for shifting or rotating any of the operands before they are used in the two Multiply instructions. Some versions of the ARM ISA accommodate double-length products (64 bits). (See Chapter 11.)

Operand Shift Operations

We noted earlier that one of the distinctive features of the ARM instruction set is that all instructions are executed conditionally. Another distinctive feature is the shifting and rotation operations that are incorporated into most instructions. In most other computer instruction sets, shifting operations are done using separate instructions. This is the case for the Motorola 68000 and the Intel IA-32 processors described in Parts II and III of this chapter. By incorporating shifting and rotation operations into instructions, as needed, the ARM architecture saves code space and can potentially improve execution time performance relative to more conventional processor designs. This feature is implemented using a *barrel shifter* circuit in the data path between the registers and the arithmetic and logic unit in the processor. Details of the shifting and rotation operations available, and their encoding in the instruction format, are given in Appendix B.

3.2.2 LOGIC INSTRUCTIONS

The logic operations AND, OR, XOR, and Bit-Clear are implemented by instructions with the OP codes AND, ORR, EOR, and BIC. They have the same format as the arithmetic instructions. The instruction

$$\text{AND} \quad \text{R}d,\text{R}n,\text{R}m$$

performs the operation

$$\text{R}d \leftarrow [\text{R}n] \wedge [\text{R}m]$$

which is a bitwise logical AND between the operands in registers Rn and Rm. For example, if register R0 contains the hexadecimal pattern 02FA62CA and R1 contains the pattern 0000FFFF, then the instruction

$$\text{AND} \quad \text{R0,R0,R1}$$

will result in the pattern 000062CA being placed in register R0.

The Bit-Clear instruction (BIC) is closely related to the AND instruction. It complements each bit in operand Rm before ANDing them with the bits in register Rn. Using the same R0 and R1 bit patterns as in the above example, the instruction

$$\text{BIC} \quad \text{R0,R0,R1}$$

results in the pattern 02FA0000 being placed in R0.

The Move Negative instruction, with the OP-code mnemonic MVN, complements the bits of the source operand and places the result in Rd. If the contents of R3 are the hexadecimal pattern 0F0F0F0F, then the instruction

$$\text{MVN} \quad \text{R0,R3}$$

places the result F0F0F0F0 in register R0.

```
LDR     R0,POINTER          Load address LOC into R0.
LDRB    R1,[R0]             Load ASCII characters
LDRB    R2,[R0,#1]             into R1 and R2.
AND     R2,R2,#&F           Clear high-order 28 bits of R2.
ORR     R2,R2,R1,LSL #4     Or [R1] shifted left into [R2].
STRB    R2,PACKED           Store packed BCD digits
                                into PACKED.
```

Figure 3.5 An ARM program for packing two 4-bit decimal digits into a byte.

Digit-Packing Program

Figure 3.5 shows an ARM program for packing two 4-bit decimal digits into a memory byte location. The generic version of this program is shown in Figure 2.31 and is described in Section 2.10.2. The decimal digits, represented in ASCII code, are stored in byte locations LOC and LOC + 1. The program packs the corresponding 4-bit BCD codes into a single byte location PACKED.

The first Load instruction in the program in Figure 3.5 assumes that the address LOC is stored in memory at address POINTER. As we will see in Section 3.4, an assembler directive can be used to place LOC in POINTER. This method of loading the address LOC into R0 is needed because a 32-bit address cannot be included as an immediate operand in an instruction. Location POINTER points to the BCD digit characters stored in successive byte locations. The two ASCII characters containing the BCD digits in their low-order four bits are loaded into the low-order byte positions of registers R1 and R2 by the next two Load instructions. The And instruction clears the high-order 28 bits of R2 to zero, leaving the second BCD digit in the four low-order bit positions. The Or instruction then shifts the first BCD digit in R1 to the left four positions and places it to the left of the second BCD digit in R2. The packed digits in the low-order byte of R2 are then stored into PACKED.

3.3 BRANCH INSTRUCTIONS

Conditional branch instructions contain a signed, 2's-complement, 24-bit offset that is added to the updated contents of the Program Counter to generate the branch target address. The format for the branch instructions is shown in Figure 3.6a, and an example is given in Figure 3.6b. The BEQ instruction (Branch if Equal to 0) causes a branch if the Z flag is set to 1.

The condition to be tested to determine whether or not branching should take place is specified in the high-order 4 bits, b_{31-28}, of the instruction word. A Branch instruction is executed in the same way as any other ARM instruction, that is, it is executed only if the current state of the condition code flags corresponds to the condition specified in the Condition field of the instruction.

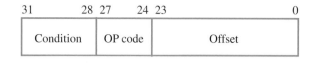

31   28 27   24 23   0

Condition	OP code	Offset

(a) Instruction format

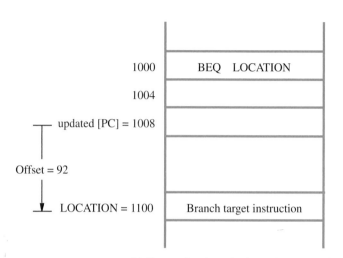

(b) Determination of a branch target address

Figure 3.6 ARM branch instructions.

At the time that the branch target address is computed, the contents of the PC have been updated to contain the address of the instruction that is two words beyond the Branch instruction itself. If the Branch instruction is at address location 1000, and the branch target address is 1100, as shown in Figure 3.6b, then the offset has to be 92 because the contents of the updated PC will be $1000 + 8 = 1008$ when address 1100 is computed.

3.3.1 SETTING CONDITION CODES

Some instructions, such as Compare, given by

$$CMP \quad Rn, Rm$$

which performs the operation

$$[Rn] - [Rm]$$

have the sole purpose of setting the condition code flags based on the result of the subtraction operation. On the other hand, the arithmetic and logic instructions affect the condition code flags only if explicitly specified to do so by a bit in the OP-code

```
         LDR    R1,N            Load count into R1.
         LDR    R2,POINTER      Load address NUM1 into R2.
         MOV    R0,#0           Clear accumulator R0.
LOOP     LDR    R3,[R2],#4      Load next number into R3.
         ADD    R0,R0,R3        Add number into R0.
         SUBS   R1,R1,#1        Decrement loop counter R1.
         BGT    LOOP            Branch back if not done.
         STR    R0,SUM          Store sum.
```

Figure 3.7   An ARM program for adding numbers.

field. This is indicated by appending the suffix S to the assembly language OP-code mnemonic. For example, the instruction

$$ADDS \quad R0,R1,R2$$

sets the condition code flags, but

$$ADD \quad R0,R1,R2$$

does not.

3.3.2   A LOOP PROGRAM FOR ADDING NUMBERS

Figure 3.7 shows a loop program for adding a list of numbers, patterned after the program in Figure 2.16. The load and store operations performed by the first, second, and last instructions use the Relative addressing mode. This assumes that the memory locations N, POINTER, and SUM are within the range reachable by the offset relative to the PC. Memory location POINTER contains the address NUM1 of the first of the numbers to be added, N contains the number of entries in the list, and SUM is used to store the sum. The Post-indexed addressing mode with writeback in the first instruction of the loop mirrors the use of the Autoincrement addressing mode in Figure 2.16.

3.4   ASSEMBLY LANGUAGE

The ARM assembly language has assembler directives to reserve storage space, assign numerical values to address labels and constant symbols, define where program and data blocks are to be placed in memory, and specify the end of the source program text. These facilities were described in general in Section 2.6.1.

We illustrate some of the ARM directives in Figure 3.8, which gives a complete source program for the program of Figure 3.7. The AREA directive, which uses the argument CODE or DATA, indicates the beginning of a block of memory that contains

	Memory address label	Operation	Addressing or data information
Assembler directives		AREA	CODE
		ENTRY	
Statements that		LDR	R1,N
generate		LDR	R2,POINTER
machine		MOV	R0,#0
instructions	LOOP	LDR	R3,[R2],#4
		ADD	R0,R0,R3
		SUBS	R1,R1,#1
		BGT	LOOP
		STR	R0,SUM
Assembler directives		AREA	DATA
	SUM	DCD	0
	N	DCD	5
	POINTER	DCD	NUM1
	NUM1	DCD	3,−17,27,−12,322
		END	

Figure 3.8   ARM assembly language source program for the program in Figure 3.7.

either program instructions or data. The AREA directive actually requires more parameters to be specified, but they are not relevant for the level of discussion here. The ENTRY directive specifies that program execution is to begin at the following LDR instruction.

In the data area, which follows the code area, the DCD directives are used to label and initialize the data operands. The word locations SUM and N are initialized to 0 and 5, respectively, by the first two DCD directives. The address NUM1 is placed in the pointer location POINTER by the next DCD directive. The last DCD directive specifies that the five numbers to be added are placed in successive memory locations, starting at NUM1.

Constants in hexadecimal notation have a & prefix, and constants in base n, for n between two and nine, are denoted as n_xxx. For example, 2_101100 denotes a binary constant. Base ten constants do not need a prefix.

An EQU directive can be used to define symbolic names for constants. For example, the statement

TEN   EQU   10

allows TEN to be used in a program instead of the decimal constant 10. When a number of registers are used in a program, it is convenient to use symbolic names for them that relate to their usage. The RN directive is used for this purpose. For example,

COUNTER   RN   3

establishes the name COUNTER for register R3. The register names R0 to R15, PC (for R15), and LR (for R14) are predefined by the assembler.

3.4.1 PSEUDO-INSTRUCTIONS

An alternative way of loading the address NUM1 into register R2 in Figure 3.8 is also provided in the assembly language. The *pseudo-instruction*

ADR   Rd,ADDRESS

loads the 32-bit value ADDRESS into Rd. This instruction is not an actual machine instruction. The assembler chooses appropriate real machine instructions to implement pseudo-instructions. For example, the combination of the machine instruction

LDR   R2,POINTER

and the data declaration directive

POINTER   DCD   NUM1

that is used in Figure 3.8 is one way to implement the pseudo-instruction

ADR   R2,NUM1

which would be placed at the position of the LDR instruction in the program. In this case, the assembler would need to allocate an appropriate data area for the DCD declaration.

　　　A more efficient way to implement the ADR instruction is possible in this particular example, and it is the one that would be chosen by the assembler. When the address value to be loaded by the ADR instruction is within 255 bytes of the current contents of the PC (R15), the instruction

ADD   Rd,R15,#offset

can be used to implement the ADR pseudo-instruction. If this is done in the example program, the location POINTER is not needed. The assembler implements the ADR pseudo-instruction with the real machine instruction

ADD   R2,R15,#28

because NUM1 is 28 bytes beyond the updated PC when the ADD instruction is executed. This assumes that the data area immediately follows the STR instruction. This is not actually true because an instruction to return control to the operating system must follow the STR instruction, but it has been omitted.

3.5   I/O OPERATIONS

The ARM architecture uses memory-mapped I/O as described in Section 2.7. Reading a character from a keyboard or sending a character to a display can be done using program-controlled I/O as described in that section.

Suppose that bit 3 in each of the device status registers INSTATUS (keyboard) and OUTSTATUS (display) contains the respective control flags SIN and SOUT. Also assume that the keyboard DATAIN and display DATAOUT registers are located at addresses INSTATUS + 4 and OUTSTATUS + 4, immediately following the status register locations. The read and write wait loops can then be implemented as follows. Assume that address INSTATUS has been loaded into register R1. The instruction sequence

```
READWAIT   LDR    R3,[R1]
           TST    R3,#8
           BEQ    READWAIT
           LDRB   R3,[R1,#4]
```

reads a character into register R3 when a key has been pressed on the keyboard. The test (TST) instruction performs the bitwise logical AND operation on its two operands and sets the condition code flags based on the result. The immediate operand 8 has a single one in the bit 3 position. Therefore, the result of the TST operation will be zero if bit 3 of INSTATUS is zero and will be nonzero if bit 3 is one, signifying that a character is available in DATAIN. The BEQ instruction branches back to READWAIT if the result is zero, looping until a key is pressed, which sets bit 3 of INSTATUS to one.

Assuming that address OUTSTATUS has been loaded into register R2, the instruction sequence

```
WRITEWAIT   LDR    R4,[R2]
            TST    R4,#8
            BEQ    WRITEWAIT
            STRB   R3,[R2,#4]
```

sends the character in register R3 to the DATAOUT register when the display is ready to receive it.

These two routines can be used to read a line of characters from a keyboard, store them in the memory, and echo them back to a display, as shown in the program in Figure 3.9. This program is patterned after the generic program in Figure 2.20. Register R0 is assumed to contain the address of the first byte in the memory area where the line is to be stored. Registers R1 through R4 have the same usage as in the READWAIT and WRITEWAIT loops described above. The first Store instruction (STRB) stores the character read from the keyboard into the memory. The Post-indexed addressing mode with writeback is used in this instruction to step through the memory area, analogous to the use of the Autoincrement addressing mode in Figure 2.20. The Test if Equal (TEQ)

```
READ    LDR     R3,[R1]         Load [INSTATUS] and
        TST     R3,#8              wait for character.
        BEQ     READ
        LDRB    R3,[R1,#4]      Read the character and
        STRB    R3,[R0],#1         store it in memory.
ECHO    LDR     R4,[R2]         Load [OUTSTATUS] and
        TST     R4,#8              wait for display
        BEQ     ECHO               to be ready.
        STRB    R3,[R2,#4]      Send character to display.
        TEQ     R3,#CR          If not carriage return,
        BNE     READ               read more characters.
```

Figure 3.9 An ARM program that reads a line of characters and displays it.

instruction tests whether or not the two operands are equal and sets the Z condition code flag accordingly.

3.6 SUBROUTINES

A Branch and Link (BL) instruction is used to call a subroutine. It operates in the same way as other branch instructions, with one added step. The return address, which is the address of the next instruction after the BL instruction, is loaded into register R14, which acts as a link register. Since subroutines may be nested, the contents of the link register must be saved on a stack by the subroutine. Register R13 is normally used as the pointer for this stack.

Figure 3.10 shows the program of Figure 3.7 rewritten as a subroutine. Parameters are passed through registers. The calling program passes the size of the number list and the address of the first number to the subroutine in registers R1 and R2; and the subroutine passes the sum back to the calling program in register R0. The subroutine also uses register R3. Therefore, its contents, along with the contents of the link register R14, are saved on the stack by the STMFD instruction. The suffix FD in this instruction specifies that the stack grows toward lower addresses and that the stack pointer R13 is to be predecremented before pushing words onto the stack. The LDMFD instruction restores the contents of register R3 and pops the saved return address into the PC (R15), performing the return operation automatically.

Figure 3.11a shows the program of Figure 3.7 rewritten as a subroutine with parameters passed on the stack. The parameters NUM1 and n are pushed onto the stack by the first four instructions of the calling program. We assume that NUM1 is contained in memory location POINTER. Registers R0 to R3 serve the same purpose inside the subroutine as in Figure 3.7. Their contents are saved on the stack by the first instruction of the subroutine along with the return address in R14. The contents of the stack at

Calling program

```
        LDR     R1,N
        LDR     R2,POINTER
        BL      LISTADD
        STR     R0,SUM
        ⋮
```

Subroutine

```
LISTADD STMFD   R13!,{R3,R14}    Save R3 and return address in R14 on
                                 stack, using R13 as the stack pointer.
        MOV     R0,#0
LOOP    LDR     R3,[R2],#4
        ADD     R0,R0,R3
        SUBS    R1,R1,#1
        BGT     LOOP
        LDMFD   R13!,{R3,R15}    Restore R3 and load return address
                                 into PC (R15).
```

Figure 3.10 Program of Figure 3.7 written as an ARM subroutine; parameters passed through registers.

various times are shown in Figure 3.11*b*. After the parameters have been pushed and the Call instruction (BL) has been executed, the top of the stack is at level 2. It is at level 3 after all registers have been saved by the first instruction of the subroutine. The next two instructions load the parameters into registers R1 and R2 using offsets of 20 and 24 bytes into the stack, which reach to *n* and NUM1, respectively, from level 3. When the sum has been accumulated in R0, it is inserted into the stack by the Store instruction (STR), overwriting NUM1.

The last example of subroutines is the case of handling nested calls. Figure 3.12 shows the ARM code for the program of Figure 2.28. The stack frames corresponding to the first and second subroutines are shown in Figure 3.13. Register R12 is used as the frame pointer. Symbolic names are used for some of the registers in this example to aid program readability. Registers R12 (frame pointer), R13 (stack pointer), R14 (link register), and R15 (program counter), are labeled as FP, SP, LR, and PC, respectively. The assembler directive RN can be used to define these names.

The structure of the calling program and the subroutines is the same as in Figure 2.28. Aspects that are specific to ARM are as follows. Both the return address and the old contents of the frame pointer are saved on the stack by the first instruction in each subroutine. The second instruction sets the frame pointer to point to its saved value, as shown in Figure 3.13. This is consistent with the frame pointer position in Figures 2.27 and 2.29. The parameters are then referenced at offsets of 8, 12, and so on, as usual.

(Assume top of stack is at level 1 below.)

Calling program

```
        LDR     R0,POINTER          Push NUM1
        STR     R0,[R13,#−4]!          on stack.
        LDR     R0,N                Push n
        STR     R0,[R13,#−4]!          on stack.
        BL      LISTADD
        LDR     R0,[R13,#4]         Move the sum into
        STR     R0,SUM                 memory location SUM.
        ADD     R13,R13,#8          Remove parameters from stack.
          .
          .
          .
```

Subroutine

```
LISTADD STMFD   R13!,{R0−R3,R14}    Save registers.
        LDR     R1,[R13,#20]        Load parameters
        LDR     R2,[R13,#24]           from stack.
        MOV     R0,#0
LOOP    LDR     R3,[R2],#4
        ADD     R0,R0,R3
        SUBS    R1,R1,#1
        BGT     LOOP
        STR     R0,[R13,#24]        Place sum on stack.
        LDMFD   R13!,{R0−R3,R15}    Restore registers and return.
```

(a) Calling program and subroutine

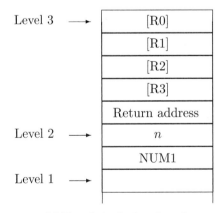

(b) Top of stack at various times

Figure 3.11   Program of Figure 3.7 written as an ARM subroutine; parameters passed on the stack.

Memory location		Instructions	Comments

Calling program

$\vdots$

2000		LDR	R10,PARAM2	Place parameters on stack.
2004		STR	R10,[SP,#−4]!	
2008		LDR	R10,PARAM1	
2012		STR	R10,[SP,#−4]!	
2016		BL	SUB1	
2020		LDR	R10,[SP]	Store SUB1 result.
2024		STR	R10,RESULT	
2028		ADD	SP,SP,#8	Remove parameters from stack.
2032		next instruction		

$\vdots$

First subroutine

2100	SUB1	STMFD	SP!,{R0−R3,FP,LR}	Save registers.
2104		ADD	FP,SP,#16	Load frame pointer.
2108		LDR	R0,[FP,#8]	Load parameters.
2112		LDR	R1,[FP,#12]	

$\vdots$

		LDR	R2,PARAM3	Place parameter on stack.
		STR	R2,[SP,#−4]!	
2160		BL	SUB2	
2164		LDR	R2,[SP],#4	Pop SUB2 result into R2.

$\vdots$

		STR	R3,[FP,#8]	Place result on stack.
		LDMFD	SP!,{R0−R3,FP,PC}	Restore registers and return.

Second subroutine

3000	SUB2	STMFD	SP!,{R0,R1,FP,LR}	Save registers.
		ADD	FP,SP,#8	Load frame pointer.
		LDR	R0,[FP,#8]	Load parameter.

$\vdots$

		STR	R1,[FP,#8]	Place result on stack.
		LDMFD	SP!,{R0,R1,FP,PC}	Restore registers and return.

Figure 3.12 Nested subroutines in ARM assembly language.

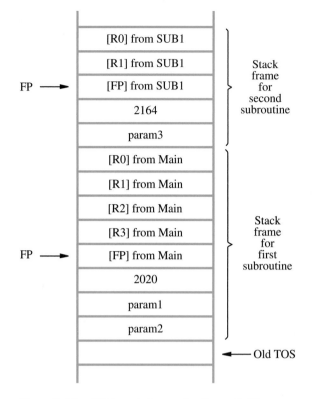

Figure 3.13 ARM stack frames for Figure 3.12.

The last instruction in each subroutine restores the old value of the frame pointer as well as the values of the other registers used, and pops the return address from the stack into the PC.

3.7 Program Examples

In this section, we give ARM versions of the programs for dot product, byte sorting, and linked-list operations that were described in Chapter 2. The programs are patterned after the generic programs shown in Figures 2.33, 2.34, 2.37, and 2.38. We will describe only those aspects of the ARM code that differ from the generic versions used in Chapter 2.

3.7.1 Vector Dot Product Program

The first two instructions in Figure 3.14 load the addresses of the A and B vectors into registers R1 and R2. They are the ADR pseudo-instructions described in Section 3.4.1. If AVEC and BVEC are close enough to the program, an Add instruction using the current

```
              ADR    R1,AVEC          R1 points to vector A.
              ADR    R2,BVEC          R2 points to vector B.
              LDR    R3,N             R3 is the loop counter.
              MOV    R0,#0            R0 accumulates the dot product.
     LOOP     LDR    R4,[R1],#4       Load A component.
              LDR    R5,[R2],#4       Load B component.
              MLA    R0,R4,R5,R0      Multiply components and
                                        accumulate into R0.
              SUBS   R3,R3,#1         Decrement the counter.
              BNE    LOOP             Branch back if not done.
              STR    R0,DOTPROD       Store dot product.
```

Figure 3.14   An ARM dot-product program.

value of the PC can be used to generate the addresses. The Relative addressing mode is used to access the contents of N and DOTPROD, and the Post-indexed addressing mode with writeback is used in the first two instructions of the loop. The Multiply-Accumulate instruction (MLA) performs the necessary arithmetic operations. It multiplies the vector elements in R4 and R5 and accumulates their product into R0.

3.7.2 BYTE-SORTING PROGRAM

Figure 3.15 shows the byte-sorting program. It follows the same structure as used in the program in Figure 2.34b. The address LIST of the first byte is loaded into register R4. It is used in the second to the last Compare instruction to determine when the inner loop (based on the k index) terminates. Correspondingly, R5 contains the address LIST + 1 and is used in the last Compare instruction to determine when the outer loop (based on the j index) terminates. The base register R2 is used to step the j index backward from the end of the list in the outer loop. Register R3 steps the k index backward through each sublist in the inner loop. The Pre-indexed addressing mode with writeback is used to load LIST(j) bytes into register R0 and to load LIST(k) bytes into R1 in the outer and inner loops, respectively.

The conditional execution feature of the ARM instruction set is used to advantage in the inner loop when LIST(k) must be interchanged with LIST(j). The three-instruction sequence STR, STR, MOV is only executed if LIST(k) is greater than LIST(j), as indicated by the GT suffixes. The forward conditional branch to NEXT in the generic program in Figure 2.34b is not needed in the ARM program.

3.7.3 LINKED-LIST INSERTION AND DELETION SUBROUTINES

The insertion and deletion subroutine programs in Figures 3.16 and 3.17 mirror the structure of the corresponding programs in Figures 2.37 and 2.38 quite closely. The forward conditional branches used in the generic programs are not needed in the ARM

```
for   (j = n−1; j > 0; j = j − 1)
      { for ( k = j−1; k >= 0; k = k − 1 )
          { if    (LIST[k] > LIST[j])
              {  TEMP = LIST[k];
                 LIST[k] = LIST[j];
                 LIST[j] = TEMP;
              }
          }
      }
```

(a) C-language program for sorting

	ADR	R4,LIST	Load list pointer register R4,
	LDR	R10,N	and initialize outer loop base
	ADD	R2,R4,R10	register R2 to LIST + n.
	ADD	R5,R4,#1	Load LIST + 1 into R5.
OUTER	LDRB	R0,[R2,#−1]!	Load LIST(j) into R0.
	MOV	R3,R2	Initialize inner loop base register
			R3 to LIST + n − 1.
INNER	LDRB	R1,[R3,#−1]!	Load LIST(k) into R1.
	CMP	R1,R0	Compare LIST(k) to LIST(j).
	STRGTB	R1,[R2]	If LIST(k) > LIST(j), interchange
	STRGTB	R0,[R3]	LIST(k) and LIST(j), and
	MOVGT	R0,R1	move (new) LIST(j) into R0.
	CMP	R3,R4	If k > 0, repeat
	BNE	INNER	inner loop.
	CMP	R2,R5	If j > 1, repeat
	BNE	OUTER	outer loop.

(b) ARM program implementation

Figure 3.15   An ARM byte-sorting program.

programs. This is a result of the use of conditional execution of instruction blocks, as done in the byte-sorting program in Figure 3.15. Parameters are passed through registers in both ARM subroutines.

Register mnemonics are used to reflect register usage, instead of the usual Ri notation. The assembler directive RN can be used to define the equivalences. As in the programs in Figures 2.37 and 2.38, RHEAD contains the address of the first record in

Subroutine

```
INSERTION   CMP      RHEAD,#0                    Check if list empty.
            MOVEQ    RHEAD,RNEWREC               If empty, insert new
            MOVEQ    PC,R14                        record as head.
            LDR      R0,[RHEAD]                  If not empty, check if
            LDR      R1,[RNEWREC]                  new record becomes
            CMP      R0,R1                         new head, and
            STRGT    RHEAD,[RNEWREC,#4]            insert if yes.
            MOVGT    RHEAD,RNEWREC
            MOVGT    PC,R14
            MOV      RCURRENT,RHEAD             If new record goes after
LOOP        LDR      RNEXT,[RCURRENT,#4]          current head,
            CMP      RNEXT,#0                     find where.
            STREQ    RNEWREC,[RCURRENT,#4]      New record becomes new tail.
            MOVEQ    PC,R14
            LDR      R0,[RNEXT]                 Go further?
            CMP      R0,R1
            MOVLT    RCURRENT,RNEXT            Yes, then loop back.
            BLT      LOOP
            STR      RNEXT,[RNEWREC,#4]        Otherwise, insert new record
            STR      RNEWREC,[RCURRENT,#4]       between current and
            MOV      PC,R14                      next records.
```

Figure 3.16 An ARM subroutine for inserting a new record into a linked list.

Subroutine

```
DELETION    LDR      R0,[RHEAD]                 Check if record to be
            CMP      R0,RIDNUM                    deleted is the head.
            LDREQ    RHEAD,[RHEAD,#4]           If yes, delete
            MOVEQ    PC,R14                       and return.
            MOV      RCURRENT,RHEAD            Otherwise, continue search.
LOOP        LDR      RNEXT,[RCURRENT,#4]       Is next record the one
            LDR      R0,[RNEXT]                 to be deleted?
            CMP      R0,RIDNUM
            LDREQ    R0,[RNEXT,#4]             If yes, delete
            STREQ    R0,[RCURRENT,#4]            and return.
            MOVEQ    PC,R14
            MOV      RCURRENT,RNEXT           Otherwise, loop back
            B        LOOP                       to continue search.
```

Figure 3.17 An ARM subroutine for deleting a record from a linked list.

the list. RNEWREC contains the address of the new record to be inserted. RIDNUM contains the ID number of the record to be deleted. The two registers RCURRENT and RNEXT contain link addresses that are used by the subroutines to walk through the list to find the insertion or deletion positions.

The insertion subroutine in Figure 3.16, patterned after the subroutine in Figure 2.37, has the following structure. The first three instructions insert the new record as the head (and tail) of a previously empty list. Recall that the new record is assumed to initially have zero in its link field. The third instruction in this block performs the return operation from the subroutine to the calling program. The next six instructions determine whether or not the new record should become the new head of the existing list. The list is ordered by increasing ID numbers. Therefore, if the ID number in the first word of the current head record is greater than the ID number of the new record, then the new record becomes the new head of the list. The conditionally executed STRGT and MOVGT instructions perform the appropriate link address operations if this is the case. Otherwise, the remaining part of the subroutine determines where the new record should be inserted in the list after the current head, including the possibility that the new record becomes the tail.

The deletion subroutine is shown in Figure 3.17. If the record to be deleted is the head of the list, the first four instructions discover this, delete it, and return. Otherwise, the remainder of the subroutine uses registers RCURRENT and RNEXT to move through the list looking for the record. The LDREQ/STREQ pair of instructions delete the record when it is found to be the one pointed to by RNEXT.

As with the generic programs in Figures 2.37 and 2.38, the insertion subroutine in Figure 3.16 assumes that the ID number of the new record does not match that of any record already in the list, and the deletion subroutine in Figure 3.17 assumes that there exists a record in the list with an ID number that does match the contents of RIDNUM. Problems 3.23 and 3.24 consider how the subroutines should be changed to signal an error if the assumptions are not true.

PART II
THE 68000 EXAMPLE

In this second part of Chapter 3, we describe the basic architecture of processors in Motorola's 680X0 family by discussing the 68000 ISA. The family includes several processors that provide different performance levels. All members of the family have the same basic architecture, but later members have additional features that enhance their performance. We use the 68000 here because it is somewhat simpler to describe, yet it portrays the salient features of the entire family. We do not provide a comprehensive description of the 68000. For such information, the reader can consult manufacturer's information [6]. Instead, we concentrate on the most important aspects of the 68000, giving sufficient detail to enable the reader to prepare, assemble, and run simple programs. The distinguishing features of various members of the 680X0 family, as well as some of the features introduced for performance enhancement, are described in Chapter 11. The programs from Chapter 2 are presented here in the 68000 assembly language to illustrate various aspects of the 68000 architecture.

3.8 REGISTERS AND ADDRESSING

The 68000 processor is characterized by a 16-bit external word length because the processor chip has 16 data pins for connection to the memory. However, data are manipulated inside the processor in registers that contain 32 bits. The more advanced models of this family are the 68020, 68030, and 68040 processors, which come in larger chip packages and have 32 external data pins. Thus, they can deal with data both internally and externally in 32-bit quantities. Tabak [7] covers these members of the 680X0 family, emphasizing the 68040.

3.8.1 THE 68000 REGISTER STRUCTURE

The 68000 register structure, shown in Figure 3.18, has 8 data registers and 8 address registers, each 32 bits long. The data registers serve as general-purpose accumulators and as counters.

The 68000 instructions deal with operands of three different lengths. A 32-bit operand is said to occupy a *long word,* a 16-bit operand constitutes a word, and an 8-bit operand is a byte. When an instruction uses a byte or a word operand in a register, the operand is in the low-order bit positions of the register. In most cases, such instructions do not affect the remaining high-order bits of the register, but some instructions extend the sign of a shorter operand into the high-order bits.

The address registers hold information used in determining the addresses of memory operands. This information may be given in either long word or word sizes. When the address of a given memory location is in an address register, the register serves as a pointer to that location. Both address and data registers can also be used as index registers. One address register, A7, has the special function of being the processor stack pointer. The role of this register is discussed in Section 3.13.

The address registers and address calculations involve 32 bits. However, in the 68000, only the least-significant 24 bits of an address are used externally to access the memory. The 68020, 68030, and 68040 processors have 32 external address lines as well as 32 data lines.

The last register shown in Figure 3.18 is the processor *status register,* SR. It contains five condition code bits, which are described in Section 3.11.1; three interrupt bits, which are discussed in Chapter 4; and two mode-select bits, which are explained in Section 3.13.

3.8.2 ADDRESSING

The memory of a 68000 computer is organized in 16-bit words and is byte addressable. Two consecutive words can be interpreted as a single 32-bit long word. Memory addresses are assigned as shown in Figure 3.19. A word must be aligned on an even boundary, that is, its address must be an even number. The big-endian address assignment is used. The byte in the high-order position of a word has the same address as the word, whereas the byte in the low-order position has the next higher address.

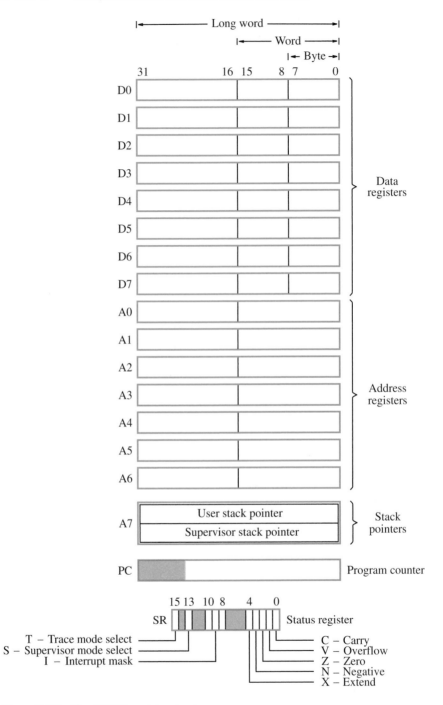

Figure 3.18   The 68000 register structure.

Word
addresses   Contents

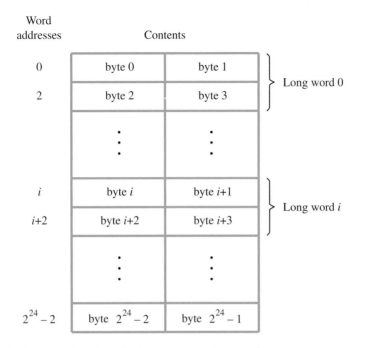

Figure 3.19 Map of addressable locations in the 68000.

Since the 68000 generates 24-bit addresses, its addressable space is 2^{24} (16,777,216 or 16M) bytes. This addressable space may be thought of as consisting of 512 (2^9) *pages* of 32K (2^{15}) bytes each. Thus, hexadecimal addresses 0 to 7FFF constitute page 0, addresses 8000 to FFFF make up page 2, and so on. The last page consists of addresses FF8000 to FFFFFF.

The 68000 has several addressing modes, including those discussed in Section 2.5. Many of the 68000's instructions fit into a 16-bit word, but some require additional words for extra addressing information. The first word of an instruction is the OP-code word, which specifies the operation to be performed and gives some addressing information. The rest of the addressing information, if any, is given in subsequent words. The available addressing modes are defined as follows:

Immediate mode — The operand is contained in the instruction. Four sizes of operands can be specified. Byte, word, and long-word operands are given following the OP-code word. The fourth size consists of very small numbers that can be included directly in the OP-code word of some instructions.

Absolute mode — The absolute address of an operand is given in the instruction, following the OP code. There are two versions of this mode — long and short. In the long mode, a 24-bit address is specified explicitly. In the short mode, a 16-bit value is given in the instruction to be used as the low-order 16 bits of an address. The sign bit of this value is extended to provide the high-order eight bits of the address. Since the sign bit is either 0 or 1, it follows that in the short mode only two pages of the addressable space can be accessed. These are the 0 page and the FF8 page, each containing 32K bytes.

Register mode — The operand is in a processor register specified in the instruction.

Register indirect mode — The effective address of the operand is in an address register specified in the instruction.

Autoincrement mode — The effective address of the operand is in an address register, An, specified in the instruction. After the operand is accessed, the contents of An are incremented by 1, 2, or 4, depending on whether a byte, a word, or a long-word operand, respectively, is involved.

Autodecrement mode — The contents of an address register, An, specified in the instruction are decremented by 1, 2, or 4, depending on whether a byte, a word, or a long-word operand, respectively, is involved. The effective address of the operand is the decremented contents of An.

Basic index mode — A 16-bit signed offset and an address register, An, are specified in the instruction. The sum of this offset and the contents of An is the effective address of the operand.

Full index mode — An 8-bit signed offset, an address register An, and an index register Rk (either an address or a data register) are given in the instruction. The effective address of the operand is the sum of the offset and the contents of registers An and Rk. Either all 32 bits or the sign-extended low-order 16 bits of Rk are used in the derivation of the address.

Basic relative mode — This is the same mode as the basic index mode except that the program counter is used instead of an address register, An.

Full relative mode — This is the same mode as the full index mode except that the program counter is used instead of an address register, An.

The addressing modes and their assembler syntax are summarized in Table 3.2.

Note that there are two versions of the index mode. The basic index mode corresponds to the mode depicted in Figure 2.13. The full index mode involves the contents of two registers and an offset constant given in the instruction. The size of the offset constant is 16 bits in the basic mode and 8 bits in the full mode.

In the full index mode, the second register, Rk, can be used in two ways: either all 32 bits are used or only the low-order 16 bits are used. The two possibilities are indicated to the assembler by appending a size indicator — L for a long word or W for a word — to the name of the register, for example, D1.L or D1.W. The latter is the default size if no indicator is given. When a 16-bit word is used in the computation of a 32-bit effective address, this word is sign extended.

In either of the two index modes, the program counter may be used in place of the address register. The resulting addressing modes are called the relative modes because the effective address is specified in terms of the distance between the operand and the instruction that refers to it. Consider the instruction

$$\text{ADD} \quad 100(\text{PC,A1}),\text{D0}$$

Table 3.2 68000 addressing modes

Name	Assembler syntax	Addressing function
Immediate	#Value	Operand = Value
Absolute Short	Value	EA = Sign Extended WValue
Absolute Long	Value	EA = Value
Register	Rn	EA = R_n that is, Operand = $[R_n]$
Register Indirect	(An)	EA = $[A_n]$
Autoincrement	(An)+	EA = $[A_n]$; Increment A_n
Autodecrement	−(An)	Decrement A_n; EA = $[A_n]$
Indexed basic	WValue(An)	EA = WValue + $[A_n]$
Indexed full	BValue(An,Rk.S)	EA = BValue + $[A_n]$ + $[R_k]$
Relative basic	WValue(PC) or Label	EA = WValue + [PC]
Relative full	BValue(PC,Rk.S) or Label (Rk)	EA = BValue + [PC] + $[R_k]$

EA = effective address
Value = a number given either explicitly or represented by a label
BValue = an 8-bit Value
WValue = a 16-bit Value
A_n = an address register
R_n = an address or a data register
S = a size indicator: W for sign-extended 16-bit word
and L for 32-bit long word

When encoded in machine form, this instruction consists of two words. The OP-code word specifies that this is an Add instruction, that the destination register is data register D0, and that the full relative addressing mode is used for the source operand. The second word, also called the *extension word*, specifies that register A1 is used as the index register and it contains the offset value 100 encoded in 8 bits.

Assume that the preceding instruction is stored in location 1000 and that register A1 contains the value 6, as shown in Figure 3.20. When the OP-code word of this instruction has been fetched and while it is being decoded by the processor, the program counter points to the extension word, which means that the program counter contains the value 1002. Therefore, the effective address of the source operand is

$$EA = [PC] + [A1] + 100$$

$$= 1002 + 6 + 100$$

$$= 1108$$

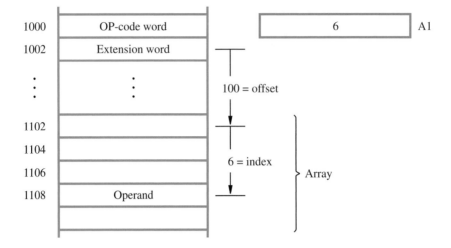

Figure 3.20   An example of 68000 full relative mode for the instruction
ADD 100(PC,A1),D0.

Figure 3.20 suggests how this addressing mode can be used to access an entry in an array. The offset value specifies the distance between the first entry in the array and the instruction. Then the index register gives the distance between that point and the desired operand, which is the fourth word in the array.

We have written the relative mode in an explicit format. Most assemblers allow this mode to be specified in a simpler way. First, the assembler must be informed that relative addressing is to be used in a given section of the program through an appropriate assembler directive. Next, after the name ARRAY has been assigned the value 1102, the instruction in Figure 3.20 can be written as

$$\text{ADD}\quad\text{ARRAY(A1),D0}$$

The assembler interprets this specification of the source operand as being in the full relative mode, and it computes the offset as indicated in the figure. The assembler does not know, and does not need to know, what the contents of register A1 will be when the instruction is executed. For example, this instruction may be inside a program loop, in which case A1 could be used to access successive elements of the array.

The full relative mode is limited by the fact that the offset is a 2's-complement 8-bit number, thus restricting its values to the range -128 to $+127$ bytes.

3.9   INSTRUCTIONS

The 68000 ISA provides an extensive set of instructions, most of which can operate on any of the three possible sizes of operands. The instruction set is summarized in Appendix C. All addressing modes can be used in a uniform way with most instructions. Instruction sets that exhibit this feature are said to be *orthogonal*.

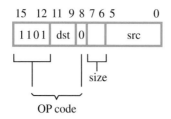

(a) Format of the OP-code word for an ADD instruction

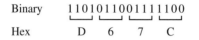

(b) Encoding of the OP-code word

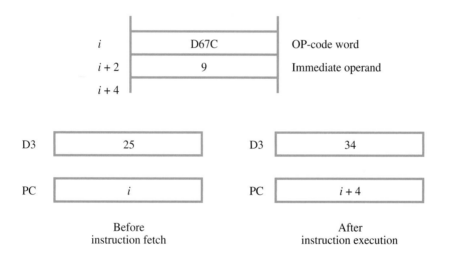

Before
instruction fetch

After
instruction execution

(c) Consequences of the execution

Figure 3.21 The 68000 instruction ADD #9,D3.

The 68000 has both one-operand and two-operand instructions. A two-operand instruction is written as

OP   src,dst

where the operation OP is performed using the source and destination operands. The result is placed in the destination location. An example is given in Figure 3.21, which shows the instruction

$$\text{ADD} \quad \#9,\text{D3}$$

This instruction performs the action

$$\text{dst} \leftarrow [\text{src}] + [\text{dst}]$$

which results in adding the value 9 to the contents of register D3 and storing the result back in D3.

Figure 3.21*a* depicts the general format of the ADD instruction. Either the source operand or the destination operand must be in a data register, Dn. The second operand may be in a register or a memory location. The allowable combinations are given in Table C.4. Since at least one of the two operands is always in one of the eight data registers, a 3-bit field suffices to identify it. The other operand is specified according to Table C.1. In our example, the destination register D3 is represented by the binary pattern 011 in bits 9 through 11, and the immediate source operand is identified with the pattern 111100 in bits 0 through 5.

The desired operand size is indicated in the 2-bit size field. In our example, the size of the operands is not stated explicitly in the assembly language statement, in which case the assembler assumes the default value of a 16-bit word. According to Table C.3, word-size operands are denoted by the pattern 01.

From the discussion above, it follows that the OP-code word for our ADD instruction is 1101011001111100, which is represented by the hex number D67C, as indicated in Figure 3.21*b*.

The immediate source operand, 9, is given in the word following the OP-code word, as shown in Figure 3.21*c*. Before fetching the instruction, the program counter points to the OP-code word at address *i*. As each word is fetched from the memory, the contents of the PC are incremented by 2. Thus, when execution of the instruction is completed, the PC points to the OP-code word of the next instruction at address $i + 4$.

A similar instruction using the same format is the Subtract instruction, SUB, which performs the operation

$$\text{dst} \leftarrow [\text{dst}] - [\text{src}]$$

As Table C.4 shows, the ADD and SUB instructions allow considerable flexibility in specifying one of the two operands. However, the second operand must be in a data register. Most other two-operand instructions have the same type of restriction. The only instruction in which both the source and the destination operands may be specified in terms of most of the addressing modes is the Move instruction, MOVE, which performs the action

$$\text{dst} \leftarrow [\text{src}]$$

Let us now consider a simple routine for the task C ← [A] + [B], shown in Figure 2.8. The required task can be performed as follows

$$\text{MOVE} \quad \text{A,D0}$$
$$\text{ADD} \quad \text{B,D0}$$
$$\text{MOVE} \quad \text{D0,C}$$

These instructions may be stored in the memory of a 68000 computer, as shown in Figure 3.22. The figure shows hexadecimal values for the addresses and operands. The operands are assumed to be 16 bits long, and their addresses are specified in the absolute mode. Note that the long version of the absolute mode is needed because the desired addresses cannot be represented in 16 bits. The high-order 16 bits of a 32-bit address are placed in the lower address word and the low-order 16 bits in the higher address word, according to the convention shown in Figure 3.19.

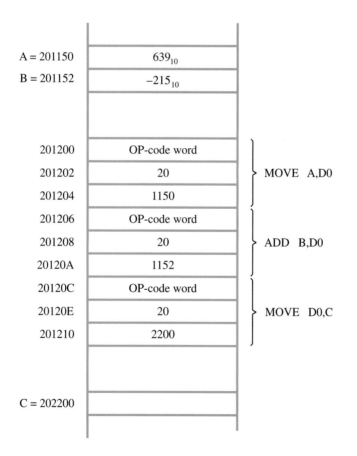

After execution, $[202200] = 424_{10}$

Figure 3.22 A 68000 routine for C ← [A] + [B].

3.10   ASSEMBLY LANGUAGE

The discussion of assembly languages in Section 2.6 applies generally to the 68000 assembly language. Some minor differences and additions are explained here.

Because 68000 instructions can deal with three different sizes of operands, the assembler instructions must indicate the desired size. This is done by appending the size indicator to the operation mnemonic. The size indicator is L for long word, W for word, and B for byte. Thus, if an Add instruction is to operate on long-word operands, its operation mnemonic is written as ADD.L. When no size indication is given, the operand size is taken to be one word. This means that the instructions ADD.W #20,D1 and ADD #20,D1 are identical.

Numbers in a source program are assumed to be in decimal representation unless marked with the prefix $ for hexadecimal or % for binary. Alphanumeric characters placed between single quotes are replaced by the assembler with their ASCII codes. Several characters may be specified in a string between quotes. For example, a valid character string is 'STRING3'.

All of the assembler directives discussed in Section 2.6 can be used with only slight differences in notation. The starting address of a block of instructions or data is specified with the ORG directives. The EQU directives equates names with numerical values. Data constants are inserted into an object program using the DC (Define Constant) directives. The size indicator is appended to specify the size of the data items, and several items may be defined in one directives. For example, the directives

ORG   100

PLACE   DC.B   23,$4F,%10110101

	Memory address label	Operation	Addressing or data information
Assembler directives	C	EQU	$202200
		ORG	$201150
	A	DC.W	639
	B	DC.W	−215
		ORG	$201200
Statements that		MOVE	A,D0
generate machine		ADD	B,D0
instructions		MOVE	D0,C
Assembler directive		END	

Figure 3.23   68000 assembly language representation for the routine in Figure 3.22.

result in hex values 17 (23_{10}), 4F, and B5 being loaded into memory locations 100, 101, and 102, respectively. The label PLACE is assigned the value 100.

A block of memory can be reserved for data by means of the DS (Define Storage) directive. For instance, the directive

ARRAY   DS.L   200

reserves 200 long words and associates the name ARRAY with the address of the first long word.

A simple example of a 68000 assembly language program that corresponds to Figure 3.22 is given in Figure 3.23.

3.11 PROGRAM FLOW CONTROL

Branch instructions are needed to implement program structures such as **if** statements and loops. In general, a branch instruction tests a branch condition and then, depending on the result, causes execution to proceed along one of two possible paths. The conditions tested relate to the result of a recently performed operation.

3.11.1 CONDITION CODE FLAGS

The 68000 has five condition code flags, stored in the status register shown in Figure 3.18. In addition to the N, Z, V, and C flags described in Section 2.4.6, the 68000 has a fifth flag, X (extend). It is set in the same way as the C flag, but it is not affected by as many instructions. This apparent duplication is convenient when dealing with multiple-precision operations, which we will discuss in Chapter 6.

Table C.4 in Appendix C shows which flags are affected by each instruction. The C and X flags are set to 1 if a carry occurs from the most-significant bit position as a result of performing an add operation. The C and X flags are set to 1 if no carry occurs as a result of performing a subtract operation, signifying a borrow signal. Since operands can be specified in any of three possible lengths, these two flags depend on the carry-out from bit positions 7, 15, and 31, for byte, word, and long-word operands, respectively. The MOVE instruction sets the N and Z flags according to the operand moved and clears the C and V flags. MOVE does not affect the X flag unless the destination specified is the status register itself.

3.11.2 BRANCH INSTRUCTIONS

A conditional branch instruction causes program execution to continue with the instruction at the branch target address if the branch condition is met. This address is determined from the branch offset in the operand field. Otherwise, if the branch condition is not met, the instruction that immediately follows the branch instruction is executed. The 68000 provides branch instructions with two types of offset. In the first type, a short offset of 8 bits is included in the OP-code word. These instructions can be used when the branch target is within $+127$ or -128 bytes of the value in the program counter at the time the branch address is computed. Recall that the PC contents are incremented as each word is fetched from the memory, which means that the offset defines the distance from the word that follows the branch instruction OP-code word. In the second type, a 16-bit offset is specified in the word that follows the OP-code word. This provides for a much greater range ($\pm32K$) within which the branch target can be located. In this case, the offset is the distance from the extension word to the branch target.

Figure 3.24 illustrates the use of a short-offset branch instruction. It shows how the program loop in Figure 2.16 can be implemented using a 68000 processor. Note that the program in Figure 2.16 uses a Decrement instruction. Since the 68000 does not have such an instruction, we have used the Subtract Quick instruction, SUBQ, which subtracts the immediate operand 1 from the contents of register D1. A 3-bit immediate operand is included within the OP-code word of the SUBQ instruction; thus, only one word is needed to represent the instruction.

The 68000 has 16 conditional branch instructions, each with 8- and 16-bit offsets. It also has an unconditional branch instruction, BRA, where the branch is always taken. Tables C.5 and C.6 give the details of these instructions.

(a) Short-offset branch instruction format

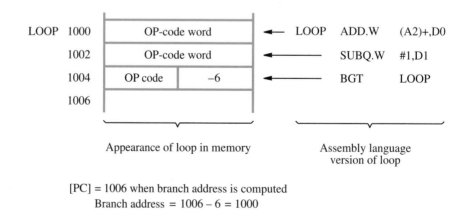

(b) Example of using a branch instruction in the loop of Figure 2.16

Figure 3.24   68000 short-offset branch instructions.

	MOVE.L	N,D1	N contains n, the number of entries to be added, and D1 is used as a counter that determines how many times to execute the loop.
	MOVEA.L	#NUM1,A2	A2 is used as a pointer to the list entries. It is initialized to NUM1, the address of the first entry.
	CLR.L	D0	D0 is used to accumulate the sum.
LOOP	ADD.W	(A2)+,D0	Successive numbers are added in D0.
	SUBQ.L	#1,D1	Decrement the counter.
	BGT	LOOP	If $[D1] \neq 0$, execute the loop again.
	MOVE.L	D0,SUM	Store the sum in SUM.

Figure 3.25   A 68000 program for the addition program in Figure 2.16.

Figure 3.25 shows a 68000 program for the program in Figure 2.16. It uses data registers D0 and D1 to accumulate the sum and to act as a counter, respectively, and uses address register A2 to point to the operands as they are fetched from the memory. Note that an address register is used because, in the Autoincrement addressing mode, only address registers are allowed.

Decrement and Branch Instructions

In addition to the normal branch instructions, the 68000 has a set of more complex branch instructions that incorporate a counting mechanism. Such a facility is useful for implementing loop control. These instructions are written in the format

$$DBcc \quad Dn,LABEL$$

where the suffix cc denotes a branch condition. For example, if GT is used in place of cc, the resultant instruction, DBGT, is the Decrement and Branch unless Greater Than instruction. The full set of possible branch conditions is given in Table C.6. The way the branch condition is used in these instructions is opposite to the way it is used in other branch instructions. The action is as follows:

* If the condition specified by cc is satisfied, then the instruction that immediately follows the DBcc instruction is executed next.
* If the condition specified by cc is not satisfied, then the least-significant 16 bits of register Dn are decremented by 1. If the result is equal to -1, the instruction that follows the DBcc instruction is executed next. If the result is not equal to -1, a branch is made to the instruction at location LABEL.

The DBcc instructions are more powerful than normal branch instructions because the decision on whether the branch is to be taken depends on two conditions rather than one. If the same action were specified using normal branch instructions, it would be necessary to use a sequence of three instructions: first, a branch instruction that tests the cc condition; next, an instruction that decrements the contents of the counter register; and finally, another branch instruction that causes a branch based on the result of the decrement operation. For example, the instructions

DBcc   D3,LOOP

next instruction

are equivalent to the sequence

Bcc   NEXT

SUBQ   #1,D3

BGE   LOOP

NEXT   next instruction

A useful way of thinking about the DBcc instructions is to view them as providing convenient means for loop control where early exit from the loop occurs when a given condition is met. The number of times that the loop can be executed is limited by the contents of the counter register, which is D3 in the preceding example.

One DBcc instruction, DBF (Decrement and Branch if False), uses a test condition that is always false. Thus, the decision on whether a branch is to be made is based solely on the result of decrementing the counter register. This instruction is useful when a loop is always executed a predetermined number of times. It is even given a second name, DBRA (Decrement and Branch Always).

To demonstrate the usefulness of decrement and branch instructions, the program of Figure 3.25 can be rewritten using the DBRA instruction, as shown in Figure 3.26. Register D1 is initialized to the value n in Figure 3.25. However, because the DBRA instruction causes a branch when the counter register contains a value equal to or greater than zero, register D1 is initialized to the value $n - 1$ in Figure 3.26. The total number of instructions in the two programs is the same, but the program in Figure 3.26 takes less time to execute because of the shorter loop.

```
          MOVE.L    N,D1          Put n − 1 into the
          SUBQ.L    #1,D1            counter register D1.
          MOVEA.L   #NUM1,A2
          CLR.L     D0
LOOP      ADD.W     (A2)+,D0
          DBRA      D1,LOOP       Loop back until [D1]= −1.
          MOVE.L    D0,SUM
```

Figure 3.26   An alternative 68000 program for the program in Figure 3.25.

3.12 I/O OPERATIONS

The 68000 processor requires that all status and data buffers in the interfaces of I/O devices be addressable as if they were memory locations. This means that program-controlled I/O in a 68000 computer can be achieved as described in the general discussion in Section 2.7.

Assume that bit b_3 of the keyboard status register INSTATUS contains the input control flag SIN. An input operation from the keyboard is accomplished with the instruction sequence

```
READWAIT   BTST.W   #3,INSTATUS
           BEQ      READWAIT
           MOVE.B   DATAIN,D1
```

The bit test instruction, BTST, tests the state of one bit of the destination operand and sets condition code flag Z to be the complement of the bit tested. The position of the bit to be tested, b_3 in our example, is specified by the first operand.

Assuming that bit b_3 in the display status register OUTSTATUS contains the output control flag SOUT, the character in register D1 can be sent to the display by the instruction sequence

```
WRITEWAIT   BTST.W   #3,OUTSTATUS
            BEQ      WRITEWAIT
            MOVE.B   D1,DATAOUT
```

A 68000 program that reads one line of characters from a keyboard, stores them in the memory, and echoes them back to the display is shown in Figure 3.27. This

	MOVEA.L	#LOC,A1	Initialize pointer register A1 to contain the address of the first location in memory where the characters are to be stored.
READ	BTST.W	#3, INSTATUS	Wait for a character to be entered
	BEQ	READ	in the keyboard buffer DATAIN.
	MOVE.B	DATAIN,(A1)	Transfer the character from DATAIN into the memory (this clears SIN to 0).
ECHO	BTST.W	#3,OUTSTATUS	Wait for the display to become ready.
	BEQ	ECHO	
	MOVE.B	(A1),DATAOUT	Move the character just read to the output buffer register (this clears SOUT to 0).
	CMPI.B	#CR,(A1)+	Check if the character just read is CR (carriage return). If it is not CR, then
	BNE	READ	branch back and read another character. Also, increment the pointer to store the next character.

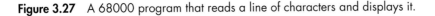

Figure 3.27 A 68000 program that reads a line of characters and displays it.

program is patterned after the program in Figure 2.20. It assumes that a line ends when the return key is pressed. The characters are stored in memory byte locations starting with location LOC.

3.13 STACKS AND SUBROUTINES

A stack can be implemented, as explained in Section 2.8, using any of the address registers as a pointer. The Autoincrement and Autodecrement addressing modes facilitate this process. One specific register, register A7, is designated as the processor stack pointer, and the stack this register points to is called the *processor stack*. This is the stack used in all stack operations that the processor performs automatically, as in the case of subroutine linkage.

Figure 3.18 shows two different 32-bit registers called A7. The 68000 provides for two different modes of operation, called the user and supervisor modes. Each mode has its own version of the processor stack pointer, A7. In the *supervisor mode,* the processor can execute all machine instructions. In the *user mode,* some instructions, called *privileged* instructions, cannot be executed. Application programs are normally run in the user mode, and the system software uses the supervisor mode. Bit S in the processor status register determines which of the two modes is active, and, hence, which of the two A7 registers is used.

A Branch-to-Subroutine (BSR) instruction is used to call a subroutine. It is implemented in the same way as any other branch instruction, but it also causes the contents of the program counter to be pushed onto the stack. Its branch target is the first instruction in the subroutine. When the subroutine is completed, a Return-from-Subroutine (RTS) instruction is used to return to the calling program. It pops the return address at the top of the stack into the program counter. The BSR and RTS instructions allow the subroutine linkage mechanism, described in general terms in Section 2.9, to be implemented.

Figure 3.28 shows how the program in Figure 3.26 can be written as a subroutine, passing parameters through registers. The list address and the number of entries in the list are passed to the subroutine using registers A2 and D1. After performing the addition, the subroutine returns the sum in register D0.

Figure 3.29 shows how the program in Figure 3.26 can be written as a subroutine, passing parameters on the processor stack pointed to by address register A7. The MOVEM (Move multiple registers) instructions save and restore registers A2, D1, and D0. The order in which these registers are stored on the stack is shown in Figure 3.29*b.* The first MOVEM instruction, which uses the Autodecrement addressing mode, pushes the specified registers onto the stack. The second MOVEM instruction uses the Autoincrement addressing mode to pop the stored values off the stack and store them into the registers in the reverse order.

Consider now the case of nested subroutines, in which one subroutine calls another, as shown in Figure 2.28. Figure 3.30 gives the 68000 code for this example, and the stack frames for subroutines SUB1 and SUB2 are shown in Figure 3.31. The main program calls subroutine SUB1. Before the call instruction BSR is executed, the main program pushes parameters param2 and param1 onto the stack for use by SUB1.

Calling program

MOVEA.L	#NUM1,A2	Put the address NUM1 in A2.
MOVE.L	N,D1	Put the number of entries n in D1.
BSR	LISTADD	Call subroutine LISTADD.
MOVE.L	D0,SUM	Store the sum in SUM.
next instruction		

$\vdots$

Subroutine

LISTADD	SUBQ.L	#1,D1	Adjust count to $n-1$.
	CLR.L	D0	
LOOP	ADD.W	(A2)+,D0	Accumulate sum in D0.
	DBRA	D1,LOOP	
	RTS		

Figure 3.28   Program of Figure 3.26 written as a 68000 subroutine; parameters passed through registers.

The subroutine begins by creating its own frame on the stack. The special instruction:

$$\text{LINK} \quad A_i, \#disp$$

sets up register A_i as the frame pointer by performing the following operations:

1. It pushes the contents of register A_i onto the processor stack.
2. It copies the contents of the processor stack pointer, A7, into register A_i.
3. It adds the specified displacement value to register A7.

If the displacement value is a negative number, it will cause the top of the stack to move upward (to a lower address location), thus creating an empty space on the stack which the subroutine can use for local variables. These variables can be accessed using indexed addressing with the frame pointer register A_i. At the end of the subroutine, the UNLK (Unlink) instruction reverses the actions of the LINK instruction. It loads A7 from A_i, thus lowering the top of the stack to its position before adding the displacement value. Then it pops the original contents of register A_i off the stack and back into A_i.

In the example in Figure 3.30, we have assumed that the subroutines can perform their tasks using only registers, so they do not require work space on the stack. Hence, each subroutine begins with the instruction

$$\text{LINK} \quad A6, \#0$$

(Assume top of stack is at level 1 below.)

Calling program

```
        MOVE.L    #NUM1,−(A7)     Push parameters onto stack.
        MOVE.L    N,−(A7)
        BSR       LISTADD
        MOVE.L    4(A7),SUM       Save result.
        ADDI.L    #8,A7           Restore top of stack.
        ⋮
```

Subroutine

```
LISTADD MOVEM.L   D0−D1/A2,−(A7)  Save registers D0, D1, and A2.
        MOVE.L    16(A7),D1       Initialize counter to n.
        SUBQ.L    #1,D1           Adjust count to use DBRA.
        MOVEA.L   20(A7),A2       Initialize pointer to the list.
        CLR.L     D0              Initialize sum to 0.
LOOP    ADD.W     (A2)+,D0        Add entry from list.
        DBRA      D1,LOOP
        MOVE.L    D0,20(A7)       Put result on the stack.
        MOVEM.L   (A7)+,D0−D1/A2  Restore registers.
        RTS
```

(a) Calling program and subroutine

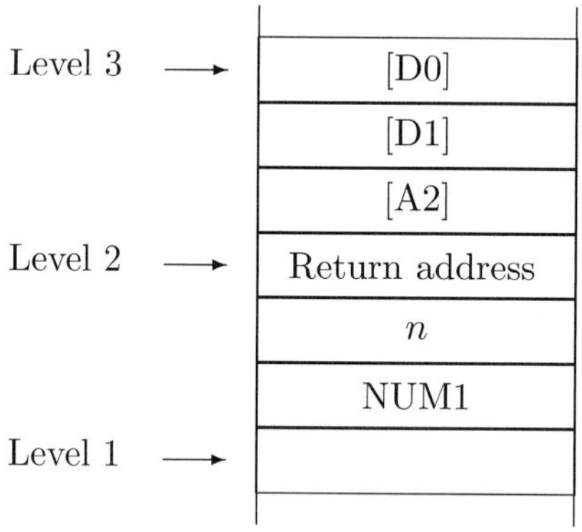

(b) Stack contents at different times

Figure 3.29   Program of Figure 3.26 written as a 68000 subroutine; parameters passed on the stack.

Memory location		Instructions		Comments

Calling program

:

2000		MOVE.L	PARAM2,−(A7)	Place parameters on stack.
2006		MOVE.L	PARAM1,−(A7)	
2012		BSR	SUB1	
2014		MOVE.L	(A7),RESULT	Store result.
2020		ADDI.L	#8,A7	Restore stack level.
2024		next instruction		

:

First subroutine

2100	SUB1	LINK	A6,#0	Set frame pointer.
2104		MOVEM.L	D0−D2/A0,−(A7)	Save registers.
		MOVEA.L	8(A6),A0	Load parameters.
		MOVE.L	12(A6),D0	

:

		MOVE.L	PARAM3,−(A7)	Place a parameter on stack.
2160		BSR	SUB2	
2164		MOVE.L	(A7)+,D1	Pop result from SUB2 into D1.

:

		MOVE.L	D2,8(A6)	Place result on stack.
		MOVEM.L	(A7)+,D0−D2/A0	Restore registers.
		UNLK	A6	Restore frame pointer.
		RTS		Return.

Second subroutine

3000	SUB2	LINK	A6,#0	Set frame pointer.
		MOVEM.L	D0−D1,−(A7)	Save registers.
		MOVE.L	8(A6),D0	Load parameter.

:

		MOVE.L	D1,8(A6)	Place result on stack.
		MOVEM.L	(A7)+,D0−D1	Restore registers.
		UNLK	A6	Restore frame pointer.
		RTS		Return.

Figure 3.30 Nested subroutines in 68000 assembly language.

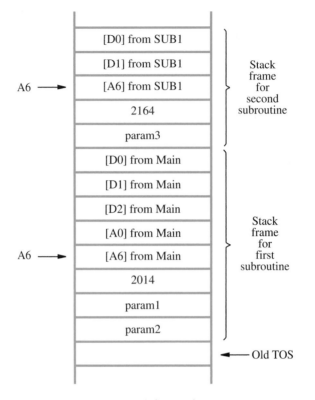

Figure 3.31 68000 stack frames for Figure 3.30.

which defines register A6 as the stack frame pointer and leaves A7 pointing to the location where the old contents of A6 are stored. This instruction performs the same operations as the first two Move instructions at the beginning of the subroutines in Figure 2.28. In each case, it is followed by a MOVEM instruction, which saves the registers needed by the subroutine on the stack.

The remainder of the program in Figure 3.30 is a straightforward implementation of the program in Figure 2.28, using 68000 instructions. As the program in Figure 3.30 is executed, the resulting items are placed on the stack as shown in Figure 3.31. The main program pushes two parameters on the stack, and then the BSR instruction causes the return address, 2014, to be pushed onto the stack. Note that the BSR instruction fits in one word at location 2012 because the offset to SUB1 is small enough to be represented in 8 bits. The LINK and MOVEM instructions in SUB1 save the contents of the frame pointer, A6, and four other registers.

Before subroutine SUB1 calls SUB2, it pushes one parameter, param3, onto the stack. The return address, 2164, is pushed onto the stack by the BSR instruction. The BSR instruction occupies two words because the offset to the target address is larger than can be represented in 8 bits. When each subroutine completes its task, it restores the saved register contents and then returns. After control is returned to the main program, the result placed on the stack by SUB1 (overwriting param1) is stored in memory location RESULT. Then, the stack pointer A7 is returned to its original value, pointing to the old TOS element in Figure 3.31, by the ADDI.L instruction.

3.14   Logic Instructions

In previous sections, we described instructions that move operands and perform arithmetic operations such as addition or subtraction. The operands involved in these instructions have a fixed length of 32, 16, or 8 bits. In some applications it is necessary to manipulate other sizes of data, perhaps only individual bits, and perform logic operations on these data. The 68000 has several instructions for such purposes. In particular, the 68000 has instructions that perform logical AND, OR, and XOR operations as well as instructions that shift and rotate operands in several different ways.

To illustrate the use of logic instructions, let us consider two examples. Suppose that register D1 contains some 32-bit binary pattern, and we want to determine if the pattern in bit positions b_{18} through b_{14} is 11001. This can be done using the instructions

$$\begin{aligned}
&\text{AND.L} \quad \#\$7\text{C000,D1} \\
&\text{CMPI.L} \quad \#\$64000,\text{D1} \\
&\text{BEQ} \qquad \text{YES}
\end{aligned}$$

The first instruction performs the logical AND of individual bits of the source and destination operands, leaving the result in register D1. The hex number 7C000 has ones in bit positions b_{18} through b_{14} and zeros elsewhere. Thus, as a result of the AND operation, the five bits in positions b_{18} through b_{14} in register D1 retain their original values and the remaining bits are cleared to 0. The subsequent Compare instruction tests whether these five bits correspond to the desired pattern.

Digit-Packing Program

As a second example, consider again the BCD digit-packing program shown in Figure 2.31. The 68000 code for this routine is shown in Figure 3.32. The two ASCII bytes are brought into registers D0 and D1. The LSL instruction shifts the byte in

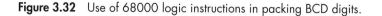

```
MOVEA.L   #LOC,A0      A0 points to data.
MOVE.B    (A0)+,D0     Load first byte into D0.
LSL.B     #4,D0        Shift left by 4 bit positions.
MOVE.B    (A0),D1      Load second byte into D1.
ANDI.B    #$F,D1       Clear high-order 4 bits to zero.
OR.B      D0,D1        Concatenate the digits.
MOVE.B    D1,PACKED    Store the result.
```

Figure 3.32   Use of 68000 logic instructions in packing BCD digits.

D0 four bit positions to the left, filling the low-order four bits with zeros. The first entry in the operand field of this instruction is a count that indicates the number of bit positions by which the operand is to be shifted. Table C.4 shows that the count may also be specified in another data register. Hence, the same effect can be achieved with

LSL.B   D2,D0

if the contents of D2 have been set to 4 earlier. The ANDI instruction sets the high-order four bits of the second byte to 0. Finally, the 4-bit patterns that are the desired BCD codes are combined in D1 with the OR instruction and stored in memory location PACKED.

3.15   PROGRAM EXAMPLES

In this section, we give the 68000 version of the programs for dot product, byte sorting, and linked-list operations that were described in Chapter 2.

3.15.1   VECTOR DOT PRODUCT PROGRAM

The program in Figure 2.33 computes the dot product of two vectors, AVEC and BVEC. The 68000 version is shown in Figure 3.33. The two programs are identical except for the use of the DBRA instruction to control the loop. Using this instruction necessitates reducing the contents of the count register D0 by 1, as explained in Section 3.11.2.

Note that the MULS instruction multiplies two signed 16-bit numbers and produces a 32-bit product. We have assumed that the vector elements are represented in 16-bit words and that the dot product fits in 16 bits. All addresses are treated as 32-bit values.

```
         MOVEA.L  #AVEC,A1      Address of first vector.
         MOVEA.L  #BVEC,A2      Address of second vector.
         MOVE     N,D0          Number of elements.
         SUBQ     #1,D0         Adjust count to use DBRA.
         CLR      D1            Use D1 as accumulator.
LOOP     MOVE     (A1)+,D2      Get element from vector A.
         MULS     (A2)+,D2      Multiply element from vector B.
         ADD      D2,D1         Accumulate product.
         DBRA     D0,LOOP
         MOVE     D1,DOTPROD
```

Figure 3.33   A 68000 program for computing the dot product of two vectors.

3.15.2 BYTE-SORTING PROGRAM

Now let us consider the program to sort a list of bytes given in Figure 2.34. This program performs an in-place sort using the straight selection algorithm to put a list of characters in alphabetic order. The list is stored in memory locations LIST through LIST $+ n - 1$, with each character represented in the ASCII code and occupying one byte. The value n is a 16-bit value stored at address N.

The C-language program for this task is reproduced in Figure 3.34a. The 68000 implementation of this task is given in Figure 3.34b. This program closely parallels the program in Figure 2.34b. The programs differ in some minor respects, as follows.

```
for   (j = n−1; j > 0; j = j − 1)
        { for ( k = j−1; k >= 0; k = k − 1 )
            { if    (LIST[k] > LIST[j])
                { TEMP = LIST[k];
                    LIST[k] = LIST[j];
                    LIST[j] = TEMP;
                }
            }
        }
```

(a) C-language program for sorting

```
        MOVEA.L  #LIST,A1        Pointer to the start of the list.
        MOVE     N,D1            Initialize outer loop
        SUBQ     #1,D1               index j in D1.
OUTER   MOVE     D1,D2           Initialize inner loop
        SUBQ     #1,D2               index k in D2.
        MOVE.B   (A1,D1),D3      Current maximum value in D3.
INNER   CMP.B    D3,(A1,D2)      If LIST(k) ≤ [D3],
        BLE      NEXT            do not exchange.
        MOVE.B   (A1,D2),(A1,D1) Interchange LIST(k)
        MOVE.B   D3,(A1,D2)          and LIST(j) and load
        MOVE.B   (A1,D1),D3         new maximum into D3.
NEXT    DBRA     D2,INNER        Decrement counters k and j
        SUBQ     #1,D1               and branch back
        BGT      OUTER               if not finished.
```

(b) 68000 program implementation

Figure 3.34 A 68000 byte-sorting program.

The MOVE instruction of the 68000 allows both the source and the destination operands to be in the memory. Hence, when interchanging two entries, the value of LIST(k) is copied directly into LIST(j). This eliminates the need for the temporary register R4 used in Figure 2.34 and leads to a slight reorganization of the program instructions.

Another difference is that we have used the DBRA instruction to terminate the inner loop in the program because the index k runs down to 0. Note that it is not possible to use the DBRA instruction in the outer loop because the final value for j is 1 rather than 0.

3.15.3 LINKED-LIST INSERTION AND DELETION SUBROUTINES

Figure 3.35 gives a 68000 subroutine to insert a record in linked list. This program is identical to the program in Figure 2.37. Note that the CMPA version of the Compare instruction is used to compare address values, and the CMP version is used for data values.

A 68000 program to delete a record from a linked list is given in Figure 3.36. This program corresponds directly to the program given in Figure 2.38.

Subroutine

INSERTION	CMPA.L	#0,A0	A0 is RHEAD.
	BGT	HEAD	
	MOVEA.L	A1,A0	A1 is RNEWREC.
	RTS		
HEAD	CMP.L	(A0),(A1)	Compare ID of new record to head.
	BGT	SEARCH	
	MOVE.L	A0,4(A1)	New record becomes head.
	MOVEA.L	A1,A0	
	RTS		
SEARCH	MOVEA.L	A0,A2	A2 is RCURRENT.
LOOP	MOVEA.L	4(A2),A3	A3 is RNEXT.
	CMPA.L	#0,A3	
	BEQ	TAIL	
	CMP.L	(A3),(A1)	
	BLT	INSERT	
	MOVEA.L	A3,A2	Go to next record.
	BRA	LOOP	
INSERT	MOVE.L	A2,4(A1)	
TAIL	MOVE.L	A1,4(A2)	
	RTS		

Figure 3.35   A 68000 subroutine to insert a record in a linked list.

Subroutine

DELETION	CMP.L	(A0),D1	D1 is RIDNUM.
	BGT	SEARCH	
	MOVEA.L	4(A0),A0	Delete head record.
	RTS		
SEARCH	MOVEA.L	A0,A2	A2 is RCURRENT.
LOOP	MOVEA.L	4(A2),A3	A3 is RNEXT.
	CMP.L	(A3),D1	
	BEQ	DELETE	
	MOVEA.L	A3,A2	
	BRA	LOOP	
DELETE	MOVE.L	4(A3),D2	D2 is RTEMP.
	MOVE.L	D2,4(A2)	
	RTS		

Figure 3.36   A 68000 subroutine to delete a record from a linked list.

As with the generic subroutines in Figures 2.37 and 2.38, the insertion subroutine in Figure 3.35 assumes that the ID number of the new record does not match that of any record already in the list, and the deletion subroutine in Figure 3.36 assumes that there exists a record in the list with an ID number that does match the contents of RIDNUM. Problems 3.49 and 3.50 consider how the subroutines should be changed to signal an error if the assumptions are not true.

PART III
THE IA-32 PENTIUM EXAMPLE

The Intel Corporation uses the generic name Intel Architecture (IA) for processors in its product line. We will describe IA processors that operate with 32-bit memory addresses and 32-bit data operands. They are referred to as IA-32 processors, and the most recent is the Pentium series. The first IA-32 processor was the 80386, introduced in 1985. Since then, the 80486 (1989), Pentium (1993), Pentium Pro (1995), Pentium II (1997), Pentium III (1999), and Pentium 4 (2000) have been implemented. These processors have increasing levels of performance, achieved through a number of architectural and microelectronic technology improvements. The evolution of the IA family will be explained in Chapter 11. The latest members of the family have specialized instructions for handling multimedia graphical information and for vector data processing. These aspects of the instruction set will be considered briefly here and also in Chapter 11. The IA-32 instruction set is very large. We will restrict our attention to the basic instructions and addressing modes. Detailed information on the IA-32 instruction set architecture and assembly language can be found at the Intel web site [8] and in the books by Brey [9], Dandamudi [10], and Tabak [7].

3.16   REGISTERS AND ADDRESSING

In the IA-32 architecture, memory is byte addressable using 32-bit addresses, and instructions operate on data operands of 8 or 32 bits. These operand sizes are called byte and doubleword in Intel terminology. A 16-bit operand was called a word in earlier 16-bit Intel processors. Little-endian addressing is used, as described in Section 2.2.2. Multiple-byte data operands may start at any byte address location. They need not be aligned with any particular address boundaries in the memory.

3.16.1   IA-32 REGISTER STRUCTURE

The processor registers are shown in Figure 3.37. While there are some exceptions, the eight 32-bit registers labeled R0 through R7 are general-purpose registers that can be used to hold either data operands or addressing information. There are eight floating-point registers for holding doubleword or quadword (64 bits) floating-point data operands. The floating-point registers have an extension field to provide a total length of 80 bits, not shown in Figure 3.37. The extra bits are used for increased accuracy while floating-point numbers are operated on in the processor. Chapter 6 provides a discussion of floating-point number representation and operations. This topic is not discussed here in Chapter 3.

IA-32 architectures are based on a memory model that associates different areas of the memory, called *segments,* with different usages. The *code segment* holds the instructions of a program. The *stack segment* contains the processor stack, and four *data segments* are provided for holding data operands. The six segment registers shown in Figure 3.37 contain selector values that are used in locating these segments in the memory address space. The detailed function of these registers will be explained in Chapter 11 where we discuss the IA family. Here, we will not need to know these details. A 32-bit address in the IA-32 architecture can be presumed to access memory locations anywhere in the program, processor stack, or data areas.

The two registers shown at the bottom of Figure 3.37 are the Instruction Pointer, which serves as the program counter and contains the address of the next instruction to be executed, and the Status Register, which holds the condition code flags (CF, ZF, SF, OF). These flags contain information about the results of arithmetic operations, as will be discussed in Section 3.19. The program execution mode bits (IOPL, IF, TF) are associated with input/output operations and interrupts, discussed in Chapter 4.

The IA-32 general-purpose registers allow for compatibility with the registers of earlier 8-bit and 16-bit Intel processors. In those processors, some restrictions applied to the specific usage of the different registers in programs. Figure 3.38 shows the association between the IA-32 registers and the registers in earlier processors. The eight general-purpose registers are grouped into three different types: data registers for holding operands, and pointer and index registers for holding addresses and address indices used to determine the effective address of a memory operand.

In Intel's original 8-bit processors, the data registers were called A, B, C, and D. In later 16-bit processors, these registers were labeled AX, BX, CX, and DX. The high- and low-order bytes in each register are identified by suffixes H and L. For example,

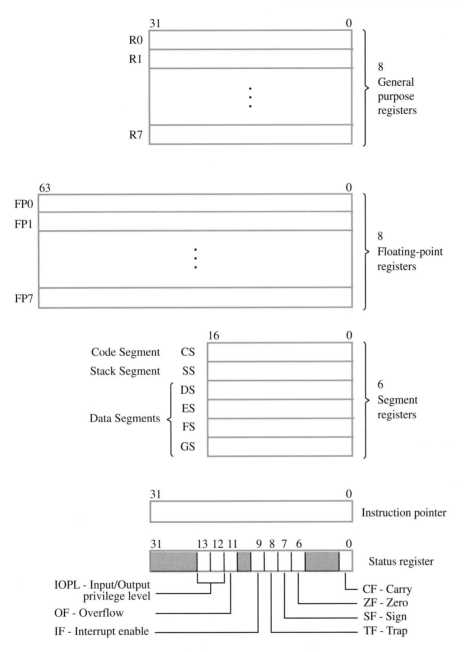

Figure 3.37 IA-32 register structure.

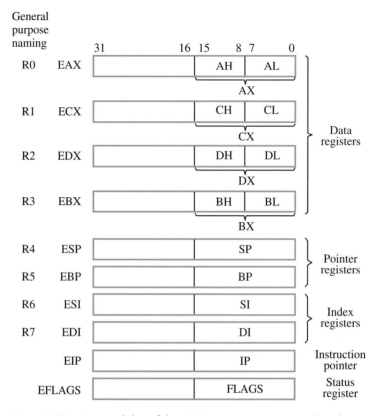

Figure 3.38   Compatibility of the IA-32 register structure with earlier
Intel processor register structures.

the two bytes in register AX are referred to as AH and AL. In IA-32 processors, the
prefix E is used to identify the corresponding "extended" 32-bit registers: EAX, EBX,
ECX, and EDX. The E-prefix labeling is also used for the other 32-bit registers shown
in Figure 3.38. They are the extended versions of the corresponding 16-bit registers
used in earlier processors.

This register labeling is used in Intel technical documents and in other descriptions
of Intel processors. The reason that the historical labeling has been retained is that
Intel has maintained upward compatibility over its processor line. That is, programs in
machine language representation developed for the earlier 16-bit processors will run
correctly on current IA-32 processors without change if the processor state is set to
do so. We will use the E-prefix register labeling in giving examples of assembly language programs because these mnemonics are used in current versions of the assembly
language for IA-32 processors. The AL, BL, etc. labeling will also be used for byte
operands when they are operated on in the low-order eight bits of the corresponding
32-bit register.

The IA-32 processor state can be switched dynamically between 32-bit operation
and 16-bit operation during program execution on an instruction by instruction basis
by the use of instruction prefix bytes. We will discuss this feature in Chapter 11.

3.16.2 IA-32 ADDRESSING MODES

The IA-32 architecture has a large and flexible set of addressing modes. They are designed to access individual data items or data items that are members of an ordered list that begins at a specified memory address. We give full definitions for these modes, along with the way that they are expressed in assembly language.

The basic modes, which are available in most processors, have been described in Section 2.5. They are: Immediate, Absolute, Register, and Register indirect. Intel uses the term Direct for the Absolute mode, so we will do the same here. There are also several addressing modes that provide more flexibility in accessing data operands in the memory. The most flexible mode described in Section 2.5 is the Index mode that has the general notation $X(Ri, Rj)$. The effective address of the operand, EA, is calculated as

$$EA = [Ri] + [Rj] + X$$

where Ri and Rj are general-purpose registers and X is a constant. The registers Ri and Rj are called *base* and *index* registers, respectively, and the constant X is called a *displacement*. The IA-32 addressing modes include this mode and simpler variations of it.

The full set of IA-32 addressing modes is defined as follows:

Immediate mode — The operand is contained in the instruction. It is a signed 8-bit or 32-bit number, with the length being specified by a bit in the OP code of the instruction. This bit is 0 for the short version and 1 for the long version.

Direct mode — The memory address of the operand is given by a 32-bit value in the instruction.

Register mode — The operand is contained in one of the eight general-purpose registers specified in the instruction.

Register indirect mode — The memory address of the operand is contained in one of the eight general-purpose registers specified in the instruction.

Base with displacement mode — An 8-bit or 32-bit signed displacement and one of the eight general-purpose registers to be used as a base register are specified in the instruction. The effective address of the operand is the sum of the contents of the base register and the displacement.

Index with displacement mode — A 32-bit signed displacement, one of the eight general-purpose registers to be used as an index register, and a scale factor of 1, 2, 4, or 8, are specified in the instruction. To obtain the effective address of the operand, the contents of the index register are multiplied by the scale factor and then added to the displacement.

Base with index mode — Two of the eight general-purpose registers and a scale factor of 1, 2, 4, or 8, are specified in the instruction. The registers are used as base and index registers, and the effective address of the operand is calculated as follows. The contents of the index register are multiplied by the scale factor and added to the contents of the base register.

Base with index and displacement mode — An 8-bit or 32-bit signed displacement, two of the eight general-purpose registers, and a scale factor of 1, 2, 4, or 8, are specified in the instruction. The registers are used as base and index registers, and the effective address of the operand is calculated as follows. The contents of the index register are multiplied by the scale factor and then added to the contents of the base register and the displacement.

The IA-32 addressing modes and the way that they are expressed in assembly language are given in Table 3.3. The calculation of the effective address of the operand is also specified in the table. As specified in the footnotes, register ESP cannot be used as an index register. As we will see later, it is used as the processor stack pointer. We will now give some examples of how the addressing modes are used to access operands.

In two-operand instructions, the source (src) and destination (dst) operands are specified in the assembly language in the order

$$\text{OPcode} \quad \text{dst,src}$$

This ordering is the same as in the ARM architecture described in Part I of this chapter, but it is opposite to that used in Chapter 2 and in the Motorola 68000 processor described in Part II of this chapter. For example, the Move instruction

$$\text{MOV} \quad \text{dst,src}$$

performs the operation

$$\text{dst} \leftarrow [\text{src}]$$

Table 3.3   IA-32 addressing modes

Name	Assembler syntax	Addressing function
Immediate	Value	Operand = Value
Direct	Location	EA = Location
Register	Reg	EA = Reg that is, Operand = [Reg]
Register indirect	[Reg]	EA = [Reg]
Base with displacement	[Reg + Disp]	EA = [Reg] + Disp
Index with displacement	[Reg $*$ S + Disp]	EA = [Reg] $\times$ S + Disp
Base with index	[Reg1 + Reg2 $*$ S]	EA = [Reg1] + [Reg2] $\times$ S
Base with index and displacement	[Reg1 + Reg2 $*$ S + Disp]	EA = [Reg1] + [Reg2] $\times$ S + Disp

Value	= an 8- or 32-bit signed number
Location	= a 32-bit address
Reg, Reg1, Reg2	= one of the general purpose registers EAX, EBX, ECX, EDX, ESP, EBP, ESI, EDI, with the exception that ESP cannot be used as an index register
Disp	= an 8- or 32-bit signed number, except that in the Index with displacement mode it can only be 32 bits.
S	= a scale factor of 1, 2, 4, or 8

It is convenient to use the Move instruction to illustrate the IA-32 addressing modes. The instruction

MOV   EAX,25

uses the Immediate addressing mode to move the decimal value 25 into the EAX register. A number given in this form using the digits 0 through 9 is assumed to be in decimal notation. The suffixes B and H are used to specify binary and hexadecimal numbers, respectively. For example, the instruction

MOV   EAX,3FA00H

moves the hex number 3FA00 into EAX.

The instruction

MOV   EAX,LOCATION

uses the Direct addressing mode to move the doubleword at the memory location specified by the address label LOCATION into register EAX. This assumes that LOCATION has been defined as an address label for a memory location in the data declaration section of the assembly language program. We will see how to do this in Section 3.18. If LOCATION represents the address 1000, then this instruction moves the doubleword at 1000 into EAX.

The distinction between the Immediate addressing mode and the Direct addressing mode in IA-32 assembly language programs warrants some discussion because it can be somewhat confusing. Consider the following case: It is sometimes useful to give symbolic names to numerical constants that are used as immediate operands. The assembler directive

NUMBER   EQU   25

is used to associate the symbolic name NUMBER with the decimal value 25, as described in Section 2.6.1. If this is done, the instruction

MOV   EAX,NUMBER

is interpreted by the assembler to mean that NUMBER is an immediate operand to be moved into register EAX. On the other hand, if NUMBER is defined as an address label, this instruction is interpreted as using the Direct addressing mode.

In many assembly languages, this potentially confusing situation is avoided by using a special symbol, such as #, as a prefix to denote the Immediate addressing mode. In the IA-32 assembly language, square brackets can be used to explicitly indicate the Direct addressing mode, as in the instruction

MOV   EAX,[LOCATION]

However, the brackets are not needed if LOCATION has been defined as an address label.

When it is necessary to treat an address label as an immediate operand, the assembler directive OFFSET is used. For example, the instruction

MOV   EBX, OFFSET LOCATION

moves the value of the address label LOCATION, for example 1000, using the Immediate addressing mode, into the EBX register. The EBX register can then be used in the Register indirect mode in the instruction

$$MOV \quad EAX,[EBX]$$

to move the contents of the memory location whose address, LOCATION, is contained in register EBX into register EAX. The word OFFSET as an assembler directive is chosen to indicate that an address is always considered as a relative distance away from the starting point of the memory segment containing the location. In all of these examples, the Register mode has been used to specify the destination.

These examples have illustrated the basic addressing modes: Immediate, Direct, Register, and Register indirect. The remaining four addressing modes provide more flexibility in accessing data operands in the memory.

The Base with displacement mode is illustrated in Figure 3.39a. Register EBP is used as the base register. A doubleword operand that is 60 byte locations away from the base address of 1000, that is, at address 1060, can be moved into register EAX by the instruction

$$MOV \quad EAX,[EBP + 60]$$

The IA-32 instructions and addressing modes can be used to operate on byte operands as well as doubleword operands. For example, still assuming that the base register EBP contains the address 1000, the byte operand at address 1010 can be loaded into the low-order byte position in the EAX register by the instruction

$$MOV \quad AL,[EBP + 10]$$

The assembler selects the version of the Move OP code that is used for byte data because the destination, AL, is the low-order byte position of the EAX register.

The addressing mode that provides the most flexibility is the Base with index and displacement mode. An example is shown in Figure 3.39b, using EBP and ESI as the base and index registers. This example shows how the mode is used to access a particular doubleword operand in a list of doubleword operands. The list begins at a displacement of 200 away from the base address 1000. Using a scale factor of 4 on the index register contents, successive doubleword operands at addresses 1200, 1204, 1208, ... can be accessed by using the sequence of indices 0, 1, 2, ... in the index register ESI. In the example shown in the figure, the doubleword at address 1360 (that is, $1000 + 200 + 4 \times 40$) is accessed when the index register contains 40. This operand can be loaded into register EAX by the instruction

$$MOV \quad EAX,[EBP + ESI*4 + 200]$$

The use of a scale factor of 4 in this addressing mode makes it easy to access successive doubleword operands of the list in a program loop by simply incrementing the index register by 1 on each pass through the loop. Having discussed these two modes in some detail, the closely related Index with displacement mode and Base with index mode should be easy to understand.

Before leaving this discussion of addressing modes, a comment on an aspect of the Table 3.3 entries is useful. It would appear that the Base with displacement mode is

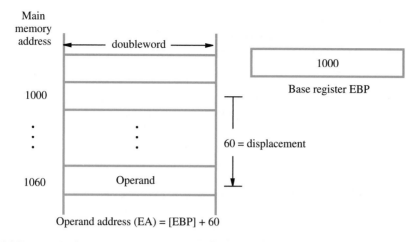

Operand address (EA) = [EBP] + 60

(a) Base with displacement mode, expressed as [EBP + 60]

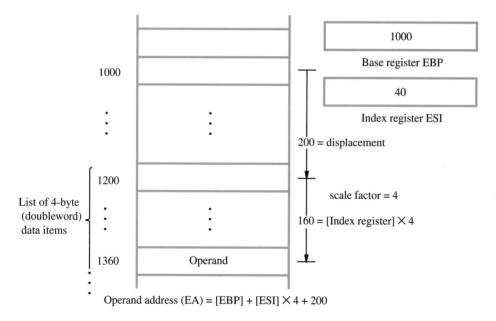

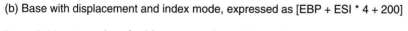

Operand address (EA) = [EBP] + [ESI] × 4 + 200

(b) Base with displacement and index mode, expressed as [EBP + ESI * 4 + 200]

Figure 3.39 Examples of addressing modes in the IA-32 architecture.

redundant because the same effect could be obtained by using the Index with displacement mode with a scale factor of 1. But the former mode is useful because it is encoded with one less byte. In addition, the displacement size in the Index with displacement mode can only be 32 bits.

A discussion of how the addressing modes are encoded into machine instructions is included in the next section. More detail is provided in Appendix D.

3.17 IA-32 INSTRUCTIONS

The IA-32 instruction set is extensive. It is encoded in a variable-length instruction format that does not have a fully regular layout. We will examine the instruction format in Section 3.17.1. Most of the IA-32 instructions have either one or two operands. In the two-operand case, only one of the operands can be in the memory. The other must be in a processor register. In addition to the usual instructions for moving data between the memory and the processor registers, and for performing arithmetic operations, the instruction set includes a number of different logical and shift/rotate operations on data. Byte string instructions are included for nonnumeric data processing. Push and pop operations for manipulating the processor stack are directly supported in the instruction set.

We will begin by introducing a small set of instructions and show how they can be used in a simple complete program. The instruction

$$\text{ADD} \quad \text{dst,src}$$

performs the operation

$$\text{dst} \leftarrow [\text{dst}] + [\text{src}]$$

and, as we have seen earlier,

$$\text{MOV} \quad \text{dst,src}$$

performs the operation

$$\text{dst} \leftarrow [\text{src}]$$

Suppose that two data operands are in registers EAX and EBX. Their sum can be computed in EAX and stored in the memory at location SUM by the two-instruction sequence

$$\text{ADD} \quad \text{EAX,EBX}$$

$$\text{MOV} \quad \text{SUM,EAX}$$

Since only one operand can be in memory in the two-operand instructions, the operation

$$C \leftarrow [A] + [B]$$

involving three memory locations A, B, and C, can be performed using the instruction sequence

MOV   EAX,A

ADD   EAX,B

MOV   C,EAX

The subtract instruction

SUB   dst,src

performs the operation

$$dst \leftarrow [dst] - [src]$$

Useful one-operand instructions INC and DEC are provided for incrementing or decrementing their operand by 1.

We need a few other instructions before we can give an example of a complete loop program for adding numbers. One of these is a conditional branch instruction. The branch instruction

JG   LOOPSTART

causes a branch to the instruction at memory location LOOPSTART if the result of the most recent arithmetic operation was greater than 0. All conditional branch instructions start with the letter J, for Jump, and the following letters specify the condition. In this example, the G stands for greater than 0. Other conditional branch instructions will be discussed later.

In order to use a general-purpose register for Register indirect addressing, it is first necessary to load the address of the memory location to be accessed into the register. The IA-32 instruction set provides two ways to do this. If the address is known explicitly as an address label, say LOCATION, it can be loaded into the register by using the Immediate addressing mode in a Move instruction such as

MOV   EBX, OFFSET LOCATION

This instruction loads the address represented by the label LOCATION into register EBX. Alternatively, an instruction called Load Effective Address, with the mnemonic LEA, may be used. The instruction

LEA   EBX,LOCATION

has exactly the same effect. The LEA instruction can be used to load any address that is computed dynamically during program execution. For example, suppose there is a need to load the address of a data operand that is referenced by the Base with displacement mode into register EBX. The instruction

LEA   EBX,[EBP + 12]

loads the address of the operand at location [EBP] + 12 into register EBX. This address depends on the contents of register EBP when the instruction is executed.

A Loop Program for Adding Numbers

Using the instructions just introduced, we can now give a program for adding numbers using a loop. Assume that memory location N contains the number of 32-bit integers in a list that starts at memory location NUM1. The assembly language program shown in Figure 3.40a can be used to add the numbers and place their sum in memory location SUM.

Register EBX is loaded with the address value NUM1. It is used as the base register in the Base with index addressing mode in the instruction at the location STARTADD, which is the first instruction of the loop. Register EDI is used as the index register. It is cleared by loading it with zero before the loop is entered. On the first pass through the loop, the first number at location [EBX] = NUM1 is added into the EAX register, which was initially cleared to zero. The index register is then incremented by 1. Thus, on the second pass, the scale factor of 4 in the Add instruction causes the second 32-bit number at byte address NUM1 + 4 to be added into EAX. Subsequent passes will add the numbers at NUM1 + 8, NUM1 + 12, ... Register ECX is used as a counter register. It is initially loaded with the contents of memory location N in the second instruction of the program and is decremented by 1 during each pass through the loop. The conditional

```
               LEA    EBX,NUM1              Initialize base (EBX) and
               MOV    ECX,N                    counter (ECX) registers.
               MOV    EAX,0                 Clear accumulator (EAX)
               MOV    EDI,0                    and index (EDI) registers.
STARTADD:      ADD    EAX,[EBX + EDI *4]    Add next number into EAX.
               INC    EDI                   Increment index register.
               DEC    ECX                   Decrement counter register.
               JG     STARTADD             Branch back if [ECX] > 0.
               MOV    SUM,EAX               Store sum in memory.
```

(a) Straightforward approach

```
               LEA    EBX,NUM1              Load base register EBX and
               SUB    EBX,4                    adjust to hold NUM1−4.
               MOV    ECX,N                 Initialize counter/index (ECX).
               MOV    EAX,0                 Clear the accumulator (EAX).
STARTADD:      ADD    EAX,[EBX + ECX * 4]  Add next number into EAX.
               LOOP   STARTADD             Decrement ECX and branch
                                              back if [ECX] > 0.
               MOV    SUM,EAX               Store sum in memory.
```

(b) More compact program

Figure 3.40 IA-32 program for adding numbers.

branch instruction JG causes a branch back to STARTADD while [ECX] > 0. When the contents of ECX reach zero, all the numbers have been added. The branch is not taken, and the Move instruction stores the sum in register EAX into memory location SUM.

A more compact program for the same task can be developed by making the following two observations on the program in Figure 3.40a. The two-instruction sequence

DEC   ECX

JG   STARTADD

occurs often at the end of program loops. Hence, the IA-32 instruction set includes a single instruction that combines the operations of these two instructions. The instruction

LOOP   STARTADD

first decrements the ECX register and then branches to the target address STARTADD if the contents of ECX have not reached zero.

The second observation is that we have used two registers, EDI and ECX, as counters. If we scan the list of numbers to be added in the opposite direction, starting with the last number in the list, only one counter register is needed. We will use register ECX because it is the register referenced implicitly by the LOOP instruction. Assuming $[N] = n$, the first program accesses the numbers using the address sequence NUM1, NUM1 + 4, NUM1 + 8, . . . , NUM1 + 4(n − 1), as EDI contains the sequence of values 0, 1, 2, . . . , (n − 1). The new program, shown in Figure 3.40b, uses the address sequence (NUM1 − 4) + 4n, (NUM1 − 4) + 4(n − 1), . . . , (NUM1 − 4) + 4(1), as ECX contains the sequence $n, n − 1, . . . , 1$. Hence, the value in the base register EBX needs to be changed from NUM1 to NUM1 − 4 in the new program in order to account for the difference between the EDI sequence and the ECX sequence. On the last pass through the loop in the new program, before the LOOP instruction is executed, [ECX] = 1 and the last number to be added is accessed at memory location NUM1.

The reader should note that this type of detailed reasoning in properly accounting for 0-origin and 1-origin indexing and for the correct choice for branch conditions often arises when dealing with lists and arrays. It can be the source of subtle errors. The difficulty is mitigated somewhat in high-level languages where list variables are explicitly referenced as LIST(0), LIST(1), . . . , LIST(n − 1), and loop ranges are related to index values using expressions such as

FOR   i   FROM   0   UPTO   (n − 1)

or

FOR   i   FROM   (n − 1)   DOWNTO   0

This brief discussion of some commonly used IA-32 instructions, along with the addition loop program example, provides an introduction to the basic features of the instruction set and the assembly language used with it. We will now describe the format for machine representation of instructions.

3.17.1 MACHINE INSTRUCTION FORMAT

The general format for machine instructions is shown in Figure 3.41. The instructions are variable in length, ranging from one byte (only an OP code, which is always required) to 12 bytes, consisting of up to four fields. The OP-code field consists of one or two bytes, with most instructions requiring only one byte. The addressing mode information is contained in one or two bytes immediately following the OP code. For instructions that involve the use of only one register in generating the effective address of an operand, only one byte is needed in the addressing mode field. Two bytes are needed for encoding the last two addressing modes in Table 3.3. Those modes use two registers to generate the effective address of a memory operand.

If a displacement value is needed in computing an effective address for a memory operand, it is encoded into either one or four bytes in a field that immediately follows the addressing mode field. If one of the operands is an immediate value, then it is placed in the last field of an instruction and it occupies either one or four bytes.

For some simple instructions, such as those that we will discuss first below, the code for a register involved in the instruction is given in the OP-code byte. However, for most instructions and addressing modes, the registers used are specified in the addressing mode field.

In any instruction set, when instructions are encoded in a variable-length format, the bit pattern for an instruction, when read from left to right, must determine the total length of the instruction. This is necessary because successive instructions in a program are placed one after another in the memory, and there is no other information available to indicate the boundaries between them.

One-Byte Instructions

Registers can be incremented or decremented by instructions that occupy only one byte. Examples are

INC   EDI

and

DEC   ECX

in which the general-purpose registers EDI and ECX are specified by 3-bit codes in the single OP-code byte.

OP code	Addressing mode	Displacement	Immediate
1 or 2 bytes	1 or 2 bytes	1 or 4 bytes	1 or 4 bytes

Figure 3.41   IA-32 instruction format.

Immediate Mode Encoding

The OP code specifies when the Immediate addressing mode is used. For example, the instruction

$$\text{MOV} \quad \text{EAX,820}$$

is encoded into 5 bytes. A one-byte OP code specifies the Move operation, the fact that a 32-bit immediate operand is used, and the name of the destination register. The OP-code byte is directly followed by the 4-byte immediate value of 820. When an 8-bit immediate operand is used, as in the instruction

$$\text{MOV} \quad \text{DL,5}$$

only two bytes are needed to encode the instruction.

Addressing Mode and Displacement Fields

As a general rule, one operand of a two-operand instruction must be in a register. The other operand can also be in a register, or it can be in the memory. There are two exceptions where both operands can be in the memory. The first is the case where the source operand is an immediate operand, and the destination operand is in the memory. The second is the case of instructions for Push and Pop operations on the processor stack. The stack is located in the stack segment of memory, and it is possible to push a memory operand onto the stack or to pop an operand from the stack into the memory. We will discuss this later in Section 3.22.

When both operands are in registers, only one addressing mode byte is needed. For example, the instruction

$$\text{ADD} \quad \text{EAX,EDX}$$

is encoded into two bytes. The first byte contains the OP code and the other byte is an addressing mode byte that specifies the two registers.

Now let us consider a few examples of instruction encoding where one operand is in a register and the other is in memory. The instruction

$$\text{MOV} \quad \text{ECX,N}$$

in the programs in Figure 3.40 is encoded in six bytes: one for the OP code, one for the addressing mode byte that specifies both the Direct mode and the destination register ECX, and four bytes for the address of memory location N.

The instruction

$$\text{ADD} \quad \text{EAX,[EBX + EDI*4]}$$

in the same programs requires two addressing mode bytes because two registers are used to generate the effective address of the source operand. The scale factor of 4 is also included in the second of these two bytes. Thus, the instruction requires a total of three bytes, including the OP-code byte.

As a third example, consider the instruction

$$\text{MOV} \quad \text{DWORD PTR [EBP + ESI*4 + DISP],10}$$

The assembly language directive DWORD PTR is needed to specify that the operand length is 32 bits for the immediate operand with the value 10. In other assembly languages, specification of the size of the operand is often included in the OP-code mnemonic. For example, in the Motorola 68000, discussed in Part II of this chapter, MOVE.B specifies a 1-byte operand, and MOVE.L specifies a 4-byte long-word operand. If a 32-bit displacement value DISP is used, a total of 11 bytes is needed to encode this instruction: one byte for the OP code, two for the addressing mode field, and four bytes each for the displacement and immediate fields. It is noted in Table 3.3 that displacements can have a length of either 8 bits or 32 bits. The size is specified in the first of the two addressing mode bytes.

In the encoding of two-operand instructions, the specifications of the register operand and the memory operand are placed in a fixed order, with the register operand always being specified first. In order to distinguish between the instructions

$$\text{MOV} \quad \text{EAX,LOCATION}$$

which loads the contents of memory location LOCATION into register EAX, and the instruction

$$\text{MOV} \quad \text{LOCATION,EAX}$$

which stores the contents of EAX into LOCATION, the OP-code byte contains a bit called the *direction bit*. This bit indicates which operand is the source.

The encoding of OP codes and addressing modes in the IA-32 architecture is somewhat complex and has a number of nonuniformities and exceptions. While this makes it difficult for a compiler to take advantage of all of the features of the instruction set and addressing modes, there is no doubt that the IA-32 architecture has very powerful and flexible features.

Appendix D contains a summary of the IA-32 instructions and a guide to entering and running assembly language programs on a personal computer.

3.18 IA-32 ASSEMBLY LANGUAGE

Basic aspects of the IA-32 assembly language for specifying OP codes, addressing modes, and instruction address labels are illustrated by the programs in Figure 3.40. As discussed in Section 2.6.1, assembler directives are needed to define the data area of a program and to define the correspondence between symbolic names for data locations and the actual physical address values.

A complete assembly language program for the program in Figure 3.40b is shown in Figure 3.42. The .data and .code assembler directives define the beginning of the data and code (instruction) sections of the program. In the data section, the DD directives allocate 4-byte doubleword data locations. NUM1 is the label assigned to the address of the first of five doublewords initialized to the decimal values 17, 3, −51, 242, and −113. The next two doubleword locations, initialized to 5 and 0, are given the address labels N and SUM.

$$
\text{Assembler directives}
\begin{cases}
\begin{array}{lll}
\text{.data} & & \\
\text{NUM1} & \text{DD} & 17, 3, \text{-}51, 242, \text{-}113 \\
\text{N} & \text{DD} & 5 \\
\text{SUM} & \text{DD} & 0 \\
\\
\text{.code} & &
\end{array}
\end{cases}
$$

$$
\begin{array}{l}
\text{Statements that generate} \\
\text{machine instructions}
\end{array}
\begin{cases}
\begin{array}{lll}
\text{MAIN}: & \text{LEA} & \text{EBX, NUM1} \\
& \text{SUB} & \text{EBX, 4} \\
& \text{MOV} & \text{ECX, N} \\
& \text{MOV} & \text{EAX, 0} \\
\text{STARTADD}: & \text{ADD} & \text{EAX, [EBX+ECX} * 4] \\
& \text{LOOP} & \text{STARTADD} \\
& \text{MOV} & \text{SUM, EAX}
\end{array}
\end{cases}
$$

Assembler directive   END   MAIN

Figure 3.42 Complete IA-32 assembly language representation for the program in Figure 3.40*b*.

The three symbolic names declared in the data section are used in the addressing modes of the instructions in the code section. The MAIN label is used to specify the location where instruction execution is to begin, and this label is used in the END assembler directive that terminates the text file for the program. Other assembler directives, such as EQU which was discussed in Section 2.6.1, are also available.

3.19 PROGRAM FLOW CONTROL

There are two main ways in which the flow of executing instructions varies from straight-line sequencing. Calls to subroutines and returns from them break straight-line sequencing, as will be discussed in Section 3.22. Also, branch instructions, either conditional or unconditional, can cause a break. We will now discuss branch instructions. In IA-32 terminology, branch instructions are called Jumps.

3.19.1 CONDITIONAL JUMPS AND CONDITION CODE FLAGS

The instruction

JG   STARTADD

in Figure 3.40*a* is an example of a conditional jump instruction. The condition is "Greater than 0," as signified by the G suffix in the OP code. This condition is related to the results of the most recently executed data manipulation instruction, which is the

DEC   ECX

instruction in this example. Properties of the results generated by instructions such as Decrement, Add, or others that perform arithmetic and comparison operations are recorded in four condition code flags in the processor Status Register, as shown in Figure 3.37. These flags, called SF (sign), ZF (zero), OF (overflow), and CF (carry), are set to 1 or cleared to 0 as described in Section 2.4.6, where they were called N, Z, V, and C, respectively, with one exception. On a subtract operation, the CF bit is set to 1 if no carry occurs, signifying a borrow signal. The flags can be tested in subsequent conditional jump instructions to determine whether or not the jump should be taken. In our example, execution control switches to the instruction at the jump target address STARTADD if the condition [ECX] > 0 holds.

Conditional jump instructions do not contain the jump target address as an absolute address. They contain a signed number that is added to the contents of the Instruction Pointer register to determine the target address. Thus, the target address is given relative to the address in the Instruction Pointer. The first step performed after an instruction is fetched is to advance the Instruction Pointer to point to the next instruction. Hence, the Instruction Pointer contains the address of the instruction that immediately follows the jump instruction when the relative offset to the jump target address is added to it. In our example, assume that the address STARTADD is 1000. A total of seven bytes is needed to encode the four instructions ADD, INC, DEC, and JG in Figure 3.40*a*. The updated contents of the Instruction Pointer register, EIP, will be 1007, which is the address of the last MOV instruction in the program. Therefore, the relative distance to the jump target address is −7, and that is the value stored in the conditional jump instruction. This small negative number can be represented in one byte. Hence, including the OP-code byte, only two bytes are needed to encode a conditional jump instruction when the relative address of the target is in the range −128 through +127. When the jump target is farther away, a 4-byte offset is used.

In this example, the result of decrementing the ECX register is tested to see if it is greater than zero. Other arithmetic properties of a result can be tested by different conditional jump instructions. For example, Jump if equal to 0, and Jump if sign bit is 1 (negative) are done by instructions with the OP codes JZ (or JE) and JS, respectively.

Compare Instructions

It is often necessary to make conditional jumps in a program based on the result of comparing two numbers. The Compare instruction

CMP   dst,src

performs the operation

$$[dst] - [src]$$

and sets the condition code flags based on the result obtained. Neither of the operands is changed. The first operand is always compared to the second. For example, if we follow the Compare instruction by a conditional jump that is based on the "greater than" condition, then we wish to take the jump to the target address if the destination operand is greater than the source operand.

3.19.2 UNCONDITIONAL JUMP

An unconditional jump instruction, JMP, always causes a branch to the instruction at the target address. In addition to using short (one byte) or long (four bytes) relative signed offsets to determine the target address, as is done in conditional jump instructions, the JMP instruction also allows the use of other addressing modes. This flexibility in generating the target address can be very useful. Consider the Case statement that is found in many high-level languages. At some point in a program, exactly one of a number of alternative calculations is to be performed. Each of these is referred to as a case. Suppose that the 4-byte addresses of the first instruction for each of the routines corresponding to the cases are stored in a table in the memory, starting at a location labeled JUMPTABLE. If the cases are numbered with indices 0, 1, 2, ... and the index of the case to be executed is loaded into index register ESI, then a jump to the selected case can be performed by executing the instruction

$$\text{JMP} \quad [\text{JUMPTABLE} + \text{ESI*4}]$$

which uses the Index with displacement addressing mode.

3.20 LOGIC AND SHIFT/ROTATE INSTRUCTIONS

3.20.1 LOGIC OPERATIONS

The IA-32 architecture has instructions that perform the logic operations AND, OR, and XOR. The operation is performed bitwise on two operands, and the result is placed in the destination location. For example, suppose register EAX contains the hexadecimal pattern 0000FFFF and register EBX contains the pattern 02FA62CA. Then the instruction

$$\text{AND} \quad \text{EBX,EAX}$$

will clear the left half of EBX to all zeros, and leave the right half unchanged. The result in EBX will be 000062CA.

There is also a NOT instruction which generates the logical complement of all bits of the operand, that is, it changes all 1s to 0s and all 0s to 1s.

3.20.2 SHIFT AND ROTATE OPERATIONS

An operand can be shifted right or left, using either logical or arithmetic shifts, by a number of bit positions determined by a specified count. The format of the shift instructions is

$$\text{OPcode} \quad \text{dst,count}$$

where the destination operand to be shifted is specified by the general addressing modes and the count is given either as an 8-bit immediate value or is contained in the 8-bit

```
LEA    EBP,LOC        EBP points to first byte.
MOV    AL,[EBP]       Load first byte into AL.
SHL    AL,4           Shift left by 4 bit positions.
MOV    BL,[EBP+1]     Load second byte into BL.
AND    BL,0FH         Clear high-order 4 bits to zero.
OR     AL,BL          Concatenate the BCD digits.
MOV    PACKED,AL      Store the result.
```

Figure 3.43   An IA-32 routine to pack two BCD digits into a byte.

register CL. There are four shift instructions:

SHL   Shift left logical

SHR   Shift right logical

SAL   Shift left arithmetic (same as SHL)

SAR   Shift right arithmetic

Shift operations are discussed in Section 2.10 and illustrated in Figure 2.30.

There are also four rotate instructions. They are ROL and ROR for left and right rotate without the carry flag CF, and RCL and RCR for rotations that include CF. All four operations are illustrated in Figure 2.32.

Digit-Packing Program

As a simple application of these instructions, consider the BCD digit-packing program shown in Figure 2.31. The IA-32 code for this routine is shown in Figure 3.43. The two ASCII bytes are loaded into registers AL and BL. The SHL instruction shifts the byte in AL four bit positions to the left, filling the low-order four bits with zeros. The second entry in the operand field of this instruction is a count that indicates the number of bit positions to be shifted. The AND instruction clears the high-order four bit positions of the second byte to zeros. Finally, the 4-bit patterns that are the desired BCD codes are combined in AL with the OR instruction and then stored in memory byte location PACKED.

3.21   I/O OPERATIONS

3.21.1   MEMORY-MAPPED I/O

Input/Output device buffer registers are most commonly accessed in modern computer systems by the memory-mapped I/O method as described in Section 2.7. The IA-32 Move instruction can be used to transfer directives to I/O devices, and to transfer data and status information to and from devices. For example, suppose that keyboard and display devices have their synchronization flags SIN and SOUT (see Figure 2.19) stored in bit 3 of device status registers INSTATUS and OUTSTATUS, respectively. Using program-controlled I/O, a byte can be read from the keyboard buffer register DATAIN into register AL using the wait loop

```
READWAIT:   BT    INSTATUS,3
            JNC   READWAIT
            MOV   AL,DATAIN
```

The instruction BT is a bit-test instruction. The value in the destination bit position specified by the source operand (in this case, the immediate value 3) is loaded into the carry flag CF. The conditional jump JNC (jump if no carry) causes a jump to READWAIT if $CF = 0$.

Similarly, an output operation to send a byte from register AL to the display buffer register DATAOUT is performed by

```
WRITEWAIT:   BT    OUTSTATUS,3
             JNC   WRITEWAIT
             MOV   DATAOUT,AL
```

An IA-32 program that reads one line of characters from a keyboard, stores them in memory starting at address LOC, and echoes them back out to the display, is shown in Figure 3.44. This program is patterned after the generic program in Figure 2.20. Register EBP points to the memory area where the line is to be stored.

3.21.2 ISOLATED I/O

The IA-32 instruction set also has two instructions, with OP codes IN and OUT, that are used only for I/O purposes. The addresses issued by these instructions are in an address space that is separate from the memory address space used by the other instructions.

```
            LEA    EBP,LOC        EBP points to memory area.
READ:   BT     INSTATUS,3     Wait for character to be
            JNC    READ               entered into DATAIN.
            MOV    AL,DATAIN      Transfer character into AL.
            MOV    [EBP],AL       Store the character in memory
            INC    EBP                and increment pointer.
ECHO:   BT     OUTSTATUS,3    Wait for display to
            JNC    ECHO               be ready.
            MOV    DATAOUT,AL     Send character to display.
            CMP    AL,CR          If not carriage return,
            JNE    READ               read more characters.
```

Figure 3.44 An IA-32 program that reads a line of characters and displays it.

This arrangement is called *isolated I/O* to distinguish it from memory-mapped I/O in which the addressable locations in I/O devices are in the same address space as memory locations. The same address and data lines on Intel processor chips are used for both address spaces. An output control line is used to indicate which address space is referenced by the current instruction.

Sixteen-bit addresses are used in the byte-addressable I/O address space. There are 8-bit and 32-bit I/O device operand locations that hold data, status, and command information. The first 256 addresses can be specified directly using an 8-bit field in the In and Out instructions. The format for the input instruction using this mode is

IN   REG,DEVADDR

where the destination REG must be register AL or EAX, denoting an 8-bit or a 32-bit operand transfer, respectively. The last field in the instruction contains the 8-bit device address DEVADDR. The corresponding output instruction is

OUT   DEVADDR,REG

Since the address space is byte addressable, a keyboard device that can send an 8-bit ASCII character to the processor could have its data buffer register at byte address DEVADDR and its 8-bit status register at address DEVADDR + 1.

The full 16-bit I/O address space spans 64K locations; it can be referenced through the DX register using the input instruction

IN   REG,DX

where, as before, REG must be AL or EAX. The 16-bit device address is contained in the DX register, which is the low-order 16 bits of the EDX register, and the width of the data transfer is determined by the size of the REG operand. The corresponding output instruction is

OUT   DX,REG

3.21.3 BLOCK TRANSFERS

In addition to the instructions IN and OUT that transfer a single item of information between the processor and an I/O device, the IA-32 architecture also has two block transfer I/O instructions: REPINS and REPOUTS. They transfer a block of data items serially, one item at a time, between the memory and an I/O device. The S suffix in the OP codes stands for string, and the REP prefix stands for "repeat the item by item transfer until the complete block has been transferred". The instructions themselves do not specify the parameters needed to describe the transfer. These parameters are specified implicitly by processor registers DX, EDI, and ECX as follows:

DX contains a 16-bit I/O device address.

EDI contains a 32-bit address for the beginning of a block in memory.

ECX contains the number of data items to be transferred.

A suffix B or D in the OP-code mnemonic indicates that the item size is either of byte or doubleword length. Thus, REPINSB is a byte-block transfer, and REPINSD is a doubleword-block transfer. The block transfer instructions operate as follows: After each data item is transferred, the index register EDI is incremented by 1 or 4, depending on the size of the data items, and the ECX register is decremented by 1. The transfers are repeated until the contents of the counter register ECX have been decremented to 0. The effect of these single instructions is equivalent to a program loop that uses register ECX as the loop counter.

As an example, suppose that a block of 128 doublewords is to be transferred from a disk storage device into the memory. Assume that the addressable data buffer register in the disk device contains a doubleword data item, and has the I/O address DISKDATA. The data block is to be written into the memory beginning at address MEMBLOCK. The counter register ECX has to be initialized to 128. The instruction sequence

```
LEA      EDI,MEMBLOCK
MOV      DX,DISKDATA
MOV      ECX,128
REPINSD
```

can be used to accomplish the transfer. This assumes that MEMBLOCK has been defined as an address label, and DISKDATA has been defined by an EQU assembler directive to represent the 16-bit address of the device data buffer register.

This discussion illustrates how isolated I/O can be organized. It also shows how a multi-item block transfer can be performed by a single instruction with the use of an address counter (EDI) and a data item counter (ECX).

3.22 SUBROUTINES

As explained in Section 2.9, the processor stack data structure is convenient for handling entry to and return from subroutines. In the IA-32 architecture, register ESP is used as the stack pointer, which points to the current top element (TOS) in the processor stack. The stack grows toward lower numbered addresses. This arrangement is the same as discussed in Section 2.8 and illustrated in Figures 2.21 and 2.22. The width of the stack is 32 bits, that is, all stack entries are doublewords.

There are four instructions for pushing elements onto the stack and for popping them off. The instruction

$$\text{PUSH} \quad src$$

decrements ESP by 4, and then stores the doubleword at location src into the memory location pointed to by ESP. The instruction

$$\text{POP} \quad dst$$

reverses this process by retrieving the TOS doubleword from the location pointed to by ESP, storing it at location dst, and then incrementing ESP by 4, thus effectively removing the TOS element from the stack. These instructions implicitly use ESP as the stack pointer. The source and destination operands are specified using the IA-32 addressing modes. Two instructions push or pop multiple register contents. The instruction

PUSHAD

pushes the contents of all eight general-purpose registers EAX through EDI onto the stack, and the instruction

POPAD

pops them off in the reverse order. When POPAD reaches the old stored value of ESP, it discards those four bytes without loading them into ESP and continues to pop the remaining values into their respective registers. These two instructions are used to efficiently save and restore the contents of all registers as part of implementing subroutines.

The list addition program in Figure 3.40*a* can be written as a subroutine as shown in Figure 3.45. Parameters are passed through registers. Memory address NUM1 of the first of the numbers to be added is loaded into register EBX by the calling program, and the number of values to be added, contained in memory location N, is loaded into register ECX. The calling program expects to get the sum of the numbers in the list passed back to it in register EAX. Thus, the registers EBX, ECX, and EAX are used for passing parameters. Register EDI is used by the subroutine as an index register in performing the addition, so its contents have to be saved and restored in the subroutine by PUSH and POP instructions.

The subroutine is called by the instruction

CALL   LISTADD

which first pushes the return address onto the stack and then branches to LISTADD. The contents of the stack after the subroutine has saved (PUSHed) EDI are shown in Figure 3.45*b*. The return address is the address of the MOV instruction that immediately follows the CALL instruction in the calling program. The instruction RET returns execution control to the calling program by popping the TOS element into the Instruction Pointer (program counter), EIP.

Figure 3.46 shows the program of Figure 3.40*a* rewritten as a subroutine with parameters passed on the stack. The parameters NUM1 and *n* are pushed onto the stack by the two PUSH instructions in the calling program. The top of the stack is at level 2 after the Call instruction has been executed. Registers EDI, EAX, EBX, and ECX serve the same purpose in this subroutine as in the subroutine in Figure 3.45. Their values are saved and they are loaded with initial values and parameters by the first eight instructions in the subroutine. At this point, the top of the stack is at level 3. When the numbers have been added by the four-instruction loop, the sum is placed into the stack, overwriting the parameter NUM1. After the Return instruction is executed, the ADD and POP instructions in the calling program remove the parameter *n* from the stack and pop the result sum into the memory location SUM, restoring the top of the stack to level 1.

Calling program

```
            ⋮
        LEA    EBX,NUM1        Load parameters
        MOV    ECX,N              into EBX,ECX.
        CALL   LISTADD         Branch to subroutine.
        MOV    SUM,EAX         Store sum into memory.
            ⋮
```

Subroutine

```
LISTADD:    PUSH   EDI             Save EDI.
            MOV    EDI,0           Use EDI as index register.
            MOV    EAX,0           Use EAX as accumulator register.

STARTADD:   ADD    EAX, [EBX + EDI * 4]   Add next number.
            INC    EDI             Increment index.
            DEC    ECX             Decrement counter.
            JG     STARTADD        Branch back if [ECX] > 0.
            POP    EDI             Restore EDI.
            RET                    Branch back to Calling program.
```

(a) Calling program and subroutine

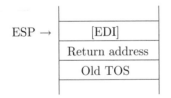

(b) Stack contents after saving EDI in subroutine

Figure 3.45   Program of Figure 3.40*a* written as an IA-32 subroutine; parameters passed through registers.

The last example of subroutines that we will discuss is the case of handling nested calls. Figure 3.47 shows the IA-32 code for the program in Figure 2.28. The stack frames corresponding to the first and second subroutines are shown in Figure 3.48. Register EBP is used as the frame pointer. The structures of the calling program and the subroutines are very close to those in Figure 2.28. The essential differences in Figure 3.47 are that multiple PUSH and POP instructions are used for saving and

(Assume top of stack is at level 1 below.)

Calling program

PUSH	OFFSET NUM1	Push parameters onto the stack.
PUSH	N	
CALL	LISTADD	Branch to the subroutine.
ADD	ESP,4	Remove n from the stack.
POP	SUM	Pop the sum into SUM.

.
.
.

Subroutine

LISTADD:	PUSH	EDI	Save EDI and use
	MOV	EDI,0	as index register.
	PUSH	EAX	Save EAX and use as
	MOV	EAX,0	as accumulator register.
	PUSH	EBX	Save EBX and load
	MOV	EBX,[ESP+20]	address NUM1.
	PUSH	ECX	Save ECX and
	MOV	ECX,[ESP+20]	load count n.
STARTADD:	ADD	EAX,[EBX+EDI*4]	Add next number.
	INC	EDI	Increment index.
	DEC	ECX	Decrement counter.
	JG	STARTADD	Branch back if not done.
	MOV	[ESP+24],EAX	Overwrite NUM1 in stack with sum.
	POP	ECX	Restore registers.
	POP	EBX	
	POP	EAX	
	POP	EDI	
	RET		Return.

(a) Calling program and subroutine

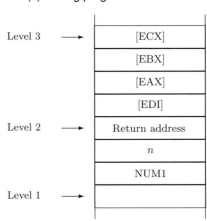

(b) Stack contents at different times

Figure 3.46   Program of Figure 3.40*a* written as an IA-32 subroutine; parameters passed on the stack.

Address		Instructions		Comments

Calling program

⋮

2000		PUSH	PARAM2	Place parameters
2006		PUSH	PARAM1	on stack.
2012		CALL	SUB1	
2017		POP	RESULT	Store result.
		ADD	ESP,4	Restore stack level.

⋮

First subroutine

2100	SUB1:	PUSH	EBP	Save frame pointer register.
		MOV	EBP,ESP	Load frame pointer.
		PUSH	EAX	Save registers.
		PUSH	EBX	
		PUSH	ECX	
		PUSH	EDX	
		MOV	EAX,[EBP+8]	Get first parameter.
		MOV	EBX,[EBP+12]	Get second parameter.

⋮

		PUSH	PARAM3	Place parameter on stack.
2160		CALL	SUB2	
2165		POP	ECX	Pop SUB2 result into ECX.

⋮

		MOV	[EBP+8],EDX	Place answer on stack.
		POP	EDX	Restore registers.
		POP	ECX	
		POP	EBX	
		POP	EAX	
		POP	EBP	Restore frame pointer register.
		RET		Return to Main program.

Second subroutine

3000	SUB2:	PUSH	EBP	Save frame pointer register.
		MOV	EBP,ESP	Load frame pointer.
		PUSH	EAX	Save registers.
		PUSH	EBX	
		MOV	EAX,[EBP+8]	Get parameter.

⋮

		MOV	[EBP+8],EBX	Place SUB2 result on stack.
		POP	EBX	Restore registers.
		POP	EAX	
		POP	EBP	Restore frame pointer register.
		RET		Return to first subroutine.

Figure 3.47 Nested subroutines in IA-32 assembly language.

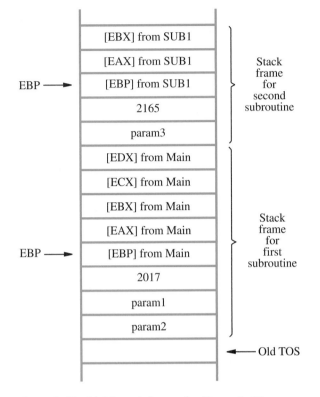

Figure 3.48   IA-32 stack frames for Figure 3.47.

restoring registers in place of the MoveMultiple instructions in Figure 2.28. The IA-32 instruction set has instructions PUSHAD and POPAD that can be used to push and pop all eight general-purpose registers, as described earlier in this section, but we have chosen to use individual PUSH and POP instructions in Figure 3.47 because only half of the register set is used by the subroutines.

3.23   OTHER INSTRUCTIONS

We have described only a small part of the full set of IA-32 instructions. Here, we will describe a few more important instructions.

3.23.1   MULTIPLY AND DIVIDE INSTRUCTIONS

In addition to the Add and Subtract instructions for signed integer numbers, discussed in Section 3.17, there are instructions for integer multiply and divide, as well as instructions for operations on floating-point numbers.

In general, the multiplication of two 32-bit integers produces a double-length product of 64 bits. However, in many applications, it may be known that the product is only a single-length 32-bit result. Different instructions are used for these two cases. For the latter case, which is more common, the instruction

IMUL   REG,src

places the single-length product into the destination location, which must be a general-purpose register REG. The source operand can be in a register or in the memory. For the first case, the instruction

IMUL   src

uses the EAX register as the destination. The source can be in a register or in the memory. The double-length product is placed in registers EDX (high-order half) and EAX (low-order half).

The instruction for integer divide has the format

IDIV   src

The source operand (src) is the divisor. The dividend is assumed to be in register EAX. The quotient result is placed in EAX and the remainder is placed in EDX. The dividend in EAX must be sign-extended into EDX before the instruction is executed. This is done by the instruction CDQ (convert doubleword to quadword), which has no operands because the registers involved are assumed to be EAX and EDX.

Floating-point numbers, which are described in Chapter 6, have a much larger range than integers and are needed for scientific calculations. Instructions for the full range of arithmetic operations on these numbers are provided. The operands and results are held in the floating-point registers shown in Figure 3.37. Both single-precision (32-bit) and double-precision (64-bit) formats are supported in the instruction set.

3.23.2 MULTIMEDIA EXTENSION (MMX) INSTRUCTIONS

A two-dimensional graphic or video image can be represented by an array of a large number of sampled image points. The color and brightness of each point, called a *pixel* (picture element), can be encoded into an 8-bit data item. Processing of such data has two main characteristics. The first is that manipulations of individual pixels often involve very simple arithmetic or logic operations. The second is that very high computational rates may be needed for some real-time display applications. The same characteristics apply to sampled audio signals or speech processing, where a sequence of signed numbers represents samples of a continuous analog signal taken at periodic intervals.

In both of these applications, processing efficiency is achieved if the individual data items, which are usually bytes or 16-bit words, are packed into small groups that can be processed in parallel. The IA-32 instruction set has a number of instructions that operate in parallel on such data packed into 64-bit quadwords. (A quadword contains eight bytes or four 16-bit words.) These instructions are called *multimedia extension* (MMX) instructions. The operands can be in the memory or in the eight floating-point registers. Thus, these registers serve a dual purpose. They can hold either floating-point numbers or MMX operands. When used by MMX instructions, the registers are referred to as MM0 through MM7.

Move instructions are provided for transferring 64-bit MMX operands between the memory and the MMX registers. The instruction

$$\text{PADDB} \quad \text{MMi,src}$$

adds the corresponding bytes of two 8-byte operands individually and places eight sums in the destination register. The source can be in the memory or in an MMX register, but the destination must be an MMX register. Similar instructions are provided for subtraction and for logic operations.

A common operation in signal processing applications is to multiply a short time sequence of input signal samples by constants, called *weights,* and add the products together to produce an output signal sample. An MMX instruction that combines the multiply and add operations is provided. It operates on 64-bit MMX operands that contain four 16-bit signal sample data items.

3.23.3 VECTOR (SIMD) INSTRUCTIONS

A set of instructions that are used to perform arithmetic operations on small groups of floating-point numbers is provided. SIMD (single-instruction multiple-data) instructions are useful for vector and matrix calculations in scientific applications. In Intel terminology, these instructions are called *streaming SIMD extension* (SSE) instructions. They handle compound operands that are 128 bits long, each consisting of four 32-bit floating-point numbers. Eight 128-bit registers are available for holding these operands. (These registers are not shown in Figure 3.37.) Add and Multiply are two of the basic instructions provided in this group. They operate on the four corresponding pairs of 32-bit operands in the 128-bit compound source and destination operands and place the four individual results in the 128-bit destination location.

3.24 PROGRAM EXAMPLES

This section presents the IA-32 code for the example programs described in Section 2.11.

3.24.1 VECTOR DOT PRODUCT PROGRAM

Figure 3.49 shows an IA-32 program for computing the dot product of two vectors of numbers stored in the memory starting at addresses AVEC and BVEC. This program is patterned after the generic program in Figure 2.33. In Figure 3.49, the Base with index addressing mode is used to access successive elements of each vector. Register EDI is used as the index register. A scale factor of 4 is used because the vector elements are assumed to be doubleword (4-byte) numbers. Register ECX is used as the loop counter,

```
                 LEA    EBP,AVEC             EBP points to vector A.
                 LEA    EBX,BVEC             EBX points to vector B.
                 MOV    ECX,N                ECX is the loop counter.
                 MOV    EAX,0                EAX accumulates the dot product.
                 MOV    EDI,0                EDI is an index register.
LOOPSTART:       MOV    EDX,[EBP+EDI*4]      Compute the product
                 IMUL   EDX,[EBX+EDI*4]        of next components.
                 INC    EDI                  Increment index.
                 ADD    EAX,EDX              Add to previous sum.
                 LOOP   LOOPSTART            Branch back if not done.
                 MOV    DOTPROD,EAX          Store dot product in memory.
```

Figure 3.49 An IA-32 dot product program.

initialized to n. This allows the use of the LOOP instruction (see Section 3.17 and Figure 3.40b) that first decrements ECX and then branches conditionally to the target address LOOPSTART if the contents of ECX have not reached zero. The product of two vector elements is assumed to fit into a doubleword, so the Multiply instruction IMUL explicitly specifies the desired destination register EDX, as discussed in Section 3.23.

3.24.2 BYTE-SORTING PROGRAM

Figure 3.50b shows the IA-32 code for the byte-sorting program of Figure 2.34b. Register EAX is loaded with the address LIST and serves as a base register in accessing bytes of the list by using the Base with index addressing mode. Register EDI serves as an index register for the j index in the outer loop, and register ECX serves as an index register for the k index in the inner loop. Register DL holds the current largest byte as each sublist is traversed. The IA-32 program in Figure 3.50b matches the generic program in Figure 2.34b instruction for instruction except for the interchange of LIST(k) with LIST(j). The single instruction XCHG achieves this in the IA-32 code, while three instructions and a temporary register are needed in the generic code.

3.24.3 LINKED-LIST INSERTION AND DELETION SUBROUTINES

The insertion and deletion subroutines in Figures 3.51 and 3.52 mirror the corresponding generic programs in Figures 2.37 and 2.38 very closely. Parameters are passed through registers, and register names RHEAD, RNEWREC, RIDNUM, RCURRENT, and RNEXT correspond to the same usage as in the generic routines. These names have been used instead of the IA-32 names EAX, EBX, and so on. A sixth register, RNEWID, has been used to hold the ID number of the new record to be inserted. It is loaded with the ID number of the new record by the first instruction of the subroutine

```
for   (j = n−1; j > 0; j = j − 1)
       { for ( k = j−1; k >= 0; k = k − 1 )
           { if    (LIST[k] > LIST[j])
               {  TEMP = LIST[k];
                  LIST[k] = LIST[j];
                  LIST[j] = TEMP;
               }
           }
       }
```

(a) C-language program for sorting

	LEA	EAX,LIST	Load list pointer base
	MOV	EDI,N	register (EAX), and initialize
	DEC	EDI	outer loop index register
			(EDI) to j = n − 1.
OUTER:	MOV	ECX,EDI	Initialize inner loop index
	DEC	ECX	register (ECX) to k = j − 1.
	MOV	DL,[EAX + EDI]	Load LIST(j) into register DL.
INNER:	CMP	[EAX + ECX],DL	Compare LIST(k) to LIST(j).
	JLE	NEXT	If LIST(k) ≤ LIST(j), go to
			next lower k index entry;
	XCHG	[EAX + ECX],DL	Otherwise, interchange LIST(k)
			and LIST(j), leaving
	MOV	[EAX + EDI],DL	new LIST(j) in DL.
NEXT:	DEC	ECX	Decrement inner loop index k.
	JGE	INNER	Repeat or terminate inner loop.
	DEC	EDI	Decrement outer loop index j.
	JG	OUTER	Repeat or terminate outer loop.

(b) IA-32 program implementation

Figure 3.50   An IA-32 byte-sorting program using straight-selection sort.

in Figure 3.51. The rest of the subroutine is an instruction for instruction match with the subroutine in Figure 2.37. The subroutine for deleting a record, shown in Figure 3.52, is also an instruction for instruction match with the subroutine in Figure 2.38.

As with the generic programs in Figures 2.37 and 2.38, the IA-32 insertion subroutine assumes that the ID number of the new record does not match that of any record already in the list, and the IA-32 deletion subroutine assumes that there exists a record in the list with an ID number that matches the contents of RIDNUM. Problems 3.72

Subroutine

INSERTION:	MOV	RNEWID,[RNEWREC]	
	CMP	RHEAD,0	Check if list empty.
	JG	HEAD	
	MOV	RHEAD,RNEWREC	If yes, new record becomes
	RET		one-entry list.
HEAD:	CMP	RNEWID,[RHEAD]	Check if new record
			becomes head.
	JG	SEARCH	
	MOV	[RNEWREC+4],RHEAD	If yes, make new record
	MOV	RHEAD,RNEWREC	the head.
	RET		
SEARCH:	MOV	RCURRENT,RHEAD	Otherwise, use
LOOPSTART:	MOV	RNEXT,[RCURRENT+4]	RCURRENT
	CMP	RNEXT,0	and RNEXT
	JE	TAIL	to move through
	CMP	RNEWID,[RNEXT]	the list to find
	JL	INSERT	the insertion point.
	MOV	RCURRENT,RNEXT	
	JMP	LOOPSTART	
INSERT:	MOV	[RNEWREC+4],RNEXT	
TAIL:	MOV	[RCURRENT+4],RNEWREC	
	RET		

Figure 3.51 An IA-32 subroutine for inserting a new record into a linked list.

Subroutine

DELETION:	CMP	RIDNUM,[RHEAD]	Check if head.
	JG	SEARCH	
	MOV	RHEAD,[RHEAD+4]	If yes, remove.
	RET		
SEARCH:	MOV	RCURRENT,RHEAD	Otherwise,
LOOPSTART:	MOV	RNEXT,[RCURRENT+4]	use RCURRENT
	CMP	RIDNUM,[RNEXT]	and RNEXT
	JE	DELETE	to move through
	MOV	RCURRENT,RNEXT	the list to
	JMP	LOOPSTART	find the record.
DELETE:	MOV	RTEMP,[RNEXT+4]	
	MOV	[RCURRENT+4],RTEMP	
	RET		

Figure 3.52 An IA-32 subroutine for deleting a record from a linked list.

and 3.73 consider how the subroutines should be changed to signal an error if the assumptions are not true.

3.25 CONCLUDING REMARKS

Three different instruction set architectures — ARM, Motorola 68000, and Intel IA-32 — were discussed in this chapter. The ARM and 68000 instruction sets provide basic illustrations of the RISC and CISC design styles, respectively. The IA-32 instruction set is a very extensive CISC design.

Any instruction in the ARM instruction set is encoded into one 32-bit word. Operations on data can only be performed when the data are contained in processor registers. Load and Store instructions are used to transfer operands between the processor registers and the memory. We explained how conditional execution of all instructions and extensive options for shifting operands in most instructions lead to efficient implementation of common programming tasks.

The 68000 is a traditional example of an instruction set whose instructions are encoded into a variable number of memory words, depending on the complexity of the operation to be performed and the amount of information needed to generate the effective addresses of any required memory operands. Both register and memory operands can be referenced in individual instructions.

The Intel IA-32 instruction set was seen to have extensive facilities for a broad range of operations on different types of data.

PROBLEMS

PART I: ARM

3.1 Assume the following register and memory contents in an ARM computer:

Register R0 contains 1000.
Register R1 contains 2000.
Register R2 contains 1016.
Register R6 contains 20.
Register R7 contains 30.

The numbers 1, 2, 3, 4, 5, and 6, are stored in successive word locations starting at memory address 1000. What is the effect of executing each of the following three short instruction blocks, starting each time from the given initial values?

```
(a) LDR      R8,[R0]
    LDR      R9,[R0,#4]
    ADD      R10,R8,R9
```

    (*b*) STR   R6,[R1,#−4]!

         STR   R7,[R1,#−4]!

         LDR   R8,[R1],#4

         LDR   R9,[R1],#4

         SUB   R10,R8,R9

    (*c*) LDMIA   R2!,{R4,R5}

         ADD   R4,R4,R5

3.2 Which of the following ARM instructions would cause the assembler to issue a syntax error message? Why?

    (*a*) ADD   R2,R2,R2

    (*b*) SUB   R0,R1,[R2,#4]

    (*c*) MOV   R0,#2_1010101

    (*d*) MOV   R0,#257

    (*e*) ADD   R0,R1,R11,LSL #8

3.3 When a byte is loaded from memory into an ARM processor register using the Load instruction, the high-order 24 bits are cleared to 0s. (See Section 3.1.2.) If the loaded byte represents an 8-bit signed integer in 2's-complement representation, it must be sign-extended to 32 bits in the register before it can be used in arithmetic operations. Assuming such a byte has been loaded into register R0, write a short routine to sign-extend it to the 32-bit register length. (Hint: Use MOV instructions to move the contents of R0 back into R0 after appropriate shifts from the possibilities LSL, LSR, and ASR, as described in Section 2.10.2 and shown in Figure 2.30.)

3.4 Write an ARM program to reverse the order of bits in register R2. For example, if the starting pattern in R2 is 1110 . . . 0100, the result left in R2 should be 0010 . . . 0111. (Hint: Use shift and rotate operations.)

3.5 A *program trace* is a listing of the contents of certain registers and memory locations at different times during the execution of a program. List the contents of registers R0, R1, and R2 after each of the first three executions of the BGT instruction in the program in Figure 3.7. Present the results in a table that has the three registers as column headers. Use three rows to list the contents of the registers after each execution of the BGT instruction. The program data are as given in Figure 3.8.

3.6 Write an ARM program that compares the corresponding bytes of two lists of bytes and places the larger byte in a third list. The two lists start at byte locations X and Y, and the larger-byte list starts at LARGER. The length of the lists is stored in memory location N.

3.7 An ARM program is required for the following character manipulation task: A string of *n* characters is stored in the memory in consecutive byte locations, beginning at location STRING. Another shorter string of *m* characters is stored in consecutive byte locations, beginning at location SUBSTRING. The program must search the string that begins at

STRING to determine whether or not it contains a contiguous substring identical to the string that begins at SUBSTRING. The length parameters n and m, where $n > m$, are stored in memory locations N and M, respectively. If a matching substring is found, the address of its first byte is to be stored in register R0; otherwise, the contents of R0 are to be cleared to 0. The program does not need to determine multiple occurrences of the substring. Only the address of the first matching substring is required.

3.8 Write an ARM program that generates the first n numbers of the Fibonacci series. In this series, the first two numbers are 0 and 1, and each subsequent number is generated by adding the preceding two numbers. For example, for $n = 8$, the series is

$$0, 1, 1, 2, 3, 5, 8, 13$$

Your program should store the numbers in successive memory word locations starting at MEMLOC. Assume that the value n is stored in location N.

3.9 Write an ARM program to convert a word of text from lowercase to uppercase. The word consists of ASCII characters stored in successive byte locations in the memory, starting at location WORD and ending with a space character. (See Appendix E for the ASCII code.)

3.10 The list of student marks shown in Figure 2.14 is changed to contain j test scores for each student. Assume that there are n students. Write an ARM program for computing the sums of the scores on each test and store these sums in the memory word locations at addresses SUM, SUM + 4, SUM + 8, ... The number of tests, j, is larger than the number of registers in the processor, so the type of program shown in Figure 2.15 for the 3-test case cannot be used. Use two nested loops, as suggested in Section 2.5.3. The inner loop should accumulate the sum for a particular test, and the outer loop should run over the number of tests, j. Assume that j is stored in memory location J, placed ahead of location N.

3.11 Consider an array of numbers $A(i, j)$, where $i = 0$ through $n - 1$ is the row index and $j = 0$ through $m - 1$ is the column index. The array is stored in the memory of an ARM computer one row after another, with elements of each row occupying m successive word locations. Write an ARM subroutine for adding column x to column y, element by element, leaving the sum elements in column y. The indices x and y are passed to the subroutine in registers R1 and R2. The parameters n and m are passed to the subroutine in registers R3 and R4, and the address of element $A(0,0)$ is passed in register R0. Any of the addressing modes in Table 3.1 can be used.

3.12 Write an ARM program that reads n characters from a keyboard and echoes them back to a display after pushing them onto a user stack as they are read. Use register R6 as the stack pointer. The count value n is contained in memory word location N.

3.13 Assume that the average time taken to fetch and execute an instruction in the program in Figure 3.9 is 20 nanoseconds. If keyboard characters are entered at the rate of 10 per second, approximately how many times is the BEQ READ instruction executed per character entered? Assume that the time taken to display each character is much less than the time between the entry of successive characters at the keyboard.

3.14 In the ARM program in Figure 3.9, "in-line" code is used to read a line of characters and display them. Rewrite this program in the form of a main program that calls a subroutine named GETCHAR to read a single character and calls another subroutine named PUTCHAR to display a single character. The address INSTATUS is passed to GETCHAR in register R1, and the main program expects to get the character passed back in register R3. The address OUTSTATUS and the character to be displayed are passed to PUTCHAR in registers R2 and R3, respectively. Any other registers used by either subroutine must be saved and restored by the subroutine using a stack whose pointer is register R13. Storing the characters in memory and checking for the end-of-line character CR is to be done in the main program.

3.15 Repeat Problem 3.14 using the stack to pass parameters.

3.16 Write an ARM program to accept three decimal digits from a keyboard. Each digit is represented in the ASCII code (see Appendix E). Assume that these three digits represent a decimal integer in the range 0 to 999 and convert the integer into a binary number representation. The high-order digit is received first. To aid in this conversion, two tables of words are stored in the memory. Each table has 10 entries. The first table, starting at word location TENS, contains the binary representations for the decimal values 0, 10, 20, ... , 90. The second table starts at word location HUNDREDS and contains the decimal values 0, 100, 200, ... , 900 in binary representation.

3.17 The decimal-to-binary conversion program of Problem 3.16 is to be implemented using two nested subroutines. The main program that calls the first subroutine passes two parameters by pushing them onto the stack whose pointer register is R13. The first parameter is the address of a 3-byte memory buffer area for storing the input decimal-digit characters. The second parameter is the address of the location where the converted binary value is to be stored. The first subroutine reads in the three characters from the keyboard and then calls the second subroutine to perform the conversion. The necessary parameters are passed to this subroutine via the processor registers. Both subroutines must save the contents of any registers that they use on the stack.

(*a*) Write the two subroutines for the ARM processor.

(*b*) Give the contents of the stack immediately after the execution of the instruction that calls the second subroutine.

3.18 Consider the queue structure described in Problem 2.18. Write ARM APPEND and REMOVE routines that transfer data between a processor register and the queue. Be careful to inspect and update the state of the queue and the pointers each time an operation is attempted and performed.

3.19 Using the format for presenting results that is described in Problem 3.5, give a program trace for the byte-sorting program in Figure 3.15*b*. Show the contents of registers R0, R2, and R3, and list byte locations LIST, LIST + 1, ... , LIST + 4 for a 5-byte list after each execution of the last instruction in the program. Assume that LIST = 1000 and that the initial list of byte values is 120, 13, 106, 45, and 67, where [LIST] = 120.

3.20 Rewrite the byte-sorting program in Figure 3.15b as a subroutine that sorts a list of 32-bit positive integers. The calling program should pass the list address to the subroutine. The first 32-bit quantity at that location is the number of entries in the list, followed by the numbers to be sorted.

3.21 Consider the byte-sorting program of Figure 3.15b. During each pass through a sublist, LIST(j) through LIST(0), list entries are swapped whenever LIST(k) > LIST(j). An alternative strategy is to keep track of the address of the largest value in the sublist and to perform, at most, one swap at the end of the sublist search. Rewrite the program using this approach. What is the advantage of this approach?

3.22 Assume that the list of student test scores shown in Figure 2.14 is stored in the memory as a linked list as shown in Figure 2.36. Write an ARM program that accomplishes the same thing as the program in Figure 2.15. The head record is stored at memory location 1000.

3.23 The linked-list insertion subroutine in Figure 3.16 does not check if the ID of the new record matches that of a record already in the list. What happens in the execution of the subroutine if this is the case? Modify the subroutine to return the address of the matching record in register R10 if this occurs or to return a zero if the insertion is successful.

3.24 The linked-list deletion subroutine in Figure 3.17 assumes that a record with the ID contained in register RIDNUM is in the list. What happens in the execution of the subroutine if there is no record with this ID? Modify the subroutine to return a zero in RIDNUM if deletion is successful, or leave RIDNUM unchanged if the record is not in the list.

PART II: 68000

3.25 Consider the following state of the 68000 processor:

> Register D0 contains $1000.
> Register A0 contains $2000.
> Register A1 contains $1000.
> Memory location $1000 contains the long word $2000.
> Memory location $2000 contains the long word $3000.

What is the effect of executing each of the following three instructions, starting each time from this initial state? How many bytes does each instruction occupy? How many memory accesses does the fetching and execution of each instruction require?

> (a) ADD.L   D0,(A0)
> (b) ADD.L   (A1,D0),D0
> (c) ADD.L   #$2000,(A0)

3.26 Find the syntax errors in the following 68000 instructions:

> (a) ADDX   −(A2),D3
>
> (b) LSR.L   #9,D2
>
> (c) MOVE.B   520(A2,D2)
>
> (d) SUBA.L   12(A2,PC),A0
>
> (e) CMP.B   #254,$12(A2,D1.B)

3.27 A *program trace* is a listing of the contents of certain registers and memory locations at different times during the execution of a program. List the contents of registers D0, D1, and A2 and memory locations N, NUM1, and SUM after each of five executions of the ADD.W instruction and after execution of the last MOVE.L instruction in the program in Figure 3.25. Present the results in a table that has the registers and memory locations as column headers. Use six rows to list the contents of the registers and memory locations after execution of each of the instructions. Assume the following initial values: [SUM] = 0, [N] = 5, NUM1 = 2400, and the five numbers are 83, 45, 156, −250, and 100.

3.28 Consider the following 68000 program:

```
        MOVEA.L   MEM1,A0
        MOVEA.L   MEM2,A2
        ADDA.L    A0,A1
        MOVEA.L   A0,A2
        MOVE.B    (A0) +,D0
LOOP    CMP.B     (A0) +,D0
        BLE       NXT
        LEA       −1(A0),A2
        MOVE.B    (A2),D0
NXT     CMPA.L    A0,A1
        BGT       LOOP
        MOVE.L    A2,DESIRED
```

(a) What does this program do?

(b) How many 16-bit words are needed to store this program in the memory?

(c) Give an expression for the number of memory accesses required. The expression should be of the form $T = a + bn + cm$, where n is the number of times the loop is executed, m is the number of times the branch to NXT is not taken, and a, b, and c are constants.

3.29 Consider the two 68000 programs given in Figure P3.1.

(a) Do these programs leave the same value in location RSLT?

(b) What task(s) do they accomplish?

	Program 1			Program 2	
	CLR.L	D0		MOVE.W	#$FFFF,D0
	MOVEA.L	#LIST,A0		MOVEA.L	#LIST,A0
LOOP	MOVE.W	(A0)+,D1	LOOP	LSL.W	(A0)+
	BGE	LOOP		BCC	LOOP
	ADDQ.L	#1,D0		LSL.W	#1,D0
	CMPI	#17,D0		BCS	LOOP
	BLT	LOOP		MOVE.W	−2(A0),RSLT
	MOVE.W	−2(A0),RSLT			

Figure P3.1   Two 68000 programs for Problem 3.29.

(*c*) How many bytes of memory are needed to store each program?

(*d*) Which program requires the larger number of memory accesses?

(*e*) What are the advantages and disadvantages of these programs?

3.30 Write a 68000 program that compares the corresponding bytes of two lists of bytes and places the larger byte in a third list. The two lists start at byte locations X and Y, and the larger-byte list starts at LARGER. The length of the lists is stored in memory location N.

3.31 A 68000 program is required for the following character manipulation task: A string of *n* characters is stored in the memory in consecutive byte locations, beginning at location STRING. Another, shorter string of *m* characters is stored in consecutive byte locations, beginning at location SUBSTRING. The program must search the string that begins at STRING to determine whether or not it contains a contiguous substring identical to the string that begins at SUBSTRING. The length parameters *n* and *m*, where $n > m$, are stored in memory locations N and M, respectively. If a matching substring is found, the address of its first byte is to be stored in register D0; otherwise, the contents of D0 are to be cleared to 0. The program does not need to determine multiple occurrences of the substring. Only the address of the first matching substring is required.

3.32 Write a 68000 program that generates the first *n* numbers of the Fibonacci series. In this series, the first two numbers are 0 and 1, and each subsequent number is generated by adding the preceding two numbers. For example, for $n = 8$, the series is

$$0, 1, 1, 2, 3, 5, 8, 13$$

Your program should store the numbers in memory byte locations starting at MEMLOC. Assume that the value *n* is stored in location N. What is the largest *n* that your program can handle?

3.33 Write a 68000 program to convert a word of text from lowercase to uppercase. The word consists of ASCII characters stored in successive byte locations in the memory, starting at location WORD and ending with a space character. (See Appendix E for the ASCII code.)

3.34 The list of student marks shown in Figure 2.14 is changed to contain j test scores for each student. Each entry in the list is a 16-bit word, so the increments on LIST are by 2. Assume that there are n students. Write a 68000 program for computing the sums of the scores on each test and store these sums in the memory word locations at addresses SUM, SUM + 2, SUM + 4, ... The number of tests, j, is larger than the number of registers in the processor, so the type of program shown in Figure 2.15 for the 3-test case cannot be used. Use two nested loops, as suggested in Section 2.5.3. The inner loop should accumulate the sum for a particular test, and the outer loop should run over the number of tests, j. Assume that j is stored in memory location J, placed ahead of N.

3.35 Write a 68000 program that reads n characters from a keyboard and echoes them back to a display after pushing them onto a user stack as they are read. Use register A0 as the stack pointer. The count value n is stored in memory word location N.

3.36 Assume that the average time taken to fetch and execute an instruction in the program in Figure 3.27 is 20 nanoseconds. If keyboard characters are entered at the rate of 10 per second, approximately how many times is the BEQ READ instruction executed per character entered? Assume that the time taken to display each character is much less than the time between the entry of successive characters at the keyboard.

3.37 In the 68000 program in Figure 3.27, "in-line" code is used to read a line of characters and display them. Rewrite this program in the form of a main program that calls a subroutine named GETCHAR to read a single character and calls another subroutine named PUTCHAR to display a single character. The addresses INSTATUS and DATAIN are passed to GETCHAR in registers A0 and A1; and the main program expects to get the character passed back in register D0. The addresses OUTSTATUS and DATAOUT and the character to be displayed are passed to PUTCHAR in registers A2, A3, and D0, respectively. Any other registers used by either subroutine must be saved and restored by the subroutine using the processor stack whose pointer is register A7. Storing the characters in memory and checking for the end-of-line character CR is to be done in the main program.

3.38 Repeat problem 3.37 using the stack to pass parameters.

3.39 Consider the queue structure described in Problem 2.18. Write 68000 APPEND and REMOVE routines that transfer data between a processor register and the queue. Be careful to inspect and update the state of the queue and the pointers each time an operation is attempted and performed.

3.40 Write a 68000 program to accept three decimal digits from a keyboard. Each digit is represented in the ASCII code (see Appendix E). Assume that these three digits represent a decimal integer in the range 0 to 999 and convert the integer into a binary number representation. The high-order digit is received first. To aid in this conversion, two tables of words are stored in the memory. Each table has 10 entries. The first table, starting at word location TENS, contains the binary representations for the decimal values 0, 10, 20, . . . , 90. The second table starts at word location HUNDREDS and contains the decimal values 0, 100, 200, . . . , 900 in binary representation.

3.41 The decimal-to-binary conversion program of Problem 3.40 is to be implemented as two nested subroutines. The main program that calls the first subroutine passes two parameters by pushing them onto the processor stack. The first parameter is the address of a 3-byte memory buffer area for storing the input decimal-digit characters. The second parameter is the address of the location for the converted binary value. The first subroutine reads in the three characters from the keyboard and then calls the second subroutine to perform the conversion. The necessary parameters are passed to this subroutine via the processor registers. Both subroutines must save the contents of any registers that they use on the processor stack.

(*a*) Write the two subroutines for the 68000 processor.

(*b*) Give the contents of the processor stack immediately after the execution of the instruction that calls the second subroutine.

3.42 Consider an array of 16-bit numbers $A(i, j)$, where $i = 0$ through $n - 1$ is the row index and $j = 0$ through $m - 1$ is the column index. The array is stored in the memory of a 68000 computer one row after another, with elements of each row occupying m successive word locations. Write a 68000 subroutine for adding column x to column y, element by element, leaving the sum elements in column y. The indices x and y are passed to the subroutine in registers D1 and D2. The parameters n and m are passed to the subroutine in registers D3 and D4, and the address of element $A(0,0)$ is passed in register A0. Any of the addressing modes in Table 3.2 can be used.

3.43 Write a 68000 program to reverse the order of bits in register D2. For example, if the starting pattern in D2 is 1110 ... 0100, the result left in D2 should be 0010 ... 0111. (Hint: Use shift and rotate operations.)

3.44 How many bytes of memory are needed to store the program in Figure 3.32? How many memory accesses take place during execution of this program?

3.45 Using the format for presenting results that is described in Problem 3.27, give a program trace for the byte-sorting program in Figure 3.34*b*. Show the contents of registers D1, D2, and D3, and the list byte locations LIST, LIST + 1, ... , LIST + 4 for a 5-byte list after each execution of the last instruction in the program. Assume that LIST = 1000, and that the initial list of byte values is 120, 13, 106, 45, and 67, where [LIST] = 120.

3.46 Rewrite the byte-sorting program in Figure 3.34*b* as a subroutine that sorts a list of 16-bit positive integers. The calling program should pass the list address to the subroutine. The first 16-bit quantity at that location is the number of entries in the list, followed by the numbers to be sorted.

3.47 Consider the byte-sorting program of Figure 3.34*b*. During each pass through a sublist, LIST(j) through LIST(0), list entries are swapped whenever LIST(k) > LIST(j). An alternative strategy is to keep track of the address of the largest value in the sublist and to perform, at most, one swap at the end of the sublist search. Rewrite the program using this approach. What is the advantage of this approach?

3.48 Assume that the list of student test scores shown in Figure 2.14 is stored in the memory as a linked list as shown in Figure 2.36. Write a 68000 program that accomplishes the same thing as the program in Figure 2.15. The head record is stored at memory location 1000. Assume that all list entries are long words.

3.49 The linked-list insertion subroutine in Figure 3.35 does not check if the ID of the new record matches that of a record already in the list. What happens in the execution of the subroutine if this is the case? Modify the subroutine to return the address of the matching record in register A6 if this occurs, or return a zero if the insertion is successful.

3.50 The linked-list deletion subroutine in Figure 3.36 assumes that a record with the ID contained in register RIDNUM is in the list. What happens in the execution of the subroutine if there is no record with this ID? Modify the subroutine to return a zero in RIDNUM if deletion is successful, or leave RIDNUM unchanged if the record is not in the list.

PART III: Intel IA-32

3.51 Assume the following register and memory contents in an IA-32 computer:

Register EBX contains 1000.

Register ESI contains 2.

The numbers 1, 2, 3, 4, 5, and 6, are stored in successive doubleword locations starting at memory address 1000.

The address label LOC represents address 1008.

What is the effect of executing each of the following three short instruction blocks, starting each time from the given initial values?

(a)	MOV	EAX,10
	ADD	EAX,[EBX + ESI*4 + 8]
(b)	PUSH	20
	PUSH	30
	POP	EAX
	POP	EBX
	SUB	EAX,EBX
(c)	LEA	EAX,LOC
	MOV	EBX,[EAX]

3.52 Which of the following IA-32 instructions would cause the assembler to issue a syntax error message? Why?

(a)	ADD	EAX,EAX
(b)	ADD	[EAX],[EBX + 4]
(c)	SUB	EAX,[EBX + ESI*4 + 20]
(d)	SUB	EAX,[EBX + ESI*10]
(e)	ADD	EAX,−31728542
(f)	MOV	20,EAX
(g)	MOV	EAX,[EBP + ESP*4]

3.53   A *program trace* is a listing of the contents of certain registers and memory locations at different times during the execution of a program. List the contents of registers EAX, EBX, and ECX after each of the first three executions of the LOOP instruction in the program in Figure 3.40*b*. Present the results in a table that has the three registers as column headers. Use three rows to list the contents of the registers after each execution of the LOOP instruction. The program data is as given in Figure 3.42.

3.54   Write an IA-32 program that compares the corresponding bytes of two lists of bytes and places the larger byte in a third list. The two lists start at byte locations X and Y, and the larger-byte list starts at LARGER. The length of the lists is stored in memory location N.

3.55   An IA-32 program is required for the following character manipulation task: A string of n characters is stored in the memory in consecutive byte locations, beginning at location STRING. Another, shorter string of m characters is stored in consecutive byte locations, beginning at location SUBSTRING. The program must search the string that begins at STRING to determine whether or not it contains a contiguous substring identical to the string that begins at SUBSTRING. The length parameters n and m, where $n > m$, are stored in memory locations N and M, respectively. If a matching substring is found, the address of its first byte is to be stored in register EAX; otherwise, the contents of EAX are to be cleared to 0. The program does not need to determine multiple occurrences of the substring. Only the address of the first matching substring is required.

3.56   Write an IA-32 program that generates the first n numbers of the Fibonacci series. In this series, the first two numbers are 0 and 1, and each subsequent number is generated by adding the preceding two numbers. For example, for $n = 8$, the series is

$$0, 1, 1, 2, 3, 5, 8, 13$$

Your program should store the numbers in successive memory doubleword locations starting at MEMLOC. Assume that the value n is stored in location N.

3.57   Write an IA-32 program to convert a word of text from lowercase to uppercase. The word consists of ASCII characters stored in successive byte locations in the memory, starting at location WORD and ending with a space character. (See Appendix E for the ASCII code.)

3.58   The list of student marks shown in Figure 2.14 is changed to contain j test scores for each student. Assume that there are n students. Write an IA-32 program for computing the sums of the scores on each test and store these sums in the memory doubleword locations at addresses SUM, SUM + 4, SUM + 8, ... The number of tests, j, is larger than the number of registers in the processor, so the type of program shown in Figure 2.15 for the 3-test case cannot be used. Use two nested loops, as suggested in Section 2.5.3. The inner loop should accumulate the sum for a particular test, and the outer loop should run over the number of tests, j. Assume that j is stored in memory location J, placed ahead of location N.

3.59   Write an IA-32 program to reverse the order of bits in register EAX. For example, if the starting pattern in EAX is 1110 . . . 0100, the result left in EAX should be 0010 . . . 0111. (Hint: Use shift and rotate operations.)

3.60   Consider the queue structure described in Problem 2.18. Write IA-32 APPEND and REMOVE routines that transfer data between a processor register and the queue. Be careful to inspect and update the state of the queue and the pointers each time an operation is attempted and performed.

3.61   Write an IA-32 program that reads n characters from a keyboard and echoes them back to a display after pushing them onto a user stack as they are read. Use register EBX as the stack pointer. The count value n is stored in memory doubleword location N.

3.62   Assume that the average time taken to fetch and execute an instruction in the program in Figure 3.44 is 10 nanoseconds. If keyboard characters are entered at the rate of 10 per second, approximately how many times is the   JNC   READ   instruction executed per character entered? Assume that the time taken to display each character is much less than the time between the entry of successive characters at the keyboard.

3.63   In the IA-32 program in Figure 3.44, "in-line" code is used to read a line of characters and display them. Rewrite this program in the form of a main program that calls a subroutine named GETCHAR to read a single character and calls another subroutine named PUTCHAR to display a single character. The addresses INSTATUS and DATAIN are passed to GETCHAR in registers EBX and EDX; and the main program expects to get the character passed back in register AL. The addresses OUTSTATUS and DATAOUT and the character to be displayed are passed to PUTCHAR in registers ESI, EDI, and AL, respectively. Any other registers used by either subroutine must be saved and restored by the subroutine using the processor stack, whose pointer is register ESP. Storing the characters in memory and checking for the end-of-line character CR is to be done in the main program.

3.64   Repeat problem 3.63, passing parameters on the processor stack.

3.65   Write an IA-32 program to accept three decimal digits from a keyboard. Each digit is represented in the ASCII code (see Appendix E). Assume that these three digits represent a decimal integer in the range 0 to 999 and convert the integer into a binary number representation. The high-order digit is received first. To aid in this conversion, two tables of doublewords are stored in the memory. Each table has 10 entries. The first table, starting at doubleword location TENS, contains the binary representations for the decimal values 0, 10, 20, . . . , 90. The second table starts at doubleword location HUNDREDS and contains the decimal values 0, 100, 200, . . . , 900 in binary representation.

3.66   The decimal-to-binary conversion program of Problem 3.65 is to be implemented using two nested subroutines. The main program that calls the first subroutine passes two parameters by pushing them onto the processor stack. The first parameter is the address of a 3-byte memory buffer area for storing the input decimal-digit characters. The second parameter is the address of the location for the converted binary value. The first subroutine reads in the three characters from the keyboard and then calls the second subroutine to perform the conversion. The necessary parameters are passed to this subroutine via the processor registers. Both subroutines must save the contents of any registers that they use on the processor stack.

(*a*) Write the two subroutines for the IA-32 processor.

(*b*) Give the contents of the processor stack immediately after the execution of the instruction that calls the second subroutine.

3.67 Consider an array of numbers $A(i, j)$, where $i = 0$ through $n - 1$ is the row index and $j = 0$ through $m - 1$ is the column index. The array is stored in the memory of a IA-32 computer one row after another, with elements of each row occupying m successive doubleword locations. Write an IA-32 subroutine for adding column x to column y, element by element, leaving the sum elements in column y. The indices x and y are passed to the subroutine in registers ESI and EDI. The parameters n and m are passed to the subroutine in registers EAX and EBX, and the address of element $A(0,0)$ is passed in register EDX. Any of the addressing modes in Table 3.3 can be used.

3.68 Using the format for presenting results that is described in Problem 3.53, give a program trace for the byte-sorting program in Figure 3.50*b*. Show the contents of registers EDI, ECX, and DL, and list byte locations LIST, LIST + 1, ... , LIST + 4 for a 5-byte list after each execution of the last instruction in the program. Assume that LIST = 1000 and that the initial list of byte values is 120, 13, 106, 45, and 67, where [LIST] = 120.

3.69 Rewrite the byte-sorting program in Figure 3.50*b* as a subroutine that sorts a list of 32-bit positive integers. The calling program should pass the list address to the subroutine. The first 32-bit quantity at that location is the number of entries in the list, followed by the numbers to be sorted.

3.70 Consider the byte-sorting program of Figure 3.50*b*. During each pass through a sublist, LIST(j) through LIST(0), list entries are swapped whenever LIST(k) > LIST(j). An alternative strategy is to keep track of the address of the largest value in the sublist, and to perform, at most, one swap at the end of the sublist search. Rewrite the program using this approach. What is the advantage of this approach?

3.71 Assume that the list of student test scores shown in Figure 2.14 is stored in the memory as a linked list as shown in Figure 2.36. Write an IA-32 program that accomplishes the same thing as the program in Figure 2.15. The head record is stored at memory location 1000.

3.72 The linked-list insertion subroutine in Figure 3.51 does not check if the ID of the new record matches that of a record already in the list. What happens in the execution of the subroutine if this is the case? Modify the subroutine to return the address of the matching record in register EDX if this occurs or to return a zero if the insertion is successful.

3.73 The linked-list deletion subroutine in Figure 3.52 assumes that a record with the ID contained in register RIDNUM is in the list. What happens in the execution of the subroutine if there is no record with this ID? Modify the subroutine to return a zero in RIDNUM if deletion is successful, or leave RIDNUM unchanged if the record is not in the list.

REFERENCES

1. D. Jaggar, "ARM Architecture and Systems," *IEEE Micro,* 17(4): 9–11, July/August 1997.

2. S. Furber, *ARM System-on-Chip Architecture,* Addison-Wesley, Harlow, England, 2000.

3. A. Clements, *The Principles of Computer Hardware,* 3rd ed., Oxford University Press, New York, 2000.

4. A. van Someren and C. Atack, *The ARM RISC Chip — A Programmer's Guide,* Addison-Wesley, Wokingham, England, 1994.

5. http://www.arm.com

6. http://www.motorola.com

7. D. Tabak, *Advanced Microprocessors,* McGraw-Hill, New York, 1991.

8. http://www.intel.com

9. B.B. Brey, *The Intel Microprocessors,* 5th ed., Prentice-Hall, Upper Saddle River, New Jersey, 2000.

10. S.P. Dandamudi, *Introduction to Assembly Language Programming — From 8086 to Pentium Processors,* Springer-Verlag, New York, 1998.

CHAPTER

4

INPUT/OUTPUT ORGANIZATION

CHAPTER OBJECTIVES

In this chapter you will learn about:

- How program-controlled I/O is performed using polling
- The idea of interrupts and the hardware and software needed to support them
- Direct memory access as an I/O mechanism for high-speed devices
- Data transfer over synchronous and asynchronous buses
- The design of I/O interface circuits
- Commercial bus standards, in particular the PCI, SCSI, and USB buses

One of the basic features of a computer is its ability to exchange data with other devices. This communication capability enables a human operator, for example, to use a keyboard and a display screen to process text and graphics. We make extensive use of computers to communicate with other computers over the Internet and access information around the globe. In other applications, computers are less visible but equally important. They are an integral part of home appliances, manufacturing equipment, transportation systems, banking and point-of-sale terminals. In such applications, input to a computer may come from a sensor switch, a digital camera, a microphone, or a fire alarm. Output may be a sound signal to be sent to a speaker or a digitally coded command to change the speed of a motor, open a valve, or cause a robot to move in a specified manner. In short, a general-purpose computer should have the ability to exchange information with a wide range of devices in varying environments.

In this chapter, we will consider in detail various ways in which I/O operations are performed. First, we will consider the problem from the point of view of the programmer. Then, we will discuss some of the hardware details associated with buses and I/O interfaces and introduce some commonly used bus standards.

4.1   ACCESSING I/O DEVICES

A simple arrangement to connect I/O devices to a computer is to use a single bus arrangement, as shown in Figure 4.1. The bus enables all the devices connected to it to exchange information. Typically, it consists of three sets of lines used to carry address, data, and control signals. Each I/O device is assigned a unique set of addresses. When the processor places a particular address on the address lines, the device that recognizes this address responds to the commands issued on the control lines. The processor requests either a read or a write operation, and the requested data are transferred over the data lines. As mentioned in Section 2.7, when I/O devices and the memory share the same address space, the arrangement is called *memory-mapped I/O*.

With memory-mapped I/O, any machine instruction that can access memory can be used to transfer data to or from an I/O device. For example, if DATAIN is the address

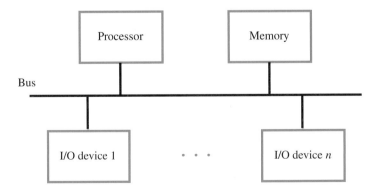

Figure 4.1   A single-bus structure.

of the input buffer associated with the keyboard, the instruction

Move   DATAIN,R0

reads the data from DATAIN and stores them into processor register R0. Similarly, the instruction

Move   R0,DATAOUT

sends the contents of register R0 to location DATAOUT, which may be the output data buffer of a display unit or a printer.

Most computer systems use memory-mapped I/O. Some processors have special In and Out instructions to perform I/O transfers. For example, processors in the Intel family described in Chapter 3 have special I/O instructions and a separate 16-bit address space for I/O devices. When building a computer system based on these processors, the designer has the option of connecting I/O devices to use the special I/O address space or simply incorporating them as part of the memory address space. The latter approach is by far the most common as it leads to simpler software. One advantage of a separate I/O address space is that I/O devices deal with fewer address lines. Note that a separate I/O address space does not necessarily mean that the I/O address lines are physically separate from the memory address lines. A special signal on the bus indicates that the requested read or write transfer is an I/O operation. When this signal is asserted, the memory unit ignores the requested transfer. The I/O devices examine the low-order bits of the address bus to determine whether they should respond.

Figure 4.2 illustrates the hardware required to connect an I/O device to the bus. The address decoder enables the device to recognize its address when this address appears on the address lines. The data register holds the data being transferred to or from the processor. The status register contains information relevant to the operation of the I/O device. Both the data and status registers are connected to the data bus and

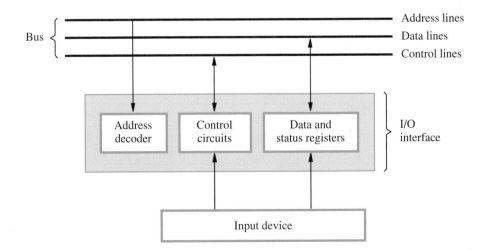

Figure 4.2 I/O interface for an input device.

assigned unique addresses. The address decoder, the data and status registers, and the control circuitry required to coordinate I/O transfers constitute the device's *interface circuit*.

I/O devices operate at speeds that are vastly different from that of the processor. When a human operator is entering characters at a keyboard, the processor is capable of executing millions of instructions between successive character entries. An instruction that reads a character from the keyboard should be executed only when a character is available in the input buffer of the keyboard interface. Also, we must make sure that an input character is read only once.

The basic ideas used for performing input and output operations were introduced in Section 2.7. For an input device such as a keyboard, a status flag, SIN, is included in the interface circuit as part of the status register. This flag is set to 1 when a character is entered at the keyboard and cleared to 0 once this character is read by the processor. Hence, by checking the SIN flag, the software can ensure that it is always reading valid data. This is often accomplished in a program loop that repeatedly reads the status register and checks the state of SIN. When SIN becomes equal to 1, the program reads the input data register. A similar procedure can be used to control output operations using an output status flag, SOUT.

Example 4.1   To review the basic concepts, let us consider a simple example of I/O operations involving a keyboard and a display device in a computer system. The four registers shown in Figure 4.3 are used in the data transfer operations. Register STATUS contains two control flags, SIN and SOUT, which provide status information for the keyboard and the display unit, respectively. The two flags KIRQ and DIRQ in this register are used in conjunction with interrupts. They, and the KEN and DEN bits in register CONTROL, will be discussed in Section 4.2. Data from the keyboard are made available

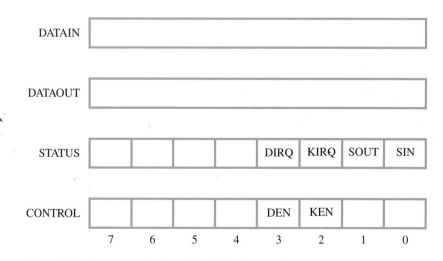

Figure 4.3 Registers in keyboard and display interfaces.

	Move	#LINE,R0	Initialize memory pointer.
WAITK	TestBit	#0,STATUS	Test SIN.
	Branch=0	WAITK	Wait for character to be entered.
	Move	DATAIN,R1	Read character.
WAITD	TestBit	#1,STATUS	Test SOUT.
	Branch=0	WAITD	Wait for display to become ready.
	Move	R1,DATAOUT	Send character to display.
	Move	R1,(R0)+	Store charater and advance pointer.
	Compare	#$0D,R1	Check if Carriage Return.
	Branch≠0	WAITK	If not, get another character.
	Move	#$0A,DATAOUT	Otherwise, send Line Feed.
	Call	PROCESS	Call a subroutine to process the
			the input line.

Figure 4.4 A program that reads one line from the keyboard, stores it in memory buffer, and echoes it back to the display.

in the DATAIN register, and data sent to the display are stored in the DATAOUT register.

The program in Figure 4.4 is similar to that in Figure 2.20. This program reads a line of characters from the keyboard and stores it in a memory buffer starting at location LINE. Then, it calls a subroutine PROCESS to process the input line. As each character is read, it is *echoed back* to the display. Register R0 is used as a pointer to the memory buffer area. The contents of R0 are updated using the Autoincrement addressing mode so that successive characters are stored in successive memory locations.

Each character is checked to see if it is the Carriage Return (CR) character, which has the ASCII code 0D (hex). If it is, a Line Feed character (ASCII code 0A) is sent to move the cursor one line down on the display and subroutine PROCESS is called. Otherwise, the program loops back to wait for another character from the keyboard.

This example illustrates *program-controlled I/O*, in which the processor repeatedly checks a status flag to achieve the required synchronization between the processor and an input or output device. We say that the processor *polls* the device. There are two other commonly used mechanisms for implementing I/O operations: interrupts and direct memory access. In the case of interrupts, synchronization is achieved by having the I/O device send a special signal over the bus whenever it is ready for a data transfer operation. Direct memory access is a technique used for high-speed I/O devices. It involves having the device interface transfer data directly to or from the memory, without continuous involvement by the processor. We will discuss these mechanisms in the next three sections. Then, we will examine the hardware involved, which includes the processor bus and the I/O device interface.

4.2 INTERRUPTS

In the example of Figure 4.4, the program enters a wait loop in which it repeatedly tests the device status. During this period, the processor is not performing any useful computation. There are many situations where other tasks can be performed while waiting for an I/O device to become ready. To allow this to happen, we can arrange for the I/O device to alert the processor when it becomes ready. It can do so by sending a hardware signal called an *interrupt* to the processor. At least one of the bus control lines, called an *interrupt-request* line, is usually dedicated for this purpose. Since the processor is no longer required to continuously check the status of external devices, it can use the waiting period to perform other useful functions. Indeed, by using interrupts, such waiting periods can ideally be eliminated.

Example 4.2

Consider a task that requires some computations to be performed and the results to be printed on a line printer. This is followed by more computations and output, and so on. Let the program consist of two routines, COMPUTE and PRINT. Assume that COMPUTE produces a set of *n* lines of output, to be printed by the PRINT routine.

The required task may be performed by repeatedly executing first the COMPUTE routine and then the PRINT routine. The printer accepts only one line of text at a time. Hence, the PRINT routine must send one line of text, wait for it to be printed, then send the next line, and so on, until all the results have been printed. The disadvantage of this simple approach is that the processor spends a considerable amount of time waiting for the printer to become ready. If it is possible to overlap printing and computation, that is, to execute the COMPUTE routine while printing is in progress, a faster overall speed of execution will result. This may be achieved as follows. First, the COMPUTE routine is executed to produce the first *n* lines of output. Then, the PRINT routine is executed to send the first line of text to the printer. At this point, instead of waiting for the line to be printed, the PRINT routine may be temporarily suspended and execution of the COMPUTE routine continued. Whenever the printer becomes ready, it alerts the processor by sending an interrupt-request signal. In response, the processor interrupts execution of the COMPUTE routine and transfers control to the PRINT routine. The PRINT routine sends the second line to the printer and is again suspended. Then the interrupted COMPUTE routine resumes execution at the point of interruption. This process continues until all *n* lines have been printed and the PRINT routine ends.

The PRINT routine will be restarted whenever the next set of *n* lines is available for printing. If COMPUTE takes longer to generate *n* lines than the time required to print them, the processor will be performing useful computations all the time.

This example illustrates the concept of interrupts. The routine executed in response to an interrupt request is called the *interrupt-service routine,* which is the PRINT routine in our example. Interrupts bear considerable resemblance to subroutine calls. Assume that an interrupt request arrives during execution of instruction *i* in Figure 4.5. The

Program 1
COMPUTE routine

Program 2
PRINT routine

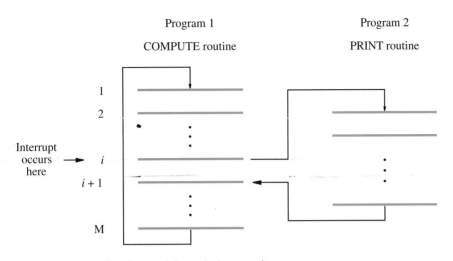

1

2

Interrupt
occurs → i
here

$i + 1$

M

Figure 4.5 Transfer of control through the use of interrupts.

processor first completes execution of instruction i. Then, it loads the program counter with the address of the first instruction of the interrupt-service routine. For the time being, let us assume that this address is hardwired in the processor. After execution of the interrupt-service routine, the processor has to come back to instruction $i + 1$. Therefore, when an interrupt occurs, the current contents of the PC, which point to instruction $i + 1$, must be put in temporary storage in a known location. A Return-from-interrupt instruction at the end of the interrupt-service routine reloads the PC from that temporary storage location, causing execution to resume at instruction $i + 1$. In many processors, the return address is saved on the processor stack. Alternatively, it may be saved in a special location, such as a register provided for this purpose.

We should note that as part of handling interrupts, the processor must inform the device that its request has been recognized so that it may remove its interrupt-request signal. This may be accomplished by means of a special control signal on the bus. An *interrupt-acknowledge* signal, used in some of the interrupt schemes to be discussed later, serves this function. A common alternative is to have the transfer of data between the processor and the I/O device interface accomplish the same purpose. The execution of an instruction in the interrupt-service routine that accesses a status or data register in the device interface implicitly informs the device that its interrupt request has been recognized.

So far, treatment of an interrupt-service routine is very similar to that of a subroutine. An important departure from this similarity should be noted. A subroutine performs a function required by the program from which it is called. However, the interrupt-service routine may not have anything in common with the program being executed at the time the interrupt request is received. In fact, the two programs often belong to different users. Therefore, before starting execution of the interrupt-service routine, any information that may be altered during the execution of that routine must be saved. This information must be restored before execution of the interrupted program is resumed. In this way, the original program can continue execution without being affected in any way by the interruption, except for the time delay. The information that needs to be saved and restored typically includes the condition code flags and the contents of any registers used by both the interrupted program and the interrupt-service routine.

The task of saving and restoring information can be done automatically by the processor or by program instructions. Most modern processors save only the minimum amount of information needed to maintain the integrity of program execution. This is because the process of saving and restoring registers involves memory transfers that increase the total execution time, and hence represent execution overhead. Saving registers also increases the delay between the time an interrupt request is received and the start of execution of the interrupt-service routine. This delay is called *interrupt latency*. In some applications, a long interrupt latency is unacceptable. For these reasons, the amount of information saved automatically by the processor when an interrupt request is accepted should be kept to a minimum. Typically, the processor saves only the contents of the program counter and the processor status register. Any additional information that needs to be saved must be saved by program instructions at the beginning of the interrupt-service routine and restored at the end of the routine.

In some earlier processors, particularly those with a small number of registers, all registers are saved automatically by the processor hardware at the time an interrupt request is accepted. The data saved are restored to their respective registers as part of the execution of the Return-from interrupt instruction. Some computers provide two types of interrupts. One saves all register contents, and the other does not. A particular I/O device may use either type, depending upon its response-time requirements. Another interesting approach is to provide duplicate sets of processor registers. In this case, a different set of registers can be used by the interrupt-service routine, thus eliminating the need to save and restore registers.

An interrupt is more than a simple mechanism for coordinating I/O transfers. In a general sense, interrupts enable transfer of control from one program to another to be initiated by an event external to the computer. Execution of the interrupted program resumes after the execution of the interrupt-service routine has been completed. The concept of interrupts is used in operating systems and in many control applications where processing of certain routines must be accurately timed relative to external events. The latter type of application is referred to as *real-time processing*.

4.2.1 INTERRUPT HARDWARE

We pointed out that an I/O device requests an interrupt by activating a bus line called interrupt-request. Most computers are likely to have several I/O devices that can request an interrupt. A single interrupt-request line may be used to serve n devices as depicted in Figure 4.6. All devices are connected to the line via switches to ground. To request an interrupt, a device closes its associated switch. Thus, if all interrupt-request signals $INTR_1$ to $INTR_n$ are inactive, that is, if all switches are open, the voltage on the interrupt-request line will be equal to V_{dd}. This is the inactive state of the line. When a device requests an interrupt by closing its switch, the voltage on the line drops to 0, causing the interrupt-request signal, INTR, received by the processor to go to 1. Since the closing of one or more switches will cause the line voltage to drop to 0, the value

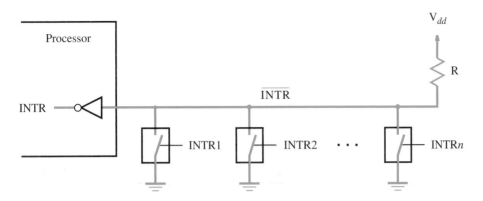

Figure 4.6 An equivalent circuit for an open-drain bus used to implement a common interrupt-request line.

of INTR is the logical OR of the requests from individual devices, that is,

$$\text{INTR} = \text{INTR}_1 + \cdots + \text{INTR}_n$$

It is customary to use the complemented form, $\overline{\text{INTR}}$, to name the interrupt-request signal on the common line, because this signal is active when in the low-voltage state.

In the electronic implementation of the circuit in Figure 4.6, special gates known as *open-collector* (for bipolar circuits) or *open-drain* (for MOS circuits) are used to drive the $\overline{\text{INTR}}$ line. The output of an open-collector or an open-drain gate is equivalent to a switch to ground that is open when the gate's input is in the 0 state and closed when it is in the 1 state. The voltage level, hence the logic state, at the output of the gate is determined by the data applied to all the gates connected to the bus, according to the equation given above. Resistor R is called a *pull-up resistor* because it pulls the line voltage up to the high-voltage state when the switches are open.

4.2.2 ENABLING AND DISABLING INTERRUPTS

The facilities provided in a computer must give the programmer complete control over the events that take place during program execution. The arrival of an interrupt request from an external device causes the processor to suspend the execution of one program and start the execution of another. Because interrupts can arrive at any time, they may alter the sequence of events from that envisaged by the programmer. Hence, the interruption of program execution must be carefully controlled. A fundamental facility found in all computers is the ability to enable and disable such interruptions as desired. We will now examine this and related facilities in some detail.

There are many situations in which the processor should ignore interrupt requests. For example, in the case of the Compute-Print program of Figure 4.5, an interrupt request from the printer should be accepted only if there are output lines to be printed. After printing the last line of a set of n lines, interrupts should be disabled until another set becomes available for printing. In another case, it may be necessary to guarantee that a particular sequence of instructions is executed to the end without interruption because the interrupt-service routine may change some of the data used by the instructions in question. For these reasons, some means for enabling and disabling interrupts must be available to the programmer. A simple way is to provide machine instructions, such as Interrupt-enable and Interrupt-disable, that perform these functions.

Let us consider in detail the specific case of a single interrupt request from one device. When a device activates the interrupt-request signal, it keeps this signal activated until it learns that the processor has accepted its request. This means that the interrupt-request signal will be active during execution of the interrupt-service routine, perhaps until an instruction is reached that accesses the device in question. It is essential to ensure that this active request signal does not lead to successive interruptions, causing the system to enter an infinite loop from which it cannot recover. Several mechanisms are available to solve this problem. We will describe three possibilities here; other schemes that can handle more than one interrupting device will be presented later.

The first possibility is to have the processor hardware ignore the interrupt-request line until the execution of the first instruction of the interrupt-service routine has been completed. Then, by using an Interrupt-disable instruction as the first instruction in the interrupt-service routine, the programmer can ensure that no further interruptions will occur until an Interrupt-enable instruction is executed. Typically, the Interrupt-enable instruction will be the last instruction in the interrupt-service routine before the Return-from-interrupt instruction. The processor must guarantee that execution of the Return-from-interrupt instruction is completed before further interruption can occur.

The second option, which is suitable for a simple processor with only one interrupt-request line, is to have the processor automatically disable interrupts before starting the execution of the interrupt-service routine. After saving the contents of the PC and the processor status register (PS) on the stack, the processor performs the equivalent of executing an Interrupt-disable instruction. It is often the case that one bit in the PS register, called *Interrupt-enable*, indicates whether interrupts are enabled. An interrupt request received while this bit is equal to 1 will be accepted. After saving the contents of the PS on the stack, with the Interrupt-enable bit equal to 1, the processor clears the Interrupt-enable bit in its PS register, thus disabling further interrupts. When a Return-from-interrupt instruction is executed, the contents of the PS are restored from the stack, setting the Interrupt-enable bit back to 1. Hence, interrupts are again enabled.

In the third option, the processor has a special interrupt-request line for which the interrupt-handling circuit responds only to the leading edge of the signal. Such a line is said to be *edge-triggered*. In this case, the processor will receive only one request, regardless of how long the line is activated. Hence, there is no danger of multiple interruptions and no need to explicitly disable interrupt requests from this line.

Before proceeding to study more complex aspects of interrupts, let us summarize the sequence of events involved in handling an interrupt request from a single device. Assuming that interrupts are enabled, the following is a typical scenario:

1. The device raises an interrupt request.
2. The processor interrupts the program currently being executed.

3. Interrupts are disabled by changing the control bits in the PS (except in the case of edge-triggered interrupts).

4. The device is informed that its request has been recognized, and in response, it deactivates the interrupt-request signal.

5. The action requested by the interrupt is performed by the interrupt-service routine.

6. Interrupts are enabled and execution of the interrupted program is resumed.

4.2.3 HANDLING MULTIPLE DEVICES

Let us now consider the situation where a number of devices capable of initiating interrupts are connected to the processor. Because these devices are operationally independent, there is no definite order in which they will generate interrupts. For example, device X may request an interrupt while an interrupt caused by device Y is being serviced, or several devices may request interrupts at exactly the same time. This gives rise to a number of questions:

1. How can the processor recognize the device requesting an interrupt?

2. Given that different devices are likely to require different interrupt-service routines, how can the processor obtain the starting address of the appropriate routine in each case?

3. Should a device be allowed to interrupt the processor while another interrupt is being serviced?

4. How should two or more simultaneous interrupt requests be handled?

The means by which these problems are resolved vary from one computer to another, and the approach taken is an important consideration in determining the computer's suitability for a given application.

When a request is received over the common interrupt-request line in Figure 4.6, additional information is needed to identify the particular device that activated the line. Furthermore, if two devices have activated the line at the same time, it must be possible to break the tie and select one of the two requests for service. When the interrupt-service routine for the selected device has been completed, the second request can be serviced.

The information needed to determine whether a device is requesting an interrupt is available in its status register. When a device raises an interrupt request, it sets to 1 one of the bits in its status register, which we will call the IRQ bit. For example, bits KIRQ and DIRQ in Figure 4.3 are the interrupt request bits for the keyboard and the display, respectively. The simplest way to identify the interrupting device is to have the interrupt-service routine poll all the I/O devices connected to the bus. The first device encountered with its IRQ bit set is the device that should be serviced. An appropriate subroutine is called to provide the requested service.

The polling scheme is easy to implement. Its main disadvantage is the time spent interrogating the IRQ bits of all the devices that may not be requesting any service. An alternative approach is to use vectored interrupts, which we describe next.

Most commonly used

Vectored Interrupts

To reduce the time involved in the polling process, a device requesting an interrupt may identify itself directly to the processor. Then, the processor can immediately start executing the corresponding interrupt-service routine. The term *vectored interrupts* refers to all interrupt-handling schemes based on this approach.

A device requesting an interrupt can identify itself by sending a special code to the processor over the bus. This enables the processor to identify individual devices even if they share a single interrupt-request line. The code supplied by the device may represent the starting address of the interrupt-service routine for that device. The code length is typically in the range of 4 to 8 bits. The remainder of the address is supplied by the processor based on the area in its memory where the addresses for interrupt-service routines are located.

This arrangement implies that the interrupt-service routine for a given device must always start at the same location. The programmer can gain some flexibility by storing in this location an instruction that causes a branch to the appropriate routine. In many computers, this is done automatically by the interrupt-handling mechanism. The location pointed to by the interrupting device is used to store the starting address of the interrupt-service routine. The processor reads this address, called the *interrupt vector,* and loads it into the PC. The interrupt vector may also include a new value for the processor status register.

In most computers, I/O devices send the interrupt-vector code over the data bus, using the bus control signals to ensure that devices do not interfere with each other. When a device sends an interrupt request, the processor may not be ready to receive the interrupt-vector code immediately. For example, it must first complete the execution of the current instruction, which may require the use of the bus. There may be further delays if interrupts happen to be disabled at the time the request is raised. The interrupting device must wait to put data on the bus only when the processor is ready to receive it. When the processor is ready to receive the interrupt-vector code, it activates the interrupt-acknowledge line, INTA. The I/O device responds by sending its interrupt-vector code and turning off the INTR signal.

Interrupt Nesting

We suggested in Section 4.2.1 that interrupts should be disabled during the execution of an interrupt-service routine, to ensure that a request from one device will not cause more than one interruption. The same arrangement is often used when several devices are involved, in which case execution of a given interrupt-service routine, once started, always continues to completion before the processor accepts an interrupt request from a second device. Interrupt-service routines are typically short, and the delay they may cause is acceptable for most simple devices.

For some devices, however, a long delay in responding to an interrupt request may lead to erroneous operation. Consider, for example, a computer that keeps track of the time of day using a real-time clock. This is a device that sends interrupt requests to the processor at regular intervals. For each of these requests, the processor executes a short interrupt-service routine to increment a set of counters in the memory that keep track of time in seconds, minutes, and so on. Proper operation requires that the delay in responding to an interrupt request from the real-time clock be small in comparison with the interval between two successive requests. To ensure that this requirement is satisfied in the presence of other interrupting devices, it may be necessary to accept an interrupt request from the clock during the execution of an interrupt-service routine for another device.

This example suggests that I/O devices should be organized in a priority structure. An interrupt request from a high-priority device should be accepted while the processor is servicing another request from a lower-priority device.

A multiple-level priority organization means that during execution of an interrupt-service routine, interrupt requests will be accepted from some devices but not from others, depending upon the device's priority. To implement this scheme, we can assign a priority level to the processor that can be changed under program control. The priority level of the processor is the priority of the program that is currently being executed. The processor accepts interrupts only from devices that have priorities higher than its own. At the time the execution of an interrupt-service routine for some device is started, the priority of the processor is raised to that of the device. This action disables interrupts from devices at the same level of priority or lower. However, interrupt requests from higher-priority devices will continue to be accepted.

The processor's priority is usually encoded in a few bits of the processor status word. It can be changed by program instructions that write into the PS. These are *privileged* instructions, which can be executed only while the processor is running in the supervisor mode. The processor is in the supervisor mode only when executing operating system routines. It switches to the user mode before beginning to execute application programs. Thus, a user program cannot accidentally, or intentionally, change the priority of the processor and disrupt the system's operation. An attempt to execute a privileged instruction while in the user mode leads to a special type of interrupt called a *privilege exception,* which we describe in Section 4.2.5.

A multiple-priority scheme can be implemented easily by using separate interrupt-request and interrupt-acknowledge lines for each device, as shown in Figure 4.7. Each of the interrupt-request lines is assigned a different priority level. Interrupt requests received over these lines are sent to a priority arbitration circuit in the processor. A request is accepted only if it has a higher priority level than that currently assigned to the processor.

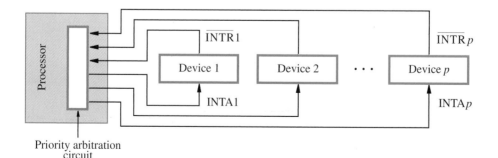

Figure 4.7   Implementation of interrupt priority using individual interrupt-request and acknowledge lines.

Simultaneous Requests

Let us now consider the problem of simultaneous arrivals of interrupt requests from two or more devices. The processor must have some means of deciding which request to service first. Using a priority scheme such as that of Figure 4.7, the solution is straightforward. The processor simply accepts the request having the highest priority. If several devices share one interrupt-request line, as in Figure 4.6, some other mechanism is needed.

Polling the status registers of the I/O devices is the simplest such mechanism. In this case, priority is determined by the order in which the devices are polled. When vectored interrupts are used, we must ensure that only one device is selected to send its interrupt vector code. A widely used scheme is to connect the devices to form a *daisy chain,* as shown in Figure 4.8*a*. The interrupt-request line $\overline{\text{INTR}}$ is common to all devices. The interrupt-acknowledge line, INTA, is connected in a daisy-chain fashion, such that the INTA signal propagates serially through the devices. When several devices raise an interrupt request and the $\overline{\text{INTR}}$ line is activated, the processor responds by setting the INTA line to 1. This signal is received by device 1. Device 1 passes the signal on to device 2 only if it does not require any service. If device 1 has a pending request for

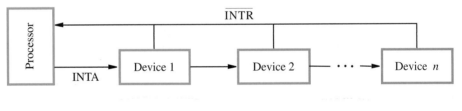

(a) Daisy chain

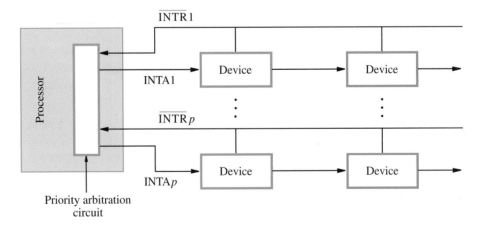

(b) Arrangement of priority groups

Figure 4.8   Interrupt priority schemes.

interrupt, it blocks the INTA signal and proceeds to put its identifying code on the data lines. Therefore, in the daisy-chain arrangement, the device that is electrically closest to the processor has the highest priority. The second device along the chain has second highest priority, and so on.

The scheme in Figure 4.8a requires considerably fewer wires than the individual connections in Figure 4.7. The main advantage of the scheme in Figure 4.7 is that it allows the processor to accept interrupt requests from some devices but not from others, depending upon their priorities. The two schemes may be combined to produce the more general structure in Figure 4.8b. Devices are organized in groups, and each group is connected at a different priority level. Within a group, devices are connected in a daisy chain. This organization is used in many computer systems.

4.2.4 CONTROLLING DEVICE REQUESTS

Until now, we have assumed that an I/O device interface generates an interrupt request whenever it is ready for an I/O transfer, for example whenever the SIN flag in Figure 4.3 is equal to 1. It is important to ensure that interrupt requests are generated only by those I/O devices that are being used by a given program. Idle devices must not be allowed to generate interrupt requests, even though they may be ready to participate in I/O transfer operations. Hence, we need a mechanism in the interface circuits of individual devices to control whether a device is allowed to generate an interrupt request.

The control needed is usually provided in the form of an interrupt-enable bit in the device's interface circuit. The keyboard interrupt-enable, KEN, and display interrupt-enable, DEN, flags in register CONTROL in Figure 4.3 perform this function. If either of these flags is set, the interface circuit generates an interrupt request whenever the corresponding status flag in register STATUS is set. At the same time, the interface circuit sets bit KIRQ or DIRQ to indicate that the keyboard or display unit, respectively, is requesting an interrupt. If an interrupt-enable bit is equal to 0, the interface circuit will not generate an interrupt request, regardless of the state of the status flag.

To summarize, there are two independent mechanisms for controlling interrupt requests. At the device end, an interrupt-enable bit in a control register determines whether the device is allowed to generate an interrupt request. At the processor end, either an interrupt enable bit in the PS register or a priority structure determines whether a given interrupt request will be accepted.

Consider a processor that uses the vectored interrupt scheme, where the starting address of the interrupt-service routine is stored at memory location INTVEC. Interrupts are enabled by setting to 1 an interrupt-enable bit, IE, in the processor status word, which we assume is bit 9. A keyboard and a display unit connected to this processor have the status, control, and data registers shown in Figure 4.3.

Assume that at some point in a program called Main we wish to read an input line from the keyboard and store the characters in successive byte locations in the

Example 4.3

memory, starting at location LINE. To perform this operation using interrupts, we need to initialize the interrupt process. This may be accomplished as follows:

1. Load the starting address of the interrupt-service routine in location INTVEC.
2. Load the address LINE in a memory location PNTR. The interrupt-service routine will use this location as a pointer to store the input characters in the memory.
3. Enable keyboard interrupts by setting bit 2 in register CONTROL to 1.
4. Enable interrupts in the processor by setting to 1 the IE bit in the processor status register, PS.

Once this initialization is completed, typing a character on the keyboard will cause an interrupt request to be generated by the keyboard interface. The program being executed at that time will be interrupted and the interrupt-service routine will be executed. This routine has to perform the following tasks:

1. Read the input character from the keyboard input data register. This will cause the interface circuit to remove its interrupt request.
2. Store the character in the memory location pointed to by PNTR, and increment PNTR.
3. When the end of the line is reached, disable keyboard interrupts and inform program Main.
4. Return from interrupt.

The instructions needed to perform these tasks are shown in Figure 4.9. When, the end of the input line is detected, the interrupt-service routine clears the KEN bit in register CONTROL as no further input is expected. It also sets to 1 the variable EOL (End Of Line). This variable is initially set to 0. We assume that it is checked periodically by program Main to determine when the input line is ready for processing.

Input/output operations in a computer system are usually much more involved than this simple example suggests. As we will describe in Section 4.2.5, the operating system of the computer performs these operations on behalf of user programs.

4.2.5 EXCEPTIONS

An interrupt is an event that causes the execution of one program to be suspended and the execution of another program to begin. So far, we have dealt only with interrupts caused by requests received during I/O data transfers. However, the interrupt mechanism is used in a number of other situations.

The term *exception* is often used to refer to any event that causes an interruption. Hence, I/O interrupts are one example of an exception. We now describe a few other kinds of exceptions.

Recovery from Errors

Computers use a variety of techniques to ensure that all hardware components are operating properly. For example, many computers include an error-checking code in

Main Program

Move	#LINE,PNTR	Initialize buffer pointer.
Clear	EOL	Clear end-of-line indicator.
BitSet	#2,CONTROL	Enable keyboard interrupts.
BitSet	#9,PS	Set interrupt-enable bit in the PS.

⋮

Interrupt-service routine

READ	MoveMultiple	R0–R1,−(SP)	Save registers R0 and R1 on stack.
	Move	PNTR,R0	Load address pointer.
	MoveByte	DATAIN,R1	Get input character and
	MoveByte	R1,(R0)+	store it in memory.
	Move	R0,PNTR	Update pointer.
	CompareByte	#$0D,R1	Check if Carriage Return.
	Branch≠0	RTRN	
	Move	#1,EOL	Indicate end of line.
	BitClear	#2,CONTROL	Disable keyboard interrupts.
RTRN	MoveMultiple	(SP)+,R0–R1	Restore registers R0 and R1.
	Return-from-interrupt		

Figure 4.9 Using interrupts to read a line of characters from a keyboard via the registers in Figure 4.3.

the main memory, which allows detection of errors in the stored data. If an error occurs, the control hardware detects it and informs the processor by raising an interrupt.

The processor may also interrupt a program if it detects an error or an unusual condition while executing the instructions of this program. For example, the OP-code field of an instruction may not correspond to any legal instruction, or an arithmetic instruction may attempt a division by zero.

When exception processing is initiated as a result of such errors, the processor proceeds in exactly the same manner as in the case of an I/O interrupt request. It suspends the program being executed and starts an exception-service routine. This routine takes appropriate action to recover from the error, if possible, or to inform the user about it. Recall that in the case of an I/O interrupt, the processor completes execution of the instruction in progress before accepting the interrupt. However, when an interrupt is caused by an error, execution of the interrupted instruction cannot usually be completed, and the processor begins exception processing immediately.

Debugging

Another important type of exception is used as an aid in debugging programs. System software usually includes a program called a *debugger*, which helps the programmer find errors in a program. The debugger uses exceptions to provide two important facilities called trace and breakpoints.

When a processor is operating in the *trace* mode, an exception occurs after execution of every instruction, using the debugging program as the exception-service routine. The debugging program enables the user to examine the contents of registers, memory locations, and so on. On return from the debugging program, the next instruction in the program being debugged is executed, then the debugging program is activated again. The trace exception is disabled during the execution of the debugging program.

Breakpoints provide a similar facility, except that the program being debugged is interrupted only at specific points selected by the user. An instruction called Trap or Software-interrupt is usually provided for this purpose. Execution of this instruction results in exactly the same actions as when a hardware interrupt request is received. While debugging a program, the user may wish to interrupt program execution after instruction i. The debugging routine saves instruction $i + 1$ and replaces it with a software interrupt instruction. When the program is executed and reaches that point, it is interrupted and the debugging routine is activated. This gives the user a chance to examine memory and register contents. When the user is ready to continue executing the program being debugged, the debugging routine restores the saved instruction that was at location $i + 1$ and executes a Return-from-interrupt instruction.

Privilege Exception

To protect the operating system of a computer from being corrupted by user programs, certain instructions can be executed only while the processor is in the supervisor mode. These are called *privileged instructions.* For example, when the processor is running in the user mode, it will not execute an instruction that changes the priority level of the processor or that enables a user program to access areas in the computer memory that have been allocated to other users. An attempt to execute such an instruction will produce a privilege exception, causing the processor to switch to the supervisor mode and begin executing an appropriate routine in the operating system.

4.2.6 USE OF INTERRUPTS IN OPERATING SYSTEMS

The operating system (OS) is responsible for coordinating all activities within a computer. It makes extensive use of interrupts to perform I/O operations and communicate with and control the execution of user programs. The interrupt mechanism enables the operating system to assign priorities, switch from one user program to another, implement security and protection features, and coordinate I/O activities. We will discuss some of these aspects briefly. A discussion of operating systems is outside the scope of this book. Our objective here is to illustrate how interrupts are used.

The operating system incorporates the interrupt-service routines for all devices connected to a computer. Application programs do not perform I/O operations themselves. When an application program needs an input or an output operation, it points to the data to be transferred and asks the OS to perform the operation. The OS suspends the execution of that program temporarily and performs the requested I/O operation. When the operation is completed, the OS transfers control back to the application program. The OS and the application program pass control back and forth using software interrupts.

An operating system provides a variety of services to application programs. To facilitate the implementation of these services, most processors have several different software interrupt instructions, each with its own interrupt vector. They can be used to call different parts of the OS, depending on the service being requested. Alternatively, a processor may have only one software interrupt instruction, with an immediate operand that can be used to specify the desired service. *aka privileged mode*

In a computer that has both a supervisor and a user mode, the processor switches its operation to supervisor mode at the time it accepts an interrupt request. It does so by setting a bit in the processor status register after saving the old contents of that register on the stack. Thus, when an application program calls the OS by a software interrupt instruction, the processor automatically switches to supervisor mode, giving the OS complete access to the computer's resources. When the OS executes a Return-from-interrupt instruction, the processor status word belonging to the application program is restored from the stack. As a result, the processor switches back to the user mode.

To illustrate the interaction between application programs and the operating system, let us consider an example that involves multitasking. *Multitasking* is a mode of operation in which a processor executes several user programs at the same time. A common OS technique that makes this possible is called *time slicing*. With this technique, each program runs for a short period called a time slice, τ, then another program runs for its time slice, and so on. The period τ is determined by a continuously running hardware clock, which generates an interrupt every τ seconds.

Figure 4.10 describes the routines needed to implement some of the essential functions in a multitasking environment. At the time the operating system is started, an initialization routine, called OSINIT in the figure, is executed. Among other things, this routine loads the appropriate values in the interrupt vector locations in the memory. These values are the starting addresses of the interrupt service routines for the corresponding interrupts. For example, OSINIT loads the starting address of a routine called SCHEDULER in the interrupt vector corresponding to the timer interrupt. Hence, at the end of each time slice, the timer interrupt causes this routine to be executed.

A program, together with any information that describes its current state of execution, is regarded by the OS as an entity called a *process*. A process can be in one of three states: Running, Runnable, or Blocked. The Running state means that the program is currently being executed. The process is Runnable if the program is ready for execution but is waiting to be selected by the scheduler. The third state, Blocked, means that the program is not ready to resume execution for some reason. For example, it may be waiting for completion of an I/O operation that it requested earlier.

Assume that program A is in the Running state during a given time slice. At the end of that time slice, the timer interrupts the execution of this program and starts the execution of SCHEDULER. This is an operating system routine whose function is to determine which user program should run in the next time slice. It starts by saving all the information that will be needed later when execution of program A is resumed. The information saved, which is called the *program state*, includes register contents, the program counter, and the processor status word. Registers must be saved because they may contain intermediate results for any computation in progress at the time of interruption. The program counter points to the location where execution is to resume

OSINIT	Set interrupt vectors:
	Time-slice clock ← SCHEDULER
	Software interrupt ← OSSERVICES
	Keyboard interrupts ← IOData
	$\vdots$
OSSERVICES	Examine stack to determine requested operation.
	Call appropriate routine.
SCHEDULER	Save program state.
	Select a runnable process.
	Restore saved context of new process.
	Push new values for PS and PC on stack.
	Return from interrupt.

(a) OS initialization, services, and scheduler

IOINIT	Set process status to Blocked.
	Initialize memory buffer address pointer and counter.
	Call device driver to initialize device
	and enable interrupts in the device interface.
	Return from subroutine.
IODATA	Poll devices to determine source of interrupt.
	Call appropriate driver.
	If END = 1, then set process status to Runnable.
	Return from interrupt.

(b) I/O routines

KBDINIT	Enable interrupts.
	Return from subroutine.
KBDDATA	Check device status.
	If ready, then transfer character.
	If character = CR, then {set END = 1; Disable interrupts}
	else set END = 0.
	Return from subroutine.

(c) Keyboard driver

Figure 4.10   A few operating system routines.

later. The processor status word is needed because it contains the condition code flags and other information such as priority level.

Then, SCHEDULER selects for execution some other program, B, that was suspended earlier and is in the Runnable state. It restores all information saved at the time program B was suspended, including the contents of PS and PC, and executes a Return-from-interrupt instruction. As a result, program B resumes execution for τ seconds, at the end of which the timer clock raises an interrupt again, and a *context switch* to another runnable process takes place.

Suppose that program A needs to read an input line from the keyboard. Instead of performing the operation itself, it requests I/O service from the operating system. It uses the stack or the processor registers to pass information to the OS describing the required operation, the I/O device, and the address of a buffer in the program data area where the line should be placed. Then it executes a software interrupt instruction. The interrupt vector for this instruction points to the OSSERVICES routine in Figure 4.10*a*. This routine examines the information on the stack and initiates the requested operation by calling an appropriate OS routine. In our example, it calls IOINIT in Figure 4.10*b*, which is a routine responsible for starting I/O operations.

While an I/O operation is in progress, the program that requested it cannot continue execution. Hence, the IOINIT routine sets the process associated with program A into the Blocked state, indicating to the scheduler that the program cannot resume execution at this time. The IOINIT routine carries out any preparations needed for the I/O operation, such as initializing address pointers and byte count, then calls a routine that performs the I/O transfers.

It is common practice in operating system design to encapsulate all software pertaining to a particular device into a self-contained module called the *device driver*. Such a module can be easily added to or deleted from the OS. We have assumed that the device driver for the keyboard consists of two routines, KBDINIT and KBDDATA, as shown in Figure 4.10*c*. The IOINIT routine calls KBDINIT, which performs any initialization operations needed by the device or its interface circuit. KBDINIT also enables interrupts in the interface circuit by setting the appropriate bit in its control register, and then it returns to IOINIT, which returns to OSSERVICES. The keyboard is now ready to participate in a data transfer operation. It will generate an interrupt request whenever a key is pressed.

Following the return to OSSERVICES, the SCHEDULER routine selects another user program to run. Of course, the scheduler will not select program A, because that program is now in the Blocked state. The Return-from-interrupt instruction that causes the selected user program to begin execution will also enable interrupts in the processor by loading new contents into the processor status register. Thus, an interrupt request generated by the keyboard's interface will be accepted. The interrupt vector for this interrupt points to an OS routine called IODATA. Because there could be several devices connected to the same interrupt request line, IODATA begins by polling these devices to determine the one requesting service. Then, it calls the appropriate device driver to service the request. In our example, the driver called will be KBDDATA, which will transfer one character of data. If the character is a Carriage Return, it will also set to 1 a flag called END, to inform IODATA that the requested I/O operation has been completed. At this point, the IODATA routine changes the state of process A from Blocked to Runnable, so that the scheduler may select it for execution in some future time slice.

4.3 PROCESSOR EXAMPLES

We have discussed the organization of interrupts in general in the previous section. Commercial processors provide many of the features and control mechanisms described, but not necessarily all of them. For example, vectored interrupts may be supported to enable the processor to branch quickly to the interrupt-service routine for a particular device. Alternatively, the task of identifying the device and determining the starting address of the appropriate interrupt-service routine may be left for implementation in software using polling. In the following sections we describe the interrupt-handling mechanisms of the three processors described in Chapter 3.

4.3.1 ARM INTERRUPT STRUCTURE

The ARM processor has a simple yet powerful exception-handling mechanism. There are five sources for exceptions, only two of which are external interrupt-request lines, IRQ and FIQ (Fast Interrupt Request). There is one software interrupt instruction, SWI, and two exceptions that may be caused by abnormal conditions encountered during program execution. These exceptions are an external abort following a bus error and an attempt to execute an undefined instruction. Exceptions are handled according to the following priority structure:

1. Reset (highest priority)
2. Data abort
3. FIQ
4. IRQ
5. Prefetch abort
6. Undefined instruction (lowest priority)

The Reset condition is included in this structure because it must override all other conditions to bring the processor to a known starting condition. Also note that there are two abort conditions. *Data Abort* arises from an error in reading or writing data, and *Prefetch Abort* arises from an error when prefetching instructions from the memory.

Figure 3.1 shows the status register of the ARM processor, CPSR (Current Program Status Register). The low-order byte of this register is shown in Figure 4.11. There are two interrupt mask bits, one each for IRQ and FIQ. When either of these bits is equal to 1, the corresponding interrupt is disabled. The register also contains five mode bits,

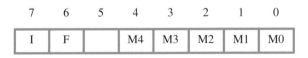

7	6	5	4	3	2	1	0
I	F		M4	M3	M2	M1	M0

Figure 4.11   Low-order byte of the ARM processor status register.

M_{4-0}, which indicate the mode in which the processor is running. There are six modes — a User mode and five privileged modes, one for each of the five types of exception.

When the processor switches to a different mode, it also switches some of the registers accessible to the program. The register set that is accessible in each mode is shown in Figure 4.12. Registers R0 to R7, R15 (the PC), and CPSR are accessible in all modes. In all privileged modes, except FIQ, registers R8 to R12 are also accessible.

General-purpose registers and program counter

User	FIQ	IRQ	Supervisor	Abort	Undefined
R0	R0	R0	R0	R0	R0
R1	R1	R1	R1	R1	R1
R2	R2	R2	R2	R2	R2
R3	R3	R3	R3	R3	R3
R4	R4	R4	R4	R4	R4
R5	R5	R5	R5	R5	R5
R6	R6	R6	R6	R6	R6
R7	R7	R7	R7	R7	R7
R8	R8_fiq	R8	R8	R8	R8
R9	R9_fiq	R9	R9	R9	R9
R10	R10_fiq	R10	R10	R10	R10
R11	R11_fiq	R11	R11	R11	R11
R12	R12_fiq	R12	R12	R12	R12
R13	R13_fiq	R13_irq	R13-svc	R13_abt	R13_und
R14	R14_fiq	R14_irq	R14_svc	R14_abt	R14_und
R15	R15	R15	R15	R15	R15

Processor status register

CPSR	CPSR	CPSR	CPSR	CPSR	CPSR
	SPSR_fiq	SPSR_irq	SPSR_svc	SPSR_abt	SPSR_und

Figure 4.12 Accessible registers in different modes of the ARM processor.

Table 4.1   Interrupt vector addresses for ARM processor

Address (hex)	Exception	Mode entered
0	Reset	Supervisor
4	Undefined instruction	Undefined
8	Software interrupt	Supervisor
C	Abort during prefetch	Abort
10	Abort during data	Abort
14	Reserved	
18	IRQ	IRQ
1C	FIQ	FIQ

However, two new registers replace R13 and R14 in each of the modes: IRQ, Supervisor, Abort, and Undefined. In the case of FIQ, registers R8 to R14 are replaced by R8_fiq to R14_fiq. The registers that replace user mode registers are called *banked registers*. They can be used by interrupt-service routines without the need to save the contents of their User mode counterparts. For example, when an instruction refers to R13 while the processor is in the IRQ mode, the register accessed is R13_irq rather than User mode register R13. Also, each mode other than the User mode has a dedicated register called Saved Processor Status Register (SPSR_svc, SPRS_irq, etc.) for saving the contents of CPSR at the time the interruption occurs.

Exception-handling routines start at fixed locations in memory, as shown in Table 4.1. Following an interrupt, the processor enters the mode indicated and begins execution at the corresponding vector address. Since there is only space for one instruction at all but the last address (FIQ), these locations should contain branch instructions to the service routines. In the case of FIQ, the service routine does not need to use a branch instruction and may continue from the starting location shown.

When the processor accepts an interrupt, it takes the following actions:

1. It saves the return address of the interrupted program in register 14 of the corresponding mode. For example, in the case of FIQ, it saves the return address in R14_fiq. The exact value saved depends on the type of exception, as will be explained shortly.

2. It saves the contents of the processor status register, CPSR, in the corresponding SPSR.

3. It changes the mode bits in CPSR according to the type of interrupt, as shown in the last column of Table 4.1. For FIQ and IRQ, it also sets the corresponding mask bit in CPSR to 1, thus disabling further interrupts on the same line.

4. It branches to the interrupt-service routine starting at the appropriate vector address.

The ARM processor uses a pipelined structure. As we will explain in Chapter 8, this means that an instruction is fetched before the execution of the preceding instruction is completed. Suppose that the processor fetches instruction I_1 at some address A. The processor increments the contents of the PC to A+4 and begins executing instruction I_1. Before completing execution of that instruction, it fetches instruction I_2 at address A+4, then it increments the PC to A+8. Let us now assume that at the end of execution of instruction I_1 the processor detects that an IRQ interrupt has been received, and it begins to perform the actions described above. It copies the contents of the PC, which are now equal to A+8, into register R14_irq. Instruction I_2, which has been fetched but not yet executed, is discarded. This is the instruction to which the interrupt-service routine must return.

In the scenario described above, the address saved in R14_irq is A+8, but the return address of the interrupt-service routine must be A+4. This means that the interrupt-service routine must subtract 4 from R14_irq before using its contents as the return address. That is, the return instruction must load the value [R14_irq] − 4 into the PC. It must also copy the contents of SPSR_irq into CPSR. The latter action restores the processor to its operating mode before the interruption occurred, and it clears the interrupt mask so that interrupts are once again enabled. The required actions are carried out by the instruction:

$$\text{SUBS} \quad \text{PC,R14\_irq, \#4}$$

This instruction subtracts 4 from R14_irq and stores the result into R15. The suffix S normally means set condition codes. When the target register of the instruction is the PC, the S suffix causes the processor to copy the contents of SPSR_irq into CPSR, thus completing the actions required to return to the interrupted program.

The amount that needs to be subtracted from R14 to obtain the correct return address depends on the details of instruction execution in the processor pipeline. Hence, it differs from one type of exception to another. For example, in the case of a software interrupt triggered by the SWI instruction, the value saved in R14_svc is the correct return address. Hence, return from an SWI service routine could be accomplished using the instruction

$$\text{MOVS} \quad \text{PC,R14\_svc}$$

Table 4.2 gives the correct value for the return address and the instruction that can be used to return to the interrupted program for each of the exceptions in Table 4.1. Note that for an abort interrupt, which may be caused by a bus error, the desired return address is shown as the address of the instruction that caused the error. It is assumed that the controlling software may wish to retry this instruction.

When running in a privileged mode, two special MOV instructions called MSR and MRS transfer data to or from either the current or the saved PSR. For example,

$$\text{MRS} \quad \text{R0,CPSR}$$

copies the contents of CPSR into R0. Similarly,

$$\text{MSR} \quad \text{SPSR,R0}$$

Table 4.2 Address correction during return from exception

Exception	Saved address*	Desired return address	Return instruction
Undefined instruction	PC+4	PC+4	MOVS PC,R14_und
Software interrupt	PC+4	PC+4	MOVS PC,R14_svc
Prefetch Abort	PC+4	PC	SUBS PC,R14_abt,#4
Data Abort	PC+8	PC	SUBS PC,R14_abt,#8
IRQ	PC+4	PC	SUBS PC,R14_irq,#4
FIQ	PC+4	PC	SUBS PC,R14_fiq,#4

*PC is the address of the instruction that caused the exception. For IRQ and FIQ, it is the address of the first instruction not executed because of the interrupt.

loads SPSR from register R0. These instructions are useful when the operating system needs to enable or disable interrupts, as we will see in Example 4.4.

Stacks and Nesting

The ARM interrupt mechanism stores the return address in a register and does not automatically implement a stacking mechanism to allow subroutine or interrupt nesting. The facilities provided have been carefully thought out to allow the programmer to implement such features when needed and to avoid unnecessary overhead when they are not needed. First, let us observe that nesting is possible when it is caused by different sources. For example, the IRQ interrupt-service routine, whose return address is in R14_irq, may be interrupted by the higher priority FIQ interrupt. The new return address will be stored in R14_fiq.

To allow nesting of interrupts from the same source, the contents of the corresponding R14 and SPSR must be saved on a stack. This can be readily done by program instructions using R13 as the stack pointer. For this reason, dedicated registers R13 and R14 are available in every mode. The interrupt-service routine can save R14 and SPSR on its private stack, then clear the interrupt mask in CPSR. It may also save other registers on the stack to create additional working space, as needed. For FIQ, which is intended as a fast interrupt, some dedicated register space is available, R8_fiq to R13_fiq, without the need to save registers on the stack.

We pointed out in Chapter 3 that the LDM and STM instructions, which transfer multiple words, are convenient for handling stack operations. For example, using R13 as a stack pointer, a subroutine or an interrupt-service routine may save some registers and the return address as follows:

STMFD   R13!,{R0,R1,R2,R14}

Similarly, an LDMFD instruction can be used to restore the saved values. In the case of an SWI or instruction prefetch exception, the value restored to R14 is also the correct return address. Hence, it can be restored directly to R15, thus effecting a return to the interrupted program, as follows:

$$\text{LDMFD} \quad \text{R13!,}\{\text{R0,R1,R2,R15}\}^{\wedge}$$

The "$^{\wedge}$" symbol at the end of the instruction has the same effect as the S suffix in the case of the SUBS instruction used earlier. It causes the processor to copy SPSR into CSPR at the same time it loads R15. Note that LDM cannot be used to return from an IRQ or FIQ interrupt because the contents of R14 must be corrected first, as shown in Table 4.2.

An example of the use of interrupts is given in Figure 4.13, which shows the program in Figure 4.9 rewritten for ARM. We have assumed that the keyboard is connected to interrupt line IRQ and that the corresponding interrupt vector location contains a branch instruction to READ. We have also assumed that at the time this code segment is entered the memory buffer address, LINE, has been loaded into location PNTR. Locations PNTR and EOL are assumed to be sufficiently close in the address space that they can be reached using the Relative addressing mode. The Main program enables interrupts in both the keyboard interface and the processor by setting the KEN flag in the keyboard's CONTROL register and clearing the I mask in the processor status register. The I mask, bit 7, is cleared by loading the value $50 into CPSR using the MSR instruction.

Example 4.4

In the interrupt-service routine, we use the LDM and STM instructions to save and restore registers and the SUBS instruction to return to the interrupted program. The address of the keyboard's DATAIN register in Figure 4.3 is loaded in a processor register using the ADR instruction described in Section 3.4.1. We have assumed that the address of the control register, CONTROL, is equal to DATAIN+3.

4.3.2 68000 INTERRUPT STRUCTURE

The 68000 has eight interrupt priority levels. The priority at which the processor is running at any given time is encoded in three bits of the processor status word, as shown in Figure 4.14, with level 0 being the lowest priority. I/O devices are connected to the 68000 using an arrangement similar to that in Figure 4.8*b*, in which interrupt requests are assigned priorities in the range 1 through 7. A request is accepted only if its priority is higher than that of the processor, with one exception: An interrupt request at level 7 is always accepted. This is an edge-triggered *nonmaskable* interrupt. When the processor accepts an interrupt request, the priority level indicated in the PS register is automatically raised to that of the request before the interrupt-service routine is executed. Thus, requests of equal or lower priority are disabled, except for level-7 interrupts, which are always enabled.

The processor automatically saves the contents of the program counter and the processor status word at the time of interruption. The PC is pushed onto the processor

Main program

```
MOV     R0,#0
STR     R0,EOL          Clear EOL flag.
ADR     R1,DATAIN       Load address of register DATAIN.
LDRB    R0,[R1,#3]      Get contents of CONTROL register.
ORR     R0,R0,#4        Set bit KEN in register CONTROL
STRB    R0,[R1,#3]        to enable keyboard interrupts.
MOV     R0,#&50         Enable IRQ interrupts in processor
MSR     CPSR,R0           and switch to user mode.
          ⋮
```

IRQ Interrupt-service routine

```
READ   STMFD    R13!,{R0-R2,R14_irq}   Save R0, R1, and R14_irq on the stack.
       ADR      R1,DATAIN              Load address of register DATAIN.
       LDRB     R0,[R1]                Get input character.
       LDR      R2,PNTR                Load pointer value.
       STRB     R0,[R2],#1             Store character and increment pointer.
       STR      R2,PNTR                Update pointer value in the memory.
       CMPB     R0,#&0D                Check if Carriage Return.
       LDMNEFD  R13!,{R0-R2,R14_irq}   If not, restore registers
       SUBNES   PC,R14_irq,#4            and return.
       LDRB     R0,[R1,#3]             Otherwise, get CONTROL register.
       AND      R0,R0,#&FB             Clear bit KEN
       STRB     R0,[R1,#3]               to disable keyboard interrupts.
       MOV      R0,#1                  Set EOL flag.
       STR      R0,EOL
       LDMFD    R13!,{R0-R2,R14}       Restore registers
       SUBS     PC,R14_irq,#4            and return.
```

Figure 4.13   An ARM interrupt-service routine to read an input line from a keyboard, based on Figure 4.9.

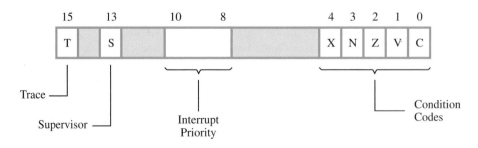

Figure 4.14   Processor status register in the 68000 processor.

stack followed by the PS, using register A7 as the stack pointer. A Return-from-interrupt instruction, called Return-from-exception (RTE) in the 68000 assembly language, pops the top element of the stack into the PS and pops the next element into the PC. As shown in Figure 4.14, the PS register contains a Supervisor bit, S, and a Trace bit, T. The S bit determines whether the processor is running in the Supervisor mode (S = 1) or User mode (S = 0). The T bit enables a special type of interrupt called a trace exception, as described in Section 4.2.4. This information is saved automatically at the time an interrupt is accepted and restored at the end of interrupt servicing. Any additional information to be saved, such as the contents of general-purpose registers, must be saved and restored explicitly inside the interrupt-service routine.

The 68000 processor uses vectored interrupts. When it accepts an interrupt request, it obtains the starting address of the interrupt-service routine from an interrupt vector stored in the main memory. There are 256 interrupt vectors, numbered 0 through 255. Each vector consists of 32 bits that constitute the required starting address. When a device requests an interrupt, it may point to the vector that should be used by sending an 8-bit vector number to the processor in response to the interrupt-acknowledge signal. As an alternative, the 68000 also provides an *autovector* facility. Instead of sending a vector number, the device can activate a special bus control line to indicate that it wishes to use the autovector facility. In this case, the processor chooses one of seven vectors provided for this purpose, based on the priority level of the interrupt request.

An example of the use of interrupts in the 68000 is shown in Figure 4.15. This is the program given in Figure 4.9 rewritten for the 68000. We have assumed that the keyboard interface uses the autovector facility and generates interrupt requests at level 2. Hence, to enable interrupts, the processor priority must be set at a level less than 2. When the bit pattern $100 is loaded into register PS, it sets the processor's priority to 1.

Example 4.5

4.3.3 PENTIUM INTERRUPT STRUCTURE

The IA-32 architecture, of which the Pentium processors are examples, uses two interrupt-request lines, a nonmaskable interrupt (NMI) and a maskable interrupt, also called user interrupt request, INTR. Interrupt requests on NMI are always accepted by the processor. Requests on INTR are accepted only if they have a higher privilege level than the program currently executing, as we will explain shortly. INTR interrupts can also be enabled or disabled by setting an interrupt-enable bit in the processor status register.

In addition to external interrupts, there are many events that arise during program execution that can cause an exception. These include invalid opcodes, division errors, overflow, and many others. They also include trace and breakpoint interrupts.

Main program

MOVE.L	#LINE,PNTR	Initialize buffer pointer.
CLR	EOL	Clear end-of-line indicator.
ORI.B	#4,CONTROL	Set bit KEN.
MOVE	#$100,SR	Set processor priority to 1.

⋮

Interrupt-service routine

READ	MOVEM.L	A0/D0,−(A7)	Save registers A0, D0 on stack.
	MOVEA.L	PNTR,A0	Load address pointer.
	MOVE.B	DATAIN,D0	Get input character.
	MOVE.B	D0,(A0)+	Store it in memory buffer.
	MOVE.L	A0,PNTR	Update pointer.
	CMPI.B	#$0D,D0	Check if Carriage Return.
	BNE	RTRN	
	MOVE	#1,EOL	Indicate end of line.
	ANDI.B	#$FB,CONTROL	Clear bit KEN.
RTRN	MOVEM.L	(A7)+,A0/D0	Restore registers D0, A0.
	RTE		

Figure 4.15 A 68000 interrupt-service routine to read an input line from a keyboard, based on Figure 4.9.

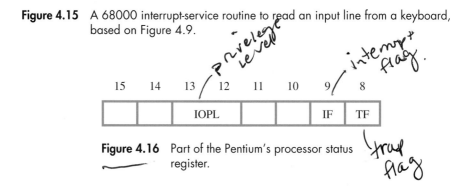

Figure 4.16 Part of the Pentium's processor status register.

The occurrence of any of these events causes the processor to branch to an interrupt-service routine. Each interrupt or exception is assigned a vector number. In the case of INTR, the vector number is sent by the I/O device over the bus when the interrupt request is acknowledged. For all other exceptions, the vector number is preassigned. Based on the vector number, the processor determines the starting address of the interrupt-service routine from a table called the Interrupt Descriptor Table.

A companion chip to the Pentium processor is called the Advanced Programmable Interrupt Controller (APIC). Various I/O devices are connected to the processor through this chip. The interrupt controller implements a priority structure among different devices and sends an appropriate vector number to the processor for each device.

The processor status register, which is called EFLAGS in Intel literature, is shown in Figure 3.37. Figure 4.16 shows bits 8 to 15 of this register, which contain the Interrupt Enable Flag (IF), the Trap flag (TF) and the I/O Privilege Level (IOPL). When IF = 1, INTR interrupts are accepted. The Trap flag enables trace interrupts after every instruction.

The Pentium processor has a sophisticated privilege structure, whereby different parts of the operating system execute at one of four levels of privilege. A different segment in the processor address space is used for each level. Switching from one level to another involves a number of checks implemented in a mechanism called a gate. This enables a highly secure OS to be constructed. It is also possible for the processor to run in a simple mode in which no privileges are implemented and all programs run in the same segment. We will only discuss this simple case here.

When an interrupt request is received or when an exception occurs, the processor takes the following actions:

1. It pushes the processor status register, the current segment register (CS), and the instruction pointer (EIP) onto the processor stack pointed to by the processor stack pointer, ESP.

2. In the case of an exception resulting from an abnormal execution condition, it pushes a code on the stack describing the cause of the exception.

3. It clears the corresponding interrupt-enable flag, if appropriate, so that further interrupts from the same source are disabled.

4. It fetches the starting address of the interrupt-service routine from the Interrupt Descriptor Table based on the vector number of the interrupt and loads this value into EIP, then resumes execution.

After servicing the interrupt request, for example, by transferring input or output data, the interrupt-service routine returns to the interrupted program using a return from interrupt instruction, IRET. This instruction pops EIP, CS, and the processor status register from the stack into the corresponding registers, thus restoring the processor state.

As in the case of subroutines, the interrupt-service routine may create temporary work space by saving registers or using the stack frame for local variables. It must restore any saved registers and ensure that the stack pointer ESP is pointing to the return address before executing the IRET instruction.

The example in Figure 4.9 rewritten for the Pentium is shown in Figure 4.17. We have assumed that the keyboard sends an interrupt request with vector number 32 and that the corresponding entry in the Interrupt Descriptor Table has been loaded with the starting address READ of the interrupt-service routine. Interrupts are enabled in the processor using the STI instruction, which sets to 1 the IF flag in the processor status register.

Example 4.6

Main program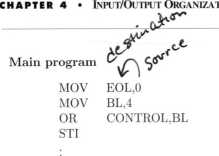

```
        MOV    EOL,0
        MOV    BL,4
        OR     CONTROL,BL          Set KEN to enable keyboard interrupts.
        STI                        Set interrupt flag in processor register.
        ⋮
```

Interrupt-service routine

```
READ    PUSH   EAX                 Save register EAX on stack.
        PUSH   EBX                 Save register EBX on stack.
        MOV    EAX,PNTR            Load address pointer.
        MOV    BL,DATAIN           Get input character.
        MOV    [EAX],BL            Store character.
        INC    DWORD PTR [EAX]     Increment PNTR.
        CMP    BL,0DH              Check if character is CR.
        JNE    RTRN
        MOV    BL,4
        XOR    CONTROL,BL          Clear bit KEN.
        MOV    EOL,1               Set EOL flag.
RTRN    POP    EBX                 Restore register EBX.
        POP    EAX                 Restore register EAX.
        IRET
```

Figure 4.17   An interrupt-servicing routine to read one line from a keyboard using interrupts on IA-32 processors.

4.4   DIRECT MEMORY ACCESS

The discussion in the previous sections concentrates on data transfer between the processor and I/O devices. Data are transferred by executing instructions such as

$$\text{Move}\quad \text{DATAIN,R0}$$

An instruction to transfer input or output data is executed only after the processor determines that the I/O device is ready. To do this, the processor either polls a status flag in the device interface or waits for the device to send an interrupt request. In either case, considerable overhead is incurred, because several program instructions must be executed for each data word transferred. In addition to polling the status register of the device, instructions are needed for incrementing the memory address and keeping track of the word count. When interrupts are used, there is the additional overhead associated with saving and restoring the program counter and other state information.

To transfer large blocks of data at high speed, an alternative approach is used. A special control unit may be provided to allow transfer of a block of data directly between an external device and the main memory, without continuous intervention by the processor. This approach is called *direct memory access,* or DMA.

DMA transfers are performed by a control circuit that is part of the I/O device interface. We refer to this circuit as a *DMA controller.* The DMA controller performs the functions that would normally be carried out by the processor when accessing the main memory. For each word transferred, it provides the memory address and all the bus signals that control data transfer. Since it has to transfer blocks of data, the DMA controller must increment the memory address for successive words and keep track of the number of transfers.

Although a DMA controller can transfer data without intervention by the processor, its operation must be under the control of a program executed by the processor. To initiate the transfer of a block of words, the processor sends the starting address, the number of words in the block, and the direction of the transfer. On receiving this information, the DMA controller proceeds to perform the requested operation. When the entire block has been transferred, the controller informs the processor by raising an interrupt signal.

While a DMA transfer is taking place, the program that requested the transfer cannot continue, and the processor can be used to execute another program. After the DMA transfer is completed, the processor can return to the program that requested the transfer.

I/O operations are always performed by the operating system of the computer in response to a request from an application program. The OS is also responsible for suspending the execution of one program and starting another. Thus, for an I/O operation involving DMA, the OS puts the program that requested the transfer in the Blocked state (see Section 4.2.6), initiates the DMA operation, and starts the execution of another program. When the transfer is completed, the DMA controller informs the processor by sending an interrupt request. In response, the OS puts the suspended program in the Runnable state so that it can be selected by the scheduler to continue execution.

Figure 4.18 shows an example of the DMA controller registers that are accessed by the processor to initiate transfer operations. Two registers are used for storing the

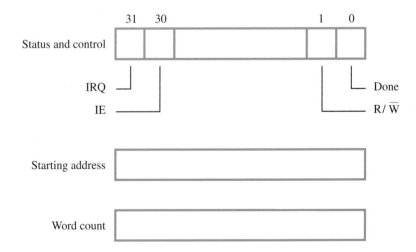

Figure 4.18 Registers in a DMA interface.

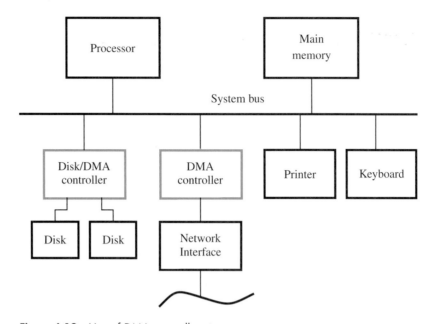

Figure 4.19 Use of DMA controllers in a computer system.

starting address and the word count. The third register contains status and control flags. The $\overline{\text{R/W}}$ bit determines the direction of the transfer. When this bit is set to 1 by a program instruction, the controller performs a read operation, that is, it transfers data from the memory to the I/O device. Otherwise, it performs a write operation. When the controller has completed transferring a block of data and is ready to receive another command, it sets the Done flag to 1. Bit 30 is the Interrupt-enable flag, IE. When this flag is set to 1, it causes the controller to raise an interrupt after it has completed transferring a block of data. Finally, the controller sets the IRQ bit to 1 when it has requested an interrupt.

An example of a computer system is given in Figure 4.19, showing how DMA controllers may be used. A DMA controller connects a high-speed network to the computer bus. The disk controller, which controls two disks, also has DMA capability and provides two DMA channels. It can perform two independent DMA operations, as if each disk had its own DMA controller. The registers needed to store the memory address, the word count, and so on are duplicated, so that one set can be used with each device.

To start a DMA transfer of a block of data from the main memory to one of the disks, a program writes the address and word count information into the registers of the corresponding channel of the disk controller. It also provides the disk controller with information to identify the data for future retrieval. The DMA controller proceeds independently to implement the specified operation. When the DMA transfer is completed, this fact is recorded in the status and control register of the DMA channel by setting the Done bit. At the same time, if the IE bit is set, the controller sends an interrupt request to the processor and sets the IRQ bit. The status register can also be used to record other information, such as whether the transfer took place correctly or errors occurred.

Memory accesses by the processor and the DMA controllers are interwoven. Requests by DMA devices for using the bus are always given higher priority than processor requests. Among different DMA devices, top priority is given to high-speed peripherals such as a disk, a high-speed network interface, or a graphics display device. Since the processor originates most memory access cycles, the DMA controller can be said to "steal" memory cycles from the processor. Hence, this interweaving technique is usually called *cycle stealing*. Alternatively, the DMA controller may be given exclusive access to the main memory to transfer a block of data without interruption. This is known as *block* or *burst* mode.

Most DMA controllers incorporate a data storage buffer. In the case of the network interface in Figure 4.19, for example, the DMA controller reads a block of data from the main memory and stores it into its input buffer. This transfer takes place using burst mode at a speed appropriate to the memory and the computer bus. Then, the data in the buffer are transmitted over the network at the speed of the network.

A conflict may arise if both the processor and a DMA controller or two DMA controllers try to use the bus at the same time to access the main memory. To resolve these conflicts, an arbitration procedure is implemented on the bus to coordinate the activities of all devices requesting memory transfers.

4.4.1 BUS ARBITRATION

The device that is allowed to initiate data transfers on the bus at any given time is called the *bus master*. When the current master relinquishes control of the bus, another device can acquire this status. Bus arbitration is the process by which the next device to become the bus master is selected and bus mastership is transferred to it. The selection of the bus master must take into account the needs of various devices by establishing a priority system for gaining access to the bus.

There are two approaches to bus arbitration: centralized and distributed. In centralized arbitration, a single *bus arbiter* performs the required arbitration. In distributed arbitration, all devices participate in the selection of the next bus master.

Centralized Arbitration

The bus arbiter may be the processor or a separate unit connected to the bus. Figure 4.20 illustrates a basic arrangement in which the processor contains the bus arbitration circuitry. In this case, the processor is normally the bus master unless it grants bus mastership to one of the DMA controllers. A DMA controller indicates that it needs to become the bus master by activating the Bus-Request line, $\overline{\text{BR}}$. This is an open-drain line for the same reasons that the Interrupt-Request line in Figure 4.6 is an open-drain line. The signal on the Bus-Request line is the logical OR of the bus requests from all the devices connected to it. When Bus-Request is activated, the processor activates the Bus-Grant signal, BG1, indicating to the DMA controllers that they may use the bus when it becomes free. This signal is connected to all DMA controllers using a daisy-chain arrangement. Thus, if DMA controller 1 is requesting the bus, it blocks the propagation of the grant signal to other devices. Otherwise, it passes the grant downstream by asserting BG2. The current bus master indicates to all

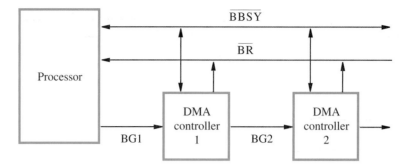

Figure 4.20   A simple arrangement for bus arbitration using a daisy chain.

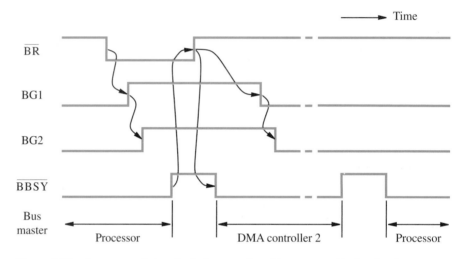

Figure 4.21   Sequence of signals during transfer of bus mastership for the devices in Figure 4.20.

devices that it is using the bus by activating another open-collector line called Bus-Busy, $\overline{\text{BBSY}}$. Hence, after receiving the Bus-Grant signal, a DMA controller waits for Bus-Busy to become inactive, then assumes mastership of the bus. At this time, it activates Bus-Busy to prevent other devices from using the bus at the same time.

The timing diagram in Figure 4.21 shows the sequence of events for the devices in Figure 4.20 as DMA controller 2 requests and acquires bus mastership and later releases the bus. During its tenure as the bus master, it may perform one or more data transfer operations, depending on whether it is operating in the cycle stealing or block mode. After it releases the bus, the processor resumes bus mastership. This figure shows the causal relationships among the signals involved in the arbitration process. Details of timing, which vary significantly from one computer bus to another, are not shown.

Figure 4.20 shows one bus-request line and one bus-grant line forming a daisy chain. Several such pairs may be provided, in an arrangement similar to that used for multiple interrupt requests in Figure 4.8*b*. This arrangement leads to considerable flexibility in determining the order in which requests from different devices are serviced. The arbiter circuit ensures that only one request is granted at any given time, according to a predefined priority scheme. For example, if there are four bus request lines, BR1 through BR4, a fixed priority scheme may be used in which BR1 is given top priority and BR4 is given lowest priority. Alternatively, a rotating priority scheme may be used to give all devices an equal chance of being serviced. Rotating priority means that after a request on line BR1 is granted, the priority order becomes 2, 3, 4, 1.

Distributed Arbitration

Distributed arbitration means that all devices waiting to use the bus have equal responsibility in carrying out the arbitration process, without using a central arbiter. A simple method for distributed arbitration is illustrated in Figure 4.22. Each device on the bus is assigned a 4-bit identification number. When one or more devices request the bus, they assert the $\overline{\text{Start-Arbitration}}$ signal and place their 4-bit ID numbers on four open-collector lines, $\overline{\text{ARB0}}$ through $\overline{\text{ARB3}}$. A winner is selected as a result of the interaction among the signals transmitted over these lines by all contenders. The net outcome is that the code on the four lines represents the request that has the highest ID number.

The drivers are of the open-collector type. Hence, if the input to one driver is equal to one and the input to another driver connected to the same bus line is equal to 0 the

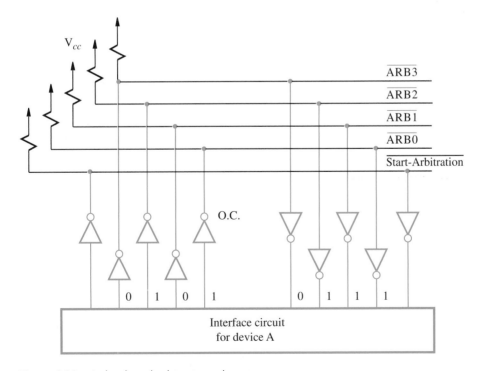

Figure 4.22   A distributed arbitration scheme.

bus will be in the low-voltage state. In other words, the connection performs an OR function in which logic 1 wins.

Assume that two devices, A and B, having ID numbers 5 and 6, respectively, are requesting the use of the bus. Device A transmits the pattern 0101, and device B transmits the pattern 0110. The code seen by both devices is 0111. Each device compares the pattern on the arbitration lines to its own ID, starting from the most significant bit. If it detects a difference at any bit position, it disables its drivers at that bit position and for all lower-order bits. It does so by placing a 0 at the input of these drivers. In the case of our example, device A detects a difference on line $\overline{ARB1}$. Hence, it disables its drivers on lines $\overline{ARB1}$ and $\overline{ARB0}$. This causes the pattern on the arbitration lines to change to 0110, which means that B has won the contention. Note that, since the code on the priority lines is 0111 for a short period, device B may temporarily disable its driver on line $\overline{ARB0}$. However, it will enable this driver again once it sees a 0 on line $\overline{ARB1}$ resulting from the action by device A.

Decentralized arbitration has the advantage of offering higher reliability, because operation of the bus is not dependent on any single device. Many schemes have been proposed and used in practice to implement distributed arbitration. The SCSI bus described in Section 4.7.2 provides another example.

4.5 BUSES

The processor, main memory, and I/O devices can be interconnected by means of a common bus whose primary function is to provide a communications path for the transfer of data. The bus includes the lines needed to support interrupts and arbitration. In this section, we discuss the main features of the bus protocols used for transferring data. A bus protocol is the set of rules that govern the behavior of various devices connected to the bus as to when to place information on the bus, assert control signals, and so on. After describing bus protocols, we will present examples of interface circuits that use these protocols.

The bus lines used for transferring data may be grouped into three types: data, address, and control lines. The control signals specify whether a read or a write operation is to be performed. Usually, a single a $R/\overline{W}$ line is used. It specifies Read when set to 1 and Write when set to 0. When several operand sizes are possible, such as byte, word, or long word, the required size of data is indicated.

The bus control signals also carry timing information. They specify the times at which the processor and the I/O devices may place data on the bus or receive data from the bus. A variety of schemes have been devised for the timing of data transfers over a bus. These can be broadly classified as either synchronous or asynchronous schemes.

Recall from Section 4.4.1 that in any data transfer operation, one device plays the role of a *master*. This is the device that initiates data transfers by issuing read or write commands on the bus; hence, it may be called an *initiator*. Normally, the processor acts as the master, but other devices with DMA capability may also become bus masters. The device addressed by the master is referred to as a *slave* or *target*.

4.5.1 SYNCHRONOUS BUS

In a *synchronous* bus, all devices derive timing information from a common clock line. Equally spaced pulses on this line define equal time intervals. In the simplest form of a synchronous bus, each of these intervals constitutes a *bus cycle* during which one data transfer can take place. Such a scheme is illustrated in Figure 4.23. The address and data lines in this and subsequent figures are shown as high and low at the same time. This is a common convention indicating that some lines are high and some low, depending on the particular address or data pattern being transmitted. The crossing points indicate the times at which these patterns change. A signal line in an indeterminate or high impedance state is represented by an intermediate level half-way between the low and high signal levels.

Let us consider the sequence of events during an input (read) operation. At time t_0, the master places the device address on the address lines and sends an appropriate command on the control lines. In this case, the command will indicate an input operation and specify the length of the operand to be read, if necessary. Information travels over the bus at a speed determined by its physical and electrical characteristics. The clock pulse width, $t_1 - t_0$, must be longer than the maximum propagation delay between two devices connected to the bus. It also has to be long enough to allow all devices to decode the address and control signals so that the addressed device (the slave) can respond at time t_1. It is important that slaves take no action or place any data on the bus before t_1. The information on the bus is unreliable during the period t_0 to t_1 because signals are changing state. The addressed slave places the requested input data on the data lines at time t_1.

At the end of the clock cycle, at time t_2, the master *strobes* the data on the data lines into its input buffer. In this context, "strobe" means to capture the values of the

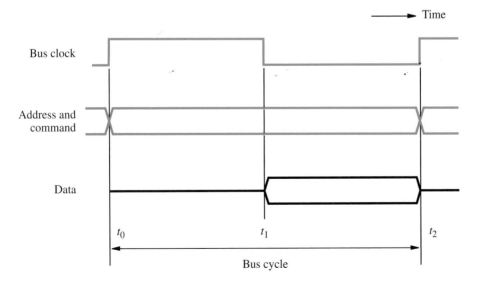

Figure 4.23 Timing of an input transfer on a synchronous bus.

data at a given instant and store them into a buffer. For data to be loaded correctly into any storage device, such as a register built with flip-flops, the data must be available at the input of that device for a period greater than the setup time of the device (see Appendix A). Hence, the period $t_2 - t_1$ must be greater than the maximum propagation time on the bus plus the setup time of the input buffer register of the master.

A similar procedure is followed for an output operation. The master places the output data on the data lines when it transmits the address and command information. At time t_2, the addressed device strobes the data lines and loads the data into its data buffer.

The timing diagram in Figure 4.23 is an idealized representation of the actions that take place on the bus lines. The exact times at which signals actually change state are somewhat different from those shown because of propagation delays on bus wires and in the circuits of the devices. Figure 4.24 gives a more realistic picture of what happens in practice. It shows two views of each signal, except the clock. Because signals take time to travel from one device to another, a given signal transition is seen by different devices at different times. One view shows the signal as seen by the master and the other as seen by the slave. We assume that the clock changes are seen at the same time by all devices on the bus. System designers spend considerable effort to ensure that the clock signal satisfies this condition.

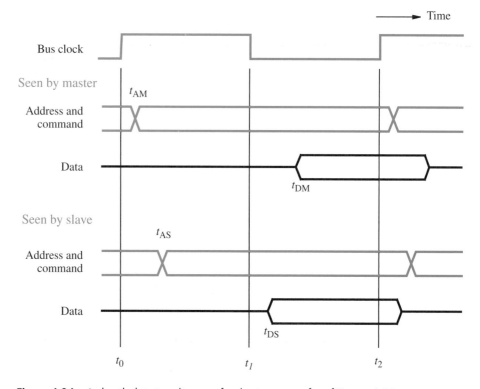

Figure 4.24 A detailed timing diagram for the input transfer of Figure 4.23.

The master sends the address and command signals on the rising edge at the beginning of clock period 1 (t_0). However, these signals do not actually appear on the bus until t_{AM}, largely due to the delay in the bus driver circuit. A while later, at t_{AS}, the signals reach the slave. The slave decodes the address and at t_1 sends the requested data. Here again, the data signals do not appear on the bus until t_{DS}. They travel toward the master and arrive at t_{DM}. At t_2, the master loads the data into its input buffer. Hence the period $t_2 - t_{DM}$ is the setup time for the master's input buffer. The data must continue to be valid after t_2 for a period equal to the hold time of that buffer.

Timing diagrams in the literature often give only the simplified picture in Figure 4.23, particularly when the intent is to give a conceptual overview of how data are transferred. But, actual signals will always involve delays as shown in Figure 4.24.

Multiple-Cycle Transfers

The scheme described above results in a simple design for the device interface. *trouble w/* However, it has some limitations. Because a transfer has to be completed within one clock cycle, the clock period, $t_2 - t_0$, must be chosen to accommodate the longest delays on the bus and the slowest device interface. This forces all devices to operate at the speed of the slowest device.

Also, the processor has no way of determining whether the addressed device has actually responded. It simply assumes that, at t_2, the output data have been received by the I/O device or the input data are available on the data lines. If, because of a malfunction, the device does not respond, the error will not be detected.

To overcome these limitations, most buses incorporate control signals that represent a response from the device. These signals inform the master that the slave has recognized its address and that it is ready to participate in a data-transfer operation. They also make it possible to adjust the duration of the data-transfer period to suit the needs of the participating devices. To simplify this process, a high-frequency clock signal is used such that a complete data transfer cycle would span several clock cycles. Then, the number of clock cycles involved can vary from one device to another.

An example of this approach is shown in Figure 4.25. During clock cycle 1, the master sends address and command information on the bus, requesting a read operation. The slave receives this information and decodes it. On the following active edge of the clock, that is, at the beginning of clock cycle 2, it makes a decision to respond and begins to access the requested data. We have assumed that some delay is involved in getting the data, and hence the slave cannot respond immediately. The data become ready and are placed on the bus in clock cycle 3. At the same time, the slave asserts a control signal called Slave-ready. The master, which has been waiting for this signal, strobes the data into its input buffer at the end of clock cycle 3. The bus transfer operation is now complete, and the master may send a new address to start a new transfer in clock cycle 4.

The Slave-ready signal is an acknowledgment from the slave to the master, confirming that valid data have been sent. In the example in Figure 4.25, the slave responds in cycle 3. Another device may respond sooner or later. The Slave-ready signal allows the duration of a bus transfer to change from one device to another. If the addressed device does not respond at all, the master waits for some predefined maximum number of clock cycles, then aborts the operation. This could be the result of an incorrect address or a device malfunction.

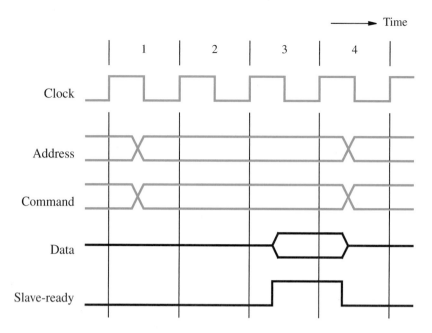

Figure 4.25 An input transfer using multiple clock cycles.

Note that the clock signal used on a computer bus is not necessarily the same as the processor clock. The latter is often much faster because it controls internal operation on the processor chip. The delays encountered by signals internal to a chip are much less than on a bus that interconnects chips on a printed circuit board, for example. Clock frequencies are highly technology dependent. In modern processor chips, clock frequencies above 500 MHz are typical. On memory and I/O buses, the clock frequency may be in the range 50 to 150 MHz.

Many computer buses, such as the processor buses of Pentium and ARM, use a scheme similar to that illustrated in Figure 4.25 to control the transfer of data. The PCI bus standard described in Section 4.7.1 is also very similar. We will now present a different approach that does not use a clock signal at all.

4.5.2 ASYNCHRONOUS BUS

An alternative scheme for controlling data transfers on the bus is based on the use of a *handshake* between the master and the slave. The concept of a handshake is a generalization of the idea of the Slave-ready signal in Figure 4.25. The common clock is replaced by two timing control lines, Master-ready and Slave-ready. The first is asserted by the master to indicate that it is ready for a transaction, and the second is a response from the slave.

In principle, a data transfer controlled by a handshake protocol proceeds as follows. The master places the address and command information on the bus. Then it indicates

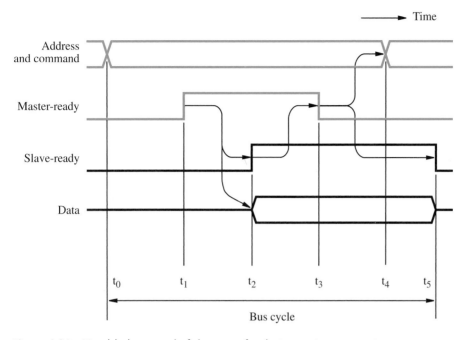

Time

Address
and command

Master-ready

Slave-ready

Data

t_0 t_1 t_2 t_3 t_4 t_5

Bus cycle

Figure 4.26 Handshake control of data transfer during an input operation.

to all devices that it has done so by activating the Master-ready line. This causes all devices on the bus to decode the address. The selected slave performs the required operation and informs the processor it has done so by activating the Slave-ready line. The master waits for Slave-ready to become asserted before it removes its signals from the bus. In the case of a read operation, it also strobes the data into its input buffer.

An example of the timing of an input data transfer using the handshake scheme is given in Figure 4.26, which depicts the following sequence of events:

t_0 — The master places the address and command information on the bus, and all devices on the bus begin to decode this information.

t_1 — The master sets the Master-ready line to 1 to inform the I/O devices that the address and command information is ready. The delay $t_1 - t_0$ is intended to allow for any *skew* that may occur on the bus. Skew occurs when two signals simultaneously transmitted from one source arrive at the destination at different times. This happens because different lines of the bus may have different propagation speeds. Thus, to guarantee that the Master-ready signal does not arrive at any device ahead of the address and command information, the delay $t_1 - t_0$ should be larger than the maximum possible bus skew. (Note that, in the synchronous case, bus skew is accounted for as a part of the maximum propagation delay.) When the address information arrives at any device, it is decoded by the interface circuitry. Sufficient time should be allowed for the interface circuitry to decode the address. The delay needed can be included in the period $t_1 - t_0$.

t_2 — The selected slave, having decoded the address and command information, performs the required input operation by placing the data from its data register on the data lines. At the same time, it sets the Slave-ready signal to 1. If extra delays are introduced by the interface circuitry before it places the data on the bus, the slave must delay the Slave-ready signal accordingly. The period $t_2 - t_1$ depends on the distance between the master and the slave and on the delays introduced by the slave's circuitry. It is this variability that gives the bus its asynchronous nature.

t_3 — The Slave-ready signal arrives at the master, indicating that the input data are available on the bus. However, since it was assumed that the device interface transmits the Slave-ready signal at the same time that it places the data on the bus, the master should allow for bus skew. It must also allow for the setup time needed by its input buffer. After a delay equivalent to the maximum bus skew and the minimum setup time, the master strobes the data into its input buffer. At the same time, it drops the Master-ready signal, indicating that it has received the data.

t_4 — The master removes the address and command information from the bus. The delay between t_3 and t_4 is again intended to allow for bus skew. Erroneous addressing may take place if the address, as seen by some device on the bus, starts to change while the Master-ready signal is still equal to 1.

t_5 — When the device interface receives the 1 to 0 transition of the Master-ready signal, it removes the data and the Slave-ready signal from the bus. This completes the input transfer.

The timing for an output operation, illustrated in Figure 4.27, is essentially the same as for an input operation. In this case, the master places the output data on the data lines

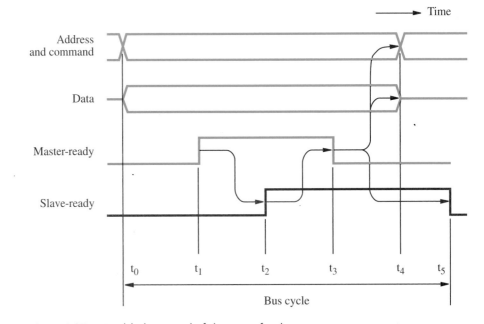

Figure 4.27 Handshake control of data transfer during an output operation.

at the same time that it transmits the address and command information. The selected slave strobes the data into its output buffer when it receives the Master-ready signal and indicates that it has done so by setting the Slave-ready signal to 1. The remainder of the cycle is identical to the input operation.

In the timing diagrams in Figures 4.26 and 4.27, it is assumed that the master compensates for bus skew and address decoding delay. It introduces the delays from t_0 to t_1 and from t_3 to t_4 for this purpose. If this delay provides sufficient time for the I/O device interface to decode the address, the interface circuit can use the Master-ready signal directly to gate other signals to or from the bus, This point will become clearer when we study the interface circuit examples in the next section.

The handshake signals in Figures 4.26 and 4.27 are fully interlocked. A change of state in one signal is followed by a change in the other signal. Hence this scheme is known as a *full handshake*. It provides the highest degree of flexibility and reliability.

4.5.3 DISCUSSION

Many variations of the bus techniques just described are found in commercial computers. For example, the bus in the 68000 family of processors has two modes of operation, one asynchronous and one synchronous. The choice of a particular design involves trade-offs among factors such as:

- Simplicity of the device interface
- Ability to accommodate device interfaces that introduce different amounts of delay
- Total time required for a bus transfer
- Ability to detect errors resulting from addressing a nonexistent device or from an interface malfunction

The main advantage of the asynchronous bus is that the handshake process eliminates the need for synchronization of the sender and receiver clocks, thus simplifying timing design. Delays, whether introduced by the interface circuits or by propagation over the bus wires, are readily accommodated. When these delays change, for example, due to a change in load when an interface circuit is added or removed, the timing of data transfer adjusts automatically based on the new conditions. For a synchronous bus, clock circuitry must be designed carefully to ensure proper synchronization, and delays must be kept within strict bounds.

The rate of data transfer on an asynchronous bus controlled by a full handshake is limited by the fact that each transfer involves two round-trip delays (four end-to-end delays). This can be readily seen in Figures 4.26 and 4.27 as each transition on Slave-ready must wait for the arrival of a transition on Master-ready, and vice versa. On synchronous buses, the clock period need only accommodate one end-to-end propagation delay. Hence, faster transfer rates can be achieved. To accommodate a slow device, additional clock cycles are used, as described above. Most of today's high-speed buses use this approach.

4.6   INTERFACE CIRCUITS

An I/O interface consists of the circuitry required to connect an I/O device to a computer bus. On one side of the interface we have the bus signals for address, data, and control. On the other side we have a data path with its associated controls to transfer data between the interface and the I/O device. This side is called a *port,* and it can be classified as either a parallel or a serial port. A parallel port transfers data in the form of a number of bits, typically 8 or 16, simultaneously to or from the device. A serial port transmits and receives data one bit at a time. Communication with the bus is the same for both formats; the conversion from the parallel to the serial format, and vice versa, takes place inside the interface circuit.

In the case of a parallel port, the connection between the device and the computer uses a multiple-pin connector and a cable with as many wires, typically arranged in a flat configuration. The circuits at either end are relatively simple, as there is no need to convert between parallel and serial formats. This arrangement is suitable for devices that are physically close to the computer. For longer distances, the problem of timing skew mentioned earlier limits the data rates that can be used. The serial format is much more convenient and cost-effective where longer cables are needed. Serial transmission formats will be discussed in Chapter 10.

Before discussing a specific interface circuit example, let us recall the functions of an I/O interface. According to the discussion in Section 4.1, an I/O interface does the following:

1. Provides a storage buffer for at least one word of data (or one byte, in the case of byte-oriented devices)
2. Contains status flags that can be accessed by the processor to determine whether the buffer is full (for input) or empty (for output)
3. Contains address-decoding circuitry to determine when it is being addressed by the processor
4. Generates the appropriate timing signals required by the bus control scheme
5. Performs any format conversion that may be necessary to transfer data between the bus and the I/O device, such as parallel-serial conversion in the case of a serial port

4.6.1   PARALLEL PORT

We now explain the key aspects of interface design with a practical example. First, we describe circuits for an 8-bit input port and an 8-bit output port. Then, we combine the two circuits to show how the interface for a general-purpose 8-bit parallel port can be designed. We assume that the interface circuit is connected to a 32-bit processor that uses memory-mapped I/O and the asynchronous bus protocol depicted in Figures 4.26 and 4.27. We will also show how the design can be modified to suit the bus protocol in Figure 4.25.

Figure 4.28 shows the hardware components needed for connecting a keyboard to a processor. A typical keyboard consists of mechanical switches that are normally

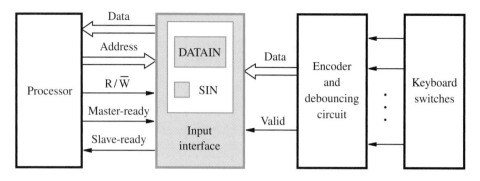

Figure 4.28 Keyboard to processor connection.

open. When a key is pressed, its switch closes and establishes a path for an electrical signal. This signal is detected by an encoder circuit that generates the ASCII code for the corresponding character. A difficulty with such push-button switches is that the contacts bounce when a key is pressed. Although bouncing may last only one or two milliseconds, this is long enough for the computer to observe a single pressing of a key as several distinct electrical events; this single pressing could be erroneously interpreted as the key being pressed and released rapidly several times. The effect of bouncing must be eliminated. We can do this in two ways: A simple debouncing circuit can be included, or a software approach can be used. When debouncing is implemented in software, the I/O routine that reads a character from the keyboard waits long enough to ensure that bouncing has subsided. Figure 4.28 illustrates the hardware approach; debouncing circuits are included as a part of the encoder block.

The output of the encoder consists of the bits that represent the encoded character and one control signal called Valid, which indicates that a key is being pressed. This information is sent to the interface circuit, which contains a data register, DATAIN, and a status flag, SIN. When a key is pressed, the Valid signal changes from 0 to 1, causing the ASCII code to be loaded into DATAIN and SIN to be set to 1. The status flag SIN is cleared to 0 when the processor reads the contents of the DATAIN register. The interface circuit is connected to an asynchronous bus on which transfers are controlled using the handshake signals Master-ready and Slave-ready, as indicated in Figure 4.26. The third control line, R/$\overline{\text{W}}$ distinguishes read and write transfers.

Figure 4.29 shows a suitable circuit for an input interface. The output lines of the DATAIN register are connected to the data lines of the bus by means of three-state drivers, which are turned on when the processor issues a read instruction with the address that selects this register. The SIN signal is generated by a status flag circuit. This signal is also sent to the bus through a three-state driver. It is connected to bit D0, which means it will appear as bit 0 of the status register. Other bits of this register do not contain valid information. An address decoder is used to select the input interface when the high-order 31 bits of an address correspond to any of the addresses assigned to this interface. Address bit A0 determines whether the status or the data registers is to be read when the Master-ready signal is active. The control handshake is accomplished by activating the Slave-ready signal when either Read-status or Read-data is equal to 1.

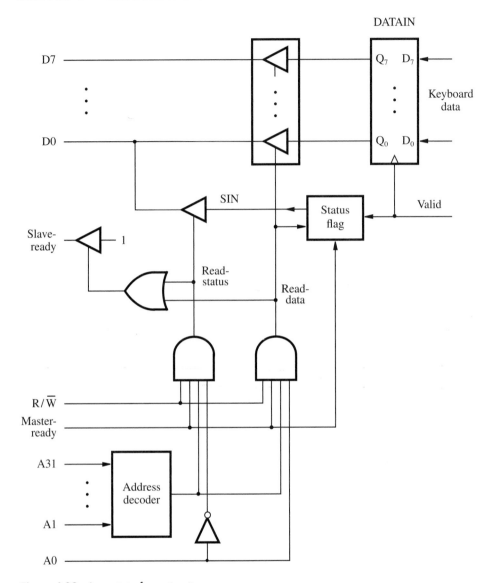

Figure 4.29   Input interface circuit.

A possible implementation of the status flag circuit is shown in Figure 4.30. An edge-triggered D flip-flop is set to 1 by a rising edge on the Valid signal line. This event changes the state of the NOR latch such that SIN is set to 1. The state of this latch must not change while SIN is being read by the processor. Hence, the circuit ensures that SIN can be set only while Master-ready is equal to 0. Both the flip-flop and the latch are reset to 0 when Read-data is set to 1 to read the DATAIN register.

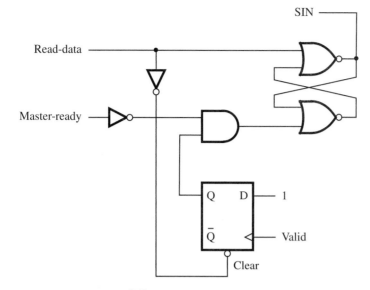

Figure 4.30 Circuit for the status flag block in Figure 4.29.

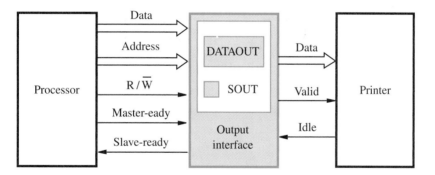

Figure 4.31 Printer to processor connection.

Let us now consider an output interface that can be used to connect an output device, such as a printer, to a processor, as shown in Figure 4.31. The printer operates under control of the handshake signals Valid and Idle in a manner similar to the handshake used on the bus with the Master-ready and Slave-ready signals. When it is ready to accept a character, the printer asserts its Idle signal. The interface circuit can then place a new character on the data lines and activate the Valid signal. In response, the printer starts printing the new character and negates the Idle signal, which in turn causes the interface to deactivate the Valid signal.

The interface contains a data register, DATAOUT, and a status flag, SOUT. The SOUT flag is set to 1 when the printer is ready to accept another character, and it is cleared to 0 when a new character is loaded into DATAOUT by the processor. Figure 4.32

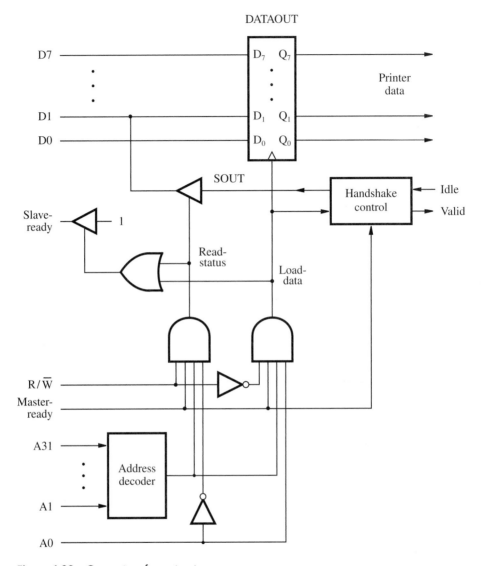

Figure 4.32 Output interface circuit.

shows an implementation of this interface. Its operation is similar to the input interface of Figure 4.29. The only significant difference is the handshake control circuit, the detailed design of which we leave as an exercise for the reader.

The input and output interfaces just described can be combined into a single interface, as shown in Figure 4.33. In this case, the overall interface is selected by the high-order 30 bits of the address. Address bits A1 and A0 select one of the three addressable locations in the interface, namely, the two data registers and the status register. The status register contains the flags SIN and SOUT in bits 0 and 1, respectively. Since

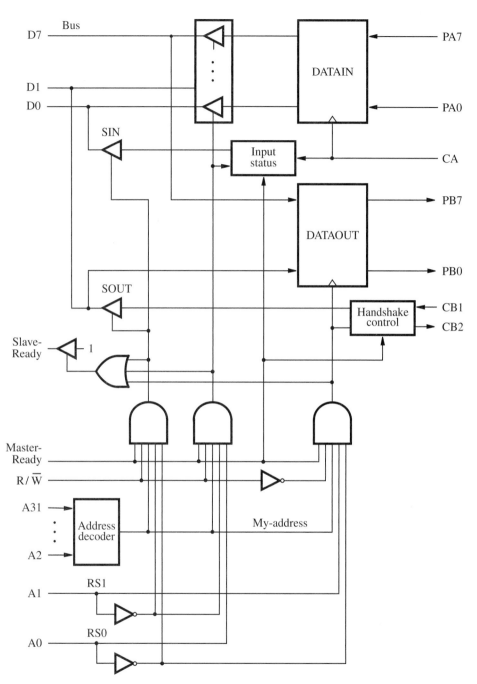

Figure 4.33 Combined input/output interface circuit.

such locations in I/O interfaces are often referred to as registers, we have used the labels RS1 and RS0 (for Register Select) to denote the two inputs that determine the register being selected.

The circuit in Figure 4.33 has separate input and output data lines for connection to an I/O device. A more flexible parallel port is created if the data lines to I/O devices are bidirectional. Figure 4.34 shows a general-purpose parallel interface circuit that can be configured in a variety of ways. Data lines P7 through P0 can be used for either input or output purposes. For increased flexibility, the circuit makes it possible for some lines to serve as inputs and some lines to serve as outputs, under program control. The

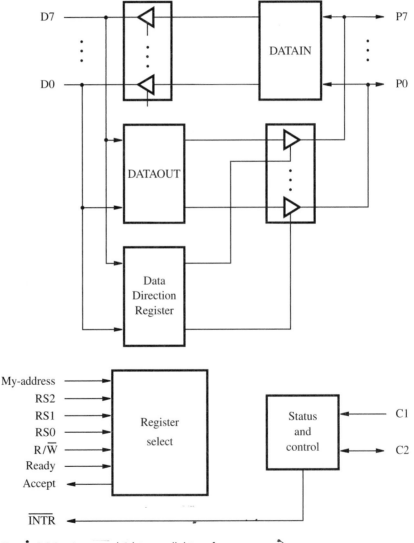

Figure 4.34 A general 8-bit parallel interface.

DATAOUT register is connected to these lines via three-state drivers that are controlled by a data direction register, DDR. The processor can write any 8-bit pattern into DDR. For a given bit, if the DDR value is 1, the corresponding data line acts as an output line; otherwise, it acts as an input line.

Two lines, C1 and C2, are provided to control the interaction between the interface circuit and the I/O device it serves. These lines are also programmable. Line C2 is bidirectional to provide several different modes of signaling, including the handshake. Not all the internal details are shown in the figure, but we can see how they may correspond to those in Figure 4.33. The Ready and Accept lines are the handshake control lines on the processor bus side, and hence would be connected to Master-ready and Slave-ready. The input signal My-address should be connected to the output of an address decoder that recognizes the address assigned to the interface. There are three register select lines, allowing up to eight registers in the interface, input and output data, data direction, and control and status registers for various modes of operation. An interrupt request output, $\overline{\text{INTR}}$, is also provided. It should be connected to the interrupt-request line on the computer bus.

Parallel interface circuits that have the features illustrated in Figure 4.34 are often encountered in practice. An example of their use in an embedded system is described in Chapter 9. Instead of having just one port for connecting an I/O device, two or more ports may be provided.

Let us now examine how the interface circuits in Figures 4.28 to 4.34 can be changed to work with the bus protocol of Figure 4.25. A modified circuit for the interface in Figure 4.32 is shown in Figure 4.35. We have introduced the Timing logic block to generate the Load-data and Read-status signals. The state diagram for this block is given at the bottom of the figure. Initially, the machine is in the Idle state. When the output of the address decoder, My-address, shows that this interface is being addressed, the machine changes state to Respond. As a result it asserts Go, which in turn asserts either Load-data or Read-status, depending on address bit A0 and the state of the $R/\overline{W}$ line.

A timing diagram for an output operation is shown in Figure 4.36. The processor sends the data at the same time as the address, in clock cycle 1. The Timing logic sets Go to 1 at the beginning of clock cycle 2, and the rising edge of that signal loads the output data into register DATAOUT. An input operation that reads the status register follows a similar timing pattern. The Timing logic block moves to the Respond state directly from the Idle state because the requested data are available in a register and can be transmitted immediately. As a result, the transfer is one clock cycle shorter than that shown in Figure 4.25. In a situation where some time is needed before the data becomes available, the state machine should enter a wait state first and move to Respond only when the data are ready.

In concluding the discussion of these interface circuit examples, we should point out that we have used simplified representations of some signals to help in readability and understanding of the ideas. In practice, the Slave-ready signal is likely to be an open-drain signal and would be called $\overline{\text{Slave-ready}}$, for the same reasons as for $\overline{\text{INTR}}$. This line must have a pull-up resistor connected to ensure that it is always in the negated (high-voltage) state except when it is asserted (pulled down) by some device.

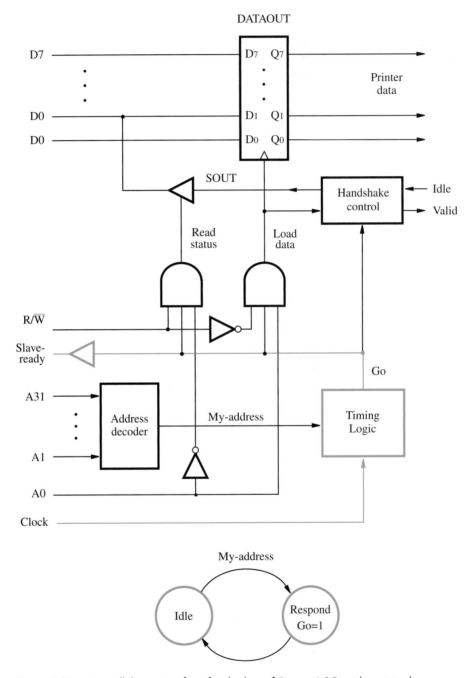

Figure 4.35 A parallel port interface for the bus of Figure 4.25, with a state-diagram for the timing logic.

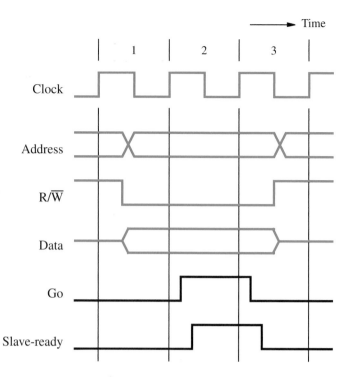

Figure 4.36 Timing for the output interface in Figure 4.35.

4.6.2 SERIAL PORT

A serial port is used to connect the processor to I/O devices that require transmission of data one bit at a time. The key feature of an interface circuit for a serial port is that it is capable of communicating in a bit-serial fashion on the device side and in a bit-parallel fashion on the bus side. The transformation between the parallel and serial formats is achieved with shift registers that have parallel access capability. A block diagram of a typical serial interface is shown in Figure 4.37. It includes the familiar DATAIN and DATAOUT registers. The input shift register accepts bit-serial input from the I/O device. When all 8 bits of data have been received, the contents of this shift register are loaded in parallel into the DATAIN register. Similarly, output data in the DATAOUT register are loaded into the output shift register, from which the bits are shifted out and sent to the I/O device.

The part of the interface that deals with the bus is the same as in the parallel interface described earlier. The status flags SIN and SOUT serve similar functions. The SIN flag is set to 1 when new data are loaded in DATAIN; it is cleared to 0 when the processor reads the contents of DATAIN. As soon as the data are transferred from the input shift register into the DATAIN register, the shift register can start accepting the next 8-bit character from the I/O device. The SOUT flag indicates whether the output buffer is available. It is cleared to 0 when the processor writes new data into the DATAOUT

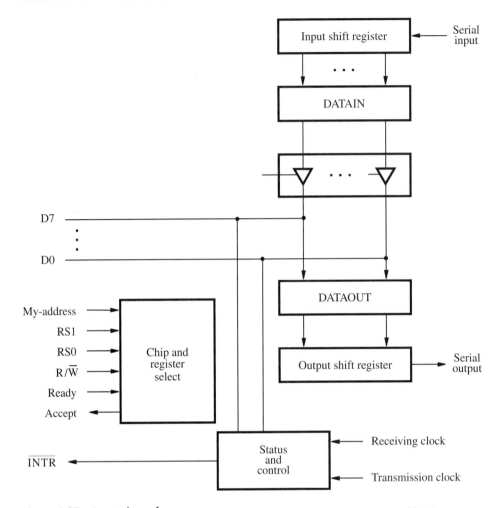

Figure 4.37   A serial interface.

register and set to 1 when data are transferred from DATAOUT into the output shift register.

The double buffering used in the input and output paths is important. A simpler interface could be implemented by turning DATAIN and DATAOUT into shift registers and eliminating the shift registers in Figure 4.37. However, this would impose awkward restrictions on the operation of the I/O device; after receiving one character from the serial line, the device cannot start receiving the next character until the processor reads the contents of DATAIN. Thus, a pause would be needed between two characters to allow the processor to read the input data. With the double buffer, the transfer of the second character can begin as soon as the first character is loaded from the shift register into the DATAIN register. Thus, provided the processor reads the contents of DATAIN before the serial transfer of the second character is completed, the interface can receive a continuous stream of serial data. An analogous situation occurs in the output path of the interface.

Because it requires fewer wires, serial transmission is convenient for connecting devices that are physically far away from the computer. The speed of transmission, often given as a *bit rate,* depends on the nature of the devices connected. To accommodate a range of devices, a serial interface must be able to use a range of clock speeds. The circuit in Figure 4.37 allows separate clock signals to be used for input and output operations for increased flexibility.

Because serial interfaces play a vital role in connecting I/O devices, several widely used standards have been developed. A standard circuit that includes the features of our example in Figure 4.37 is known as a Universal Asynchronous Receiver Transmitter (UART). It is intended for use with low-speed serial devices. Data transmission is performed using the asynchronous start-stop format, which we discuss in Chapter 10. To facilitate connection to communication links, a popular standard known as RS-232-C was developed. It is also described in Chapter 10.

4.7 STANDARD I/O INTERFACES

The previous sections point out that there are several alternative designs for the bus of a computer. This variety means that I/O devices fitted with an interface circuit suitable for one computer may not be usable with other computers. A different interface may have to be designed for every combination of I/O device and computer, resulting in many different interfaces. The most practical solution is to develop standard interface signals and protocols.

It is helpful at this point to understand how a computer system is put together. A typical personal computer, for example, includes a printed circuit board called the motherboard. This board houses the processor chip, the main memory, and some I/O interfaces. It also has a few connectors into which additional interfaces can be plugged.

The processor bus is the bus defined by the signals on the processor chip itself. Devices that require a very high speed connection to the processor, such as the main memory, may be connected directly to this bus. For electrical reasons, only a few devices can be connected in this manner. The motherboard usually provides another bus that can support more devices. The two buses are interconnected by a circuit, which we will call a *bridge,* that translates the signals and protocols of one bus into those of the other. Devices connected to the expansion bus appear to the processor as if they were connected directly to the processor's own bus. The only difference is that the bridge circuit introduces a small delay in data transfers between the processor and those devices.

It is not possible to define a uniform standard for the processor bus. The structure of this bus is closely tied to the architecture of the processor. It is also dependent on the electrical characteristics of the processor chip, such as its clock speed. The expansion bus is not subject to these limitations, and therefore it can use a standardized signaling scheme. A number of standards have been developed. Some have evolved by default, when a particular design became commercially successful. For example, IBM developed a bus they called <u>ISA (Industry Standard Architecture)</u> for their personal computer known at the time as PC AT. The popularity of that computer led to other manufacturers producing ISA-compatible interfaces for their I/O devices, thus making ISA into a de facto standard.

Some standards have been developed through industrial cooperative efforts, even among competing companies driven by their common self-interest in having compatible products. In some cases, organizations such as the IEEE (Institute of Electrical and Electronics Engineers), ANSI (American National Standards Institute), or international bodies such as ISO (International Standards Organization) have blessed these standards and given them an official status.

In this section, we present three widely used bus standards, <u>PCI (Peripheral Component Interconnect)</u>, <u>SCSI (Small Computer System Interface)</u>, and <u>USB (Universal Serial Bus)</u>. The way these standards are used in a typical computer system is illustrated in Figure 4.38. The PCI standard defines an expansion bus on the motherboard. SCSI and USB are used for connecting additional devices, both inside and outside the

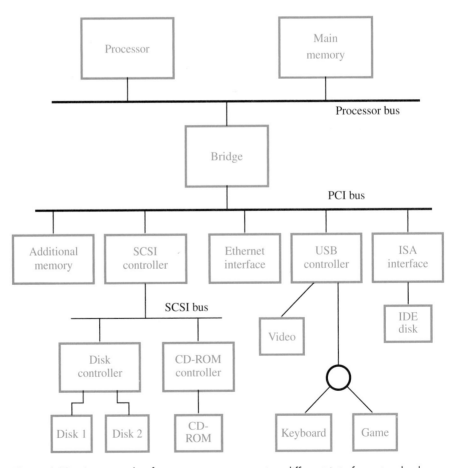

Figure 4.38   An example of a computer system using different interface standards.

computer box. The SCSI bus is a high-speed parallel bus intended for devices such as disks and video displays. The USB bus uses serial transmission to suit the needs of equipment ranging from keyboards to game controls to internet connections. The figure shows an interface circuit that enables devices compatible with the earlier ISA standard, such as the popular IDE (Integrated Device Electronics) disk, to be connected. It also shows a connection to an Ethernet. The Ethernet is a widely used local area network, providing a high-speed connection among computers in a building or a university campus.

A given computer may use more than one bus standard. A typical Pentium computer has both a PCI bus and an ISA bus, thus providing the user with a wide range of devices to choose from.

4.7.1 PERIPHERAL COMPONENT INTERCONNECT (PCI) BUS

The PCI bus [1] is a good example of a system bus that grew out of the need for standardization. It supports the functions found on a processor bus but in a standardized format that is independent of any particular processor. Devices connected to the PCI bus appear to the processor as if they were connected directly to the processor bus. They are assigned addresses in the memory address space of the processor.

The PCI follows a sequence of bus standards that were used primarily in IBM PCs. Early PCs used the 8-bit XT bus, whose signals closely mimicked those of Intel's $80x86$ processors. Later, the 16-bit bus used on the PC AT computers became known as the ISA bus. Its extended 32-bit version is known as the EISA bus. Other buses developed in the eighties with similar capabilities are the Microchannel used in IBM PCs and the NuBus used in Macintosh computers.

The PCI was developed as a low-cost bus that is truly processor independent. Its design anticipated a rapidly growing demand for bus bandwidth to support high-speed disks and graphic and video devices, as well as the specialized needs of multiprocessor systems. As a result, the PCI is still popular as an industry standard almost a decade after it was first introduced in 1992.

An important feature that the PCI pioneered is a plug-and-play capability for connecting I/O devices. To connect a new device, the user simply connects the device interface board to the bus. The software takes care of the rest. We will discuss this feature after we describe how the PCI bus operates.

Data Transfer

In today's computers, most memory transfers involve a burst of data rather than just one word. The reason is that modern processors include a cache memory (see Figure 1.6). Data are transferred between the cache and the main memory in bursts of several words each, as we will explain in Chapter 5. The words involved in such a transfer are stored at successive memory locations. When the processor (actually the cache controller) specifies an address and requests a read operation from the main memory, the memory responds by sending a sequence of data words starting at that address. Similarly, during a write operation, the processor sends a memory address followed by a sequence of data words, to be written in successive memory locations starting at that address. The PCI is designed primarily to support this mode of operation. A read or a write operation involving a single word is simply treated as a burst of length one.

The bus supports three independent address spaces: memory, I/O, and configuration. The first two are self-explanatory. The I/O address space is intended for use with processors, such as Pentium, that have a separate I/O address space. However, as noted in Chapter 3, the system designer may choose to use memory-mapped I/O even when a separate I/O address space is available. In fact, this is the approach recommended by the PCI standard for wider compatibility. The configuration space is intended to give the PCI its plug-and-play capability, as we will explain shortly. A 4-bit command that accompanies the address identifies which of the three spaces is being used in a given data transfer operation.

Figure 4.38 shows the main memory of the computer connected directly to the processor bus. An alternative arrangement that is used often with the PCI bus is shown in Figure 4.39. The PCI bridge provides a separate physical connection for the main memory. For electrical reasons, the bus may be further divided into segments connected via bridges. However, regardless of which bus segment a device is connected to, it may still be mapped into the processor's memory address space.

The signaling convention on the PCI bus is similar to the one used in Figure 4.25. In that figure, we assumed that the master maintains the address information on the bus until data transfer is completed. But, this is not necessary. The address is needed only long enough for the slave to be selected. The slave can store the address in its internal buffer. Thus, the address is needed on the bus for one clock cycle only, freeing the address lines to be used for sending data in subsequent clock cycles. The result is

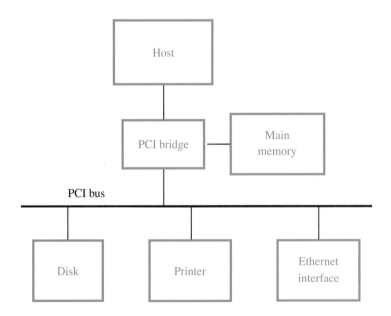

Figure 4.39 Use of a PCI bus in a computer system.

Table 4.3 Data transfer signals on the PCI bus.

Name	Function
CLK	A 33-MHz or 66-MHz clock.
FRAME#	Sent by the initiator to indicate the duration of a transaction.
AD	32 address/data lines, which may be optionally increased to 64.
C/BE#	4 command/byte-enable lines (8 for a 64-bit bus).
IRDY#, TRDY#	Initiator-ready and Target-ready signals.
DEVSEL#	A response from the device indicating that it has recognized its address and is ready for a data transfer transaction.
IDSEL#	Initialization Device Select.

a significant cost reduction because the number of wires on a bus is an important cost factor. This approach is used in the PCI bus.

At any given time, one device is the bus master. It has the right to initiate data transfers by issuing read and write commands. A master is called an *initiator* in PCI terminology. This is either a processor or a DMA controller. The addressed device that responds to read and write commands is called a *target.*

To understand the operation of the bus and its various features, we will examine a typical bus transaction. The main bus signals used for transferring data are listed in Table 4.3. Signals whose name ends with the symbol # are asserted when in the low-voltage state. The main difference between the PCI protocol and Figure 4.25 is that in addition to a Target-ready signal, PCI also uses an Initiator-ready signal, IRDY#. The latter is needed to support burst transfers.

Consider a bus transaction in which the processor reads four 32-bit words from the memory. In this case, the initiator is the processor and the target is the memory. A complete transfer operation on the bus, involving an address and a burst of data, is called a *transaction*. Individual word transfers within a transaction are called *phases*. The sequence of events on the bus is shown in Figure 4.40. A clock signal provides the timing reference used to coordinate different phases of a transaction. All signal transitions are triggered by the rising edge of the clock. As in the case of Figure 4.25, we show the signals changing later in the clock cycle to indicate the delays they encounter.

In clock cycle 1, the processor asserts FRAME# to indicate the beginning of a transaction. At the same time, it sends the address on the AD lines and a command on the C/BE# lines. In this case, the command will indicate that a read operation is requested and that the memory address space is being used.

Clock cycle 2 is used to turn the AD bus lines around. The processor removes the address and disconnects its drivers from the AD lines. The selected target enables its drivers on the AD lines, and fetches the requested data to be placed on the bus during clock cycle 3. It asserts DEVSEL# and maintains it in the asserted state until the end of the transaction.

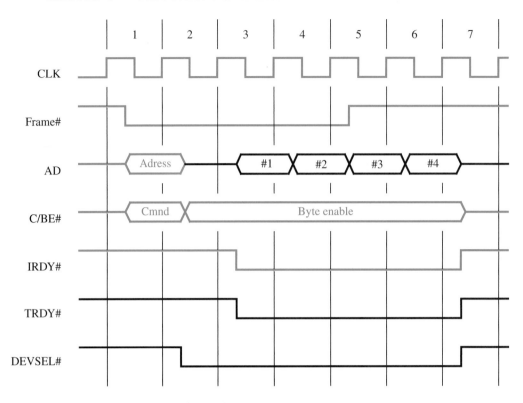

Figure 4.40 A read operation on the PCI bus.

The C/BE# lines, which were used to send a bus command in clock cycle 1, are used for a different purpose during the rest of the transaction. Each of these four lines is associated with one byte on the AD lines. The initiator sets one or more of the C/BE# lines to indicate which byte lines are to be used for transferring data. Assuming that the target is capable of transferring 32 bits at a time, all four C/BE# lines are asserted.

During clock cycle 3, the initiator asserts the initiator ready signal, IRDY#, to indicate that it is ready to receive data. If the target has data ready to send at this time, it asserts target ready, TRDY#, and sends a word of data. The initiator loads the data into its input buffer at the end of the clock cycle. The target sends three more words of data in clock cycles 4 to 6.

The initiator uses the FRAME# signal to indicate the duration of the burst. It negates this signal during the second last word of the transfer. Since it wishes to read four words, the initiator negates FRAME# during clock cycle 5, the cycle in which it receives the third word. After sending the fourth word in clock cycle 6, the target disconnects its drivers and negates DEVSEL# at the beginning of clock cycle 7.

Figure 4.41 gives an example of a more general input transaction. It shows how the IRDY# and TRDY# signals can be used by the initiator and target, respectively, to indicate a pause in the middle of a transaction. The read operation starts the same way as in Figure 4.40, and the first two words are transferred. The target sends the third

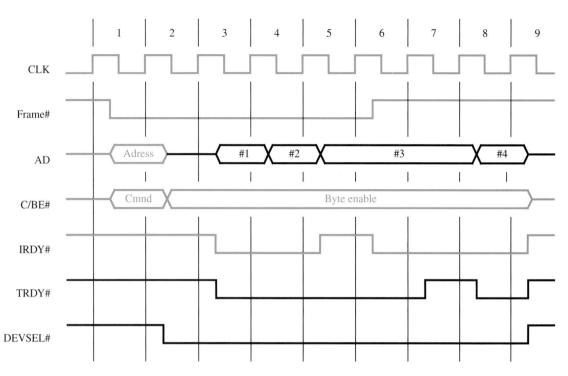

Figure 4.41 A read operation showing the role of IRDY#/TRDY#.

word in cycle 5. However, we assume that the initiator is not able to receive it. Hence, it negates IRDY#. In response, the target maintains the third data word on the AD lines until IRDY# is asserted again. In cycle 6, the initiator asserts IRDY# and loads the data into its input buffer at the end of the clock cycle. At this point, we assume that the target is not ready to transfer the fourth word immediately; hence, it negates TRDY# at the beginning of cycle 7. In cycle 8, it sends the fourth word and asserts TRDY#. Since Frame# was negated with the third data word, the transaction ends after the fourth word has been transferred.

Device Configuration

When an I/O device is connected to a computer, several actions are needed to configure both the device and the software that communicates with it. A typical device interface card for an ISA bus, for example, has a number of jumpers or switches that have to be set by the user to select certain options. Once the device is connected, the software needs to know the address of the device. It may also need to know relevant device characteristics, such as the speed of the transmission link, whether parity bits are used, and so on.

The PCI simplifies this process by incorporating in each I/O device interface a small configuration ROM memory that stores information about that device. The configuration ROMs of all devices are accessible in the configuration address space. The PCI initialization software reads these ROMs whenever the system is powered up or reset. In each case, it determines whether the device is a printer, a keyboard, an Ethernet interface, or a disk controller. It can further learn about various device options and characteristics.

Devices are assigned addresses during the initialization process. This means that during the bus configuration operation, devices cannot be accessed based on their address, as they have not yet been assigned one. Hence, the configuration address space uses a different mechanism. Each device has an input signal called Initialization Device Select, IDSEL#. During a configuration operation, it is this signal, rather than the address applied to the AD inputs of the device, that causes the device to be selected. The motherboard in which device connectors are plugged typically has the IDSEL# pin of each device connected to one of the upper 21 address lines, AD11 to AD31. Hence, a device can be selected for a configuration operation by issuing a configuration command and an address in which the corresponding AD line is set to 1 and the remaining 20 lines set to 0. The lower address lines, AD10 to AD00, are used to specify the type of operation and to access the contents of the device configuration ROM. This arrangement limits the number of I/O devices to 21.

The configuration software scans all 21 locations in the configuration address space to identify which devices are present. Each device may request an address in the I/O space or in the memory space. The device is then assigned an address by writing that address into the appropriate device register. The configuration software also sets such parameters as the device interrupt priority. The PCI bus has four interrupt-request lines. By writing into a device configuration register, the software instructs the device as to which of these lines it can use to request an interrupt. If a device requires initialization, the initialization code is stored in a ROM in the device interface. (This is a different ROM from that used in the configuration process.) The PCI software reads this code and executes it to perform the required initialization.

This process relieves the user from having to be involved in the configuration process. The user simply plugs in the interface board and turns on the power. The software does the rest. The device is ready to use.

The PCI bus has gained great popularity in the PC world. It is also used in many other computers, such as SUNs, to benefit from the wide range of I/O devices for which a PCI interface is available. In the case of some processors, such as the Compaq Alpha, the PCI-processor bridge circuit is built on the processor chip itself, further simplifying system design and packaging.

Electrical Characteristics

The PCI bus has been defined for operation with either a 5- or 3.3-V power supply. The motherboard may be designed to operate with either signaling system. Connectors on expansion boards are designed to ensure that they can be plugged only in a compatible motherboard.

4.7.2 SCSI BUS

The acronym SCSI stands for Small Computer System Interface. It refers to a standard bus defined by the American National Standards Institute (ANSI) under the designation X3.131 [2]. In the original specifications of the standard, devices such as disks are connected to a computer via a 50-wire cable, which can be up to 25 meters in length and can transfer data at rates up to 5 megabytes/s.

The SCSI bus standard has undergone many revisions, and its data transfer capability has increased very rapidly, almost doubling every two years. SCSI-2 and SCSI-3 have been defined, and each has several options. A SCSI bus may have eight data lines, in which case it is called a narrow bus and transfers data one byte at a time. Alternatively, a wide SCSI bus has 16 data lines and transfers data 16 bits at a time. There are also several options for the electrical signaling scheme used. The bus may use single-ended transmission (SE), where each signal uses one wire, with a common ground return for all signals. In another option, differential signaling is used, where a separate return wire is provided for each signal. In this case, two voltage levels are possible. Earlier versions use 5 V (TTL levels) and are known as High Voltage Differential (HVD). More recently, a 3.3 V version has been introduced and is known as Low Voltage Differential (LVD).

Because of these various options, the SCSI connector may have 50, 68, or 80 pins. The maximum transfer rate in commercial devices that are currently available varies from 5 megabytes/s to 160 megabytes/s. The most recent version of the standard is intended to support transfer rates up to 320 megabytes/s, and 640 megabytes/s is anticipated a little later. The maximum transfer rate on a given bus is often a function of the length of the cable and the number of devices connected, with higher rates for a shorter cable and fewer devices. To achieve the top data transfer rate, the bus length is typically limited to 1.6 m for SE signaling and 12 m for LVD signaling. However, manufacturers often provide special bus expanders to connect devices that are farther away. The maximum capacity of the bus is 8 devices for a narrow bus and 16 devices for a wide bus.

Devices connected to the SCSI bus are not part of the address space of the processor in the same way as devices connected to the processor bus. The SCSI bus is connected to the processor bus through a SCSI controller, as shown in Figure 4.38. This controller uses DMA to transfer data packets from the main memory to the device, or vice versa. A packet may contain a block of data, commands from the processor to the device, or status information about the device.

To illustrate the operation of the SCSI bus, let us consider how it may be used with a disk drive. Communication with a disk drive differs substantially from communication with the main memory. As described in Chapter 5, data are stored on a disk in blocks called *sectors,* where each sector may contain several hundred bytes. These data may not necessarily be stored in contiguous sectors. Some sectors may already contain previously stored data; others may be defective and must be skipped. Hence, a read or write request may result in accessing several disk sectors that are not necessarily contiguous. Because of the constraints of the mechanical motion of the disk, there is a long delay, on the order of several milliseconds, before reaching the first sector to or from which data are to be transferred. Then, a burst of data are transferred at high speed. Another delay may ensue, followed by a burst of data. A single read or write request may involve several such bursts. The SCSI protocol is designed to facilitate this mode of operation.

A controller connected to a SCSI bus is one of two types — an *initiator* or a *target.* An initiator has the ability to select a particular target and to send commands specifying the operations to be performed. Clearly, the controller on the processor side, such as the SCSI controller in Figure 4.38, must be able to operate as an initiator. The disk controller operates as a target. It carries out the commands it receives from the initiator. The initiator establishes a *logical connection* with the intended target.

Once this connection has been established, it can be suspended and restored as needed to transfer commands and bursts of data. While a particular connection is suspended, other devices can use the bus to transfer information. This ability to overlap data transfer requests is one of the key features of the SCSI bus that leads to its high performance.

Data transfers on the SCSI bus are always controlled by the target controller. To send a command to a target, an initiator requests control of the bus and, after winning arbitration, selects the controller it wants to communicate with and hands control of the bus over to it. Then the controller starts a data transfer operation to receive a command from the initiator.

Let us examine a complete disk read operation as an example. In this discussion, even though we refer to the initiator controller as taking certain actions, it should be clear that it performs these actions after receiving appropriate commands from the processor. Assume that the processor wishes to read a block of data from a disk drive and that these data are stored in two disk sectors that are not contiguous. The processor sends a command to the SCSI controller, which causes the following sequence of events to take place:

1. The SCSI controller, acting as an initiator, contends for control of the bus.

2. When the initiator wins the arbitration process, it selects the target controller and hands over control of the bus to it.

3. The target starts an output operation (from initiator to target); in response to this, the initiator sends a command specifying the required read operation.

4. The target, realizing that it first needs to perform a disk seek operation, sends a message to the initiator indicating that it will temporarily suspend the connection between them. Then it releases the bus.

5. The target controller sends a command to the disk drive to move the read head to the first sector involved in the requested read operation. Then, it reads the data stored in that sector and stores them in a data buffer. When it is ready to begin transferring data to the initiator, the target requests control of the bus. After it wins arbitration, it reselects the initiator controller, thus restoring the suspended connection.

6. The target transfers the contents of the data buffer to the initiator and then suspends the connection again. Data are transferred either 8 or 16 bits in parallel, depending on the width of the bus.

7. The target controller sends a command to the disk drive to perform another seek operation. Then, it transfers the contents of the second disk sector to the initiator, as before. At the end of this transfer, the logical connection between the two controllers is terminated.

8. As the initiator controller receives the data, it stores them into the main memory using the DMA approach.

9. The SCSI controller sends an interrupt to the processor to inform it that the requested operation has been completed.

This scenario shows that the messages exchanged over the SCSI bus are at a higher level than those exchanged over the processor bus. In this context, a "higher level" means that the messages refer to operations that may require several steps to complete, depending on the device. Neither the processor nor the SCSI controller need be aware of the details of operation of the particular device involved in a data transfer. In the preceding example, the processor need not be involved in the disk seek operations.

The SCSI bus standard defines a wide range of control messages that can be exchanged between the controllers to handle different types of I/O devices. Messages are also defined to deal with various error or failure conditions that might arise during device operation or data transfer.

Bus Signals

We now describe the operation of the SCSI bus from the hardware point of view. The bus signals are summarized in Table 4.4. For simplicity we show the signals for a narrow bus (8 data lines). Note that all signal names are preceded by a minus sign. This indicates that the signals are active, or that a data line is equal to 1, when they are in the low-voltage state. The bus has no address lines. Instead, the data lines are used to identify the bus controllers involved during the selection or reselection process and during bus arbitration. For a narrow bus, there are eight possible controllers, numbered 0 through 7, and each is associated with the data line that has the same number. A wide bus accommodates up to 16 controllers. A controller places its own address or the address of another controller on the bus by activating the corresponding data line. Thus, it is possible to have more than one address on the bus at the same time, as in the arbitration process we describe next. Once a connection is established between two

Table 4.4 The SCSI bus signals

Category	Name	Function
Data	−DB(0) to −DB(7)	Data lines: Carry one byte of information during the information transfer phase and identify device during arbitration, selection and reselection phases
	−DB(P)	Parity bit for the data bus
Phase	−BSY	Busy: Asserted when the bus is not free
	−SEL	Selection: Asserted during selection and reselection
Information type	−C/D	Control/Data: Asserted during transfer of control information (command, status or message)
	−MSG	Message: indicates that the information being transferred is a message
Handshake	−REQ	Request: Asserted by a target to request a data transfer cycle
	−ACK	Acknowledge: Asserted by the initiator when it has completed a data transfer operation
Direction of transfer	−I/O	Input/Output: Asserted to indicate an input operation (relative to the initiator)
Other	−ATN	Attention: Asserted by an initiator when it wishes to send a message to a target
	−RST	Reset: Causes all device controls to disconnect from the bus and assume their start-up state

controllers, there is no further need for addressing, and the data lines are used to carry data.

The main phases involved in the operation of the SCSI bus are arbitration, selection, information transfer, and reselection. We now examine each of these phases.

Arbitration

The bus is free when the $-$BSY signal is in the inactive (high-voltage) state. Any controller can request the use of the bus while it is in this state. Since two or more controllers may generate such a request at the same time, an arbitration scheme must be implemented. A controller requests the bus by asserting the $-$BSY signal and by asserting its associated data line to identify itself. The SCSI bus uses a simple distributed arbitration scheme. It is illustrated by the example in Figure 4.42, in which controllers 2 and 6 request the use of the bus simultaneously.

Each controller on the bus is assigned a fixed priority, with controller 7 having the highest priority. When $-$BSY becomes active, all controllers that are requesting the bus examine the data lines and determine whether a higher-priority device is requesting the bus at the same time. The controller using the highest-numbered line realizes that it has won the arbitration process. All other controllers disconnect from the bus and wait for $-$BSY to become inactive again.

In Figure 4.42, we have assumed that controller 6 is an initiator that wishes to establish a connection to controller 5. After winning arbitration, controller 6 proceeds to the selection phase, in which it identifies the target.

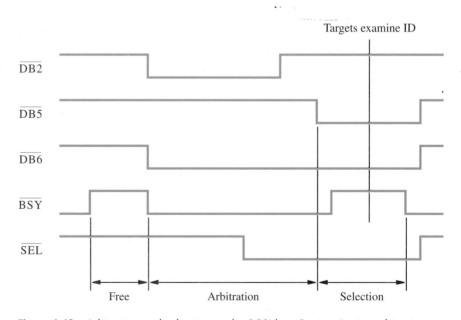

Figure 4.42   Arbitration and selection on the SCSI bus. Device 6 wins arbitration and selects device 2.

Selection

Having won arbitration, controller 6 continues to assert −BSY and −DB6 (its address). It indicates that it wishes to select controller 5 by asserting the −SEL and then the −DB5 lines. Any other controller that may have been involved in the arbitration phase, such as controller 2 in the figure, must stop driving the data lines once the −SEL line becomes active, if it has not already done so. After placing the address of the target controller on the bus, the initiator releases the −BSY line.

The selected target controller responds by asserting −BSY. This informs the initiator that the connection it is requesting has been established, so that it may remove the address information from the data lines. The selection process is now complete, and the target controller (controller 5) is asserting −BSY. From this point on, controller 5 has control of the bus, as required for the information transfer phase.

Information Transfer

The information transferred between two controllers may consist of commands from the initiator to the target, status responses from the target to the initiator, or data being transferred to or from the I/O device. Handshake signaling is used to control information transfers in the same manner as described in Section 4.5.2, with the target controller taking the role of the bus master. The −REQ and −ACK signals replace the Master-ready and Slave-ready signals in Figures 4.26 and 4.27. The target asserts −I/O during an input operation (target to initiator), and it asserts −C/D to indicate that the information being transferred is either a command or a status response rather than data.

We should point out that high-speed versions of the SCSI bus use a technique known as double-edge clocking or Double Transitions (DT). In Figures 4.26 and 4.27, each data transfer requires a high-to-low transition followed by a low-to-high transition on the two handshake signals. Double-edge clocking means that data are transferred on both the rising and falling edges of these signals, thus doubling the transfer rate.

At the end of the transfer, the target controller releases the −BSY signal, thus freeing the bus for use by other devices. Later, it may reestablish the connection to the initiator controller when it is ready to transfer more data. This is done in the reselection operation described next.

Reselection

When a logical connection is suspended and the target is ready to restore it, the target must first gain control of the bus. It starts an arbitration cycle, and after winning arbitration, it selects the initiator controller in exactly the same manner as described above. But with the roles of the target and initiator reversed, the initiator is now asserting −BSY. Before data transfer can begin, the initiator must hand control over to the target. This is achieved by having the target controller assert −BSY after selecting the initiator. Meanwhile, the initiator waits for a short period after being selected to make sure that the target has asserted −BSY, and then it releases the −BSY line. The connection between the two controllers has now been reestablished, with the target in control of the bus as required for data transfer to proceed.

The bus signaling scheme described above provides the mechanisms needed for two controllers to establish a logical connection and exchange messages. The connection may be suspended and reestablished at any time. The SCSI standard defines the structure and contents of various types of packets that the controllers exchange to handle different situations. The initiator uses these packets to send the commands it receives from the processor to the target. The target responds with status information, and data transfer operations. The latter are controlled by the target, because it is the target that knows when data are available, when to suspend and reestablish connections, etc.

Additional information on the SCSI bus and various SCSI products is available on the web from the standards committee [2].

4.7.3 UNIVERSAL SERIAL BUS (USB)

The synergy between computers and communications is at the heart of today's information technology revolution. A modern computer system is likely to involve a wide variety of devices such as keyboards, microphones, cameras, speakers, and display devices. Most computers also have a wired or wireless connection to the Internet. A key requirement in such an environment is the availability of a simple, low-cost mechanism to connect these devices to the computer, and an important recent development in this regard is the introduction of the Universal Serial Bus (USB) [3]. This is an industry standard developed through a collaborative effort of several computer and communications companies, including Compaq, Hewlett-Packard, Intel, Lucent, Microsoft, Nortel Networks, and Philips.

The USB supports two speeds of operation, called low-speed (1.5 megabits/s) and full-speed (12 megabits/s). The most recent revision of the bus specification (USB 2.0) introduced a third speed of operation, called high-speed (480 megabits/s). The USB is quickly gaining acceptance in the market place, and with the addition of the high-speed capability it may well become the interconnection method of choice for most computer devices.

The USB has been designed to meet several key objectives:

- Provide a simple, low-cost, and easy to use interconnection system that overcomes the difficulties due to the limited number of I/O ports available on a computer
- Accommodate a wide range of data transfer characteristics for I/O devices, including telephone and Internet connections
- Enhance user convenience through a "plug-and-play" mode of operation

We will elaborate on these objectives before discussing the technical details of the USB.

Port Limitation

The parallel and serial ports described in Section 4.6 provide a general-purpose point of connection through which a variety of low- to medium-speed devices can be connected to a computer. For practical reasons, only a few such ports are provided in a typical computer. To add new ports, a user must open the computer box to gain access to the internal expansion bus and install a new interface card. The user may also need to know how to configure the device and the software. An objective of the USB is to make it possible to add many devices to a computer system at any time, without opening the computer box.

Device Characteristics

The kinds of devices that may be connected to a computer cover a wide range of functionality. The speed, volume, and timing constraints associated with data transfers to and from such devices vary significantly.

In the case of a keyboard, one byte of data is generated every time a key is pressed, which may happen at any time. These data should be transferred to the computer promptly. Since the event of pressing a key is not synchronized to any other event in a computer system, the data generated by the keyboard are called *asynchronous*. Furthermore, the rate at which the data are generated is quite low. It is limited by the speed of the human operator to about 100 bytes per second, which is less than 1000 bits per second.

A variety of simple devices that may be attached to a computer generate data of a similar nature — low speed and asynchronous. Computer mice and the controls and manipulators used with video games are good examples.

Let us consider a different source of data. Many computers have a microphone either externally attached or built in. The sound picked up by the microphone produces an analog electrical signal, which must be converted into a digital form before it can be handled by the computer. This is accomplished by sampling the analog signal periodically. For each sample, an analog-to-digital (A/D) converter generates an n-bit number representing the magnitude of the sample. The number of bits, n, is selected based on the desired precision with which to represent each sample. Later, when these data are sent to a speaker, a digital-to-analog (D/A) converter is used to restore the original analog signal from the digital format.

The sampling process yields a continuous stream of digitized samples that arrive at regular intervals, synchronized with the sampling clock. Such a data stream is called *isochronous*, meaning that successive events are separated by equal periods of time.

A signal must be sampled quickly enough to track its highest-frequency components. In general, if the sampling rate is s samples per second, the maximum frequency component that will be captured by the sampling process is $s/2$. For example, human speech can be captured adequately with a sampling rate of 8 kHz, which will record sound signals having frequencies up to 4 kHz. For a higher-quality sound, as needed in a music system, higher sampling rates are used. A standard rate for digital sound is 44.1 kHz. Each sample is represented by 4 bytes of data to accommodate the wide range in sound volume (dynamic range) that is necessary for high-quality sound reproduction. This yields a data rate of about 1.4 megabits/s.

An important requirement in dealing with sampled voice or music is to maintain precise timing in the sampling and replay processes. A high degree of jitter (variability in sample timing) is unacceptable. Hence, the data transfer mechanism between a computer and a music system must maintain consistent delays from one sample to the next. Otherwise, complex buffering and retiming circuitry would be needed. On the other hand, occasional errors or missed samples can be tolerated. They either go unnoticed by the listener or they may cause an unobtrusive click. No sophisticated mechanisms are needed to ensure perfectly correct data delivery.

Data transfers for images and video have similar requirements, but at much higher data transfer bandwidth. The term bandwidth refers to the total data transfer capacity of a communications channel, measured in a suitable unit such as bits or bytes per second. To maintain the picture quality of commercial television, an image should be represented by about 160 kilobytes and transmitted 30 times per second, for a total bandwidth of 44 megabits/s. Higher-quality images, as in HDTV (High Definition TV), require higher rates.

Large storage devices such as hard disks and CD-ROMs present different requirements. These devices are part of the computer's memory hierarchy, as will be discussed in Chapter 5. Their connection to the computer must provide a data transfer bandwidth of at least 40 or 50 megabits/s. Delays on the order of a millisecond are introduced by the disk mechanism. Hence, a small additional delay introduced while transferring data to or from the computer is not important, and jitter is not an issue.

Plug-and-Play

As computers become part of everyday life, their existence should become increasingly transparent. For example, when operating a home theater system, which includes at least one computer, the user should not find it necessary to turn the computer off or to restart the system to connect or disconnect a device.

The *plug-and-play* feature means that a new device, such as an additional speaker, can be connected at any time while the system is operating. The system should detect the existence of this new device automatically, identify the appropriate device-driver software and any other facilities needed to service that device, and establish the appropriate addresses and logical connections to enable them to communicate.

The plug-and-play requirement has many implications at all levels in the system, from the hardware to the operating system and the applications software. One of the primary objectives of the design of the USB has been to provide a plug-and-play capability.

USB Architecture

The discussion above points to the need for an interconnection system that combines low cost, flexibility, and high data-transfer bandwidth. Also, I/O devices may be located at some distance from the computer to which they are connected. The requirement for high bandwidth would normally suggest a wide bus that carries 8, 16, or more bits in parallel. However, a large number of wires increases cost and complexity and is inconvenient to the user. Also, it is difficult to design a wide bus that carries data for a long distance because of the data skew problem discussed in Section 4.5.2. The amount of skew increases with distance and limits the data rate that can be used.

A serial transmission format has been chosen for the USB because a serial bus satisfies the low-cost and flexibility requirements. Clock and data information are encoded together and transmitted as a single signal. Hence, there are no limitations on clock frequency or distance arising from data skew. Therefore, it is possible to provide a high data transfer bandwidth by using a high clock frequency. As pointed out earlier, the USB offers three bit rates, ranging from 1.5 to 480 megabits/s, to suit the needs of different I/O devices.

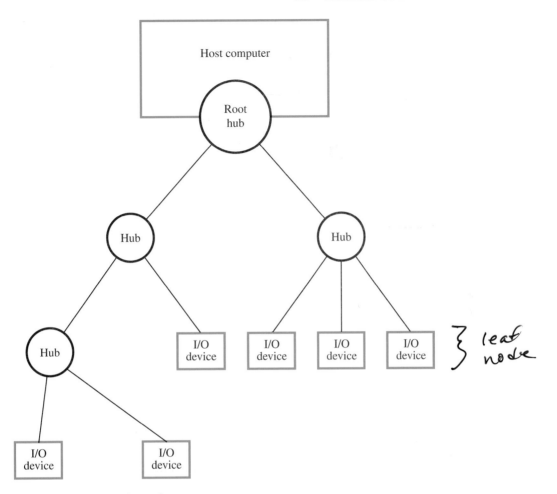

Figure 4.43 Universal Serial Bus tree structure.

To accommodate a large number of devices that can be added or removed at any time, the USB has the tree structure shown in Figure 4.43. Each node of the tree has a device called a *hub*, which acts as an intermediate control point between the host and the I/O devices. At the root of the tree, a *root hub* connects the entire tree to the host computer. The leaves of the tree are the I/O devices being served (for example, keyboard, Internet connection, speaker, or digital TV), which are called *functions* in USB terminology. For consistency with the rest of the discussion in the book, we will refer to these devices as I/O devices.

The tree structure enables many devices to be connected while using only simple point-to-point serial links. Each hub has a number of ports where devices may be connected, including other hubs. In normal operation, a hub copies a message that it receives from its upstream connection to all its downstream ports. As a result, a message sent by the host computer is broadcast to all I/O devices, but only the addressed device will respond to that message. In this respect, the USB functions in the same way as the bus in Figure 4.1. However, unlike the bus in Figure 4.1, a message from an I/O device is sent only upstream towards the root of the tree and is not seen by other devices. Hence, the USB enables the host to communicate with the I/O devices, but it does not enable these devices to communicate with each other.

Note how the tree structure helps meet the USB's design objectives. The tree makes it possible to connect a large number of devices to a computer through a few ports (the root hub). At the same time, each I/O device is connected through a serial point-to-point connection. This is an important consideration in facilitating the plug-and-play feature, as we will see shortly. Also, because of electrical transmission considerations, serial data transmission on such a connection is much easier than parallel transmission on buses of the form represented in Figure 4.1. Much higher data rates and longer cables can be used.

The USB operates strictly on the basis of polling. A device may send a message only in response to a poll message from the host. Hence, upstream messages do not encounter conflicts or interfere with each other, as no two devices can send messages at the same time. This restriction allows hubs to be simple, low-cost devices.

The mode of operation described above is observed for all devices operating at either low speed or full speed. However, one exception has been necessitated by the introduction of high-speed operation in USB version 2.0. Consider the situation in Figure 4.44. Hub A is connected to the root hub by a high-speed link. This hub serves

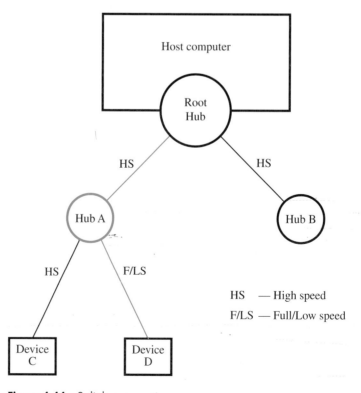

Figure 4.44 Split bus operation.

one high-speed device, C, and one low-speed device, D. Normally, a message to device D would be sent at low speed from the root hub. At 1.5 megabits/s, even a short message takes several tens of microseconds. For the duration of this message, no other data transfers can take place, thus reducing the effectiveness of the high-speed links and introducing unacceptable delays for high-speed devices. To mitigate this problem, the USB protocol requires that a message transmitted on a high-speed link is always transmitted at high speed, even when the ultimate receiver is a low-speed device. Hence, a message intended for device D is sent at high speed from the root hub to hub A, then forwarded at low speed to device D. The latter transfer will take a long time, during which high-speed traffic to other nodes is allowed to continue. For example, the root hub may exchange several messages with device C while the low-speed message is being sent from hub A to device D. During this period, the bus is said to be split between high-speed and low-speed traffic. The message to device D is preceded and followed by special commands to hub A to start and end the split-traffic mode of operation, respectively.

The USB standard specifies the hardware details of USB interconnections as well as the organization and requirements of the host software. The purpose of the USB software is to provide bidirectional communication links between application software and I/O devices. These links are called *pipes*. Any data entering at one end of a pipe is delivered at the other end. Issues such as addressing, timing, or error detection and recovery are handled by the USB protocols.

We mentioned in Section 4.2.6 that the software that transfers data to or from a given I/O device is called the device driver for that device. The device drivers depend on the characteristics of the devices they support. Hence, a more precise description of the USB pipe is that it connects an I/O device to its device driver. It is established when a device is connected and assigned a unique address by the USB software. Once established, data may flow through the pipe at any time.

We will now examine how devices are addressed on the USB. Then we will discuss the various ways in which data transfer can take place.

Addressing

In earlier discussions of input and output operations, we explained that I/O devices are normally identified by assigning them a unique memory address. In fact, a device usually has several addressable locations to enable the software to send and receive control and status information and to transfer data.

When a USB is connected to a host computer, its root hub is attached to the processor bus, where it appears as a single device. The host software communicates with individual devices attached to the USB by sending packets of information, which the root hub forwards to the appropriate device in the USB tree.

Each device on the USB, whether it is a hub or an I/O device, is assigned a 7-bit address. This address is local to the USB tree and is not related in any way to the addresses used on the processor bus. A hub may have any number of devices or other hubs connected to it, and addresses are assigned arbitrarily. When a device is first connected to a hub, or when it is powered on, it has the address 0. The hardware of the hub to which this device is connected is capable of detecting that the device has been connected, and it records this fact as part of its own status information. Periodically, the host polls each hub to collect status information and learn about new devices that may have been added or disconnected. When the host is informed that a new device has been connected, it uses a sequence of commands to send a reset signal on the corresponding hub port, read information from the device about its capabilities, send configuration information to the device, and assign the device a unique USB address. Once this sequence is completed the device begins normal operation and responds only to the new address.

The initial connection procedure just described is a key feature that helps give the USB its plug-and-play capability. The host software is in complete control of the procedure. It is able to sense that a device has been connected, to read information about the device, which is typically stored in a small read-only memory in the device hardware, to send commands that will configure the device by enabling or disabling certain features or capabilities, and finally to assign a unique USB address to the device. The only action required from the user is to plug the device into a hub port and to turn on its power switch.

When a device is powered off, a similar procedure is followed. The corresponding hub reports this fact to the USB system software, which in turn updates its tables. Of course, if the device that has been disconnected is itself a hub, all devices connected through that hub must also be recorded as disconnected. The USB software must maintain a complete picture of the bus topology and the connected devices at all times.

Locations in the device to or from which data transfer can take place, such as status, control, and data registers, are called *endpoints*. They are identified by a 4-bit number. Actually, each 4-bit value identifies a pair of endpoints, one for input and one for output. Thus, a device may have up to 16 input/output pairs of endpoints. A USB pipe, which is a bidirectional data transfer channel, is connected to one such pair. The pipe connected to endpoints number 0 exists all the time, including immediately after a device is powered on or reset. This is the control pipe that the USB software uses in the power-on procedure. As part of that procedure, other pipes using other endpoint pairs may be established, depending on the needs and complexity of the device. The 4-bit endpoint number is part of the addressing information sent by the host, as we will see shortly.

USB Protocols

All information transferred over the USB is organized in packets, where a packet consists of one or more bytes of information. There are many types of packets that perform a variety of control functions. We illustrate the operation of the USB by giving a few examples of the key packet types and show how they are used.

The information transferred on the USB can be divided into two broad categories: control and data. Control packets perform such tasks as addressing a device to initiate data transfer, acknowledging that data have been received correctly, or indicating an error. Data packets carry information that is delivered to a device. For example, input and output data are transferred inside data packets.

A packet consists of one or more fields containing different kinds of information. The first field of any packet is called the packet identifier, PID, which identifies the type of that packet. There are four bits of information in this field, but they are transmitted twice. The first time they are sent with their true values, and the second time with each

(a) Packet identifier field

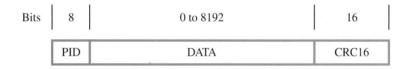

(b) Token packet, IN or OUT

Bits	8	0 to 8192	16
	PID	DATA	CRC16

(c) Data packet

Figure 4.45 USB packet formats.

bit complemented, as shown in Figure 4.45a. This enables the receiving device to verify that the PID byte has been received correctly.

The four PID bits identify one of 16 different packet types. Some control packets, such as ACK (Acknowledge), consist only of the PID byte. Control packets used for controlling data transfer operations are called token packets. They have the format shown in Figure 4.45b. A token packet starts with the PID field, using one of two PID values to distinguish between an IN packet and an OUT packet, which control input and output transfers, respectively. The PID field is followed by the 7-bit address of a device and the 4-bit endpoint number within that device. The packet ends with 5 bits for error checking, using a method called cyclic redundancy check (CRC). The CRC bits are computed based on the contents of the address and endpoint fields. By performing an inverse computation, the receiving device can determine whether the packet has been received correctly.

Data packets, which carry input and output data, have the format shown in Figure 4.45c. The packet identifier field is followed by up to 8192 bits of data, then 16 error-checking bits. Three different PID patterns are used to identify data packets, so that data packets may be numbered 0, 1, or 2. Note that data packets do not carry a

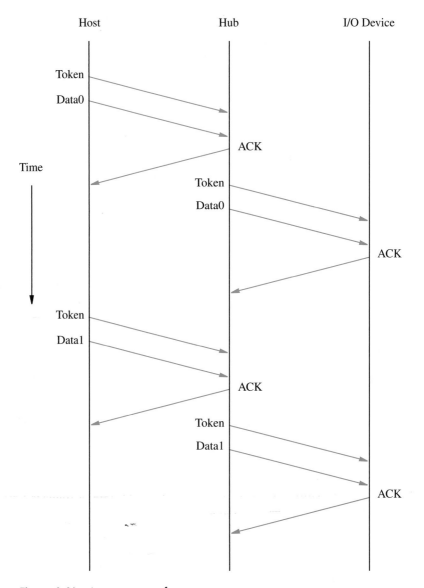

Figure 4.46 An output transfer.

device address or an endpoint number. This information is included in the IN or OUT token packet that initiates the transfer.

Consider an output device connected to a USB hub, which in turn is connected to a host computer. An example of an output operation is shown in Figure 4.46. The host computer sends a token packet of type OUT to the hub, followed by a data packet containing the output data. The PID field of the data packet identifies it as data packet number 0. The hub verifies that the transmission has been error free by checking the error control bits, then sends an acknowledgment packet (ACK) back to the host. The hub forwards the token and data packets downstream. All I/O devices receive this sequence of packets, but only the device that recognizes its address in the token packet accepts the data in the packet that follows. After verifying that transmission has been error free, it sends an ACK packet to the hub.

Successive data packets on a full-speed or low-speed pipe carry the numbers 0 and 1, alternately. This simplifies recovery from transmission errors. If a token, data, or acknowledgment packet is lost as a result of a transmission error, the sender resends the entire sequence. By checking the data packet number in the PID field, the receiver can detect and discard duplicate packets. High-speed data packets are sequentially numbered 0, 1, 2, 0, and so on.

Input operations follow a similar procedure. The host sends a token packet of type IN containing the device address. In effect, this packet is a poll asking the device to send any input data it may have. The device responds by sending a data packet followed by an ACK. If it has no data ready, it responds by sending a negative acknowledgment (NAK) instead.

In earlier discussion, we pointed out that a bus that has a mix of full/low-speed links and high-speed links uses the split-traffic mode of operation in order not to delay messages on high-speed links. In such cases, an IN or an OUT packet intended for a full- or low-speed device is preceded by a special control packet that starts the split-traffic mode.

This discussion should give the reader an idea about the data transfer protocols used on the USB. There are many different ways in which such transactions take place and many protocol rules governing the behavior of the devices involved. A detailed description of these protocols can be found in the USB specification document [3].

Isochronous Traffic on USB

One of the key objectives of the USB is to support the transfer of isochronous data, such as sampled voice, in a simple manner. Devices that generate or receive isochronous data require a time reference to control the sampling process. To provide this reference, transmission over the USB is divided into *frames* of equal length. A frame is 1 ms long for low- and full-speed data. The root hub generates a Start Of Frame control packet (SOF) precisely once every 1 ms to mark the beginning of a new frame.

The arrival of an SOF packet at any device constitutes a regular clock signal that the device can use for its own purposes. To assist devices that may need longer periods of time, the SOF packet carries an 11-bit frame number, as shown in Figure 4.47a. Following each SOF packet, the host carries out input and output transfers for isochronous devices. This means that each device will have an opportunity for an input or output transfer once every 1 ms.

The main requirement for isochronous traffic is consistent timing. An occasional error can be tolerated. Hence, there is no need to retransmit packets that are lost or to send acknowledgments. Figure 4.47b shows the first two transmissions following SOF. A control packet carrying device address 3 is followed by data for that device. This may be input or output data, depending on whether the control packet is an IN or OUT control packet. There is no acknowledgment packet. The next transmission sequence is for device 7.

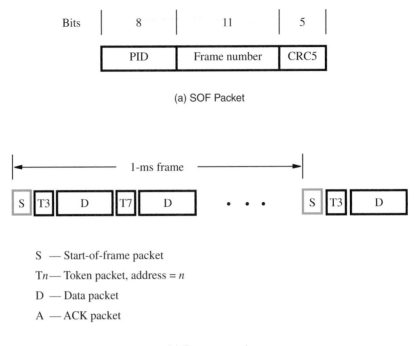

Bits	8	11	5

| PID | Frame number | CRC5 |

(a) SOF Packet

S — Start-of-frame packet
Tn— Token packet, address = n
D — Data packet
A — ACK packet

(b) Frame example

Figure 4.47   USB frames.

As an example, the data packet for device 3 may contain 8 bytes of data. One such packet is sent in each frame, providing a 64-kilobits/s isochronous channel. Such a channel may be used for a voice connection. The transmission of 8 bytes of data requires a 3-byte token packet followed by an 11-byte data packet (including the PID and CRC fields), for a total of 132 bits. A minimum of three more bytes are needed for clock synchronization and to mark the end of a packet sequence. At a speed of 12 megabits/s, this takes about 13 μs. Clearly, there is room in a frame to support several such devices. After serving all isochronous devices on the bus, whatever time is left in a frame is used to service asynchronous devices and exchange control and status information.

Isochronous data are allowed only on full-speed and high-speed links. For high-speed links, the SOF packet is repeated eight times at equal intervals within the 1-ms frame to create eight microframes of 125 μs each.

Electrical Characteristics

The cables used for USB connections consist of four wires. Two are used to carry power, +5 V and Ground. Thus, a hub or an I/O device may be powered directly from the bus, or it may have its own external power connection. The other two wires are used to carry data. Different signaling schemes are used for different speeds of transmission. At low speed, 1s and 0s are transmitted by sending a high voltage state (5 V) on one or the other of the two signal wires. For high-speed links, differential transmission is used.

4.8 CONCLUDING REMARKS

In this chapter, we discussed three basic approaches to I/O transfers. The simplest technique is programmed I/O, in which the processor performs all the necessary control functions under direct control of program instructions. The second approach is based on the use of interrupts; this mechanism makes it possible to interrupt normal execution of programs in order to service higher-priority requests that require more urgent attention. Although all computers have a mechanism for dealing with such situations, the complexity and sophistication of interrupt-handling schemes vary from one computer to another. The third I/O scheme involves direct memory access; the DMA controller transfers data between an I/O device and the main memory without continuous processor intervention. Access to memory is shared between the DMA controller and the processor.

Three popular interconnection standards are described, the PCI, SCSI, and USB. They represent different approaches that meet the needs of various devices and reflect the increasing importance of plug-and-play features that increase user convenience.

PROBLEMS

4.1 The input status bit in an interface circuit is cleared as soon as the input data buffer is read. Why is this important?

4.2 Write a program that displays the contents of 10 bytes of the main memory in hexadecimal format on a video display. Use either the assembler instructions of a processor of your choice or pseudo-instructions. Start at location LOC in the memory, and use two hex characters per byte. The contents of successive bytes should be separated by a space.

4.3 The address bus of a computer has 16 address lines, A_{15-0}. If the address assigned to one device is $7CA4_{16}$ and the address decoder for that device ignores lines A_8 and A_9, what are all the addresses to which this device will respond?

4.4 What is the difference between a subroutine and an interrupt-service routine?

4.5 The discussion in this chapter assumed that interrupts are not acknowledged until the current machine instruction completes execution. Consider the possibility of suspending operation of the processor in the middle of executing an instruction in order to acknowledge an interrupt. Discuss the difficulties that may arise.

4.6 Three devices, A, B, and C, are connected to the bus of a computer. I/O transfers for all three devices use interrupt control. Interrupt nesting for devices A and B is not allowed, but interrupt requests from C may be accepted while either A or B is being serviced. Suggest different ways in which this can be accomplished in each of the following cases:

(*a*) The computer has one interrupt-request line.

(*b*) Two interrupt-request lines, INTR1 and INTR2, are available, with INTR1 having higher priority.

Specify when and how interrupts are enabled and disabled in each case.

4.7   Consider a computer in which several devices are connected to a common interrupt-request line, as in Figure 4.8a. Explain how you would arrange for interrupts from device j to be accepted before the execution of the interrupt-service routine for device i is completed. Comment in particular on the times at which interrupts must be enabled and disabled at various points in the system.

4.8   Consider the daisy chain arrangement in Figure 4.8a. Assume that after a device generates an interrupt request, it turns off that request as soon as it receives the interrupt-acknowledge signal. Is it still necessary to disable interrupts in the processor before entering the interrupt-service routine? Why?

4.9   Successive data blocks of N bytes each are to be read from a character-oriented input device, and program PROG is to perform some computation on each block of data. Write a control program, CONTROL, for the 68000, ARM, or Pentium processors that will perform the following functions.

(*a*) Read data block 1.

(*b*) Activate PROG and point it to the location of block 1 in the main memory.

(*c*) Read block 2 using interrupts while PROG is performing computations on block 1.

(*d*) Start PROG on block 2, and meanwhile start reading block 3, and so on.

Note that CNTRL must maintain correct buffer pointers, keep track of the character count, and correctly transfer control to PROG, whether PROG takes more or less time than block input.

4.10 A computer is required to accept characters from 20 video terminals. The main memory area to be used for storing data for each terminal is pointed to by a pointer PNTRn, where $n = 1$ through 20. Input data must be collected from the terminals while another program PROG is being executed. This may be accomplished in one of two ways:

(*a*) Every T seconds, program PROG calls a polling subroutine POLL. This subroutine checks the status of each of the 20 terminals in sequence and transfers any input characters to the memory. Then it returns to PROG.

(*b*) Whenever a character is ready in any of the interface buffers of the terminals, an interrupt request is generated. This causes the interrupt routine INTERRUPT to be executed. After polling the status registers, INTERRUPT transfers the input character and then returns to PROG.

Write the routines POLL and INTERRUPT using either pseudocode or the assembler language of the processor of your choice. Let the maximum character rate for any terminal be c characters per second, with an average rate equal to rc, where $r \leq 1$. In method (*a*), what is the maximum value of T for which it is still possible to guarantee that no input characters will be lost? What is the equivalent value for method (*b*)? Estimate, on the average, the percentage of time spent in servicing the terminals for methods (*a*) and (*b*), for $c = 100$ characters per second and $r = 0.01, 0.1, 0.5$, and 1. Assume that POLL takes 800 ns to poll all 20 devices and that an interrupt from a device requires 200 ns to process.

4.11 Consider an I/O device that uses the vectored-interrupt capability of the 68000 processor.

(*a*) Describe the sequence of steps that take place when the processor receives an interrupt request, and give the number of bus transfers required during each of these steps. Do not give details of bus signals or the microprogram.

(*b*) When an interrupt request is received, the processor completes execution of the current instruction before accepting the interrupt. Examine the instruction table in Appendix C, and estimate the maximum possible number of memory transfers that can take place during that period.

(*c*) Estimate the number of bus transfers that can occur from the instant a device requests an interrupt until the first instruction of the interrupt-service routine is fetched for execution.

4.12 A logic circuit is needed to implement the priority network shown in Figure 4.8*b*. The network handles three interrupt request lines. When a request is received on line INTR*i*, the network generates an acknowledgment on line INTA*i*. If more than one request is received, only the highest-priority request is acknowledged, where the ordering of priorities is

priority of INTR1 > priority of INTR2 > priority of INTR3

(*a*) Give a truth table for each of the outputs INTA1, INTA2, and INTA3.

(*b*) Give a logic circuit for implementing this priority network.

(*c*) Can your design be easily extended for more interrupt-request lines?

(*d*) By adding inputs DECIDE and RESET, modify your design such that INTA*i* is set to 1 when a pulse is received on the input DECIDE and is reset to 0 when a pulse is received on the input RESET.

4.13 Interrupts and bus arbitration require means for selecting one of several requests based on their priority. Design a circuit that implements a rotating-priority scheme for four input lines, REQ1 through REQ4. Initially, REQ1 has the highest and REQ4 the lowest priority. After some line receives service, it becomes the lowest priority line, and the next line receives highest priority. For example, after REQ2 has been serviced, the priority order, starting with the highest, becomes REQ3, REQ4, REQ1, REQ2. Your circuit should generate four output grant signals, GR1 through GR4, one for each input request line. One of these outputs should be asserted when a pulse is received on a line called DECIDE.

4.14 The 68000 processor has a set of three lines called IPL2–0 that are used to signal interrupt requests. The 3-bit binary number on these lines is interpreted by the processor as representing the highest-priority device requesting an interrupt. Design a priority encoder circuit that accepts interrupt requests from as many as seven devices and generates a 3-bit code representing the request with the highest priority.

4.15 (This problem is suitable for use as a laboratory experiment.) Given a video terminal connected to the computer in your laboratory, complete the following two assignments.

(*a*) Write an I/O routine A that prints letters in alphabetical order. It prints two lines as follows, and then stops:

$$ABC \ldots YZ$$

$$ABC \ldots YZ$$

(*b*) Write an I/O routine B that prints the numeric characters 0 through 9 in increasing order three times. Its output should have the following format:

$$012 \ldots 9012 \ldots 9012 \ldots 9$$

Use program A as the main program and program B as an interrupt-service routine whose execution is initiated by entering any character on the keyboard. Execution of program B can also be interrupted by entering another character on the keyboard. When program B is completed, execution of the most recently interrupted program should be resumed at the point of interruption. Program B should start a new line as appropriate so that the printed output may appear as follows:

$$ABC$$

$$012 \ldots 901$$

$$012 \ldots 9012 \ldots 9012 \ldots 9$$

$$2 \ldots 9012 \ldots 9$$

$$DE \ldots YZ$$

To start a new line, the program needs to send two characters: CR ($0D_{16}$) and LF ($0A_{16}$). Show how you can use the processor priority to either enable or inhibit interrupt nesting.

4.16   (This problem is suitable for use as a laboratory experiment.) In Problem 4.15, when the printing of a sequence is interrupted and later resumed, the sequence continues at the beginning of a new line. It is desired to add cursor movement control functions such that when printing of a sequence is resumed, the characters are printed on a new line, at the same character position where they would have been had the interruption not occurred. Thus, the printed output would appear as follows:

$$ABC$$

$$012 \ldots 901$$

$$012 \ldots 9012 \ldots 9012 \ldots 9$$

$$2 \ldots 9012 \ldots 9$$

$$DE \ldots YZ$$

Rearrange the software you prepared in Problem 4.15 so that a third controller routine, C, is entered when interruption occurs. This routine calls program B to print the number sequence. Then, before returning to the interrupted program, the routine issues cursor movement commands as appropriate.

4.17   Consider the breakpoint scheme described in Section 4.2.5. A software-interrupt instruction replaces a program instruction where the breakpoint is inserted. Before it returns to the original program, the debugging software puts the original program instruction back in its place, thus removing the breakpoint. Explain how the debugger can put the original program instruction in its place, execute it, then install the breakpoint again before any other program instruction is executed.

4.18 The software interrupt instruction, SWI, of the ARM can be used by a program to call the operating system to request some service. The service being requested is specified in the low-order 8 bits of the instruction. Each of the services provided by the operating system is performed by a separate subroutine, and the starting addresses of these routines are stored in a table.

(*a*) Give one or more instructions that the operating system can use to copy the low-order 8 bits of the SWI instruction into a register.

(*b*) Give one or more instructions to call the appropriate service routine.

4.19 The interrupt-request line, which uses the open-collector scheme, carries a signal that is the logical OR of the requests from all the devices connected to it. In a different application, it is required to generate a signal that indicates that all devices connected to the bus are ready. Explain how you can use the open-collector scheme for this purpose.

4.20 In some computers, the processor responds only to the leading edge of the interrupt-request signal on one of its interrupt-request lines. What happens if two independent devices are connected to this line?

4.21 In the arrangement in Figure 4.20, a device becomes the bus master only when it receives a low-to-high transition on its bus grant input. Assume that device 1 requests the bus and receives a grant. While it is still using the bus, device 3 asserts its BR output. Draw a timing diagram showing how device 3 becomes the bus master after device 1 releases the bus.

4.22 Assume that in the bus arbitration arrangement in Figure 4.20, the processor keeps asserting BG1 as long as $\overline{\text{BR}}$ is asserted. When device *i* is requesting the bus, it becomes the bus master only when it receives a low-to-high transition on its BG*i* input.

(*a*) Assume that devices are allowed to assert the BR signal at any time. Give a sequence of events to show that the system can enter a deadlock situation, in which one or more devices are requesting the bus, the bus is free, and no device can become the bus master.

(*b*) Suggest a rule for the devices to observe in order to prevent this deadlock situation from occurring.

4.23 Consider the daisy-chain arrangement shown in Figure P4.1, in which the bus-request signal is fed back directly as the bus grant. Assume that device 3 requests the bus and

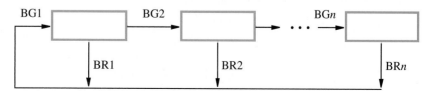

Figure P4.1 A decentralized bus assignment scheme.

begins using it. When device 3 is finished, it deactivates BR3. Assume that the delay from BGi to BG$(i + 1)$ in any device is d. Show that a spurious bus grant pulse will travel downstream from device 3 (spurious because it is not a response to any request). Estimate the width of this pulse.

4.24 Shortly after device 3 in Problem 4.23 releases the bus, devices 1 and 5 request the bus simultaneously. Show that they can both receive a bus grant.

4.25 Consider the bus arbitration scheme shown in Figure 4.20. Assume that a local signal called BUSREQ in the device interface circuit is equal to 1 whenever the device needs to use the bus. Design the part of the interface circuit that has BUSREQ, BGi, and $\overline{\text{BBSY}}$ as inputs and that generates $\overline{\text{BR}}$, BG$(i + 1)$, and $\overline{\text{BBSY}}$ as outputs.

4.26 Consider the arbitration circuit shown in Figure 4.22. Assume that the priority code for a device is stored in a register in the interface circuit. Design a circuit to implement this arbitration scheme. Arbitration begins when $\overline{\text{Start-Arbitration}}$ is asserted. A little later, the arbitration circuit should activate an output called Winner if it wins the arbitration cycle.

4.27 How would the timing diagram in Figure 4.26 be affected if the distance between the processor and the I/O device is increased? How can this increased distance be accommodated in the case of Figure 4.24?

4.28 An industrial plant uses several limit sensors for monitoring temperature, pressure, and other factors. The output of each sensor consists of an ON/OFF switch, and eight such sensors need to be connected to the bus of a small computer. Design an appropriate interface so that the state of all eight switches can be read simultaneously as a single byte at address FE10$_{16}$. Assume the bus is synchronous and that it uses the timing sequence of Figure 4.24.

4.29 Design an appropriate interface for connecting a seven-segment display as an output device on a synchronous bus. (See Figure A.37 in Appendix A for a description of a seven-segment display.)

4.30 Add an interrupt capability to the interface in Figure 4.29. Show how you can introduce an interrupt-enable bit, which can be set or cleared by the processor as bit 6 of the status register of the interface. The interface should assert an interrupt request line, $\overline{\text{INTR}}$, when interrupts are enabled and input data are available to be read by the processor.

4.31 The bus of a processor uses the multiple-cycle scheme described in Section 4.5.1. The speed of a memory unit is such that a read operation follows the timing diagram shown in Figure 4.25. Design an interface circuit to connect this memory unit to the bus.

4.32 Consider a write operation on a bus that uses the multiple-cycle scheme described in Section 4.5.1. Assume that the processor can send both address and data in the first clock cycle of a bus transaction. But the memory requires two clock cycles after that to store the data.

(*a*) Can the bus be used for other transactions during that period?

(*b*) Can we do away with the memory's response in this case? (*Hint:* Examine carefully the case in which the processor attempts another write operation to the same memory module while that module is still busy completing a previous request. Explain how this situation can be handled.)

4.33 Figures 4.24 to 4.26 provide three different approaches to bus design. What happens in each case if the addressed device does not respond due to a malfunction? What problems would this cause and what remedies are possible?

4.34 In the timing diagram in Figure 4.25, the processor maintains the address on the bus until it receives a response from the device. Is this necessary? What additions are needed on the device side if the processor sends an address for one cycle only?

4.35 Consider a synchronous bus that operates according to the timing diagram in Figure 4.24. The address transmitted by the processor appears on the bus after 4 ns. The propagation delay on the bus wires between the processor and different devices connected varies from 1 to 5 ns, address decoding takes 6 ns, and the addressed device takes between 5 and 10 ns to place the requested data on the bus. The input buffer needs 3 ns of setup time. What is the maximum clock speed at which this bus can operate?

4.36 The time required for a complete bus transfer in the case of Figure 4.26 varies depending on the delays involved. Consider a bus having the same parameters as in Problem 4.35. What is the minimum and maximum bus cycle time?

REFERENCES

1. *PCI Local Bus Specifications,* available at www.pcisig.com/developers.

2. *SCSI-3 Architecture Model (SAM),* ANSI Standard X3.270, 1996. This and other SCSI documents are available on the web at www.ansi.org.

3. *Universal Serial Bus Specification,* available at www.usb.org/developers.

THE MEMORY SYSTEM

Programs and the data they operate on are held in the memory of the computer. In this chapter, we discuss how this vital part of the computer operates. By now, the reader appreciates that the execution speed of programs is highly dependent on the speed with which instructions and data can be transferred between the processor and the memory. It is also important to have a large memory to facilitate execution of programs that are large and deal with huge amounts of data.

Ideally, the memory would be fast, large, and inexpensive. Unfortunately, it is impossible to meet all three of these requirements simultaneously. Increased speed and size are achieved at increased cost. To solve this problem, much work has gone into developing clever structures that improve the apparent speed and size of the memory, yet keep the cost reasonable.

First, we describe the most common components and organizations used to implement the memory. Then we examine memory speed and discuss how the apparent speed of the memory can be increased by means of caches. Next, we present the virtual memory concept, which increases the apparent size of the memory. Finally, we discuss the secondary storage devices, which provide much larger storage capability.

5.1 SOME BASIC CONCEPTS

The maximum size of the memory that can be used in any computer is determined by the addressing scheme. For example, a 16-bit computer that generates 16-bit addresses is capable of addressing up to $2^{16} = 64K$ memory locations. Similarly, machines whose instructions generate 32-bit addresses can utilize a memory that contains up to $2^{32} = 4G$ (giga) memory locations, whereas machines with 40-bit addresses can access up to $2^{40} = 1T$ (tera) locations. The number of locations represents the size of the address space of the computer.

Most modern computers are byte addressable. Figure 2.7 shows the possible address assignments for a byte-addressable 32-bit computer. The big-endian arrangement is used in the 68000 processor. The little-endian arrangement is used in Intel processors. The ARM architecture can be configured to use either arrangement. As far as the memory structure is concerned, there is no substantial difference between the two schemes.

The memory is usually designed to store and retrieve data in word-length quantities. In fact, the number of bits actually stored or retrieved in one memory access is the most common definition of the word length of a computer. Consider, for example, a byte-addressable computer whose instructions generate 32-bit addresses. When a 32-bit address is sent from the processor to the memory unit, the high-order 30 bits determine which word will be accessed. If a byte quantity is specified, the low-order 2 bits of the address specify which byte location is involved. In a Read operation, other bytes may be fetched from the memory, but they are ignored by the processor. If the byte operation is a Write, however, the control circuitry of the memory must ensure that the contents of other bytes of the same word are not changed.

Modern implementations of computer memory are rather complex and difficult to understand on first encounter. To simplify our introduction to memory structures, we

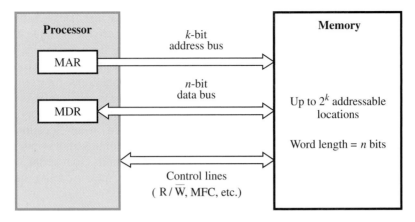

Figure 5.1 Connection of the memory to the processor.

will first present a traditional architecture. Then, in later sections, we will discuss the latest approaches.

From the system standpoint, we can view the memory unit as a black box. Data transfer between the memory and the processor takes place through the use of two processor registers, usually called MAR (memory address register) and MDR (memory data register), as introduced in Section 1.2. If MAR is k bits long and MDR is n bits long, then the memory unit may contain up to 2^k addressable locations. During a memory cycle, n bits of data are transferred between the memory and the processor. This transfer takes place over the processor bus, which has k address lines and n data lines. The bus also includes the control lines Read/$\overline{\text{Write}}$ (R/$\overline{\text{W}}$) and Memory Function Completed (MFC) for coordinating data transfers. Other control lines may be added to indicate the number of bytes to be transferred. The connection between the processor and the memory is shown schematically in Figure 5.1.

The processor reads data from the memory by loading the address of the required memory location into the MAR register and setting the R/$\overline{\text{W}}$ line to 1. The memory responds by placing the data from the addressed location onto the data lines, and confirms this action by asserting the MFC signal. Upon receipt of the MFC signal, the processor loads the data on the data lines into the MDR register.

The processor writes data into a memory location by loading the address of this location into MAR and loading the data into MDR. It indicates that a write operation is involved by setting the R/$\overline{\text{W}}$ line to 0.

If read or write operations involve consecutive address locations in the main memory, then a "block transfer" operation can be performed in which the only address sent to the memory is the one that identifies the first location. We will encounter a need for such block transfers in Section 5.5.

Memory accesses may be synchronized using a clock, or they may be controlled using special signals that control transfers on the bus, using the bus signaling schemes described in Section 4.5.1. Memory read and write operations are controlled as input and output bus transfers, respectively.

A useful measure of the speed of memory units is the time that elapses between the initiation of an operation and the completion of that operation, for example, the time between the Read and the MFC signals. This is referred to as the *memory access time.* Another important measure is the *memory cycle time,* which is the minimum time delay required between the initiation of two successive memory operations, for example, the time between two successive Read operations. The cycle time is usually slightly longer than the access time, depending on the implementation details of the memory unit.

A memory unit is called *random-access memory* (RAM) if any location can be accessed for a Read or Write operation in some fixed amount of time that is independent of the location's address. This distinguishes such memory units from serial, or partly serial, access storage devices such as magnetic disks and tapes. Access time on the latter devices depends on the address or position of the data.

The basic technology for implementing the memory uses semiconductor integrated circuits. The sections that follow present some basic facts about the internal structure and operation of such memories. We then discuss some of the techniques used to increase the effective speed and size of the memory.

The processor of a computer can usually process instructions and data faster than they can be fetched from a reasonably priced memory unit. The memory cycle time, then, is the bottleneck in the system. One way to reduce the memory access time is to use a *cache memory.* This is a small, fast memory that is inserted between the larger, slower main memory and the processor. It holds the currently active segments of a program and their data.

Virtual memory is another important concept related to memory organization. So far, we have assumed that the addresses generated by the processor directly specify physical locations in the memory. This may not always be the case. For reasons that will become apparent later in this chapter, data may be stored in physical memory locations that have addresses different from those specified by the program. The memory control circuitry translates the address specified by the program into an address that can be used to access the physical memory. In such a case, an address generated by the processor is referred to as a *virtual* or *logical address.* The virtual address space is mapped onto the physical memory where data are actually stored. The mapping function is implemented by a special memory control circuit, often called the *memory management unit.* This mapping function can be changed during program execution according to system requirements.

Virtual memory is used to increase the apparent size of the physical memory. Data are addressed in a virtual address space that can be as large as the addressing capability of the processor. But at any given time, only the active portion of this space is mapped onto locations in the physical memory. The remaining virtual addresses are mapped onto the bulk storage devices used, which are usually magnetic disks. As the active portion of the virtual address space changes during program execution, the memory management unit changes the mapping function and transfers data between the disk and the memory. Thus, during every memory cycle, an address-processing mechanism determines whether the addressed information is in the physical memory unit. If it is, then the proper word is accessed and execution proceeds. If it is not, a *page* of words containing the desired word is transferred from the disk to the memory, as explained in Section 5.7.1. This page displaces some page in the memory that is currently inactive.

Because of the time required to move pages between the disk and the memory, there is a speed degradation if pages are moved frequently. By judiciously choosing which page to replace in the memory, however, there may be reasonably long periods when the probability is high that the words accessed by the processor are in the physical memory unit.

This section has briefly introduced several organizational features of memory systems. These features have been developed to help provide a computer system with as large and as fast a memory as can be afforded in relation to the overall cost of the system. We do not expect the reader to grasp all the ideas or their implications now; more detail is given later. We introduce these terms together to establish that they are related; a study of their interrelationships is as important as a detailed study of their individual features.

5.2 SEMICONDUCTOR RAM MEMORIES

Semiconductor memories are available in a wide range of speeds. Their cycle times range from 100 ns to less than 10 ns. When first introduced in the late 1960s, they were much more expensive than the magnetic-core memories they replaced. Because of rapid advances in VLSI (Very Large Scale Integration) technology, the cost of semiconductor memories has dropped dramatically. As a result, they are now used almost exclusively in implementing memories. In this section, we discuss the main characteristics of semiconductor memories. We start by introducing the way that a number of memory cells are organized inside a chip.

5.2.1 INTERNAL ORGANIZATION OF MEMORY CHIPS

Memory cells are usually organized in the form of an array, in which each cell is capable of storing one bit of information. A possible organization is illustrated in Figure 5.2. Each row of cells constitutes a memory word, and all cells of a row are connected to a common line referred to as the *word line,* which is driven by the address decoder on the chip. The cells in each column are connected to a Sense/Write circuit by two *bit lines.* The Sense/Write circuits are connected to the data input/output lines of the chip. During a Read operation, these circuits sense, or read, the information stored in the cells selected by a word line and transmit this information to the output data lines. During a Write operation, the Sense/Write circuits receive input information and store it in the cells of the selected word.

Figure 5.2 is an example of a very small memory chip consisting of 16 words of 8 bits each. This is referred to as a 16×8 organization. The data input and the data output of each Sense/Write circuit are connected to a single bidirectional data line that can be connected to the data bus of a computer. Two control lines, $R/\overline{W}$ and CS, are provided in addition to address and data lines. The $R/\overline{W}$ (Read/$\overline{W}$rite) input specifies the required operation, and the CS (Chip Select) input selects a given chip in a multichip memory system. This will be discussed in Section 5.2.4.

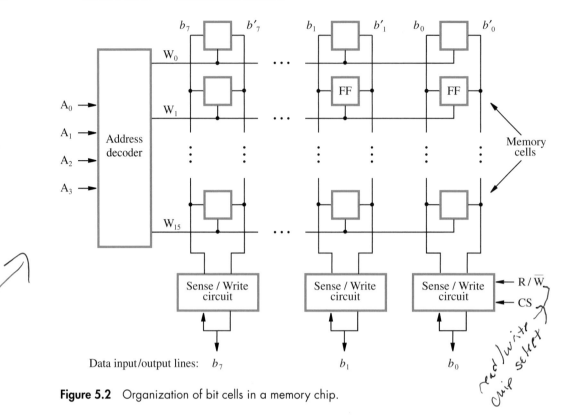

Figure 5.2   Organization of bit cells in a memory chip.

The memory circuit in Figure 5.2 stores 128 bits and requires 14 external connections for address, data, and control lines. Of course, it also needs two lines for power supply and ground connections. Consider now a slightly larger memory circuit, one that has 1K (1024) memory cells. This circuit can be organized as a 128×8 memory, requiring a total of 19 external connections. Alternatively, the same number of cells can be organized into a $1K \times 1$ format. In this case, a 10-bit address is needed, but there is only one data line, resulting in 15 external connections. Figure 5.3 shows such an organization. The required 10-bit address is divided into two groups of 5 bits each to form the row and column addresses for the cell array. A row address selects a row of 32 cells, all of which are accessed in parallel. However, according to the column address, only one of these cells is connected to the external data line by the output multiplexer and input demultiplexer.

Commercially available memory chips contain a much larger number of memory cells than the examples shown in Figures 5.2 and 5.3. We use small examples to make the figures easy to understand. Large chips have essentially the same organization as Figure 5.3 but use a larger memory cell array and have more external connections. For example, a 4M-bit chip may have a $512K \times 8$ organization, in which case 19 address and 8 data input/output pins are needed. Chips with a capacity of hundreds of megabits are now available.

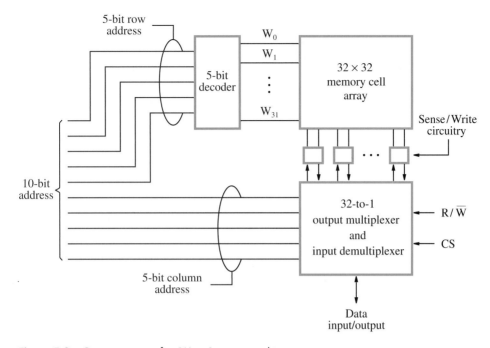

Figure 5.3 Organization of a 1K × 1 memory chip.

5.2.2 STATIC MEMORIES   *faster than dynamic Ram cells*

Memories that consist of circuits capable of retaining their state as long as power is applied are known as *static memories*. Figure 5.4 illustrates how a *static RAM* (SRAM) cell may be implemented. Two inverters are cross-connected to form a latch. The latch is connected to two bit lines by transistors T_1 and T_2. These transistors act as switches that can be opened or closed under control of the word line. When the word line is at ground level, the transistors are turned off and the latch retains its state. For example, let us assume that the cell is in state 1 if the logic value at point X is 1 and at point Y is 0. This state is maintained as long as the signal on the word line is at ground level.

Read Operation

In order to read the state of the SRAM cell, the word line is activated to close switches T_1 and T_2. If the cell is in state 1, the signal on bit line b is high and the signal on bit line b' is low. The opposite is true if the cell is in state 0. Thus, b and b' are complements of each other. Sense/Write circuits at the end of the bit lines monitor the state of b and b' and set the output accordingly.

Write Operation

The state of the cell is set by placing the appropriate value on bit line b and its complement on b', and then activating the word line. This forces the cell into the corresponding state. The required signals on the bit lines are generated by the Sense/Write circuit.

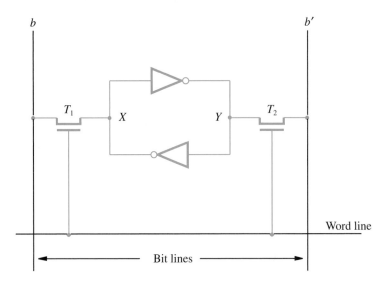

Figure 5.4   A static RAM cell.

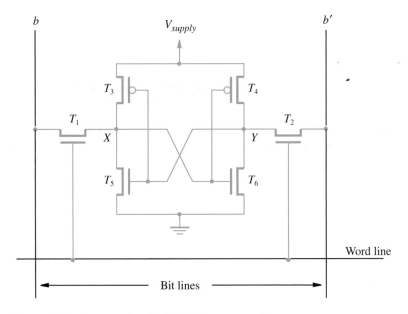

Figure 5.5   An example of a CMOS memory cell.

CMOS Cell

A CMOS realization of the cell in Figure 5.4 is given in Figure 5.5. Transistor pairs (T_3, T_5) and (T_4, T_6) form the inverters in the latch (see Appendix A). The state of the cell is read or written as just explained. For example, in state 1, the voltage at point X is maintained high by having transistors T_3 and T_6 on, while T_4 and T_5 are off. Thus, if T_1 and T_2 are turned on (closed), bit lines b and b' will have high and low signals, respectively.

The power supply voltage, V_{supply}, is 5 V in older CMOS SRAMs or 3.3 V in new low-voltage versions. Note that continuous power is needed for the cell to retain its state. If power is interrupted, the cell's contents will be lost. When power is restored, the latch will settle into a stable state, but it will not necessarily be the same state the cell was in before the interruption. Hence, SRAMs are said to be *volatile* memories because their contents are lost when power is interrupted.

A major advantage of CMOS SRAMs is their very low power consumption because current flows in the cell only when the cell is being accessed. Otherwise, T_1, T_2, and one transistor in each inverter are turned off, ensuring that there is no active path between V_{supply} and ground.

Static RAMs can be accessed very quickly. Access times of just a few nanoseconds are found in commercially available chips. SRAMs are used in applications where speed is of critical concern.

5.2.3 ASYNCHRONOUS DRAMS

Dynamic Ram cell

Static RAMs are fast, but they come at a high cost because their cells require several transistors. Less expensive RAMs can be implemented if simpler cells are used. However, such cells do not retain their state indefinitely; hence, they are called *dynamic RAMs* (DRAMs).

Information is stored in a dynamic memory cell in the form of a charge on a capacitor, and this charge can be maintained for only tens of milliseconds. Since the cell is required to store information for a much longer time, its contents must be periodically refreshed by restoring the capacitor charge to its full value.

An example of a dynamic memory cell that consists of a capacitor, C, and a transistor, T, is shown in Figure 5.6. In order to store information in this cell, transistor

→ Stores electric charge

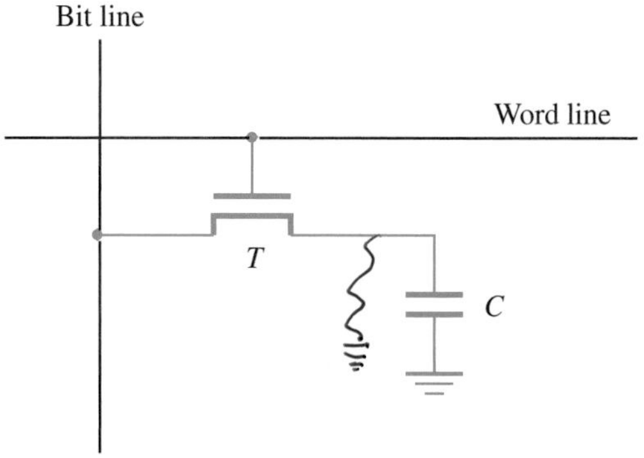

Bit line

Word line

T

C

Figure 5.6 A single-transistor dynamic memory cell.

in reality there is a trickle / leak of charge of C to ground C ca. 64 milli sec. For this reason "volitill".

∴ Refresh memory more frequently than dissipation

T is turned on and an appropriate voltage is applied to the bit line. This causes a known amount of charge to be stored in the capacitor.

After the transistor is turned off, the capacitor begins to discharge. This is caused by the capacitor's own leakage resistance and by the fact that the transistor continues to conduct a tiny amount of current, measured in picoamperes, after it is turned off. Hence, the information stored in the cell can be retrieved correctly only if it is read before the charge on the capacitor drops below some threshold value. During a Read operation, the transistor in a selected cell is turned on. A sense amplifier connected to the bit line detects whether the charge stored on the capacitor is above the threshold value. If so, it drives the bit line to a full voltage that represents logic value 1. This voltage recharges the capacitor to the full charge that corresponds to logic value 1. If the sense amplifier detects that the charge on the capacitor is below the threshold value, it pulls the bit line to ground level, which ensures that the capacitor will have no charge, representing logic value 0. Thus, reading the contents of the cell automatically refreshes its contents. All cells in a selected row are read at the same time, which refreshes the contents of the entire row. The detailed implementation of the sense amplifier circuit is beyond the scope of this book.

A 16-megabit DRAM chip, configured as 2M × 8, is shown in Figure 5.7. The cells are organized in the form of a 4K × 4K array. The 4096 cells in each row are divided into 512 groups of 8, so that a row can store 512 bytes of data. Therefore, 12 address bits are needed to select a row. Another 9 bits are needed to specify a group of 8 bits in the selected row. Thus, a 21-bit address is needed to access a byte in this memory. The high-order 12 bits and the low-order 9 bits of the address constitute

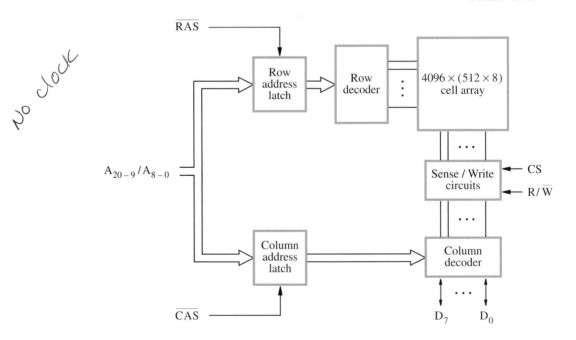

Figure 5.7   Internal organization of a 2M × 8 dynamic memory chip.

the row and column addresses of a byte, respectively. To reduce the number of pins needed for external connections, the row and column addresses are multiplexed on 12 pins. During a Read or a Write operation, the row address is applied first. It is loaded into the row address latch in response to a signal pulse on the Row Address Strobe (RAS) input of the chip. Then a Read operation is initiated, in which all cells on the selected row are read and refreshed. Shortly after the row address is loaded, the column address is applied to the address pins and loaded into the column address latch under control of the Column Address Strobe (CAS) signal. The information in this latch is decoded and the appropriate group of 8 Sense/Write circuits are selected. If the $R/\overline{W}$ control signal indicates a Read operation, the output values of the selected circuits are transferred to the data lines, D_{7-0}. For a Write operation, the information on the D_{7-0} lines is transferred to the selected circuits. This information is then used to overwrite the contents of the selected cells in the corresponding 8 columns. We should note that in commercial DRAM chips, the RAS and CAS control signals are active low so that they cause the latching of addresses when they change from high to low. To indicate this fact, these signals are shown on diagrams as RAS and CAS.

Applying a row address causes all cells on the corresponding row to be read and refreshed during both Read and Write operations. To ensure that the contents of a DRAM are maintained, each row of cells must be accessed periodically. A *refresh circuit* usually performs this function automatically. Many dynamic memory chips incorporate a refresh facility within the chips themselves. In this case, the dynamic nature of these memory chips is almost invisible to the user.

In the DRAM described in this section, the timing of the memory device is controlled asynchronously. A specialized memory controller circuit provides the necessary control signals, RAS and CAS, that govern the timing. The processor must take into account the delay in the response of the memory. Such memories are referred to as *asynchronous DRAMs*.

Because of their high density and low cost, DRAMs are widely used in the memory units of computers. Available chips range in size from 1M to 256M bits, and even larger chips are being developed. To reduce the number of memory chips needed in a given computer, a DRAM chip is organized to read or write a number of bits in parallel, as indicated in Figure 5.7. To provide flexibility in designing memory systems, these chips are manufactured in different organizations. For example, a 64-Mbit chip may be organized as 16M × 4, 8M × 8, or 4M × 16.

Fast Page Mode

When the DRAM in Figure 5.7 is accessed, the contents of all 4096 cells in the selected row are sensed, but only 8 bits are placed on the data lines D_{7-0}. This byte is selected by the column address bits A_{8-0}. A simple modification can make it possible to access the other bytes in the same row without having to reselect the row. A latch can be added at the output of the sense amplifier in each column. The application of a row address will load the latches corresponding to all bits in the selected row. Then, it is only necessary to apply different column addresses to place the different bytes on the data lines.

The most useful arrangement is to transfer the bytes in sequential order, which is achieved by applying a consecutive sequence of column addresses under the control of successive CAS signals. This scheme allows transferring a block of data at a much faster rate than can be achieved for transfers involving random addresses. The block transfer capability is referred to as the *fast page mode* feature. (Popular jargon refers to small groups of bytes as blocks, and larger groups as pages.)

The faster rate attainable in block transfers can be exploited in applications in which memory accesses follow regular patterns, such as in graphics terminals. This feature is also beneficial in general-purpose computers for transferring data blocks between the main memory and a cache, as we will explain in Section 5.5.

5.2.4 SYNCHRONOUS DRAMS

More recent developments in memory technology have resulted in DRAMs whose operation is directly synchronized with a clock signal. Such memories are known as *synchronous DRAMs* (SDRAMs). Figure 5.8 indicates the structure of an SDRAM. The cell array is the same as in asynchronous DRAMs. The address and data connections are buffered by means of registers. We should particularly note that the output of each

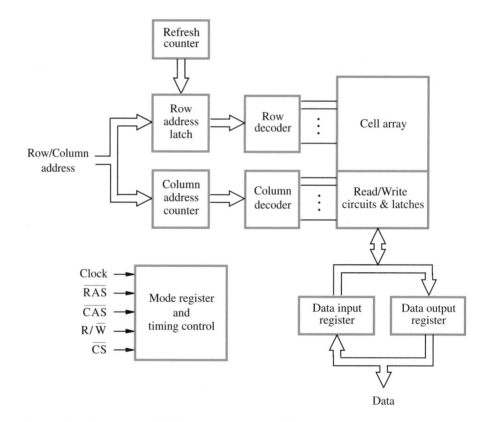

Figure 5.8 Synchronous DRAM.

sense amplifier is connected to a latch. A Read operation causes the contents of all cells in the selected row to be loaded into these latches. But, if an access is made for refreshing purposes only, it will not change the contents of these latches; it will merely refresh the contents of the cells. Data held in the latches that correspond to the selected column(s) are transferred into the data output register, thus becoming available on the data output pins.

SDRAMs have several different modes of operation, which can be selected by writing control information into a *mode* register. For example, burst operations of different lengths can be specified. The burst operations use the block transfer capability described above as the fast page mode feature. In SDRAMs, it is not necessary to provide externally generated pulses on the CAS line to select successive columns. The necessary control signals are provided internally using a column counter and the clock signal. New data can be placed on the data lines in each clock cycle. All actions are triggered by the rising edge of the clock.

Figure 5.9 shows a timing diagram for a typical burst read of length 4. First, the row address is latched under control of the $\overline{RAS}$ signal. The memory typically takes 2 or 3 clock cycles (we use 2 in the figure) to activate the selected row. Then, the column address is latched under control of the $\overline{CAS}$ signal. After a delay of one clock cycle, the first set of data bits is placed on the data lines. The SDRAM automatically increments the column address to access the next three sets of bits in the selected row, which are placed on the data lines in the next 3 clock cycles.

SDRAMs have built-in refresh circuitry. A part of this circuitry is a refresh counter, which provides the addresses of the rows that are selected for refreshing. In a typical SDRAM, each row must be refreshed at least every 64 ms.

Commercial SDRAMs can be used with clock speeds above 100 MHz. These chips are designed to meet the requirements of commercially available processors that are used

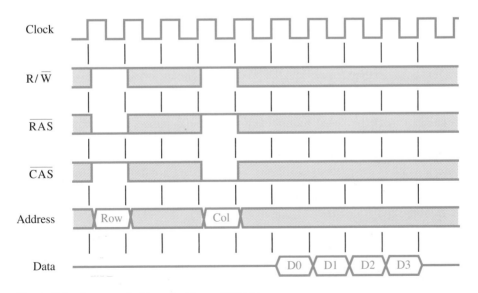

Figure 5.9 Burst read of length 4 in an SDRAM.

in large volume. For example, Intel has defined PC100 and PC133 bus specifications in which the system bus (to which the main memory is connected) is controlled by a 100 or 133 MHz clock, respectively. Therefore, major manufacturers of memory chips produce 100 and 133 MHz SDRAM chips.

Latency and Bandwidth

Transfers between the memory and the processor involve single words of data or small blocks of words (to or from the processor caches which are discussed in Section 5.5). Large blocks, constituting a page of data, are transferred between the memory and the disks, as described in Section 5.7. The speed and efficiency of these transfers have a large impact on the performance of a computer system. A good indication of the performance is given by two parameters: latency and bandwidth.

The term *memory latency* is used to refer to the amount of time it takes to transfer a word of data to or from the memory. In the case of reading or writing a single word of data, the latency provides a complete indication of memory performance. But, in the case of burst operations that transfer a block of data, the time needed to complete the operation depends also on the rate at which successive words can be transferred and on the size of the block. In block transfers, the term latency is used to denote the time it takes to transfer the first word of data. This time is usually substantially longer than the time needed to transfer each subsequent word of a block. For instance, in the timing diagram in Figure 5.9, the access cycle begins with the assertion of the $\overline{RAS}$ signal. The first word of data is transferred five clock cycles later. Thus, the latency is five clock cycles. If the clock rate is 100 MHz, then the latency is 50 ns. The remaining three words are transferred in consecutive clock cycles.

When transferring blocks of data, it is of interest to know how much time is needed to transfer an entire block. Since blocks can be variable in size, it is useful to define a performance measure in terms of the number of bits or bytes that can be transferred in one second. This measure is often referred to as the memory *bandwidth*. The bandwidth of a memory unit (consisting of one or more memory chips) depends on the speed of access to the stored data and on the number of bits that can be accessed in parallel. However, the effective bandwidth in a computer system (involving data transfers between the memory and the processor) is not determined solely by the speed of the memory; it also depends on the transfer capability of the links that connect the memory and the processor, typically the speed of the bus. Memory chips are usually designed to meet the speed requirements of popular buses. The bandwidth clearly depends on the speed of access and transmission along a single wire, as well as on the number of bits that can be transferred in parallel, namely the number of wires. Thus, the bandwidth is the product of the rate at which data are transferred (and accessed) and the width of the data bus.

Double-Data-Rate SDRAM

In the continuous quest for improved performance, a faster version of SDRAM has been developed. The standard SDRAM performs all actions on the rising edge of the clock signal. A similar memory device is available, which accesses the cell array in the same way, but transfers data on both edges of the clock. The latency of these devices is the same as for standard SDRAMs. But, since they transfer data on both edges of the clock, their bandwidth is essentially doubled for long burst transfers. <u>Such devices are</u> known as *double-data-rate SDRAMs* (DDR SDRAMs).

To make it possible to access the data at a high enough rate, the cell array is organized in two banks. Each bank can be accessed separately. Consecutive words of a given block are stored in different banks. Such *interleaving* of words allows simultaneous access to two words that are transferred on successive edges of the clock. We will consider the concept of interleaving in more detail in Section 5.6.1.

DDR SDRAMs and standard SDRAMs are most efficiently used in applications where block transfers are prevalent. This is the case in general-purpose computers in which main memory transfers are primarily to and from processor caches, as we will see in Section 5.5. Block transfers are also done in high-quality video displays.

5.2.5 STRUCTURE OF LARGER MEMORIES

We have discussed the basic organization of memory circuits as they may be implemented on a single chip. Next, we should examine how memory chips may be connected to form a much larger memory.

Static Memory Systems

Consider a memory consisting of 2M (2,097,152) words of 32 bits each. Figure 5.10 shows how we can implement this memory using 512K × 8 static memory chips. Each column in the figure consists of four chips, which implement one byte position. Four of these sets provide the required 2M × 32 memory. Each chip has a control input called Chip Select. When this input is set to 1, it enables the chip to accept data from or to place data on its data lines. The data output for each chip is of the three-state type (see Section A.5.4). Only the selected chip places data on the data output line, while all other outputs are in the high-impedance state. Twenty one address bits are needed to select a 32-bit word in this memory. The high-order 2 bits of the address are decoded to determine which of the four Chip Select control signals should be activated, and the remaining 19 address bits are used to access specific byte locations inside each chip of the selected row. The R/$\overline{\text{W}}$ inputs of all chips are tied together to provide a common Read/$\overline{\text{Write}}$ control (not shown in the figure).

Dynamic Memory Systems

The organization of large dynamic memory systems is essentially the same as the memory shown in Figure 5.10. However, physical implementation is often done more conveniently in the form of *memory modules.*

Modern computers use very large memories; even a small personal computer is likely to have at least 32M bytes of memory. Typical workstations have at least 128M bytes of memory. A large memory leads to better performance because more of the programs and data used in processing can be held in the memory, thus reducing the frequency of accessing the information in secondary storage. However, if a large memory is built by placing DRAM chips directly on the main system printed-circuit board that contains the processor, often referred to as a *motherboard,* it will occupy an unacceptably large amount of space on the board. Also, it is awkward to provide for future

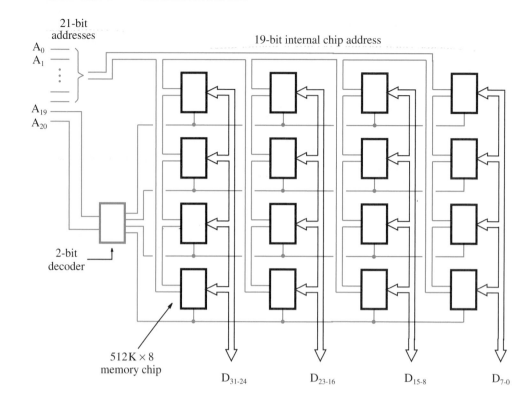

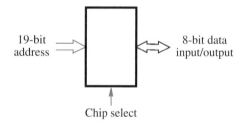

512K × 8 memory chip

Figure 5.10   Organization of a 2M × 32 memory module using 512K × 8 static
memory chips.

expansion of the memory, because space must be allocated and wiring provided for
the maximum expected size. These packaging considerations have led to the development of larger memory units known as *SIMM*s (Single In-line Memory Modules)
and *DIMM*s (Dual In-line Memory Modules). Such a module is an assembly of several
memory chips on a separate small board that plugs vertically into a single socket on the
motherboard. SIMMs and DIMMs of different sizes are designed to use the same size
socket. For example, 4M × 32, 16M × 32, and 32M × 32 bit DIMMs all use the same

100-pin socket. Similarly, 8M × 64, 16M × 64, 32M × 64, and 64M × 72 DIMMs use a 168-pin socket. Such modules occupy a smaller amount of space on a motherboard, and they allow easy expansion by replacement if a larger module uses the same socket as the smaller one.

5.2.6 MEMORY SYSTEM CONSIDERATIONS

The choice of a RAM chip for a given application depends on several factors. Foremost among these factors are the cost, speed, power dissipation, and size of the chip.

Static RAMs are generally used only when very fast operation is the primary requirement. Their cost and size are adversely affected by the complexity of the circuit that realizes the basic cell. They are used mostly in cache memories. Dynamic RAMs are the predominant choice for implementing computer main memories. The high densities achievable in these chips make large memories economically feasible.

Memory Controller

To reduce the number of pins, the dynamic memory chips use multiplexed address inputs. The address is divided into two parts. The high-order address bits, which select a row in the cell array, are provided first and latched into the memory chip under control of the RAS signal. Then, the low-order address bits, which select a column, are provided on the same address pins and latched using the CAS signal.

A typical processor issues all bits of an address at the same time. The required multiplexing of address bits is usually performed by a *memory controller* circuit, which is interposed between the processor and the dynamic memory as shown in Figure 5.11. The controller accepts a complete address and the R/$\overline{\text{W}}$ signal from the processor, under control of a *Request* signal which indicates that a memory access operation is needed. The controller then forwards the row and column portions of the address to the memory and generates the $\overline{\text{RAS}}$ and $\overline{\text{CAS}}$ signals. Thus, the controller provides the RAS-CAS timing, in addition to its address multiplexing function. It also sends the R/$\overline{\text{W}}$ and CS

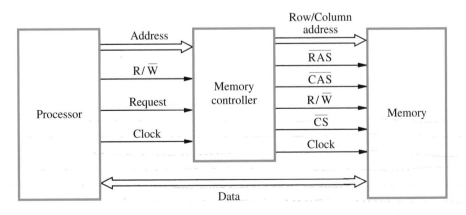

Figure 5.11 Use of a memory controller.

signals to the memory. The CS signal is usually active low, hence it is shown as $\overline{CS}$ in Figure 5.11. Data lines are connected directly between the processor and the memory. Note that the clock signal is needed in SDRAM chips.

When used with DRAM chips, which do not have self-refreshing capability, the memory controller has to provide all the information needed to control the refreshing process. It contains a refresh counter that provides successive row addresses. Its function is to cause the refreshing of all rows to be done within the period specified for a particular device.

Refresh Overhead

All dynamic memories have to be refreshed. In older DRAMs, a typical period for refreshing all rows was 16 ms. In typical SDRAMs, a typical period is 64 ms.

Consider an SDRAM whose cells are arranged in 8K (=8192) rows. Suppose that it takes four clock cycles to access (read) each row. Then, it takes $8192 \times 4 = 32,768$ cycles to refresh all rows. At a clock rate of 133 MHz, the time needed to refresh all rows is $32,768/(133 \times 10^6) = 246 \times 10^{-6}$ seconds. Thus, the refreshing process occupies 0.246 ms in each 64-ms time interval. Therefore, the refresh overhead is $0.246/64 = 0.0038$, which is less than 0.4 percent of the total time available for accessing the memory.

5.2.7 RAMBUS MEMORY

The performance of a dynamic memory is characterized by its latency and bandwidth. Since all dynamic memory chips use similar organizations for their cell arrays, their latencies tend to be similar if the chips are produced using the same manufacturing process. On the other hand, the effective bandwidth of a memory system depends not only on the structure of the memory chips, but also on the nature of the connecting path to the processor. DDR SDRAMs and standard SDRAMs are connected to the processor bus. Thus, the speed of transfers is not just a function of the speed of the memory device — it also depends on the speed of the bus. A bus clocked at 133 MHz allows at most one transfer every 7.5 ns, or two transfers if both edges of the clock are used. The only way to increase the amount of data that can be transferred on a speed-limited bus is to increase the width of the bus by providing more data lines, thus widening the bus.

A very wide bus is expensive and requires a lot of space on a motherboard. An alternative approach is to implement a narrow bus that is much faster. This approach was used by Rambus Inc. to develop a proprietary design known as *Rambus*. The key feature of Rambus technology is a fast signaling method used to transfer information between chips. Instead of using signals that have voltage levels of either 0 or V_{supply} to represent the logic values, the signals consist of much smaller voltage swings around a reference voltage, V_{ref}. The reference voltage is about 2 V, and the two logic values are represented by 0.3 V swings above and below V_{ref}. This type of signaling is generally known as *differential signaling*. Small voltage swings make it possible to have short transition times, which allows for a high speed of transmission.

Differential signaling and high transmission rates require special techniques for the design of wire connections that serve as communication links. These requirements make it difficult to make the bus wide. It is also necessary to design special circuit interfaces to deal with the differential signals. Rambus provides a complete specification for the design of such communication links, called the *Rambus channel*. Present designs of Rambus allow for a clock frequency of 400 MHz. Moreover, data are transmitted on both edges of the clock, so that the effective data transfer rate is 800 MHz.

Rambus requires specially designed memory chips. These chips use cell arrays based on the standard DRAM technology. Multiple banks of cell arrays are used to access more than one word at a time. Circuitry needed to interface to the Rambus channel is included on the chip. Such chips are known as *Rambus DRAMs* (RDRAMs).

The original specification of Rambus provided for a channel consisting of 9 data lines and a number of control and power supply lines. Eight of the data lines are intended for transferring a byte of data. The ninth data line can be used for purposes such as parity checking. Subsequent specifications allow for additional channels. A two-channel Rambus, also known as *Direct RDRAM,* has 18 data lines intended to transfer two bytes of data at a time. There are no separate address lines.

Communication between the processor, or some other device that can serve as a *master,* and RDRAM modules, which serve as *slaves,* is carried out by means of *packets* transmitted on the data lines. There are three types of packets: request, acknowledge, and data. A request packet issued by the master indicates the type of operation that is to be performed. It contains the address of the desired memory location and includes an 8-bit count that specifies the number of bytes involved in the transfer. The operation types include memory reads and writes, as well as reading and writing of various control registers in the RDRAM chips. When the master issues a request packet, the addressed slave responds by returning a positive acknowledgement packet if it can immediately satisfy the request. Otherwise, the slave indicates that it is "busy" by returning a negative acknowledgement packet, in which case the master will try again.

The number of bits in a request packet exceeds the number of data lines, which means that several clock cycles are needed to transmit the entire packet. Using a narrow communication link is compensated by the very high rate of transmission.

RDRAM chips can be assembled into larger modules, similar to SIMMs and DIMMs. One such module, called RIMM, can hold up to 16 RDRAMs.

Rambus technology competes directly with the DDR SDRAM technology. Each has certain advantages and disadvantages. A nontechnical consideration is that the specification of DDR SDRAM is an open standard, while RDRAM is a proprietary design of Rambus Inc. for which the manufacturers of chips have to pay a royalty. Finally, we should note that in the memory market, assuming that the performance is adequate, the decisive factor is often the price of components.

5.3   READ-ONLY MEMORIES

Both SRAM and DRAM chips are volatile, which means that they lose the stored information if power is turned off. There are many applications that need memory devices which retain the stored information if power is turned off. For example, in a typical computer a hard disk drive is used to store a large amount of information, including the operating system software. When a computer is turned on, the operating system software has to be loaded from the disk into the memory. This requires execution of a program that "boots" the operating system. Since the boot program is quite large, most of it is stored on the disk. The processor must execute some instructions that load the boot program into the memory. If the entire memory consisted of only volatile memory chips, the processor would have no means of accessing these instructions. A practical solution is to provide a small amount of nonvolatile memory that holds the instructions whose execution results in loading the boot program from the disk.

Nonvolatile memory is used extensively in embedded systems, which are presented in Chapter 9. Such systems typically do not use disk storage devices. Their programs are stored in nonvolatile semiconductor memory devices.

Different types of nonvolatile memory have been developed. Generally, the contents of such memory can be read as if they were SRAM or DRAM memories. But, a special writing process is needed to place the information into this memory. Since its normal operation involves only reading of stored data, a memory of this type is called *read-only memory* (ROM).

5.3.1 ROM

Figure 5.12 shows a possible configuration for a ROM cell. A logic value 0 is stored in the cell if the transistor is connected to ground at point P; otherwise, a 1 is stored. The bit line is connected through a resistor to the power supply. To read the state of the cell, the word line is activated. Thus, the transistor switch is closed and the voltage on the bit line drops to near zero if there is a connection between the transistor and ground. If there is no connection to ground, the bit line remains at the high voltage, indicating a 1. A sense circuit at the end of the bit line generates the proper output value. Data are written into a ROM when it is manufactured.

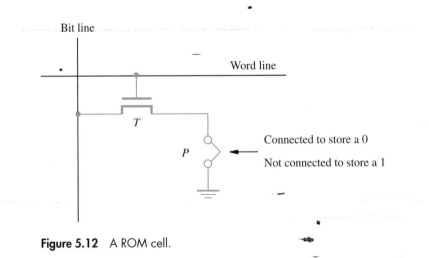

Figure 5.12   A ROM cell.

5.3.2 PROM

Some ROM designs allow the data to be loaded by the user, thus providing a *programmable ROM* (PROM). Programmability is achieved by inserting a fuse at point *P* in Figure 5.12. Before it is programmed, the memory contains all 0s. The user can insert 1s at the required locations by burning out the fuses at these locations using high-current pulses. Of course, this process is irreversible.

PROMs provide flexibility and convenience not available with ROMs. The latter are economically attractive for storing fixed programs and data when high volumes of ROMs are produced. However, the cost of preparing the masks needed for storing a particular information pattern in ROMs makes them very expensive when only a small number are required. In this case, PROMs provide a faster and considerably less expensive approach because they can be programmed directly by the user.

5.3.3 EPROM

Another type of ROM chip allows the stored data to be erased and new data to be loaded. Such an erasable, reprogrammable ROM is usually called an *EPROM*. It provides considerable flexibility during the development phase of digital systems. Since EPROMs are capable of retaining stored information for a long time, they can be used in place of ROMs while software is being developed. In this way, memory changes and updates can be easily made.

An EPROM cell has a structure similar to the ROM cell in Figure 5.12. In an EPROM cell, however, the connection to ground is always made at point *P* and a special transistor is used, which has the ability to function either as a normal transistor or as a disabled transistor that is always turned off. This transistor can be programmed to behave as a permanently open switch, by injecting charge into it that becomes trapped inside. Thus, an EPROM cell can be used to construct a memory in the same way as the previously discussed ROM cell.

The important advantage of EPROM chips is that their contents can be erased and reprogrammed. Erasure requires dissipating the charges trapped in the transistors of memory cells; this can be done by exposing the chip to ultraviolet light. For this reason, EPROM chips are mounted in packages that have transparent windows.

5.3.4 EEPROM

A significant disadvantage of EPROMs is that a chip must be physically removed from the circuit for reprogramming and that its entire contents are erased by the ultraviolet light. It is possible to implement another version of erasable PROMs that can be both programmed and erased electrically. Such chips, called EEPROMs, do not have to be removed for erasure. Moreover, it is possible to erase the cell contents selectively. The only disadvantage of EEPROMs is that different voltages are needed for erasing, writing, and reading the stored data.

5.3.5 FLASH MEMORY

An approach similar to EEPROM technology has more recently given rise to *flash memory* devices. A flash cell is based on a single transistor controlled by trapped charge, just like an EEPROM cell. While similar in some respects, there are also substantial differences between flash and EEPROM devices. In EEPROM it is possible to read and write the contents of a single cell. In a flash device it is possible to read the contents of a single cell, but it is only possible to write an entire block of cells. Prior to writing, the previous contents of the block are erased. Flash devices have greater density, which leads to higher capacity and a lower cost per bit. They require a single power supply voltage, and consume less power in their operation.

The low power consumption of flash memory makes it attractive for use in portable equipment that is battery driven. Typical applications include hand-held computers, cell phones, digital cameras, and MP3 music players. In hand-held computers and cell phones, flash memory holds the software needed to operate the equipment, thus obviating the need for a disk drive. In digital cameras, flash memory is used to store picture image data. In MP3 players, flash memory stores the data that represent sound. Cell phones, digital cameras, and MP3 players are good examples of embedded systems, which will be discussed in detail in Chapter 9.

Single flash chips do not provide sufficient storage capacity for the applications mentioned above. Larger memory modules consisting of a number of chips are needed. There are two popular choices for the implementation of such modules: flash cards and flash drives.

Flash Cards

One way of constructing a larger module is to mount flash chips on a small card. Such flash cards have a standard interface that makes them usable in a variety of products. A card is simply plugged into a conveniently accessible slot. Flash cards come in a variety of memory sizes. Typical sizes are 8, 32, and 64 Mbytes. A minute of music can be stored in about 1 Mbyte of memory, using the MP3 encoding format. Hence, a 64-MB flash card can store an hour of music.

Flash Drives

Larger flash memory modules have been developed to replace hard disk drives. These flash drives are designed to fully emulate the hard disks, to the point that they can be fitted into standard disk drive bays. However, the storage capacity of flash drives is significantly lower. Currently, the capacity of flash drives is less than one gigabyte. In contrast, hard disks can store many gigabytes.

The fact that flash drives are solid state electronic devices that have no movable parts provides some important advantages. They have shorter seek and access times, which results in faster response. (Seek and access times are discussed in the context of disks in Section 5.9.) They have lower power consumption, which makes them attractive for battery driven applications, and they are also insensitive to vibration.

The disadvantages of flash drives vis-a-vis hard disk drives are their smaller capacity and higher cost per bit. Disks provide an extremely low cost per bit. Another disadvantage is that the flash memory will deteriorate after it has been written a number of times. Fortunately, this number is high, typically at least one million times.

5.4 SPEED, SIZE, AND COST

We have already stated that an ideal memory would be fast, large, and inexpensive. From the discussion in Section 5.2, it is clear that a very fast memory can be implemented if SRAM chips are used. But these chips are expensive because their basic cells have six transistors, which precludes packing a very large number of cells onto a single chip. Thus, for cost reasons, it is impractical to build a large memory using SRAM chips. The alternative is to use Dynamic RAM chips, which have much simpler basic cells and thus are much less expensive. But such memories are significantly slower.

Although dynamic memory units in the range of hundreds of megabytes can be implemented at a reasonable cost, the affordable size is still small compared to the demands of large programs with voluminous data. A solution is provided by using secondary storage, mainly magnetic disks, to implement large memory spaces. Very large disks are available at a reasonable price, and they are used extensively in computer systems. However, they are much slower than the semiconductor memory units. So we conclude the following: A huge amount of cost-effective storage can be provided by magnetic disks. A large, yet affordable, main memory can be built with dynamic RAM technology. This leaves SRAMs to be used in smaller units where speed is of the essence, such as in cache memories.

All of these different types of memory units are employed effectively in a computer. The entire computer memory can be viewed as the hierarchy depicted in Figure 5.13. The fastest access is to data held in processor registers. Therefore, if we consider the registers to be part of the memory hierarchy, then the processor registers are at the top in terms of the speed of access. Of course, the registers provide only a minuscule portion of the required memory.

At the next level of the hierarchy is a relatively small amount of memory that can be implemented directly on the processor chip. This memory, called a *processor cache*, holds copies of instructions and data stored in a much larger memory that is provided externally. The cache memory concept was introduced in Figure 1.6 and is examined in detail in Section 5.5. There are often two levels of caches. A primary cache is always located on the processor chip. This cache is small because it competes for space on the processor chip, which must implement many other functions. The primary cache is referred to as *level 1* (L1) cache. A larger, secondary cache is placed between the primary cache and the rest of the memory. It is referred to as *level 2* (L2) cache. It is usually implemented using SRAM chips.

Including a primary cache on the processor chip and using a larger, off-chip, secondary cache is currently the most common way of designing computers. However, other arrangements can be found in practice. It is possible not to have a cache on the processor chip at all. Also, it is possible to have both L1 and L2 caches on the processor chip.

The next level in the hierarchy is called the *main memory*. This rather large memory is implemented using dynamic memory components, typically in the form of SIMMs,

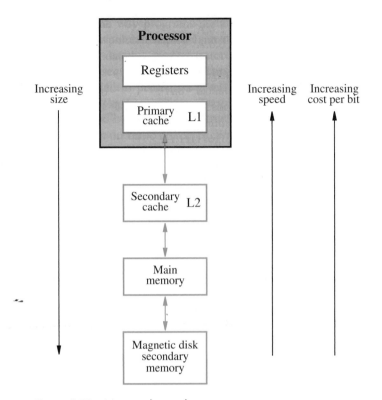

Figure 5.13   Memory hierarchy.

DIMMs, or RIMMs. The main memory is much larger but significantly slower than the cache memory. In a typical computer, the access time for the main memory is about ten times longer than the access time for the L1 cache.

   Disk devices provide a huge amount of inexpensive storage. They are very slow compared to the semiconductor devices used to implement the main memory. We will discuss disk technology in Section 5.9.

   During program execution, the speed of memory access is of utmost importance. The key to managing the operation of the hierarchical memory system in Figure 5.13 is to bring the instructions and data that will be used in the near future as close to the processor as possible. This can be done by using the mechanisms presented in the sections that follow. We begin with a detailed discussion of cache memories.

5.5   CACHE MEMORIES

The speed of the main memory is very low in comparison with the speed of modern processors. For good performance, the processor cannot spend much of its time waiting to access instructions and data in main memory. Hence, it is important to devise a scheme that reduces the time needed to access the necessary information. Since the speed of the main memory unit is limited by electronic and packaging constraints, the solution must be sought in a different architectural arrangement. An efficient solution is to use a fast *cache memory* which essentially makes the main memory appear to the processor to be faster than it really is.

The effectiveness of the cache mechanism is based on a property of computer programs called locality of reference. Analysis of programs shows that most of their execution time is spent on routines in which many instructions are executed repeatedly. These instructions may constitute a simple loop, nested loops, or a few procedures that repeatedly call each other. The actual detailed pattern of instruction sequencing is not important — the point is that many instructions in localized areas of the program are executed repeatedly during some time period, and the remainder of the program is accessed relatively infrequently. This is referred to as *locality of reference*. It manifests itself in two ways: temporal and spatial. The first means that a recently executed instruction is likely to be executed again very soon. The spatial aspect means that instructions in close proximity to a recently executed instruction (with respect to the instructions' addresses) are also likely to be executed soon.

If the active segments of a program can be placed in a fast cache memory, then the total execution time can be reduced significantly. Conceptually, operation of a cache memory is very simple. The memory control circuitry is designed to take advantage of the property of locality of reference. The temporal aspect of the locality of reference suggests that whenever an information item (instruction or data) is first needed, this item should be brought into the cache where it will hopefully remain until it is needed again. The spatial aspect suggests that instead of fetching just one item from the main memory to the cache, it is useful to fetch several items that reside at adjacent addresses as well. We will use the term *block* to refer to a set of contiguous address locations of some size. Another term that is often used to refer to a cache block is *cache line*.

Consider the simple arrangement in Figure 5.14. When a Read request is received from the processor, the contents of a block of memory words containing the location specified are transferred into the cache one word at a time. Subsequently, when the program references any of the locations in this block, the desired contents are read directly from the cache. Usually, the cache memory can store a reasonable number of blocks at any given time, but this number is small compared to the total number of

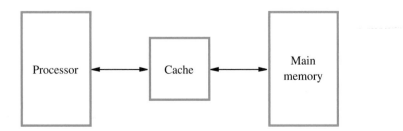

Figure 5.14 Use of a cache memory.

blocks in the main memory. The correspondence between the main memory blocks and those in the cache is specified by a mapping function. When the cache is full and a memory word (instruction or data) that is not in the cache is referenced, the cache control hardware must decide which block should be removed to create space for the new block that contains the referenced word. The collection of rules for making this decision constitutes the *replacement algorithm*.

The processor does not need to know explicitly about the existence of the cache. It simply issues Read and Write requests using addresses that refer to locations in the memory. The cache control circuitry determines whether the requested word currently exists in the cache. If it does, the Read or Write operation is performed on the appropriate cache location. In this case, a *read* or *write hit* is said to have occurred. In a Read operation, the main memory is not involved. For a Write operation, the system can proceed in two ways. In the first technique, called the *write-through* protocol, the cache location and the main memory location are updated simultaneously. The second technique is to update only the cache location and to mark it as updated with an associated flag bit, often called the *dirty* or *modified* bit. The main memory location of the word is updated later, when the block containing this marked word is to be removed from the cache to make room for a new block. This technique is known as the *write-back*, or *copy-back*, protocol. The write-through protocol is simpler, but it results in unnecessary Write operations in the main memory when a given cache word is updated several times during its cache residency. Note that the write-back protocol may also result in unnecessary Write operations because when a cache block is written back to the memory all words of the block are written back, even if only a single word has been changed while the block was in the cache.

When the addressed word in a Read operation is not in the cache, a *read miss* occurs. The block of words that contains the requested word is copied from the main memory into the cache. After the entire block is loaded into the cache, the particular word requested is forwarded to the processor. Alternatively, this word may be sent to the processor as soon as it is read from the main memory. The latter approach, which is called *load-through*, or *early restart*, reduces the processor's waiting period somewhat, but at the expense of more complex circuitry.

During a Write operation, if the addressed word is not in the cache, a *write miss* occurs. Then, if the write-through protocol is used, the information is written directly into the main memory. In the case of the write-back protocol, the block containing the addressed word is first brought into the cache, and then the desired word in the cache is overwritten with the new information.

5.5.1 MAPPING FUNCTIONS

To discuss possible methods for specifying where memory blocks are placed in the cache, we use a specific small example. Consider a cache consisting of 128 blocks of 16 words each, for a total of 2048 (2K) words, and assume that the main memory is addressable by a 16-bit address. The main memory has 64K words, which we will view as 4K blocks of 16 words each. For simplicity, we will assume that consecutive addresses refer to consecutive words.

Direct Mapping

The simplest way to determine cache locations in which to store memory blocks is the *direct-mapping* technique. In this technique, block *j* of the main memory maps onto block *j* modulo 128 of the cache, as depicted in Figure 5.15. Thus, whenever one of the main memory blocks 0, 128, 256, . . . is loaded in the cache, it is stored in cache block 0. Blocks 1, 129, 257, . . . are stored in cache block 1, and so on. Since more than one memory block is mapped onto a given cache block position, contention may arise for that position even when the cache is not full. For example, instructions of a

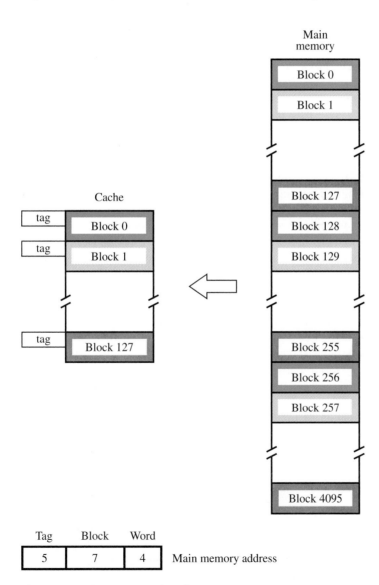

Figure 5.15   Direct-mapped cache.

program may start in block 1 and continue in block 129, possibly after a branch. As this program is executed, both of these blocks must be transferred to the block-1 position in the cache. Contention is resolved by allowing the new block to overwrite the currently resident block. In this case, the replacement algorithm is trivial.

Placement of a block in the cache is determined from the memory address. The memory address can be divided into three fields, as shown in Figure 5.15. The low-order 4 bits select one of 16 words in a block. When a new block enters the cache, the 7-bit cache block field determines the cache position in which this block must be stored. The high-order 5 bits of the memory address of the block are stored in 5 *tag* bits associated with its location in the cache. They identify which of the 32 blocks that are mapped into this cache position are currently resident in the cache. As execution proceeds, the 7-bit cache block field of each address generated by the processor points to a particular block location in the cache. The high-order 5 bits of the address are compared with the tag bits associated with that cache location. If they match, then the desired word is in that block of the cache. If there is no match, then the block containing the required word must first be read from the main memory and loaded into the cache. The direct-mapping technique is easy to implement, but it is not very flexible.

Associative Mapping

Figure 5.16 shows a much more flexible mapping method, in which a main memory block can be placed into any cache block position. In this case, 12 tag bits are required to identify a memory block when it is resident in the cache. The tag bits of an address received from the processor are compared to the tag bits of each block of the cache to see if the desired block is present. This is called the *associative-mapping* technique. It gives complete freedom in choosing the cache location in which to place the memory block. Thus, the space in the cache can be used more efficiently. A new block that has to be brought into the cache has to replace (eject) an existing block only if the cache is full. In this case, we need an algorithm to select the block to be replaced. Many replacement algorithms are possible, as we discuss in Section 5.5.2. The cost of an associative cache is higher than the cost of a direct-mapped cache because of the need to search all 128 tag patterns to determine whether a given block is in the cache. A search of this kind is called an *associative search*. For performance reasons, the tags must be searched in parallel.

Set-Associative Mapping

A combination of the direct- and associative-mapping techniques can be used. Blocks of the cache are grouped into sets, and the mapping allows a block of the main memory to reside in any block of a specific set. Hence, the contention problem of the direct method is eased by having a few choices for block placement. At the same time, the hardware cost is reduced by decreasing the size of the associative search. An example of this *set-associative-mapping* technique is shown in Figure 5.17 for a cache with two blocks per set. In this case, memory blocks 0, 64, 128, ..., 4032 map into cache set 0, and they can occupy either of the two block positions within this set. Having 64 sets means that the 6-bit set field of the address determines which set of the cache might contain the desired block. The tag field of the address must then be associatively compared to the tags of the two blocks of the set to check if the desired block is present. This two-way associative search is simple to implement.

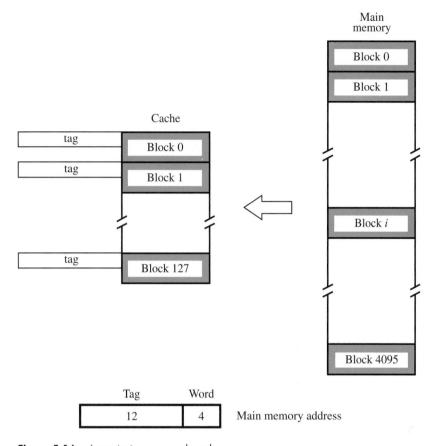

Main
memory

Block 0

Block 1

Block *i*

Block 4095

Cache

tag

Block 0

tag

Block 1

tag

Block 127

Tag	Word
12	4

Main memory address

Figure 5.16   Associative-mapped cache.

The number of blocks per set is a parameter that can be selected to suit the requirements of a particular computer. For the main memory and cache sizes in Figure 5.17, four blocks per set can be accommodated by a 5-bit set field, eight blocks per set by a 4-bit set field, and so on. The extreme condition of 128 blocks per set requires no set bits and corresponds to the fully associative technique, with 12 tag bits. The other extreme of one block per set is the direct-mapping method. A cache that has k blocks per set is referred to as a k-way set-associative cache.

One more control bit, called the *valid bit,* must be provided for each block. This bit indicates whether the block contains valid data. It should not be confused with the modified, or dirty, bit mentioned earlier. The dirty bit, which indicates whether the block has been modified during its cache residency, is needed only in systems that do not use the write-through method. The valid bits are all set to 0 when power is initially applied to the system or when the main memory is loaded with new programs and data from the disk. Transfers from the disk to the main memory are carried out by a DMA mechanism. Normally, they bypass the cache for both cost and performance reasons. The valid bit of a particular cache block is set to 1 the first time this block is loaded

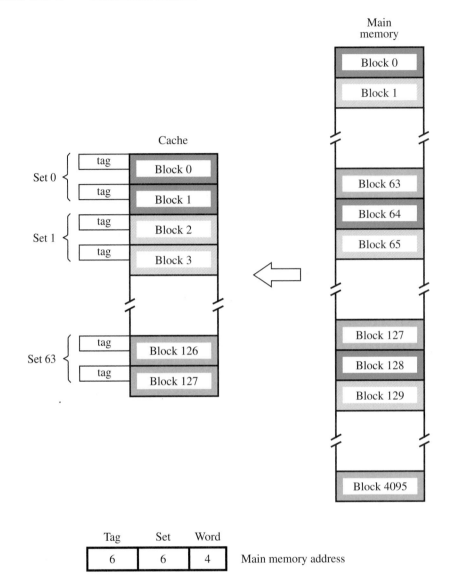

Figure 5.17   Set-associative-mapped cache with two blocks per set.

from the main memory. Whenever a main memory block is updated by a source that bypasses the cache, a check is made to determine whether the block being loaded is currently in the cache. If it is, its valid bit is cleared to 0. This ensures that *stale* data will not exist in the cache.

A similar difficulty arises when a DMA transfer is made from the main memory to the disk, and the cache uses the write-back protocol. In this case, the data in the memory might not reflect the changes that may have been made in the cached copy.

One solution to this problem is to *flush* the cache by forcing the dirty data to be written back to the memory before the DMA transfer takes place. The operating system can do this easily, and it does not affect performance greatly, because such disk transfers do not occur often. This need to ensure that two different entities (the processor and DMA subsystems in this case) use the same copies of data is referred to as a *cache-coherence* problem.

5.5.2 REPLACEMENT ALGORITHMS

In a direct-mapped cache, the position of each block is predetermined; hence, no replacement strategy exists. In associative and set-associative caches there exists some flexibility. When a new block is to be brought into the cache and all the positions that it may occupy are full, the cache controller must decide which of the old blocks to overwrite. This is an important issue because the decision can be a strong determining factor in system performance. In general, the objective is to keep blocks in the cache that are likely to be referenced in the near future. However, it is not easy to determine which blocks are about to be referenced. The property of locality of reference in programs gives a clue to a reasonable strategy. Because programs usually stay in localized areas for reasonable periods of time, there is a high probability that the blocks that have been referenced recently will be referenced again soon. Therefore, when a block is to be overwritten, it is sensible to overwrite the one that has gone the longest time without being referenced. This block is called the *least recently used* (LRU) block, and the technique is called the *LRU replacement algorithm*.

To use the LRU algorithm, the cache controller must track references to all blocks as computation proceeds. Suppose it is required to track the LRU block of a four-block set in a set-associative cache. A 2-bit counter can be used for each block. When a hit occurs, the counter of the block that is referenced is set to 0. Counters with values originally lower than the referenced one are incremented by one, and all others remain unchanged. When a *miss* occurs and the set is not full, the counter associated with the new block loaded from the main memory is set to 0, and the values of all other counters are increased by one. When a miss occurs and the set is full, the block with the counter value 3 is removed, the new block is put in its place, and its counter is set to 0. The other three block counters are incremented by one. It can be easily verified that the counter values of occupied blocks are always distinct.

The LRU algorithm has been used extensively. Although it performs well for many access patterns, it can lead to poor performance in some cases. For example, it produces disappointing results when accesses are made to sequential elements of an array that is slightly too large to fit into the cache (see Section 5.5.3 and Problem 5.12). Performance of the LRU algorithm can be improved by introducing a small amount of randomness in deciding which block to replace.

Several other replacement algorithms are also used in practice. An intuitively reasonable rule would be to remove the "oldest" block from a full set when a new block must be brought in. However, because this algorithm does not take into account the recent pattern of access to blocks in the cache, it is generally not as effective as the LRU algorithm in choosing the best blocks to remove. The simplest algorithm is to randomly choose the block to be overwritten. Interestingly enough, this simple algorithm has been found to be quite effective in practice.

5.5.3 EXAMPLE OF MAPPING TECHNIQUES

We now consider a detailed example to illustrate the effects of different cache mapping techniques. Assume that a processor has separate instruction and data caches. To keep the example simple, assume the data cache has space for only eight blocks of data. Also assume that each block consists of only one 16-bit word of data and the memory is word-addressable with 16-bit addresses. (These parameters are not realistic for actual computers, but they allow us to illustrate mapping techniques clearly.) Finally, assume the LRU replacement algorithm is used for block replacement in the cache.

Let us examine changes in the data cache entries caused by running the following application: A 4 × 10 array of numbers, each occupying one word, is stored in main memory locations 7A00 through 7A27 (hex). The elements of this array, A, are stored in column order, as shown in Figure 5.18. The figure also indicates how tags for different cache mapping techniques are derived from the memory address. Note that no bits are needed to identify a word within a block, as was done in Figures 5.15 through 5.17, because we have assumed that each block contains only one word. The application normalizes the elements of the first row of A with respect to the average value of the elements in the row. Hence, we need to compute the average of the elements in the row

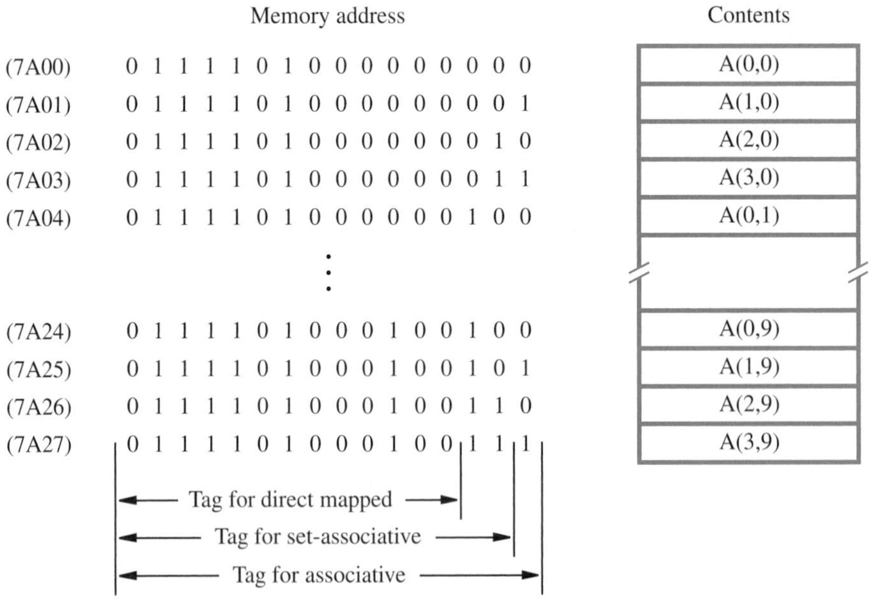

Figure 5.18 An array stored in the main memory.

```
SUM := 0
for j:= 0 to 9 do
        SUM := SUM + A(0,j)
end
AVE := SUM / 10
for i:= 9 downto 0 do
        A(0,i) := A(0,i) / AVE
end
```

Figure 5.19 Task for example in Section 5.5.3.

Block position	Contents of data cache after pass:								
	$j = 1$	$j = 3$	$j = 5$	$j = 7$	$j = 9$	$i = 6$	$i = 4$	$i = 2$	$i = 0$
0	A(0,0)	A(0,2)	A(0,4)	A(0,6)	A(0,8)	A(0,6)	A(0,4)	A(0,2)	A(0,0)
1									
2									
3									
4	A(0,1)	A(0,3)	A(0,5)	A(0,7)	A(0,9)	A(0,7)	A(0,5)	A(0,3)	A(0,1)
5									
6									
7									

Figure 5.20 Contents of a direct-mapped data cache.

and divide each element by that average. The required task can be expressed as

$$A(0, i) \leftarrow \frac{A(0, i)}{\left(\sum_{j=0}^{9} A(0, j)\right) / 10} \qquad \text{for } i = 0, 1, \dots, 9$$

Figure 5.19 gives the structure of a program that corresponds to this task. In a machine language implementation of this program, the array elements will be addressed as memory locations. We use the variables SUM and AVE to hold the sum and average values, respectively. These variables, as well as index variables i and j, will be held in processor registers during the computation.

Direct-Mapped Cache

In a direct-mapped data cache, the contents of the cache change as shown in Figure 5.20. The columns in the table indicate the cache contents after various passes through the two program loops in Figure 5.19 are completed. For example, after the second pass through the first loop ($j = 1$), the cache holds the elements $A(0, 0)$ and

$A(0, 1)$. These elements are in block positions 0 and 4, as determined by the three least-significant bits of the address. During the next pass, the $A(0, 0)$ element is replaced by $A(0, 2)$, which maps into the same block position. Note that the desired elements map into only two positions in the cache, thus leaving the contents of the other six positions unchanged from whatever they were before the normalization task was executed.

After the tenth pass through the first loop ($j = 9$), the elements $A(0, 8)$ and $A(0, 9)$ are found in the cache. Since the second loop reverses the order in which the elements are handled, the first two passes through this loop ($i = 9, 8$) will find the required data in the cache. When $i = 7$, the element $A(0, 9)$ is replaced with $A(0, 7)$. When $i = 6$, element $A(0, 8)$ is replaced with $A(0, 6)$, and so on. Thus, eight elements are replaced while the second loop is executed.

The reader should keep in mind that the tags must be kept in the cache for each block. We have not shown them in the figure for space reasons.

Associative-Mapped Cache

Figure 5.21 presents the changes if the cache is associative-mapped. During the first eight passes through the first loop, the elements are brought into consecutive block positions, assuming that the cache was initially empty. During the ninth pass ($j = 8$), the LRU algorithm chooses $A(0, 0)$ to be overwritten by $A(0, 8)$. The next and last pass through the j loop sees $A(0, 1)$ replaced by $A(0, 9)$. Now, for the first eight passes through the second loop ($i = 9, 8, \ldots, 2$) all required elements are found in the cache. When $i = 1$, the element needed is $A(0, 1)$, so it replaces the least recently used element, $A(0, 9)$. During the last pass, $A(0, 0)$ replaces $A(0, 8)$.

In this case, when the second loop is executed, only two elements are not found in the cache. In the direct-mapped case, eight of the elements had to be reloaded during the second loop. Obviously, the associative-mapped cache benefits from the complete freedom in mapping a memory block into any position in the cache. Good utilization

Block position	Contents of data cache after pass:				
	$j = 7$	$j = 8$	$j = 9$	$i = 1$	$i = 0$
0	A(0,0)	A(0,8)	A(0,8)	A(0,8)	A(0,0)
1	A(0,1)	A(0,1)	A(0,9)	A(0,1)	A(0,1)
2	A(0,2)	A(0,2)	A(0,2)	A(0,2)	A(0,2)
3	A(0,3)	A(0,3)	A(0,3)	A(0,3)	A(0,3)
4	A(0,4)	A(0,4)	A(0,4)	A(0,4)	A(0,4)
5	A(0,5)	A(0,5)	A(0,5)	A(0,5)	A(0,5)
6	A(0,6)	A(0,6)	A(0,6)	A(0,6)	A(0,6)
7	A(0,7)	A(0,7)	A(0,7)	A(0,7)	A(0,7)

Figure 5.21   Contents of an associative-mapped data cache.

Contents of data cache after pass:					
$j = 3$	$j = 7$	$j = 9$	$i = 4$	$i = 2$	$i = 0$
A(0,0)	A(0,4)	A(0,8)	A(0,4)	A(0,4)	A(0,0)
A(0,1)	A(0,5)	A(0,9)	A(0,5)	A(0,5)	A(0,1)
A(0,2)	A(0,6)	A(0,6)	A(0,6)	A(0,2)	A(0,2)
A(0,3)	A(0,7)	A(0,7)	A(0,7)	A(0,3)	A(0,3)

Set 0 (rows 1–4), Set 1 (rows 5–8)

Figure 5.22 Contents of a set-associative-mapped data cache.

of this cache also occurred because we chose to reverse the order in which the elements are handled in the second loop of the program. It is interesting to consider what would happen if the second loop dealt with the elements in the same order as in the first loop (see Problem 5.12). Using the LRU algorithm, all elements would be overwritten before they are used in the second loop. This degradation in performance would not occur if a random replacement algorithm were used.

Set-Associative-Mapped Cache

For this example, we assume that a set-associative data cache is organized into two sets, each capable of holding four blocks. Thus, the least-significant bit of an address determines which set the corresponding memory block maps into. The high-order 15 bits constitute the tag.

Changes in the cache contents are depicted in Figure 5.22. Since all the desired blocks have even addresses, they map into set 0. Note that, in this case, six elements must be reloaded during execution of the second loop.

Even though this is a simplified example, it illustrates that in general, associative mapping performs best, set-associative mapping is next best, and direct mapping is the worst. However, fully associative mapping is expensive to implement, so set-associative mapping is a good practical compromise.

5.5.4 EXAMPLES OF CACHES IN COMMERCIAL PROCESSORS

We now consider the implementation of caches in the 68040, ARM710T, and Pentium III and 4 processors.

68040 Caches

Motorola's 68040 has two caches included on the processor chip — one used for instructions and the other for data. Each cache has a capacity of 4K bytes and uses a four-way set-associative organization illustrated in Figure 5.23. The cache has 64 sets, each of which can hold 4 blocks. Each block has 4 long words, and each long word has 4 bytes. For mapping purposes, an address is interpreted as shown in the blue box in the figure. The least-significant 4 bits specify a byte position within a block. The next 6 bits identify one of 64 sets. The high-order 22 bits constitute the tag. To keep the notation in the figure compact, the contents of each of these fields are shown in hex coding.

The cache control mechanism includes one *valid* bit per block and one *dirty* bit for each long word in the block. These bits are explained in Section 5.5.1. The valid bit is set to 1 when a corresponding block is first loaded into the cache. An individual dirty bit is associated with each long word, and it is set to 1 when the long-word data are changed during a write operation. The dirty bit remains set until the contents of the block are written back into the main memory.

When the cache is accessed, the tag bits of the address are compared with the four tags in the specified set. If one of the tags matches the desired address and if the valid bit for the corresponding block is equal to 1, then a hit has occurred. Figure 5.23 gives an example in which the addressed data are found in the third long word of the fourth block in set 0.

The data cache can use either the write-back or the write-through protocol, under control of the operating system software. The contents of the instruction cache are changed only when new instructions are loaded as a result of a read miss. When a new block must be brought into a cache set that is already full, the replacement algorithm chooses at random the block to be ejected. Of course, if one or more of the dirty bits in this block are equal to 1, then a write-back must be performed first.

ARM710T Cache

The ARM family comprises processors that have an efficient RISC-type architecture, characterized by low cost and low power consumption. The ARM710T is one of the processors in this family. It has a single cache for both instructions and data.

The organization of the ARM710T cache is similar to the cache depicted in Figure 5.23. It is arranged as a four-way set-associative cache. Each block comprises 16 bytes, composed of four 32-bit words.

The write-through protocol is used when the processor writes to the cache. A random-replacement algorithm is used to decide which cache block is to be overwritten when space for a new block is needed.

The ARM710T cache structure is consistent with the low cost and low power consumption objective. A single unified cache, holding both instructions and data, is simpler than two separate caches. The write-through protocol and the random-replacement algorithm are also conducive to simple implementations.

Pentium III Caches

Pentium III is a high performance processor. Since high performance depends on fast access to instructions and data, Pentium III employs two cache levels. Level 1 consists of a 16-Kbyte instruction cache and a 16-Kbyte data cache. The data cache has a four-way set-associative organization, and it can use either the write-back or the write-through policy. The instruction cache has a two-way set-associative organization.

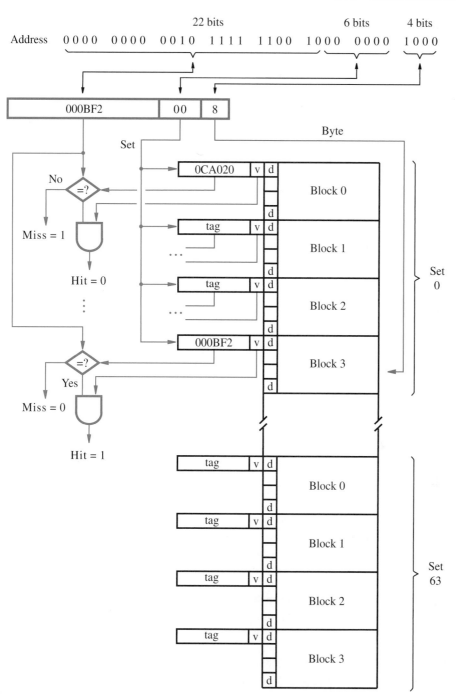

Figure 5.23 Data cache organization in the 68040 microprocessor.

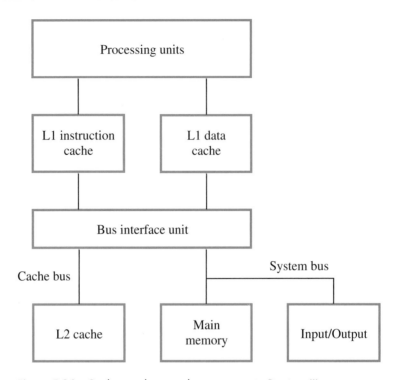

Figure 5.24   Caches and external connections in Pentium III processor.

Since instructions are normally not modified during execution of a program, there is no need for a write policy for the instruction cache.

The L2 cache is much larger. It holds both instructions and data. It is connected to the rest of the system as shown in Figure 5.24. A bus interface unit interconnects the caches, the main memory, and the I/O devices. Two separate buses are used: a fast *cache bus* connects the L2 cache to the processor, while a slower *system bus* connects the main memory and I/O devices.

The L2 cache can be implemented external to the processor chip, as is done in the Pentium III version known as Katmai. In this case, the cache contains 512 Kbytes and is implemented using SRAM memory. Its organization is four-way set-associative. It uses either the write-back or the write-through protocol, programmable on a per-block basis. The cache bus is 64 bits wide.

Improvements in VLSI technology have made it possible to integrate the L2 cache on the processor chip. This was done in the Pentium III version known as Coppermine. In this case, the cache size is 256 Kbytes. An eight-way set-associative organization is used. Since the L2 cache is on the processor chip, it is possible to use a wider 256-bit cache bus.

These examples raise an interesting question — is it better to implement the L2 cache externally or on the processor chip? External implementation allows for a larger cache. However, it is not conducive to a wide data path connection to the processor because of the pins needed and increased power consumption of the output drivers. Also, external caches have lower clock speeds. The Katmai L2 cache is driven at half the speed of the processor clock, while Coppermine L2 cache is driven at full processor clock speed. Placing the L2 cache on the processor chip reduces the latency of access and increases the bandwidth because data are transferred using a wider path. This results in superior performance. The main drawback of integrating the L2 cache is that the processor chip becomes much larger, which makes it more difficult to fabricate.

Pentium 4 Caches

The Pentium 4 processor can have up to three levels of caches. The L1 cache consists of separate data and instruction caches. The data cache has a capacity of 8K bytes, organized in a 4-way set-associative manner. Each cache block has 64 bytes. The write-through policy is used on writes to the cache. Integer data can be accessed from the data cache in two clock cycles. Pentium 4 chips can use clock signals in excess of 1.3 GHz, which means that the data can be accessed in less than 2 ns. The instruction cache does not hold normal machine instructions. Instead, it holds already decoded versions of instructions, as will be discussed in Chapter 11.

The L2 cache is a unified cache with a capacity of 256K bytes, organized in an 8-way set-associative manner. Each of its blocks comprises 128 bytes. The write-back policy is used on writes to the cache. The access latency of this cache is seven clock cycles.

Both L1 and L2 caches are implemented on the processor chip. The architecture also allows for inclusion of an on-chip L3 cache. However, this cache is not implemented in the Pentium 4 chips targeted for desktop computers. It is intended for processor chips used in server systems.

5.6 PERFORMANCE CONSIDERATIONS

Two key factors in the commercial success of a computer are performance and cost; the best possible performance at the lowest cost is the objective. The challenge in considering design alternatives is to improve the performance without increasing the cost. A common measure of success is the *price/performance ratio*. In this section, we discuss some specific features of memory design that lead to superior performance.

Performance depends on how fast machine instructions can be brought into the processor for execution and how fast they can be executed. We will discuss the speed of execution in Chapters 7 and 8, and show how additional circuitry can be used to speed up the execution phase of instruction processing. In this chapter, we focus on the memory subsystem.

The memory hierarchy described in Section 5.4 results from the quest for the best price/performance ratio. The main purpose of this hierarchy is to create a memory that the processor sees as having a short access time and a large capacity. Each level of the hierarchy plays an important role. The speed and efficiency of data transfer between various levels of the hierarchy are also of great significance. It is beneficial if transfers to and from the faster units can be done at a rate equal to that of the faster unit. This is not possible if both the slow and the fast units are accessed in the same manner, but it can be achieved when parallelism is used in the organization of the slower unit. An effective way to introduce parallelism is to use an interleaved organization.

5.6.1 INTERLEAVING

If the main memory of a computer is structured as a collection of physically separate modules, each with its own address buffer register (ABR) and data buffer register (DBR), memory access operations may proceed in more than one module at the same

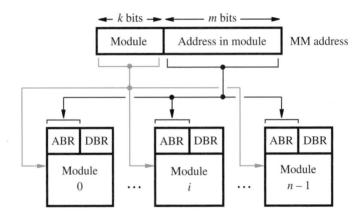

(a) Consecutive words in a module

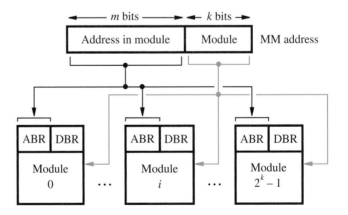

(b) Consecutive words in consecutive modules

Figure 5.25 Addressing multiple-module memory systems.

time. Thus, the aggregate rate of transmission of words to and from the main memory system can be increased.

How individual addresses are distributed over the modules is critical in determining the average number of modules that can be kept busy as computations proceed. Two methods of address layout are indicated in Figure 5.25. In the first case, the memory address generated by the processor is decoded as shown in Figure 5.25a. The high-order k bits name one of n modules, and the low-order m bits name a particular word in that module. When consecutive locations are accessed, as happens when a block of data is transferred to a cache, only one module is involved. At the same time, however, devices with direct memory access (DMA) ability may be accessing information in other memory modules.

The second and more effective way to address the modules is shown in Figure 5.25b. It is called *memory interleaving*. The low-order k bits of the memory address select a module, and the high-order m bits name a location within that module. In this way, consecutive addresses are located in successive modules. Thus, any component of the system that generates requests for access to consecutive memory locations can keep several modules busy at any one time. This results in both faster access to a block of data and higher average utilization of the memory system as a whole. To implement the interleaved structure, there must be 2^k modules; otherwise, there will be gaps of nonexistent locations in the memory address space.

The effect of interleaving is substantial. Consider the time needed to transfer a block of data from the main memory to the cache when a read miss occurs. Suppose that a cache with 8-word blocks is used, similar to our examples in Section 5.5. On a read miss, the block that contains the desired word must be copied from the memory into the cache. Assume that the hardware has the following properties. It takes one clock cycle to send an address to the main memory. The memory is built with relatively slow DRAM chips that allow the first word to be accessed in 8 cycles, but subsequent words of the block are accessed in 4 clock cycles per word. (Recall from Section 5.2.3 that, when consecutive locations in a DRAM are read from a given row of cells, the row address is decoded only once. Addresses of consecutive columns of the array are then applied to access the desired words, which takes only half the time per access.) Also, one clock cycle is needed to send one word to the cache.

If a single memory module is used, then the time needed to load the desired block into the cache is

$$1 + 8 + (7 \times 4) + 1 = 38 \text{ cycles}$$

Suppose now that the memory is constructed as four interleaved modules, using the scheme in Figure 5.25b. When the starting address of the block arrives at the memory, all four modules begin accessing the required data, using the high-order bits of the address. After 8 clock cycles, each module has one word of data in its DBR. These words are transferred to the cache, one word at a time, during the next 4 clock cycles. During this time, the next word in each module is accessed. Then it takes another 4 cycles to transfer these words to the cache. Therefore, the total time needed to load the

Example 5.1

block from the interleaved memory is

$$1 + 8 + 4 + 4 = 17 \text{ cycles}$$

Thus, interleaving reduces the block transfer time by more than a factor of 2.

In Section 5.2.4, we mentioned that interleaving is used within SDRAM chips to improve the speed of accessing successive words of data. The memory array in most SDRAM chips is organized as two or four banks of smaller interleaved arrays. This improves the rate at which a block of data can be transferred to or from the main memory.

5.6.2   HIT RATE AND MISS PENALTY

An excellent indicator of the effectiveness of a particular implementation of the memory hierarchy is the success rate in accessing information at various levels of the hierarchy. Recall that a successful access to data in a cache is called a hit. The number of hits stated as a fraction of all attempted accesses is called the *hit rate,* and the *miss rate* is the number of misses stated as a fraction of attempted accesses.

Ideally, the entire memory hierarchy would appear to the processor as a single memory unit that has the access time of a cache on the processor chip and the size of a magnetic disk. How close we get to this ideal depends largely on the hit rate at different levels of the hierarchy. High hit rates, well over 0.9, are essential for high-performance computers.

Performance is adversely affected by the actions that must be taken after a miss. The extra time needed to bring the desired information into the cache is called the *miss penalty*. This penalty is ultimately reflected in the time that the processor is stalled because the required instructions or data are not available for execution. In general, the miss penalty is the time needed to bring a block of data from a slower unit in the memory hierarchy to a faster unit. The miss penalty is reduced if efficient mechanisms for transferring data between the various units of the hierarchy are implemented. The previous section shows how an interleaved memory can reduce the miss penalty substantially.

Example 5.2   Consider now the impact of the cache on the overall performance of the computer. Let h be the hit rate, M the miss penalty, that is, the time to access information in the main memory, and C the time to access information in the cache. The average access time experienced by the processor is

$$t_{ave} = hC + (1 - h)M$$

We use the same parameters as in Example 5.1. If the computer has no cache, then, using a fast processor and a typical DRAM main memory, it takes 10 clock cycles for each memory read access. Suppose the computer has a cache that holds 8-word blocks and an interleaved main memory. Then, as we showed in Section 5.6.1, 17 cycles are needed to load a block into the cache. Assume that 30 percent of the instructions in a typical program perform a read or a write operation, which means that there are 130 memory accesses for every 100 instructions executed. Assume that the hit rates in the cache are 0.95 for instructions and 0.9 for data. Let us further assume that the miss penalty is the same for both read and write accesses. Then, a rough estimate of the improvement in performance that results from using the cache can be obtained as follows:

$$\frac{Time\ without\ cache}{Time\ with\ cache} = \frac{130 \times 10}{100(0.95 \times 1 + 0.05 \times 17) + 30(0.9 \times 1 + 0.1 \times 17)} = 5.04$$

This result suggests that the computer with the cache performs five times better.

It is also interesting to consider how effective this cache is compared to an ideal cache that has a hit rate of 100 percent (in which case, all memory references take one cycle). Our rough estimate of relative performance for these caches is

$$\frac{100(0.95 \times 1 + 0.05 \times 17) + 30(0.9 \times 1 + 0.1 \times 17)}{130} = 1.98$$

This means that the actual cache provides an environment in which the processor effectively works with a large DRAM-based main memory that appears to be only two times slower than the circuits in the cache.

In this example, we made a simplifying assumption that the same clock is used to access the on-chip cache and the main memory via the system bus. A high-performance processor is likely to operate under the control of a clock that is much faster than the system bus clock, perhaps up to ten times faster. Let us consider the impact of a cache in a system of this type.

Example 5.3

Suppose that there is a single cache that is implemented on the processor chip and that the main memory is realized using SDRAM chips. Assume that the system bus clock is four times slower than the processor clock. As in Example 5.2, assume that a cache block contains 8 words, and that the hit rates in the cache are 0.95 for instructions and 0.9 for data. The SDRAM timing diagram is similar to Figure 5.9. The only difference is that there is a burst of 8 data words rather than four. Thus, according to Figure 5.9, it will take 14 clock cycles from when the RAS signal is asserted to transfer a block of data between the main memory and the cache. Since the RAS and CAS signals are generated by the memory controller, as indicated in Figure 5.11, one more cycle is needed during which the processor sends the address of the first word in a block to the memory controller. Therefore, a total of 15 cycles is needed to transfer a block. The cycles shown in Figure 5.9 are the system bus clock cycles. If the processor clock is four times faster, then it takes 60 processor cycles to transfer an 8-word block to or from the main memory. Note also that Figure 5.9 indicates that the processor can read or write a single word in the main memory in 9 bus clock cycles, consisting of the 8 cycles indicated in Figure 5.9 plus one cycle needed to send an address to the memory controller. Hence, 36 processor cycles are needed to access a single word in the main memory. Yet, the processor accesses a word in the cache in one processor cycle!

Repeating the calculation in Example 5.2 gives:

$$\frac{Time\ without\ cache}{Time\ with\ cache} = \frac{130 \times 36}{100(0.95 \times 1 + 0.05 \times 60) + 30(0.9 \times 1 + 0.1 \times 60)} = 7.77$$

Thus, accounting for the differences between processor and system bus clock speeds shows that the cache has an even greater positive effect on the performance.

In the preceding examples, we distinguish between instructions and data as far as the hit rate is concerned. Although hit rates above 0.9 are achievable for both, the hit rate for instructions is usually higher than that for data. The hit rates depend on the design of the cache and on the instruction and data access patterns of the programs being executed.

How can the hit rate be improved? An obvious possibility is to make the cache larger, but this entails increased cost. Another possibility is to increase the block size while keeping the total cache size constant, to take advantage of spatial locality. If all items in a larger block are needed in a computation, then it is better to load these items into the cache as a consequence of a single miss, rather than loading several smaller blocks as a result of several misses. The efficiency of parallel access to blocks in an interleaved memory is the basic reason for this advantage. Larger blocks are effective up to a certain size, but eventually any further improvement in the hit rate tends to be offset by the fact that, in a larger block, some items may not be referenced before the block is ejected (replaced). The miss penalty increases as the block size increases. Since the performance of a computer is affected positively by increased hit rate and negatively by increased miss penalty, the block sizes that are neither very small nor very large give the best results. In practice, block sizes in the range of 16 to 128 bytes have been the most popular choices.

Finally, we note that the miss penalty can be reduced if the load-through approach is used when loading new blocks into the cache. Then, instead of waiting for the completion of the block transfer, the processor can continue as soon as the required word is loaded in the cache.

5.6.3 CACHES ON THE PROCESSOR CHIP

When information is transferred between different chips, considerable delays are introduced in driver and receiver gates on the chips. Thus, from the speed point of view, the optimal place for a cache is on the processor chip. Unfortunately, space on the processor chip is needed for many other functions; this limits the size of the cache that can be accommodated.

All high-performance processor chips include some form of a cache. Some manufacturers have chosen to implement two separate caches, one for instructions and another for data, as in the 68040, Pentium III, and Pentium 4 processors. Others have implemented a single cache for both instructions and data, as in the ARM710T processor.

A combined cache for instructions and data is likely to have a somewhat better hit rate because it offers greater flexibility in mapping new information into the cache. However, if separate caches are used, it is possible to access both caches at the same time, which leads to increased parallelism and, hence, better performance. The disadvantage of separate caches is that the increased parallelism comes at the expense of more complex circuitry.

In high-performance processors two levels of caches are normally used. The L1 cache(s) is on the processor chip. The L2 cache, which is much larger, may be implemented externally using SRAM chips. But, a somewhat smaller L2 cache may also be implemented on the processor chip, as illustrated by the Coppermine version of Pentium III processors described in Section 5.5.4.

If both L1 and L2 caches are used, the L1 cache should be designed to allow very fast access by the processor because its access time will have a large effect on the clock rate of the processor. A cache cannot be accessed at the same speed as a register file because the cache is much bigger and, hence, more complex. A practical way to speed up access to the cache is to access more than one word simultaneously and then let the processor use them one at a time. This technique is used in many commercial processors.

The L2 cache can be slower, but it should be much larger to ensure a high hit rate. Its speed is less critical because it only affects the miss penalty of the L1 cache. A workstation computer may include an L1 cache with the capacity of tens of kilobytes and an L2 cache of several megabytes.

Including an L2 cache further reduces the impact of the main memory speed on the performance of a computer. The average access time experienced by the processor in a system with two levels of caches is

$$t_{ave} = h_1 C_1 + (1 - h_1)h_2 C_2 + (1 - h_1)(1 - h_2)M$$

where

h_1 is the hit rate in the L1 cache.

h_2 is the hit rate in the L2 cache.

C_1 is the time to access information in the L1 cache.

C_2 is the time to access information in the L2 cache.

M is the time to access information in the main memory.

The number of misses in the L2 cache, given by the term $(1 - h_1)(1 - h_2)$, should be low. If both h_1 and h_2 are in the 90 percent range, then the number of misses will be less than 1 percent of the processor's memory accesses. Thus, the miss penalty M will be less critical from a performance point of view. See Problem 5.18 for a quantitative examination of this issue.

5.6.4   OTHER ENHANCEMENTS

In addition to the main design issues just discussed, several other possibilities exist for enhancing performance. We discuss three of them in this section.

Write Buffer

When the write-through protocol is used, each write operation results in writing a new value into the main memory. If the processor must wait for the memory function to be completed, as we have assumed until now, then the processor is slowed down by all write requests. Yet the processor typically does not immediately depend on the result of a write operation, so it is not necessary for the processor to wait for the write request to be completed. To improve performance, a *write buffer* can be included for temporary storage of write requests. The processor places each write request into this buffer and continues execution of the next instruction. The write requests stored in the write buffer are sent to the main memory whenever the memory is not responding to read requests. Note that it is important that the read requests be serviced immediately because the processor usually cannot proceed without the data that are to be read from the memory. Hence, these requests are given priority over write requests.

The write buffer may hold a number of write requests. Thus, it is possible that a subsequent read request may refer to data that are still in the write buffer. To ensure correct operation, the addresses of data to be read from the memory are compared with the addresses of the data in the write buffer. In case of a match, the data in the write buffer are used.

A different situation occurs with the write-back protocol. In this case, the write operations are simply performed on the corresponding word in the cache. But consider what happens when a new block of data is to be brought into the cache as a result of a read miss, which replaces an existing block that has some dirty data. The dirty block has to be written into the main memory. If the required write-back is performed first, then the processor will have to wait longer for the new block to be read into the cache. It is more prudent to read the new block first. This can be arranged by providing a fast write buffer for temporary storage of the dirty block that is ejected from the cache while the new block is being read. Afterward, the contents of the buffer are written into the main memory. Thus, the write buffer also works well for the write-back protocol.

Prefetching

In the previous discussion of the cache mechanism, we assumed that new data are brought into the cache when they are first needed. A read miss occurs, and the desired data are loaded from the main memory. The processor has to pause until the new data arrive, which is the effect of the miss penalty.

To avoid stalling the processor, it is possible to prefetch the data into the cache before they are needed. The simplest way to do this is through software. A special prefetch instruction may be provided in the instruction set of the processor. Executing this instruction causes the addressed data to be loaded into the cache, as in the case of a read miss. However, the processor does not wait for the referenced data. A prefetch instruction is inserted in a program to cause the data to be loaded in the cache by the time they are needed in the program. The hope is that prefetching will take place while the processor is busy executing instructions that do not result in a read miss, thus allowing accesses to the main memory to be overlapped with computation in the processor.

Prefetch instructions can be inserted into a program either by the programmer or by the compiler. It is obviously preferable to have the compiler insert these instructions, which can be done with good success for many applications. Note that software prefetching entails a certain overhead because inclusion of prefetch instructions increases the length of programs. Moreover, some prefetches may load into the cache data that will not be used by the instructions that follow. This can happen if the prefetched data are ejected from the cache by a read miss involving other data. However, the overall effect of software prefetching on performance is positive, and many processors have machine instructions to support this feature. See Reference [1] for a thorough discussion of software prefetching.

Prefetching can also be done through hardware. This involves adding circuitry that attempts to discover a pattern in memory references and then prefetches data according to this pattern. A number of schemes have been proposed for this purpose, but they are beyond the scope of this book. A description of these schemes is found in References [2] and [3].

Intel's Pentium 4 processor has facilities for prefetching information into its caches using both software and hardware approaches. There are special prefetch instructions that can be included in programs to bring a block of data into a desired level of cache. Harware-controlled prefetching brings cache blocks into the L2 cache based on the patterns of previous usage.

Lockup-Free Cache

The software prefetching scheme just discussed does not work well if it interferes significantly with the normal execution of instructions. This is the case if the action of prefetching stops other accesses to the cache until the prefetch is completed. A cache of this type is said to be locked while it services a miss. We can solve this problem by modifying the basic cache structure to allow the processor to access the cache while a miss is being serviced. In fact, it is desirable that more than one outstanding miss can be supported.

A cache that can support multiple outstanding misses is called *lockup-free*. Since it can service only one miss at a time, it must include circuitry that keeps track of all outstanding misses. This may be done with special registers that hold the pertinent information about these misses. Lockup-free caches were first used in the early 1980s in the Cyber series of computers manufactured by Control Data company [4].

We have used software prefetching as an obvious motivation for a cache that is not locked by a read miss. A much more important reason is that, in a processor that uses a pipelined organization, which overlaps the execution of several instructions, a read miss caused by one instruction could stall the execution of other instructions. A lockup-free cache reduces the likelihood of such stalling. We return to this topic in Chapter 8, where the pipelined organization is examined in detail.

5.7 VIRTUAL MEMORIES

In most modern computer systems, the physical main memory is not as large as the address space spanned by an address issued by the processor. For example, a processor that issues 32-bit addresses has an addressable space of 4G bytes. The size of the main memory in a typical computer ranges from a few hundred megabytes to 1G bytes. When a program does not completely fit into the main memory, the parts of it not currently being executed are stored on secondary storage devices, such as magnetic disks. Of course, all parts of a program that are eventually executed are first brought into the main memory. When a new segment of a program is to be moved into a full memory, it must replace another segment already in the memory. In modern computers, the operating system moves programs and data automatically between the main memory and secondary storage. Thus, the application programmer does not need to be aware of limitations imposed by the available main memory.

Techniques that automatically move program and data blocks into the physical main memory when they are required for execution are called *virtual-memory* techniques. Programs, and hence the processor, reference an instruction and data space that is independent of the available physical main memory space. The binary addresses that the processor issues for either instructions or data are called *virtual* or *logical addresses*. These addresses are translated into physical addresses by a combination of hardware and software components. If a virtual address refers to a part of the program or data space that is currently in the physical memory, then the contents of the appropriate location in the main memory are accessed immediately. On the other hand, if the referenced address is not in the main memory, its contents must be brought into a suitable location in the memory before they can be used.

Figure 5.26 shows a typical organization that implements virtual memory. A special hardware unit, called the *Memory Management Unit* (MMU), translates virtual

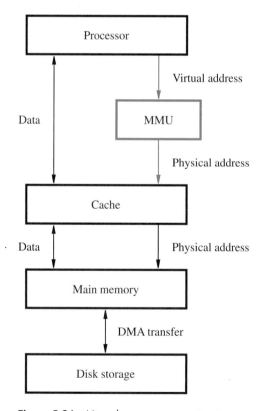

Figure 5.26 Virtual memory organization.

addresses into physical addresses. When the desired data (or instructions) are in the main memory, these data are fetched as described in our presentation of the cache mechanism. If the data are not in the main memory, the MMU causes the operating system to bring the data into the memory from the disk. Transfer of data between the disk and the main memory is performed using the DMA scheme discussed in Chapter 4.

5.7.1   ADDRESS TRANSLATION

A simple method for translating virtual addresses into physical addresses is to assume that all programs and data are composed of fixed-length units called *pages*, each of which consists of a block of words that occupy contiguous locations in the main memory. Pages commonly range from 2K to 16K bytes in length. They constitute the basic unit of information that is moved between the main memory and the disk whenever the translation mechanism determines that a move is required. Pages should not be too small, because the access time of a magnetic disk is much longer (several milliseconds) than the access time of the main memory. The reason for this is that it takes a considerable amount of time to locate the data on the disk, but once located, the data can be transferred at a rate of several megabytes per second. On the other hand, if pages are too large it is possible that a substantial portion of a page may not be used, yet this unnecessary data will occupy valuable space in the main memory.

This discussion clearly parallels the concepts introduced in Section 5.5 on cache memory. The cache bridges the speed gap between the processor and the main memory and is implemented in hardware. The virtual-memory mechanism bridges the size and speed gaps between the main memory and secondary storage and is usually implemented in part by software techniques. Conceptually, cache techniques and virtual-memory techniques are very similar. They differ mainly in the details of their implementation.

A virtual-memory address translation method based on the concept of fixed-length pages is shown schematically in Figure 5.27. Each virtual address generated by the processor, whether it is for an instruction fetch or an operand fetch/store operation, is interpreted as a *virtual page number* (high-order bits) followed by an *offset* (low-order bits) that specifies the location of a particular byte (or word) within a page. Information about the main memory location of each page is kept in a *page table*. This information includes the main memory address where the page is stored and the current status of the page. An area in the main memory that can hold one page is called a *page frame*. The starting address of the page table is kept in a *page table base register*. By adding the virtual page number to the contents of this register, the address of the corresponding entry in the page table is obtained. The contents of this location give the starting address of the page if that page currently resides in the main memory.

Each entry in the page table also includes some control bits that describe the status of the page while it is in the main memory. One bit indicates the validity of the page, that is, whether the page is actually loaded in the main memory. This bit allows the operating system to invalidate the page without actually removing it. Another bit indicates whether the page has been modified during its residency in the memory. As in cache memories,

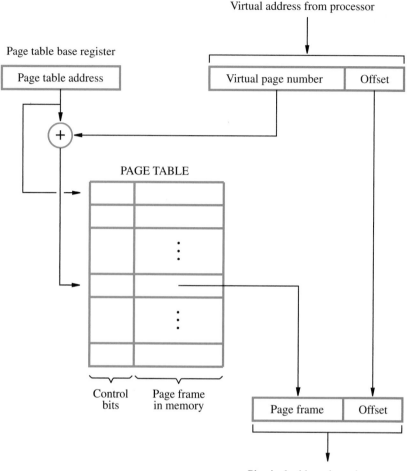

Figure 5.27 Virtual-memory address translation.

this information is needed to determine whether the page should be written back to the disk before it is removed from the main memory to make room for another page. Other control bits indicate various restrictions that may be imposed on accessing the page. For example, a program may be given full read and write permission, or it may be restricted to read accesses only.

The page table information is used by the MMU for every read and write access, so ideally, the page table should be situated within the MMU. Unfortunately, the page table may be rather large, and since the MMU is normally implemented as part of the processor chip (along with the primary cache), it is impossible to include a complete page table on this chip. Therefore, the page table is kept in the main memory. However, a copy of a small portion of the page table can be accommodated within the MMU.

This portion consists of the page table entries that correspond to the most recently accessed pages. A small cache, usually called the *Translation Lookaside Buffer* (TLB) is incorporated into the MMU for this purpose. The operation of the TLB with respect to the page table in the main memory is essentially the same as the operation we have discussed in conjunction with the cache memory. In addition to the information that constitutes a page table entry, the TLB must also include the virtual address of the entry. Figure 5.28 shows a possible organization of a TLB where the associative-mapping technique is used. Set-associative mapped TLBs are also found in commercial products.

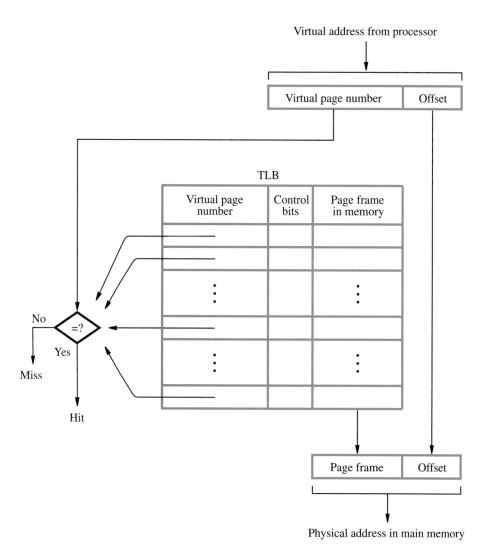

Figure 5.28 Use of an associative-mapped TLB.

An essential requirement is that the contents of the TLB be coherent with the contents of page tables in the memory. When the operating system changes the contents of page tables, it must simultaneously invalidate the corresponding entries in the TLB. One of the control bits in the TLB is provided for this purpose. When an entry is invalidated, the TLB will acquire the new information as part of the MMU's normal response to access misses.

Address translation proceeds as follows. Given a virtual address, the MMU looks in the TLB for the referenced page. If the page table entry for this page is found in the TLB, the physical address is obtained immediately. If there is a miss in the TLB, then the required entry is obtained from the page table in the main memory and the TLB is updated.

When a program generates an access request to a page that is not in the main memory, a *page fault* is said to have occurred. The whole page must be brought from the disk into the memory before access can proceed. When it detects a page fault, the MMU asks the operating system to intervene by raising an exception (interrupt). Processing of the active task is interrupted, and control is transferred to the operating system. The operating system then copies the requested page from the disk into the main memory and returns control to the interrupted task. Because a long delay occurs while the page transfer takes place, the operating system may suspend execution of the task that caused the page fault and begin execution of another task whose pages are in the main memory.

It is essential to ensure that the interrupted task can continue correctly when it resumes execution. A page fault occurs when some instruction accesses a memory operand that is not in the main memory, resulting in an interruption before the execution of this instruction is completed. Hence, when the task resumes, either the execution of the interrupted instruction must continue from the point of interruption, or the instruction must be restarted. The design of a particular processor dictates which of these options should be used.

If a new page is brought from the disk when the main memory is full, it must replace one of the resident pages. The problem of choosing which page to remove is just as critical here as it is in a cache, and the idea that programs spend most of their time in a few localized areas also applies. Because main memories are considerably larger than cache memories, it should be possible to keep relatively larger portions of a program in the main memory. This will reduce the frequency of transfers to and from the disk. Concepts similar to the LRU replacement algorithm can be applied to page replacement, and the control bits in the page table entries can indicate usage. One simple scheme is based on a control bit that is set to 1 whenever the corresponding page is referenced (accessed). The operating system occasionally clears this bit in all page table entries, thus providing a simple way of determining which pages have not been used recently.

A modified page has to be written back to the disk before it is removed from the main memory. It is important to note that the write-through protocol, which is useful in the framework of cache memories, is not suitable for virtual memory. The access time of the disk is so long that it does not make sense to access it frequently to write small amounts of data.

The address translation process in the MMU requires some time to perform, mostly dependent on the time needed to look up entries in the TLB. Because of locality of reference, it is likely that many successive translations involve addresses on the same page. This is particularly evident in fetching instructions. Thus, we can reduce the average translation time by including one or more special registers that retain the virtual page number and the physical page frame of the most recently performed translations. The information in these registers can be accessed more quickly than the TLB.

5.8   MEMORY MANAGEMENT REQUIREMENTS

In our discussion of virtual-memory concepts, we have tacitly assumed that only one large program is being executed. If all of the program does not fit into the available physical memory, parts of it (pages) are moved from the disk into the main memory when they are to be executed. Although we have alluded to software routines that are needed to manage this movement of program segments, we have not been specific about the details.

Management routines are part of the operating system of the computer. It is convenient to assemble the operating system routines into a virtual address space, called the *system space,* that is separate from the virtual space in which user application programs reside. The latter space is called the *user space*. In fact, there may be a number of user spaces, one for each user. This is arranged by providing a separate page table for each user program. The MMU uses a page table base register to determine the address of the table to be used in the translation process. Hence, by changing the contents of this register, the operating system can switch from one space to another. The physical main memory is thus shared by the active pages of the system space and several user spaces. However, only the pages that belong to one of these spaces are accessible at any given time.

In any computer system in which independent user programs coexist in the main memory, the notion of *protection* must be addressed. No program should be allowed to destroy either the data or instructions of other programs in the memory. Such protection can be provided in several ways. Let us first consider the most basic form of protection. Recall that in the simplest case, the processor has two states, the *supervisor state* and the *user state*. As the names suggest, the processor is usually placed in the supervisor state when operating system routines are being executed and in the user state to execute user programs. In the user state, some machine instructions cannot be executed. These *privileged instructions,* which include such operations as modifying the page table base register, can only be executed while the processor is in the supervisor state. Hence, a user program is prevented from accessing the page tables of other user spaces or of the system space.

It is sometimes desirable for one application program to have access to certain pages belonging to another program. The operating system can arrange this by causing these pages to appear in both spaces. The shared pages will therefore have entries in two different page tables. The control bits in each table entry can be set to control the access privileges granted to each program. For example, one program may be allowed to read and write a given page, while the other program may be given only read access.

5.9 SECONDARY STORAGE

Semiconductor memories discussed in the previous sections cannot be used to provide all of the storage capability needed in computers. Their main limitation is the cost per bit of stored information. Large storage requirements of most computer systems are economically realized in the form of magnetic disks, optical disks, and magnetic tapes, which are usually referred to as secondary storage devices.

5.9.1 MAGNETIC HARD DISKS

As the name implies, the storage medium in a magnetic-disk system consists of one or more disks mounted on a common spindle. A thin magnetic film is deposited on each disk, usually on both sides. The disks are placed in a rotary drive so that the magnetized surfaces move in close proximity to read/write heads, as shown in Figure 5.29a. The disks rotate at a uniform speed. Each head consists of a magnetic yoke and a magnetizing coil, as indicated in Figure 5.29b.

Digital information can be stored on the magnetic film by applying current pulses of suitable polarity to the magnetizing coil. This causes the magnetization of the film in the area immediately underneath the head to switch to a direction parallel to the applied field. The same head can be used for reading the stored information. In this case, changes in the magnetic field in the vicinity of the head caused by the movement of the film relative to the yoke induce a voltage in the coil, which now serves as a sense coil. The polarity of this voltage is monitored by the control circuitry to determine the state of magnetization of the film. Only changes in the magnetic field under the head can be sensed during the Read operation. Therefore, if the binary states 0 and 1 are represented by two opposite states of magnetization, a voltage is induced in the head only at 0-to-1 and at 1-to-0 transitions in the bit stream. A long string of 0s or 1s causes an induced voltage only at the beginning and end of the string. To determine the number of consecutive 0s or 1s stored, a clock must provide information for synchronization. In some early designs, a clock was stored on a separate track, where a change in magnetization is forced for each bit period. Using the clock signal as a reference, the data stored on other tracks can be read correctly.

The modern approach is to combine the clocking information with the data. Several different techniques have been developed for such encoding. One simple scheme, depicted in Figure 5.29c, is known as *phase encoding* or *Manchester encoding*. In this scheme, changes in magnetization occur for each data bit, as shown in the figure. Note that a change in magnetization is guaranteed at the midpoint of each bit period, thus providing the clocking information. The drawback of Manchester encoding is its poor bit-storage density. The space required to represent each bit must be large enough to accommodate two changes in magnetization. We use the Manchester encoding example to illustrate how a *self-clocking* scheme may be implemented, because it is easy to understand. Other, more compact codes have been developed. They are much more efficient and provide better storage density. They also require more complex control circuitry. The discussion of such codes is beyond the scope of this book.

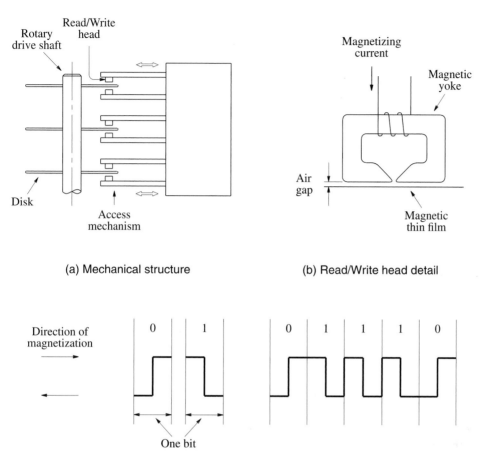

(a) Mechanical structure

(b) Read/Write head detail

(c) Bit representation by phase encoding

Figure 5.29 Magnetic disk principles.

Read/write heads must be maintained at a very small distance from the moving disk surfaces in order to achieve high bit densities and reliable read/write operations. When the disks are moving at their steady rate, air pressure develops between the disk surface and the head and forces the head away from the surface. This force can be counteracted by a spring-loaded mounting arrangement for the head that allows it to be pressed toward the surface. The flexible spring connection between the head and its arm mounting permits the head to fly at the desired distance away from the surface in spite of any small variations in the flatness of the surface.

In most modern disk units, the disks and the read/write heads are placed in a sealed, air-filtered enclosure. This approach is known as *Winchester technology*. In such units, the read/write heads can operate closer to the magnetized track surfaces because dust particles, which are a problem in unsealed assemblies, are absent. The closer the heads are to a track surface, the more densely the data can be packed along the track, and the closer the tracks can be to each other. Thus, Winchester disks have a larger capacity for a given physical size compared to unsealed units. Another advantage of Winchester technology is that data integrity tends to be greater in sealed units where the storage medium is not exposed to contaminating elements.

The read/write heads of a disk system are movable. There is one head per surface. All heads are mounted on a comb-like arm that can move radially across the stack of disks to provide access to individual tracks, as shown in Figure 5.29*a*. To read or write data on a given track, the arm holding the read/write heads must first be positioned to that track.

The disk system consists of three key parts. One part is the assembly of disk platters, which is usually referred to as the *disk*. The second part comprises the electromechanical mechanism that spins the disk and moves the read/write heads; it is called the *disk drive*. The third part is the electronic circuitry that controls the operation of the system, which is called the *disk controller*. The disk controller may be implemented as a separate module, or it may be incorporated into the enclosure that contains the entire disk system. We should note that the term disk is often used to refer to the combined package of the disk drive and the disk it contains. We will do so in the sections that follow when there is no ambiguity in the meaning of the term.

Organization and Accessing of Data on a Disk

The organization of data on a disk is illustrated in Figure 5.30. Each surface is divided into concentric *tracks,* and each track is divided into *sectors*. The set of corresponding tracks on all surfaces of a stack of disks forms a logical *cylinder*. The data on all tracks of a cylinder can be accessed without moving the read/write heads. The data are accessed by specifying the surface number, the track number, and the sector number. The Read and Write operations start at sector boundaries.

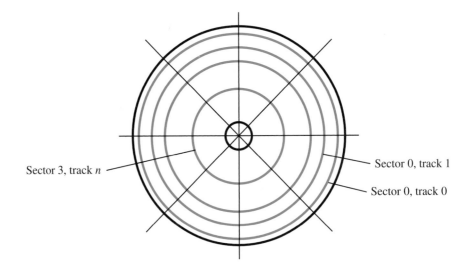

Figure 5.30 Organization of one surface of a disk.

Data bits are stored serially on each track. Each sector usually contains 512 bytes of data, but other sizes may be used. The data are preceded by a *sector header* that contains identification (addressing) information used to find the desired sector on the selected track. Following the data, there are additional bits that constitute an *error-correcting code* (ECC). The ECC bits are used to detect and correct errors that may have occurred in writing or reading of the 512 data bytes. To easily distinguish between two consecutive sectors, there is a small *intersector gap*.

An unformatted disk has no information on its tracks. The formatting process divides the disk physically into tracks and sectors. This process may discover some defective sectors or even whole tracks. The disk controller keeps a record of such defects and excludes them from use. The capacity of a formatted disk is a proper indicator of the storage capability of the given disk. The formatting information accounts for about 15 percent of the total information that can be stored on a disk. It comprises the sector headers, the ECC bits, and intersector gaps. In a typical computer, the disk is subsequently divided into logical partitions. There must be at least one such partition, called the primary partition. There may be a number of additional partitions.

Figure 5.30 indicates that each track has the same number of sectors. So all tracks have the same storage capacity. Thus, the stored information is packed more densely on inner tracks than on outer tracks. This arrangement is used in many disks because it simplifies the electronic circuits needed to access the data. But, it is possible to increase the storage density by placing more sectors on outer tracks, which have longer circumference, at the expense of more complicated access circuitry. This scheme is used in large disks.

Access Time

There are two components involved in the time delay between receiving an address and the beginning of the actual data transfer. The first, called the *seek time,* is the time required to move the read/write head to the proper track. This depends on the initial position of the head relative to the track specified in the address. Average values are in the 5- to 8-ms range. The second component is the *rotational delay,* also called *latency time*. This is the amount of time that elapses after the head is positioned over the correct track until the starting position of the addressed sector passes under the read/write head. On average, this is the time for half a rotation of the disk. The sum of these two delays is called the disk *access time*. If only a few sectors of data are moved in a single operation, the access time is at least an order of magnitude longer than the actual data transfer period.

Typical Disks

A 3.5-inch (diameter) high-capacity, high-data-rate disk available today may have the following representative parameters. There are 20 data-recording surfaces with 15,000 tracks per surface. There is an average of 400 sectors per track, and each sector contains 512 bytes of data. Hence, the total capacity of the formatted disk is $20 \times 15,000 \times 400 \times 512 \approx 60 \times 10^9 = 60$ gigabytes. The average seek time is 6 ms. The platters rotate at 10,000 revolutions per minute, so that the average latency is 3 ms, which is the time for a half-rotation. The average internal transfer rate, from a track to the data buffer in the disk controller, is 34 Mbytes/s. When connected to a SCSI bus, a drive of this type may have an external transfer rate of 160 Mbytes/s. Thus, a buffering scheme is needed to deal with the difference in transfer speeds, as explained in the next section.

There are also some very small disks. For example, a one-inch disk may store one gigabyte of data. Its physical size is comparable to a matchbook and it weighs less than an ounce. Such disks are attractive for use in portable equipment and hand-held devices. In a digital camera, such a disk could store 1000 photographs. It is interesting to observe that the first disk drive that had a 1-gigabyte capacity was produced by IBM in 1980. It was the size of a kitchen appliance. It weighed 250 kilograms and cost $40,000.

Data Buffer/Cache

A disk drive is connected to the rest of a computer system using some standard interconnection scheme. Normally, a standard bus, such as the SCSI bus discussed in Section 4.7.2, is used. A disk drive that incorporates the required SCSI interface circuitry is usually referred to as a SCSI drive. The SCSI bus is capable of transferring data at much higher rates than the rate at which data can be read from disk tracks. An efficient way to deal with the possible differences in transfer rates between the disk and the SCSI bus is to include a *data buffer* in the disk unit. This buffer is a semiconductor memory, capable of storing a few megabytes of data. The requested data are transferred between the disk tracks and the buffer at a rate dependent on the rotational speed of the disk. Transfers between the data buffer and other devices connected to the bus, normally the main memory, can then take place at the maximum rate allowed by the bus.

The data buffer can also be used to provide a caching mechanism for the disk. When a read request arrives at the disk, the controller can first check to see if the desired data are already available in the cache (buffer). If so, the data can be accessed and placed on the SCSI bus in microseconds rather than milliseconds. Otherwise, the data are read from a disk track in the usual way and stored in the cache. Since it is likely that a subsequent read request will be for data that sequentially follow the currently accessed data, the disk controller can cause more data than needed to be read and placed into the cache, thus potentially shortening the response time for the next request. The cache is typically large enough to store entire tracks of data, so a possible strategy is to begin transferring the contents of the track into the data buffer as soon as the read/write head is positioned over the desired track.

Disk Controller

Operation of a disk drive is controlled by a *disk controller* circuit, which also provides an interface between the disk drive and the bus that connects it to the rest of the computer system. The disk controller may be used to control more than one drive. Figure 5.31 shows a disk controller which controls two disk drives.

A disk controller that is connected directly to the processor system bus, or to an expansion bus such as PCI, contains a number of registers that can be read and written by the operating system. Thus, communication between the OS and the disk controller is achieved in the same manner as with any I/O interface, as discussed in Chapter 4. The disk controller uses the DMA scheme to transfer data between the disk and the main memory. Actually, these transfers are from/to the data buffer, which is implemented

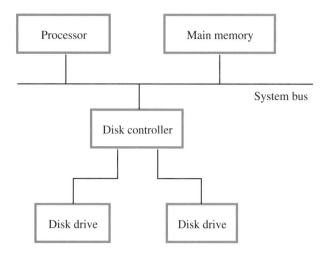

Figure 5.31   Disks connected to the system bus.

as a part of the disk controller module. The OS initiates the transfers by issuing Read and Write requests, which entail loading the controller's registers with the necessary addressing and control information, typically:

Main memory address — The address of the first main memory location of the block of words involved in the transfer.

Disk address — The location of the sector containing the beginning of the desired block of words.

Word count — The number of words in the block to be transferred.

The disk address issued by the OS is a logical address. The corresponding physical address on the disk may be different. For example, bad sectors may be detected when the disk is formatted. The disk controller keeps track of such sectors and substitutes other sectors instead. Normally, a few spare sectors are kept on each track, or on another track in the same cylinder, to be used as substitutes for the bad sectors.

On the disk drive side, the controller's major functions are:

Seek — Causes the disk drive to move the read/write head from its current position to the desired track.

Read — Initiates a Read operation, starting at the address specified in the disk address register. Data read serially from the disk are assembled into words and placed into the data buffer for transfer to the main memory. The number of words is determined by the word count register.

Write — Transfers data to the disk, using a control method similar to that for the Read operations.

Error checking — Computes the error correcting code (ECC) value for the data read from a given sector and compares it with the corresponding ECC value read from the disk. In case of a mismatch, it corrects the error if possible; otherwise, it raises an interrupt to inform the OS that an error has occurred. During a write operation, the controller computes the ECC value for the data to be written and stores this value on the disk.

If a disk drive is connected to a bus that uses packetized transfers, then the controller must be capable of handling such transfers. For example, a controller for a SCSI drive conforms to the SCSI bus protocol described in Chapter 4.

Software and Operating System Implications

All data transfer activities involving disks are initiated by the operating system. The disk is a nonvolatile storage medium, so the OS itself is stored on a disk. During normal operation of a computer, parts of the OS are loaded into the main memory and executed as needed.

When power is turned off, the contents of the main memory are lost. When the power is turned on again, the OS has to be loaded into the main memory, which takes place as part of a process known as *booting*. To initiate booting, a tiny part of main memory is implemented as a nonvolatile ROM. This ROM stores a small *monitor* program that can read and write main memory locations as well as read one block of data stored on the disk at address 0. This block, referred to as the *boot block,* contains a loader program. After the boot block is loaded into memory by the ROM monitor program, it loads the main parts of the OS into the main memory.

Disk accesses are very slow compared to main memory accesses, mostly due to long seek times. After the OS initiates a disk transfer operation, it normally attempts to switch execution to some other task, to make use of the time it would otherwise spend waiting for the transfer to complete. The disk controller informs the OS when the transfer is completed by raising an interrupt.

In a computer system that has multiple disks, the OS may require transfers from several disks. Efficient operation is achieved if the DMA transfer from/to one disk occurs while another disk is doing a seek. The OS can schedule such overlapped I/O activities.

Floppy Disks

The devices previously discussed are known as hard or rigid disk units. *Floppy disks* are smaller, simpler, and cheaper disk units that consist of a flexible, removable, plastic *diskette* coated with magnetic material. The diskette is enclosed in a plastic jacket, which has an opening where the read/write head makes contact with the diskette. A hole in the center of the diskette allows a spindle mechanism in the disk drive to position and rotate the diskette.

One of the simplest schemes used in the first floppy disks for recording data is phase or Manchester encoding mentioned earlier. Disks encoded in this way are said to have *single density*. A more complicated variant of this scheme, called *double density,* is most often used in current standard floppy disks. It increases the storage density by a factor of 2 but also requires more complex circuits in the disk controller.

The main feature of floppy disks is their low cost and shipping convenience. However, they have much smaller storage capacities, longer access times, and higher failure rates than hard disks. Current standard floppy disks are 3.25 inches in diameter and store

1.44 or 2 Mbytes of data. Larger super-floppy disks are also available. One type of such disks, known as the *zip* disk, can store more than 100 Mbytes. In recent years, the attraction of floppy-disk technology has been diminished by the emergence of rewritable compact disks, which we discuss below.

RAID Disk Arrays

Processor speeds have increased dramatically during the past decade. Processor performance has doubled every 18 months. Semiconductor memory speeds have improved more modestly. The smallest relative improvement in terms of speed has been in disk storage devices, for which access times are still on the order of milliseconds. Of course, there has been a spectacular improvement in the storage capacity of these devices.

High-performance devices tend to be expensive. Sometimes it is possible to achieve very high performance at a reasonable cost by using a number of low-cost devices operating in parallel. In Chapter 12 we will see how many commodity processors can be used to implement a high-performance multiprocessor computer system. Multiple magnetic disk drives can be used to provide a high-performance storage unit.

In 1988, researchers at the University of California-Berkeley proposed a storage system based on multiple disks [5]. They called it RAID, for Redundant Array of Inexpensive Disks. Using multiple disks also makes it possible to improve the reliability of the overall system. Six different configurations were proposed. They are known as RAID levels even though there is no hierarchy involved.

RAID 0 is the basic configuration intended to enhance performance. A single large file is stored in several separate disk units by breaking the file up into a number of smaller pieces and storing these pieces on different disks. This is called *data striping*. When the file is accessed for a read, all disks can deliver their data in parallel. The total transfer time of the file is equal to the transfer time that would be required in a single-disk system divided by the number of disks used in the array. However, access time, that is, the seek and rotational delay needed to locate the beginning of the data on each disk, is not reduced. In fact, since each disk operates independently of the others, access times vary, and buffering of the accessed pieces of data is needed so that the complete file can be reassembled and sent to the requesting processor as a single entity. This is the simplest possible disk array operation in which only data-flow-time performance is improved.

RAID 1 is intended to provide better reliability by storing identical copies of data on two disks rather than just one. The two disks are said to be mirrors of each other. Then, if one disk drive fails, all read and write operations are directed to its mirror drive. This is a costly way to improve the reliability because all disks are duplicated.

RAID 2, RAID 3, and RAID 4 levels achieve increased reliability through various parity checking schemes without requiring a full duplication of disks. All of the parity information is kept on one disk.

RAID 5 also makes use of a parity-based error-recovery scheme. However, the parity information is distributed among all disks, rather than being stored on one disk.

Some hybrid arrangements have subsequently been developed. For example, RAID 10 is an array that combines the features of RAID 0 and RAID 1. A more detailed treatment of RAID schemes can be found in References [6] to [10].

* hot swapable spares

The RAID concept has gained commercial acceptance. For example, the Dell Computer Corporation offers products based on RAID 0, RAID 1, RAID 5, and RAID 10. Finally, we should note that as the price of magnetic disk drives has decreased greatly during the past few years, it may be inappropriate to refer to "inexpensive" disks in RAID. Indeed, the term RAID has been redefined by the industry to refer to "independent" disks.

Commodity Disk Considerations

Most disk units are designed to connect to standard buses. The performance of a disk unit depends on its internal structure and the interface used to connect it to the rest of the system. The cost depends largely on the storage capacity, but it is also affected greatly by the sales volume of a particular product.

ATA/EIDE Disks The most widely used computers are the personal computers (PCs) introduced by IBM in 1980, familiarly known as IBM PCs. A disk interface suitable for connection to the IBM PC bus was developed. Its present (enhanced) version has become a standard known as EIDE (Enhanced Integrated Drive Electronics) or as ATA (Advanced Technology Attachment). Many disk manufacturers have a range of disks that have EIDE/ATA interfaces. Such disks can be connected directly to the PCI bus (discussed in Section 4.7.1), which is used in many PCs. In fact, Intel's Pentium chip sets include a controller that allows EIDE/ATA disks to be connected directly to the motherboard. A significant advantage of EIDE/ATA drives is their low price, due to their use in the PC market. One of their main drawbacks is that a separate controller is needed for each drive if two drives are to be used concurrently to improve performance.

SCSI Disks As we have already explained in a previous example, many disks have an interface designed for connection to a standard SCSI bus. These disks tend to be more expensive, but they exhibit better performance, made possible by the advantages of the SCSI bus in comparison with the PCI bus. Concurrent accesses can be made to multiple disk drives because the drive's interface is actively connected to the SCSI bus only when the drive is ready for a data transfer. This is especially useful in applications where there is a large number of requests for small files, which is often the case in computers used as file servers.

RAID Disks RAID disks offer excellent performance and provide a large and reliable storage. They are used either in high-performance computers, or in systems where a higher than normal degree of reliability is required. However, as their price drops to a more affordable level, they are becoming attractive for use even in average-size computer systems.

5.9.2 OPTICAL DISKS

Large storage devices can also be implemented using optical means. The familiar compact disk (CD), used in audio systems, was the first practical application of this technology. Soon after, the optical technology was adapted to the computer environment to provide high-capacity read-only storage referred to as CD-ROM.

The first generation of CDs was developed in the mid-1980s by the Sony and Philips companies, which also published a complete specification for these devices. The technology exploited the possibility of using digital representation of analog sound signals. To provide high-quality sound recording and reproduction, 16-bit samples of the analog signal are taken at a rate of 44,100 samples per second. This sampling rate is twice the highest frequency in the original sound signal, thus allowing for accurate reconstruction. The CDs were required to hold at least an hour of music. The first version was designed to hold up to 75 minutes, which requires a total of about 3×10^9 bits (3 gigabits) of storage. Since then, higher-capacity devices have been developed. A video CD is capable of storing a full-length movie. This requires approximately an order of magnitude more bit-storage capacity than that of audio CDs. Multimedia CDs are also suitable for storing large amounts of computer data.

CD Technology

The optical technology that is used for CD systems is based on a laser light source. A laser beam is directed onto the surface of the spinning disk. Physical indentations in the surface are arranged along the tracks of the disk. They reflect the focused beam toward a photodetector, which detects the stored binary patterns.

The laser emits a coherent light beam that is sharply focussed on the surface of the disk. Coherent light consists of synchronized waves that have the same wavelength. If a coherent light beam is combined with another beam of the same kind, and the two beams are in phase, then the result will be a brighter beam. But, if the waves of the two beams are 180 degrees out of phase, they will cancel each other. Thus, if a photodetector is used to detect the beams, it will detect a bright spot in the first case and a dark spot in the second case.

A cross-section of a small portion of a CD is shown in Figure 5.32a. The bottom layer is polycarbonate plastic, which functions as a clear glass base. The surface of this plastic is programmed to store data by indenting it with *pits*. The unindented parts are called *lands*. A thin layer of reflecting aluminum material is placed on top of a programmed disk. The aluminum is then covered by a protective acrylic. Finally, the topmost layer is deposited and stamped with a label. The total thickness of the disk is 1.2 mm. Almost all of it is contributed by the polycarbonate plastic. The other layers are very thin.

The laser source and the photodetector are positioned below the polycarbonate plastic. The emitted beam travels through this plastic, reflects off the aluminum layer, and travels back toward the photodetector. Note that from the laser side, the pits actually appear as bumps with respect to the lands.

Figure 5.32b shows what happens as the laser beam scans across the disk and encounters a transition from a pit to a land. Three different positions of the laser source and the detector are shown, as would occur when the disk is rotating. When the light reflects solely from the pit, or solely from the land, the detector will see the reflected beam as a bright spot. But, a different situation arises when the beam moves through the edge where the pit changes to the land, and vice versa. The pit is recessed one quarter of the wavelength of the light. Thus, the reflected wave from the pit will be 180 degrees out of phase with the wave reflected from the land, cancelling each other. Hence, at

The hills are alive with the sound of music!

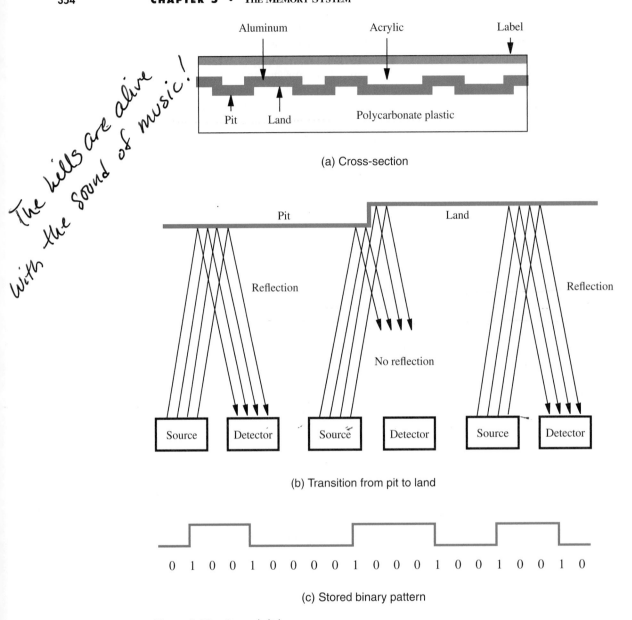

(a) Cross-section

(b) Transition from pit to land

0 1 0 0 1 0 0 0 0 1 0 0 0 1 0 0 1 0 0 1 0

(c) Stored binary pattern

Figure 5.32 Optical disk.

the pit-land and land-pit transitions the detector will not see a reflected beam and will detect a dark spot.

Figure 5.32c depicts several transitions between lands and pits. If each transition, detected as a dark spot, is taken to denote the binary value 1, and the flat portions represent 0s, then the detected binary pattern will be as shown in the figure. This pattern is not a direct representation of the stored data. CDs use a complex encoding scheme to represent data. Each byte of data is represented by a 14-bit code, which provides considerable error detection capability. We will not delve into details of this code.

The pits are arranged along tracks on the surface of the disk. Actually, there is just one physical track, spiraling from the middle of the disk toward the outer edge. But, it is customary to refer to each circular path spanning 360 degrees as a separate track, which is analogous to the terminology used for magnetic disks. The CD is 120 mm in diameter. There is a 15-mm hole in the center. Data are stored on tracks that cover the area from 25-mm radius to 58-mm radius. The space between the tracks is 1.6 microns. Pits are 0.5 microns wide and 0.8 to 3 microns long. There are more than 15,000 tracks on a disk. If the entire track spiral were unraveled, it would be over 5 km long!

These numbers indicate a track density of about 6000 tracks/cm, which is much higher than the density achievable in magnetic disks. The density ranges from 800 to 2000 tracks/cm in hard disks, and is less than 40 tracks/cm in floppy disks.

CD-ROM

Since information is stored in binary form in CDs, they are suitable for use as a storage medium in computer systems. The biggest problem is to ensure the integrity of stored data. Because the pits are very small, it is difficult to implement all of the pits perfectly. In audio and video applications, some errors in data can be tolerated because they are unlikely to affect the reproduced sound or image in a perceptible way. However, such errors are not acceptable in computer applications. Since physical imperfections cannot be avoided, it is necessary to use additional bits to provide error checking and correcting capability. CDs used in computer applications have such capability. They are called *CD-ROMs,* because after manufacture their contents can only be read, as with semiconductor ROM chips. ↳ read only memory

Stored data are organized on CD-ROM tracks in the form of blocks that are called *sectors*. There are several different formats for a sector. One format, known as Mode 1, uses 2352-byte sectors. There is a 16-byte header that contains a synchronization field used to detect the beginning of the sector and addressing information used to identify the sector. This is followed by 2048 bytes of stored data. At the end of the sector, there are 288 bytes used to implement the error-correcting scheme. The number of sectors per track is variable; there are more sectors on the longer outer tracks.

Error detection and correction is done at more than one level. As mentioned in the introduction to CDs, each byte of stored information is encoded using a 14-bit code that has some error-correcting capability. This code can correct single-bit errors. Errors that occur in short bursts, affecting several bits, are detected and corrected using the error-checking bits at the end of the sector.

CD-ROM drives operate at a number of different rotational speeds. The basic speed, known as 1X, is 75 sectors per second. This provides a data rate of 153,600 bytes/s (150 Kbytes/s), using the Mode 1 format. With this speed and format, a CD-ROM based on the standard CD designed for 75 minutes of music has a data storage capacity of about 650 Mbytes. Note that the speed of the drive affects only the data transfer rate but not the storage capacity of the disk. Higher speed CD-ROM drives are identified in relation to the basic speed. Thus, a 40X CD-ROM has a data transfer rate that is 40 times higher than that of the 1X CD-ROM. Observe that this transfer rate (<6 Mbytes/s) is considerably lower than the transfer rates in magnetic hard disks, which are in the range of tens of megabytes per second. Another big difference in performance is the seek time, which in CD-ROMs may be several hundred milliseconds. So, in terms of performance, CD-ROMs are clearly inferior to magnetic disks. Their attraction lies in the small physical size, low cost, and ease of handling as a removable and transportable mass-storage medium.

The importance of CD ROMs for computer systems stems from their large storage capacity and fast access times compared to other inexpensive portable media, such as floppy disks and magnetic tapes. They are widely used for the distribution of software, databases, large texts (books), application programs, and video games.

CD-Recordables

Previously described CDs are read-only devices in which the information is stored using a special procedure. First, a master disk is produced using a high-power laser to burn holes that correspond to the required pits. A mold is then made from the master disk, which has bumps in the place of holes. This is followed by injecting molten polycarbonate plastic into the mold to make a CD that has the same pattern of holes (pits) as the master disk. This process is clearly suitable only for volume production of CDs.

A new type of CD was developed in the late 1990s on which data can be easily recorded by a computer user. It is known as CD-Recordable (CD-R). A spiral track is implemented on a disk during the manufacturing process. A laser in a CD-R drive is used to burn pits into an organic dye on the track. When a burned spot is heated beyond a critical temperature, it becomes opaque. Such burned spots reflect less light when subsequently read. The written data are stored permanently. Unused portions of a disk can be used to store additional data at a later time.

CD-ReWritables

The most flexible CDs are those that can be written multiple times by the user. They are known as CD-RWs (CD-ReWritables).

The basic structure of CD-RWs is similar to the structure of CD-Rs. Instead of using an organic dye in the recording layer, an alloy of silver, indium, antimony and tellurium is used. This alloy has interesting and useful behavior when it is heated and cooled. If it is heated above its melting point (500 degrees C) and then cooled down, it goes into an amorphous state in which it absorbs light. But, if it is heated only to about 200 degrees C and this temperature is maintained for an extended period, a process known as *annealing* takes place, which leaves the alloy in a crystalline state that allows light to pass through. If the crystalline state represents land area, pits can be created by heating selected spots past the melting point. The stored data can be erased using the annealing process, which returns the alloy to a uniform crystalline state. A reflective material is placed above the recording layer to reflect the light when the disk is read.

The CD-RW drive uses three different laser powers. The highest power is used to record the pits. The middle power is used to put the alloy into its crystalline state; it is referred to as the "erase power." The lowest power is used to read the stored information. There is a limit on how many times a CD-RW disk can be rewritten. Presently, this can be done up to 1000 times.

CD-RW drives can usually also deal with other compact disk media. They can read CD-ROMs, and both read and write CD-Rs. They are designed to meet the requirements of standard interconnection interfaces, such as EIDE, SCSI, and USB.

CD-RWs provide a low-cost storage medium. They are suitable for archival storage of information that may range from databases to photographic images. They can be used for low-volume distribution of information, just like CD-Rs. The CD-RW drives are now fast enough to be used for daily hard disk backup purposes. The CD-RW technology has made CD-Rs less relevant because it offers superior capability at only slightly higher cost.

DVD Technology

The success of CD technology and the continuing quest for greater storage capability has led to the development of DVD (Digital Versatile Disk) technology. The first DVD standard was defined in 1996 by a consortium of companies. The objective is to be able to store a full-length movie on one side of a DVD disk.

The physical size of a DVD disk is the same as for CDs. The disk is 1.2 mm thick, and it is 120 mm in diameter. Its storage capacity is made much larger than that of CDs by several design changes:

- A red light laser with a wavelength of 635 nm is used instead of the infrared light laser used in CDs, which has a wavelength of 780 nm. The shorter wavelength makes it possible to focus the light to a smaller spot.
- Pits are smaller, having a minimum length of 0.4 micron.
- Tracks are placed closer together; the distance between tracks is 0.74 micron.

Using these improvements leads to a DVD capacity of 4.7 Gbytes.

Further increases in capacity have been achieved by going to two-layered and two-sided disks. The single-layered single-sided disk, defined in the standard as DVD-5, has a structure that is almost the same as the CD in Figure 5.32a. A double-layered disk makes use of two layers on which tracks are implemented on top of each other. The first layer is the clear base, as in CD disks. But, instead of using reflecting aluminum, the lands and pits of this layer are covered by a translucent material that acts as a semireflector. The surface of this material is then also programmed with indented pits to store data. A reflective material is placed on top of the second layer of pits and lands. The disk is read by focusing the laser beam on the desired layer. When the beam is focused on the first layer, sufficient light is reflected by the translucent material to detect the stored binary patterns. When the beam is focused on the second layer, the light reflected by the reflective material corresponds to the information stored on this layer. In both cases, the layer on which the beam is not focused reflects a much smaller amount of light, which is eliminated by the detector circuit as noise. The total storage capacity of both layers is 8.5 Gbytes. This disk is called DVD-9 in the standard.

Two single-sided disks can be put together to form a sandwich-like structure where the top disk is turned upside down. This can be done with single-layered disks, as specified in DVD-10, giving a composite disk with a capacity of 9.4 Gbytes. It can also be done with the double-layered disks, as specified in DVD-18, yielding a capacity of 17 Gbytes.

Access times for DVD drives are similar to CD drives. However, when the DVD disks rotate at the same speed, the data transfer rates are much higher because of the higher density of pits.

DVD-RAM

A rewritable version of DVD devices, known as DVD-RAM, has also been developed. It provides a large storage capacity. Its only disadvantages are the higher price and the relatively slow writing speed. To ensure that the data have been recorded correctly on the disk, a process known as write verification is performed. This is done by the DVD-RAM drive, which reads the stored contents and checks them against the original data. A detailed discussion of optical disk technology can be found in Reference [11].

5.9.3 MAGNETIC TAPE SYSTEMS

Magnetic tapes are suited for off-line storage of large amounts of data. They are typically used for hard disk backup purposes and for archival storage. Magnetic-tape recording uses the same principle as used in magnetic-disk recording. The main difference is that the magnetic film is deposited on a very thin 0.5- or 0.25-inch wide plastic tape. Seven or 9 bits (corresponding to one character) are recorded in parallel across the width of the tape, perpendicular to the direction of motion. A separate read/write head is provided for each bit position on the tape, so that all bits of a character can be read or written in parallel. One of the character bits is used as a parity bit.

Data on the tape are organized in the form of *records* separated by gaps, as shown in Figure 5.33. Tape motion is stopped only when a record gap is underneath the read/write heads. The record gaps are long enough to allow the tape to attain its normal speed before the beginning of the next record is reached. If a coding scheme such as that in Figure 5.29*c* is used for recording data on the tape, record gaps are identified as areas where there is no change in magnetization. This allows record gaps to be detected independently of the recorded data. To help users organize large amounts of data, a group of related records is called a *file*. The beginning of a file is identified by a *file mark*, as shown in Figure 5.33. The file mark is a special single- or multiple-character

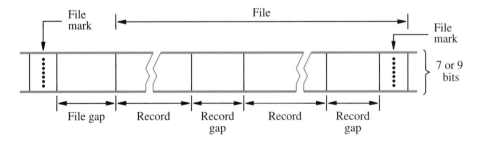

Figure 5.33 Organization of data on magnetic tape.

record, usually preceded by a gap longer than the interrecord gap. The first record following a file mark can be used as a *header* or *identifier* for this file. This allows the user to search a tape containing a large number of files for a particular file.

The controller of a magnetic tape drive enables the execution of a number of control commands in addition to read and write commands. Control commands include the following operations:

- Rewind tape
- Rewind and unload tape
- Erase tape
- Write tape mark
- Forward space one record
- Backspace one record
- Forward space one file
- Backspace one file

The tape mark referred to in the operation "Write tape mark" is similar to a file mark except that it is used for identifying the beginning of the tape. The end of the tape is sometimes identified by the EOT (end of tape) character (see Appendix E).

Two methods of formatting and using tapes are available. In the first method, the records are variable in length. This allows efficient use of the tape, but it does not permit updating or overwriting of records in place. The second method is to use fixed-length records. In this case, it is possible to update records in place. Although this may seem to be a significant advantage, in practice it has turned out to be of little importance. The most common uses of tapes are backing up information on magnetic disks and archival storage of data. In these applications, a tape is written from the beginning to the end so that the size of the records is irrelevant.

Cartridge Tape System

Tape systems have been developed for backup of on-line disk storage. One such system uses an 8-mm video format tape housed in a cassette. These units are called cartridge tapes. They have capacities in the range of 2 to 5 gigabytes and handle data transfers at the rate of a few hundred kilobytes per second. Reading and writing is done by a helical scan system operating across the tape, similar to that used in video cassette tape drives. Bit densities of tens of millions of bits per square inch are achievable. Multiple-cartridge systems are available that automate the loading and unloading of cassettes so that tens of gigabytes of on-line storage can be backed up unattended.

5.10   CONCLUDING REMARKS

The memory is a major component in any computer. Its capacity and speed characteristics are important in determining the performance of a computer. In this chapter, we presented the most important technological and organizational details of memory design.

Developments in semiconductor technology have led to spectacular improvements in the speed and capacity of memory chips, accompanied by a large decrease in the cost per bit. But processor chips have evolved even more spectacularly. In particular, improvement in the operating speed of processor chips has outpaced that of memory chips. To exploit fully the capability of a modern processor, the computer must have a large and fast memory. Since cost is also important, the memory cannot be designed simply by using fast SRAM components. As we saw in this chapter, the solution lies in the memory hierarchy.

Today, an affordable large main memory is implemented with dynamic memory chips. Such a memory may be an order of magnitude slower than a fast processor, in terms of clock cycles, which makes it imperative to use an SRAM cache memory to reduce the effective memory access time seen by the processor. Memory latency is an important parameter in determining the performance of a computer. Much research effort has focused on developing schemes that minimize the effect of memory latency. We described how write buffers and prefetching can reduce the impact of latency by performing less urgent memory accesses at times when no higher-priority memory accesses (caused by read misses) are required. The effect of memory latency can also be reduced if blocks of consecutive words are accessed at one time; new memory chips are being developed to exploit this fact.

Secondary storage, in the form of magnetic and optical disks, provides the largest capacity in the memory hierarchy. The virtual memory mechanism makes interaction between the disk and the main memory transparent to the user. Hardware support for virtual memory has become a standard feature of modern processors.

Magnetic disks are a fascinating example of evolution in computer technology. They have always been the slow part of the memory hierarchy. At various times, the continued viability of magnetic disks has been questioned as new technologies appeared to have greater promise for future development. In the early 1980s, it seemed that "magnetic bubble" memories would pose a large threat. More recent contenders are flash drives and optical disks. However, instead of being pushed aside, the magnetic disk technology keeps getting better. The disk drives are continuously becoming larger in storage capacity, smaller in physical size, and cheaper in terms of the cost per bit stored.

PROBLEMS

5.1   Give a block diagram similar to the one in Figure 5.10 for a 8M × 32 memory using 512K × 8 memory chips.

5.2   Consider the dynamic memory cell of Figure 5.6. Assume that $C = 50$ femtofarads $(10^{-15}$ F) and that leakage current through the transistor is about 9 picoamperes $(10^{-12}$ A). The voltage across the capacitor when it is fully charged is equal to 4.5 V. The cell must be refreshed before this voltage drops below 3 V. Estimate the minimum refresh rate.

5.3   In the bottom right corner of Figure 5.8 there are data input and data output registers. Draw a circuit that can implement one bit of each of these registers, and show the required connections to the block "Read/Write circuits & latches" on one side and the data bus on the other side.

5.4 Consider a main memory constructed with SDRAM chips that have timing requirements depicted in Figure 5.9, except that the burst length is 8. Assume that 32 bits of data are transferred in parallel. If a 133-MHz clock is used, how much time does it take to transfer:

(a) 32 bytes of data

(b) 64 bytes of data

What is the latency in each case?

5.5 Criticize the following statement: "Using a faster processor chip results in a corresponding increase in performance of a computer even if the main memory speed remains the same."

5.6 A program consists of two nested loops — a small inner loop and a much larger outer loop. The general structure of the program is given in Figure P5.1. The decimal memory addresses shown delineate the location of the two loops and the beginning and end of the total program. All memory locations in the various sections, 17–22, 23–164, 165–239, and so on, contain instructions to be executed in straight-line sequencing. The program is to be run on a computer that has an instruction cache organized in the direct-mapped manner (see Figure 5.15) and that has the following parameters:

Main memory size	64K words
Cache size	1K words
Block size	128 words

Figure P5.1   A program structure for Problem 5.6.

The cycle time of the main memory is 10τ s, and the cycle time of the cache is 1τ s.

(a) Specify the number of bits in the TAG, BLOCK, and WORD fields in main memory addresses.

(b) Compute the total time needed for instruction fetching during execution of the program in Figure P5.1.

5.7 A computer uses a small direct-mapped cache between the main memory and the processor. The cache has four 16-bit words, and each word has an associated 13-bit tag, as shown in Figure P5.2a. When a miss occurs during a read operation, the requested word is read from the main memory and sent to the processor. At the same time, it is copied into the cache, and its block number is stored in the associated tag. Consider the following loop in a program where all instructions and operands are 16 bits long:

$$
\begin{array}{lll}
\text{LOOP} & \text{Add} & \text{(R1)+,R0} \\
& \text{Decrement} & \text{R2} \\
& \text{BNE} & \text{LOOP}
\end{array}
$$

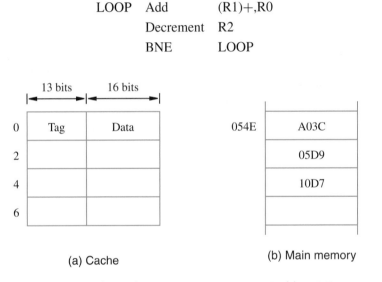

(a) Cache

(b) Main memory

Figure P5.2 Cache and main memory contents in Problem 5.7.

Assume that, before this loop is entered, registers R0, R1, and R2 contain 0, 054E, and 3, respectively. Also assume that the main memory contains the data shown in Figure P5.2b, where all entries are given in hexadecimal notation. The loop starts at location LOOP = 02EC.

(a) Show the contents of the cache at the end of each pass through the loop.

(b) Assume that the access time of the main memory is 10τ and that of the cache is 1τ. Calculate the execution time for each pass. Ignore the time taken by the processor between memory cycles.

5.8 Repeat Problem 5.7, assuming only instructions are stored in the cache. Data operands are fetched directly from the main memory and not copied into the cache. Why does this choice lead to faster execution than when both instructions and data are written into the cache?

5.9 A block-set-associative cache consists of a total of 64 blocks divided into 4-block sets. The main memory contains 4096 blocks, each consisting of 128 words.

(*a*) How many bits are there in a main memory address?

(*b*) How many bits are there in each of the TAG, SET, and WORD fields?

5.10 A computer system has a main memory consisting of 1M 16-bit words. It also has a 4K-word cache organized in the block-set-associative manner, with 4 blocks per set and 64 words per block.

(*a*) Calculate the number of bits in each of the TAG, SET, and WORD fields of the main memory address format.

(*b*) Assume that the cache is initially empty. Suppose that the processor fetches 4352 words from locations 0, 1, 2, ... , 4351, in that order. It then repeats this fetch sequence nine more times. If the cache is 10 times faster than the main memory, estimate the improvement factor resulting from the use of the cache. Assume that the LRU algorithm is used for block replacement.

5.11 Repeat Problem 5.10, assuming that whenever a block is to be brought from the main memory and the corresponding set in the cache is full, the new block replaces the most recently used block of this set.

5.12 Section 5.5.3 illustrates the effect of different cache-mapping techniques, using the program in Figure 5.19. Suppose that this program is changed so that in the second loop the elements are handled in the same order as in the first loop, that is, the control for the second loop is specified as

for $i := 0$ **to** 9 **do**

Derive the equivalents of Figures 5.20 through 5.22 for this program. What conclusions can be drawn from this exercise?

5.13 A byte-addressable computer has a small data cache capable of holding eight 32-bit words. Each cache block consists of one 32-bit word. When a given program is executed, the processor reads data from the following sequence of hex addresses:

200, 204, 208, 20C, 2F4, 2F0, 200, 204, 218, 21C, 24C, 2F4

This pattern is repeated four times.

(*a*) Show the contents of the cache at the end of each pass through this loop if a direct-mapped cache is used. Compute the hit rate for this example. Assume that the cache is initially empty.

(*b*) Repeat part (*a*) for an associative-mapped cache that uses the LRU replacement algorithm.

(*c*) Repeat part (*a*) for a four-way set-associative cache.

5.14 Repeat Problem 5.13, assuming that each cache block consists of two 32-bit words. For part (*c*), use a two-way set-associative cache.

5.15 How might the value of k in the interleaved memory system of Figure 5.25*b* influence block size in the design of a cache memory to be used with the system?

5.16 In many computers the cache block size is in the range of 32 to 128 bytes. What would be the main advantages and disadvantages of making the size of cache blocks larger or smaller?

5.17 Consider the effectiveness of interleaving with respect to the size of cache blocks. Using calculations similar to those in Section 5.6.2, estimate the performance improvement for block sizes of 16, 8, and 4 words. Assume that all words loaded into the cache are accessed by the processor at least once.

5.18 Assume a computer has L1 and L2 caches, as discussed in Section 5.6.3. The cache blocks consist of 8 words. Assume that the hit rate is the same for both caches and that it is equal to 0.95 for instructions and 0.90 for data. Assume also that the times needed to access an 8-word block in these caches are $C_1 = 1$ cycle and $C_2 = 10$ cycles.

    (*a*) What is the average access time experienced by the processor if the main memory uses interleaving? Assume that the memory access parameters are as described in Section 5.6.1.

    (*b*) What is the average access time if the main memory is not interleaved?

    (*c*) What is the improvement obtained with interleaving?

5.19 Repeat Problem 5.18, assuming that a cache block consists of 4 words. Estimate an appropriate value for C_2, assuming that the L2 cache is implemented with SRAM chips.

5.20 Consider the following analogy for the concept of caching. A serviceman comes to a house to repair the heating system. He carries a toolbox that contains a number of tools that he has used recently in similar jobs. He uses these tools repeatedly, until he reaches a point where other tools are needed. It is likely that he has the required tools in his truck outside the house. But, if the needed tools are not in the truck, he must go to his shop to get them.

    Suppose we argue that the toolbox, the truck, and the shop correspond to the L1 cache, the L2 cache, and the main memory of a computer. How good is this analogy? Discuss its correct and incorrect features.

5.21 A 1024 × 1024 array of 32-bit numbers is to be "normalized" as follows. For each column, the largest element is found and all elements of the column are divided by this maximum value. Assume that each page in the virtual memory consists of 4K bytes, and that 1M bytes of the main memory are allocated for storing data during this computation. Suppose that it takes 40 ms to load a page from the disk into the main memory when a page fault occurs.

    (*a*) How many page faults would occur if the elements of the array are stored in column order in the virtual memory?

    (*b*) How many page faults would occur if the elements are stored in row order?

    (*c*) Estimate the total time needed to perform this normalization for both arrangements (*a*) and (*b*).

5.22 Consider a computer system in which the available pages in the physical memory are divided among several application programs. When all the pages allocated to a program are full and a new page is needed, the new page must replace one of the resident pages. The operating system monitors the page transfer activity and dynamically adjusts the page allocation to various programs. Suggest a suitable strategy that the operating system can use to minimize the overall rate of page transfers.

5.23 In a computer with a virtual-memory system, the execution of an instruction may be interrupted by a page fault. What state information has to be saved so that this instruction can be resumed later? Note that bringing a new page into the main memory involves a DMA transfer, which requires execution of other instructions. Is it simpler to abandon the interrupted instruction and completely reexecute it later? Can this be done?

5.24 When a program generates a reference to a page that does not reside in the physical main memory, execution of the program is suspended until the requested page is loaded into the main memory. What difficulties might arise when an instruction in one page has an operand in a different page? What capabilities must the processor have to handle this situation?

5.25 A disk unit has 24 recording surfaces. It has a total of 14,000 cylinders. There is an average of 400 sectors per track. Each sector contains 512 bytes of data.

(a) What is the maximum number of bytes that can be stored in this unit?

(b) What is the data transfer rate in bytes per second at a rotational speed of 7200 rpm?

(c) Using a 32-bit word, suggest a suitable scheme for specifying the disk address, assuming that there are 512 bytes per sector.

5.26 The seek time plus rotational delay in accessing a particular data block on a disk is usually much longer than the data flow period for most disk transfers. Consider a long sequence of accesses to the 3.5-inch disk given as an example in Section 5.9.1, for either Read or Write operations in which the average block being accessed is 8K bytes long.

(a) Assuming that the blocks are randomly located on the disk, estimate the average percentage of the total time occupied by seek operations and rotational delays.

(b) Repeat part (a) for the situation in which the disk accesses have been arranged so that in 90 percent of the cases, the next access will be to a data block on the same cylinder.

5.27 The average seek time and rotational delay in a disk system are 6 ms and 3 ms, respectively. The rate of data transfer to or from the disk is 30 Mbytes/sec and all disk accesses are for 8 Kbytes of data. Disk DMA controllers, the processor, and the main memory are all attached to a single bus. The bus data width is 32 bits, and a bus transfer to or from the main memory takes 10 nanoseconds.

(a) What is the maximum number of disk units that can be simultaneously transferring data to or from the main memory?

(b) What percentage of main memory cycles are stolen by a disk unit, on average, over a long period of time during which a sequence of independent 8K-byte transfers takes place?

5.28 Given that magnetic disks are used as the secondary storage for program and data files in a virtual-memory system, which disk parameter(s) should influence the choice of page size?

5.29 A tape drive has the following parameters:

Bit density	2000 bits/cm
Tape speed	800 cm/s
Time to reverse direction of motion	225 ms
Minimum time spent at an interrecord gap	3 ms
Average record length	4000 characters

Estimate the percentage gain in time resulting from the ability to read records in both the forward and backward directions. Assume that records are accessed at random and that on average, the distance between two records accessed in sequence is four records.

REFERENCES

1. T.C. Mowry, "Tolerating Latency through Software-Controlled Data Prefetching," *Tech. Report CSL-TR-94-628,* Stanford University, Calif., 1994.

2. J.L. Baer and T.F. Chen, "An Effective On-Chip Preloading Scheme to Reduce Data Access Penalty," *Proceedings of Supercomputing '91,* 1991, pp. 176–186.

3. J.W.C. Fu and J.H. Patel, "Stride Directed Prefetching in Scalar Processors," *Proceedings of the 24th International Symposium on Microarchitecture,* 1992, pp. 102–110.

4. D. Kroft, "Lockup-Free Instruction Fetch/Prefetch Cache Organization," *Proceedings of the 8th Annual International Symposium on Computer Architecture,* 1981, pp. 81–85.

5. D.A. Patterson, G.A. Gibson, and R.H. Katz, "A case for redundant arrays of inexpensive disks (RAID)," *Proceedings of the ACM SIGMOD International Conference on Management of Data,* 1988, pp. 109–166.

6. P.M. Chen, E.K. Lee, G.A. Gibson, R.H. Katz, and D.A. Patterson, "RAID: High-Performance, Reliable Secondary Storage," *ACM Computing Surveys,* vol. 26, no. 2, June 1994, pp. 145–185.

7. D.A. Patterson and J.L. Hennessy, *Computer Architecture — A Quantitative Approach,* 2nd ed., Morgan Kaufmann, San Francisco, CA, 1996.

8. A.S. Tannenbaum, *Structured Computer Organization,* 4th ed. Prentice Hall, Upper Saddle River, NJ, 1999.

9. "RAID Technology White Paper," Dell Computer Corporation, 1999.

10. A. Clements, *The Principles of Computer Hardware,* 3rd ed., Oxford University Press, 2000.

CHAPTER

6

ARITHMETIC

CHAPTER OBJECTIVES

In this chapter you will learn about:

- High-speed adders, implemented in a hierarchical structure, using carry-lookahead logic to generate carry signals in parallel

- The Booth algorithm, used to determine how multiplicand summands are selected by the multiplier bit patterns in performing multiplication of signed numbers

- High-speed multipliers, which use carry-save addition to add summands in parallel

- Circuits that perform division operations

- The representation of floating-point numbers in the IEEE standard format, and how to perform basic arithmetic operations on them

A basic operation in all digital computers is the addition or subtraction of two numbers. Arithmetic operations occur at the machine instruction level. They are implemented, along with basic logic functions such as AND, OR, NOT, and EXCLUSIVE-OR (XOR), in the arithmetic and logic unit (ALU) subsystem of the processor, as discussed in Chapter 1. In this chapter, we present the logic circuits used to implement arithmetic operations. The time needed to perform an addition operation affects the processor's performance. Multiply and divide operations, which require more complex circuitry than either addition or subtraction operations, also affect performance. We present some of the techniques used in modern computers to perform arithmetic operations at high speed.

Compared with arithmetic operations, logic operations are simple to implement using combinational circuitry. They require only independent Boolean operations on individual bit positions of the operands, whereas carry/borrow lateral signals are required in arithmetic operations.

In Section 2.1, we described the representation of signed binary numbers, and showed that 2's-complement is the best representation from the standpoint of performing addition and subtraction operations. The examples in Figure 2.4 show that two, n-bit, signed numbers can be added using n-bit binary addition, treating the sign bit the same as the other bits. In other words, a logic circuit that is designed to add unsigned binary numbers can also be used to add signed numbers in 2's-complement. If overflow does not occur, the sum is correct, and any output carry can be ignored. The first two sections of this chapter present logic circuit networks for addition and subtraction.

6.1 ADDITION AND SUBTRACTION OF SIGNED NUMBERS

Figure 6.1 shows the logic truth table for the sum and carry-out functions for adding equally weighted bits x_i and y_i in two numbers X and Y. The figure also shows logic expressions for these functions, along with an example of addition of the 4-bit unsigned numbers 7 and 6. Note that each stage of the addition process must accommodate a carry-in bit. We use c_i to represent the carry-in to the ith stage, which is the same as the carry-out from the $(i - 1)$st stage.

The logic expression for s_i in Figure 6.1 can be implemented with a 3-input XOR gate, used in Figure 6.2a as part of the logic required for a single stage of binary addition. The carry-out function, c_{i+1}, is implemented with a two-level AND-OR logic circuit. A convenient symbol for the complete circuit for a single stage of addition, called a *full adder* (FA), is also shown in the figure.

A cascaded connection of n full adder blocks, as shown in Figure 6.2b, can be used to add two n-bit numbers. Since the carries must propagate, or ripple, through this cascade, the configuration is called an *n-bit ripple-carry adder*.

The carry-in, c_0, into the *least-significant-bit* (LSB) position provides a convenient means of adding 1 to a number. For instance, forming the 2's-complement of a number involves adding 1 to the 1's-complement of the number. The carry signals are also useful for interconnecting k adders to form an adder capable of handling input numbers that are kn bits long, as shown in Figure 6.2c.

x_i	y_i	Carry-in c_i	Sum s_i	Carry-out c_{i+1}
0	0	0	0	0
0	0	1	1	0
0	1	0	1	0
0	1	1	0	1
1	0	0	1	0
1	0	1	0	1
1	1	0	0	1
1	1	1	1	1

$$s_i = \overline{x_i}\overline{y_i}c_i + \overline{x_i}y_i\overline{c_i} + x_i\overline{y_i}\overline{c_i} + x_iy_ic_i = x_i \oplus y_i \oplus c_i$$
$$c_{i+1} = y_ic_i + x_ic_i + x_iy_i$$

Example:

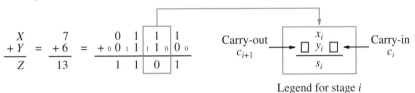

Legend for stage i

Figure 6.1 Logic specification for a stage of binary addition.

6.1.1 ADDITION/SUBTRACTION LOGIC UNIT

The n-bit adder in Figure 6.2b can be used to add 2's-complement numbers X and Y, where the x_{n-1} and y_{n-1} bits are the sign bits. In this case, the carry-out bit, c_n, is not part of the answer. In section 2.1.4, arithmetic overflow was discussed. Overflow can only occur when the signs of the two operands are the same. In this case, overflow obviously occurs if the sign of the result is different. Therefore, a circuit to detect overflow can be added to the n-bit adder by implementing the logic expression

$$\text{Overflow} = x_{n-1}y_{n-1}\overline{s}_{n-1} + \overline{x}_{n-1}\overline{y}_{n-1}s_{n-1}$$

It can also be shown that overflow occurs when the carry bits c_n and c_{n-1} are different. (See Problem 6.9.) Therefore, a simpler alternative circuit for detecting overflow can be obtained by implementing the expression $c_n \oplus c_{n-1}$ with an XOR gate.

In order to perform the subtraction operation $X - Y$ on 2's-complement numbers X and Y, we form the 2's-complement of Y and add it to X. The logic circuit network shown in Figure 6.3 can be used to perform either addition or subtraction based on the value applied to the Add/Sub input control line. This line is set to 0 for addition, applying the Y vector unchanged to one of the adder inputs along with a carry-in signal, c_0,

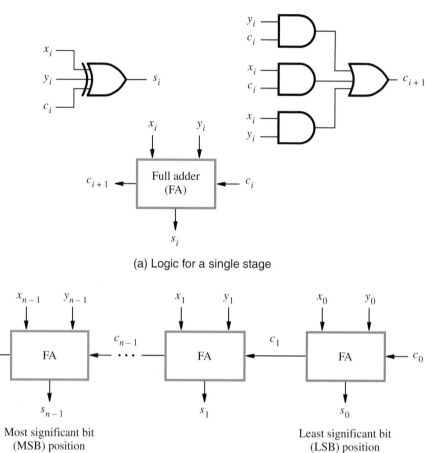

(a) Logic for a single stage

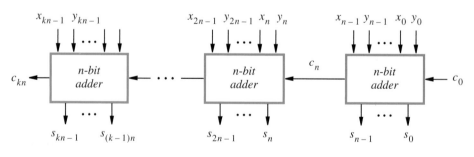

Most significant bit
(MSB) position

Least significant bit
(LSB) position

(b) An *n*-bit ripple-carry adder

(c) Cascade of *k n*-bit adders

Figure 6.2   Logic for addition of binary vectors.

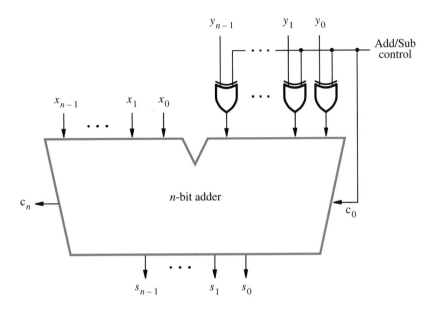

Figure 6.3 Binary addition-subtraction logic network.

of 0. When the Add/Sub control line is set to 1, the Y vector is 1's-complemented (that is, bit complemented) by the XOR gates and c_0 is set to 1 to complete the 2's-complementation of Y. Remember that 2's-complementing a negative number is done in exactly the same manner as for a positive number. An XOR gate can be added to Figure 6.3 to detect the overflow condition $c_n \oplus c_{n-1}$.

6.2 DESIGN OF FAST ADDERS

If an n-bit ripple-carry adder is used in the addition/subtraction unit of Figure 6.3, it may have too much delay in developing its outputs, s_0 through s_{n-1} and c_n. Whether or not the delay incurred is acceptable can be decided only in the context of the speed of other processor components and the data transfer times of registers and cache memories. The delay through a network of logic gates depends on the integrated circuit electronic technology (see Appendix A) used in fabricating the network and on the number of gates in the paths from inputs to outputs. The delay through any combinational logic network constructed from gates in a particular technology is determined by adding up the number of logic-gate delays along the longest signal propagation path through the network. In the case of the n-bit ripple-carry adder, the longest path is from inputs x_0, y_0, and c_0 at the LSB position to outputs c_n and s_{n-1} at the *most-significant-bit* (MSB) position.

Using the logic implementation indicated in Figure 6.2a, c_{n-1} is available in $2(n-1)$ gate delays, and s_{n-1} is correct one XOR gate delay later. The final carry-out, c_n, is available after $2n$ gate delays. Therefore, if a ripple-carry adder is used to implement the addition/subtraction unit shown in Figure 6.3, all sum bits are available in $2n$ gate delays, including the delay through the XOR gates on the Y input. Using the implementation $c_n \oplus c_{n-1}$ for overflow, this indicator is available after $2_n + 2$ gate delays.

Two approaches can be taken to reduce delay in adders. The first approach is to use the fastest possible electronic technology in implementing the ripple-carry logic design or variations of it. The second approach is to use an augmented logic gate network structure that is larger than that shown in Figure 6.2b. We will describe an easily understood version of the second approach in the next section. In practice, a number of design techniques have been used to implement high-speed adders. They include electronic circuit designs for fast propagation of carry signals as well as variations on the basic network structure presented in the next section.

6.2.1 CARRY-LOOKAHEAD ADDITION

A fast adder circuit must speed up the generation of the carry signals. The logic expressions for s_i (sum) and c_{i+1} (carry-out) of stage i (see Figure 6.1) are

$$s_i = x_i \oplus y_i \oplus c_i$$

and

$$c_{i+1} = x_i y_i + x_i c_i + y_i c_i$$

Factoring the second equation into

$$c_{i+1} = x_i y_i + (x_i + y_i)c_i$$

we can write

$$c_{i+1} = G_i + P_i c_i$$

where

$$G_i = x_i y_i \quad \text{and} \quad P_i = x_i + y_i$$

The expressions G_i and P_i are called the *generate* and *propagate* functions for stage i. If the generate function for stage i is equal to 1, then $c_{i+1} = 1$, independent of the input carry, c_i. This occurs when both x_i and y_i are 1. The propagate function means that an input carry will produce an output carry when either x_i is 1 or y_i is 1. All G_i and P_i functions can be formed independently and in parallel in one logic-gate delay after the X and Y vectors are applied to the inputs of an n-bit adder. Each bit stage contains an AND gate to form G_i, an OR gate to form P_i, and a three-input XOR gate to form s_i. A simpler circuit can be derived by observing that an adequate propagate function can be realized as $P_i = x_i \oplus y_i$, which differs from $P_i = x_i + y_i$ only when $x_i = y_i = 1$. But, in this case $G_i = 1$, so it does not matter whether P_i is 0 or 1. Then, using a cascade of two 2-input XOR gates to realize the 3-input XOR function, the basic cell B in Figure 6.4a can be used in each bit stage.

Expanding c_i in terms of $i - 1$ subscripted variables and substituting into the c_{i+1} expression, we obtain

$$c_{i+1} = G_i + P_i G_{i-1} + P_i P_{i-1} c_{i-1}$$

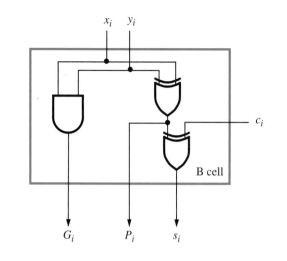

(a) Bit-stage cell

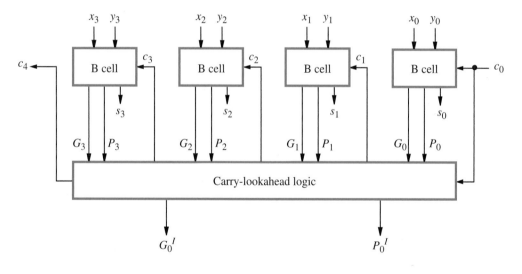

(b) 4-bit adder

Figure 6.4 4-bit carry-lookahead adder.

Continuing this type of expansion, the final expression for any carry variable is

$$c_{i+1} = G_i + P_i G_{i-1} + P_i P_{i-1} G_{i-2} + \cdots + P_i P_{i-1} \cdots P_1 G_0 + P_i P_{i-1} \cdots P_0 c_0 \qquad [6.1]$$

Thus, all carries can be obtained three gate delays after the input signals X, Y, and c_0 are applied because only one gate delay is needed to develop all P_i and G_i signals, followed by two gate delays in the AND-OR circuit for c_{i+1}. After a further XOR gate delay, all sum bits are available. Therefore, independent of n, the n-bit addition process requires only four gate delays.

Let us consider the design of a 4-bit adder. The carries can be implemented as

$$c_1 = G_0 + P_0 c_0$$

$$c_2 = G_1 + P_1 G_0 + P_1 P_0 c_0$$

$$c_3 = G_2 + P_2 G_1 + P_2 P_1 G_0 + P_2 P_1 P_0 c_0$$

$$c_4 = G_3 + P_3 G_2 + P_3 P_2 G_1 + P_3 P_2 P_1 G_0 + P_3 P_2 P_1 P_0 c_0$$

The complete 4-bit adder is shown in Figure 6.4b. The carries are implemented in the block labeled carry-lookahead logic. An adder implemented in this form is called a *carry-lookahead adder*. Delay through the adder is 3 gate delays for all carry bits and 4 gate delays for all sum bits. In comparison, note that a 4-bit ripple-carry adder requires 7 gate delays for s_3 and 8 gate delays for c_4.

If we try to extend the carry-lookahead adder of Figure 6.4b for longer operands, we run into a problem of gate fan-in constraints. From Expression 6.1, we see that the last AND gate and the OR gate require a fan-in of $i + 2$ in generating c_{i+1}. For c_4 in the 4-bit adder, a fan-in of 5 is required. This is about the limit for practical gates. So the adder design shown in Figure 6.4b cannot be directly extended to longer operand sizes. However, if we cascade a number of 4-bit adders, as shown in Figure 6.2c, it is possible to build longer adders.

Eight 4-bit carry-lookahead adders can be connected as in Figure 6.2c to form a 32-bit adder. The delays in generating sum bits $s_{31}, s_{30}, s_{29}, s_{28}$, and c_{32} in the high-order 4-bit adder in this cascade are calculated as follows. The carry-out c_4 from the low-order adder is available 3 gate delays after the input operands X, Y, and c_0 are applied to the 32-bit adder. Then, c_8 is available at the output of the second adder after a further 2 gate delays, c_{12} is available after a further 2 gate delays, and so on. Finally, c_{28}, the carry-in to the high-order 4-bit adder, is available after a total of $(6 \times 2) + 3 = 15$ gate delays. Then, c_{32} and all carries inside the high-order adder are available after a further 2 gate delays, and all 4 sum bits are available after 1 more gate delay, for a total of 18 gate delays. This should be compared to total delays of 63 and 64 for s_{31} and c_{32} if a ripple-carry adder is used.

In the next section, we show how it is possible to improve upon the cascade structure just discussed, leading to further reduction in adder delay. The key idea is to generate the carries $c_4, c_8, \ldots$ in parallel, similar to the way that c_1, c_2, c_3, and c_4, are generated in parallel in the 4-bit carry-lookahead adder.

Higher-Level Generate and Propagate Functions

In the 32-bit adder just discussed, the carries $c_4, c_8, c_{12}, \ldots$ ripple through the 4-bit adder blocks with two gate delays per block, analogous to the way that individual carries ripple through each bit stage in a ripple-carry adder. By using higher-level block generate and propagate functions, it is possible to use the lookahead approach to develop the carries $c_4, c_8, c_{12}, \ldots$ in parallel, in a higher-level carry-lookahead circuit.

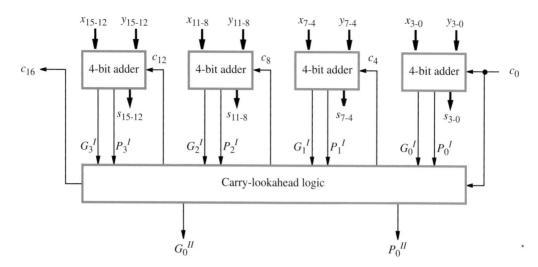

Figure 6.5 16-bit carry-lookahead adder built from 4-bit adders (see Figure 6.4b).

Figure 6.5 shows a 16-bit adder built from four 4-bit adder blocks. These blocks provide new output functions defined as G_k^I and P_k^I, where $k = 0$ for the first 4-bit block, as shown in Figure 6.4b, $k = 1$ for the second 4-bit block, and so on. In the first block,

$$P_0^I = P_3 P_2 P_1 P_0$$

and

$$G_0^I = G_3 + P_3 G_2 + P_3 P_2 G_1 + P_3 P_2 P_1 G_0$$

In words, we say that the first-level G_i and P_i functions determine whether bit stage i generates or propagates a carry, and that the second-level G_k^I and P_k^I functions determine whether block k generates or propagates a carry. With these new functions available, it is not necessary to wait for carries to ripple through the 4-bit blocks. Carry c_{16} is formed by one of the carry-lookahead circuits in Figure 6.5 as

$$c_{16} = G_3^I + P_3^I G_2^I + P_3^I P_2^I G_1^I + P_3^I P_2^I P_1^I G_0^I + P_3^I P_2^I P_1^I P_0^I c_0$$

The input carries to the 4-bit blocks are formed in parallel by similar shorter expressions. These expressions for c_{16}, c_{12}, c_8, and c_4, are identical in form to the expressions for c_4, c_3, c_2, and c_1, respectively, implemented in the carry-lookahead circuits in Figure 6.4b. Only the variable names are different. Therefore, the structure of the carry-lookahead circuits in Figure 6.5 is identical to the carry-lookahead circuits in Figure 6.4b. We should note, however, that the carries c_4, c_8, c_{12}, and c_{16}, generated internally by the 4-bit adder blocks, are not needed in Figure 6.5 because they are generated by the higher-level carry-lookahead circuits.

Now, consider the delay in producing outputs from the 16-bit carry-lookahead adder. The delay in developing the carries produced by the carry-lookahead circuits is two gate delays more than the delay needed to develop the G_k^I and P_k^I functions. The latter require two gate delays and one gate delay, respectively, after the generation of G_i and P_i. Therefore, all carries produced by the carry-lookahead circuits are available 5 gate delays after X, Y, and c_0 are applied as inputs. The carry c_{15} is generated inside the high-order 4-bit block in Figure 6.5 in two gate delays after c_{12}, followed by s_{15} in one further gate delay. Therefore, s_{15} is available after 8 gate delays. Note that if a 16-bit adder is built by cascading 4-bit carry-lookahead adder blocks, the delays in developing c_{16} and s_{15} are 9 and 10 gate delays, respectively, as compared to 5 and 8 gate delays for the configuration in Figure 6.5.

Two 16-bit adder blocks can be cascaded to implement a 32-bit adder. In this configuration, the output c_{16} from the low-order block is the carry input to the high-order block. The delay is much lower than the delay through the 32-bit adder that we discussed earlier, which was built by cascading eight 4-bit adders. In that configuration, recall that s_{31} is available after 18 gate delays and c_{32} is available after 17 gate delays. The delay analysis for the cascade of two 16-bit adders is as follows. The carry c_{16} out of the low-order block is available after 5 gate delays, as calculated above. Then, both c_{28} and c_{32} are available in the high-order block after a further 2 gate delays, and c_{31} is available 2 gate delays after c_{28}. Therefore, c_{31} is available after a total of 9 gate delays, and s_{31} is available in 10 gate delays. Recapitulating, s_{31} and c_{32} are available after 10 and 7 gate delays, respectively, compared to 18 and 17 gate delays for the same outputs if the 32-bit adder is built from a cascade of eight 4-bit adders.

The same reasoning used in developing second-level G_k^I and P_k^I functions from first-level G_i and P_i functions can be used to develop third-level G_k^{II} and P_k^{II} functions from G_k^I and P_k^I functions. Two such third-level functions are shown as outputs from the carry-lookahead logic in Figure 6.5. A 64-bit adder can be built from four of the 16-bit adders shown in Figure 6.5 along with additional carry-lookahead logic circuits that produces carries c_{16}, c_{32}, c_{48}, and c_{64}. Delay through this adder can be shown to be 12 gate delays for s_{63} and 7 gate delays for c_{64}, using an extension of the reasoning used above for the 16-bit adder. (See Problem 6.10.)

6.3 MULTIPLICATION OF POSITIVE NUMBERS

The usual algorithm for multiplying integers by hand is illustrated in Figure 6.6a for the binary system. This algorithm applies to unsigned numbers and to positive signed numbers. The product of two n-digit numbers can be accommodated in $2n$ digits, so the product of the two 4-bit numbers in this example fits into 8 bits, as shown. In the binary system, multiplication of the multiplicand by one bit of the multiplier is easy. If the multiplier bit is 1, the multiplicand is entered in the appropriate position to be added to the partial product. If the multiplier bit is 0, then 0s are entered, as in the third row of the example.

Binary multiplication of positive operands can be implemented in a combinational, two-dimensional logic array, as shown in Figure 6.6b. The main component in each cell is a full adder FA. The AND gate in each cell determines whether a multiplicand bit, m_j, is added to the incoming partial-product bit, based on the value of the multiplier

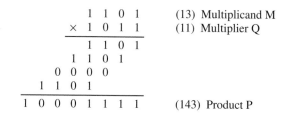

(a) Manual multiplication algorithm

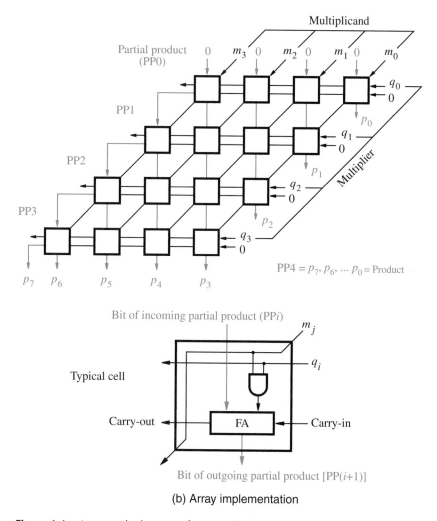

(b) Array implementation

Figure 6.6 Array multiplication of positive binary operands.

bit, q_i. Each row i, where $0 \leq i \leq 3$, adds the multiplicand (appropriately shifted) to the incoming partial product, PPi, to generate the outgoing partial product, PP$(i + 1)$, if $q_i = 1$. If $q_i = 0$, PPi is passed vertically downward unchanged. PP0 is all 0s, and PP4 is the desired product. The multiplicand is shifted left one position per row by the diagonal signal path.

The worst case signal propagation delay path is from the upper right corner of the array to the high-order product bit output at the bottom left corner of the array. The path consists of the staircase pattern that includes the two cells at the right end of each row, followed by all the cells in the bottom row. Assuming that there are two gate delays from the inputs to the outputs of a full adder block, the path has a total of $6(n - 1) - 1$ gate delays, including the initial AND gate delay in all cells, for the $n \times n$ array. (See Problem 6.12.) Only the AND gates are actually needed in the first row of the array because the incoming partial product PP0 is zero. This has been taken into account in developing the delay expression.

Multiplication is usually provided in the machine instruction set of a processor. High-performance processor chips use an appreciable area of the chip to perform arithmetic functions on both integer and floating-point operands. (Floating-point operations are discussed later in this chapter.) Although the preceding combinational multiplier is easy to understand, it uses many gates for multiplying numbers of practical size, such as 32- or 64-bit numbers. Multiplication can also be performed using a mixture of combinational array techniques, similar to those shown in Figure 6.6, and sequential techniques requiring less combinational logic.

The simplest way to perform multiplication is to use the adder circuitry in the ALU for a number of sequential steps. The block diagram in Figure 6.7a shows the hardware arrangement for sequential multiplication. This circuit performs multiplication by using a single n-bit adder n times to implement the spatial addition performed by the n rows of ripple-carry adders of Figure 6.6b. Registers A and Q combined hold PPi while multiplier bit q_i generates the signal Add/Noadd. This signal controls the addition of the multiplicand, M, to PPi to generate PP$(i + 1)$. The product is computed in n cycles. The partial product grows in length by one bit per cycle from the initial vector, PP0, of n 0s in register A. The carry-out from the adder is stored in flip-flop C, shown at the left end of register A. At the start, the multiplier is loaded into register Q, the multiplicand into register M, and C and A are cleared to 0. At the end of each cycle, C, A, and Q are shifted right one bit position to allow for growth of the partial product as the multiplier is shifted out of register Q. Because of this shifting, multiplier bit q_i appears at the LSB position of Q to generate the Add/Noadd signal at the correct time, starting with q_0 during the first cycle, q_1 during the second cycle, and so on. After they are used, the multiplier bits are discarded by the right-shift operation. Note that the carry-out from the adder is the leftmost bit of PP$(i + 1)$, and it must be held in the C flip-flop to be shifted right with the contents of A and Q. After n cycles, the high-order half of the product is held in register A and the low-order half is in register Q. The multiplication example of Figure 6.6a is shown in Figure 6.7b as it would be performed by this hardware arrangement.

Using this sequential hardware structure, it is clear that a Multiply instruction takes much more time to execute than an Add instruction. Several techniques have been used to speed up multiplication; we discuss some of them in the next few sections.

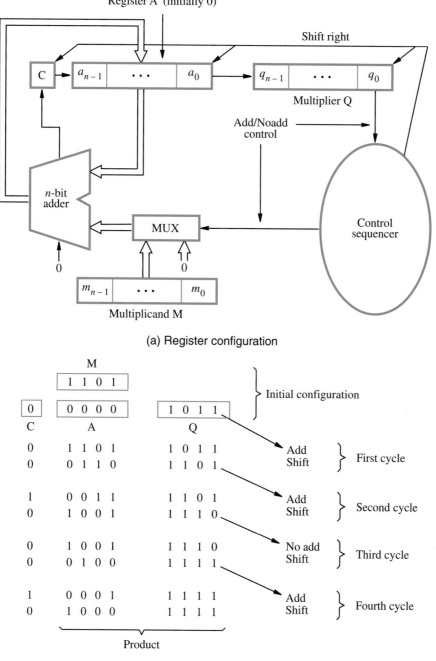

(a) Register configuration

(b) Multiplication example

Figure 6.7 Sequential circuit binary multiplier.

6.4 SIGNED-OPERAND MULTIPLICATION

We now discuss multiplication of 2's-complement signed operands, generating a double-length product. The general strategy is still to accumulate partial products by adding versions of the multiplicand as selected by the multiplier bits.

First, consider the case of a positive multiplier and a negative multiplicand. When we add a negative multiplicand to a partial product, we must extend the sign-bit value of the multiplicand to the left as far as the product will extend. In Figure 6.8, for example, the 5-bit signed operand, -13, is the multiplicand, and it is multiplied by $+11$, the multiplier, to get the 10-bit product, -143. The sign extension of the multiplicand is shown in blue. Thus, the hardware discussed earlier can be used for negative multiplicands if it provides for sign extension of the partial products.

For a negative multiplier, a straightforward solution is to form the 2's-complement of both the multiplier and the multiplicand and proceed as in the case of a positive multiplier. This is possible because complementation of both operands does not change the value or the sign of the product. A technique that works equally well for both negative and positive multipliers, called the Booth algorithm, is described next.

6.4.1 BOOTH ALGORITHM

The Booth algorithm generates a $2n$-bit product and treats both positive and negative 2's-complement n-bit operands uniformly. To understand the essence of this algorithm, consider a multiplication operation in which the multiplier is positive and has a single block of 1s, for example, 0011110. To derive the product, we could add four appropriately shifted versions of the multiplicand, as in the standard procedure. However, we can reduce the number of required operations by regarding this multiplier as the

						1	0	0	1	1	(-13)
					×	0	1	0	1	1	$(+11)$
	1	1	1	1	1	1	0	0	1	1	
	1	1	1	1	1	0	0	1	1		
Sign extension is shown in blue	0	0	0	0	0	0	0	0			
	1	1	1	0	0	1	1				
	0	0	0	0	0	0					
	1	1	0	1	1	1	0	0	0	1	(-143)

Figure 6.8 Sign extension of negative multiplicand.

```
                  0   1   0   1   1   0   1
                  0  0+1 +1  +1  +1   0
                  0   0   0   0   0   0   0
              0   1   0   1   1   0   1
          0   1   0   1   1   0   1
      0   1   0   1   1   0   1
  0   1   0   1   1   0   1
0   0   0   0   0   0   0
0   0   0   0   0   0   0
0   0   0   1   0   1   0   1   0   0   0   1   1   0


                  0   1   0   1   1   0   1
                  0  +1   0   0   0  -1   0
0   0   0   0   0   0   0   0   0   0   0   0   0   0
1   1   1   1   1   1   1   0   1   0   0   1   1      ◀── 2's complement of
0   0   0   0   0   0   0   0   0   0   0   0              the multiplicand
0   0   0   0   0   0   0   0   0   0   0
0   0   0   0   0   0   0   0   0   0
0   0   0   1   0   1   1   0   1
0   0   0   0   0   0   0   0
0   0   0   1   0   1   0   1   0   0   0   1   1   0
```

Figure 6.9 Normal and Booth multiplication schemes.

difference between two numbers:

$$0100000 \quad (32)$$
$$-0000010 \quad (2)$$
$$\overline{0011110 \quad (30)}$$

This suggests that the product can be generated by adding 2^5 times the multiplicand to the 2's-complement of 2^1 times the multiplicand. For convenience, we can describe the sequence of required operations by recoding the preceding multiplier as $0\ +1000\ -10$.

In general, in the Booth scheme, -1 times the shifted multiplicand is selected when moving from 0 to 1, and $+1$ times the shifted multiplicand is selected when moving from 1 to 0, as the multiplier is scanned from right to left. Figure 6.9 illustrates the normal and the Booth algorithms for the example just discussed. The Booth algorithm clearly extends to any number of blocks of 1s in a multiplier, including the situation in which a single 1 is considered a block. See Figure 6.10 for another example of recoding a multiplier. The case when the least significant bit of the multiplier is 1 is handled by assuming that an implied 0 lies to its right. The Booth algorithm can also be used directly for negative multipliers, as shown in Figure 6.11.

To demonstrate the correctness of the Booth algorithm for negative multipliers, we use the following property of negative-number representations in the 2's-complement

$$0 \quad 0 \quad 1 \quad 0 \quad 1 \quad 1 \quad 0 \quad 0 \quad 1 \quad 1 \quad 1 \quad 0 \quad 1 \quad 0 \quad 1 \quad 1 \quad 0 \quad 0$$

$\Downarrow$

$$0 \; +1 \; -1 \; +1 \quad 0 \; -1 \quad 0 \; +1 \quad 0 \quad 0 \; -1 \; +1 \; -1 \; +1 \quad 0 \; -1 \quad 0 \quad 0$$

Figure 6.10   Booth recoding of a multiplier.

$$
\begin{array}{rl}
0 \; 1 \; 1 \; 0 \; 1 & (+13) \\
\times \; 1 \; 1 \; 0 \; 1 \; 0 & (-6)
\end{array}
\qquad \Longrightarrow \qquad
\begin{array}{l}
0 \; 1 \; 1 \; 0 \; 1 \\
0 \; -1 \; +1 \; -1 \; 0
\end{array}
$$

$$
\begin{array}{r}
0 \; 0 \; 0 \; 0 \; 0 \; 0 \; 0 \; 0 \; 0 \; 0 \\
1 \; 1 \; 1 \; 1 \; 1 \; 0 \; 0 \; 1 \; 1 \\
0 \; 0 \; 0 \; 0 \; 1 \; 1 \; 0 \; 1 \\
1 \; 1 \; 1 \; 0 \; 0 \; 1 \; 1 \\
0 \; 0 \; 0 \; 0 \; 0 \; 0 \\
\hline
1 \; 1 \; 1 \; 0 \; 1 \; 1 \; 0 \; 0 \; 1 \; 0 \quad (-78)
\end{array}
$$

Figure 6.11   Booth multiplication with a negative multiplier.

system: Let the leftmost 0 of a negative number, X, be at bit position k, that is,

$$X = 11 \ldots 10 x_{k-1} \ldots x_0$$

Then the value of X is given by

$$V(X) = -2^{k+1} + x_{k-1} \times 2^{k-1} + \cdots + x_0 \times 2^0$$

The correctness of this expression for $V(X)$ is shown by observing that if X is formed as the sum of two numbers

$$
\begin{array}{r}
11 \ldots 100000 \ldots 0 \\
+ \quad 00 \ldots 00 x_{k-1} \ldots x_0 \\
\hline
X = 11 \ldots 10 x_{k-1} \ldots x_0
\end{array}
$$

then the top number is the 2's-complement representation of -2^{k+1}. The recoded multiplier now consists of the part corresponding to the second number, with -1 added in position $k + 1$. For example, the multiplier 110110 is recoded as $0 -1 +1 0 -1 0$.

The Booth technique for recoding multipliers is summarized in Figure 6.12. The transformation $011 \ldots 110 \Rightarrow +100 \ldots 0 -10$ is called *skipping over 1s*. This term is derived from the case in which the multiplier has its 1s grouped into a few contiguous blocks. Only a few versions of the shifted multiplicand (the summands) must be added to generate the product, thus speeding up the multiplication operation. However, in the worst case — that of alternating 1s and 0s in the multiplier — each bit of the multiplier selects a summand. In fact, this results in more summands than if the Booth algorithm were not used. A 16-bit, worst-case multiplier, an ordinary multiplier, and a good multiplier are shown in Figure 6.13.

Multiplier		Version of multiplicand selected by bit i
Bit i	Bit $i-1$	
0	0	$0 \times M$
0	1	$+1 \times M$
1	0	$-1 \times M$
1	1	$0 \times M$

Figure 6.12 Booth multiplier recoding table.

Worst-case multiplier

0 1 0 1 0 1 0 1 0 1 0 1 0 1 0 1

⇓

+1 −1 +1 −1 +1 −1 +1 −1 +1 −1 +1 −1 +1 −1 +1 −1

Ordinary multiplier

1 1 0 0 0 1 0 1 1 0 1 1 1 1 0 0

⇓

0 −1 0 0 +1 −1 +1 0 −1 +1 0 0 0 −1 0 0

Good multiplier

0 0 0 0 1 1 1 1 1 0 0 0 0 1 1 1

⇓

0 0 0 +1 0 0 0 0 −1 0 0 0 +1 0 0 −1

Figure 6.13 Booth recoded multipliers.

The Booth algorithm has two attractive features. First, it handles both positive and negative multipliers uniformly. Second, it achieves some efficiency in the number of additions required when the multiplier has a few large blocks of 1s. The speed gained by skipping over 1s depends on the data. On average, the speed of doing multiplication with the Booth algorithm is the same as with the normal algorithm.

6.5 FAST MULTIPLICATION

We now describe two techniques for speeding up the multiplication operation. The first technique guarantees that the maximum number of summands (versions of the multiplicand) that must be added is $n/2$ for n-bit operands. The second technique reduces the time needed to add the summands.

6.5.1 BIT-PAIR RECODING OF MULTIPLIERS

A technique called *bit-pair recoding* halves the maximum number of summands. It is derived directly from the Booth algorithm. Group the Booth-recoded multiplier bits in pairs, and observe the following: The pair $(+1 \ -1)$ is equivalent to the pair $(0 \ +1)$. That is, instead of adding -1 times the multiplicand M at shift position i to $+1 \times M$ at position $i + 1$, the same result is obtained by adding $+1 \times M$ at position i. Other examples are: $(+1 \ 0)$ is equivalent to $(0 \ +2)$, $(-1 \ +1)$ is equivalent to $(0 \ -1)$, and so on. Thus, if the Booth-recoded multiplier is examined two bits at a time, starting from the right, it can be rewritten in a form that requires at most one version of the multiplicand to be added to the partial product for each pair of multiplier bits. Figure 6.14*a* shows an example of bit-pair recoding of the multiplier in Figure 6.11, and

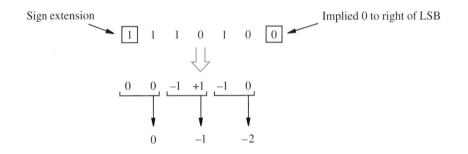

(a) Example of bit-pair recoding derived from Booth recoding

Multiplier bit-pair		Multiplier bit on the right	Multiplicand selected at position i
$i + 1$	i	$i - 1$	
0	0	0	$0 \times M$
0	0	1	$+1 \times M$
0	1	0	$+1 \times M$
0	1	1	$+2 \times M$
1	0	0	$-2 \times M$
1	0	1	$-1 \times M$
1	1	0	$-1 \times M$
1	1	1	$0 \times M$

(b) Table of multiplicand selection decisions

Figure 6.14 Multiplier bit-pair recoding.

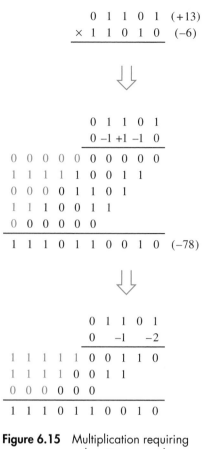

Figure 6.15 Multiplication requiring only $n/2$ summands.

Figure 6.14*b* shows a table of the multiplicand selection decisions for all possibilities. The multiplication operation in Figure 6.11 is shown in Figure 6.15 as it would be computed using bit-pair recoding of the multiplier.

6.5.2 CARRY-SAVE ADDITION OF SUMMANDS

Multiplication requires the addition of several summands. A technique called *carry-save addition* (CSA) speeds up the addition process. Consider the array for 4×4 multiplication shown in Figure 6.16*a*. This structure is the general array shown in Figure 6.6, with the first row consisting of just the AND gates that implement the bit products m_3q_0, m_2q_0, m_1q_0, and m_0q_0.

Instead of letting the carries ripple along the rows, they can be "saved" and introduced into the next row, at the correct weighted positions, as shown in Figure 6.16*b*. This frees up an input to three full adders in the first row. These inputs are used to

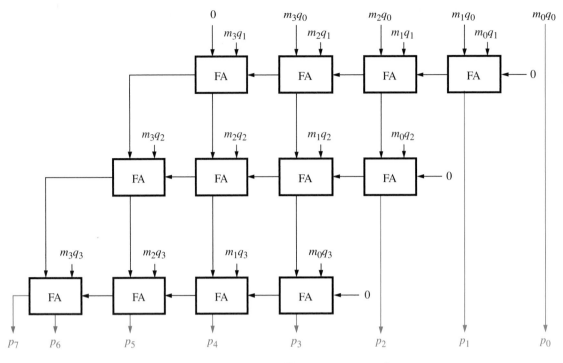

(a) Ripple-carry array (Figure 6.6 structure)

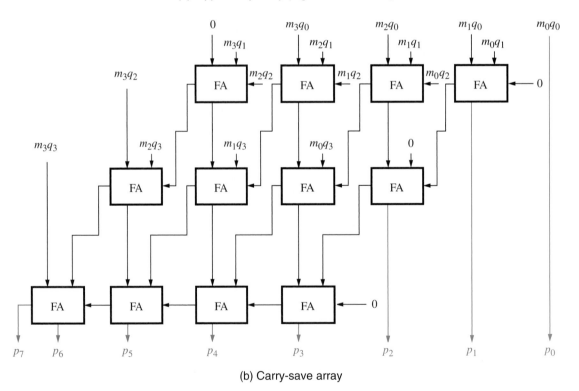

(b) Carry-save array

Figure 6.16 Ripple-carry and carry-save arrays for the multiplication operation $M \times Q = P$ for 4-bit operands.

```
              1   0   1   1   0   1      (45)       M
          x   1   1   1   1   1   1      (63)       Q
         ─────────────────────────
              1   0   1   1   0   1       A
          1   0   1   1   0   1           B
      1   0   1   1   0   1               C
  1   0   1   1   0   1                   D
1   0   1   1   0   1                     E
0   1   1   0   1                         F
─────────────────────────────────────
1 0 1 1 0 0 0 1 0 0 1 1                   (2,835)    Product
```

Figure 6.17   A multiplication example used to illustrate carry-save addition as shown in Figure 6.18.

introduce the third summand bit products m_2q_2, m_1q_2, and m_0q_2. Now, two inputs of each full adder in the second row are fed by sum and carry outputs from the first row. The third input is used to introduce the bit products m_2q_3, m_1q_3, and m_0q_3 of the fourth summand. The high-order bit products m_3q_2 and m_3q_3 of the third and fourth summands are introduced into the remaining free inputs at the left end in the second and third rows. The saved carry bits and the sum bits from the second row are now added in the third row to produce the final product bits.

Delay through the carry-save array is somewhat less than delay through the ripple-carry array. This is because the S and C vector outputs from each row are produced in parallel in one full-adder delay. The amount of reduction in delay is considered in Problem 6.22.

A more significant reduction in delay can be achieved as follows. Consider the addition of many summands, as required in the multiplication of longer operands. We can group the summands in threes and perform carry-save addition on each of these groups in parallel to generate a set of S and C vectors in one full-adder delay. Next, we group all of the S and C vectors into threes, and perform carry-save addition on them, generating a further set of S and C vectors in one more full-adder delay. We continue with this process until there are only two vectors remaining. They can then be added in a ripple-carry or a carry-lookahead adder to produce the desired product.

Consider the example of adding the six shifted versions of the multiplicand for the case of multiplying two 6-bit unsigned numbers where all six bits of the multiplier are equal to 1. Such an example is shown in Figure 6.17. The six summands, $A, B, \ldots, F$ are added by carry-save addition in Figure 6.18. The "blue boxes" in these two figures indicate the same operand bits, and show how they are reduced to sum and carry bits in Figure 6.18 by carry-save addition. Three levels of carry-save addition are performed, as shown schematically in Figure 6.19. It is clear from this figure that the final two vectors S_4 and C_4 are available in three full-adder delays after the six input summands

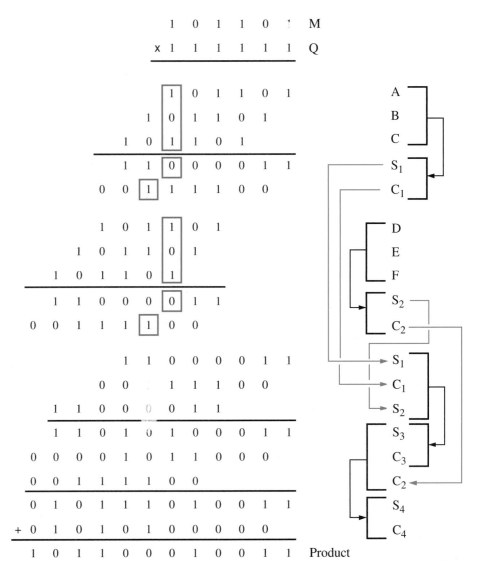

Figure 6.18 The multiplication example from Figure 6.17 performed using carry-save addition.

are applied to level 1. The final regular addition operation on S_4 and C_4, which produces the product, can be done with either a ripple-carry or a carry-lookahead adder.

Let us compute the total logic gate delay required to perform the 6×6 multiplication as shown in Figures 6.18 and 6.19. After one AND gate delay, used to select the summands based on the multiplier bits, all six summands are available as inputs to CSA level 1. The outputs S_4 and C_4 from the third CSA level are available 6 gate delays later, assuming two gate delays per CSA level. The final two vectors can be added in a further

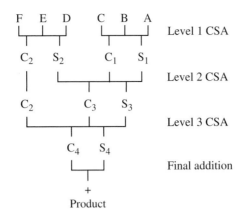

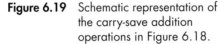

Figure 6.19 Schematic representation of the carry-save addition operations in Figure 6.18.

8 gate delays using a carry-lookahead adder of the form shown in Figure 6.5. The total gate delay is therefore 15. By comparison, the total gate delay in performing multiplication by using an $n \times n$ array of the type shown in Figure 6.6 is $6(n - 1) - 1$; so the 6×6 case has a gate delay of 29. This halving of delay is a result of using both carry-save addition of summands in parallel and carry-lookahead addition of the final two vectors.

When the number of summands is large, the time saved is proportionally much greater. For example, the addition of 32 numbers using the carry-save addition method, following the pattern shown in Figure 6.19, requires only 8 levels of CSA steps before the final Add operation. In general, it can be shown that approximately $1.7log_2k - 1.7$ levels of CSA steps are needed to reduce k summands to 2 vectors, which, when added, produce the desired sum. (See Problem 6.23.) A 64-bit carry-lookahead adder can be used to add the final 2 vectors. Total delay for 32×32 multiplication is calculated as follows: one gate delay for the initial AND gates, whose outputs produce the 32 summands; 16 gate delays for 8 levels of CSA steps; and 12 gate delays for the longest path (to s_{63}) through the 64-bit adder. The total delay is thus 29 gate delays. In comparison, an array multiplier for the 32×32 case requires 185 gate delays to generate the last bit of the product.

Some issues have been omitted in discussing the use of carry-save addition for speeding up the multiplication operation. First, when negative summands are involved, as they are for signed-operand multiplication using the Booth algorithm, it is necessary to accommodate sign-extension in the CSA logic. Full extension to the double-length product distance is not actually required. Only a few bits of extension at each CSA level are needed. Second, we have assumed that a $2n$-bit carry-lookahead adder is needed to add the final two S and C vectors for $n \times n$ multiplication. Somewhat fewer bits are actually involved in this final addition because some of the low-order product bits are determined earlier. But this is not a big factor; and the delay analysis that we have used is correct because the adder is not significantly shorter. Finally, we have used n summands for an $n \times n$ multiplication. But if bit-pair recoding of the multiplier is done, the number of summands is reduced to $n/2$. This reduces the number of CSA levels required from $1.7log_2n - 1.7$ to $1.7log_2n - 3.4$.

Summary of Fast Multiplication

We now summarize the techniques for high-speed multiplication. Bit-pair recoding of the multiplier, derived from the Booth algorithm, reduces the number of summands by a factor of 2. These summands can then be reduced to only 2 by using a relatively small number of carry-save addition steps. The final product can be generated by an addition operation that uses a carry-lookahead adder. All three of these techniques — bit-pair recoding of the multiplier, carry-save addition of the summands, and lookahead addition — have been used in various ways by the designers of high-performance processors to reduce the time needed to perform multiplication.

6.6 I̲ɴᴛᴇɢᴇʀ D̲ɪᴠɪsɪᴏɴ

In Section 6.4, we discussed positive-number multiplication by relating the way the multiplication operation is done manually to the way it is done in a logic circuit. We use the same approach here in discussing integer division. We discuss positive-number division in detail, and then make some general comments on the signed-operand case.

Figure 6.20 shows examples of decimal division and binary division of the same values. Consider the decimal version first. The 2 in the quotient is determined by the following reasoning: First, we try to divide 13 into 2, and it does not work. Next, we try to divide 13 into 27. We go through the trial exercise of multiplying 13 by 2 to get 26, and, knowing that $27 - 26 = 1$ is less than 13, we enter 2 as the quotient and perform the required subtraction. The next digit of the dividend, 4, is brought down, and we finish by deciding that 13 goes into 14 once, and the remainder is 1. We can discuss binary division in a similar way, with the simplification that the only possibilities for the quotient bits are 0 and 1.

A circuit that implements division by this longhand method operates as follows: It positions the divisor appropriately with respect to the dividend and performs a subtraction. If the remainder is zero or positive, a quotient bit of 1 is determined, the remainder is extended by another bit of the dividend, the divisor is repositioned, and another subtraction is performed. On the other hand, if the remainder is negative, a quotient bit of 0 is determined, the dividend is restored by adding back the divisor, and the divisor is repositioned for another subtraction.

```
            21                              10101
       13 ) 274                   1101 ) 100010010
            26                              1101
           ────                           ─────
            14                             10000
            13                              1101
           ────                           ─────
             1                              1110
                                           1101
                                          ─────
                                              1
```

Figure 6.20 Longhand division examples.

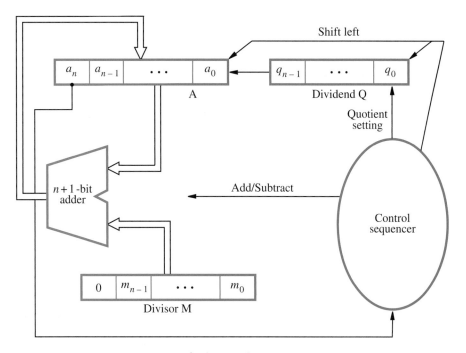

Figure 6.21 Circuit arrangement for binary division.

Restoring Division

Figure 6.21 shows a logic circuit arrangement that implements *restoring division.* Note its similarity to the structure for multiplication that was shown in Figure 6.7. An *n*-bit positive divisor is loaded into register M and an *n*-bit positive dividend is loaded into register Q at the start of the operation. Register A is set to 0. After the division is complete, the *n*-bit quotient is in register Q and the remainder is in register A. The required subtractions are facilitated by using 2's-complement arithmetic. The extra bit position at the left end of both A and M accommodates the sign bit during subtractions. The following algorithm performs restoring division.

Do the following *n* times:

1. Shift A and Q left one binary position.
2. Subtract M from A, and place the answer back in A.
3. If the sign of A is 1, set q_0 to 0 and add M back to A (that is, restore A); otherwise, set q_0 to 1.

Figure 6.22 shows a 4-bit example as it would be processed by the circuit in Figure 6.21.

Nonrestoring Division

The restoring-division algorithm can be improved by avoiding the need for restoring A after an unsuccessful subtraction. Subtraction is said to be unsuccessful if the result

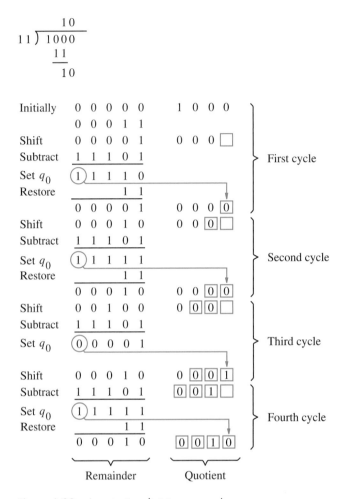

Figure 6.22   A restoring-division example.

is negative. Consider the sequence of operations that takes place after the subtraction operation in the preceding algorithm. If A is positive, we shift left and subtract M, that is, we perform $2A - M$. If A is negative, we restore it by performing $A + M$, and then we shift it left and subtract M. This is equivalent to performing $2A + M$. The q_0 bit is appropriately set to 0 or 1 after the correct operation has been performed. We can summarize this in the following algorithm for *nonrestoring division*.

Step 1: Do the following n times:

1. If the sign of A is 0, shift A and Q left one bit position and subtract M from A; otherwise, shift A and Q left and add M to A.

2. Now, if the sign of A is 0, set q_0 to 1; otherwise, set q_0 to 0.

Step 2: If the sign of A is 1, add M to A.

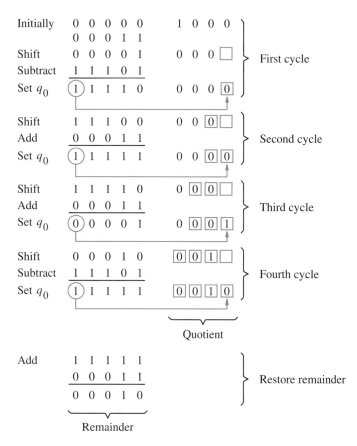

Figure 6.23 A nonrestoring-division example.

Step 2 is needed to leave the proper positive remainder in A at the end of the n cycles of Step 1. The logic circuitry in Figure 6.21 can also be used to perform this algorithm. Note that the Restore operations are no longer needed, and that exactly one Add or Subtract operation is performed per cycle. Figure 6.23 shows how the division example in Figure 6.22 is executed by the nonrestoring-division algorithm.

There are no simple algorithms for directly performing division on signed operands that are comparable to the algorithms for signed multiplication. In division, the operands can be preprocessed to transform them into positive values. After using one of the algorithms just discussed, the results are transformed to the correct signed values, as necessary.

6.7 FLOATING-POINT NUMBERS AND OPERATIONS

Until now, we have dealt exclusively with fixed-point numbers and have considered them as integers, that is, as having an implied binary point at the right end of the number. It is also possible to assume that the binary point is just to the right of the sign bit, thus representing a fraction. In the 2's-complement system, the signed value F, represented by the n-bit binary fraction

$$B = b_0.b_{-1}b_{-2}\ldots b_{-(n-1)}$$

is given by

$$F(B) = -b_0 \times 2^0 + b_{-1} \times 2^{-1} + b_{-2} \times 2^{-2} + \cdots + b_{-(n-1)} \times 2^{-(n-1)}$$

where the range of F is

$$-1 \le F \le 1 - 2^{-(n-1)}$$

Consider the range of values representable in a 32-bit, signed, fixed-point format. Interpreted as integers, the value range is approximately 0 to $\pm 2.15 \times 10^9$. If we consider them to be fractions, the range is approximately $\pm 4.55 \times 10^{-10}$ to ± 1. Neither of these ranges is sufficient for scientific calculations, which might involve parameters like Avogadro's number (6.0247×10^{23} mole^{-1}) or Planck's constant (6.6254×10^{-27} erg·s). Hence, we need to easily accommodate both very large integers and very small fractions. To do this, a computer must be able to represent numbers and operate on them in such a way that the position of the binary point is variable and is automatically adjusted as computation proceeds. In such a case, the binary point is said to float, and the numbers are called *floating-point numbers*. This distinguishes them from fixed-point numbers, whose binary point is always in the same position.

Because the position of the binary point in a floating-point number is variable, it must be given explicitly in the floating-point representation. For example, in the familiar decimal scientific notation, numbers may be written as 6.0247×10^{23}, 6.6254×10^{-27}, -1.0341×10^2, -7.3000×10^{-14}, and so on. These numbers are said to be given to five *significant digits*. The *scale factors* (10^{23}, 10^{-27}, and so on) indicate the position of the decimal point with respect to the significant digits. By convention, when the decimal point is placed to the right of the first (nonzero) significant digit, the number is said to be *normalized*. Note that the base, 10, in the scale factor is fixed and does not need to appear explicitly in the machine representation of a floating-point number. The sign, the significant digits, and the exponent in the scale factor constitute the representation. We are thus motivated to define a floating-point number representation as one in which a number is represented by its sign, a string of significant digits, commonly called the *mantissa,* and an exponent to an implied base for the scale factor.

6.7.1 IEEE STANDARD FOR FLOATING-POINT NUMBERS

We start with a general form and size for floating-point numbers in the decimal system, and then relate this form to a comparable binary representation. A useful form is

$$\pm X_1.X_2X_3X_4X_5X_6X_7 \times 10^{\pm Y_1Y_2}$$

where X_i and Y_i are decimal digits. Both the number of significant digits (7) and the exponent range (± 99) are sufficient for a wide range of scientific calculations. It is possible to approximate this mantissa precision and scale factor range in a binary representation that occupies 32 bits, which is a standard computer word length. A 24-bit mantissa can approximately represent a 7-digit decimal number, and an 8-bit exponent to an implied base of 2 provides a scale factor with a reasonable range. One bit is needed for the sign of the number. Since the leading nonzero bit of a normalized binary mantissa must be a 1, it does not have to be included explicitly in the representation. Therefore, a total of 32 bits is needed.

This standard for representing floating-point numbers in 32 bits has been developed and specified in detail by the Institute of Electrical and Electronics Engineers (IEEE) [1]. The standard describes both the representation and the way in which the four basic arithmetic operations are to be performed. The 32-bit representation is given in Figure 6.24a. The sign of the number is given in the first bit, followed by a representation for the exponent (to the base 2) of the scale factor. Instead of the signed exponent, E, the value actually stored in the exponent field is an unsigned integer $E' = E + 127$.

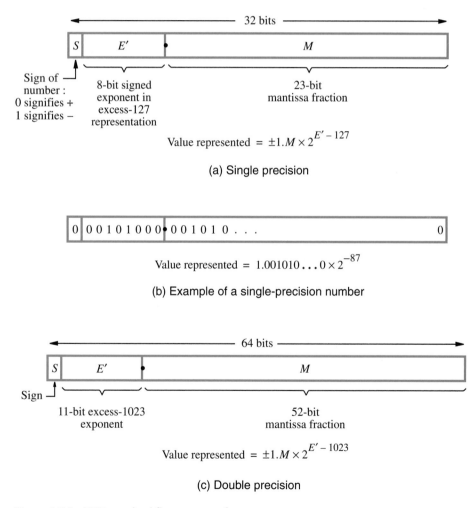

(a) Single precision

(b) Example of a single-precision number

Value represented $= 1.001010\ldots 0 \times 2^{-87}$

(c) Double precision

Value represented $= \pm 1.M \times 2^{E' - 1023}$

Figure 6.24 IEEE standard floating-point formats.

This is called the excess-127 format. Thus, E' is in the range $0 \leq E' \leq 255$. The end values of this range, 0 and 255, are used to represent special values, as described below. Therefore, the range of E' for normal values is $1 \leq E' \leq 254$. This means that the actual exponent, E, is in the range $-126 \leq E \leq 127$. The *excess-x* representation for exponents enables efficient comparison of the relative sizes of two floating-point numbers. (See Problem 6.27.)

The last 23 bits represent the mantissa. Since binary normalization is used, the most significant bit of the mantissa is always equal to 1. This bit is not explicitly represented; it is assumed to be to the immediate left of the binary point. Hence, the 23 bits stored in the M field actually represent the fractional part of the mantissa, that is, the bits to the right of the binary point. An example of a single-precision floating-point number is shown in Figure 6.24*b*.

The 32-bit standard representation in Figure 6.24*a* is called a *single-precision* representation because it occupies a single 32-bit word. The scale factor has a range of 2^{-126} to 2^{+127}, which is approximately equal to $10^{\pm 38}$. The 24-bit mantissa provides approximately the same precision as a 7-digit decimal value. To provide more precision and range for floating-point numbers, the IEEE standard also specifies a *double-precision* format, as shown in Figure 6.24*c*. The double-precision format has increased exponent and mantissa ranges. The 11-bit excess-1023 exponent E' has the range $1 \leq E' \leq 2046$ for normal values, with 0 and 2047 used to indicate special values, as before. Thus, the actual exponent E is in the range $-1022 \leq E \leq 1023$, providing scale factors of 2^{-1022} to 2^{1023} (approximately $10^{\pm 308}$). The 53-bit mantissa provides a precision equivalent to about 16 decimal digits.

A computer must provide at least single-precision representation to conform to the IEEE standard. Double-precision representation is optional. The standard also specifies certain optional extended versions of both of these formats. The extended versions are intended to provide increased precision and increased exponent range for the representation of intermediate values in a sequence of calculations. For example, the dot product of two vectors of numbers can be computed by accumulating the sum of products in extended precision. The inputs are given in a standard precision, either single or double, and the answer is truncated to the same precision. The use of extended formats helps to reduce the size of the accumulated round-off error in a sequence of calculations. Extended formats also enhance the accuracy of evaluation of elementary functions such as sine, cosine, and so on. In addition to requiring the four basic arithmetic operations, the standard requires that the operations of remainder, square root, and conversion between binary and decimal representations be provided.

We note two basic aspects of operating with floating-point numbers. First, if a number is not normalized, it can always be put in normalized form by shifting the fraction and adjusting the exponent. Figure 6.25 shows an unnormalized value, $0.0010110 \ldots \times 2^9$, and its normalized version, $1.0110 \ldots \times 2^6$. Since the scale factor is in the form 2^i, shifting the mantissa right or left by one bit position is compensated by an increase or a decrease of 1 in the exponent, respectively. Second, as computations proceed, a number that does not fall in the representable range of normal numbers might be generated. In single precision, this means that its normalized representation requires an exponent less than -126 or greater than $+127$. In the first case, we say that *underflow* has occurred, and in the second case, we say that *overflow* has occurred. Both underflow and overflow are arithmetic exceptions that are considered below.

excess-127 exponent

(There is no implicit 1 to the left of the binary point.)

$$\text{Value represented} = +0.0010110\ldots \times 2^9$$

(a) Unnormalized value

$$\text{Value represented} = +1.0110\ldots \times 2^6$$

(b) Normalized version

Figure 6.25 Floating-point normalization in IEEE single-precision format.

Special Values

The end values 0 and 255 of the excess-127 exponent E' are used to represent special values. When $E' = 0$ and the mantissa fraction M is zero, the value exact 0 is represented. When $E' = 255$ and $M = 0$, the value ∞ is represented, where ∞ is the result of dividing a normal number by zero. The sign bit is still part of these representations, so there are ± 0 and $\pm \infty$ representations.

When $E' = 0$ and $M \neq 0$, *denormal* numbers are represented. Their value is $\pm 0.M \times 2^{-126}$. Therefore, they are smaller than the smallest normal number. There is no implied one to the left of the binary point, and M is any nonzero 23-bit fraction. The purpose of introducing denormal numbers is to allow for *gradual underflow*, providing an extension of the range of normal representable numbers that is useful in dealing with very small numbers in certain situations. When $E' = 255$ and $M \neq 0$, the value represented is called *Not a Number* (NaN). A NaN is the result of performing an invalid operation such as $0/0$ or $\sqrt{-1}$.

Exceptions

In conforming to the IEEE Standard, a processor must set *exception* flags if any of the following occur in performing operations: underflow, overflow, divide by zero, inexact, invalid. We have already mentioned the first three. *Inexact* is the name for a result that requires rounding in order to be represented in one of the normal formats. An *invalid* exception occurs if operations such as $0/0$ or $\sqrt{-1}$ are attempted. When exceptions occur, the results are set to special values.

If interrupts are enabled for any of the exception flags, system or user-defined routines are entered when the associated exception occurs. Alternatively, the application program can test for the occurrence of exceptions, as necessary, and decide how to proceed.

A more detailed discussion of the floating-point issues raised here and in the next two sections is given in Appendix A of Hennessy and Patterson [2].

6.7.2 ARITHMETIC OPERATIONS ON FLOATING-POINT NUMBERS

In this section, we outline the general procedures for addition, subtraction, multiplication, and division of floating-point numbers. The rules we give apply to the single-precision IEEE standard format. These rules specify only the major steps needed to perform the four operations; for example, the possibility that overflow or underflow might occur is not discussed. Furthermore, intermediate results for both mantissas and exponents might require more than 24 and 8 bits, respectively. These and other aspects of the operations must be carefully considered in designing an arithmetic unit that meets the standard. Although we do not provide full details in specifying the rules, we consider some aspects of implementation, including rounding, in later sections.

If their exponents differ, the mantissas of floating-point numbers must be shifted with respect to each other before they are added or subtracted. Consider a decimal example in which we wish to add 2.9400×10^2 to 4.3100×10^4. We rewrite 2.9400×10^2 as 0.0294×10^4 and then perform addition of the mantissas to get 4.3394×10^4. The rule for addition and subtraction can be stated as follows:

Add/Subtract Rule

1. Choose the number with the smaller exponent and shift its mantissa right a number of steps equal to the difference in exponents.
2. Set the exponent of the result equal to the larger exponent.
3. Perform addition/subtraction on the mantissas and determine the sign of the result.
4. Normalize the resulting value, if necessary.

Multiplication and division are somewhat easier than addition and subtraction, in that no alignment of mantissas is needed.

Multiply Rule

1. Add the exponents and subtract 127.
2. Multiply the mantissas and determine the sign of the result.
3. Normalize the resulting value, if necessary.

Divide Rule

1. Subtract the exponents and add 127.
2. Divide the mantissas and determine the sign of the result.
3. Normalize the resulting value, if necessary.

The addition or subtraction of 127 in the multiply and divide rules results from using the excess-127 notation for exponents.

6.7.3 GUARD BITS AND TRUNCATION

Let us consider some important aspects of implementing the steps in the preceding algorithms. Although the mantissas of initial operands and final results are limited to 24 bits, including the implicit leading 1, it is important to retain extra bits, often called *guard* bits, during the intermediate steps. This yields maximum accuracy in the final results.

Removing guard bits in generating a final result requires that the extended mantissa be *truncated* to create a 24-bit number that approximates the longer version. This operation also arises in other situations, for instance, in converting from decimal to binary numbers. We should mention that the general term rounding is also used for the truncation operation, but we will use a more restrictive definition of rounding as one of the forms of truncation.

There are several ways to truncate. The simplest way is to remove the guard bits and make no changes in the retained bits. This is called *chopping*. Suppose we want to truncate a fraction from six to three bits by this method. All fractions in the range $0.b_{-1}b_{-2}b_{-3}000$ to $0.b_{-1}b_{-2}b_{-3}111$ are truncated to $0.b_{-1}b_{-2}b_{-3}$. The error in the 3-bit result ranges from 0 to 0.000111. In other words, the error in chopping ranges from 0 to almost 1 in the least significant position of the retained bits. In our example, this is the b_{-3} position. The result of chopping is a *biased* approximation because the error range is not symmetrical about 0.

The next simplest method of truncation is *Von Neumann rounding*. If the bits to be removed are all 0s, they are simply dropped, with no changes to the retained bits. However, if any of the bits to be removed are 1, the least significant bit of the retained bits is set to 1. In our 6-bit to 3-bit truncation example, all 6-bit fractions with $b_{-4}b_{-5}b_{-6}$ not equal to 000 are truncated to $0.b_{-1}b_{-2}1$. The error in this truncation method ranges between -1 and $+1$ in the LSB position of the retained bits. Although the range of error is larger with this technique than it is with chopping, the maximum magnitude is the same, and the approximation is *unbiased* because the error range is symmetrical about 0.

Unbiased approximations are advantageous if many operands and operations are involved in generating a result, because positive errors tend to offset negative errors as the computation proceeds. Statistically, we can expect the results of a complex computation to have a high probability of accuracy.

The third truncation method is a *rounding* procedure. Rounding achieves the closest approximation to the number being truncated and is an unbiased technique. The procedure is as follows: A 1 is added to the LSB position of the bits to be retained if there is a 1 in the MSB position of the bits being removed. Thus, $0.b_{-1}b_{-2}b_{-3}1\ldots$ is rounded to $0.b_{-1}b_{-2}b_{-3} + 0.001$, and $0.b_{-1}b_{-2}b_{-3}0\ldots$ is rounded to $0.b_{-1}b_{-2}b_{-3}$. This provides the desired approximation, except for the case in which the bits to be removed are $10\ldots0$. This is a tie situation; the longer value is halfway between the two closest truncated representations. To break the tie in an unbiased way, one possibility is to choose the retained bits to be the nearest even number. In terms of our 6-bit example, the value $0.b_{-1}b_{-2}0100$ is truncated to the value $0.b_{-1}b_{-2}0$, and $0.b_{-1}b_{-2}1100$ is truncated to $0.b_{-1}b_{-2}1 + 0.001$. The descriptive phrase "round to the nearest number or nearest even number in case of a tie" is sometimes used to refer to this truncation technique.

The error range is approximately $-\frac{1}{2}$ to $+\frac{1}{2}$ in the LSB position of the retained bits. Clearly, this is the best method. However, it is also the most difficult to implement because it requires an addition operation and a possible renormalization. This rounding technique is the default mode for truncation specified in the IEEE floating-point standard. The standard also specifies other truncation methods, referring to all of them as rounding modes.

This discussion of errors that are introduced when guard bits are removed by truncation has treated the case of a single truncation operation. When a long series of calculations involving floating-point numbers is performed, the analysis that determines error ranges or bounds for the final results can be a complicated study. We do not discuss this aspect of numerical computation further, except to make a few comments on the way that guard bits and rounding are handled in the IEEE floating-point standard.

Results of single operations must be computed to be accurate within half a unit in the LSB position. In general, this requires that rounding be used as the truncation method. Implementing this rounding scheme requires only three guard bits to be carried along during the intermediate steps in performing the operations described. The first two of these bits are the two most significant bits of the section of the mantissa to be removed. The third bit is the logical OR of all bits beyond these first two bits in the full representation of the mantissa. This bit is relatively easy to maintain during the intermediate steps of the operations to be performed. It should be initialized to 0. If a 1 is shifted out through this position, the bit becomes 1 and retains that value; hence, it is usually called the *sticky bit*.

6.7.4   IMPLEMENTING FLOATING-POINT OPERATIONS

The hardware implementation of floating-point operations involves a considerable amount of logic circuitry. These operations can also be implemented by software routines. In either case, the computer must be able to convert input and output from and to the user's decimal representation of numbers. In most general-purpose processors, floating-point operations are available at the machine-instruction level, implemented in hardware.

An example of the implementation of floating-point operations is shown in Figure 6.26. This is a block diagram of a hardware implementation for the addition and subtraction of 32-bit floating-point operands that have the format shown in Figure 6.24a. Following the Add/Subtract rule given in Section 6.7.2, we see that the first step is to compare exponents to determine how far to shift the mantissa of the number with the smaller exponent. The shift-count value, n, is determined by the 8-bit subtractor circuit in the upper left corner of the figure. The magnitude of the difference $E'_A - E'_B$, or n, is sent to the SHIFTER unit. If n is larger than the number of significant bits of the operands, then the answer is essentially the larger operand (except for guard and sticky-bit considerations in rounding), and shortcuts can be taken in deriving the result. We do not explore this in detail.

The sign of the difference that results from comparing exponents determines which mantissa is to be shifted. Therefore, in step 1, the sign is sent to the SWAP network in

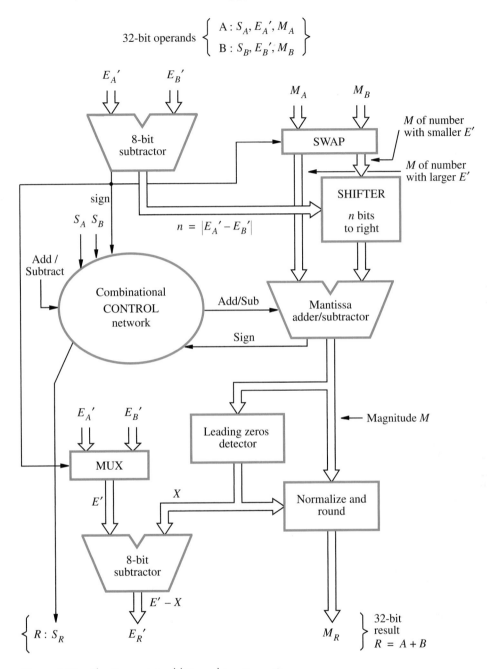

Figure 6.26   Floating-point addition-subtraction unit.

the upper right corner of Figure 6.26. If the sign is 0, then $E'_A \geq E'_B$ and the mantissas M_A and M_B are sent straight through the SWAP network. This results in M_B being sent to the SHIFTER, to be shifted n positions to the right. The other mantissa, M_A, is sent directly to the mantissa adder/subtractor. If the sign is 1, then $E'_A < E'_B$ and the mantissas are swapped before they are sent to the SHIFTER.

Step 2 is performed by the two-way multiplexer, MUX, near the bottom left corner of the figure. The exponent of the result, E', is tentatively determined as E'_A if $E'_A \geq E'_B$, or E'_B if $E'_A < E'_B$, based on the sign of the difference resulting from comparing exponents in step 1.

Step 3 involves the major component, the mantissa adder/subtractor in the middle of the figure. The CONTROL logic determines whether the mantissas are to be added or subtracted. This is decided by the signs of the operands (S_A and S_B) and the operation (Add or Subtract) that is to be performed on the operands. The CONTROL logic also determines the sign of the result, S_R. For example, if A is negative ($S_A = 1$), B is positive ($S_B = 0$), and the operation is $A - B$, then the mantissas are added and the sign of the result is negative ($S_R = 1$). On the other hand, if A and B are both positive and the operation is $A - B$, then the mantissas are subtracted. The sign of the result, S_R, now depends on the mantissa subtraction operation. For instance, if $E'_A > E'_B$, then $M_A - $ (shifted M_B) is positive and the result is positive. But if $E'_B > E'_A$, then $M_B - $ (shifted M_A) is positive and the result is negative. This example shows that the sign from the exponent comparison is also required as an input to the CONTROL network. When $E'_A = E'_B$ and the mantissas are subtracted, the sign of the mantissa adder/subtractor output determines the sign of the result. The reader should now be able to construct the complete truth table for the CONTROL network.

Step 4 of the Add/Subtract rule consists of normalizing the result of step 3, mantissa M. The number of leading zeros in M determines the number of bit shifts, X, to be applied to M. The normalized value is truncated to generate the 24-bit mantissa, M_R, of the result. The value X is also subtracted from the tentative result exponent E' to generate the true result exponent, E'_R. Note that only a single right shift might be needed to normalize the result. This would be the case if two mantissas of the form $1.xx\ldots$ were added. The vector M would then have the form $1x.xx\ldots$. This would correspond to an X value of -1 in the figure.

We have not given any details on the guard bits that must be carried along with intermediate mantissa values. In the IEEE standard, only a few bits are needed, as discussed earlier, to generate the 24-bit normalized mantissa of the result.

Let us consider the actual hardware that is needed to implement the blocks in Figure 6.26. The two 8-bit subtractors and the mantissa adder/subtractor can be implemented by combinational logic, as discussed earlier in this chapter. Because their outputs must be in sign-and-magnitude form, we must modify some of our earlier discussions. A combination of 1's-complement arithmetic and sign-and-magnitude representation is often used. Considerable flexibility is allowed in implementing the SHIFTER and the output normalization operation. If a design with a modest logic gate count is required, the operations can be implemented with shift registers. However, they can also be built as combinational logic units for high-performance, but in that case, a significant number of logic gates is needed. In high-performance processors, a significant portion of the chip area is assigned to floating-point operations.

6.8 CONCLUDING REMARKS

Computer arithmetic poses several interesting logic design problems. This chapter discussed some of the techniques that have proven useful in designing binary arithmetic units. The carry-lookahead technique is one of the major ideas in high-performance adder design. In the design of fast multipliers, bit-pair recoding of the multiplier, derived from the Booth algorithm, reduces the number of summands that must be added to generate the product. Carry-save addition substantially reduces the time needed to add the summands.

The IEEE floating-point number representation standard was described, and a set of rules for performing the four standard operations was given. As an example of the circuit complexity required to implement floating-point operations, the block diagram of an addition/subtraction unit was described.

PROBLEMS

6.1 Consider the binary numbers in the following addition and subtraction problems to be signed, 6-bit values in the 2's-complement representation. Perform the operations indicated, specify whether or not arithmetic overflow occurs, and check your answers by converting operands and results to decimal sign-and-magnitude representation.

ι	010110	101011	111111
	+001001	+100101	+000111
$\checkmark$	011001	110111	010101
	+010000	+111001	+101011
γ	010110	111110	100001
	−011111	−100101	−011101
$\iota\sigma$	111111	000111	011010
	−000111	−111000	−100010

6.2 Signed binary fractions in 2's-complement representation are discussed at the beginning of Section 6.7.

(*a*) Express the decimal values 0.5, −0.123, −0.75, and −0.1 as signed 6-bit fractions. (See Appendix E for decimal-to-binary fraction conversion.)

(*b*) What is the maximum representation error, *e*, involved in using only 5 significant bits after the binary point?

(*c*) Calculate the number of bits needed after the binary point so that

$$(a)\ e < \tfrac{1}{10}$$
$$(b)\ e < \tfrac{1}{100}$$
$$(c)\ e < \tfrac{1}{1000}$$
$$(d)\ e < \tfrac{1}{10^6}$$

6.3 The 1's-complement and 2's-complement binary representation methods are special cases of the $(b-1)$'s-complement and b's-complement representation techniques in base b number systems. For example, consider the decimal system. The sign-and-magnitude values $+526$, -526, $+70$, and -70 have 4-digit signed-number representations in each of the two complement systems, as shown in Figure P6.1. The 9's-complement is formed by taking the complement of each digit position with respect to 9. The 10's-complement is formed by adding 1 to the 9's-complement. In each of the latter two representations, the leftmost digit is zero for a positive number and 9 for a negative number.

Representation	Examples			
Sign and magnitude	+526	−526	+70	−70
9's complement	0526	9473	0070	9929
10's complement	0526	9474	0070	9930

Figure P6.1   Signed numbers in base 10 used in Problem 6.3.

Now consider the base-3 (ternary) system, in which the unsigned, 5-digit number $t_4t_3t_2t_1t_0$ has the value $t_4 \times 3^4 + t_3 \times 3^3 + t_2 \times 3^2 + t_1 \times 3^1 + t_0 \times 3^0$, with $0 \le t_i \le 2$. Express the ternary sign-and-magnitude numbers $+11011$, -10222, $+2120$, -1212, $+10$, and -201 as 6-digit, signed, ternary numbers in the 3's-complement system.

6.4 Represent each of the decimal values 56, -37, 122, and -123 as signed 6-digit numbers in the 3's-complement ternary format, perform addition and subtraction on them in all possible pairwise combinations, and state whether or not arithmetic overflow occurs for each operation performed. (See Problem 6.3 for a definition of the ternary number system, and use a technique analogous to that given in Appendix E for decimal-to-ternary integer conversion.)

6.5 A half adder is a combinational logic circuit that has two inputs, x and y, and two outputs, s and c, that are the sum and carry-out, respectively, resulting from the binary addition of x and y.

(*a*) Design a half adder as a two-level AND-OR circuit.

(*b*) Show how to implement a full adder, as shown in Figure 6.2*a*, by using two half adders and external logic gates, as necessary.

(*c*) Compare the longest logic delay path through the network derived in Part (*b*) to that of the logic delay of the adder network shown in Figure 6.2*a*.

6.6 Write a 68000 or IA-32 program to transform a 16-bit positive binary number into a 5-digit decimal number in which each digit of the number is coded in the binary-coded decimal (BCD) code. These BCD digit codes are to occupy the low-order 4 bits of five successive byte locations in the main memory. Use the conversion technique based on successive division by 10. This method is analogous to successive division by 2 when converting decimal-to-binary, as discussed in Appendix E. Consult Appendix C (68000) or D (IA-32) for the format and operation of the Divide instruction.

6.7 Assume that four BCD digits, representing a decimal integer in the range 0 to 9999, are packed into the lower half of a 32-bit memory location DECIMAL. Write an ARM, 68000, or IA-32 subroutine to convert the decimal integer stored at DECIMAL into binary representation and to store it in the memory location BINARY.

6.8 A modulo 10 adder is needed for adding BCD digits. Modulo 10 addition of two BCD digits, $A = A_3 A_2 A_1 A_0$ and $B = B_3 B_2 B_1 B_0$, can be achieved as follows: Add A to B (binary addition). Then, if the result is an illegal code that is greater than or equal to 10_{10}, add 6_{10}. (Ignore overflow from this addition.)

(*a*) When is the output carry equal to 1?

(*b*) Show that this algorithm gives correct results for

$$(1)\ A = 0101 \quad \text{and} \quad B = 0110$$
$$(2)\ A = 0011 \quad \text{and} \quad B = 0100$$

(*c*) Design a BCD digit adder using a 4-bit binary adder and external logic gates as needed. The inputs are $A_3 A_2 A_1 A_0$, $B_3 B_2 B_1 B_0$, and a carry-in. The outputs are the sum digit $S_3 S_2 S_1 S_0$ and the carry-out. A cascade of such blocks can form a ripple-carry BCD adder.

6.9 Show that the logic expression $c_n \oplus c_{n-1}$ is a correct indicator of overflow in the addition of 2's-complement integers, by using an appropriate truth table.

6.10 (*a*) Design a 64-bit adder that uses four of the 16-bit carry-lookahead adders shown in Figure 6.5 along with additional logic to generate c_{16}, c_{32}, c_{48}, and c_{64}, from c_0 and the G_i^{II} and P_i^{II} variables shown in this figure. What is the relationship of the additional logic to the logic inside each lookahead circuit in the figure?

(*b*) Show that the delay through the 64-bit adder is 12 gate delays for s_{63} and 7 gate delays for c_{64}, as claimed at the end of Section 6.2.1.

(*c*) Compare the gate delays to produce s_{31} and c_{32} in the 64-bit adder of part (*a*) to the gate delays for the same variables in the 32-bit adder built from a cascade of two 16-bit adders, as discussed in Section 6.2.1.

6.11 (*a*) How many logic gates are needed to build the 4-bit carry-lookahead adder shown in Figure 6.4?

(*b*) Use appropriate parts of the result from Part (*a*) to calculate how many logic gates are needed to build the 16-bit carry-lookahead adder shown in Figure 6.5.

6.12 Show that the worst case delay through an $n \times n$ array of the type shown in Figure 6.6*b* is $6(n-1) - 1$ gate delays, as claimed in Section 6.3.

6.13 Using manual methods, perform the operations $A \times B$ and $A \div B$ on the 5-bit unsigned numbers $A = 10101$ and $B = 00101$.

6.14 Show how the multiplication and division operations in Problem 6.13 would be performed by the hardware in Figures 6.7*a* and 6.21, respectively, by constructing charts similar to those in Figures 6.7*b* and 6.23.

6.15 Write an ARM, 68000, or IA-32 program for the multiplication of two 32-bit unsigned numbers that is patterned after the technique used in Figure 6.7. Assume that the multiplier and multiplicand are in registers R_2 and R_3, respectively. The product is to be developed in registers R_1 (high-order half) and R_2 (low-order half). (*Hint:* Use a combination of Shift and Rotate operations for a double-register shift.)

6.16 Write an ARM, 68000, or IA-32 program for integer division based on the nonrestoring-division algorithm. Assume that both operands are positive, that is, the leftmost bit is zero for both the dividend and the divisor.

6.17 Multiply each of the following pairs of signed 2's-complement numbers using the Booth algorithm. In each case, assume that A is the multiplicand and B is the multiplier.

$$(a)\ A = 010111\ \text{ and }\ B = 110110$$
$$(b)\ A = 110011\ \text{ and }\ B = 101100$$
$$(c)\ A = 110101\ \text{ and }\ B = 011011$$
$$(d)\ A = 001111\ \text{ and }\ B = 001111$$

6.18 Repeat Problem 6.17 using bit-pairing of the multipliers.

6.19 Indicate generally how to modify the circuit diagram in Figure 6.7*a* to implement multiplication of signed, 2's-complement, *n*-bit numbers using the Booth algorithm, by clearly specifying inputs and outputs for the Control sequencer and any other changes needed around the adder and *A* register.

6.20 If the product of two, *n*-bit, signed numbers in the 2's-complement representation can be represented in *n* bits, the manual multiplication algorithm shown in Figure 6.6*a* can be used directly, treating the sign bits the same as the other bits. Try this on each of the following pairs of 4-bit signed numbers:

$$(a)\ \text{Multiplicand} = 1110\ \text{ and }\ \text{Multiplier} = 1101$$
$$(b)\ \text{Multiplicand} = 0010\ \text{ and }\ \text{Multiplier} = 1110$$

Why does this work correctly?

6.21 An integer arithmetic unit that can perform addition and multiplication of 16-bit unsigned numbers is to be used to multiply two 32-bit unsigned numbers. All operands, intermediate results, and final results are held in 16-bit registers labeled R_0 through R_{15}. The hardware multiplier multiplies the contents of R_i (multiplicand) by R_j (multiplier) and stores the double-length 32-bit product in registers R_j and R_{j+1}, with the low-order half in R_j. When $j = i - 1$, the product overwrites both operands. The hardware adder adds the contents of R_i and R_j and puts the result in R_j. The input carry to an Add operation is 0, and the input carry to an Add-with-carry operation is the contents of a carry flag C. The output carry from the adder is always stored in C.

   Specify the steps of a procedure for multiplying two 32-bit operands in registers R_1, R_0, and R_3, R_2, high-order halves first, leaving the 64-bit product in registers

R_{15}, R_{14}, R_{13}, and R_{12}. Any of the registers R_{11} through R_4 may be used for intermediate values, if necessary. Each step in the procedure can be a multiplication, or an addition, or a register transfer operation.

6.22 (a) Calculate the delay, in terms of logic gate delays, for the product bit p_7 in each of the arrays in Figure 6.16. Assume that each output from a full adder is available two gate delays after the inputs are available. Include the AND gate delay to generate all $m_i q_j$ products at the beginning.

(b) The delay for the extension of Figure 6.16a to the $n \times n$ case has been stated as $6(n-1) - 1$ in Section 6.4. Develop a similar expression for the extension of Figure 6.16b to the $n \times n$ case.

6.23 Develop the derivation for the formula $1.7 log_2 k - 1.7$ for the number of carry-save addition steps needed to reduce k summands to two vectors. (This formula is stated without derivation in Section 6.5.2.)

6.24 (a) How many CSA levels are needed to reduce 16 summands to 2 using a pattern similar to that shown in Figure 6.19?

(b) Draw the pattern for reducing 32 summands to 2 to prove that the claim of 8 levels in Section 6.5.2 is correct.

(c) Compare the exact answers in Parts (a) and (b) to the results derived from the approximation $1.7 log_2 k - 1.7$.

6.25 In Section 6.7, we used the practical-sized 32-bit IEEE standard format for floating-point numbers. Here, we use a shortened format that retains all the pertinent concepts but is manageable for working through numerical exercises. Consider that floating-point numbers are represented in a 12-bit format as shown in Figure P6.2. The scale factor has an implied base of 2 and a 5-bit, excess-15 exponent, with the two end values of 0 and 31 used to signify exact 0 and infinity, respectively. The 6-bit mantissa is normalized as in the IEEE format, with an implied 1 to the left of the binary point.

(a) Represent the numbers $+1.7$, -0.012, $+19$, and $\frac{1}{8}$ in this format.

(b) What are the smallest and largest numbers representable in this format?

(c) How does the range calculated in Part (b) compare to the ranges of a 12-bit signed integer and a 12-bit signed fraction?

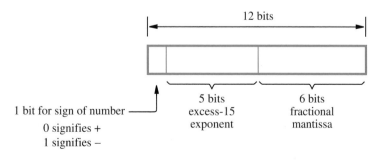

Figure P6.2 Floating-point format used in Problem 6.25.

(*d*) Perform Add, Subtract, Multiply, and Divide operations on the operands

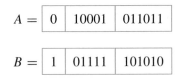

$$A = \boxed{0} \; \boxed{10001} \; \boxed{011011}$$

$$B = \boxed{1} \; \boxed{01111} \; \boxed{101010}$$

6.26   Consider a 16-bit, floating-point number in a format similar to that discussed in Problem 6.25, with a 6-bit exponent and a 9-bit normalized fractional mantissa. The base of the scale factor is 2 and the exponent is represented in excess-31 format.

(*a*) Add the numbers *A* and *B*, formatted as follows:

$$A = \boxed{0} \; \boxed{100001} \; \boxed{111111110}$$

$$B = \boxed{0} \; \boxed{011111} \; \boxed{001010101}$$

Give the answer in normalized form. Remember that an implicit 1 is to the left of the binary point but is not included in the *A* and *B* formats. Use rounding when producing the final normalized 9-bit mantissa.

(*b*) Using decimal numbers *w*, *x*, *y*, and *z*, express the magnitude of the largest and smallest (nonzero) values representable in the preceding normalized floating-point format. Use the following form:

$$\text{Largest} = w \times 2^x$$
$$\text{Smallest} = y \times 2^{-z}$$

6.27   How does the excess-*x* representation for exponents of the scale factor in the floating-point number representation of Figure 6.24*a* facilitate the comparison of the relative sizes of two floating-point numbers? (*Hint:* Assume that a combinational logic network that compares the relative sizes of two, 32-bit, unsigned integers is available. Use this network, along with external logic gates, as necessary, to design the required network for the comparison of floating-point numbers.)

6.28   In Problem 6.25*a*, conversion of the simple decimal numbers into binary floating-point format is straightforward. However, if the decimal numbers are given in floating-point format, conversion is not straightforward because we cannot separately convert the mantissa and the exponent of the scale factor because $10^x = 2^y$ does not, in general, allow both *x* and *y* to be integers. Suppose a table of binary, floating-point numbers t_i, such that $t_i = 10^{x_i}$ for x_i in the representable range, is stored in a computer. Give a procedure in general terms for converting a given decimal floating-point number into binary floating-point format. You may use both the integer and floating-point instructions available in the computer.

6.29 Consider the representation of the decimal number 0.1 as a signed, 8-bit, binary fraction in the representation discussed at the beginning of Section 6.7. If the number does not convert exactly into this 8-bit format, approximate the number using all three of the truncation methods discussed in Section 6.7.3.

6.30 Construct an example to show that three guard bits are needed to produce the correct answer when two positive numbers are subtracted.

6.31 Which of the four 6-bit answers to Problem 6.2a are not exact? For each of these cases, give the three 6-bit values that correspond to the three types of truncation defined in Section 6.7.3.

6.32 Derive logic equations that specify the Add/Sub and S_R outputs of the combinational CONTROL network in Figure 6.26.

6.33 If gate fan-in is limited to four, how can the SHIFTER in Figure 6.26 be implemented combinationally?

6.34 (a) Sketch a logic-gate network that implements the multiplexer MUX in Figure 6.26.
(b) Relate the structure of the SWAP network in Figure 6.26 to your solution to Part (a).

6.35 How can the leading zeros detector in Figure 6.26 be implemented combinationally?

6.36 The mantissa adder-subtractor in Figure 6.26 operates on positive, unsigned binary fractions and must produce a sign-and-magnitude result. In the discussion accompanying Figure 6.26, we state that 1's-complement arithmetic is convenient because of the required format for input and output operands. When adding two signed numbers in 1's-complement notation, the carry-out from the sign position must be added to the result to obtain the correct signed answer. This is called *end-around carry correction*. Consider the two examples in Figure P6.3, which illustrate addition using signed, 4-bit encodings of operands and answers in the 1's-complement system.

The 1's-complement arithmetic system is convenient when a sign-and-magnitude result is to be generated because a negative number in 1's-complement notation can be converted to sign-and-magnitude form by complementing the bits to the right of the sign-bit position. Using 2's-complement arithmetic, addition of +1 is needed to convert a negative value into sign-and-magnitude notation. If a carry-lookahead adder is used, it is possible to incorporate the end-around carry operation required by 1's-complement arithmetic into the lookahead logic. With this discussion as a guide, give the complete design of the 1's-complement adder-subtractor required in Figure 6.26.

Figure P6.3 1's-complement addition used in Problem 6.36.

REFERENCES

1. Institute of Electrical and Electronics Engineers, *IEEE Standard for Binary Floating-Point Arithmetic,* ANSI/IEEE Standard 754-1985, August 1985.

2. J.L. Hennessy and D.A. Patterson, *Computer Architecture — A Quantitative Approach,* 2nd ed., Morgan Kaufmann, San Francisco, CA, 1996.

BASIC PROCESSING UNIT

CHAPTER OBJECTIVES

In this chapter you will learn about:

- How a processor executes instructions
- The internal functional units of a processor and how they are interconnected
- Hardware for generating internal control signals
- The microprogramming approach
- Microprogram organization

In this and the next chapter we focus on the processing unit, which executes machine instructions and coordinates the activities of other units. This unit is often called the *Instruction Set Processor* (ISP), or simply the *processor*. We examine its internal structure and how it performs the tasks of fetching, decoding, and executing instructions of a program. The processing unit used to be called the *central processing unit* (CPU). The term "central" is less appropriate today because many modern computer systems include several processing units.

The organization of processors has evolved over the years, driven by developments in technology and the need to provide high performance. A common strategy in the development of high-performance processors is to make various functional units operate in parallel as much as possible. High-performance processors have a pipelined organization where the execution of one instruction is started before the execution of the preceding instruction is completed. In another approach, known as superscalar operation, several instructions are fetched and executed at the same time. Pipelining and superscalar architectures are discussed in Chapter 8. In this chapter, we concentrate on the basic ideas that are common to all processors.

A typical computing task consists of a series of steps specified by a sequence of machine instructions that constitute a program. An instruction is executed by carrying out a sequence of more rudimentary operations. These operations and the means by which they are controlled are the main topic of this chapter.

7.1 SOME FUNDAMENTAL CONCEPTS

To execute a program, the processor fetches one instruction at a time and performs the operations specified. Instructions are fetched from successive memory locations until a branch or a jump instruction is encountered. The processor keeps track of the address of the memory location containing the next instruction to be fetched using the program counter, PC. After fetching an instruction, the contents of the PC are updated to point to the next instruction in the sequence. A branch instruction may load a different value into the PC.

Another key register in the processor is the instruction register, IR. Suppose that each instruction comprises 4 bytes, and that it is stored in one memory word. To execute an instruction, the processor has to perform the following three steps:

1. Fetch the contents of the memory location pointed to by the PC. The contents of this location are interpreted as an instruction to be executed. Hence, they are loaded into the IR. Symbolically, this can be written as

$$IR \leftarrow [[PC]]$$

2. Assuming that the memory is byte addressable, increment the contents of the PC by 4, that is,

$$PC \leftarrow [PC] + 4$$

3. Carry out the actions specified by the instruction in the IR.

In cases where an instruction occupies more than one word, steps 1 and 2 must be repeated as many times as necessary to fetch the complete instruction. These two steps are usually referred to as the *fetch phase;* step 3 constitutes the *execution phase.*

To study these operations in detail, we first need to examine the internal organization of the processor. The main building blocks of a processor were introduced in Figure 1.2. They can be organized and interconnected in a variety of ways. We will start with a very simple organization. Later in this chapter and in Chapter 8 we will present more complex structures that provide high performance. Figure 7.1 shows an organization

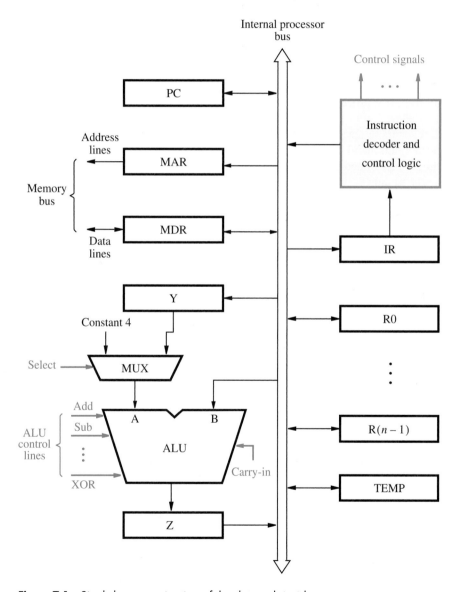

Figure 7.1   Single-bus organization of the datapath inside a processor.

in which the arithmetic and logic unit (ALU) and all the registers are interconnected via a single common bus. This bus is internal to the processor and should not be confused with the external bus that connects the processor to the memory and I/O devices.

The data and address lines of the external memory bus are shown in Figure 7.1 connected to the internal processor bus via the memory data register, MDR, and the memory address register, MAR, respectively. Register MDR has two inputs and two outputs. Data may be loaded into MDR either from the memory bus or from the internal processor bus. The data stored in MDR may be placed on either bus. The input of MAR is connected to the internal bus, and its output is connected to the external bus. The control lines of the memory bus are connected to the instruction decoder and control logic block. This unit is responsible for issuing the signals that control the operation of all the units inside the processor and for interacting with the memory bus.

The number and use of the processor registers R0 through R($n - 1$) vary considerably from one processor to another. Registers may be provided for general-purpose use by the programmer. Some may be dedicated as special-purpose registers, such as index registers or stack pointers. Three registers, Y, Z, and TEMP in Figure 7.1, have not been mentioned before. These registers are transparent to the programmer, that is, the programmer need not be concerned with them because they are never referenced explicitly by any instruction. They are used by the processor for temporary storage during execution of some instructions. These registers are never used for storing data generated by one instruction for later use by another instruction.

The multiplexer MUX selects either the output of register Y or a constant value 4 to be provided as input A of the ALU. The constant 4 is used to increment the contents of the program counter. We will refer to the two possible values of the MUX control input Select as Select4 and SelectY for selecting the constant 4 or register Y, respectively.

As instruction execution progresses, data are transferred from one register to another, often passing through the ALU to perform some arithmetic or logic operation. The instruction decoder and control logic unit is responsible for implementing the actions specified by the instruction loaded in the IR register. The decoder generates the control signals needed to select the registers involved and direct the transfer of data. The registers, the ALU, and the interconnecting bus are collectively referred to as the *datapath*.

With few exceptions, an instruction can be executed by performing one or more of the following operations in some specified sequence:

•   Transfer a word of data from one processor register to another or to the ALU

•   Perform an arithmetic or a logic operation and store the result in a processor register

•   Fetch the contents of a given memory location and load them into a processor register

•   Store a word of data from a processor register into a given memory location

We now consider in detail how each of these operations is implemented, using the simple processor model in Figure 7.1.

7.1.1 REGISTER TRANSFERS

Instruction execution involves a sequence of steps in which data are transferred from one register to another. For each register, two control signals are used to place the contents of that register on the bus or to load the data on the bus into the register. This is represented symbolically in Figure 7.2. The input and output of register Ri are connected to the bus via switches controlled by the signals Ri_{in} and Ri_{out}, respectively. When Ri_{in} is set to 1, the data on the bus are loaded into Ri. Similarly, when Ri_{out} is set to 1, the contents of register Ri are placed on the bus. While Ri_{out} is equal to 0, the bus can be used for transferring data from other registers.

Suppose that we wish to transfer the contents of register R1 to register R4. This can be accomplished as follows:

- Enable the output of register R1 by setting R1$_{out}$ to 1. This places the contents of R1 on the processor bus.

- Enable the input of register R4 by setting R4$_{in}$ to 1. This loads data from the processor bus into register R4.

All operations and data transfers within the processor take place within time periods defined by the *processor clock*. The control signals that govern a particular transfer are asserted at the start of the clock cycle. In our example, R1$_{out}$ and R4$_{in}$ are set to 1. The registers consist of edge-triggered flip-flops. Hence, at the next active edge of the clock, the flip-flops that constitute R4 will load the data present at their inputs. At the same time, the control signals R1$_{out}$ and R4$_{in}$ will return to 0. We will use this simple model of the timing of data transfers for the rest of this chapter. However, we should point out that other schemes are possible. For example, data transfers may use both the rising and falling edges of the clock. Also, when edge-triggered flip-flops are not used, two or more clock signals may be needed to guarantee proper transfer of data. This is known as *multiphase clocking*.

An implementation for one bit of register Ri is shown in Figure 7.3 as an example. A two-input multiplexer is used to select the data applied to the input of an edge-triggered D flip-flop. When the control input Ri_{in} is equal to 1, the multiplexer selects the data on the bus. This data will be loaded into the flip-flop at the rising edge of the clock. When Ri_{in} is equal to 0, the multiplexer feeds back the value currently stored in the flip-flop.

The Q output of the flip-flop is connected to the bus via a tri-state gate. When Ri_{out} is equal to 0, the gate's output is in the high-impedance (electrically disconnected) state. This corresponds to the open-circuit state of a switch. When R$i_{out} = 1$, the gate drives the bus to 0 or 1, depending on the value of Q.

7.1.2 PERFORMING AN ARITHMETIC OR LOGIC OPERATION

The ALU is a combinational circuit that has no internal storage. It performs arithmetic and logic operations on the two operands applied to its A and B inputs. In Figures 7.1 and 7.2, one of the operands is the output of the multiplexer MUX and the other operand

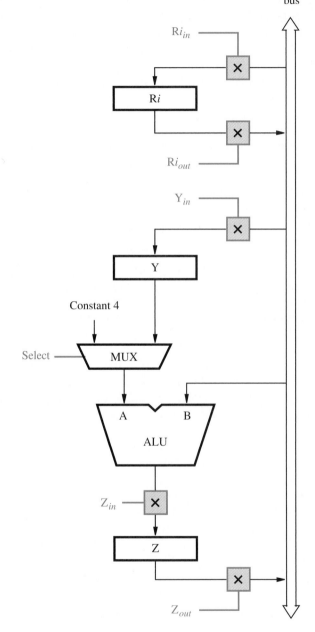

Figure 7.2 Input and output gating for the registers in Figure 7.1.

Bus

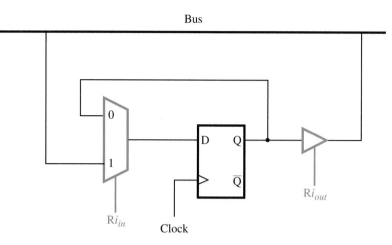

Figure 7.3 Input and output gating for one register bit.

is obtained directly from the bus. The result produced by the ALU is stored temporarily in register Z. Therefore, a sequence of operations to add the contents of register R1 to those of register R2 and store the result in register R3 is

1. $R1_{out}$, Y_{in}
2. $R2_{out}$, SelectY, Add, Z_{in}
3. Z_{out}, $R3_{in}$

The signals whose names are given in any step are activated for the duration of the clock cycle corresponding to that step. All other signals are inactive. Hence, in step 1, the output of register R1 and the input of register Y are enabled, causing the contents of R1 to be transferred over the bus to Y. In step 2, the multiplexer's Select signal is set to SelectY, causing the multiplexer to gate the contents of register Y to input A of the ALU. At the same time, the contents of register R2 are gated onto the bus and, hence, to input B. The function performed by the ALU depends on the signals applied to its control lines. In this case, the Add line is set to 1, causing the output of the ALU to be the sum of the two numbers at inputs A and B. This sum is loaded into register Z because its input control signal is activated. In step 3, the contents of register Z are transferred to the destination register, R3. This last transfer cannot be carried out during step 2, because only one register output can be connected to the bus during any clock cycle.

In this introductory discussion, we assume that there is a dedicated signal for each function to be performed. For example, we assume that there are separate control signals to specify individual ALU operations, such as Add, Subtract, XOR, and so on. In reality, some degree of encoding is likely to be used. For example, if the ALU can perform eight different operations, three control signals would suffice to specify the required operation. We will discuss the limitations and pros and cons of control signal encoding in Section 7.5.1.

7.1.3 Fetching a Word from Memory

To fetch a word of information from memory, the processor has to specify the address of the memory location where this information is stored and request a Read operation. This applies whether the information to be fetched represents an instruction in a program or an operand specified by an instruction. The processor transfers the required address to the MAR, whose output is connected to the address lines of the memory bus. At the same time, the processor uses the control lines of the memory bus to indicate that a Read operation is needed. When the requested data are received from the memory they are stored in register MDR, from where they can be transferred to other registers in the processor.

The connections for register MDR are illustrated in Figure 7.4. It has four control signals: MDR_{in} and MDR_{out} control the connection to the internal bus, and MDR_{inE} and MDR_{outE} control the connection to the external bus. The circuit in Figure 7.3 is easily modified to provide the additional connections. A three-input multiplexer can be used, with the memory bus data line connected to the third input. This input is selected when $MDR_{inE} = 1$. A second tri-state gate, controlled by MDR_{outE} can be used to connect the output of the flip-flop to the memory bus.

During memory Read and Write operations, the timing of internal processor operations must be coordinated with the response of the addressed device on the memory bus. The processor completes one internal data transfer in one clock cycle. The speed of operation of the addressed device, on the other hand, varies with the device. We saw in Chapter 5 that modern processors include a cache memory on the same chip as the processor. Typically, a cache will respond to a memory read request in one clock cycle. However, when a cache miss occurs, the request is forwarded to the main memory, which introduces a delay of several clock cycles. A read or write request may also be intended for a register in a memory-mapped I/O device.

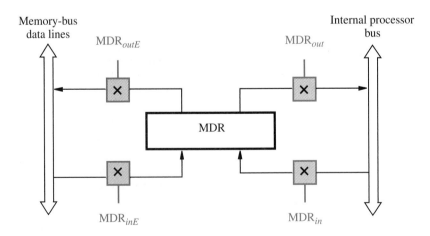

Figure 7.4   Connection and control signals for register MDR.

Such I/O registers are not cached, so their accesses always take a number of clock cycles.

To accommodate the variability in response time, the processor waits until it receives an indication that the requested Read operation has been completed. We will assume that a control signal called Memory-Function-Completed (MFC) is used for this purpose. The addressed device sets this signal to 1 to indicate that the contents of the specified location have been read and are available on the data lines of the memory bus. (We encountered several examples of such a signal in conjunction with the buses discussed in Chapter 4, such as Slave-ready in Figure 4.25 and TRDY# in Figure 4.41.)

As an example of a read operation, consider the instruction Move (R1),R2. The actions needed to execute this instruction are:

1. MAR ← [R1]
2. Start a Read operation on the memory bus
3. Wait for the MFC response from the memory
4. Load MDR from the memory bus
5. R2 ← [MDR]

These actions may be carried out as separate steps, but some can be combined into a single step. Each action can be completed in one clock cycle, except action 3 which requires one or more clock cycles, depending on the speed of the addressed device.

For simplicity, let us assume that the output of MAR is enabled all the time. Thus, the contents of MAR are always available on the address lines of the memory bus. This is the case when the processor is the bus master. When a new address is loaded into MAR, it will appear on the memory bus at the beginning of the next clock cycle, as shown in Figure 7.5. A Read control signal is activated at the same time MAR is loaded. This signal will cause the bus interface circuit to send a read command, MR, on the bus. With this arrangement, we have combined actions 1 and 2 above into a single control step. Actions 3 and 4 can also be combined by activating control signal MDR_{inE} while waiting for a response from the memory. Thus, the data received from the memory are loaded into MDR at the end of the clock cycle in which the MFC signal is received. In the next clock cycle, MDR_{out} is activated to transfer the data to register R2. This means that the memory read operation requires three steps, which can be described by the signals being activated as follows:

1. $R1_{out}$, MAR_{in}, Read
2. MDR_{inE}, WMFC
3. MDR_{out}, $R2_{in}$

where WMFC is the control signal that causes the processor's control circuitry to wait for the arrival of the MFC signal.

Figure 7.5 shows that MDR_{inE} is set to 1 for exactly the same period as the read command, MR. Hence, in subsequent discussion, we will not specify the value of MDR_{inE} explicitly, with the understanding that it is always equal to MR.

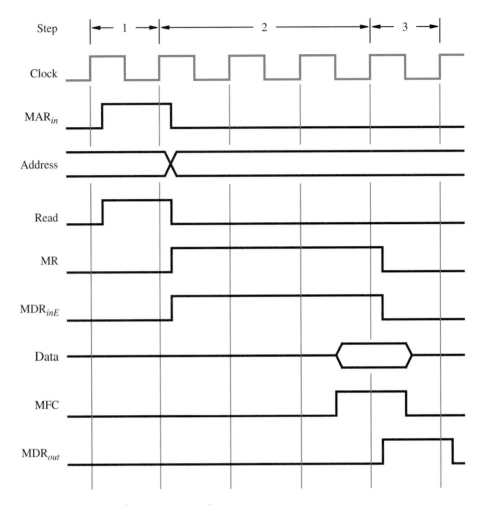

Figure 7.5 Timing of a memory Read operation.

7.1.4 STORING A WORD IN MEMORY

Writing a word into a memory location follows a similar procedure. The desired address is loaded into MAR. Then, the data to be written are loaded into MDR, and a Write command is issued. Hence, executing the instruction Move R2,(R1) requires the following sequence:

1. $R1_{out}$, MAR_{in}
2. $R2_{out}$, MDR_{in}, Write
3. MDR_{outE}, WMFC

As in the case of the read operation, the Write control signal causes the memory bus interface hardware to issue a Write command on the memory bus. The processor remains in step 3 until the memory operation is completed and an MFC response is received.

7.2 EXECUTION OF A COMPLETE INSTRUCTION

Let us now put together the sequence of elementary operations required to execute one instruction. Consider the instruction

Add   (R3),R1

which adds the contents of a memory location pointed to by R3 to register R1. Executing this instruction requires the following actions:

1. Fetch the instruction.
2. Fetch the first operand (the contents of the memory location pointed to by R3).
3. Perform the addition.
4. Load the result into R1.

Figure 7.6 gives the sequence of control steps required to perform these operations for the single-bus architecture of Figure 7.1. Instruction execution proceeds as follows. In step 1, the instruction fetch operation is initiated by loading the contents of the PC into the MAR and sending a Read request to the memory. The Select signal is set to Select4, which causes the multiplexer MUX to select the constant 4. This value is added to the operand at input B, which is the contents of the PC, and the result is stored in register Z. The updated value is moved from register Z back into the PC during step 2, while waiting for the memory to respond. In step 3, the word fetched from the memory is loaded into the IR.

Steps 1 through 3 constitute the instruction fetch phase, which is the same for all instructions. The instruction decoding circuit interprets the contents of the IR at the beginning of step 4. This enables the control circuitry to activate the control signals for steps 4 through 7, which constitute the execution phase. The contents of register R3 are transferred to the MAR in step 4, and a memory read operation is initiated. Then

Step	Action
1	PC_{out}, MAR_{in}, Read, Select4, Add, Z_{in}
2	Z_{out}, PC_{in}, Y_{in}, WMFC
3	MDR_{out}, IR_{in}
4	$R3_{out}$, MAR_{in}, Read
5	$R1_{out}$, Y_{in}, WMFC
6	MDR_{out}, SelectY, Add, Z_{in}
7	Z_{out}, $R1_{in}$, End

Figure 7.6   Control sequence for execution of the instruction Add (R3),R1.

the contents of R1 are transferred to register Y in step 5, to prepare for the addition operation. When the Read operation is completed, the memory operand is available in register MDR, and the addition operation is performed in step 6. The contents of MDR are gated to the bus, and thus also to the B input of the ALU, and register Y is selected as the second input to the ALU by choosing SelectY. The sum is stored in register Z, then transferred to R1 in step 7. The End signal causes a new instruction fetch cycle to begin by returning to step 1.

This discussion accounts for all control signals in Figure 7.6 except Y_{in} in step 2. There is no need to copy the updated contents of PC into register Y when executing the Add instruction. But, in Branch instructions the updated value of the PC is needed to compute the Branch target address. To speed up the execution of Branch instructions, this value is copied into register Y in step 2. Since step 2 is part of the fetch phase, the same action will be performed for all instructions. This does not cause any harm because register Y is not used for any other purpose at that time.

7.2.1 BRANCH INSTRUCTIONS

A branch instruction replaces the contents of the PC with the branch target address. This address is usually obtained by adding an offset X, which is given in the branch instruction, to the updated value of the PC. Figure 7.7 gives a control sequence that implements an unconditional branch instruction. Processing starts, as usual, with the fetch phase. This phase ends when the instruction is loaded into the IR in step 3. The offset value is extracted from the IR by the instruction decoding circuit, which will also perform sign extension if required. Since the value of the updated PC is already available in register Y, the offset X is gated onto the bus in step 4, and an addition operation is performed. The result, which is the branch target address, is loaded into the PC in step 5.

The offset X used in a branch instruction is usually the difference between the branch target address and the address immediately following the branch instruction.

Step	Action
1	PC_{out}, MAR_{in}, Read, Select4, Add, Z_{in}
2	Z_{out}, PC_{in}, Y_{in}, WMFC
3	MDR_{out}, IR_{in}
4	Offset-field-of-IR_{out}, Add, Z_{in}
5	Z_{out}, PC_{in}, End

Figure 7.7 Control sequence for an unconditional Branch instruction.

For example, if the branch instruction is at location 2000 and if the branch target address is 2050, the value of X must be 46. The reason for this can be readily appreciated from the control sequence in Figure 7.7. The PC is incremented during the fetch phase, before knowing the type of instruction being executed. Thus, when the branch address is computed in step 4, the PC value used is the updated value, which points to the instruction following the branch instruction in the memory.

Consider now a conditional branch. In this case, we need to check the status of the condition codes before loading a new value into the PC. For example, for a Branch-on-negative (Branch<0) instruction, step 4 in Figure 7.7 is replaced with

$$\text{Offset-field-of-IR}_{out}, \text{Add}, Z_{in}, \text{If } N = 0 \text{ then End}$$

Thus, if $N = 0$ the processor returns to step 1 immediately after step 4. If $N = 1$, step 5 is performed to load a new value into the PC, thus performing the branch operation.

7.3 MULTIPLE-BUS ORGANIZATION

We used the simple single-bus structure of Figure 7.1 to illustrate the basic ideas. The resulting control sequences in Figures 7.6 and 7.7 are quite long because only one data item can be transferred over the bus in a clock cycle. To reduce the number of steps needed, most commercial processors provide multiple internal paths that enable several transfers to take place in parallel.

Figure 7.8 depicts a three-bus structure used to connect the registers and the ALU of a processor. All general-purpose registers are combined into a single block called the *register file*. In VLSI technology, the most efficient way to implement a number of registers is in the form of an array of memory cells similar to those used in the implementation of random-access memories (RAMs) described in Chapter 5. The register file in Figure 7.8 is said to have three ports. There are two outputs, allowing the contents of two different registers to be accessed simultaneously and have their contents placed on buses A and B. The third port allows the data on bus C to be loaded into a third register during the same clock cycle.

Buses A and B are used to transfer the source operands to the A and B inputs of the ALU, where an arithmetic or logic operation may be performed. The result is transferred to the destination over bus C. If needed, the ALU may simply pass one of its two input operands unmodified to bus C. We will call the ALU control signals for such an operation R=A or R=B. The three-bus arrangement obviates the need for registers Y and Z in Figure 7.1.

A second feature in Figure 7.8 is the introduction of the Incrementer unit, which is used to increment the PC by 4. Using the Incrementer eliminates the need to add 4 to the PC using the main ALU, as was done in Figures 7.6 and 7.7. The source for the constant 4 at the ALU input multiplexer is still useful. It can be used to increment other addresses, such as the memory addresses in LoadMultiple and StoreMultiple instructions.

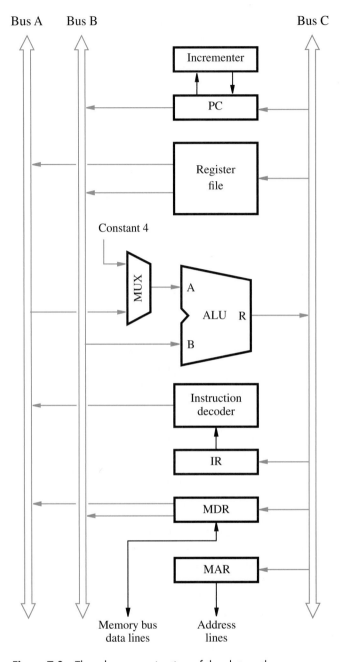

Figure 7.8   Three-bus organization of the datapath.

Step	Action
1	PC_{out}, R=B, MAR_{in}, Read, IncPC
2	WMFC
3	MDR_{outB}, R=B, IR_{in}
4	$R4_{outA}$, $R5_{outB}$, SelectA, Add, $R6_{in}$, End

Figure 7.9 Control sequence for the instruction Add R4,R5,R6 for the three-bus organization in Figure 7.8.

Consider the three-operand instruction

Add   R4,R5,R6

The control sequence for executing this instruction is given in Figure 7.9. In step 1, the contents of the PC are passed through the ALU, using the R=B control signal, and loaded into the MAR to start a memory read operation. At the same time the PC is incremented by 4. Note that the value loaded into MAR is the original contents of the PC. The incremented value is loaded into the PC at the end of the clock cycle and will not affect the contents of MAR. In step 2, the processor waits for MFC and loads the data received into MDR, then transfers them to IR in step 3. Finally, the execution phase of the instruction requires only one control step to complete, step 4.

By providing more paths for data transfer a significant reduction in the number of clock cycles needed to execute an instruction is achieved.

7.4 HARDWIRED CONTROL

To execute instructions, the processor must have some means of generating the control signals needed in the proper sequence. Computer designers use a wide variety of techniques to solve this problem. The approaches used fall into one of two categories: hardwired control and microprogrammed control. We discuss each of these techniques in detail, starting with hardwired control in this section.

Consider the sequence of control signals given in Figure 7.6. Each step in this sequence is completed in one clock period. A counter may be used to keep track of the control steps, as shown in Figure 7.10. Each state, or count, of this counter corresponds to one control step. The required control signals are determined by the following information:

• Contents of the control step counter
• Contents of the instruction register
• Contents of the condition code flags
• External input signals, such as MFC and interrupt requests

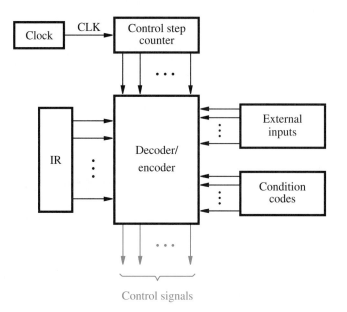

Figure 7.10 Control unit organization.

To gain insight into the structure of the control unit, we start with a simplified view of the hardware involved. The decoder/encoder block in Figure 7.10 is a combinational circuit that generates the required control outputs, depending on the state of all its inputs. By separating the decoding and encoding functions, we obtain the more detailed block diagram in Figure 7.11. The step decoder provides a separate signal line for each step, or time slot, in the control sequence. Similarly, the output of the instruction decoder consists of a separate line for each machine instruction. For any instruction loaded in the IR, one of the output lines INS_1 through INS_m is set to 1, and all other lines are set to 0. (For design details of decoders, refer to Appendix A.) The input signals to the encoder block in Figure 7.11 are combined to generate the individual control signals Y_{in}, PC_{out}, Add, End, and so on. An example of how the encoder generates the Z_{in} control signal for the processor organization in Figure 7.1 is given in Figure 7.12. This circuit implements the logic function

$$Z_{in} = T_1 + T_6 \cdot ADD + T_4 \cdot BR + \cdots \qquad [7.1]$$

This signal is asserted during time slot T_1 for all instructions, during T_6 for an Add instruction, during T_4 for an unconditional branch instruction, and so on. The logic function for Z_{in} is derived from the control sequences in Figures 7.6 and 7.7. As another example, Figure 7.13 gives a circuit that generates the End control signal from the logic function

$$End = T_7 \cdot ADD + T_5 \cdot BR + (T_5 \cdot N + T_4 \cdot \overline{N}) \cdot BRN + \cdots \qquad [7.2]$$

The End signal starts a new instruction fetch cycle by resetting the control step counter to its starting value. Figure 7.11 contains another control signal called RUN. When

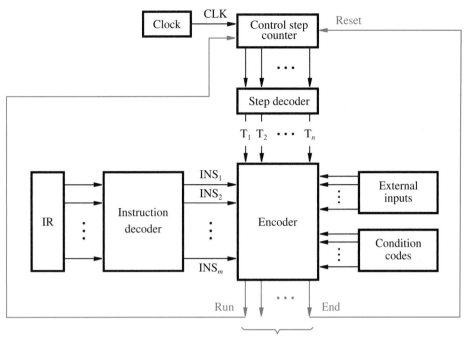

Figure 7.11   Separation of the decoding and encoding functions.

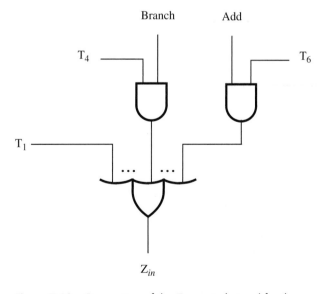

Figure 7.12   Generation of the Z_{in} control signal for the processor in Figure 7.1.

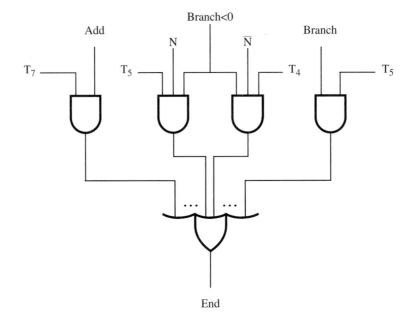

Figure 7.13   Generation of the End control signal.

set to 1, RUN causes the counter to be incremented by one at the end of every clock cycle. When RUN is equal to 0, the counter stops counting. This is needed whenever the WMFC signal is issued, to cause the processor to wait for the reply from the memory.

The control hardware shown in Figure 7.10 or 7.11 can be viewed as a state machine that changes from one state to another in every clock cycle, depending on the contents of the instruction register, the condition codes, and the external inputs. The outputs of the state machine are the control signals. The sequence of operations carried out by this machine is determined by the wiring of the logic elements, hence the name "hardwired." A controller that uses this approach can operate at high speed. However, it has little flexibility, and the complexity of the instruction set it can implement is limited.

7.4.1   A COMPLETE PROCESSOR

A complete processor can be designed using the structure shown in Figure 7.14. This structure has an instruction unit that fetches instructions from an instruction cache or from the main memory when the desired instructions are not already in the cache. It has separate processing units to deal with integer data and floating-point data. Each of these units can be organized as shown in Figure 7.8. A data cache is inserted between these units and the main memory. Using separate caches for instructions and data is common practice in many processors today. Other processors use a single cache that

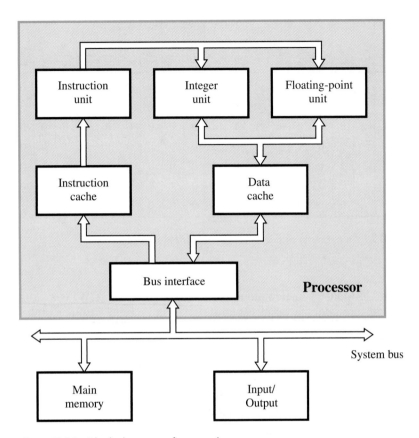

Figure 7.14 Block diagram of a complete processor.

stores both instructions and data. The processor is connected to the system bus and, hence, to the rest of the computer, by means of a bus interface.

Although we have shown just one integer and one floating-point unit in Figure 7.14, a processor may include several units of each type to increase the potential for concurrent operations. The way in which multiple units can be organized to increase the rate of instruction execution will be discussed in Chapter 8.

7.5 MICROPROGRAMMED CONTROL

In Section 7.4, we saw how the control signals required inside the processor can be generated using a control step counter and a decoder/encoder circuit. Now we discuss an alternative scheme, called *microprogrammed control*, in which control signals are generated by a program similar to machine language programs.

Micro - instruction	..	PC_{in}	PC_{out}	MAR_{in}	Read	MDR_{out}	IR_{in}	Y_{in}	Select	Add	Z_{in}	Z_{out}	$R1_{out}$	$R1_{in}$	$R3_{out}$	WMFC	End	..
1		0	1	1	1	0	0	0	1	1	1	0	0	0	0	0	0	
2		1	0	0	0	0	0	1	0	0	0	1	0	0	0	1	0	
3		0	0	0	0	1	1	0	0	0	0	0	0	0	0	0	0	
4		0	0	1	1	0	0	0	0	0	0	0	0	0	1	0	0	
5		0	0	0	0	0	0	1	0	0	0	0	1	0	0	1	0	
6		0	0	0	0	1	0	0	0	1	1	0	0	0	0	0	0	
7		0	0	0	0	0	0	0	0	0	0	1	0	1	0	0	1	

Figure 7.15   An example of microinstructions for Figure 7.6.

First, we introduce some common terms. A *control word* (CW) is a word whose individual bits represent the various control signals in Figure 7.11. Each of the control steps in the control sequence of an instruction defines a unique combination of 1s and 0s in the CW. The CWs corresponding to the 7 steps of Figure 7.6 are shown in Figure 7.15. We have assumed that SelectY is represented by Select = 0 and Select4 by Select = 1. A sequence of CWs corresponding to the control sequence of a machine instruction constitutes the *microroutine* for that instruction, and the individual control words in this microroutine are referred to as *microinstructions.*

The microroutines for all instructions in the instruction set of a computer are stored in a special memory called the *control store.* The control unit can generate the control signals for any instruction by sequentially reading the CWs of the corresponding microroutine from the control store. This suggests organizing the control unit as shown in Figure 7.16. To read the control words sequentially from the control store, a *microprogram counter* (μPC) is used. Every time a new instruction is loaded into the IR, the output of the block labeled "starting address generator" is loaded into the μPC. The μPC is then automatically incremented by the clock, causing successive microinstructions to be read from the control store. Hence, the control signals are delivered to various parts of the processor in the correct sequence.

One important function of the control unit cannot be implemented by the simple organization in Figure 7.16. This is the situation that arises when the control unit is required to check the status of the condition codes or external inputs to choose between alternative courses of action. In the case of hardwired control, this situation is handled by including an appropriate logic function, as in Equation 7.2, in the encoder circuitry. In microprogrammed control, an alternative approach is to use conditional branch microinstructions. In addition to the branch address, these microinstructions specify which of the external inputs, condition codes, or, possibly, bits of the instruction register, should be checked as a condition for branching to take place.

The instruction Branch<0 may now be implemented by a microroutine such as that shown in Figure 7.17. After loading this instruction into IR, a branch microinstruction

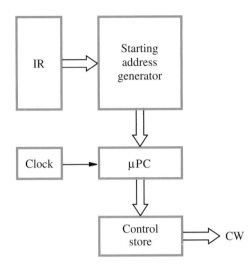

Figure 7.16 Basic organization of a
microprogrammed control unit.

Address	Microinstruction
0	PC_{out}, MAR_{in}, Read, Select4, Add, Z_{in}
1	Z_{out}, PC_{in}, Y_{in}, WMFC
2	MDR_{out}, IR_{in}
3	Branch to starting address of appropriate microroutine
....	....
25	If N=0, then branch to microinstruction 0
26	Offset-field-of-IR_{out}, SelectY, Add, Z_{in}
27	Z_{out}, PC_{in}, End

(handwritten annotations:)
{ read instruction + increment PC
 — put branch instructor into IR

— if condition not met
— add offset to PC
— load PC w/ branch address

Figure 7.17 Microroutine for the instruction Branch < 0.

transfers control to the corresponding microroutine, which is assumed to start at location
25 in the control store. This address is the output of the starting address generator block
in Figure 7.16. The microinstruction at location 25 tests the N bit of the condition
codes. If this bit is equal to 0, a branch takes place to location 0 to fetch a new machine
instruction. Otherwise, the microinstruction at location 26 is executed to put the branch
target address into register Z, as in step 4 in Figure 7.7. The microinstruction in location
27 loads this address into the PC.

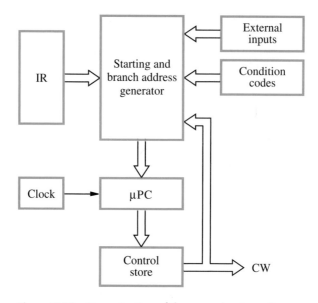

Figure 7.18 Organization of the control unit to allow
conditional branching in the microprogram.

To support microprogram branching, the organization of the control unit should be
modified as shown in Figure 7.18. The starting address generator block of Figure 7.16
becomes the starting and branch address generator. This block loads a new address
into the μPC when a microinstruction instructs it to do so. To allow implementation of
a conditional branch, inputs to this block consist of the external inputs and condition
codes as well as the contents of the instruction register. In this control unit, the μPC
is incremented every time a new microinstruction is fetched from the microprogram
memory, except in the following situations:

1. When a new instruction is loaded into the IR, the μPC is loaded with the starting
   address of the microroutine for that instruction.
2. When a Branch microinstruction is encountered and the branch condition is satisfied, the μPC is loaded with the branch address.
3. When an End microinstruction is encountered, the μPC is loaded with the address
   of the first CW in the microroutine for the instruction fetch cycle (this address is 0
   in Figure 7.17).

7.5.1 MICROINSTRUCTIONS

Having described a scheme for sequencing microinstructions, we now take a closer
look at the format of individual microinstructions. A straightforward way to structure
microinstructions is to assign one bit position to each control signal, as in Figure 7.15.

However, this scheme has one serious drawback — assigning individual bits to each control signal results in long microinstructions because the number of required signals is usually large. Moreover, only a few bits are set to 1 (to be used for active gating) in any given microinstruction, which means the available bit space is poorly used. Consider again the simple processor of Figure 7.1, and assume that it contains only four general-purpose registers, R0, R1, R2, and R3. Some of the connections in this processor are permanently enabled, such as the output of the IR to the decoding circuits and both inputs to the ALU. The remaining connections to various registers require a total of 20 gating signals. Additional control signals not shown in the figure are also needed, including the Read, Write, Select, WMFC, and End signals. Finally, we must specify the function to be performed by the ALU. Let us assume that 16 functions are provided, including Add, Subtract, AND, and XOR. These functions depend on the particular ALU used and do not necessarily have a one-to-one correspondence with the machine instruction OP codes. In total, 42 control signals are needed.

If we use the simple encoding scheme described earlier, 42 bits would be needed in each microinstruction. Fortunately, the length of the microinstructions can be reduced easily. Most signals are not needed simultaneously, and many signals are mutually exclusive. For example, only one function of the ALU can be activated at a time. The source for a data transfer must be unique because it is not possible to gate the contents of two different registers onto the bus at the same time. Read and Write signals to the memory cannot be active simultaneously. This suggests that signals can be grouped so that all mutually exclusive signals are placed in the same group. Thus, at most one *microoperation* per group is specified in any microinstruction. Then it is possible to use a binary coding scheme to represent the signals within a group. For example, four bits suffice to represent the 16 available functions in the ALU. Register output control signals can be placed in a group consisting of PC_{out}, MDR_{out}, Z_{out}, $Offset_{out}$, $R0_{out}$, $R1_{out}$, $R2_{out}$, $R3_{out}$, and $TEMP_{out}$. Any one of these can be selected by a unique 4-bit code.

Further natural groupings can be made for the remaining signals. Figure 7.19 shows an example of a partial format for the microinstructions, in which each group occupies a field large enough to contain the required codes. Most fields must include one inactive code for the case in which no action is required. For example, the all-zero pattern in F1 indicates that none of the registers that may be specified in this field should have its contents placed on the bus. An inactive code is not needed in all fields. For example, F4 contains 4 bits that specify one of the 16 operations performed in the ALU. Since no spare code is included, the ALU is active during the execution of every microinstruction. However, its activity is monitored by the rest of the machine through register Z, which is loaded only when the Z_{in} signal is activated.

Grouping control signals into fields requires a little more hardware because decoding circuits must be used to decode the bit patterns of each field into individual control signals. The cost of this additional hardware is more than offset by the reduced number of bits in each microinstruction, which results in a smaller control store. In Figure 7.19, only 20 bits are needed to store the patterns for the 42 signals.

So far we have considered grouping and encoding only mutually exclusive control signals. We can extend this idea by enumerating the patterns of required signals in all possible microinstructions. Each meaningful combination of active control signals can

Microinstruction

F1	F2	F3	F4	F5

F1 (4 bits)	F2 (3 bits)	F3 (3 bits)	F4 (4 bits)	F5 (2 bits)
0000: No transfer	000: No transfer	000: No transfer	0000: Add	00: No action
0001: PC_{out}	001: PC_{in}	001: MAR_{in}	0001: Sub	01: Read
0010: MDR_{out}	010: IR_{in}	010: MDR_{in}	$\vdots$	10: Write
0011: Z_{out}	011: Z_{in}	011: $TEMP_{in}$		
0100: $R0_{out}$	100: $R0_{in}$	100: Y_{in}	1111: XOR	
0101: $R1_{out}$	101: $R1_{in}$		$\overbrace{}$	
0110: $R2_{out}$	110: $R2_{in}$		16 ALU	
0111: $R3_{out}$	111: $R3_{in}$		functions	
1010: $TEMP_{out}$				
1011: $Offset_{out}$				

F6	F7	F8	$\cdots$

F6 (1 bit)	F7 (1 bit)	F8 (1 bit)
0: SelectY	0: No action	0: Continue
1: Select4	1: WMFC	1: End

Figure 7.19   An example of a partial format for field-encoded microinstructions.

then be assigned a distinct code that represents the microinstruction. Such full encoding is likely to further reduce the length of microwords but also to increase the complexity of the required decoder circuits.

Highly encoded schemes that use compact codes to specify only a small number of control functions in each microinstruction are referred to as a *vertical organization*. On the other hand, the minimally encoded scheme of Figure 7.15, in which many resources can be controlled with a single microinstruction, is called a *horizontal organization*. The horizontal approach is useful when a higher operating speed is desired and when the machine structure allows parallel use of resources. The vertical approach results in considerably slower operating speeds because more microinstructions are needed to perform the desired control functions. Although fewer bits are required for each microinstruction, this does not imply that the total number of bits in the control store is smaller. The significant factor is that less hardware is needed to handle the execution of microinstructions.

Horizontal and vertical organizations represent the two organizational extremes in microprogrammed control. Many intermediate schemes are also possible, in which the degree of encoding is a design parameter. The layout in Figure 7.19 is a horizontal organization because it groups only mutually exclusive microoperations in the same fields. As a result, it does not limit in any way the processor's ability to perform various microoperations in parallel.

Although we have considered only a subset of all the possible control signals, this subset is representative of actual requirements. We have omitted some details that are not essential for understanding the principles of operation.

7.5.2 MICROPROGRAM SEQUENCING

The simple microprogram example in Figure 7.15 requires only straightforward sequential execution of microinstructions, except for the branch at the end of the fetch phase. If each machine instruction is implemented by a microroutine of this kind, the microcontrol structure suggested in Figure 7.18, in which a μPC governs the sequencing, would be sufficient. A microroutine is entered by decoding the machine instruction into a starting address that is loaded into the μPC. Some branching capability within the microprogram can be introduced through special branch microinstructions that specify the branch address, similar to the way branching is done in machine-level instructions.

With this approach, writing microprograms is fairly simple because standard software techniques can be used. However, this advantage is countered by two major disadvantages. Having a separate microroutine for each machine instruction results in a large total number of microinstructions and a large control store. If most machine instructions involve several addressing modes, there can be many instruction and addressing mode combinations. A separate microroutine for each of these combinations would produce considerable duplication of common parts. We want to organize the microprogram so that the microroutines share as many common parts as possible. This requires many branch microinstructions to transfer control among the various parts. Hence, a second disadvantage arises — execution time is longer because it takes more time to carry out the required branches.

Consider a more complicated example of a complete machine instruction. In Chapter 2, we used instructions of the type

$$\text{Add} \quad \text{src,Rdst}$$

which adds the source operand to the contents of register Rdst and places the sum in Rdst, the destination register. Let us assume that the source operand can be specified in the following addressing modes: register, autoincrement, autodecrement, and indexed, as well as the indirect forms of these four modes. We now use this instruction in conjunction with the processor structure in Figure 7.1 to demonstrate a possible microprogrammed implementation.

A suitable microprogram is presented in flowchart form, for easier understanding, in Figure 7.20. Each box in the chart corresponds to a microinstruction that controls the transfers and operations indicated within the box. The microinstruction is located

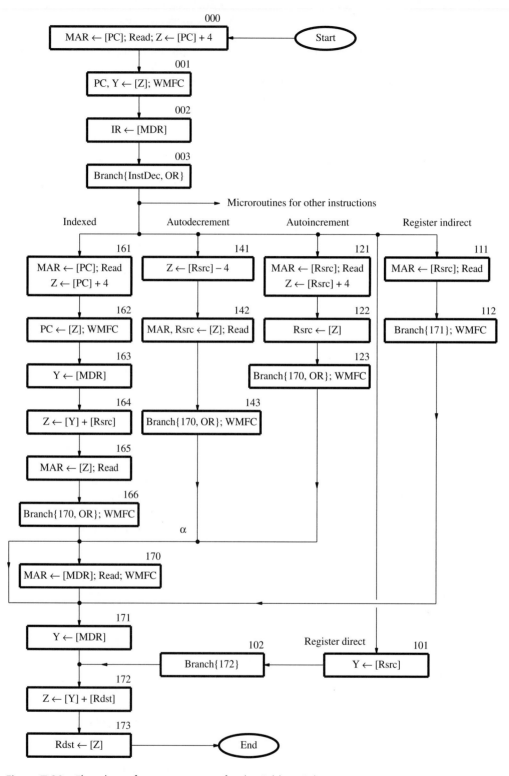

Figure 7.20 Flowchart of a microprogram for the Add src,Rdst instruction.

at the address indicated by the octal number above the upper right-hand corner of the box. Each octal digit represents three bits. We use the octal notation in this example as a convenient shorthand notation for binary numbers. Most of the flowchart in the figure is self-explanatory, but some details warrant elaboration. We will explain the issues involved first, then examine the flow of microinstructions in the figure in some detail.

Branch Address Modification Using Bit-ORing

The microprogram in Figure 7.20 shows that branches are not always made to a single branch address. This is a direct consequence of combining simple microroutines by sharing common parts. Consider the point labeled α in the figure. At this point, it is necessary to choose between actions required by direct and indirect addressing modes. If the indirect mode is specified in the instruction, then the microinstruction in location 170 is performed to fetch the operand from the memory. If the direct mode is specified, this fetch must be bypassed by branching immediately to location 171. The most efficient way to bypass microinstruction 170 is to have the preceding branch microinstructions specify the address 170 and then use an OR gate to change the least-significant bit of this address to 1 if the direct addressing mode is involved. This is known as the *bit-ORing* technique for modifying branch addresses.

An alternative to the bit-ORing approach is to use two conditional branch microinstructions at locations 123, 143, and 166. Another possibility is to include two next address fields within a branch microinstruction, one for the direct and one for the indirect address modes. Both of these alternatives are inferior to the bit-ORing technique.

7.5.3 Wide-Branch Addressing

Figure 7.20 includes a wide branch in the microinstruction at location 003. The instruction decoder, abbreviated InstDec in the figure, generates the starting address of the microroutine that implements the instruction that has just been loaded into the IR. In our example, register IR contains the Add instruction, for which the instruction decoder generates the microinstruction address 101. However, this address cannot be loaded as is into the microprogram counter.

The source operand of the Add instruction can be specified in any of several addressing modes. The figure shows five possible branches that the Add instruction may follow. From left to right these are the indexed, autodecrement, autoincrement, register direct, and register indirect addressing modes. The bit-ORing technique described above can be used at this point to modify the starting address generated by the instruction decoder to reach the appropriate path. For the addresses shown in the figure, bit-ORing should change the address 101 to one of the five possible address values, 161, 141, 121, 101, or 111, depending on the addressing mode used in the instruction.

Use of WMFC

We have assumed that it is possible to issue a wait for MFC command in a branch microinstruction. This is done in the microinstruction at location 112, for example, which causes a branch to the microinstruction in location 171. Combining these two operations introduces a subtle problem. The WMFC signal means that the microinstruction may take several clock cycles to complete. If the branch is allowed to happen in the first clock cycle, the microinstruction at location 171 would be fetched and executed prematurely. To avoid this problem, the branch must not take place until the memory transfer in progress is completed, that is, the WMFC signal must inhibit any change in the contents of the microprogram counter during the waiting period.

Detailed Examination

Let us examine one path of the flowchart in Figure 7.20 in more detail. Consider the case in which the source operand is accessed in the autoincrement mode. This is the path needed to execute the instruction

$$\text{Add} \quad (\text{Rsrc})+, \text{Rdst}$$

where Rsrc and Rdst are general-purpose registers in the machine. Figure 7.21 shows the complete microroutine for fetching and executing this instruction. We assume that the instruction has a 3-bit field used to specify the addressing mode for the source operand, as shown. Bit patterns 11, 10, 01, and 00, located in bits 10 and 9, denote the indexed, autodecrement, autoincrement, and register modes, respectively. For each of these modes, bit 8 is used to specify the indirect version. For example, 010 in the mode field specifies the direct version of the autoincrement mode, whereas 011 specifies the indirect version. We also assume that the processor has 16 registers that can be used for addressing purposes, each specified using a 4-bit code. Thus, the source operand is fully specified using the mode field and the register indicated by bits 7 through 4. The destination operand is in the register specified by bits 3 through 0.

Since any of the 16 general-purpose registers may be involved in determining the source and destination operand locations, the microinstructions refer to the respective control signals only as Rsrc_{out}, Rsrc_{in}, Rdst_{out}, and Rdst_{in}. These signals must be translated into specific register transfer signals by the decoding circuitry connected to the Rsrc and Rdst address fields of the IR. This means that there are two stages of decoding. First, the microinstruction field must be decoded to determine that an Rsrc or Rdst register is involved. The decoded output is then used to gate the contents of the Rsrc or Rdst fields in the IR into a second decoder, which produces the gating signals for the actual registers R0 to R15.

The microprogram in Figure 7.20 has been derived by combining the microroutines for all possible values in the mode field, resulting in a structure that requires many branch points. The example in Figure 7.21 has two branch points, so two branch microinstructions are required. In each case, the expression in brackets indicates the branch address that is to be loaded into the μPC and how this address is modified using the bit-ORing scheme. Consider the microinstruction at location 123 as an example. Its unmodified version causes a branch to the microinstruction at location 170, which causes another fetch from the main memory corresponding to an indirect addressing mode. For a direct addressing mode, this fetch is bypassed by ORing the inverse of the indirect bit in the src address field (bit 8 in the IR) with the 0 bit position of the μPC.

Another example of the use of bit ORing is the microinstruction in location 003. There are five starting addresses for the microroutine that implements the Add instruction in question, depending on the address mode specified for the source operand.

These addresses differ in the middle octal digit only. Hence, the required branch is implemented by using bit ORing to modify the middle octal digit of the pattern 101 obtained from the instruction decoder. The 3 bits to be ORed with this digit are supplied by the decoding circuitry connected to the src address mode field (bits 8, 9, and 10 of the IR). Microinstruction addresses have been chosen to make this modification easy to implement; bits 4 and 5 of the μPC are set directly from bits 9 and 10 in the IR. This suffices to select the appropriate microinstruction for all src address modes except one. The register indirect mode is covered by setting bit 3 of the μPC to 1 when $[\overline{IR_{10}}] \cdot [\overline{IR_9}] \cdot [IR_8]$ is equal to 1. Register indirect is a special case, because it is the only indirect mode that does not use the microinstruction at 170.

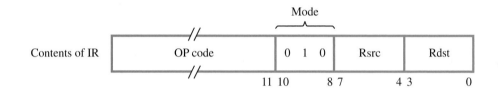

Address (octal)	Microinstruction
000	PC_{out}, MAR_{in}, Read, Select4, Add, Z_{in}
001	Z_{out}, PC_{in}, Y_{in}, WMFC
002	MDR_{out}, IR_{in}
003	μBranch {μPC $\leftarrow$ 101 (from Instruction decoder); $\mu PC_{5,4} \leftarrow [IR_{10,9}]$; $\mu PC_3 \leftarrow [\overline{IR_{10}}] \cdot [\overline{IR_9}] \cdot [IR_8]$}
121	$Rsrc_{out}$, MAR_{in}, Read, Select4, Add, Z_{in}
122	Z_{out}, $Rsrc_{in}$
123	μBranch {μPC $\leftarrow$ 170; $\mu PC_0 \leftarrow [\overline{IR_8}]$}, WMFC
170	MDR_{out}, MAR_{in}, Read, WMFC
171	MDR_{out}, Y_{in}
172	$Rdst_{out}$, SelectY, Add, Z_{in}
173	Z_{out}, $Rdst_{in}$, End

Figure 7.21 Microinstruction for Add (Rsrc)+,Rdst.

| Note: Microinstruction at location 170 is not executed for this addressing mode.

7.5.4 MICROINSTRUCTIONS WITH NEXT-ADDRESS FIELD

The microprogram in Figure 7.20 requires several branch microinstructions. These microinstructions perform no useful operation in the datapath; they are needed only to determine the address of the next microinstruction. Thus, they detract from the operating speed of the computer. The situation can become significantly worse when other microroutines are considered. The increase in branch microinstructions stems partly from limitations in the ability to assign successive addresses to all microinstructions that are generally executed in consecutive order.

This problem prompts us to reevaluate the sequencing technique built around an incrementable μPC. A powerful alternative is to include an address field as a part of every microinstruction to indicate the location of the next microinstruction to be fetched. This means, in effect, that every microinstruction becomes a branch microinstruction, in addition to its other functions.

The flexibility of this approach comes at the expense of additional bits for the address field. The severity of this penalty can be assessed as follows: In a typical computer, it is possible to design a complete microprogram with fewer than 4K microinstructions, employing perhaps 50 to 80 bits per microinstruction. This implies that an address field of 12 bits is required. Therefore, approximately one-sixth of the control store capacity would be devoted to addressing. Even if more extensive microprograms are needed, the address field would be only slightly larger.

The most obvious advantage of this approach is that separate branch microinstructions are virtually eliminated. Furthermore, there are few limitations in assigning addresses to microinstructions. These advantages more than offset any negative attributes and make the scheme very attractive. Since each instruction contains the address of the next instruction, there is no need for a counter to keep track of sequential addresses. Hence, the μPC is replaced with a *microinstruction address register* (μAR), which is loaded from the next-address field in each microinstruction. A new control structure that incorporates this feature and supports bit-ORing is shown in Figure 7.22. The next-address bits are fed through the OR gates to the μAR, so that the address can be modified on the basis of the data in the IR, external inputs, and condition codes. The decoding circuits generate the starting address of a given microroutine on the basis of the OP code in the IR.

Let us now reconsider the example of Figure 7.21 using the microprogrammed control structure of Figure 7.22. We need several control signals that are not included in the microinstruction format in Figure 7.19. Instead of referring to registers R0 to R15 explicitly, we use the names Rsrc and Rdst, which can be decoded into the actual control signals with the data in the src and dst fields of the IR. Branching with the bit-ORing technique requires that we include the appropriate commands in the microinstructions. In the flowchart of Figure 7.20, bit-ORing is needed in microinstruction 003 to determine the address of the next microinstruction based on the addressing mode of the source operand. The addressing mode is indicated by bits 8 through 10 of the instruction register, as shown in Figure 7.21. Let the signal OR_{mode} control whether or not this bit-ORing is used. In microinstructions 123, 143, and 166, bit-ORing is used to decide if indirect addressing of the source operand is to be used. We use the signal OR_{indsrc} for this purpose.

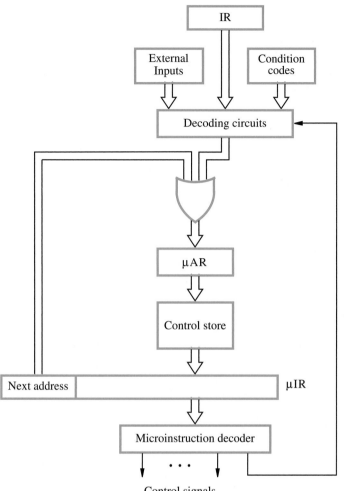

Figure 7.22 Microinstruction-sequencing organization.

For simplicity, we use separate bits in the microinstructions to denote these signals. One bit in the microinstruction is used to indicate when the output of the instruction decoder is to be gated into the μAR. Finally, each microinstruction contains an 8-bit field that holds the address of the next microinstruction. Figure 7.23 shows a complete format for these microinstructions. This format is an expansion of the format in Figure 7.19.

Using such microinstructions, we can implement the microroutine of Figure 7.21 as shown in Figure 7.24. The revised routine has one less microinstruction. The branch microinstruction at location 123 has been combined with the microinstruction immediately preceding it. When microinstruction sequencing is controlled by a μPC, the End signal is used to reset the μPC to point to the starting address of the microinstruction

Microinstruction

F0	F1	F2	F3

F0 (8 bits)	F1 (3 bits)	F2 (3 bits)	F3 (3 bits)
Address of next microinstruction	000: No transfer 001: PC_{out} 010: MDR_{out} 011: Z_{out} 100: $Rsrc_{out}$ 101: $Rdst_{out}$ 110: $TEMP_{out}$	000: No transfer 001: PC_{in} 010: IR_{in} 011: Z_{in} 100: $Rsrc_{in}$ 101: $Rdst_{in}$	000: No transfer 001: MAR_{in} 010: MDR_{in} 011: $TEMP_{in}$ 100: Y_{in}

F4	F5	F6	F7

F4 (4 bits)	F5 (2 bits)	F6 (1 bit)	F7 (1 bit)
0000: Add 0001: Sub ⋮ 1111: XOR	00: No action 01: Read 10: Write	0: SelectY 1: Select4	0: No action 1: WMFC

F8	F9	F10

F8 (1 bit)	F9 (1 bit)	F10 (1 bit)
0: NextAdrs 1: InstDec	0: No action 1: OR_{mode}	0: No action 1: OR_{indsrc}

Figure 7.23 Format for microinstructions in the example of Section 7.5.3.

that fetches the next machine instruction to be executed. In our example, this starting address is 000_8. However, the microroutine in Figure 7.24 does not terminate by producing the End signal. In an organization such as this, the starting address is not specified by a resetting mechanism triggered by the End signal — instead, it is specified explicitly in the F0 field.

Octal address	F0	F1	F2	F3	F4	F5	F6	F7	F8	F9	F10
0 0 0	0 0 0 0 0 0 0 1	0 0 1	0 1 1	0 0 1	0 0 0 0	0 1	1	0	0	0	0
0 0 1	0 0 0 0 0 0 1 0	0 1 1	0 0 1	1 0 0	0 0 0 0	0 0	0	1	0	0	0
0 0 2	0 0 0 0 0 0 1 1	0 1 0	0 1 0	0 0 0	0 0 0 0	0 0	0	0	0	0	0
0 0 3	0 0 0 0 0 0 0 0	0 0 0	0 0 0	0 0 0	0 0 0 0	0 0	0	0	1	1	0
1 2 1	0 1 0 1 0 0 1 0	1 0 0	0 1 1	0 0 1	0 0 0 0	0 1	1	0	0	0	0
1 2 2	0 1 1 1 1 0 0 0	0 1 1	1 0 0	0 0 0	0 0 0 0	0 0	0	1	0	0	1
1 7 0	0 1 1 1 1 0 0 1	0 1 0	0 0 0	0 0 1	0 0 0 0	0 1	0	1	0	0	0
1 7 1	0 1 1 1 1 0 1 0	0 1 0	0 0 0	1 0 0	0 0 0 0	0 0	0	0	0	0	0
1 7 2	0 1 1 1 1 0 1 1	1 0 1	0 1 1	0 0 0	0 0 0 0	0 0	0	0	0	0	0
1 7 3	0 0 0 0 0 0 0 0	0 1 1	1 0 1	0 0 0	0 0 0 0	0 0	0	0	0	0	0

Figure 7.24 Implementation of the microroutine of Figure 7.21 using a next-microinstruction address field. (See Figure 7.23 for encoded signals.)

Figure 7.25 gives a more detailed diagram of the control structure of Figure 7.22. It shows how control signals can be decoded from the microinstruction fields and used to control sequencing. Detailed circuitry for bit-ORing is shown in Figure 7.26.

7.5.5 PREFETCHING MICROINSTRUCTIONS

One drawback of microprogrammed control is that it leads to a slower operating speed because of the time it takes to fetch microinstructions from the control store. Faster operation is achieved if the next microinstruction is prefetched while the current one is being executed. In this way, the execution time can be overlapped with the fetch time.

Prefetching microinstructions presents some organizational difficulties. Sometimes the status flags and the results of the currently executed microinstruction are needed to determine the address of the next microinstruction. Thus, straightforward prefetching occasionally prefetches a wrong microinstruction. In these cases, the fetch must be repeated with the correct address, which requires more complex hardware. However, the disadvantages are minor, and the prefetching technique is often used.

7.5.6 EMULATION

The main function of microprogrammed control is to provide a means for simple, flexible, and relatively inexpensive execution of machine instructions. However, it also offers other interesting possibilities. Its flexibility in using a machine's resources allows diverse classes of instructions to be implemented. Given a computer with a certain

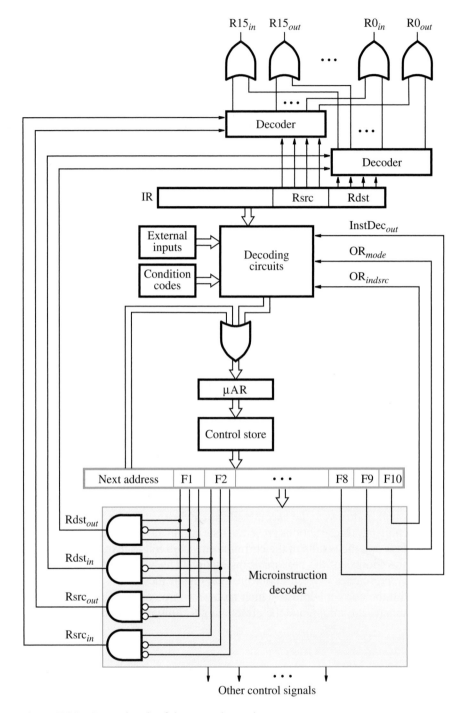

Figure 7.25 Some details of the control-signal-generating circuitry.

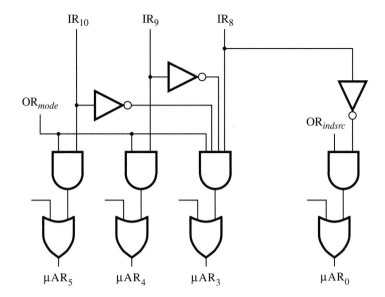

Figure 7.26 Control circuitry for bit-ORing (part of the decoding circuits in Figure 7.25).

instruction set, it is possible to define additional machine instructions and implement them with extra microroutines.

An extension of the preceding idea leads to another interesting possibility. Suppose we add to the instruction repertoire of a given computer, M_1, an entirely new set of instructions that is in fact the instruction set of a different computer, M_2. Programs written in the machine language of M_2 can then be run on computer M_1, that is, M_1 *emulates* M_2. Emulation allows us to replace obsolete equipment with more up-to-date machines. If the replacement computer fully emulates the original one, then no software changes have to be made to run existing programs. Thus, emulation facilitates transitions to new computer systems with minimal disruption.

Emulation is easiest when the machines involved have similar architectures. However, emulation can also succeed using machines with totally different architectures.

7.6 CONCLUDING REMARKS

In this chapter, we have presented an overview of the organization of the computer's central processing unit. Commercially available machines use many variations of the organizations presented here. The choice of a particular organization involves trade-offs between speed of execution and cost of implementation. Other factors also come into play, such as the technology used, the flexibility for modification, and the need for special capabilities in the instruction set of the computer.

Two approaches were presented for implementing the control unit of a processor — hardwired control and microprogrammed control. Hardwired control is the best approach when speed of operation is most important. Microprogrammed control provides considerable flexibility in implementing instruction sets.

PROBLEMS

7.1 Why is the Wait-for-Memory-Function-Completed step needed when reading from or writing to the main memory?

7.2 A processor uses a control sequence similar to that in Figure 7.6. Assume that a memory read or write operation takes the same time as one internal processor step and that both the processor and the memory are controlled by the same clock. Estimate the execution time of this sequence.

7.3 Repeat Problem 7.2 for a machine in which the memory access time is equal to twice the processor clock period.

7.4 Assume that propagation delays along the bus and through the ALU of Figure 7.1 are 0.3 and 2 ns, respectively. The setup time for the registers is 0.2 ns, and the hold time is 0. What is the minimum clock period needed?

7.5 Write the sequence of control steps required for the bus structure in Figure 7.1 for each of the following instructions:

(*a*) Add the (immediate) number NUM to register R1.

(*b*) Add the contents of memory location NUM to register R1.

(*c*) Add the contents of the memory location whose address is at memory location NUM to register R1.

Assume that each instruction consists of two words. The first word specifies the operation and the addressing mode, and the second word contains the number NUM.

7.6 The three instructions in Problem 7.5 have many common control steps. However, some of these control steps occur at different counts of the control step counter. Suggest a scheme that exploits these common steps to reduce the complexity of the encoder block in Figure 7.11.

7.7 Consider the Add instruction that has the control sequence given in Figure 7.6. The processor is driven by a continuously running clock, such that each control step is 2 ns in duration. How long will the processor have to wait in steps 2 and 5, assuming that a memory read operation takes 16 ns to complete? What percentage of time is the processor idle during execution of this instruction?

7.8 The addressing modes of a 32-bit, byte-addressable machine include autoincrement and autodecrement. In these modes, the contents of an address register are either incremented or decremented by 1, 2, or 4, depending on the length of the operand. Suggest some modification to Figure 7.1 to simplify this operation.

7.9   Show a possible control sequence for implementing the instruction

$$MUL \quad R1,R2$$

on the processor in Figure 7.1. This instruction multiplies the contents of the registers R1 and R2, and stores the result in R2. Higher-order bits in the product, if any, are discarded. Suggest additional control signals as needed, and assume that the multiplier is organized as in Figure 6.7.

7.10   Show the control steps for the Branch-on-Negative instruction for a processor that has the structure given in Figure 7.8.

7.11   Show the control steps needed to implement the Branch-to-Subroutine instruction of one of the processors described in Chapter 3. Assume that processor has the internal organization of Figure 7.1.

7.12   Repeat Problem 7.11 for the processor in Figure 7.8.

7.13   Figure 7.3 shows an edge-triggered flip-flop being used for implementing the processor registers. Consider the operation of transferring data from one register to another. Examine the timing of this operation in detail and explain any potential difficulties that may be encountered if the edge-triggered flip-flop is replaced with a simple gated latch, such as that in Figure A.27.

7.14   The multiplexer and feedback connection in Figure 7.3 eliminate the need for gating the clock input as a means for enabling and disabling register input. Using a timing diagram, explain the problems that may arise if clock gating were used.

7.15   Assume that the register file in Figure 7.8 is implemented as a RAM. At any given time, a location in this RAM can be accessed for either a read or a write operation. During the operation R1 ← [R1] + [R2], register R1 is both a source and a destination. Explain how you would use additional latches at either the input or the output of the RAM to operate the file in a master-slave mode. Use a timing diagram to explain how your new design enables register R1 to be used as both a source and a destination in the same clock cycle.

7.16   The Run signal in Figure 7.11 is set to 0 to prevent the control step counter from being advanced while waiting for a memory read or write operation to be completed. Examine the timing diagram in Figure 7.5, and prepare a state diagram for a control circuit that generates this signal. Design an appropriate circuit.

7.17   The MDR_{inE} control signal is asserted following a clock cycle in which the control signal Read is asserted and is negated when the memory transfer is completed, as shown in Figure 7.5. Design a suitable circuit to generate MDR_{inE}.

7.18   Consider a 16-bit, byte-addressable machine that has the organization of Figure 7.1. Bytes at even and odd addresses are transferred on the high- and low-order 8 bits of the memory bus, respectively. Show a suitable gating scheme for connecting register MDR to the memory bus and to the internal processor bus to allow byte transfers to occur. When a byte is being handled, it should always be in the low-order byte position inside the processor.

7.19 Design an oscillator using an inverter and a delay element. Assuming that the delay element introduces a delay T, what is the frequency of oscillation?

Modify the oscillator circuit such that oscillations can be started and stopped under the control of an asynchronous input RUN. When the oscillator is stopped, the width of the last pulse at its output must be equal to T, independent of the time at which RUN becomes inactive.

7.20 Some control steps in a processor take longer to complete than others. It is desired to generate a clock signal controlled by a signal called Long/Short such that the duration of a control step is twice as long when this signal is equal to 1. Assume that the control step counter has an Enable input and that the counter is advanced on the positive edge of the clock if Enable $= 1$. Design a circuit that generates the Enable signal to vary the size of the control steps as needed.

7.21 The output of a shift register is inverted and fed back to its input, to form a counting circuit known as a Johnson counter.

(a) What is the count sequence of a 4-bit Johnson counter, starting with the state 0000?

(b) Show how you can use a Johnson counter to generate the timing signals T_1, T_2, and so on in Figure 7.11, assuming there is a maximum of 10 timing intervals.

7.22 An ALU of a processor uses the shift register shown in Figure P7.1 to perform shift and rotate operations. Inputs to the control logic for this register consist of

ASR   Arithmetic Shift Right

LSR   Logic Shift Right

SL   Shift Left

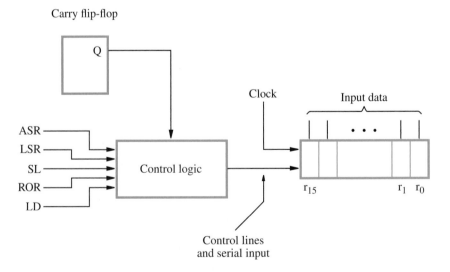

Figure P7.1   Organization of shift-register control for Problem 7.22.

ROR   Rotate Right

LD   Parallel Load

All shift and load operations are controlled by one clock input. The shift register is implemented with edge-triggered D flip-flops. Give a complete logic diagram for the control logic and for bits r_0, r_1, and r_{15} of the shift register.

7.23   The digital controller in Figure P7.2 has three outputs, X, Y, and Z, and two inputs, A and B. It is externally driven by a clock. The controller is continuously going through the following sequence of events: At the beginning of the first clock cycle, line X is set to 1. At the beginning of the second clock cycle, either line Y or Z is set to 1, depending on whether line A was equal to 1 or 0, respectively, in the previous clock cycle. The controller then waits until line B is set to 1. On the following positive edge of the clock, the controller sets output Z to 1 for the duration of one clock cycle, then resets all output signals to 0 for one clock cycle. The sequence is repeated, starting at the next positive edge of the clock. Draw a state diagram and give a suitable logic design for this controller.

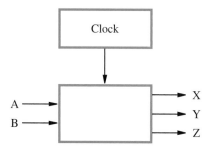

Figure P7.2   Digital controller in
Problem 7.23.

7.24   Write a microroutine, such as the one shown in Figure 7.21, for the instruction

MOV   X(Rsrc),Rdst

where the source and destination operands are specified in indexed and register addressing modes, respectively.

7.25   A BGT (Branch if > 0) machine instruction has the expression $Z + (N \oplus V) = 0$ as its branch condition, where Z, N, and V are the zero, negative, and overflow condition flags, respectively. Write a microroutine that can implement this instruction. Show the circuitry needed to test the condition codes.

7.26   Write a combined microroutine that can implement the BGT (Branch if > 0), BPL (Branch if Plus), and BR (Branch Unconditionally) instructions. The branch conditions for the BGT and BPL instructions are $Z + (N \oplus V) = 0$ and $N = 0$, respectively. What is the total number of microinstructions required? How many microinstructions are needed if a separate microroutine is used for each machine instruction?

7.27   Figure 7.21 shows an example of a microroutine in which bit-ORing is used to modify microinstruction addresses. Write an equivalent routine, without using bit-ORing, in which conditional branch microinstructions are used. How many additional microinstructions are needed? Assume that the conditional branch microinstructions can test some of the bits in the IR.

7.28   Show how the microprogram in Figure 7.20 should be modified to implement the 68000 microprocessor instruction

ADD   src,Rdst

7.29   Explain how the flowchart in Figure 7.20 can be modified to implement the general instruction

MOVE   src,dst

in which both the source and the destination can be in any of the five address modes shown.

7.30   Figure P7.3 gives part of the microinstruction sequence corresponding to one of the machine instructions of a microprogrammed computer. Microinstruction B is followed

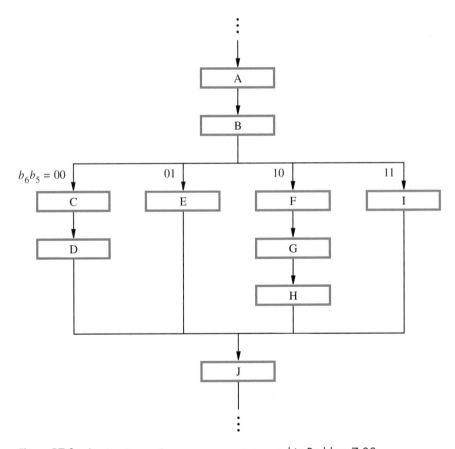

Figure P7.3   A microinstruction-sequence pattern used in Problem 7.30.

by C, E, F, or I, depending on bits b_6 and b_5 of the machine instruction register. Compare the three possible implementations described below.

(*a*) Microinstruction sequencing is accomplished by means of a microprogram counter. Branching is achieved by microinstructions of the form

$$\text{If } b_6b_5 \text{ branch to X}$$

where b_6b_5 is the branch condition and X is the branch address.

(*b*) Same as Part *a* except that the branch microinstruction has the form

$$\text{Branch to X, OR}$$

where X is a base branch address. The branch address is modified by bit-ORing of bits b_5 and b_6 with the appropriate bits within X.

(*c*) A field in each microinstruction specifies the address of the next microinstruction, which has bit-ORing capability.

Assign suitable addresses for all microinstructions in Figure P7.3 for each of the implementations in Parts *a* through *c*. Note that you may need to insert branch instructions in some cases. You may choose arbitrary addresses, as long as they are consistent with the method of sequencing used. For example, in Part *a*, you could choose addresses as follows:

Address	Microinstruction
00010	A
00011	B
00100	If $b_6b_5 = 00$ branch to XXXXX
. . .	. . .
XXXXX	C

7.31 It is desired to reduce the number of bits needed to encode the control signals in Figure 7.19. Suggest a new encoding that reduces the number of bits by two. How does the new encoding affect the number of control steps needed to implement an instruction?

7.32 Suggest a new encoding for the control signals in Figure 7.19 that reduces the number of bits needed in a microinstruction to 12. Show the effect of the new encoding on the control sequences in Figures 7.6 and 7.7.

7.33 Suggest a format for microinstructions, similar to Figure 7.19, if the processor is organized as shown in Figure 7.8.

7.34 What are the relative merits of horizontal and vertical microinstruction formats? Relate your answer to the answers to Problems 7.31 and 7.32.

7.35 What are the advantages and disadvantages of hardwired and microprogrammed control?

8

PIPELINING

CHAPTER OBJECTIVES

In this chapter you will learn about:

- Pipelining as a means for executing machine instructions concurrently
- Various hazards that cause performance degradation in pipelined processors and means for mitigating their effect
- Hardware and software implications of pipelining
- Influence of pipelining on instruction set design
- Superscalar processors

The basic building blocks of a computer are introduced in preceding chapters. In this chapter, we discuss in detail the concept of pipelining, which is used in modern computers to achieve high performance. We begin by explaining the basics of pipelining and how it can lead to improved performance. Then we examine machine instruction features that facilitate pipelined execution, and we show that the choice of instructions and instruction sequencing can have a significant effect on performance. Pipelined organization requires sophisticated compilation techniques, and *optimizing compilers* have been developed for this purpose. Among other things, such compilers rearrange the sequence of operations to maximize the benefits of pipelined execution.

8.1 BASIC CONCEPTS

The speed of execution of programs is influenced by many factors. One way to improve performance is to use faster circuit technology to build the processor and the main memory. Another possibility is to arrange the hardware so that more than one operation can be performed at the same time. In this way, the number of operations performed per second is increased even though the elapsed time needed to perform any one operation is not changed.

We have encountered concurrent activities several times before. Chapter 1 introduced the concept of multiprogramming and explained how it is possible for I/O transfers and computational activities to proceed simultaneously. DMA devices make this possible because they can perform I/O transfers independently once these transfers are initiated by the processor.

Pipelining is a particularly effective way of organizing concurrent activity in a computer system. The basic idea is very simple. It is frequently encountered in manufacturing plants, where pipelining is commonly known as an assembly-line operation. Readers are undoubtedly familiar with the assembly line used in car manufacturing. The first station in an assembly line may prepare the chassis of a car, the next station adds the body, the next one installs the engine, and so on. While one group of workers is installing the engine on one car, another group is fitting a car body on the chassis of another car, and yet another group is preparing a new chassis for a third car. It may take days to complete work on a given car, but it is possible to have a new car rolling off the end of the assembly line every few minutes.

Consider how the idea of pipelining can be used in a computer. The processor executes a program by fetching and executing instructions, one after the other. Let F_i and E_i refer to the fetch and execute steps for instruction I_i. Execution of a program consists of a sequence of fetch and execute steps, as shown in Figure 8.1a.

Now consider a computer that has two separate hardware units, one for fetching instructions and another for executing them, as shown in Figure 8.1b. The instruction fetched by the fetch unit is deposited in an intermediate storage buffer, B1. This buffer is needed to enable the execution unit to execute the instruction while the fetch unit is fetching the next instruction. The results of execution are deposited in the destination location specified by the instruction. For the purposes of this discussion, we assume that both the source and the destination of the data operated on by the instructions are inside the block labeled "Execution unit."

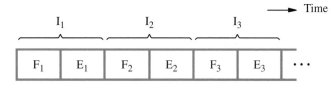

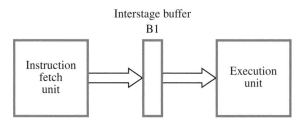

(a) Sequential execution

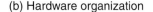

(b) Hardware organization

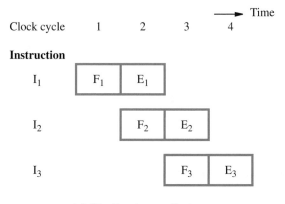

(c) Pipelined execution

Figure 8.1 Basic idea of instruction pipelining.

The computer is controlled by a clock whose period is such that the fetch and execute steps of any instruction can each be completed in one clock cycle. Operation of the computer proceeds as in Figure 8.1c. In the first clock cycle, the fetch unit fetches an instruction I_1 (step F_1) and stores it in buffer B1 at the end of the clock cycle. In the second clock cycle, the instruction fetch unit proceeds with the fetch operation for instruction I_2 (step F_2). Meanwhile, the execution unit performs the operation specified by instruction I_1, which is available to it in buffer B1 (step E_1). By the end of the second clock cycle, the execution of instruction I_1 is completed and instruction I_2 is available. Instruction I_2 is stored in B1, replacing I_1, which is no longer needed. Step E_2 is performed by the execution unit during the third clock cycle, while instruction I_3 is being fetched by the fetch unit. In this manner, both the fetch and execute units are kept busy all the time. If the pattern in Figure 8.1c can be sustained for a long time, the completion rate of instruction execution will be twice that achievable by the sequential operation depicted in Figure 8.1a.

In summary, the fetch and execute units in Figure 8.1b constitute a two-stage pipeline in which each stage performs one step in processing an instruction. An inter-stage storage buffer, B1, is needed to hold the information being passed from one stage to the next. New information is loaded into this buffer at the end of each clock cycle.

The processing of an instruction need not be divided into only two steps. For example, a pipelined processor may process each instruction in four steps, as follows:

F   Fetch: read the instruction from the memory.

D   Decode: decode the instruction and fetch the source operand(s).

E   Execute: perform the operation specified by the instruction.

W   Write: store the result in the destination location.

The sequence of events for this case is shown in Figure 8.2a. Four instructions are in progress at any given time. This means that four distinct hardware units are needed, as shown in Figure 8.2b. These units must be capable of performing their tasks simultaneously and without interfering with one another. Information is passed from one unit to the next through a storage buffer. As an instruction progresses through the pipeline, all the information needed by the stages downstream must be passed along. For example, during clock cycle 4, the information in the buffers is as follows:

- Buffer B1 holds instruction I_3, which was fetched in cycle 3 and is being decoded by the instruction-decoding unit.

- Buffer B2 holds both the source operands for instruction I_2 and the specification of the operation to be performed. This is the information produced by the decoding hardware in cycle 3. The buffer also holds the information needed for the write step of instruction I_2 (step W_2). Even though it is not needed by stage E, this information must be passed on to stage W in the following clock cycle to enable that stage to perform the required Write operation.

- Buffer B3 holds the results produced by the execution unit and the destination information for instruction I_1.

8.1.1   ROLE OF CACHE MEMORY

Each stage in a pipeline is expected to complete its operation in one clock cycle. Hence, the clock period should be sufficiently long to complete the task being performed in any stage. If different units require different amounts of time, the clock period must allow the longest task to be completed. A unit that completes its task early is idle for the remainder of the clock period. Hence, pipelining is most effective in improving

Time

Clock cycle   1   2   3   4   5   6   7

Instruction

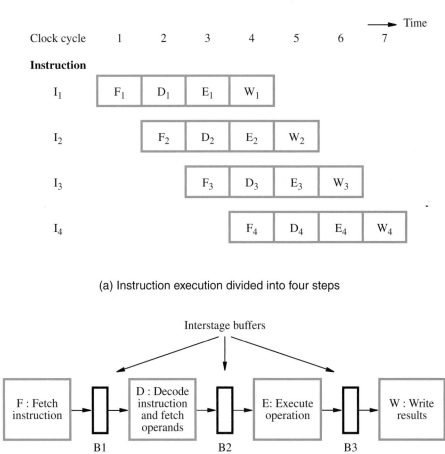

(a) Instruction execution divided into four steps

(b) Hardware organization

Figure 8.2   A 4-stage pipeline.

performance if the tasks being performed in different stages require about the same amount of time.

This consideration is particularly important for the instruction fetch step, which is assigned one clock period in Figure 8.2a. The clock cycle has to be equal to or greater than the time needed to complete a fetch operation. However, the access time of the main memory may be as much as ten times greater than the time needed to perform basic pipeline stage operations inside the processor, such as adding two numbers. Thus, if each instruction fetch required access to the main memory, pipelining would be of little value.

The use of cache memories solves the memory access problem. In particular, when a cache is included on the same chip as the processor, access time to the cache is usually the same as the time needed to perform other basic operations inside the processor. This makes it possible to divide instruction fetching and processing into steps that are more or less equal in duration. Each of these steps is performed by a different pipeline stage, and the clock period is chosen to correspond to the longest one.

8.1.2 PIPELINE PERFORMANCE

The pipelined processor in Figure 8.2 completes the processing of one instruction in each clock cycle, which means that the rate of instruction processing is four times that of sequential operation. The potential increase in performance resulting from pipelining is proportional to the number of pipeline stages. However, this increase would be achieved only if pipelined operation as depicted in Figure 8.2*a* could be sustained without interruption throughout program execution. Unfortunately, this is not the case.

For a variety of reasons, one of the pipeline stages may not be able to complete its processing task for a given instruction in the time allotted. For example, stage E in the four-stage pipeline of Figure 8.2*b* is responsible for arithmetic and logic operations, and one clock cycle is assigned for this task. Although this may be sufficient for most operations, some operations, such as divide, may require more time to complete. Figure 8.3 shows an example in which the operation specified in instruction I_2 requires three cycles to complete, from cycle 4 through cycle 6. Thus, in cycles 5 and 6, the Write stage must be told to do nothing, because it has no data to work with. Meanwhile, the information in buffer B2 must remain intact until the Execute stage has completed its operation. This means that stage 2 and, in turn, stage 1 are blocked from accepting new instructions because the information in B1 cannot be overwritten. Thus, steps D_4 and F_5 must be postponed as shown.

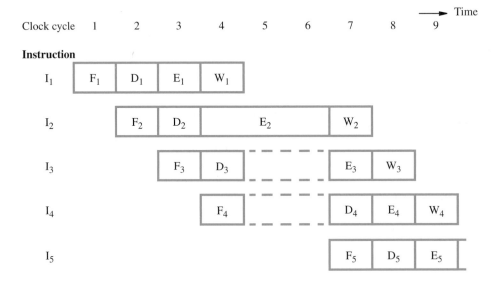

Figure 8.3 Effect of an execution operation taking more than one clock cycle.

Pipelined operation in Figure 8.3 is said to have been *stalled* for two clock cycles. Normal pipelined operation resumes in cycle 7. Any condition that causes the pipeline to stall is called a *hazard*. We have just seen an example of a *data hazard*. A data hazard is any condition in which either the source or the destination operands of an instruction are not available at the time expected in the pipeline. As a result some operation has to be delayed, and the pipeline stalls.

The pipeline may also be stalled because of a delay in the availability of an instruction. For example, this may be a result of a miss in the cache, requiring the instruction to be fetched from the main memory. Such hazards are often called *control hazards* or *instruction hazards*. The effect of a cache miss on pipelined operation is illustrated in Figure 8.4. Instruction I_1 is fetched from the cache in cycle 1, and its execution proceeds normally. However, the fetch operation for instruction I_2, which is started in cycle 2, results in a cache miss. The instruction fetch unit must now suspend any further fetch requests and wait for I_2 to arrive. We assume that instruction I_2 is received and loaded into buffer B1 at the end of cycle 5. The pipeline resumes its normal operation at that point.

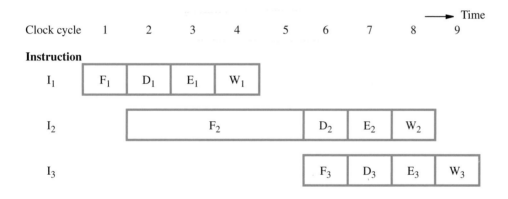

(a) Instruction execution steps in successive clock cycles

Clock cycle	1	2	3	4	5	6	7	8	9
Stage									
F: Fetch	F_1	F_2	F_2	F_2	F_2	F_3			
D: Decode		D_1	idle	idle	idle	D_2	D_3		
E: Execute			E_1	idle	idle	idle	E_2	E_3	
W: Write				W_1	idle	idle	idle	W_2	W_3

(b) Function performed by each processor stage in successive clock cycles

Figure 8.4 Pipeline stall caused by a cache miss in F2.

An alternative representation of the operation of a pipeline in the case of a cache miss is shown in Figure 8.4b. This figure gives the function performed by each pipeline stage in each clock cycle. Note that the Decode unit is idle in cycles 3 through 5, the Execute unit is idle in cycles 4 through 6, and the Write unit is idle in cycles 5 through 7. Such idle periods are called *stalls*. They are also often referred to as *bubbles* in the pipeline. Once created as a result of a delay in one of the pipeline stages, a bubble moves downstream until it reaches the last unit.

A third type of hazard that may be encountered in pipelined operation is known as a *structural hazard*. This is the situation when two instructions require the use of a given hardware resource at the same time. The most common case in which this hazard may arise is in access to memory. One instruction may need to access memory as part of the Execute or Write stage while another instruction is being fetched. If instructions and data reside in the same cache unit, only one instruction can proceed and the other instruction is delayed. Many processors use separate instruction and data caches to avoid this delay.

An example of a structural hazard is shown in Figure 8.5. This figure shows how the load instruction

$$\text{Load} \quad X(R1),R2$$

can be accommodated in our example 4-stage pipeline. The memory address, $X+[R1]$, is computed in step E_2 in cycle 4, then memory access takes place in cycle 5. The operand read from memory is written into register R2 in cycle 6. This means that the execution step of this instruction takes two clock cycles (cycles 4 and 5). It causes the pipeline to stall for one cycle, because both instructions I_2 and I_3 require access to the register file in cycle 6. Even though the instructions and their data are all available, the pipeline is

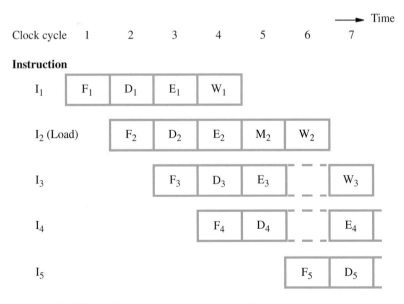

Figure 8.5   Effect of a Load instruction on pipeline timing.

stalled because one hardware resource, the register file, cannot handle two operations at once. If the register file had two input ports, that is, if it allowed two simultaneous write operations, the pipeline would not be stalled. In general, structural hazards are avoided by providing sufficient hardware resources on the processor chip.

It is important to understand that pipelining does not result in individual instructions being executed faster; rather, it is the throughput that increases, where throughput is measured by the rate at which instruction execution is completed. Any time one of the stages in the pipeline cannot complete its operation in one clock cycle, the pipeline stalls, and some degradation in performance occurs. Thus, the performance level of one instruction completion in each clock cycle is actually the upper limit for the throughput achievable in a pipelined processor organized as in Figure 8.2b.

An important goal in designing processors is to identify all hazards that may cause the pipeline to stall and to find ways to minimize their impact. In the following sections we discuss various hazards, starting with data hazards, followed by control hazards. In each case we present some of the techniques used to mitigate their negative effect on performance. We return to the issue of performance assessment in Section 8.8.

8.2 DATA HAZARDS

A data hazard is a situation in which the pipeline is stalled because the data to be operated on are delayed for some reason, as illustrated in Figure 8.3. We will now examine the issue of availability of data in some detail.

Consider a program that contains two instructions, I_1 followed by I_2. When this program is executed in a pipeline, the execution of I_2 can begin before the execution of I_1 is completed. This means that the results generated by I_1 may not be available for use by I_2. We must ensure that the results obtained when instructions are executed in a pipelined processor are identical to those obtained when the same instructions are executed sequentially. The potential for obtaining incorrect results when operations are performed concurrently can be demonstrated by a simple example. Assume that $A = 5$, and consider the following two operations:

$$A \leftarrow 3 + A$$
$$B \leftarrow 4 \times A$$

When these operations are performed in the order given, the result is $B = 32$. But if they are performed concurrently, the value of A used in computing B would be the original value, 5, leading to an incorrect result. If these two operations are performed by instructions in a program, then the instructions must be executed one after the other, because the data used in the second instruction depend on the result of the first instruction. On the other hand, the two operations

$$A \leftarrow 5 \times C$$
$$B \leftarrow 20 + C$$

can be performed concurrently, because these operations are independent.

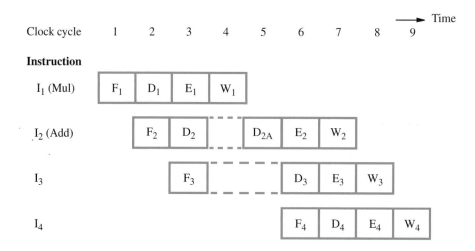

Figure 8.6   Pipeline stalled by data dependency between D_2 and W_1.

This example illustrates a basic constraint that must be enforced to guarantee correct results. When two operations depend on each other, they must be performed sequentially in the correct order. This rather obvious condition has far-reaching consequences. Understanding its implications is the key to understanding the variety of design alternatives and trade-offs encountered in pipelined computers.

Consider the pipeline in Figure 8.2. The data dependency just described arises when the destination of one instruction is used as a source in the next instruction. For example, the two instructions

$$\text{Mul} \quad \text{R2,R3,R4}$$
$$\text{Add} \quad \text{R5,R4,R6}$$

give rise to a data dependency. The result of the multiply instruction is placed into register R4, which in turn is one of the two source operands of the Add instruction. Assuming that the multiply operation takes one clock cycle to complete, execution would proceed as shown in Figure 8.6. As the Decode unit decodes the Add instruction in cycle 3, it realizes that R4 is used as a source operand. Hence, the D step of that instruction cannot be completed until the W step of the multiply instruction has been completed. Completion of step D_2 must be delayed to clock cycle 5, and is shown as step D_{2A} in the figure. Instruction I_3 is fetched in cycle 3, but its decoding must be delayed because step D_3 cannot precede D_2. Hence, pipelined execution is stalled for two cycles.

8.2.1   OPERAND FORWARDING

The data hazard just described arises because one instruction, instruction I_2 in Figure 8.6, is waiting for data to be written in the register file. However, these data are available at the output of the ALU once the Execute stage completes step E_1. Hence, the delay can be reduced, or possibly eliminated, if we arrange for the result of instruction I_1 to be forwarded directly for use in step E_2.

Figure 8.7a shows a part of the processor datapath involving the ALU and the register file. This arrangement is similar to the three-bus structure in Figure 7.8, except that registers SRC1, SRC2, and RSLT have been added. These registers constitute the

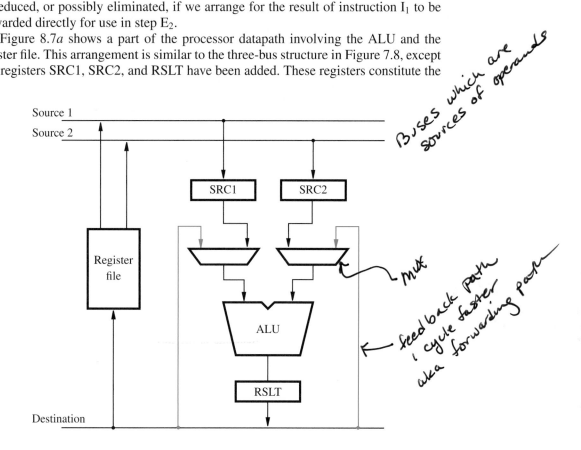

Buses which are sources of operands

mux

*feedback path
1 cycle faster
aka forwarding path*

Source 1

Source 2

SRC1   SRC2

Register file

ALU

RSLT

Destination

(a) Datapath

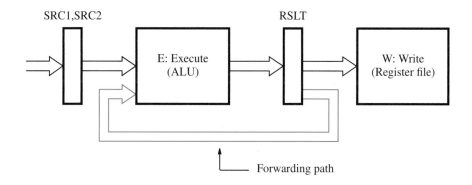

SRC1,SRC2

RSLT

E: Execute
(ALU)

W: Write
(Register file)

Forwarding path

(b) Position of the source and result registers in the processor pipeline

Figure 8.7 Operand forwarding in a pipelined processor.

interstage buffers needed for pipelined operation, as illustrated in Figure 8.7b. With reference to Figure 8.2b, registers SRC1 and SRC2 are part of buffer B2 and RSLT is part of B3. The data forwarding mechanism is provided by the blue connection lines. The two multiplexers connected at the inputs to the ALU allow the data on the destination bus to be selected instead of the contents of either the SRC1 or SRC2 register.

When the instructions in Figure 8.6 are executed in the datapath of Figure 8.7, the operations performed in each clock cycle are as follows. After decoding instruction I_2 and detecting the data dependency, a decision is made to use data forwarding. The operand not involved in the dependency, register R2, is read and loaded in register SRC1 in clock cycle 3. In the next clock cycle, the product produced by instruction I_1 is available in register RSLT, and because of the forwarding connection, it can be used in step E_2. Hence, execution of I_2 proceeds without interruption.

8.2.2 HANDLING DATA HAZARDS IN SOFTWARE

In Figure 8.6, we assumed the data dependency is discovered by the hardware while the instruction is being decoded. The control hardware delays reading register R4 until cycle 5, thus introducing a 2-cycle stall unless operand forwarding is used. An alternative approach is to leave the task of detecting data dependencies and dealing with them to the software. In this case, the compiler can introduce the two-cycle delay needed between instructions I_1 and I_2 by inserting NOP (No-operation) instructions, as follows:

$$I_1: \quad \text{Mul} \quad \text{R2,R3,R4}$$
$$\text{NOP}$$
$$\text{NOP}$$
$$I_2: \quad \text{Add} \quad \text{R5,R4,R6}$$

If the responsibility for detecting such dependencies is left entirely to the software, the compiler must insert the NOP instructions to obtain a correct result. This possibility illustrates the close link between the compiler and the hardware. A particular feature can be either implemented in hardware or left to the compiler. Leaving tasks such as inserting NOP instructions to the compiler leads to simpler hardware. Being aware of the need for a delay, the compiler can attempt to reorder instructions to perform useful tasks in the NOP slots, and thus achieve better performance. On the other hand, the insertion of NOP instructions leads to larger code size. Also, it is often the case that a given processor architecture has several hardware implementations, offering different features. NOP instructions inserted to satisfy the requirements of one implementation may not be needed and, hence, would lead to reduced performance on a different implementation.

8.2.3 SIDE EFFECTS

The data dependencies encountered in the preceding examples are explicit and easily detected because the register involved is named as the destination in instruction I_1 and as a source in I_2. Sometimes an instruction changes the contents of a register other than the one named as the destination. An instruction that uses an autoincrement or autodecrement addressing mode is an example. In addition to storing new data in its destination location, the instruction changes the contents of a source register used to access one of its operands. All the precautions needed to handle data dependencies involving the destination location must also be applied to the registers affected by an autoincrement or autodecrement operation. When a location other than one explicitly named in an instruction as a destination operand is affected, the instruction is said to have a *side effect*. For example, stack instructions, such as push and pop, produce similar side effects because they implicitly use the autoincrement and autodecrement addressing modes.

Another possible side effect involves the condition code flags, which are used by instructions such as conditional branches and add-with-carry. Suppose that registers R1 and R2 hold a double-precision integer number that we wish to add to another double-precision number in registers R3 and R4. This may be accomplished as follows:

$$\text{Add} \qquad \text{R1,R3}$$
$$\text{AddWithCarry} \quad \text{R2,R4}$$

An implicit dependency exists between these two instructions through the carry flag. This flag is set by the first instruction and used in the second instruction, which performs the operation

$$\text{R4} \leftarrow [\text{R2}] + [\text{R4}] + \text{carry}$$

Instructions that have side effects give rise to multiple data dependencies, which lead to a substantial increase in the complexity of the hardware or software needed to resolve them. For this reason, instructions designed for execution on pipelined hardware should have few side effects. Ideally, only the contents of the destination location, either a register or a memory location, should be affected by any given instruction. Side effects, such as setting the condition code flags or updating the contents of an address pointer, should be kept to a minimum. However, Chapter 2 showed that the autoincrement and autodecrement addressing modes are potentially useful. Condition code flags are also needed for recording such information as the generation of a carry or the occurrence of overflow in an arithmetic operation. In Section 8.4 we show how such functions can be provided by other means that are consistent with a pipelined organization and with the requirements of optimizing compilers.

8.3 INSTRUCTION HAZARDS

The purpose of the instruction fetch unit is to supply the execution units with a steady stream of instructions. Whenever this stream is interrupted, the pipeline stalls, as Figure 8.4 illustrates for the case of a cache miss. A branch instruction may also cause the pipeline to stall. We will now examine the effect of branch instructions and the techniques that can be used for mitigating their impact. We start with unconditional branches.

8.3.1 Unconditional Branches

Figure 8.8 shows a sequence of instructions being executed in a two-stage pipeline. Instructions I_1 to I_3 are stored at successive memory addresses, and I_2 is a branch instruction. Let the branch target be instruction I_k. In clock cycle 3, the fetch operation for instruction I_3 is in progress at the same time that the branch instruction is being decoded and the target address computed. In clock cycle 4, the processor must discard I_3, which has been incorrectly fetched, and fetch instruction I_k. In the meantime, the hardware unit responsible for the Execute (E) step must be told to do nothing during that clock period. Thus, the pipeline is stalled for one clock cycle.

The time lost as a result of a branch instruction is often referred to as the *branch penalty.* In Figure 8.8, the branch penalty is one clock cycle. For a longer pipeline, the branch penalty may be higher. For example, Figure 8.9a shows the effect of a branch instruction on a four-stage pipeline. We have assumed that the branch address is computed in step E_2. Instructions I_3 and I_4 must be discarded, and the target instruction, I_k, is fetched in clock cycle 5. Thus, the branch penalty is two clock cycles.

Reducing the branch penalty requires the branch address to be computed earlier in the pipeline. Typically, the instruction fetch unit has dedicated hardware to identify a branch instruction and compute the branch target address as quickly as possible after an instruction is fetched. With this additional hardware, both of these tasks can be performed in step D_2, leading to the sequence of events shown in Figure 8.9b. In this case, the branch penalty is only one clock cycle.

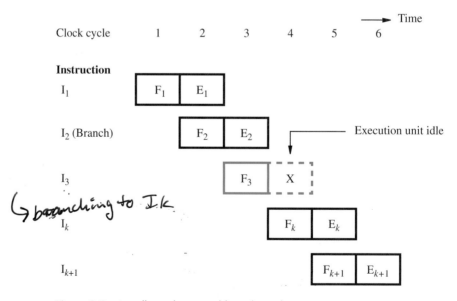

Figure 8.8 An idle cycle caused by a branch instruction.

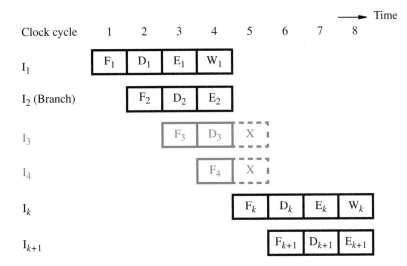

(a) Branch address computed in Execute stage

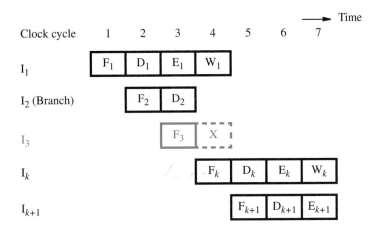

(b) Branch address computed in Decode stage

Figure 8.9 Branch timing.

added extra logic to decode unit to have it pf some to execution, thereby reducing penalty by 50%

How to handle cache misses

Instruction Queue and Prefetching

Either a cache miss or a branch instruction stalls the pipeline for one or more clock cycles. To reduce the effect of these interruptions, many processors employ sophisticated fetch units that can fetch instructions before they are needed and put them in a queue. Typically, the instruction queue can store several instructions. A separate unit, which we call the *dispatch unit,* takes instructions from the front of the queue and

Instruction fetch unit

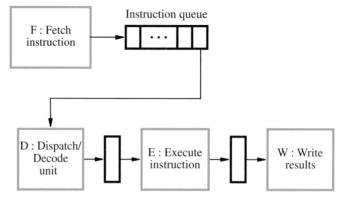

Figure 8.10   Use of an instruction queue in the hardware organization of Figure 8.2*b*.

sends them to the execution unit. This leads to the organization shown in Figure 8.10. The dispatch unit also performs the decoding function.

To be effective, the fetch unit must have sufficient decoding and processing capability to recognize and execute branch instructions. It attempts to keep the instruction queue filled at all times to reduce the impact of occasional delays when fetching instructions. When the pipeline stalls because of a data hazard, for example, the dispatch unit is not able to issue instructions from the instruction queue. However, the fetch unit continues to fetch instructions and add them to the queue. Conversely, if there is a delay in fetching instructions because of a branch or a cache miss, the dispatch unit continues to issue instructions from the instruction queue.

Figure 8.11 illustrates how the queue length changes and how it affects the relationship between different pipeline stages. We have assumed that initially the queue contains one instruction. Every fetch operation adds one instruction to the queue and every dispatch operation reduces the queue length by one. Hence, the queue length remains the same for the first four clock cycles. (There is both an F and a D step in each of these cycles.) Suppose that instruction I_1 introduces a 2-cycle stall. Since space is available in the queue, the fetch unit continues to fetch instructions and the queue length rises to 3 in clock cycle 6.

Instruction I_5 is a branch instruction. Its target instruction, I_k, is fetched in cycle 7, and instruction I_6 is discarded. The branch instruction would normally cause a stall in cycle 7 as a result of discarding instruction I_6. Instead, instruction I_4 is dispatched from the queue to the decoding stage. After discarding I_6, the queue length drops to 1 in cycle 8. The queue length will be at this value until another stall is encountered.

Now observe the sequence of instruction completions in Figure 8.11. Instructions I_1, I_2, I_3, I_4, and I_k complete execution in successive clock cycles. Hence, the branch instruction does not increase the overall execution time. This is because the instruction fetch unit has executed the branch instruction (by computing the branch address) concurrently with the execution of other instructions. This technique is referred to as *branch folding*.

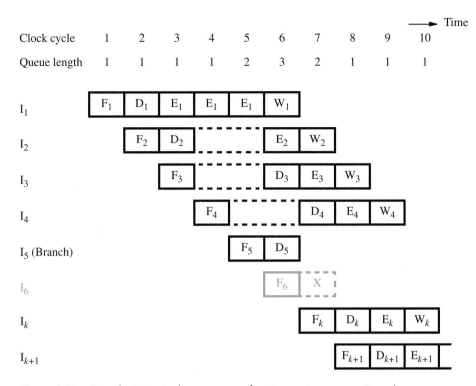

Figure 8.11 Branch timing in the presence of an instruction queue. Branch target address is computed in the D stage.

Note that branch folding occurs only if at the time a branch instruction is encountered, at least one instruction is available in the queue other than the branch instruction. If only the branch instruction is in the queue, execution would proceed as in Figure 8.9b. Therefore, it is desirable to arrange for the queue to be full most of the time, to ensure an adequate supply of instructions for processing. This can be achieved by increasing the rate at which the fetch unit reads instructions from the cache. In many processors, the width of the connection between the fetch unit and the instruction cache allows reading more than one instruction in each clock cycle. If the fetch unit replenishes the instruction queue quickly after a branch has occurred, the probability that branch folding will occur increases.

Having an instruction queue is also beneficial in dealing with cache misses. When a cache miss occurs, the dispatch unit continues to send instructions for execution as long as the instruction queue is not empty. Meanwhile, the desired cache block is read from the main memory or from a secondary cache. When fetch operations are resumed, the instruction queue is refilled. If the queue does not become empty, a cache miss will have no effect on the rate of instruction execution.

In summary, the instruction queue mitigates the impact of branch instructions on performance through the process of branch folding. It has a similar effect on stalls caused by cache misses. The effectiveness of this technique is enhanced when the instruction fetch unit is able to read more than one instruction at a time from the instruction cache.

8.3.2 CONDITIONAL BRANCHES AND BRANCH PREDICTION

A conditional branch instruction introduces the added hazard caused by the dependency of the branch condition on the result of a preceding instruction. The decision to branch cannot be made until the execution of that instruction has been completed.

Branch instructions occur frequently. In fact, they represent about 20 percent of the dynamic instruction count of most programs. (The dynamic count is the number of instruction executions, taking into account the fact that some program instructions are executed many times because of loops.) Because of the branch penalty, this large percentage would reduce the gain in performance expected from pipelining. Fortunately, branch instructions can be handled in several ways to reduce their negative impact on the rate of execution of instructions.

Delayed Branch

In Figure 8.8, the processor fetches instruction I_3 before it determines whether the current instruction, I_2, is a branch instruction. When execution of I_2 is completed and a branch is to be made, the processor must discard I_3 and fetch the instruction at the branch target. The location following a branch instruction is called a *branch delay slot*. There may be more than one branch delay slot, depending on the time it takes to execute a branch instruction. For example, there are two branch delay slots in Figure 8.9a and one delay slot in Figure 8.9b. The instructions in the delay slots are always fetched and at least partially executed before the branch decision is made and the branch target address is computed.

A technique called *delayed branching* can minimize the penalty incurred as a result of conditional branch instructions. The idea is simple. The instructions in the delay slots are always fetched. Therefore, we would like to arrange for them to be fully executed whether or not the branch is taken. The objective is to be able to place useful instructions in these slots. If no useful instructions can be placed in the delay slots, these slots must be filled with NOP instructions. This situation is exactly the same as in the case of data dependency discussed in Section 8.2.

Consider the instruction sequence given in Figure 8.12a. Register R2 is used as a counter to determine the number of times the contents of register R1 are shifted left. For a processor with one delay slot, the instructions can be reordered as shown in Figure 8.12b. The shift instruction is fetched while the branch instruction is being executed. After evaluating the branch condition, the processor fetches the instruction at LOOP or at NEXT, depending on whether the branch condition is true or false, respectively. In either case, it completes execution of the shift instruction. The sequence of events during the last two passes in the loop is illustrated in Figure 8.13. Pipelined operation is not interrupted at any time, and there are no idle cycles. Logically, the program is executed as if the branch instruction were placed after the shift instruction. That is, branching takes place one instruction later than where the branch instruction appears in the instruction sequence in the memory, hence the name "delayed branch."

LOOP	Shift_left	R1
	Decrement	R2
	Branch=0	LOOP
NEXT	Add	R1,R3

(a) Original program loop

LOOP	Decrement	R2
	Branch=0	LOOP
	Shift_left	R1
NEXT	Add	R1,R3

(b) Reordered instructions

Figure 8.12 Reordering of instructions for a delayed branch.

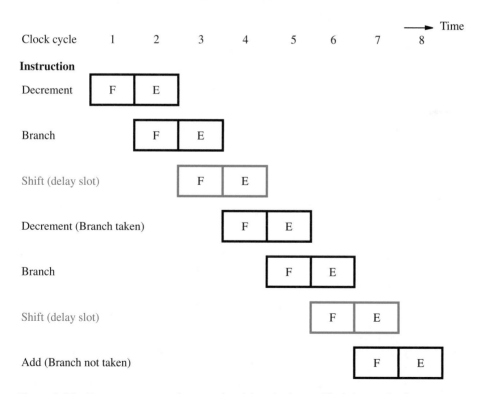

Figure 8.13 Execution timing showing the delay slot being filled during the last two passes through the loop in Figure 8.12*b*.

The effectiveness of the delayed branch approach depends on how often it is possible to reorder instructions as in Figure 8.12. Experimental data collected from many programs indicate that sophisticated compilation techniques can use one branch delay slot in as many as 85 percent of the cases. For a processor with two branch delay slots, the compiler attempts to find two instructions preceding the branch instruction that it can move into the delay slots without introducing a logical error. The chances of finding two such instructions are considerably less than the chances of finding one. Thus, if increasing the number of pipeline stages involves an increase in the number of branch delay slots, the potential gain in performance may not be fully realized.

Branch Prediction

Another technique for reducing the branch penalty associated with conditional branches is to attempt to predict whether or not a particular branch will be taken. The simplest form of branch prediction is to assume that the branch will not take place and to continue to fetch instructions in sequential address order. Until the branch condition is evaluated, instruction execution along the predicted path must be done on a speculative basis. *Speculative execution* means that instructions are executed before the processor is certain that they are in the correct execution sequence. Hence, care must be taken that no processor registers or memory locations are updated until it is confirmed that these instructions should indeed be executed. If the branch decision indicates otherwise, the instructions and all their associated data in the execution units must be purged, and the correct instructions fetched and executed.

An incorrectly predicted branch is illustrated in Figure 8.14 for a four-stage pipeline. The figure shows a Compare instruction followed by a Branch>0 instruction. Branch

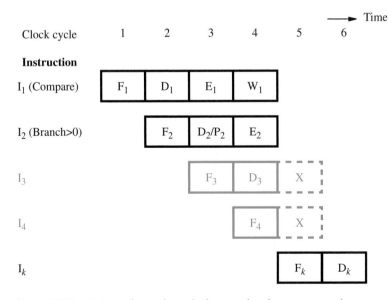

Figure 8.14   Timing when a branch decision has been incorrectly predicted as not taken.

prediction takes place in cycle 3, while instruction I_3 is being fetched. The fetch unit predicts that the branch will not be taken, and it continues to fetch instruction I_4 as I_3 enters the Decode stage. The results of the compare operation are available at the end of cycle 3. Assuming that they are forwarded immediately to the instruction fetch unit, the branch condition is evaluated in cycle 4. At this point, the instruction fetch unit realizes that the prediction was incorrect, and the two instructions in the execution pipe are purged. A new instruction, I_k, is fetched from the branch target address in clock cycle 5.

If branch outcomes were random, then half the branches would be taken. Then the simple approach of assuming that branches will not be taken would save the time lost to conditional branches 50 percent of the time. However, better performance can be achieved if we arrange for some branch instructions to be predicted as taken and others as not taken, depending on the expected program behavior. For example, a branch instruction at the end of a loop causes a branch to the start of the loop for every pass through the loop except the last one. Hence, it is advantageous to assume that this branch will be taken and to have the instruction fetch unit start to fetch instructions at the branch target address. On the other hand, for a branch instruction at the beginning of a program loop, it is advantageous to assume that the branch will not be taken.

A decision on which way to predict the result of the branch may be made in hardware by observing whether the target address of the branch is lower than or higher than the address of the branch instruction. A more flexible approach is to have the compiler decide whether a given branch instruction should be predicted taken or not taken. The branch instructions of some processors, such as SPARC, include a branch prediction bit, which is set to 0 or 1 by the compiler to indicate the desired behavior. The instruction fetch unit checks this bit to predict whether the branch will be taken or not taken.

With either of these schemes, the branch prediction decision is always the same every time a given instruction is executed. Any approach that has this characteristic is called *static branch prediction*. Another approach in which the prediction decision may change depending on execution history is called *dynamic branch prediction*.

Dynamic Branch Prediction

The objective of branch prediction algorithms is to reduce the probability of making a wrong decision, to avoid fetching instructions that eventually have to be discarded. In dynamic branch prediction schemes, the processor hardware assesses the likelihood of a given branch being taken by keeping track of branch decisions every time that instruction is executed.

In its simplest form, the execution history used in predicting the outcome of a given branch instruction is the result of the most recent execution of that instruction. The processor assumes that the next time the instruction is executed, the result is likely to be the same. Hence, the algorithm may be described by the two-state machine in Figure 8.15a. The two states are:

LT: Branch is likely to be taken

LNT: Branch is likely not to be taken

Suppose that the algorithm is started in state LNT. When the branch instruction is

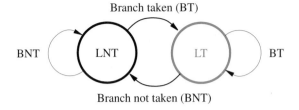

(a) A 2-state algorithm

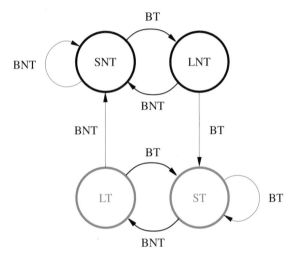

(b) A 4-state algorithm

Figure 8.15 State-machine representation of branch-prediction algorithms.

executed and if the branch is taken, the machine moves to state LT. Otherwise, it remains in state LNT. The next time the same instruction is encountered, the branch is predicted as taken if the corresponding state machine is in state LT. Otherwise it is predicted as not taken.

This simple scheme, which requires one bit of history information for each branch instruction, works well inside program loops. Once a loop is entered, the branch instruction that controls looping will always yield the same result until the last pass through the loop is reached. In the last pass, the branch prediction will turn out to be incorrect, and the branch history state machine will be changed to the opposite state. Unfortunately, this means that the next time this same loop is entered, and assuming that there will be more than one pass through the loop, the machine will lead to the wrong prediction.

Better performance can be achieved by keeping more information about execution history. An algorithm that uses 4 states, thus requiring two bits of history information for each branch instruction, is shown in Figure 8.15b. The four states are:

ST: Strongly likely to be taken

LT: Likely to be taken

LNT: Likely not to be taken

SNT: Strongly likely not to be taken

Again assume that the state of the algorithm is initially set to LNT. After the branch instruction has been executed, and if the branch is actually taken, the state is changed to ST; otherwise, it is changed to SNT. As program execution progresses and the same instruction is encountered again, the state of the branch prediction algorithm continues to change as shown. When a branch instruction is encountered, the instruction fetch unit predicts that the branch will be taken if the state is either LT or ST, and it begins to fetch instructions at the branch target address. Otherwise, it continues to fetch instructions in sequential address order.

It is instructive to examine the behavior of the branch prediction algorithm in some detail. When in state SNT, the instruction fetch unit predicts that the branch will not be taken. If the branch is actually taken, that is if the prediction is incorrect, the state changes to LNT. This means that the next time the same branch instruction is encountered, the instruction fetch unit will still predict that the branch will not be taken. Only if the prediction is incorrect twice in a row will the state change to ST. After that, the branch will be predicted as taken.

Let us reconsider what happens when executing a program loop. Assume that the branch instruction is at the end of the loop and that the processor sets the initial state of the algorithm to LNT. During the first pass, the prediction will be wrong (not taken), and hence the state will be changed to ST. In all subsequent passes the prediction will be correct, except for the last pass. At that time, the state will change to LT. When the loop is entered a second time, the prediction will be correct (branch taken).

We now add one final modification to correct the mispredicted branch at the time the loop is first entered. The cause of the misprediction in this case is the initial state of the branch prediction algorithm. In the absence of additional information about the nature of the branch instruction, we assumed that the processor sets the initial state to LNT. The information needed to set the initial state correctly can be provided by any of the static prediction schemes discussed earlier. Either by comparing addresses or by checking a prediction bit in the instruction, the processor sets the initial state of the algorithm to LNT or LT. In the case of a branch at the end of a loop, the compiler would indicate that the branch should be predicted as taken, causing the initial state to be set to LT. With this modification, branch prediction will be correct all the time, except for the final pass through the loop. Misprediction in this latter case is unavoidable.

The state information used in dynamic branch prediction algorithms may be kept by the processor in a variety of ways. It may be recorded in a look-up table, which is accessed using the low-order part of the branch instruction address. In this case, it is possible for two branch instructions to share the same table entry. This may lead to a branch being mispredicted, but it does not cause an error in execution. Misprediction only introduces a small delay in execution time. An alternative approach is to store the history bits as a tag associated with branch instructions in the instruction cache. We will see in Section 8.7 how this information is handled in the SPARC processor.

8.4 INFLUENCE ON INSTRUCTION SETS

We have seen that some instructions are much better suited to pipelined execution than others. For example, instruction side effects can lead to undesirable data dependencies. In this section, we examine the relationship between pipelined execution and machine instruction features. We discuss two key aspects of machine instructions — addressing modes and condition code flags.

8.4.1 ADDRESSING MODES

Addressing modes should provide the means for accessing a variety of data structures simply and efficiently. Useful addressing modes include index, indirect, autoincrement, and autodecrement. Many processors provide various combinations of these modes to increase the flexibility of their instruction sets. Complex addressing modes, such as those involving double indexing, are often encountered.

In choosing the addressing modes to be implemented in a pipelined processor, we must consider the effect of each addressing mode on instruction flow in the pipeline. Two important considerations in this regard are the side effects of modes such as autoincrement and autodecrement and the extent to which complex addressing modes cause the pipeline to stall. Another important factor is whether a given mode is likely to be used by compilers.

To compare various approaches, we assume a simple model for accessing operands in the memory. The load instruction Load X(R1),R2 takes five cycles to complete execution, as indicated in Figure 8.5. However, the instruction

Load   (R1),R2

can be organized to fit a four-stage pipeline because no address computation is required. Access to memory can take place in stage E. A more complex addressing mode may require several accesses to the memory to reach the named operand. For example, the instruction

Load   (X(R1)),R2

may be executed as shown in Figure 8.16a, assuming that the index offset, X, is given in the instruction word. After computing the address in cycle 3, the processor needs to access memory twice — first to read location X+[R1] in clock cycle 4 and then to read location [X+[R1]] in cycle 5. If R2 is a source operand in the next instruction, that instruction would be stalled for three cycles, which can be reduced to two cycles with operand forwarding, as shown.

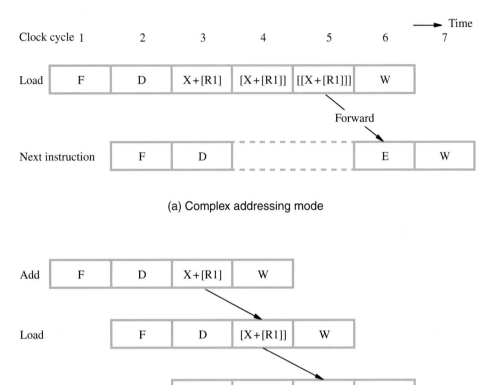

(a) Complex addressing mode

(b) Simple addressing mode

Figure 8.16 Equivalent operations using complex and simple addressing modes.

To implement the same Load operation using only simple addressing modes requires several instructions. For example, on a computer that allows three operand addresses, we can use

$$\begin{array}{ll} \text{Add} & \#X,R1,R2 \\ \text{Load} & (R2),R2 \\ \text{Load} & (R2),R2 \end{array}$$

The Add instruction performs the operation $R2 \leftarrow X+ [R1]$. The two Load instructions fetch the address and then the operand from the memory. This sequence of instructions takes exactly the same number of clock cycles as the original, single Load instruction, as shown in Figure 8.16b.

This example indicates that, in a pipelined processor, complex addressing modes that involve several accesses to the memory do not necessarily lead to faster execution. The main advantage of such modes is that they reduce the number of instructions needed to perform a given task and thereby reduce the program space needed in the main memory. Their main disadvantage is that their long execution times cause the pipeline to stall, thus reducing its effectiveness. They require more complex hardware to decode and execute them. Also, they are not convenient for compilers to work with.

The instruction sets of modern processors are designed to take maximum advantage of pipelined hardware. Because complex addressing modes are not suitable for pipelined execution, they should be avoided. The addressing modes used in modern processors often have the following features:

- Access to an operand does not require more than one access to the memory.
- Only load and store instructions access memory operands.
- The addressing modes used do not have side effects.

Three basic addressing modes that have these features are register, register indirect, and index. The first two require no address computation. In the index mode, the address can be computed in one cycle, whether the index value is given in the instruction or in a register. Memory is accessed in the following cycle. None of these modes has any side effects, with one possible exception. Some architectures, such as ARM, allow the address computed in the index mode to be written back into the index register. This is a side effect that would not be allowed under the guidelines above. Note also that relative addressing can be used; this is a special case of indexed addressing in which the program counter is used as the index register.

The three features just listed were first emphasized as part of the concept of RISC processors. The SPARC processor architecture, which adheres to these guidelines, is presented in Section 8.7.

8.4.2 CONDITION CODES

In many processors, such as those described in Chapter 3, the condition code flags are stored in the processor status register. They are either set or cleared by many instructions, so that they can be tested by subsequent conditional branch instructions to change the flow of program execution. An optimizing compiler for a pipelined processor attempts to reorder instructions to avoid stalling the pipeline when branches or data dependencies between successive instructions occur. In doing so, the compiler must ensure that reordering does not cause a change in the outcome of a computation. The dependency introduced by the condition-code flags reduces the flexibility available for the compiler to reorder instructions.

Consider the sequence of instructions in Figure 8.17a, and assume that the execution of the Compare and Branch=0 instructions proceeds as in Figure 8.14. The branch decision takes place in step E_2 rather than D_2 because it must await the result of the Compare instruction. The execution time of the Branch instruction can be reduced

Add	R1,R2
Compare	R3,R4
Branch=0	. . .

(a) A program fragment

Compare	R3,R4
Add	R1,R2
Branch=0	. . .

(b) Instructions reordered

Figure 8.17 Instruction reordering.

by interchanging the Add and Compare instructions, as shown in Figure 8.17*b*. This will delay the branch instruction by one cycle relative to the Compare instruction. As a result, at the time the Branch instruction is being decoded the result of the Compare instruction will be available and a correct branch decision will be made. There would be no need for branch prediction. However, interchanging the Add and Compare instructions can be done only if the Add instruction does not affect the condition codes.

These observations lead to two important conclusions about the way condition codes should be handled. First, to provide flexibility in reordering instructions, the condition-code flags should be affected by as few instructions as possible. Second, the compiler should be able to specify in which instructions of a program the condition codes are affected and in which they are not. An instruction set designed with pipelining in mind usually provides the desired flexibility. Figure 8.17*b* shows the instructions reordered assuming that the condition code flags are affected only when this is explicitly stated as part of the instruction OP code. The SPARC and ARM architectures provide this flexibility.

8.5 DATAPATH AND CONTROL CONSIDERATIONS

Organization of the internal datapath of a processor was introduced in Chapter 7. Consider the three-bus structure presented in Figure 7.8. To make it suitable for pipelined execution, it can be modified as shown in Figure 8.18 to support a 4-stage pipeline. The resources involved in stages F and E are shown in blue and those used in stages D and W in black. Operations in the data cache may happen during stage E or at a later stage, depending on the addressing mode and the implementation details. This section

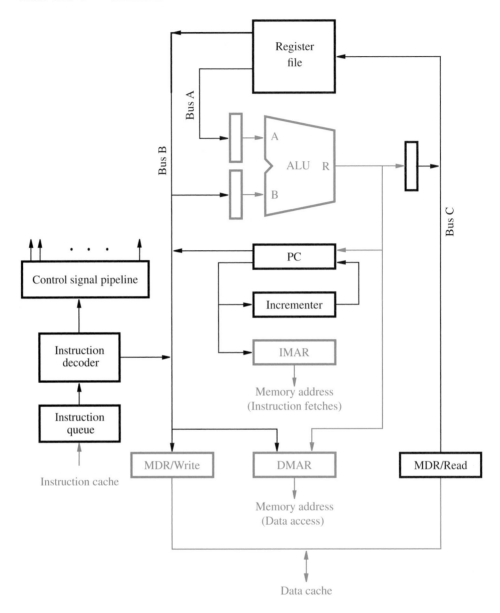

Figure 8.18 Datapath modified for pipelined execution with interstage buffers at the input and output of the ALU.

is shown in blue. Several important changes to Figure 7.8 should be noted:

1. There are separate instruction and data caches that use separate address and data connections to the processor. This requires two versions of the MAR register, IMAR for accessing the instruction cache and DMAR for accessing the data cache.

2. The PC is connected directly to the IMAR, so that the contents of the PC can be transferred to IMAR at the same time that an independent ALU operation is taking place.

3. The data address in DMAR can be obtained directly from the register file or from the ALU to support the register indirect and indexed addressing modes.

4. Separate MDR registers are provided for read and write operations. Data can be transferred directly between these registers and the register file during load and store operations without the need to pass through the ALU.

5. Buffer registers have been introduced at the inputs and output of the ALU. These are registers SRC1, SRC2, and RSLT in Figure 8.7. Forwarding connections are not included in Figure 8.18. They may be added if desired.

6. The instruction register has been replaced with an instruction queue, which is loaded from the instruction cache.

7. The output of the instruction decoder is connected to the control signal pipeline. The need for buffering control signals and passing them from one stage to the next along with the instruction is discussed in Section 8.1. This pipeline holds the control signals in buffers B2 and B3 in Figure 8.2a.

The following operations can be performed independently in the processor of Figure 8.18:

- Reading an instruction from the instruction cache
- Incrementing the PC
- Decoding an instruction
- Reading from or writing into the data cache
- Reading the contents of up to two registers from the register file
- Writing into one register in the register file
- Performing an ALU operation

Because these operations do not use any shared resources, they can be performed simultaneously in any combination. The structure provides the flexibility required to implement the four-stage pipeline in Figure 8.2. For example, let I_1, I_2, I_3, and I_4 be a sequence of four instructions. As shown in Figure 8.2a, the following actions all happen during clock cycle 4:

- Write the result of instruction I_1 into the register file
- Read the operands of instruction I_2 from the register file
- Decode instruction I_3
- Fetch instruction I_4 and increment the PC.

8.6 SUPERSCALAR OPERATION

Pipelining makes it possible to execute instructions concurrently. Several instructions are present in the pipeline at the same time, but they are in different stages of their execution. While one instruction is performing an ALU operation, another instruction is being decoded and yet another is being fetched from the memory. Instructions enter the pipeline in strict program order. In the absence of hazards, one instruction enters the pipeline and one instruction completes execution in each clock cycle. This means that the maximum throughput of a pipelined processor is one instruction per clock cycle.

A more aggressive approach is to equip the processor with multiple processing units to handle several instructions in parallel in each processing stage. With this arrangement, several instructions start execution in the same clock cycle, and the processor is said to use *multiple-issue*. Such processors are capable of achieving an instruction execution throughput of more than one instruction per cycle. They are known as *superscalar* processors. Many modern high-performance processors use this approach.

We introduced the idea of an instruction queue in Section 8.3. We pointed out that to keep the instruction queue filled, a processor should be able to fetch more than one instruction at a time from the cache. For superscalar operation, this arrangement is essential. Multiple-issue operation requires a wider path to the cache and multiple execution units. Separate execution units are provided for integer and floating-point instructions.

Figure 8.19 shows an example of a processor with two execution units, one for integer and one for floating-point operations. The Instruction fetch unit is capable of reading two instructions at a time and storing them in the instruction queue. In each clock cycle, the Dispatch unit retrieves and decodes up to two instructions from the front of the queue. If there is one integer, one floating-point instruction, and no hazards, both instructions are dispatched in the same clock cycle.

In a superscalar processor, the detrimental effect on performance of various hazards becomes even more pronounced. The compiler can avoid many hazards through judicious selection and ordering of instructions. For example, for the processor in Figure 8.19, the compiler should strive to interleave floating-point and integer instructions. This would enable the dispatch unit to keep both the integer and floating-point

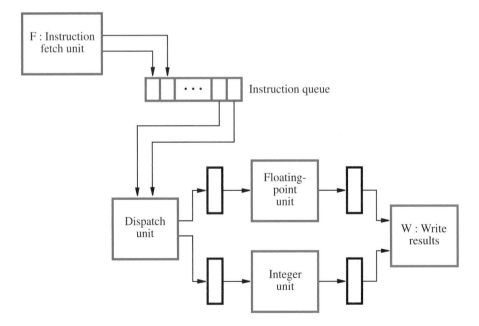

Figure 8.19   A processor with two execution units.

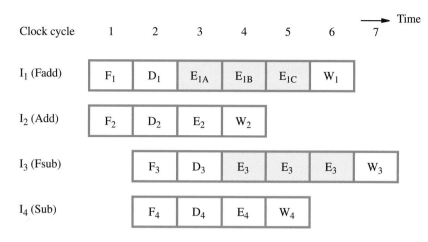

Figure 8.20   An example of instruction execution flow in the processor of Figure 8.19, assuming no hazards are encountered.

units busy most of the time. In general, high performance is achieved if the compiler is able to arrange program instructions to take maximum advantage of the available hardware units.

Pipeline timing is shown in Figure 8.20. The blue shading indicates operations in the floating-point unit. The floating-point unit takes three clock cycles to complete the floating-point operation specified in I_1. The integer unit completes execution of I_2 in one clock cycle. We have also assumed that the floating-point unit is organized internally as a three-stage pipeline. Thus, it can still accept a new instruction in each clock cycle. Hence, instructions I_3 and I_4 enter the dispatch unit in cycle 3, and both are dispatched in cycle 4. The integer unit can receive a new instruction because instruction I_2 has proceeded to the Write stage. Instruction I_1 is still in the execution phase, but it has moved to the second stage of the internal pipeline in the floating-point unit. Therefore, instruction I_3 can enter the first stage. Assuming that no hazards are encountered, the instructions complete execution as shown.

8.6.1   OUT-OF-ORDER EXECUTION

In Figure 8.20, instructions are dispatched in the same order as they appear in the program. However, their execution is completed out of order. Does this lead to any problems? We have already discussed the issues arising from dependencies among instructions. For example, if instruction I_2 depends on the result of I_1, the execution of I_2 will be delayed. As long as such dependencies are handled correctly, there is no reason to delay the execution of an instruction. However, a new complication arises when we consider the possibility of an instruction causing an exception. Exceptions may be caused by a bus error during an operand fetch or by an illegal operation, such as an attempt to divide by zero. The results of I_2 are written back into the register file in cycle 4. If instruction I_1 causes an exception, program execution is in an inconsistent state. The program counter points to the instruction in which the exception occurred. However, one or more of the succeeding instructions have been executed to completion. If such a situation is permitted, the processor is said to have *imprecise exceptions*.

To guarantee a consistent state when exceptions occur, the results of the execution of instructions must be written into the destination locations strictly in program order. This means we must delay step W_2 in Figure 8.20 until cycle 6. In turn, the integer execution unit must retain the result of instruction I_2, and hence it cannot accept instruction I_4 until cycle 6, as shown in Figure 8.21a. If an exception occurs during an instruction,

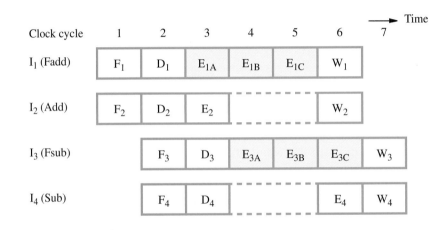

(a) Delayed write

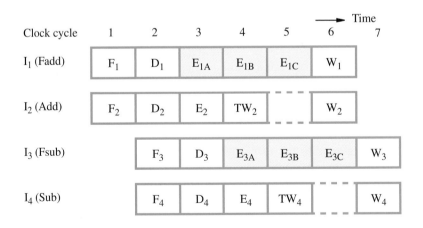

(b) Using temporary registers

Figure 8.21   Instruction completion in program order.

all subsequent instructions that may have been partially executed are discarded. This is called a *precise exception.*

It is easier to provide precise exceptions in the case of external interrupts. When an external interrupt is received, the Dispatch unit stops reading new instructions from the instruction queue, and the instructions remaining in the queue are discarded. All instructions whose execution is pending continue to completion. At this point, the processor and all its registers are in a consistent state, and interrupt processing can begin.

8.6.2 EXECUTION COMPLETION

It is desirable to use out-of-order execution, so that an execution unit is freed to execute other instructions as soon as possible. At the same time, instructions must be completed in program order to allow precise exceptions. These seemingly conflicting requirements are readily resolved if execution is allowed to proceed as shown in Figure 8.20, but the results are written into temporary registers. The contents of these registers are later transferred to the permanent registers in correct program order. This approach is illustrated in Figure 8.21b. Step TW is a write into a temporary register. Step W is the final step in which the contents of the temporary register are transferred into the appropriate permanent register. This step is often called the *commitment* step because the effect of the instruction cannot be reversed after that point. If an instruction causes an exception, the results of any subsequent instruction that has been executed would still be in temporary registers and can be safely discarded.

A temporary register assumes the role of the permanent register whose data it is holding and is given the same name. For example, if the destination register of I_2 is R5, the temporary register used in step TW_2 is treated as R5 during clock cycles 6 and 7. Its contents would be forwarded to any subsequent instruction that refers to R5 during that period. Because of this feature, this technique is called *register renaming*. Note that the temporary register is used only for instructions that *follow* I_2 in program order. If an instruction that precedes I_2 needs to read R5 in cycle 6 or 7, it would access the actual register R5, which still contains data that have not been modified by instruction I_2.

When out-of-order execution is allowed, a special control unit is needed to guarantee in-order commitment. This is called the *commitment unit*. It uses a queue called the *reorder buffer* to determine which instruction(s) should be committed next. Instructions are entered in the queue strictly in program order as they are dispatched for execution. When an instruction reaches the head of that queue and the execution of that instruction has been completed, the corresponding results are transferred from the temporary registers to the permanent registers and the instruction is removed from the queue. All resources that were assigned to the instruction, including the temporary registers, are released. The instruction is said to have been *retired* at this point. Because an instruction is retired only when it is at the head of the queue, all instructions that were dispatched before it must also have been retired. Hence, instructions may complete execution out of order, but they are retired in program order.

8.6.3 DISPATCH OPERATION

We now return to the dispatch operation. When dispatching decisions are made, the dispatch unit must ensure that all the resources needed for the execution of an instruction are available. For example, since the results of an instruction may have to be written in a temporary register, the required register must be free, and it is reserved for use by that instruction as a part of the dispatch operation. A location in the reorder buffer must also be available for the instruction. When all the resources needed are assigned, including an appropriate execution unit, the instruction is dispatched.

Should instructions be dispatched out of order? For example, if instruction I_2 in Figure 8.20b is delayed because of a cache miss for a source operand, the integer unit will be busy in cycle 4, and I_4 cannot be dispatched. Should I_5 be dispatched instead? In principle this is possible, provided that a place is reserved in the reorder buffer for instruction I_4 to ensure that all instructions are retired in the correct order. Dispatching instructions out of order requires considerable care. If I_5 is dispatched while I_4 is still waiting for some resource, we must ensure that there is no possibility of a deadlock occurring.

A *deadlock* is a situation that can arise when two units, A and B, use a shared resource. Suppose that unit B cannot complete its task until unit A completes its task. At the same time, unit B has been assigned a resource that unit A needs. If this happens, neither unit can complete its task. Unit A is waiting for the resource it needs, which is being held by unit B. At the same time, unit B is waiting for unit A to finish before it can release that resource.

If instructions are dispatched out of order, a deadlock can arise as follows. Suppose that the processor has only one temporary register, and that when I_5 is dispatched, that register is reserved for it. Instruction I_4 cannot be dispatched because it is waiting for the temporary register, which, in turn, will not become free until instruction I_5 is retired. Since instruction I_5 cannot be retired before I_4, we have a deadlock.

To prevent deadlocks, the dispatcher must take many factors into account. Hence, issuing instructions out of order is likely to increase the complexity of the Dispatch unit significantly. It may also mean that more time is required to make dispatching decisions. For these reasons, most processors use only in-order dispatching. Thus, the program order of instructions is enforced at the time instructions are dispatched and again at the time instructions are retired. Between these two events, the execution of several instructions can proceed at their own speed, subject only to any interdependencies that may exist among instructions.

In the next section, we present the UltraSPARC II as a case study of a commercially successful, superscalar, highly pipelined processor. The way in which the various issues raised in this chapter have been handled in this processor and the choices made are highly instructive.

8.7 UltraSPARC II EXAMPLE

Processor design has advanced greatly in recent years. The classification of processors as either purely RISC or CISC is no longer appropriate because modern high-performance processors contain elements of both design styles.

The early RISC processors showed how certain features can contribute to high performance. The following two observations proved to be particularly important:

- Pipelining, which enables a processor to execute several instructions at the same time, can lead to significant performance enhancements provided that the pipeline is not stalled frequently.

- A close synergy between the hardware and compiler design enables the compiler to take maximum advantage of the pipelined structure by reducing the events that lead to pipeline stalls.

It is these factors, rather than simply a reduced instruction set, that have contributed to the success of RISC processors. Of particular importance in this regard is the close co-ordination between the design of the hardware, particularly the structure of the pipeline, and the compiler. Much of the credit for today's high levels of performance goes to developments in compiler technology, which in turn have led to new hardware features that would have been of little use a few years ago.

The SPARC architecture, which is the basis for the processors used in Sun workstations, is an excellent case in point. One of Sun's implementations of the SPARC architecture is called UltraSPARC II. This is the processor we will discuss. We have chosen it instead of one of the processors presented in Chapter 3 because it illustrates very well superscalar operation as well as most of the pipeline design options and trade-offs discussed in this chapter. We will start with a brief introduction to the SPARC architecture. For a complete description, the reader should consult the SPARC Architecture Manual [1].

8.7.1 SPARC Architecture

SPARC stands for Scalable Processor ARChitecture. It is a specification of the instruction set architecture of a processor, that is, it is a specification of the processor's instruction set and register organization, regardless of how these may be implemented in hardware. Furthermore, SPARC is an "open architecture," which means that computer companies other than Sun Microsystems can develop their own hardware to implement the same instruction set.

The SPARC architecture was first announced in 1987, based on ideas developed at the University of California at Berkeley in the early eighties, in a project that coined the name reduced instruction set computer and its corresponding acronym RISC. The Sun Corporation and several other processor chip manufacturers have designed and built many processors based on this architecture, covering a wide range of performance. The SPARC architecture specifications are controlled by an international consortium, which introduces new enhanced versions every few years. The most recent version is SPARC-V9.

The instruction set of the SPARC architecture has a distinct RISC style. The architecture specifications describe a processor in which data and memory addresses are 64 bits long. Instructions are of equal length, and they are all 32 bits long. Both integer and floating-point instructions are provided.

There are two register files, one for integer data and one for floating-point data. Integer registers are 64 bits long. Their number is implementation dependent and can vary from 64 to 528. SPARC uses a scheme known as *register windows*. At any given time, an application program sees only 32 registers, called R0 to R31. Of these, the first eight are global registers that are always accessible. The remaining 24 registers are local to the current context.

Floating-point registers are only 32 bits long because this is the length of single-precision floating-point numbers according to the IEEE Standard described in Chapter 6. The instruction set includes floating-point instructions for double- and quad-precision operations. Two sequentially numbered floating-point registers are used to hold a double-precision operand and four are used for quad precision. There is a total of 64 registers, F0 to F63. Single precision operands can be stored in F0 to F31, double precision operands in F0, F2, F4, ..., F62, and quad-precision in F0, F4, F8, ..., F60.

Load and Store Instructions

Only load and store instructions access the memory, where an operand may be an 8-bit byte, a 16-bit half word, or a 32-bit word. Load and store instructions also handle 64-bit quantities, which come in two varieties: extended word or doubleword. An LDX (Load extended) instruction loads a 64-bit quantity, called an *extended* word, into one of the processor's integer registers. A *doubleword* consists of two 32-bit words. The two words are loaded into two sequentially numbered processor registers using a single LDD (Load double) instruction. They are loaded into the low-order 32 bits of each register, and the high order bits are filled with 0s. The first of the two registers, which is the register named in the instruction, must be even numbered. Load and store instructions that handle doublewords are useful for moving multiple-precision floating-point operands between the memory and floating-point registers.

Load and store instructions use one of two indexed addressing modes, as follows:

1. The effective address is the sum of the contents of two registers:

$$EA = [Radr1] + [Radr2]$$

2. The effective address is the sum of the contents of one register plus an immediate operand that is included in the instruction

$$EA = [Radr1] + Immediate$$

For most instructions, the immediate operand is a signed 13-bit value. It is sign-extended to 64 bits and then added to the contents of Radr1.

A load instruction that uses the first addressing mode is written as

$$Load \quad [Radr1+Radr2], Rdst$$

It generates the effective address [Radr1] + [Radr2] and loads the contents of that location into register Rdst. For an immediate displacement, Radr2 is replaced with the immediate operand value, which yields

Load   [Radr1+Imm], Rdst

Store instructions use a similar syntax, with the first operand specifying the source register from which data will be stored in the memory, as follows:

Store   Rsrc, [Radr1+Radr2]

Store   Rsrc, [Radr1+Imm]

In the recommended syntax for SPARC instructions, a register is specified by a % sign followed by the register number. Either %r2 or %2 refers to register number 2. However, for better readability and consistency with earlier chapters, we will use R0, R1, and so on, to refer to integer registers and F0, F1, . . . for floating-point registers.

As an example, consider the Load unsigned byte instruction

LDUB   [R2+R3], R4

This instruction loads one byte from memory location [R2] + [R3] into the low-order 8 bits of register R4, and fills the high-order 56 bits with 0s. The Load signed word instruction:

LDSW   [R2+2500], R4

reads a 32-bit word from location [R2] + 2500, sign extends it to 64 bits, and then stores it in register R4.

Arithmetic and Logic Instructions

The usual set of arithmetic and logic instructions is provided. A few examples are shown in Table 8.1. We pointed out in Section 8.4.2 that an instruction should set the condition code flags only when these flags are going to be tested by a subsequent conditional branch instruction. This maximizes the flexibility the compiler has in reordering instructions to avoid stalling the pipeline. The SPARC instruction set has been designed with this feature in mind. Arithmetic and logic instructions are available in two versions, one sets the condition code flags and the other does not. The suffix cc in an OP code is used to indicate that the flags should be set. For example, the instructions ADD, SUB, SMUL (signed multiply), OR, and XOR do not affect the flags, while ADDcc and SUBcc do.

Register R0 always contains the value 0. When it is used as the destination operand, the result of the instruction is discarded. For example, the instruction

SUBcc   R2, R3, R0

subtracts the contents of R3 from R2, sets the condition code flags, and discards the result of the subtraction operation. In effect, this is a compare instruction, and it has the alternative syntax

CMP   R2, R3

In the SPARC nomenclature, CMP is called a synthetic instruction. It is not a real

Table 8.1 Examples of SPARC instructions

	Instruction	Description
ADD	R5, R6, R7	Integer add: R7 ← [R5] + [R6]
ADDcc	R2, R3, R5	R5 ← [R2] + [R3], set condition code flags
SUB	R5, Imm, R7	Integer subtract: R7 ← [R5] − Imm(sign-extended)
AND	R3, Imm, R5	Bitwise AND: R5 ← [R3] AND Imm(sign-extended)
XOR	R3, R4, R5	Bitwise Exclusive OR: R5 ← [R3] XOR [R4]
FADDq	F4, F12, F16	Floating-point add, quad precision: F12 ← [F4] + [F12]
FSUBs	F2, F5, F7	Floating-point subtract, single precision: F7 ← [F2] − [F5]
FDIVs	F5, F10, F18	Floating-point divide, single precision, F18 ← [F5]/[F10]
LDSW	R3, R5, R7	R7 ← 32-bit word at [R3] + [R5] sign extended to a 64-bit value
LDX	R3, R5, R7	R7 ← 64-bit extended word at [R3] + [R5]
LDUB	R4, Imm, R5	Load unsigned byte from memory location [R4] + Imm, the byte is loaded into the least significant 8 bits of register R5, and all higher-order bits are filled with 0s
STW	R3, R6, R12	Store word from register R3 into memory location [R6] + [R12]
LDF	R5, R6, F3	Load a 32-bit word at address [R5] + [R6] into floating-point register F3
LDDF	R5, R6, F8	Load doubleword (two 32-bit words) at address [R5] + [R6] into floating-point registers F8 and F9
STF	F14, R6, Imm	Store word from floating-register F14 into memory location [R6] + Imm
BLE	icc, Label	Test the icc flags and branch to Label if less than or equal to zero
BZ,pn	xcc, Label	Test the xcc flags and branch to Label if equal to zero, branch is predicted not taken
BGT,a,pt	icc, Label	Test the 32-bit integer condition codes and branch to Label if greater than zero, set annul bit, branch is predicted taken
FBNE,pn	Label	Test floating-point status flags and branch if not equal, the annul bit is set to zero, and the branch is predicted not taken

instruction recognized by the hardware. It is provided only for the convenience of the programmer. The assembler replaces it with a SUBcc instruction.

A condition code register, CCR, is provided, which contains two sets of condition code flags, *icc* and *xcc,* for integer and extended condition codes, respectively. Each set consists of four flags N, Z, V, and C. Instructions that set the condition code flags, such as ADDcc, will set both the *icc* and *xcc* bits; the *xcc* flags are set based on the 64-bit result of the instruction, and the *icc* flags are set based on the low-order 32 bits only.

The condition codes for floating-point operations are held in a 64-bit register called the floating-point state register, FSR.

Branch Instructions

The way in which branches are handled is an important factor in determining performance. Branch instructions in the SPARC instruction set contain several features that are intended to enhance performance of a pipelined processor and to help the compiler in optimizing the code it emits.

A SPARC processor uses delayed branching with one delay slot (see Section 8.3.2). Branch instructions include a branch prediction bit, which the compiler can use to give the hardware a hint about the expected behavior of the branch. Branch instructions also contain an Annul bit, which is intended to increase flexibility in handling the instruction in the delay slot. This instruction is always executed, but its results are not committed until after the branch decision is known. If the branch is taken, execution of the instruction in the delay slot is completed and the results are committed. If the branch is not taken, this instruction is annulled if the Annul bit is equal to 1. Otherwise, execution of the instruction is completed.

The compiler may be able to place in the delay slot an instruction that is needed whether or not the branch is taken. This may be an instruction that logically belongs before the branch instruction but can be moved into the delay slot. The Annul bit should be set to 0 in this case. Otherwise, the delay slot should be filled with an instruction that is to be executed only if the branch is taken, in which case the Annul bit should be set to 1.

Conditional branch instructions can test the *icc, xcc,* or FSR flags. For example, the instruction

$$\text{BGT,a,pt} \quad \text{icc, Label}$$

will cause a branch to location Label if the previous instruction that set the flags in *icc* produced a greater-than-zero result. The instruction will have both the Annul bit and the branch prediction bit set to 1. The instruction

$$\text{FBGT,a,pt} \quad \text{Label}$$

is exactly the same, except that it will test the FSR flags. If neither pt (predicted taken) nor pn (predicted not taken) is specified, the assembler will default to pt.

An example that illustrates the prediction and annul facilities in branch instructions is given in Figure 8.22, which shows a program loop that adds a list of n 64-bit integers. We have assumed that the number of items in the list is stored at address LIST as a 64-bit integer, followed by the numbers to be added in successive 64-bit locations. We have also assumed that there is at least one item in the list and that the address LIST has been loaded into register R3 earlier in the program.

Figure 8.22*a* shows the desired loop as it would be written for execution on a nonpipelined processor. For execution on a SPARC processor, we should first reorganize the instructions to make effective use of the branch delay slot. Observe that the ADD instruction following LOOPSTART is executed during every pass through the loop.

```
                  LDX       R3, 0, R6          Load number of items in the list.
                  OR        R0, R0, R4         R4 to be used as offset in the list
                  OR        R0, R0, R7         Clear R7 to be used as accumulator.
LOOPSTART         LDX       R3, R4, R5         Load list item into R5.
                  ADD       R5, R7, R7         Add number to accumulator.
                  ADD       R4, 8, R4          Point to the next entry.
                  SUBcc     R6, 1, R6          Decrement R6 and set condition flags.
                  BG        xcc, LOOPSTART     Loop if more items in the list.
NEXT              ...
```

(a) Desired program loop

```
                  LDX       R3, 0, R6
                  OR        R0, R0, R4
                  OR        R0, R0, R7
LOOPSTART         LDX       R3, R4, R5
                  ADD       R4, 8, R4
                  SUBcc     R6, 1, R6
                  BG,pt     xcc, LOOPSTART     Predicted taken, Annul bit = 0
                  ADD       R5, R7, R7
NEXT              ...
```

(b) Instructions reorganized to use the delay slot

Figure 8.22   An addition loop showing the use of the branch delay slot and branch prediction.

Also, none of the instructions following it depends on its result. Hence, this instruction may be moved into the delay slot following the branch at the end of the loop, as shown in Figure 8.22*b*. Since it is to be executed regardless of the branch outcome, the Annul bit in the branch instruction is set to 0 (this is the default condition).

As for branch prediction, observe that the number of times the loop will be executed is equal to the number of items in the list. This means that, except for the trivial case of $n = 1$, the branch will be taken a number of times before exiting the loop. Hence, we have set the branch prediction bit in the BG instruction to indicate that the branch is expected to be taken.

Conditional branch instructions are not the only instructions that check the condition code flags. For example, there is a conditional move instruction, MOVcc, which copies data from one register into another only if the condition codes satisfy the condition specified in the instruction suffix, cc. Consider the two instructions

$$\text{CMP} \quad \text{R5, R6}$$
$$\text{MOVle} \quad \text{icc, R5, R6}$$

The MOVle instruction copies the contents of R5 into R6 if the condition code flags in *icc* indicate a less-than-or-equal-to condition ($Z + (N \oplus V) = 1$). The net result is to place the smaller of the two values in register R6. In the absence of a conditional move instruction, the same task would require a branch instruction, as in the following sequence

CMP	R5, R6
BG	icc, GREATER
MOVA	icc, R5, R6

GREATER ...

where MOVA is the move-always instruction. The MOVle instruction not only reduces the number of instructions needed, but more importantly, it avoids the performance degradation caused by branch instructions in pipelined execution.

The instruction set has many other features that are intended to maximize performance in a highly pipelined superscalar processor. We will discuss some of these features in the context of the UltraSPARC II processor. The ideas behind these features have already been introduced earlier in the chapter.

8.7.2 UltraSPARC II

The main building blocks of the UltraSPARC II processor are shown in Figure 8.23. The processor uses two levels of cache: an external cache (E-cache) and two internal caches, one for instructions (I-cache) and one for data (D-cache). The external cache controller is on the processor chip, as is the control hardware for memory management. The memory management unit uses two translation lookaside buffers, one for instructions, iTLB, and one for data, dTLB. The processor communicates with the memory and the I/O subsystem over the system interconnection bus.

There are two execution units, one for integer and one for floating-point operations. Each of these units contains a register set and two independent pipelines for instruction execution. Thus, the processor can simultaneously start the execution of up to four instructions, two integer and two floating-point. These four instructions proceed in parallel, each through its own pipeline. If instructions are available and none of the four pipelines is stalled, four new instructions can enter the execution phase every clock cycle.

The Prefetch and Dispatch Unit (PDU) of the processor is responsible for maintaining a continuous supply of instructions for the execution units. It does so by prefetching instructions before they are needed and placing them in a temporary storage buffer called the instruction buffer, which performs the role of the instruction queue in Figure 8.19.

8.7.3 Pipeline Structure

The UltraSPARC II has a nine-stage instruction execution pipeline, shown in Figure 8.24. The function of each stage is completed in one processor clock cycle. We will give an overview of the operation of the pipeline, then discuss each stage in detail.

The first three stages of the pipeline are common to all instructions. Instructions

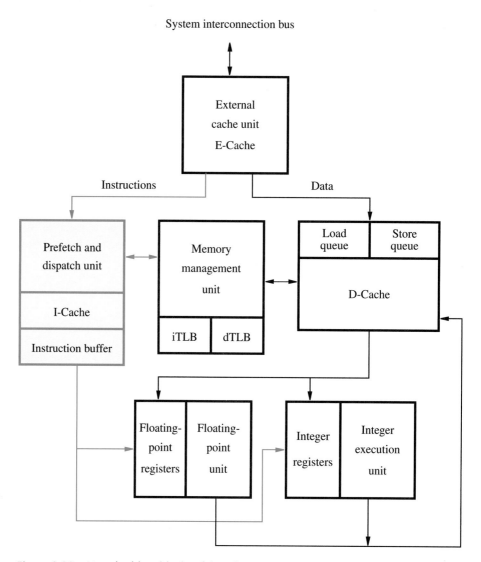

Figure 8.23 Main building blocks of the UltraSPARC II processor.

are fetched from the instruction cache in the first stage (F) and partially decoded in the second stage (D). Then, in the third stage (G), a group of up to four instructions is selected for execution in parallel. The instructions are then dispatched to the integer and floating-point execution units.

Each of the two execution units consists of two parallel pipelines with six stages each. The first four stages are available to perform the operation specified by the instruction, and the last two are used to check for exceptions and store the result of the instruction.

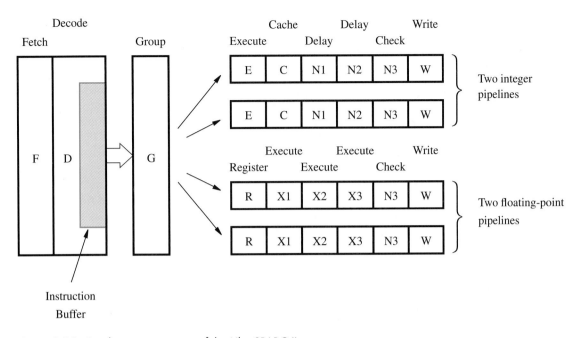

Figure 8.24 Pipeline organization of the UltraSPARC II processor.

Instruction Fetch and Decode

The PDU fetches up to four instructions from the instruction cache, partially decodes them, and stores the results in the instruction buffer, which can hold up to 12 instructions. The decoding that takes place in this stage enables the PDU to determine whether the instruction is a branch instruction. It also detects salient features that can be used to speed up the decisions to be made later in the pipeline.

A cache block in the instruction cache consists of 32 bytes. It contains eight instructions. As instructions are loaded into the cache they are stored based on their virtual addresses, so that they can be fetched quickly by the PDU without requiring address translation. The PDU can maintain the rate of four instructions per cycle as long as each group does not cross cache block boundaries. If there are fewer than four instructions left in a cache block, the unit will read only the remaining instructions in the current block.

The PDU uses a four-state branch prediction algorithm similar to that described in Figure 8.15. It uses the branch prediction bit in the branch instruction to set the initial state to either LT or LNT. For every two instructions in the instruction cache, the PDU uses two bits to record the state of the branch prediction algorithm. These bits are stored in the cache, in a tag associated with the instructions.

For each four instructions in the instruction cache, a tag field is provided called Next Address. The PDU computes the target address of a branch instruction when the instruction is first fetched for execution, and it records this address in the Next Address field. This field makes it possible to continue prefetching instructions in subsequent passes, without having to recompute the target address each time. Since there is only one Next Address field for each half of a cache line, its benefit can be fully realized only if there is at most one branch instruction in each group of four instructions.

Grouping

In the third stage of the pipeline, stage G, the Grouping Logic selects a group of up to four instructions to be executed in parallel and dispatches them to the integer and floating-point execution units. Figure 8.25 shows a short instruction sequence and the way these instructions would be dispatched. Parts *b* and *c* of the figure show the instruction grouping when the PDU predicts that the branch will be taken and not taken, respectively. Note that the instruction in the delay slot, FCMP, is included in the selected group in both cases. It will be executed, but not committed until the branch decision is made. Its results will be annulled if the branch is not taken, because the Annul bit in the branch instruction is set to 1. The first two instructions in each group are dispatched to the integer unit and the next two to the floating-point unit.

	ADDcc	R3, R4, R7	R7 ← [R3] + [R4],
			Set condition codes
	BRZ,a	Label	Branch if zero, set Annul bit to 1
	FCMP	F1, F5	FP: Compare [F2] and [F5]
	FADD	F2, F3, F6	FP: F6 ← [F2] + [F3]
	FMOVs	F3, F4	Move single precision operand from F3 to F4
	⋮		
Label	FSUB	F2, F3, F6	FP: F6 ← [F2] − [F3]
	LDSW	R3, R4, R7	Load single word at location [R3] + [R4] into R7
	⋮		

(a) Program fragment

ADDcc	R3, R4, R7
BRZ,a	Label
FCMP	F1, F5
FSUB	F2, F3, F6

(b) Instruction grouping, branch taken

ADDcc	R3, R4, R7
BRZ,a	Label
FCMP	R1, R5
FADD	R2, R3, R6

(c) Instruction grouping, branch not taken

Figure 8.25 Example of instruction grouping.

The grouping logic circuit is responsible for ensuring that the instructions it dispatches are ready for execution. For example, all the operands referenced by the instruction in a group must be available. No two instructions can be included in the same group if one of them depends on the result of the other. Branch instructions are excepted from this condition, as will be explained shortly.

Instructions are dispatched in program order. Recall that if a group includes a branch instruction, that instruction will have already been tentatively executed as a result of branch prediction in the prefetch and decode unit. Hence, the instructions in the instruction buffer will be in correct order based on this prediction. The grouping logic simply examines the instructions in the instruction buffer in order, with the objective of selecting the largest number at the head of the queue that satisfy the grouping constraints.

Some of the constraints that the grouping logic takes into account in selecting instructions to include in a group are:

1. Instructions can only be dispatched in sequence. If one instruction cannot be included in a group, no later instruction can be selected.

2. The source operand of an instruction cannot depend on the destination operand of any other instruction in the same group. There are two exceptions to this rule:

- A store instruction, which stores the contents of a register in the memory, may be grouped with an earlier instruction that has that register as a destination. This is allowed because, as we will see shortly, the store instruction does not require the data until a later stage in the pipeline.

- A branch instruction may be grouped with an earlier instruction that sets the condition codes.

3. No two instructions in a group can have the same destination operand, unless the destination is register R0. For example, the LDSW instruction in Figure 8.26*a* cannot be grouped with the ADD instruction and must be delayed to the next group as shown.

4. In some cases, certain instructions must be delayed two or three clock cycles relative to other instructions. For example, the conditional instruction

$$\text{MOVRZ} \quad \text{R1, R6, R7}$$

(Move on register condition) moves the contents of R6 into R7 if the contents of R1 are equal to zero. This instruction requires an additional clock cycle to check if the contents

| ADD | R3, R5, R6 | G | E | C | N1 | N2 | N3 | W | |
| LDSW | R4, R7, R6 | | G | E | C | N1 | N2 | N3 | W |

(a) Instructions with common destination

| MOVRZ | R1, R6, R7 | G | E | C | N1 | N2 | N3 | W | |
| OR | R7, R8, R9 | | G | E | C | N1 | N2 | N3 | W |

(b) Delay caused by MOVR instruction

Figure 8.26 Dispatch delays due to hazards.

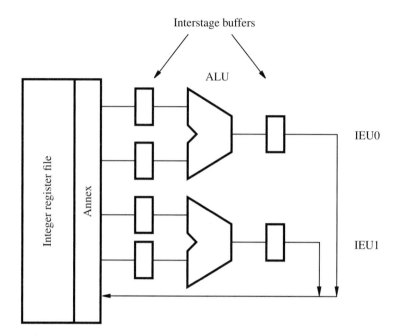

Figure 8.27   Integer execution unit.

of R1 are equal to zero. Hence, an instruction that reads register R7 cannot be in the same group or in the following group. The earliest dispatch for such an instruction is as shown in Figure 8.26*b*.

When the grouping logic dispatches an instruction to the integer unit, it also fetches the source operands of that instruction from the integer register file. The information needed to access the register file is available in the decoded bits that were entered into the instruction buffer by the prefetch and decode unit. Thus, by the end of the clock cycle of stage G, one or two integer instructions will be ready to enter the execution phase. The data read from the register file are stored in interstage buffers, as shown in Figure 8.27. Access to operands in the floating-point register file takes place in stage R, after the instruction has been forwarded to the floating-point unit.

Execution Units

The Integer execution unit consists of two similar but not identical units, IEU0 and IEU1. Only unit IEU0 is equipped to handle shift instructions, while only IEU1 can generate condition codes. Instructions that do not involve these operations can be executed in either unit.

The ALU operation for most integer instructions is completed in one clock cycle. This is stage E in the pipeline. At the end of this clock cycle, the result is stored in the buffer shown at the output of the ALU in Figure 8.27. In the next clock cycle, stage C, the contents of this buffer are transferred to a part of the register file called the Annex. The Annex contains the temporary registers used in register renaming, as explained in

Section 8.6. The contents of a temporary register are transferred to the corresponding permanent register in stage W of the pipeline.

Another action that takes place during stage C is the generation of condition codes. Of course, this is done only for instructions such as ADDcc, which specify that the condition code flags are to be set. Such instructions must be executed in unit IEU1.

Consider an instruction Icc that sets the condition code flags and a subsequent conditional branch instruction, BRcc, that checks these flags. When BRcc is encountered by the prefetch and dispatch unit, the results of execution of Icc may not yet be available. The PDU predicts the outcome of the branch and continues prefetching instructions on that basis. Later, the condition codes are generated when Icc reaches stage C of the pipeline, and they are sent to the PDU during the same clock cycle. The PDU checks whether its branch prediction was correct. If it was, execution continues without interruption. Otherwise, the contents of the pipeline and the instruction buffer are flushed, and the PDU begins to fetch the correct instructions. Aborting instructions at this point is possible because these instructions will not have reached stage W of the pipeline.

When a branch is incorrectly predicted, many instructions may be incorrectly prefetched and partially executed. The situation is illustrated in Figure 8.28. We have assumed that the grouping logic has been able to dispatch four instructions in three successive clock cycles. Instruction Icc at the beginning of the first group sets the condition codes, which are tested by the following instruction, BRcc. The test is performed when the first group reaches stage C. At this time, the third group, I_9 to I_{12}, is entering stage G of the pipeline. If the branch prediction was incorrect, the nine instructions I_4 to I_{12} will be aborted (recall that instruction I_3 in the delay slot is always executed). In addition, any instructions that may have been prefetched and loaded into the instruction buffer will also be discarded. Hence, in the extreme case, up to 21 intrustions may be discarded.

No operation is performed in pipeline stages N1 and N2. These stages introduce a delay of two clock cycles, to make the total length of the integer pipeline the same

I_1 (Icc)	G	E	C
I_2 (BRcc)	G	E	C
I_3	G	E	C
I_4	G	E	C
I_5		G	E
I_6		G	E
I_7		G	E
I_8		G	E
I_9			G
I_{10}			G
I_{11}			G
I_{12}			G

↑ Abort

Figure 8.28 Worst-case timing for an incorrectly predicted branch.

as that of the floating-point pipeline. For integer instructions that do not complete their execution in stage C, such as divide instructions, execution continues through stages N1 and N2. If more time is needed, additional clock cycles are inserted between N1 and N2. The instruction enters N2 only in the last clock cycle of its execution. For example, if the operation performed by an instruction requires 16 clock cycles, 12 clock cycles are inserted after stage N1.

The Floating-point execution unit also has two independent pipelines. Register operands are fetched in stage R, and the operation is performed in up to three pipeline stages (X1 to X3). Here also, if additional clock cycles are needed, such as for the square-root instruction, additional clock cycles are inserted between X2 and X3.

In stage N3, the processor examines various exception conditions to determine whether a trap (interrupt) should be taken. Finally, the result of an instruction is stored in the destination location, either in a register or in the data cache, during the Write stage (W). An instruction may be aborted and all its effects annulled at any time up to this stage. Once the Write stage is entered, the execution of the instruction cannot be stopped.

Load and Store Unit

The instruction

$$\text{LDUW} \quad \text{R5, R6, R7}$$

loads an unsigned 32-bit word from location [R5] + [R6] in the memory into register R7. As for other integer instructions, the contents of registers R5 and R6 are fetched during stage G of the pipeline. However, instead of this data being sent to one of the integer execution units, the instruction and its operands are forwarded to the Load and Store Unit, shown in Figure 8.29. The unit begins by adding the contents of registers R5 and R6 during stage E to generate the effective address of the memory location to be accessed. The result is a virtual address value, which is sent to the data cache. At the same time, it is sent to the data lookaside buffer, dTLB, to be translated into a physical address.

Data are stored in the cache according to their virtual address, so that they can be accessed quickly without waiting for address translation to be completed. Both the data and the corresponding tag information are read from the D-cache in stage C, and the physical address is read from the dTLB. The tag used in the D-cache is a part of the physical address of the data. During stage N1, the tag read from the D-cache is checked against the physical address obtained from the dTLB. In the case of a hit, the data are loaded into an Annex register, to be transferred to the destination register in stage W. If the tags do not match, the instruction enters the Load/store queue, where it waits for a cache block to be loaded from the external cache into the D-cache.

Once an instruction enters the Load/store queue it is no longer considered to be in the execution pipeline. Other instructions may proceed to completion while a load instruction is waiting in the queue, unless one of these instructions references the register awaiting data from the memory (R7 in the example above). Thus, the Load/store queue decouples the operation of the pipeline from external data access operations so that the two can proceed independently.

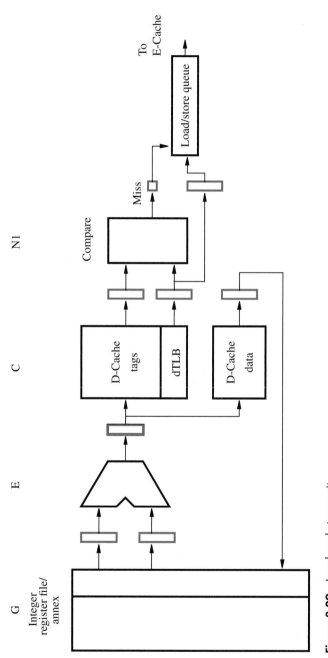

Figure 8.29 Load and store unit.

Execution Flow

It is instructive to examine the flow of instructions and data in the UltraSPARC II processor and between it and the external cache and the memory. Figure 8.30 shows the main functional units of Figure 8.23 reorganized to illustrate the flow of instructions and data and the role that the instruction and data queues play.

Instructions are fetched from the I-cache and loaded into the instruction buffer, which can store up to 12 instructions. From there, instructions are forwarded, up to four at a time, to the block labeled "Internal registers and execution units," where they are executed. On average, the speed with which the PDU can fill the instruction buffer is higher than the speed with which the grouping logic dispatches instructions. Hence, the instruction buffer tends to be full most of the time. In the absence of cache misses and mispredicted branches, the internal execution units are never starved for instructions. Similarly, the memory operands of load and store instructions are likely to be found in the data cache most of the time, where they are accessed in one clock cycle. Hence execution proceeds without delay.

When a miss occurs in the instruction cache, there is a delay of a few clock cycles while the appropriate block is loaded from the external cache. During that time, the

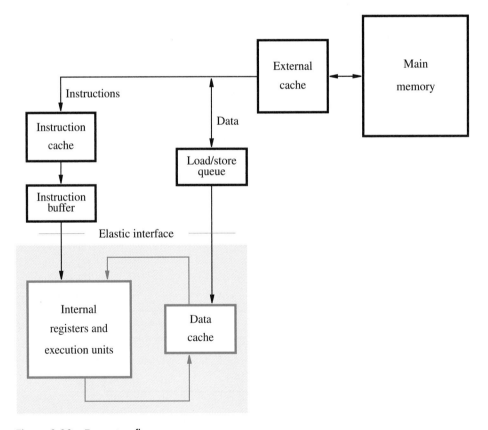

Figure 8.30   Execution flow.

grouping logic continues to dispatch instructions from the instruction buffer until the buffer becomes empty. It takes three or four clock cycles to load a cache block (eight instructions) from the external cache, depending on the processor model. This is about the same length of time it takes the grouping logic to dispatch the instructions in a full instruction buffer. (Recall that it is not always possible to dispatch four instructions in every clock cycle.) Hence, if the instruction buffer is full at the time a cache miss occurs, operation of the execution pipeline may not be interrupted at all. If a miss also occurs in the external cache, considerably more time will be needed to access the memory. In this case, it is inevitable that the pipeline will be stalled.

A load operation that causes a cache miss enters the Load/store queue and waits for a transfer from the external cache or the memory. However, as long as the destination register of the load operation is not referenced by later instructions, internal instruction execution continues. Thus, the instruction buffer and the Load/store queue isolate the internal processor pipeline from external data transfers. They act as elastic interfaces that allow the internal high-speed pipeline to continue to run while slow external data transfers are taking place.

8.8   PERFORMANCE CONSIDERATIONS

We pointed out in Section 1.6 that the execution time, T, of a program that has a dynamic instruction count N is given by

$$T = \frac{N \times S}{R}$$

where S is the average number of clock cycles it takes to fetch and execute one instruction, and R is the clock rate. This simple model assumes that instructions are executed one after the other, with no overlap. A useful performance indicator is the *instruction throughput*, which is the number of instructions executed per second. For sequential execution, the throughput, P_s is given by

$$P_s = R/S$$

In this section, we examine the extent to which pipelining increases instruction throughput. However, we should reemphasize the point made in Chapter 1 regarding performance measures. The only real measure of performance is the total execution time of a program. Higher instruction throughput will not necessarily lead to higher performance if a larger number of instructions is needed to implement the desired task. For this reason, the SPEC ratings described in Chapter 1 provide a much better indicator when comparing two processors.

Figure 8.2 shows that a four-stage pipeline may increase instruction throughput by a factor of four. In general, an n-stage pipeline has the potential to increase throughput n times. Thus, it would appear that the higher the value of n, the larger the performance gain. This leads to two questions:

- How much of this potential increase in instruction throughput can be realized in practice?
- What is a good value for n?

Any time a pipeline is stalled, the instruction throughput is reduced. Hence, the performance of a pipeline is highly influenced by factors such as branch and cache miss penalties. First, we discuss the effect of these factors on performance, and then we return to the question of how many pipeline stages should be used.

8.8.1 EFFECT OF INSTRUCTION HAZARDS

The effects of various hazards have been examined qualitatively in the previous sections. We now assess the impact of cache misses and branch penalties in quantitative terms.

Consider a processor that uses the four-stage pipeline of Figure 8.2. The clock rate, hence the time allocated to each step in the pipeline, is determined by the longest step. Let the delay through the ALU be the critical parameter. This is the time needed to add two integers. Thus, if the ALU delay is 2 ns, a clock of 500 MHz can be used. The on-chip instruction and data caches for this processor should also be designed to have an access time of 2 ns. Under ideal conditions, this pipelined processor will have an instruction throughput, P_p, given by

$$P_p = R = 500 \text{ MIPS (million instructions per second)}$$

To evaluate the effect of cache misses, we use the same parameters as in Section 5.6.2. The cache miss penalty, M_p, in that system is computed to be 17 clock cycles. Let T_I be the time between two successive instruction completions. For sequential execution, $T_I = S$. However, in the absence of hazards, a pipelined processor completes the execution of one instruction each clock cycle, thus, $T_I = 1$ cycle. A cache miss stalls the pipeline by an amount equal to the cache miss penalty. This means that the value of T_I increases by an amount equal to the cache miss penalty for the instruction in which the miss occurs. A cache miss can occur for either instructions or data. Consider a computer that has a shared cache for both instructions and data, and let d be the percentage of instructions that refer to data operands in the memory. The average increase in the value of T_I as a result of cache misses is given by

$$\delta_{miss} = ((1 - h_i) + d(1 - h_d)) \times M_p$$

where h_i and h_d are the hit ratios for instructions and data, respectively. Assume that 30 percent of the instructions access data in memory. With a 95-percent instruction hit rate and a 90-percent data hit rate, δ_{miss} is given by

$$\delta_{miss} = (0.05 + 0.3 \times 0.1) \times 17 = 1.36 \text{ cycles}$$

Taking this delay into account, the processor's throughput would be

$$P_p = \frac{R}{T_I} = \frac{R}{1 + \delta_{miss}} = 0.42R$$

Note that with R expressed in MHz, the throughput is obtained directly in millions of instructions per second. For $R = 500$ MHz, $P_p = 210$ MIPS.

Let us compare this value to the throughput obtainable without pipelining. A processor that uses sequential execution requires four cycles per instruction. Its throughput would be

$$P_s = \frac{R}{4 + \delta_{miss}} = 0.19R$$

For $R = 500$ MHz, $P_s = 95$ MIPS. Clearly, pipelining leads to significantly higher throughput. But the performance gain of $0.42/0.19 = 2.2$ is only slightly better than one-half the ideal case.

Reducing the cache miss penalty is particularly worthwhile in a pipelined processor. As Chapter 5 explains, this can be achieved by introducing a secondary cache between the primary, on-chip cache and the memory. Assume that the time needed to transfer an 8-word block from the secondary cache is 10 ns. Hence, a miss in the primary cache for which the required block is found in the secondary cache introduces a penalty, M_s, of 5 cycles. In the case of a miss in the secondary cache, the full 17-cycle penalty (M_p) is still incurred. Hence, assuming a hit rate h_s of 94 percent in the secondary cache, the average increase in T_I is

$$\delta_{miss} = ((1 - h_i) + d(1 - h_d)) \times (h_s \times M_s + (1 - h_s) \times M_p) = 0.46 \text{ cycle}$$

The instruction throughput in this case is $0.68R$, or 340 MIPS. An equivalent non-pipelined processor would have a throughput of $0.22R$, or 110 MIPS. Thus, pipelining provides a performance gain of $0.68/0.22 = 3.1$.

The values of 1.36 and 0.46 are, in fact, somewhat pessimistic, because we have assumed that every time a data miss occurs, the entire miss penalty is incurred. This is the case only if the instruction immediately following the instruction that references memory is delayed while the processor waits for the memory access to be completed. However, an optimizing compiler attempts to increase the distance between two instructions that create a dependency by placing other instructions between them whenever possible. Also, in a processor that uses an instruction queue, the cache miss penalty during instruction fetches may have a much reduced effect as the processor is able to dispatch instructions from the queue.

8.8.2 NUMBER OF PIPELINE STAGES

The fact that an n-stage pipeline may increase instruction throughput by a factor of n suggests that we should use a large number of stages. However, as the number of pipeline stages increases, so does the probability of the pipeline being stalled, because more instructions are being executed concurrently. Thus, dependencies between instructions that are far apart may still cause the pipeline to stall. Also, branch penalties may become more significant, as Figure 8.9 shows. For these reasons, the gain from increasing the value of n begins to diminish, and the associated cost is not justified.

Another important factor is the inherent delay in the basic operations performed by the processor. The most important among these is the ALU delay. In many processors, the cycle time of the processor clock is chosen such that one ALU operation can be completed in one cycle. Other operations are divided into steps that take about the same time as an add operation. It is also possible to use a pipelined ALU. For example, the ALU of the Compaq Alpha 21064 processor consists of a two-stage pipeline, in which each stage completes its operation in 5 ns.

Many pipelined processors use four to six stages. Others divide instruction execution into smaller steps and use more pipeline stages and a faster clock. For example, the UltraSPARC II uses a 9-stage pipeline and Intel's Pentium Pro uses a 12-stage pipeline. The latest Intel processor, Pentium 4, has a 20-stage pipeline and uses a clock speed in the range 1.3 to 1.5 GHz. For fast operations, there are two pipeline stages in one clock cycle.

8.9 CONCLUDING REMARKS

Two important features have been introduced in this chapter, pipelining and multiple issue. Pipelining enables us to build processors with instruction throughput approaching one instruction per clock cycle. Multiple issue makes possible superscalar operation, with instruction throughput of several instructions per clock cycle.

The potential gain in performance can only be realized by careful attention to three aspects:

- The instruction set of the processor
- The design of the pipeline hardware
- The design of the associated compiler

It is important to appreciate that there are strong interactions among all three. High performance is critically dependent on the extent to which these interactions are taken into account in the design of a processor. Instruction sets that are particularly well-suited for pipelined execution are key features of modern processors.

PROBLEMS

8.1 Consider the following sequence of instructions

> Add   #20,R0,R1
> Mul   #3,R2,R3
> And   #$3A,R2,R4
> Add   R0,R2,R5

In all instructions, the destination operand is given last. Initially, registers R0 and R2 contain 2000 and 50, respectively. These instructions are executed in a computer that has a four-stage pipeline similar to that shown in Figure 8.2. Assume that the first instruction is fetched in clock cycle 1, and that instruction fetch requires only one clock cycle.

(a) Draw a diagram similar to Figure 8.2a. Describe the operation being performed by each pipeline stage during each of clock cycles 1 through 4.

(b) Give the contents of the interstage buffers, B1, B2, and B3, during clock cycles 2 to 5.

8.2   Repeat Problem 8.1 for the following program:

> Add #20,R0,R1
> Mul #3,R2,R3
> And #$3A,R1,R4
> Add R0,R2,R5

8.3   Instruction I_2 in Figure 8.6 is delayed because it depends on the results of I_1. By occupying the Decode stage, instruction I_2 blocks I_3, which, in turn, blocks I_4. Assuming that I_3 and I_4 do not depend on either I_1 or I_2 and that the register file allows two Write steps to proceed in parallel, how would you use additional storage buffers to make it possible for I_3 and I_4 to proceed earlier than in Figure 8.6? Redraw the figure, showing the new order of steps.

8.4   The delay bubble in Figure 8.6 arises because instruction I_2 is delayed in the Decode stage. As a result, instructions I_3 and I_4 are delayed even if they do not depend on either I_1 or I_2. Assume that the Decode stage allows two Decode steps to proceed in parallel. Show that the delay bubble can be completely eliminated if the register file also allows two Write steps to proceed in parallel.

8.5   Figure 8.4 shows an instruction being delayed as a result of a cache miss. Redraw this figure for the hardware organization of Figure 8.10. Assume that the instruction queue can hold up to four instructions and that the instruction fetch unit reads two instructions at a time from the cache.

8.6   A program loop ends with a conditional branch to the beginning of the loop. How would you implement this loop on a pipelined computer that uses delayed branching with one delay slot? Under what conditions would you be able to put a useful instruction in the delay slot?

8.7   The branch instruction of the UltraSPARC II processor has an Annul bit. When set by the compiler, the instruction in the delay slot is discarded if the branch is not taken. An alternative choice is to have the instruction discarded if the branch is taken. When is each of these choices advantageous?

8.8   A computer has one delay slot. The instruction in this slot is always executed, but only on a speculative basis. If a branch does not take place, the results of that instruction are discarded. Suggest a way to implement program loops efficiently on this computer.

8.9   Rewrite the sort routine shown in Figure 2.34 for the SPARC processor. Recall that the SPARC architecture has one delay slot with an associated Annul bit and uses branch prediction. Attempt to fill the delay slots with useful instructions wherever possible.

8.10 Consider a statement of the form

> IF A>B THEN action 1 ELSE action 2

Write a sequence of assembly language instructions, first using branch instructions only, then using conditional instructions such as those available on the ARM processor.

Assume a simple two-stage pipeline, and draw a diagram similar to that in Figure 8.8 to compare execution times for the two approaches.

8.11 The feed-forward path in Figure 8.7 (blue lines) allows the content of the RSLT register to be used directly in an ALU operation. The result of that operation is stored back in the RSLT register, replacing its previous contents. What type of register is needed to make such an operation possible?

Consider the two instructions

$$I_1: \quad \text{Add} \qquad \text{R1,R2,R3}$$

$$I_2: \quad \text{Shift\_left} \quad \text{R3}$$

Assume that before instruction I_1 is executed, R1, R2, R3, and RSLT contain the values 30, 100, 45, and 198, respectively. Draw a timing diagram for a 4-stage pipeline, showing the clock signal and the contents of the RSLT register during each cycle. Use your diagram to show that correct results will be obtained during the forwarding operation.

8.12 Write the program in Figure 2.37 for a processor in which only load and store instructions access memory. Identify all dependencies in the program and show how you would optimize it for execution on a pipelined processor.

8.13 Assume that 20 percent of the dynamic count of the instructions executed on a computer are branch instructions. Delayed branching is used, with one delay slot. Estimate the gain in performance if the compiler is able to use 85 percent of the delay slots.

8.14 A pipelined processor has two branch delay slots. An optimizing compiler can fill one of these slots 85 percent of the time and can fill the second slot only 20 percent of the time. What is the percentage improvement in performance achieved by this optimization, assuming that 20 percent of the instructions executed are branch instructions?

8.15 A pipelined processor uses the delayed branch technique. You are asked to recommend one of two possibilities for the design of this processor. In the first possibility, the processor has a 4-stage pipeline and one delay slot, and in the second possibility, it has a 6-stage pipeline with two delay slots. Compare the performance of these two alternatives, taking only the branch penalty into account. Assume that 20 percent of the instructions are branch instructions and that an optimizing compiler has an 80 percent success rate in filling the single delay slot. For the second alternative, the compiler is able to fill the second slot 25 percent of the time.

8.16 Consider a processor that uses the branch prediction mechanism represented in Figure 8.15b. The initial state is either LT or LNT, depending on information provided in the branch instruction. Discuss how the compiler should handle the branch instructions used to control "do while" and "do until" loops, and discuss the suitability of the branch prediction mechanism in each case.

8.17 Assume that the instruction queue in Figure 8.10 can hold up to six instructions. Redraw Figure 8.11 assuming that the queue is full in clock cycle 1 and that the fetch unit can read up to two instructions at a time from the cache. When will the queue become full again after instruction I_k is fetched?

8.18   Redraw Figure 8.11 for the case of the mispredicted branch in Figure 8.14.

8.19   Figure 8.16 shows that one instruction that uses a complex addressing mode takes the same time to execute as an equivalent sequence of instructions that use simpler addressing modes. Yet, the use of simple addressing modes is one of the tenets of the RISC philosophy. How would you design a pipeline to handle complex addressing modes? Discuss the pros and cons of this approach.

REFERENCE

1. The SPARC Architecture Manual, Version 9, D. Weaver and T. Germond, ed., PTR Prentice Hall, Englewood Cliffs, New Jersey, 1994.

9

EMBEDDED SYSTEMS

CHAPTER OBJECTIVES

In this chapter you will learn about:

- Embedded applications
- Microcontrollers for embedded systems
- Dealing with I/O device constraints
- Using the C language to control I/O devices
- System-on-a-chip design

Computer systems are used in a myriad of applications; therefore, they come in a variety of organizations, sizes, and capabilities. The important factors that must be considered for any given application include performance, reliability, and cost. Any computer that handles large amounts of graphical information, involving pictorial images and animation, must have good real-time performance. In the case of personal computers and workstations, it is important to achieve the best performance for a cost that meets the demands of the marketplace. Exceptionally high performance inevitably implies a much costlier machine. Such machines are needed in environments where massive computations have to be performed in a reasonable time. Some examples of computationally intensive applications are: simulation of a complex system, determination of a good wiring pattern on a printed circuit board, and many computer-aided design (CAD) tasks. These applications may take many hours to run on a personal computer. It is usually necessary to run them on a *compute server,* which has much higher performance achieved at a correspondingly greater cost. Chapter 8 dealt with many issues involved in building high-performance computers.

There are many applications that do not need a high performance processor. Microprocessor control is now commonly used in cameras, cell phones, display phones, point-of-sale terminals, kitchen appliances, cars, and many toys. High performance is not crucial in these applications. Low cost and high reliability are the essential requirements. Small size and low power consumption are often of key importance. All of this can be achieved by placing on a single chip not only the processor circuitry, but also some input/output interfaces, timer circuits, and other design features to make it easy to implement a complete computer control system using very few chips. Microprocessor chips that include I/O interfaces and some memory are generally referred to as *microcontrollers*. A physical system that employs computer control for a specific purpose, rather than for general-purpose computation, is referred to as an *embedded system*. Such systems are the subject of this chapter.

9.1 EXAMPLES OF EMBEDDED SYSTEMS

In this section we present three examples of embedded systems to illustrate the processing and control capability needed in a typical embedded application.

9.1.1 MICROWAVE OVEN

Many household appliances use computer control to govern their operation. A typical example is a microwave oven. This appliance is based on a magnetron power unit that generates microwaves used to heat food in a confined space. When turned on, the magnetron generates its maximum power output. Lower power levels are achieved by turning the magnetron on and off for controlled time intervals. Thus, by controlling the power level and the total heating time, it is possible to realize a variety of user-selectable cooking options.

The specification for a microwave oven may include the following cooking options:

- Manual selection of the power level and cooking time
- A manually selected sequence of different cooking steps
- Automatic selection where the user specifies the type of food (for example, meat, vegetables, or popcorn) and the weight of the food. An appropriate power level and time are then calculated by the controller
- Automatic defrosting of meat by specifying the weight

The oven includes an output display that can show:

- Time of day clock
- Decrementing clock timer while cooking
- Information messages to the user

An audio alert signal, in the form of a beep tone, is used to indicate the end of a cooking operation. An exhaust fan and oven light are provided. Finally, a door interlock must turn the magnetron off if the door of the oven is open. All of these functions can be controlled by a microprocessor.

The input/output capability needed to communicate with the user has to include:

- Input keys that comprise the number pad 0 to 9 and function keys such as Reset, Start, Stop, Power Level, Auto Defrost, Auto Cooking, Clock Set, and Fan Control. To reduce the total number of keys, some keys may have multiple functions, for example, pressing the Fan Control key a number of times may be used to select the speed of the fan.
- Visual output in the form of a liquid crystal display (similar to the seven-segment display discussed in Section A.9).
- A small speaker that produces the beep tone.

The controller for a microwave oven can be implemented by a small microprocessor-based computer unit. The computational tasks are quite simple. They include maintaining the time of day clock, determining the actions needed in the various cooking options, and generating the control signals needed to turn on or off devices such as the magnetron and the fan, and generating display information. Therefore, it is possible to use a relatively simple processor to perform these tasks. The program needed to implement the desired actions is quite small. It must be stored in a nonvolatile read-only memory, so that it will not be lost when the power is turned off. It is also necessary to have a small RAM for use during computations and to hold the user-entered data. The most substantial requirement is to have a lot of I/O capability to deal with all of the input keys, displays, and output control signals.

From the designer's point of view, it is important to find a cost-effective solution to realize the desired controller. Parallel I/O ports provide a convenient mechanism for dealing with the external input and output signals. Figure 9.1 shows a possible organization of the microwave oven. A key point is that the amount of hardware used is quite small. A simple processor with small ROM and RAM units is sufficient, and

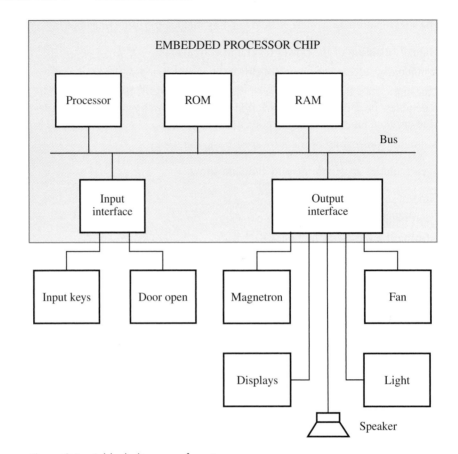

Figure 9.1 A block diagram of a microwave oven.

simple input and output interfaces are used to connect to the rest of the system. It is possible to realize most of this circuitry on a single VLSI chip.

9.1.2 DIGITAL CAMERA

Digital cameras provide an excellent example of a sophisticated embedded system in a small package. Figure 9.2 shows the main parts of a digital camera.

Traditional cameras use film to capture images. In a digital camera, an array of optical sensors is used to capture images. These sensors are based on photodiodes which convert light into electrical charge. The intensity of light determines the amount of charge that is generated. Two different types of sensors are used in commercial products. One type is known as *charge-coupled devices* (CCDs). It is the first type of sensing device used in digital cameras, and it has been refined to give high-quality images. More recently, sensors based on CMOS technology have been developed. They are less expensive, but they do not give images of quite as high quality as CCDs.

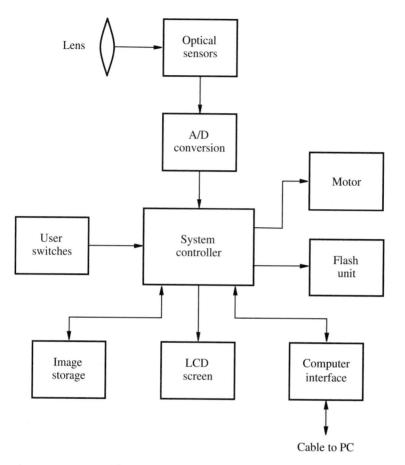

Figure 9.2 A simplified block diagram of a digital camera.

Each sensing element generates a charge that corresponds to one *pixel,* which is one point of a pictorial image. The number of pixels determines the quality of pictures that can be recorded and displayed. The charge is an analog quantity, which is converted into a digital representation using *analog-to-digital* (A/D) conversion circuits. The A/D conversion produces a digital representation of the image in which the color and intensity of each pixel is represented by a number of bits. The digital form of the image can then be manipulated using standard computer circuitry.

A key functional part is the system controller. This block contains a processor, memory (both RAM and EEPROM), and a variety of interface circuits needed to connect to other parts of the system. The processor governs the operation of the camera. It processes the raw image data obtained from the A/D circuits to generate images represented in standard formats suitable for use in computers, printers, and display devices. The main formats used are TIFF for uncompressed images and JPEG for compressed images.

The processed images are stored in a larger image storage device. Flash memory cards, discussed in Section 5.3.5, are a popular choice for storing images. Other choices include floppy disks and miniature hard disk drives.

A captured and processed image can be displayed on a liquid crystal display (LCD) screen, which is included in the camera. This allows the user to decide whether the image is worth keeping. The number of images that can be taken and saved depends on the size of the image storage unit. It also depends on the chosen quality of the images, namely on the number of pixels per image.

A standard interface provides a simple mechanism for transferring the images to a computer or a printer. This may be a simple serial or parallel interface, or a connector for a standard bus such as PCI or USB. If flash memory cards are used, images can also be transferred by physically transferring the card.

The system controller also generates the signals needed to control the operation of the motor (for focusing purposes) and the flash unit. Some of the inputs come from switches activated by the user.

A digital camera requires a considerably more powerful processor than is needed for the previously discussed microwave-oven application. The processor has to perform quite complex signal processing functions. Yet, it is essential that the processor not consume much power because the camera is a battery-powered device. Typically, the processor consumes less power than the display and flash units of a camera.

9.1.3 HOME TELEMETRY

The use of computers in the home is increasing rapidly. They are used as general-purpose computing machines and also in a host of embedded applications. In Subsection 9.1.1, we considered the microwave oven example. Similar examples can be found in other equipment, such as washers, dryers, dishwashers, cooking ranges, furnaces, and air conditioners. Another notable example is the display telephone, in which an embedded processor enables a variety of useful features. In addition to the standard telephone features, a microprocessor controlled phone can be used to provide remote access to other devices in the home that can communicate as computer equipment.

Using the telephone one can remotely perform functions such as:

- Communicate with a computer-controlled home security system
- Set a desirable temperature for a furnace or an air conditioner to maintain
- Set the start time, the cooking time, and temperature for food that has been placed in the oven at some earlier time
- Read the electricity, gas, and water meters, replacing the need for the utility companies that provide these services to send an employee to the home to read the meters

All of this is easily implementable if the device in question is controlled by a microprocessor. It is only necessary to provide a link between the device microprocessor and the microprocessor in the telephone. Such links can be realized in different ways. The simplest is to use bit-serial communication, which is easily accomplished if the controller chips include UART interfaces of the type discussed in Section 4.6.2. Using signaling from a remote location to observe and control the state of equipment is often referred to as *telemetry*.

9.2 PROCESSOR CHIPS FOR EMBEDDED APPLICATIONS

A chip that contains a processor, some memory, and I/O interface circuitry useful in embedded applications is often called an *embedded processor*. Since such chips perform important control functions in the applications, and are based on a microprocessor, they are also known as *microcontroller* chips.

An embedded processor chip should be versatile enough to serve a wide variety of applications. Figure 9.3 shows the block diagram of a typical chip. The main part is a *processor core,* which may be the basic version of a commercially available microprocessor. It is prudent to choose a microprocessor architecture that has proven to be popular in practice, because for such processors there exist numerous CAD tools, good books, and a large amount of experience and knowledge that facilitate the design of new products.

It is useful to include some memory on the chip, which may be sufficient to satisfy the memory requirements found in small applications. Some of this memory has to be

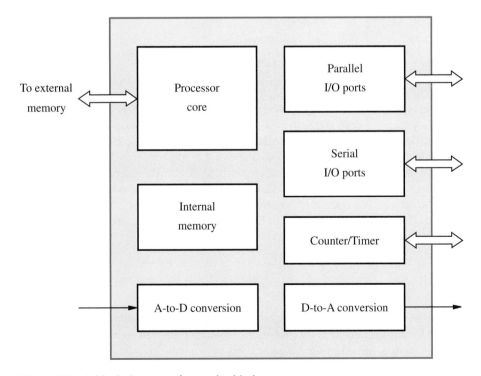

Figure 9.3   A block diagram of an embedded processor.

of RAM type to hold the data that changes during computations. Some should be of ROM type to hold the software because an embedded system usually does not include a disk drive. To allow cost-effective use in low-volume applications, it is necessary to have a field-programmable type of ROM storage. Popular choices for realization of this storage are EEPROM and Flash memory.

Several I/O ports are usually provided for both parallel and serial interfaces. These interfaces allow easy implementation of standard I/O connections. In many applications, it is necessary to generate control signals at programmable time intervals. This task is achieved easily if a timer circuit is included in the embedded processor chip. Since the timer is a circuit that counts clock pulses, it can also be used for counting purposes, for example to count the number of pulses on a given input line.

An embedded system may include some analog devices. To deal with such devices, it is necessary to be able to convert analog signals into digital representations, and vice versa. This is conveniently accomplished if the embedded controller includes A/D and D/A conversion circuits.

Many embedded processor chips are available commercially. Some of the better known examples are: Motorola's 68HC11, 683xx and MCF5xxx families, Intel's 8051 and MCS-96 family, which use CISC-type processor cores, and ARM microcontrollers which have a RISC-type processor. The nature of the processor core is not important to our discussion in this chapter. We will emphasize the system aspects of embedded applications to illustrate how the concepts presented in the previous chapters fit together in the design of a complete embedded computer system.

9.3   A SIMPLE MICROCONTROLLER

In this section we discuss a possible organization of a simple microcontroller to illustrate how some typical features may be used in practice. Figure 9.4 gives its block diagram. There is a processor core and some on-chip memory. Since the on-chip memory may not be sufficient to support all potential applications, processor bus connections are also provided on the pins of the chip so that external memory may be added.

There are two 8-bit parallel interfaces, called A and B, and one serial interface. The microcontroller also contains a 32-bit counter/timer circuit, which can be used to generate internal interrupts at programmed time intervals, to serve as a system stopwatch, to count the pulses on an input line, to generate square-wave output signals of variable duty cycle, and so on.

9.3.1   PARALLEL I/O PORTS

The parallel interface provides I/O capability similar to the scheme depicted in Figure 4.34. Individual port lines on each of the A and B ports can be used as either inputs or outputs, as determined by the bit pattern stored in a data direction register. Figure 9.5 illustrates the bidirectional control for one bit in Port A. Port pin PA_i is treated as an input if the data direction flip-flop contains a 0. In this case, an activation of the

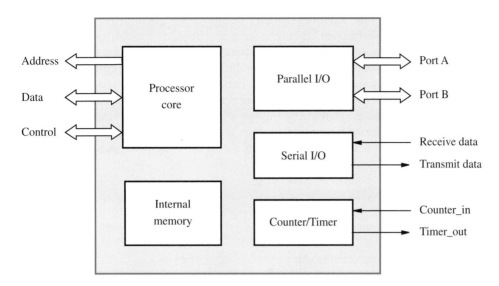

Figure 9.4 An example microcontroller.

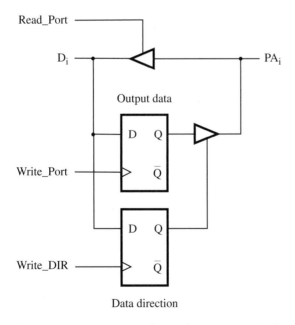

Figure 9.5 Access to one bit in Port A in Figure 9.4.

control signal Read_Port places the logic value on the port pin onto the data line D_i of the processor bus. We have chosen not to include a storage element (corresponding to DATAIN in Figure 4.34) in the input path. Hence, the processor reads the data on the pins directly. The port pin serves as an output if the data direction flip-flop is set to 1. In this case, the logic value loaded into the data output flip-flop, under control of the Write_Port signal, is placed on the pin. Since a data direction bit is provided for each pin, some pins can be programmed as inputs and others can serve as outputs.

The data transfer operations on ports A and B involve the eight 8-bit registers depicted in Figure 9.6. The figure also gives the memory-mapped addresses assigned

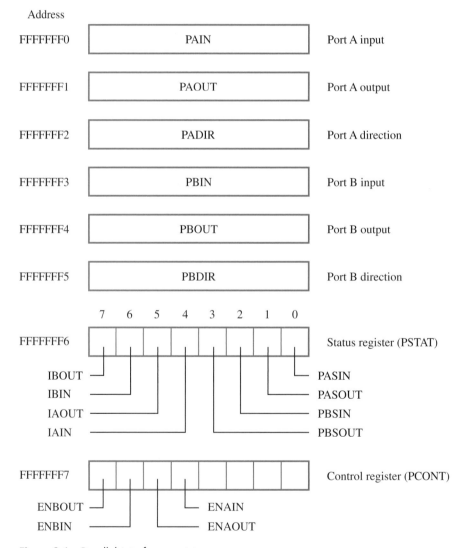

Figure 9.6 Parallel interface registers.

to these registers. We have arbitrarily chosen the addresses at the high end of a 32-bit address range.

The status register, PSTAT, contains the status flags. The PASIN flag is set to 1 when there is new data on the pins of port A. It is cleared to 0 when the processor accepts the data by reading the PAIN register. The PASOUT flag is set to 1 when the data in register PAOUT are transferred to the connected device, to indicate that the processor may now load new data into PAOUT. (The transfer to the device is signaled on a control line as described below.) The PASOUT flag is cleared to 0 when the processor writes data into PAOUT. The flags PBSIN and PBSOUT perform the same function for port B.

The status register also contains four interrupt flags. An interrupt flag, such as IAIN, is set to 1 when that interrupt is enabled and the corresponding I/O action takes place. The interrupt enable bits are held in the control register, PCONT. An enable bit is set to 1 to enable the corresponding interrupt. For example, if ENAIN = 1 and PASIN = 1, then the interrupt flag IAIN is set to 1 and an interrupt request is raised. Thus,

$$IAIN = ENAIN \cdot PASIN$$

A single interrupt request signal is used. In response to an interrupt request, the processor must examine the interrupt flags to determine the actual source of the request.

Information in the status and control registers is used for controlling the data transfers to and from the devices connected to ports A and B. Port A has two control lines, *CAIN* and *CAOUT,* which can be used to provide a signaling mechanism between the interface and the attached device as follows. When the device places new data on the port's pins, it signifies this action by activating the *CAIN* line for one clock cycle. When the interface circuit sees *CAIN* = 1, it sets the status bit PASIN to 1. Later, this bit is cleared to 0 when the processor reads the input data. This action also causes the interface to send a pulse on the *CAOUT* line to inform the device that it may send new data to the interface. For an output transfer, the processor writes the data into the PAOUT register. This action clears the PASOUT bit to 0 and sends a pulse on the *CAOUT* line to inform the device that new data are available. When the device takes the data, it sends a pulse on the *CAIN* line to signify this action, which in turn sets PASOUT to 1. This signaling mechanism is operational when all data pins of a port have the same orientation, that is when the port serves as either an input or an output port. If some pins are selected as inputs and others as outputs, then neither the control lines nor the status and control registers contain meaningful information.

9.3.2 SERIAL I/O INTERFACE

The serial interface provides the UART (Universal Asynchronous Receiver Transmitter) capability to transfer data based on the principle indicated in Figure 4.37. Double buffering is used in both the transmit and receive paths, as shown in Figure 9.7. The need for such buffering, as explained in the discussion of Figure 4.37, is to smooth out short bursts in I/O transfers.

Figure 9.8 shows the addressable registers of the serial interface. Input data are read from the 8-bit Receive buffer, and output data are loaded into the 8-bit Transmit buffer. The status register, SSTAT, provides information about the current status of the

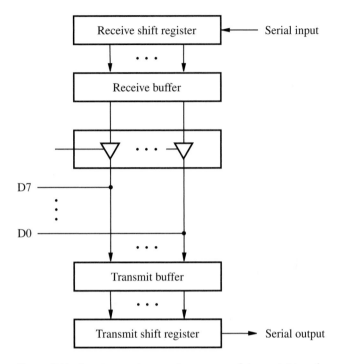

Figure 9.7   Receive and transmit structure of the serial interface.

receive and transmit units. Bit $SSTAT_0$ is set to 1 when there are valid data in the receive buffer. Bit $SSTAT_1$ is set to 1 when the transmit buffer is empty and can be loaded with new data. These bits serve the same purpose as the status flags SIN and SOUT discussed in Section 4.1. Bit $SSTAT_2$ is set to 1 if an error occurs during the receive process. For example, an error occurs if the data in the receive buffer are overwritten by a subsequently received character before the first character is read by the processor. The status register also contains the interrupt flags. Bit $SSTAT_4$ is set to 1 when the receive buffer is full and the receiver interrupt is enabled. Similarly, $SSTAT_5$ is set to 1 when the transmit buffer is empty and the transmitter interrupt is enabled. The serial interface raises an interrupt if either $SSTAT_4$ or $SSTAT_5$ is equal to 1. It also raises an interrupt if $SSTAT_6 = 1$, which occurs if $SSTAT_2 = 1$ and the error condition interrupt is enabled.

The control register, SCONT, is used to hold the interrupt enable bits. Setting $SCONT_{6-4}$ bits to 1 or 0 enables or disables the corresponding interrupts, respectively. This register also indicates how the transmit clock is generated. If $SCONT_0 = 0$, then the transmit clock is the same as the system (processor) clock. If $SCONT_0 = 1$, then the transmit clock is obtained using a clock-dividing circuit.

The last register in the serial interface is the clock-divisor register, DIV. This 32-bit register is associated with a counter circuit that divides down the system clock signal to generate the serial transmission clock. The counter generates a clock signal whose

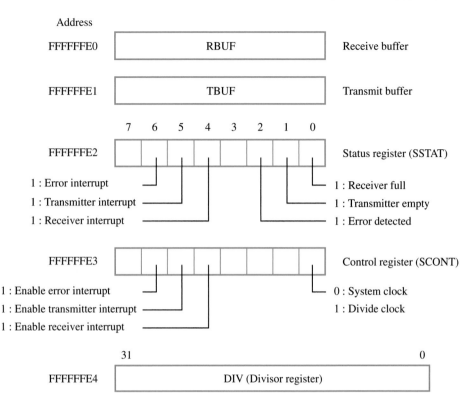

Address

Figure 9.8 Serial interface registers.

frequency is equal to the frequency of the system clock divided by the contents of this register. The value loaded into this register is transferred into the counter, which then counts down using the system clock. When the count reaches zero, the counter is reloaded using the value in the DIV register.

9.3.3 COUNTER/TIMER

A 32-bit down-counter circuit is provided for use as either a counter or a timer. The basic operation of the circuit involves loading a starting value into the counter, and then decrementing the counter contents using either the internal system clock or an external clock signal. The circuit can be programmed to raise an interrupt when the counter contents reach zero. Figure 9.9 shows the registers associated with the counter/timer circuit. The counter/timer register, CNTM, can be loaded with an initial value, which is then transferred into the counter circuit. The current contents of the counter can be read by accessing the memory address FFFFFFD4. The control register, CTCON, is used to specify the operating mode of the counter/timer circuit. It provides a mechanism for starting and stopping the counting process, and for enabling interrupts when the

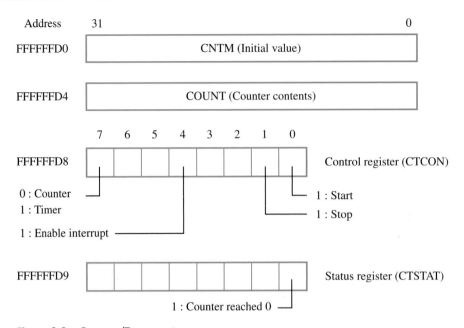

Figure 9.9   Counter/Timer registers.

counter contents are decremented to 0. The status register, CTSTAT, reflects the state of the circuit.

Counter Mode

The counter mode is selected by setting $CTCON_7$ to 0. The starting value is loaded into the counter by writing it into register CNTM. The counting process begins when bit $CTCON_0$ is set to 1 by a program instruction. Once the counter starts counting, the $CTCON_0$ bit is automatically cleared to 0. The counter is decremented by pulses on the *Counter_in* line. Upon reaching 0, the counter circuit sets the status flag $CTSTAT_0$ to 1, and will raise an interrupt if the corresponding interrupt enable bit has been set to 1. The next clock pulse causes the counter to reload the starting value, which is held in register CNTM, and counting continues. The counting process is stopped by setting $CTCON_1$ to 1.

Timer Mode

The timer mode is selected by setting $CTCON_7$ to 1. This mode is suitable for generating a square-wave signal on the output line *Timer_out* in Figure 9.4. The process starts as explained above for the counter mode. As the counter counts down, the value on the output line is held constant. Upon reaching zero, the counter is reloaded automatically with the starting value, and the output signal on the line is inverted. Thus, the period of the output signal is twice the starting counter value times the period of the controlling clock pulse. In the timer mode, the counter is decremented by the system clock.

9.3.4 INTERRUPT CONTROL MECHANISM

The microcontroller has two interrupt request lines, *IRQ* and *XRQ*. The *IRQ* line is used for interrupts raised by the I/O interfaces within the microcontroller. The *XRQ* line is used for interrupts raised by external devices. When the processor observes that the *IRQ* line has been activated, it uses the polling method to determine the source(s) of the interrupt request. This is done by examining the flags in the status registers PSTAT, SSTAT and CTSTAT. The *XRQ* interrupts have higher priority than the *IRQ* interrupts.

The processor status register, PSR, has two bits for enabling interrupts. The IRQ interrupts are enabled if $PSR_6 = 1$, and the XRQ interrupts are enabled if $PSR_7 = 1$. When the processor accepts an interrupt, it disables further interrupts at the same priority level, by clearing the corresponding PSR bit before the interrupt service routine is executed. A vectored interrupt scheme is used, with the vectors for IRQ and XRQ interrupts in memory locations $24 and $28, respectively. Each vector contains the address of the first instruction of the corresponding interrupt service routine.

Our processor has a Link register, LR, which is used for subroutine linkage as explained in Section 2.9. A subroutine Call instruction causes the updated contents of the program counter, PC, which is the required return address, to be stored in LR prior to branching to the first instruction in the subroutine. The same action takes place when an interrupt request is accepted. But, in addition to saving the return address in LR, the contents of the processor status register, PSR, are saved in a processor register IPSR.

A return from subroutine is performed by a ReturnS instruction, which transfers the contents of LR into PC. A return from interrupt is performed by a ReturnI instruction, which transfers the contents of LR and IPSR into PC and PSR, respectively. Since there is only one LR and IPSR register, nested interrupts can be implemented by saving the contents of these registers on a stack using an instruction in the interrupt service routine. This scheme is similar to the ARM approach discussed in Section 4.3.1.

9.4 PROGRAMMING CONSIDERATIONS

Having introduced the microcontroller hardware, we will now consider some software aspects. Programs can be written either in assembly language or in a high-level language. The latter choice is preferable in most applications because the desired code is easier to generate and maintain, and development time is shorter. We will show some examples in both types of languages. The examples in this section are rudimentary and are intended to illustrate the possible approaches. In Section 9.5, we will give a more elaborate example of a complete application. We have chosen the C programming language as the high-level language.

Consider the following task. Our microcontroller is used to transfer 8-bit characters from a bit-serial source to a bit-parallel destination. The source is connected to the serial interface and the destination is connected to parallel port A. The presence of a character in the receive buffer is indicated by the corresponding bit in the status register being set to 1, that is, by $SSTAT_0 = 1$. The parallel port has to be configured for output, which is accomplished by setting all bits in the data direction register to 1 ($PADIR_{7-0} =$ $FF). We will assume that the output device which receives the characters via Port A is faster than the source that delivers the characters to the serial interface. Hence, it is not necessary to poll Port A to see if it is ready to receive the next character. We will first show how to perform the desired transfer using polling. Then, we will implement the same task using interrupts.

9.4.1 POLLING APPROACH

Polling involves testing a status flag repeatedly until a character is received, as discussed in Section 2.7. In our example, it is necessary to poll the bit $SSTAT_0$.

Assembly Language Program

Figure 9.10 shows how the task may be realized using assembly language. We use the generic format used in Chapter 2. The I/O registers in the microcontroller are referred to by symbolic names associated with the register addresses. The program loop continuously checks the status bit $SSTAT_0$. Whenever $SSTAT_0 = 1$, the character in the receive buffer, RBUF, is moved to Port A. Recall that performing a read operation on RBUF automatically clears the $SSTAT_0$ bit. If $PSTAT_1 = 1$, the character is written into the PAOUT register.

The program in Figure 9.10 uses an infinite loop to transfer a continuous stream of characters. In an actual application it is not likely that one would use an infinite loop in this manner because other tasks would also be involved. We use the infinite loop merely to keep the example simple.

```
RBUF      EQU        $FFFFFFE0     Receive buffer.
SSTAT     EQU        $FFFFFFE2     Status register for serial interface.
PAOUT     EQU        $FFFFFFF1     Port A output data.
PADIR     EQU        $FFFFFFF2     Port A direction register.

* Initialization
          ORIGIN     $1000
          MoveByte   #$FF,PADIR    Configure Port A as output.

* Transfer the characters
LOOP      Testbit    #0,SSTAT      Check if new character is ready.
          Branch=0   LOOP
          MoveByte   RBUF,PAOUT    Transfer a character to Port A.
          Branch     LOOP
```

Figure 9.10 A generic assembly language program for character transfer using polling.

C Program

In a C-language program, a memory-mapped I/O location can be represented using a pointer variable, where the value of the pointer is the address of the location. If the contents of this location are to be treated as a character, the pointer should be declared to be of character type. This defines the contents as being one byte in length, which is the size of the I/O registers. The contents can be conveniently handled in hexadecimal form.

Figure 9.11 shows a C program that implements our example task. The *define* statements are used to associate the required addresses with the symbolic names of the pointers. These statements serve the same purpose as the EQU statements in Figure 9.10. They enable the preprocessor of the C compiler to replace the symbolic names in the program with their actual values. As a result, the compiled code will be similar to the code in Figure 9.10.

Note that the RBUF and SSTAT pointers are declared as being volatile. This is necessary because the program only reads the contents of the corresponding locations, but it neither writes any data into them, nor associates a specific value with them. An optimizing compiler may remove program statements that appear to have no impact, which includes statements involving variables whose values never change. Since the contents of RBUF and SSTAT registers change under influences that are external to the program, it is essential to inform the compiler of this fact. The compiler will not remove the statements that contain variables that have been declared as being volatile.

A different approach is illustrated in Figure 9.12. Instead of defining the pointers to I/O registers as constants, as in Figure 9.11, the pointers are declared as variables pointing to locations that hold character-type data. Thus, symbols such as RBUF and

```
/* Define register addresses */
#define RBUF (volatile char *) 0xFFFFFFE0
#define SSTAT (volatile char *) 0xFFFFFFE2
#define PAOUT (char *) 0xFFFFFFF1
#define PADIR (char *) 0xFFFFFFF2

void main()
{
    /* Initialize the parallel port */
    *PADIR = 0xFF;                      /* Configure Port A as output */

    /* Transfer the characters */
    while (1) {                         /* Infinite loop */
        while ((*SSTAT & 0x1) == 0);    /* Wait for a new character */
        *PAOUT = *RBUF;                 /* Move the character to Port A */
    }
}
```

Figure 9.11 C program for character transfer using polling.

```
/* Define register addresses */
volatile char *RBUF = (char *) 0xFFFFFFE0;
volatile char *SSTAT = (char *) 0xFFFFFFE2;
char *PAOUT = (char *) 0xFFFFFFF1;
char *PADIR = (char *) 0xFFFFFFF2;

void main()
{
    /* Initialize the parallel port */
    *PADIR = 0xFF;                      /* Configure Port A as output */

    /* Transfer the characters */
    while (1) {                         /* Infinite loop */
        while ((*SSTAT & 0x1) == 0);   /* Wait for a new character */
        *PAOUT = *RBUF;                /* Move the character to Port A */
    }
}
```

Figure 9.12   An alternative C program for character transfer using polling.

```
               Move        PADIR,R0
               MoveByte    #$FF,(R0)
    LOOP       Move        SSTAT,R0
               Testbit     #0,(R0)
               Branch=0    LOOP
               Move        RBUF,R0
               Move        PAOUT,R1
               Move        (R0),(R1)
               Branch      LOOP
```

Figure 9.13   Possible compiled code for
the program segment in
Figure 9.12.

PAOUT denote addresses of memory locations that hold the actual addresses of the I/O registers. In this case, the compiled code may appear as shown in Figure 9.13. To access a particular I/O register, its address is loaded into a processor register and then the Register indirect addressing mode is used to access the desired I/O register. Note that only a portion of the compiled code is shown in the figure. The compiler also indicates the memory address values that are associated with the symbols RBUF, SSTAT, PAOUT, and PADIR. The machine code generated from this figure is larger than the code derived from the program in Figure 9.11. In subsequent examples we will define the pointers as shown in Figure 9.11. Using the *define* statements to specify the addresses of I/O locations emphasizes the fact that these addresses are constants that never change in the course of execution of a program.

In the C programs in this chapter, we include the specific values that have to be loaded into registers directly in the statements that perform the desired actions. For example, in Figure 9.11 the statement

$$*PADIR = 0xFF;$$

sets all eight bits in register PADIR to 1, making Port A behave as an output port. A more usual approach in writing C programs is to declare names for such constant values and then use the names in the rest of the program. Our choice is motivated by a desire to keep the figures as small as possible and to make it easier to compare the given values with the specification of I/O registers in Figures 9.6 through 9.9.

9.4.2 INTERRUPT APPROACH

Instead of polling the bit $SSTAT_0$ to detect a new character, we can configure the I/O interface to raise an interrupt request when $SSTAT_0 = 1$. The corresponding interrupt enable bit in the SCONT register, $SCONT_4$, has to be set to 1. It is also necessary to enable IRQ interrupts in the processor by setting PSR_6 to 1. This is accomplished by loading $40 into PSR, which also disables the XRQ interrupts. The address of the interrupt service routine has to be placed in memory location $24.

Assembly Language Program

Figure 9.14 shows an assembly language program that implements the interrupt scheme for the character transfer example. An interrupt request is raised when $SSTAT_0 = 1$. In response, the interrupt service routine transfers a character from RBUF to PAOUT. The action of reading the contents of the receive buffer RBUF also causes the $SSTAT_0$ bit to be cleared to 0. Note that there is no reference to the status register SSTAT in the program. Again, as in the previous example, an infinite loop is used to wait for new characters to keep the example simple.

C Program

To write a C program that uses interrupts we need to address two issues:

- How do we access processor registers?
- How do we write an interrupt service routine?

The interrupt approach requires the interrupt control bits in the processor status register to be set appropriately. This involves writing into PSR. Variables in a high-level language, such as C, are represented in the compiled code by memory locations. Hence, memory-mapped I/O registers can be handled in a straightforward manner, as we have done in Figures 9.11 and 9.12. However, the processor registers, such as the status register PSR, do not have memory addresses associated with them. These registers can be accessed by including suitable assembly language instructions directly in the

RBUF	EQU	$FFFFFFE0	Receive buffer.
SCONT	EQU	$FFFFFFE3	Control register for serial interface.
PAOUT	EQU	$FFFFFFF1	Port A output data.
PADIR	EQU	$FFFFFFF2	Port A direction register.

* Initialization

	ORIGIN	$1000	
	MoveByte	#$FF,PADIR	Configure Port A as output.
	Move	#INTSERV,$24	Set the interrupt vector.
	Move	#$40,PSR	Processor responds to IRQ interrupts.
	MoveByte	#$10,SCONT	Enable receiver interrupts.

* Transfer loop

| LOOP | Branch | LOOP | Infinite wait loop. |

* Interrupt service routine

| INTSERV | MoveByte | RBUF,PAOUT | Transfer a character to Port A. |
| | ReturnI | | Return from interrupt. |

Figure 9.14 A generic assembly language program for character transfer using interrupts.

C program. For example, the statement

$$\text{\_\_asm\_\_(''Move \quad \#0x40,\%PSR'');}$$

causes the C compiler to insert the assembly instruction

$$\text{Move \quad \#\$40,PSR}$$

into the compiled code. This loads the pattern $40 into the PSR register.

The second issue is the interrupt service routine. This routine has to be written as a function in the C program. However, the compiler implements a function as a subroutine. Figure 9.15 gives an example. There is a main program that performs some task; we have not shown any statements of this program. There is also a function named *intserv,* which merely transfers one character from the receive buffer RBUF to the output port PAOUT. The compiler-generated code for the function *intserv* comprises the instructions

$$\text{Move \quad \$FFFFFFE0,\$FFFFFFF1}$$
$$\text{ReturnS}$$

Consider now what happens if *intserv* is an interrupt service routine. Using interrupts, the return from the interrupt service routine must be done using the return from interrupt instruction, ReturnI. It causes the contents of both the program counter and the processor status register to be restored to their previous values. Therefore, we have to insert the ReturnI instruction in the program by the statement

$$\text{\_\_asm\_\_(''ReturnI'');}$$

```
#define RBU (volatile char *) 0xFFFFFFE0
#define PAOUT (char *) 0xFFFFFFF1
    .
    .
    .


void main()
{
    .
    .
    .

}

void intserv()
{
    *PAOUT = *RBUF;   /* Move a character to Port A */
}
```

Figure 9.15 A function call in a C program.

so that the compiled code will be

Move	$FFFFFFE0,$FFFFFFF1
ReturnI	
ReturnS	

Of course, the ReturnS instruction will never be executed in this case.

We can now write the desired program that uses interrupts. Figure 9.16 gives a possible program, using the style of Figure 9.11. Note that the pointers to I/O registers are of character type because they point to locations that hold one byte of data. However, the pointer int_addr is of unsigned integer type because it points to a memory location that stores a 4-byte interrupt vector.

9.5 I/O Device Timing Constraints

The example in the previous section is made simple by the assumption that the output device connected to Port A is faster than the device that provides the characters via the serial interface. Practical systems involve devices with varying speed requirements. Suppose that we reverse our speed assumption for the previous example, namely, let the output device be slower than the input device. This means that characters cannot be sent directly from RBUF to PAOUT. Instead, it is necessary to store them temporarily in a memory buffer. This buffer may be organized as a first-in-first-out (FIFO) queue.

```
/* Define register addresses */
#define RBUF (volatile char *) 0xFFFFFFE0
#define SCONT (char *) 0xFFFFFFE3
#define PAOUT (char *) 0xFFFFFFF1
#define PADIR (char *) 0xFFFFFFF2
#define int_addr (int *) (0x24)

void intserv();

void main()
{
    /* Initialize the parallel port */
    *PADIR = 0xFF;                      /* Configure Port A as output */

    /* Initialize the interrupt mechanism */
    int_addr = &intserv;               /* Set interrupt vector */
    __asm__("Move  #0x40,%PSR");        /* Processor responds to IRQ interrupts */
    *SCONT = 0x10;                     /* Enable receiver interrupts */

    /* Transfer the characters */
    while (1);                         /* Infinite loop */
}

/* Interrupt service routine */
void intserv()
{
    *PAOUT = *RBUF;                    /* Transfer the character to Port A */
    __asm__("ReturnI");                /* Return from interrupt */
}
```

Figure 9.16   C program for character transfer using interrupts.

The problem with a simple FIFO is that the pointers that point to the head and the tail of the queue are progressively incremented, so that the queue moves through the memory as the characters are stored and retrieved. A better solution is to use a circular buffer, that is, a circular queue, which consists of a fixed number of memory locations and wraps around when the end of the buffer is reached. Of course, this buffer can overflow if the fast source generates many more characters in a burst than the output device can accept during the burst time period. To avoid dealing with the overflow problem at this point, we will assume that the source generates the characters in bursts of less than 80 characters and that the output device will accept these characters before another burst arrives. This means that the circular buffer has to be able to hold up to 80 characters.

We can implement the circular buffer as an array of 8-bit entries, using two index values to denote the current position of the head and the tail of the queue. When these indexes are equal, the queue is empty.

9.5.1 C Program for Transfer via a Circular Buffer

Figure 9.17 gives a possible C program that uses the circular buffer to transfer characters. The buffer is an array called *mbuffer,* and it has 80 entries. Characters are placed into the buffer using index *fin,* and they are retrieved using index *fout.* On each pass through the loop, the status register SSTAT is tested first to see if there is a new character

```c
/* Define register addresses */
#define RBUF (volatile char *) 0xFFFFFFE0
#define SSTAT (volatile char *) 0xFFFFFFE2
#define PAOUT (char *) 0xFFFFFFF1
#define PADIR (char *) 0xFFFFFFF2
#define PSTAT (volatile char *) 0xFFFFFFF6
#define BSIZE 80

void main()
{
    unsigned char mbuffer[BSIZE];
    unsigned char fin, fout;
    unsigned char temp;

    /* Initialize Port A and circular buffer */
    *PADIR = 0xFF;                           /* Configure Port A as output */
    fin = 0;
    fout = 0;

    /* Transfer the characters */
    while (1) {                              /* Infinite loop */
        while ((*SSTAT & 0x1) == 0) {        /* Wait for a new character */
            if (fin != fout) {               /* If circular buffer is not empty */
                if (*PSTAT & 0x2) {          /*   and output device is ready */
                    *PAOUT = mbuffer[fout];  /*   send a character to Port A */
                    if (fout < BSIZE−1)      /* Update the output index */
                        fout++;
                    else
                        fout = 0;
                }
            }
        }
        mbuffer[fin] = *RBUF;                /* Read a character from receive buffer */
        if (fin < BSIZE−1)                   /* Update the input index */
            fin++;
        else
            fin = 0;
    }
}
```

Figure 9.17 C program for transfer through a circular buffer.

in RBUF, because transfers from the faster device must be given higher priority. If there is no character in RBUF, then a transfer to Port A is performed if the circular buffer is not empty and the port is ready. The index values are updated as each transfer is made.

9.5.2 ASSEMBLY LANGUAGE PROGRAM FOR TRANSFER VIA A CIRCULAR BUFFER

Figure 9.18 shows an implementation in assembly language. The circular buffer is accessed using the indexed addressing mode. Register R0 points to the first location in

RBUF	EQU	$FFFFFFE0	Receive buffer.
SSTAT	EQU	$FFFFFFE2	Status register for serial interface.
PAOUT	EQU	$FFFFFFF1	Port A output data.
PADIR	EQU	$FFFFFFF2	Port A direction register.
PSTAT	EQU	$FFFFFFF6	Status register for parallel interface.
MBUFFER	ReserveByte	80	Define the circular buffer.
* Initialization			
	ORIGIN	$1000	
	MoveByte	#$FF,PADIR	Configure Port A as output.
	Move	#MBUFFER,R0	R0 points to the buffer.
	Move	#0,R1	Initialize head pointer.
	Move	#0,R2	Initialize tail pointer.
* Transfer the characters			
LOOP	Testbit	#0,SSTAT	Check if new character is ready.
	Branch≠0	READ	
	Compare	R1,R2	Check if queue is empty.
	Branch=0	LOOP	Queue is empty.
	Testbit	#1,PSTAT	Check if Port A is ready.
	Branch=0	LOOP	
	MoveByte	(R0,R2),PAOUT	Send a character to Port A.
	Add	#1,R2	Increment the tail pointer.
	Compare	#80,R2	Is the pointer past queue limit?
	Branch<0	LOOP	
	Move	#0,R2	Wrap around.
	Branch	LOOP	
READ	MoveByte	RBUF,(R0,R1)	Place new character into queue.
	Add	#1,R1	Increment the head pointer.
	Compare	#80,R1	Is the pointer past queue limit?
	Branch<0	LOOP	
	Move	#0,R1	Wrap around.
	Branch	LOOP	

Figure 9.18 A generic assembly language program for transfer through a circular buffer.

the queue, and registers R1 and R2 are the head and tail indexes, respectively. The flow in the program is essentially the same as in the program in Figure 9.17.

9.6 REACTION TIMER — AN EXAMPLE

Having introduced the basic features of the microcontroller, we will now show how it can be used in a simple application. Instead of using an example of a typical embedded application, which would involve considerable complexity, our choice is a simple and easily understood task.

We want to design a "reaction timer" that can be used to measure the speed of response of a person to a visual stimulus. The idea is to have the microcontroller turn on a light and then measure the reaction time that the subject takes to turn the light off by pressing a switch. The detailed operation should be as follows:

- There are two manual pushbutton switches, *Go* and *Stop,* a light-emitting diode (LED) and a three-digit seven-segment display.
- The system is activated by pressing the *Go* switch.
- Upon activation, the seven-segment display is set to 000 and the LED is turned off.
- After a three-second delay, the LED is turned on and the timing process begins.
- When the *Stop* switch is pressed, the timing process is stopped, the LED is turned off, and the elapsed time is displayed on the seven-segment display.
- The elapsed time is calculated and displayed in hundredths of a second. Since the display has only three digits, it is assumed that the elapsed time will be less than ten seconds.

Figure 9.19 depicts the hardware that can implement the desired reaction timer. The microcontroller provides all of the functionality except for the input switches and the output displays.

We will use the parallel ports, A and B, for all input/output functions. The two most-significant BCD digits of the displayed time are connected to Port A, and the least-significant digit to the upper four bits of Port B. The switches and the LED are connected to the lower four bits of Port B as shown in the figure. The counter/timer circuit is used to measure the elapsed time. It is driven by the system clock, which we assume to have a frequency of 100 MHz.

A program to realize the required task can be based on the following approach:

- The user's intention to begin a test is monitored by means of a wait loop that polls the state of the *Go* switch.
- Upon observing that the *Go* switch has been closed, that is, having detected $PB_1 = 0$, and after a further delay of three seconds, the LED is turned on.
- The counter is set to the initial value $FFFFFFFF and the counting process is activated; the count is decremented by each clock pulse.
- A wait loop polls the state of the *Stop* switch to detect when the user reacts by pressing the switch.

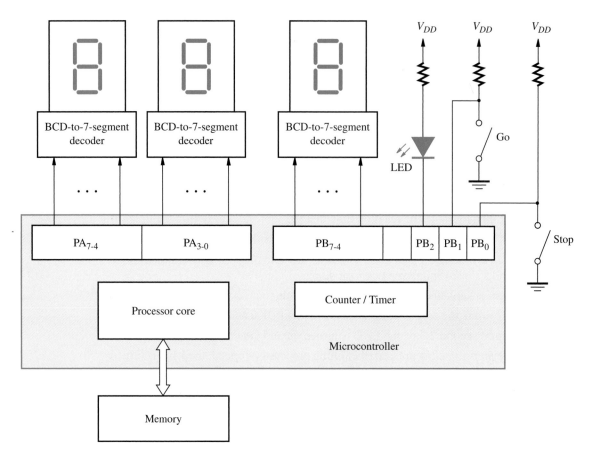

Figure 9.19   The reaction-timer circuit.

- When the *Stop* switch is pressed, the counter is stopped and the elapsed time is calculated.
- The measured delay is converted into a BCD number and sent to the seven-segment displays.

The addresses of various I/O registers in the microcontroller are as given in Figures 9.6 through 9.9. The program must configure Ports A and B as specified in Figure 9.19. All of Port A and the high-order four bits of Port B are configured as outputs. In the low-order four bits of Port B, PB_0 and PB_1 are used as inputs, while PB_2 is an output. There is no need to use the control signals available on the two ports, because the input device consists of simple switches, and the output device is a display that immediately follows any changes in signals on the port pins that drive it.

We will show how the required task can be implemented using the C programming language. Then, we will show how it may be realized in assembly language.

In both programs there are instructions that perform the following tasks. After the *Go* key is pressed, a delay of three seconds is implemented by using the timer. Since the counter/timer circuit is clocked at 100 MHz, the counter is initialized to the hex value 11E1A300, which corresponds to the decimal value 300,000,000. The process of counting down is started by setting the $CTCONT_0$ bit to 1. When the count reaches zero, the LED is turned on to begin the reaction time test. Next, the counter is set to FFFFFFFF to begin the reaction timing. Upon detecting that the *Stop* key has been pressed, the counting process is stopped by setting $CTCONT_1 = 1$. The total count is computed as

$$\text{Total count} = \text{0xFFFFFFFF} - \text{Present count}$$

Since this is the total number of clock cycles, the actual time in hundredths of seconds is

$$\text{Actual time} = (\text{Total count})/1000000$$

This binary integer can be converted to a decimal number by first dividing it by 100 to generate the most-significant digit. The remainder is then divided by 10 to generate the next digit. The final remainder is the least-significant digit.

9.6.1 C PROGRAM FOR THE REACTION TIMER

Figure 9.20 gives a possible program. Having configured Ports A and B as required, and having turned off the display and LED, the program polls the value on pin PB_1. After the *Go* key is pressed and PB_1 becomes equal to 1, a three-second delay is introduced. Then, the LED is turned on, and the reaction timing process starts. Another polling operation is used to wait for the *Stop* key to be pressed. When this key is pressed, the LED is turned off, the counter is stopped, and its contents are read. The computation of the elapsed time and the conversion to a decimal number are performed as explained above. The resulting three BCD digits are written to the port data registers according to the arrangement depicted in Figure 9.19.

9.6.2 ASSEMBLY LANGUAGE PROGRAM FOR THE REACTION TIMER

Figure 9.21 shows how the program for the reaction timer can be realized using assembly language. It is based on the general strategy outlined at the beginning of Section 9.6, and it parallels the C program in Figure 9.20. The comments given with each instruction should enable the reader to follow the flow of the program.

The conversion to BCD representation involves using the Divide instruction, discussed in Section 2.10.3. This instruction divides a dividend in register R2 by a divisor in register R1. The result of the operation is a quotient placed in R2 and a remainder placed in R3. Note that after dividing the actual time (in hundredths of seconds) by 100, only the least-significant four bits of the quotient in R2 need to be considered. We have assumed that the elapsed time will be less than ten seconds, so that only three digits have to be displayed. The first digit of the quotient is moved to R4. The remainder is moved from R3 to R2, and the division by ten is performed next.

```
/* Define register addresses */
#define PAOUT (char *) 0xFFFFFFF1
#define PADIR (char *) 0xFFFFFFF2
#define PBIN (volatile char *) 0xFFFFFFF3
#define PBOUT (char *) 0xFFFFFFF4
#define PBDIR (char *) 0xFFFFFFF5
#define CNTM (int *) 0xFFFFFFD0
#define COUNT (volatile int *) 0xFFFFFFD4
#define CTCON (char *) 0xFFFFFFD8

void main()
{
    unsigned int counter_value, total_count;
    unsigned int actual_time, seconds, tenths, hundredths;

    /* Initialize the parallel ports */
    *PADIR = 0xFF;                      /* Configure Port A */
    *PBDIR = 0xF4;                      /* Configure Port B */
    *PAOUT = 0x0;                       /* Turn off display */
    *PBOUT = 0x4;                       /* and LED */

    /* Start the test */
    while (1) {                         /* Infinite loop */
        while ((*PBIN & 0x2) == 0);     /* Wait for Go key to be pressed */

        /* Wait 3 seconds and then turn LED on */
        *CNTM = 0x11E1A300;             /* Set timer value to 300,000,000 */
        *CTCONT = 0x1;                  /* Start the timer */
        while ((*CTSTAT & 0x1) == 0);   /* Wait until timer reaches zero */
        *PBOUT = 0x0;                   /* Turn LED on */

        /* Initialize the counting process */
        counter_value = 0;
        *CNTM = 0xFFFFFFFF;             /* Set the starting counter value */
        *CTCONT = 0x1;                  /* Start counting */

        while ((*PBIN & 0x1) == 0);     /* Wait for the Stop key to be pressed */

        /* The Stop key has been pressed - stop counting */
        *PBOUT = 0x4;                   /* Turn LED off */
        *CTCONT = 0x2;                  /* Stop the counter */
        counter_value = *COUNT;         /* Read the contents of the counter */
```

Figure 9.20   C program for the reaction timer.

```
/* Compute the total count */
total_count = (0xFFFFFFFF − counter_value);

/* Convert count to time */ ;
actual_time = total_count / 1000000;        /* Time in hundredths of seconds */
seconds = actual_time / 100;
tenths = (actual_time − seconds * 100) / 10;
hundredths = actual_time − (seconds * 100 + tenths * 10);

/* Display the elapsed time */
*PAOUT = ((seconds << 4) | tenths);
*PBOUT = ((hundredths << 4) | 0x4);   /* Keep the LED turned off */
    }
}
```

Figure 9.20   (Continued)

PAOUT	EQU	$FFFFFFF1	Port A output data.
PADIR	EQU	$FFFFFFF2	Port A direction register.
PBIN	EQU	$FFFFFFF3	Port B input pins.
PBOUT	EQU	$FFFFFFF4	Port B output data.
PBDIR	EQU	$FFFFFFF5	Port B direction register.
CNTM	EQU	$FFFFFFD0	Initial counter value.
COUNT	EQU	$FFFFFFD4	Counter contents.
CTCONT	EQU	$FFFFFFD8	Control register.

```
* Initialization
            ORIGIN    $1000
            MoveByte  #$FF,PADIR        Configure Port A.
            MoveByte  #$F4,PBDIR        Configure Port B.

START       MoveByte  #0,PAOUT          Turn the display off.
            MoveByte  #4,PBOUT          Turn the LED off, by making PB2 = 1.

* Wait for Go key to be pressed
GKEY        Testbit   #1,PBIN           Go key is connected to PB1 pin.
            Branch=0   GKEY

* Delay 3 seconds before the LED is turned on
            Move      #11E1A300,CNTM    Timer value is 300,000,000.
            MoveByte  #1,CTCONT         Start the timer.
```

Figure 9.21   Assembly language program for the reaction timer using polling.

```
DELAY   Testbit     #0,CTCONT           Wait until timer
        Branch=0    DELAY                 reaches zero.
        MoveByte    #0,PBOUT            Turn the LED on.


* Initialize the counting process
        Move        #$FFFFFFFF,CNTM     Set the starting counter value.
        MoveByte    #1,CTCONT           Start counting.


* Wait for Stop key to be pressed
SKEY    Testbit     #0,PB               Stop key is connected
        Branch=0    SKEY                  to PB0 pin.


* Stop counting and read the last count
        MoveByte    #4,PBOUT            Turn the LED off, by making PB2 = 1.
        MoveByte    #2,CTCONT           Stop the counter.
        Move        COUNT,R0            Read the counter.


* Compute the total count
        Move        #$FFFFFFFF,R2       Determine the
        Subtract    R0,R2                 actual count.


* Convert the count to actual time in hundredths of seconds, and then to BCD.
* Put the 2 most-significant BCD digits in R4 and the least-significant digit in R3.
        Move        #1000000,R1         Determine the count in
        Divide      R1,R2                 hundredths of seconds.
        Move        #100,R1             Divide by 100 to find the digit that
        Divide      R1,R2                 denotes the number of seconds.
        Move        R2,R4               Save the digit in R4.
        Move        R3,R2               Use the remainder as the next dividend.
        Move        #10,R1              Divide by 10 to find the digit that
        Divide      R1,R2                 denotes 1/10th of a second.
        LShiftL     #4,R4               The first 2 BCD digits
        Or          R2,R4                 are placed in R4.


* Display the elapsed time
        MoveByte    R4,PAOUT            First 2 digits to Port A.
        LShiftL     #4,R3               Third digit to Port B
        Or          #4,R3                 and keep the LED
        MoveByte    R3,PBOUT              turned off.
        Branch      START               Ready for next test.
```

Figure 9.21 (Continued)

The BCD digits that denote the seconds and the tenths of a second of the elapsed time are placed into the least-significant byte of R4 to be sent to Port A for display. The third digit, denoting the hundredths of a second, is shifted in R3 into bit positions $R3_{7-4}$. Since the contents of R3 are sent to Port B, it is also necessary to set $R3_3 = 1$ to keep the LED turned off.

9.6.3 FINAL COMMENTS

The reaction timer is a fairly complete example of a computer-controlled application. This is in contrast to the examples in the previous chapters, which typically illustrated isolated features of a computer system.

An important aspect of software written for embedded systems is that it has to interact closely with hardware. The term *reactive system* is often used to describe the fact that the points in time at which various routines are executed are determined by events external to the processor, such as the closing of a switch or the arrival of a character at an input port. As discussed in Chapter 4, two mechanisms are available to coordinate this interaction — polling and interrupts. The software designer must decide how this interaction will be achieved.

9.7 EMBEDDED PROCESSOR FAMILIES

Having presented an example of an embedded processor in Section 9.3 and a simple application in Section 9.6, we now briefly consider the broad range of commercially available chips. Many embedded applications do not require a powerful processor. Certainly, the microwave oven discussed in Section 9.1.1 does not need a powerful controller because its computational requirements are rather modest. For such applications it is preferable to use a chip that has a simpler processor but which contains sufficient memory resources so that this is the only chip needed to implement all controller functions. The digital camera, discussed in Section 9.1.2, has much more demanding computational requirements, which dictates using a more powerful processor.

Processors may be characterized by how many data bits they handle in parallel when accessing data in the memory. The most powerful microcontrollers are likely to include a 32-bit processor, with a 32-bit-wide data bus. Such is the case with some microcontrollers based on the ARM architecture. It is also possible to have a processor that has an internal 32-bit structure, but a 16-bit-wide data bus to memory. An example is Motorola's 683xx family of microcontrollers, which use a 68000-based processor core. Such devices are classified as 16-bit microcontrollers. The most popular microcontrollers are 8-bit chips. They are much cheaper, yet powerful enough to satisfy the requirements of a large number of embedded applications. There exist even smaller 4-bit chips, which are attractive due to their simplicity and extremely low cost.

9.7.1 MICROCONTROLLERS BASED ON THE INTEL 8051

In the early 1980s, Intel Corporation introduced a microcontroller chip called the 8051. This chip has the basic architecture of Intel's 8080 microprocessor family, which used 8-bit chips for general-purpose computing applications. The 8051 chip gained rapid popularity. It has become one of the most widely used chips in practice. The 8051 has four 8-bit I/O ports, a UART, and two 16-bit counter/timer circuits. It also contains 4K bytes of ROM and 128 bytes of RAM storage. The EPROM version of the same chip, in which there are 4K bytes of EPROM rather than ROM, is available under the name 8751.

A number of other chips that are based on the 8051 architecture are available; they provide various enhancements. For example, the 8052 chip has 8K bytes of ROM and 256 bytes of RAM, as well as an extra counter/timer circuit. Its EPROM version is called 8752.

Microcontroller chips may be fabricated using either NMOS or CMOS technology. The CMOS devices have the advantage of consuming less power, hence they are particularly attractive for battery-driven applications. The CMOS versions of the above microcontrollers are known as 80C51 and 80C52.

The 8051 architecture was developed by Intel. Subsequently, a number of other semiconductor manufacturers have produced chips that are either identical to those in the 8051 family or have some enhanced features but are fully compatible. From the point of view of the designer of an embedded application, it is useful to have second sources of the chips used. This ensures a higher degree of availability of the chips and competitive prices.

9.7.2 MOTOROLA MICROCONTROLLERS

Intel and Motorola had the dominant positions as manufacturers of microprocessor chips in the 1980s. Their most popular 8-bit microprocessors became the basis for their microcontrollers. There is a wide range of Motorola microcontrollers, based on different processor cores.

68HC11 Microcontroller

Motorola's most popular 8-bit microprocessors were the 6800 and the 6809. A microcontroller chip that implements instructions that are a superset of 6800 instructions is known as the 68HC11. It has five I/O ports that can be used for a variety of purposes. The I/O structure includes two serial interfaces, one asynchronous and one synchronous. The asynchronous interface uses the start-stop protocol discussed in Section 10.3.1. The synchronous interface implements a scheme known as the *serial peripheral interface* (SPI). It is possible to connect up to eight analog inputs to the 68HC11 because the chip has the capability to perform A/D conversion. Finally, there are counter/timer circuits capable of operating in a number of different modes.

The amount of memory included on 68HC11 chips depends on the particular model. This typically ranges from an 8K-byte ROM, a 512-byte EEPROM, and a 256-byte

RAM in the original chip, to a 12K-byte ROM, a 512-byte EEPROM, and a 512-byte RAM in more advanced chips.

683xx Microcontrollers

A family of microcontrollers, known as 683xx, is based on the 68000 processor core. These chips include parallel and serial ports, counter/timer capability, and A/D conversion circuits. The amount of on-chip memory depends on the particular chip. For example, the 68376 chip has an 8K-byte EEPROM and a 4K-byte RAM.

ColdFire Microcontrollers

The 68000 instruction set architecture provides the basis for the MCF5xxx micro-controllers, known as the ColdFire embedded processors. Their distinguishing feature is a pipelined structure that leads to enhanced performance. They implement a full 32-bit bus. The ColdFire processor core is also intended for use in the system-on-a-chip environment, which is discussed in Section 9.9.

PowerPC Microcontrollers

Motorola's high-end microprocessors, known as PowerPC, are based on a RISC-style architecture. This processor architecture is also available in the microcontroller form, in chips comprising the MPC5xx family.

9.7.3 ARM MICROCONTROLLERS

The ARM architecture, presented in Chapter 3, is attractive for embedded systems where substantial computing capability is needed and the cost and power consumption have to be relatively low. A key objective has been to make the ARM processor designs suitable for use in the system-on-a-chip environment. The ARM microcontrollers are also available as separate chips.

There has been a progression of ARM processor cores intended for embedded applications, including ARM6, ARM7, ARM9, and ARM10. The basic ARM architecture uses a 32-bit organization and an instruction set in which all instructions are 32 bits long. There exists another version, known as Thumb, which uses 16-bit instructions and 16-bit data transfers. The Thumb version uses a subset of the ARM instructions, which are encoded to fit into a 16-bit format. It also has fewer registers than the ARM architecture. An advantage of Thumb is that a significantly smaller memory is needed to store programs that comprise highly encoded 16-bit instructions. At execution time, each Thumb instruction is expanded into a normal 32-bit ARM instruction. Thus, a Thumb-aware ARM core contains a *Thumb decompressor* in addition to its normal circuits.

The ARM architecture and processor cores have been developed by Advanced RISC Machines Ltd. A number of other companies are also licensed to provide these cores. Some companies, such as Atmel Corp., Sharp Electronics Corp., and Samsung Semiconductor Inc., market microcontroller chips based on ARM cores. For example, Atmel's AT91F40416 microcontroller uses the ARM7-TDMI Thumb-aware core, and it also contains 4K bytes of RAM, 526K bytes of Flash ROM, 32 programmable I/O lines, 2 serial ports, and a counter/timer circuit.

9.8 DESIGN ISSUES

The designer of an embedded system has to make many important decisions. The nature of the application or the product that has to be designed presents certain requirements and constraints. In this section, we will consider some of the most important issues that the designer faces.

Cost

The cost of electronics in many embedded applications has to be low. The cheapest solution is realized if a single microcontroller chip suffices for the implementation of all functions that must be provided. This is possible only if there is sufficient I/O capability and enough on-chip memory to hold the necessary software.

I/O Capability

Microcontroller chips provide a variety of I/O resources. This ranges from having simple parallel and serial ports to extensive support that includes counter, timer, A/D and D/A conversion circuits.

The number of available I/O lines is important. Without sufficient I/O lines it is necessary to use external circuitry to make up the shortfall. This is illustrated by the reaction-timer example in Figure 9.19, in which external decoder circuits are used to drive the 7-segment displays from the 4-bit BCD signals provided by the microcontroller. If the microcontroller had four parallel ports, rather than two, it would be possible to connect each seven-segment display to one port. The controlling program would then directly generate the output signals needed to drive the individual segments in the display.

Size

Microcontroller chips come in various sizes. If an application can be handled adequately with an 8-bit microcontroller, then it makes no sense to use a 16-bit chip which is likely to be more expensive, physically larger, and consume more power. The majority of practical applications can be handled with relatively small chips. In recent years, the largest number of chips sold have been of the 8-bit type, followed by the 4-bit and 16-bit types.

The physical size is important in terms of the area that the chip occupies on a printed circuit board. This area has significant cost implications.

Power Consumption

Power consumption is an important consideration in all computer applications. In high-performance systems the power consumption tends to be very high, requiring some mechanism to dissipate the heat generated. In many embedded applications the consumed power is low enough so that it is not necessary to worry about heat dissipation. However, these applications often involve battery powered products, so the life of the battery, determined by power consumption, is a key factor.

Power consumption is reduced if CMOS technology is used to fabricate the microcontroller chip. In CMOS technology, power consumption is proportional to clock frequency. If low performance suffices for a given application, then a lower clock frequency can be used to reduce power consumption. Another possible trade-off is with the functionality of the microcontroller chip. Reduced functionality means less circuitry on the chip, and thus lower power consumption.

On-Chip Memory

Inclusion of memory on a microcontroller chip allows single-chip implementations of simple embedded applications. The size and the type of memory have significant ramifications. A relatively small amount of RAM may be sufficient for storing data during computations. A larger read-only memory is needed to store programs. This memory may be of ROM, PROM, EPROM, EEPROM, or Flash type, characterized by increasing costs. For high-volume products, the most economical choices are microcontrollers with ROM. However, this is also the least flexible choice because the contents of the ROM are permanently implemented at the time the chip is manufactured. The PROM and EPROM types can be programmed at the time the embedded product is made. The greatest flexibility is offered by EEPROM and Flash memories, which can be programmed multiple times.

For applications that are computationally more demanding, it is necessary to use an external memory. Some microcontrollers do not have any on-chip memory. They are typically intended for sophisticated applications where a substantial amount of memory, which cannot be realized within the microcontroller chip, is needed.

Performance

Performance is not a big issue when microcontrollers are used in applications such as home appliances and toys, except in video games such as the Sony playstation. Small and inexpensive chips can be chosen in these cases. But, in applications such as cell phones and hand-held video games it is essential to have much higher performance. High performance demands more powerful chips, which results in higher cost and greater power consumption. Since the application is often battery powered, it is important to minimize power consumption. In Chapter 3, we discussed the ARM architecture. One implementation of this architecture is the StrongARM chip, which has been especially designed as a low-power processor that offers good performance. Thumb versions of the ARM architecture, discussed in Section 9.7.3, are intended for use in embedded applications in which both the cost and performance issues are critical.

Software

There are many advantages to using high-level languages for computer application programs. They facilitate the process of program development and make it easy to maintain and modify the software in the future. However, there are some instances when it may be prudent to resort to assembly language. A carefully written program in assembly language is likely to generate object code that is 10 to 20 percent more compact (in terms of the amount of storage needed) than the code produced by a compiler. If an embedded application is based on a microcontroller that has on-chip memory, it is a major advantage if the necessary code can fit into the memory provided on the chip, avoiding the need for external memory.

The designer should be careful not to overestimate the capability of the available on-chip RAM. This memory is used for storage of dynamic data, as a temporary buffer, and for implementing a stack. It is easy to write code that looks compact, for example in C language, but which requires more RAM than is available.

Instruction Set

Another significant issue is the nature of the instruction set of the processor used. CISC-like instructions lead to more compact code than RISC-like instructions. Thus, the choice of the processor has an impact on the size of the code. An interesting example is provided by the Thumb version of the ARM architecture, where a RISC-like instruction set designed for 32-bit processors has been modified into a more heavily encoded set using 16-bit instructions. Programs written for Thumb versions are up to 30 percent more compact than those written for the full ARM architecture. Recall that at execution time, the Thumb instructions are expanded into normal ARM instructions, as explained in Section 9.7.3.

Development Tools

Designers of digital systems rely heavily on development tools. These tools include software packages for computer aided design (CAD), operating system software, compilers, assemblers, and simulators for the processors. The range and the availability of tools often depends on the choice of the embedded processor. It is also attractive to have third-party support, where alternate sources of tools and documentation exist. Good documentation and helpful advice from the manufacturer (if needed) are extremely valuable.

Testability and Reliability

Printed circuit boards are often difficult to test, particularly if they are densely populated with chips. The testing process is greatly simplified if the entire system is designed to be easily testable. A microcontroller chip can include circuitry that makes it easier to test printed circuit boards that contain this chip. For example, some microcontrollers include a *test access port* that is compatible with the IEEE 1149.1 standard for a testable architecture, known as the Test Access Port and Boundary-Scan Architecture [1].

Embedded applications demand robustness and reliability. The life cycle of a typical product is expected to be at least five years. This is in contrast with personal computers, which tend to be considered obsolete in a shorter time.

9.9 S<small>YSTEM</small>-<small>ON</small>-<small>A</small>-C<small>HIP</small>

In an embedded application, it is desirable to use as few chips as possible. Ideally, a single chip would realize the entire system. In very simple applications, it is likely that some commercially available microcontrollers can realize all of the necessary functions. This is not the case in more complex applications. Some microcontroller chips are targeted for specific applications that would be difficult to implement with general-purpose microcontrollers. For example, a microcontroller intended for video games should include video and sound processing circuitry. The requirements would be quite different for microcontrollers used in a laser printer or in a cell phone.

Developing a complex microcontroller is a challenging task that takes time. Yet, the development time for most consumer products has to be short. A chip that implements an entire system for a specific application can be designed in a relatively short time if the designer makes use of some existing circuit modules that are available in an easy to use form. A microprocessor core is one of the needed modules. These cores can be obtained, through a licensing agreement, from a number of companies. Other modules that may be used to implement memory, A/D and D/A conversion circuits, or DSP (digital signal processing) circuits can also be obtained. The designer then completes the design by using the available modules and designing the rest of the required circuitry.

In Section 9.7.3, we mentioned that ARM cores have been designed to be used as modules in larger systems. Another interesting example is National Semiconductor's CompactRISC core. One of its features is the scalability from 8 to 64 bits. It has a simple 3-stage pipeline and an on-chip memory of 40K-byte ROM and 1.4K-byte RAM. A bus interface unit is added only when external memory is also needed. Thus, the complexity of the core can be adjusted to be commensurate with the functionality required by the application.

Providers of cores and other modules sell designs rather than chips. In effect, they are selling ideas rather than physical components. Their product is an example of an *intellectual property* (IP), which can be used by others to design their own chips.

9.9.1 FPGA IMPLEMENTATION

Field programmable gate arrays (FPGAs) provide an attractive medium for implementing systems on single chips. Unlike the microcontroller chips, which provide a designer with a set of predefined functional units, the FPGA devices allow complete freedom in the design process. They make it easy to include certain standard units and then build the rest of the system as desired. To illustrate the salient features of this approach, we will examine the Excalibur system available from Altera Corporation.

The functional capability of FPGAs has increased dramatically. A single large FPGA chip may implement a system that requires hundreds of thousands of logic gates. Such chips are large enough to implement the typical functionality of a microcontroller and other circuitry needed in a desired system.

The key component of any system on a chip is the processor core. The Excalibur system offers two distinct alternatives. One involves a processor that is defined in software. The other involves an FPGA chip that has a processor core implemented in silicon at the time of manufacture.

Soft Processor Core

The Excalibur system provides a software module, written in the Verilog hardware description language, which implements a processor architecture called Nios. This allows the designer to instantiate the processor as a readily available library module, which can be done using either a hardware description language, such as Verilog or

VHDL, or as a functional block using a schematic entry process. The designer can choose either a 32- or 16-bit version of the processor, depending on the performance requirements of the system.

A parallel interface module, similar to the one presented in Section 9.3.1, is available as a parameterized library module. The user can specify the parameters to suit the design requirements. The length of registers can be chosen in the range from 1 to 32 bits. The user can choose either the full bidirectional capability of the interface or a more limited version of it. For example, only the output port may be specified, in which case the output data register is provided, but the input path and the data direction register are not implemented. Thus, the FPGA resources are not wasted on unnecessary components.

A serial interface is available in the form of a UART circuit. The designer specifies the desired parameters, such as the number of data bits, the number of stop bits, and whether the parity bit should be used. The transmit/receive clock rate is selected from a predetermined standard range. This rate can later be changed by the application software, if desired, by including a divisor register that can be loaded with a value by which the clock frequency is to be divided. Again, the user is able to choose only the necessary features, and only the corresponding circuitry is implemented.

A timer module provides the counting and timing capability described in Section 9.3.3. Its operation is fully controlled by the application software.

Large FPGA chips contain a considerable amount of memory. The memory blocks can be used to implement the RAM and ROM parts of an embedded system if the memory size requirements are not too large. The designer can specify the size of the desired memory in terms of both the number of words and the number of bits per word. If the on-chip memory resources are insufficient, then an external memory interface can be instantiated, which results in the corresponding memory-bus signals being implemented on the pins of the FPGA chip.

The Excalibur CAD tools make it easy to design a system on an FPGA. They include a "wizard" which prompts the designer to enter the desired parameters and then generates the specified circuits. Thus, the processor and the I/O modules are implemented automatically. They are interconnected by a bus-like structure that implements the Nios bus protocol. We should note that a bus structure on an FPGA chip is not implemented using tri-state drivers, as discussed in Chapter 7. The FPGA is a general-purpose device that contains a large number of logic elements, interconnection wires, and switches. Tri-state drivers are useful for special purposes only; hence, they are not provided in a typical FPGA. The functionality of a tri-state bus can be implemented using multiplexer circuits. Instead of a single bidirectional path, separate multiplexers are used for each direction. While this approach requires many gates, it is a viable solution because the needed logic elements and interconnection resources are just a small fraction of the total FPGA resources.

The processor and the interface subsystem occupy a relatively small part of an FPGA chip. The rest of the chip is available for implementation of the application-specific circuitry. This circuitry can be connected either directly to the processor bus or perhaps more conveniently to the instantiated I/O ports. In the context of a system on a chip, an I/O port in the processor subsystem is not necessarily connected to an I/O pin of the FPGA device. Instead, the designer may use it to connect the application-specific circuitry implemented on the FPGA to the processor system.

The Nios processor has a RISC-like instruction set. It is capable of delivering performance up to 50 MIPS (millions of instructions per second). The designer may choose to implement more than one Nios processor on the same FPGA, thus implementing a multiprocessor system.

Hard Processor Core

An alternative to the soft processor core approach is to implement the processor in silicon, thus creating a specialized FPGA. The Excalibur system provides for such FPGAs based on different processors. One example is an FPGA that has an ARM processor core implemented in one part of the device. In addition to the processor circuits, the ARM processor bus, a RAM module, and a UART serial module are also implemented in silicon. This allows implementation of considerably higher-performance systems. The rest of the chip consists of the normal FPGA resources. Using a hard processor core, the system can deliver performance in the range of hundreds of MIPS.

Designer's View

The designer of an embedded system inevitably looks for the simplest and most cost-effective approach. A microcontroller chip that has the resources to implement an entire system may be the best choice. The situation is different if additional chips are needed to realize the system. Then, FPGA solutions become attractive because they are likely to need fewer chips to implement the system.

Another consideration is the availability of predesigned modules. A microcontroller chip contains a number of different modules, and any feature that cannot be realized using these modules has to be implemented using additional chips. An FPGA device allows the designer to design any type of digital circuit. Many practical designs involve circuits that perform commonly used tasks. Such circuits should be available as library modules. This is obviously the case with I/O interfaces and timer circuits. It is very convenient if other useful modules are available. For signal processing applications, the library should include typical filter circuits and fast multipliers. If the designed system is to be connected to another computer via a standard bus, such as PCI, the designer's task is much simpler if a PCI interface is available as a predesigned module.

9.10 CONCLUDING REMARKS

This chapter has provided an introduction to the design of a complete embedded computer system in the context of simple applications. We have not used a specific microcontroller because the principles presented are general. They deal with the key issues that face the designer of an embedded system.

It is particularly important to appreciate the close interaction of hardware and software. The design choices may involve trade-offs between polled I/O and interrupts, between different instruction sets in terms of functionality and compactness of code, between power consumption and performance, and so on.

The already large and still rapidly expanding world of embedded applications provides tremendous opportunities for creative use of computer technology. A number of books have been published that focus on embedded systems [2–4].

PROBLEMS

9.1　The microcontroller in Section 9.3 receives decimal digits (0 to 9) encoded as ASCII characters on its serial port. As each digit arrives, it has to be displayed on a 7-segment display unit connected to parallel Port A. Show the connections needed to accomplish this function. Label the segments of the display unit as indicated in Figure A.33. Write a C-language program to perform the required task. Use polling to detect the arrival of each ASCII character.

9.2　Write an assembly language program to implement the task of Problem 9.1.

9.3　Solve Problem 9.1 by using interrupts to detect the arrival of each ASCII character.

9.4　Write an assembly language program for Problem 9.3.

9.5　The microcontroller in Section 9.3 receives decimal numbers on its serial port. Each number consists of two digits encoded as ASCII characters. In order to distinguish between successive 2-digit numbers, a delimiter character H is used. Thus, if two successive numbers are 43 and 28, the received sequence will be H43H28. Each number is to be displayed on two 7-segment displays connected to parallel ports A and B. The delimiter character should not be displayed. The displayed number should change only when both digits of the next number have been received. Show the connections needed to accomplish this function. Label the segments of the display unit as indicated in Figure A.33. Write a C-language program to perform the required task. Use polling to detect the arrival of each ASCII character.

9.6　Write an assembly language program to implement the task of Problem 9.5.

9.7　Solve Problem 9.5 by using interrupts to detect the arrival of each ASCII character.

9.8　Write an assembly language program for Problem 9.7.

9.9　The microcontroller in Section 9.3 receives decimal numbers on its serial port. Each number consists of four digits encoded as ASCII characters. In order to distinguish between successive 4-digit numbers, a delimiter character H is used. Thus, if two successive numbers are 2143 and 6292, the received sequence will be H2143H6292. Each number is to be displayed on four 7-segment display units. Assume that each display unit has a BCD-to-7-segment decoder circuit associated with it, as shown in Figure P9.1.

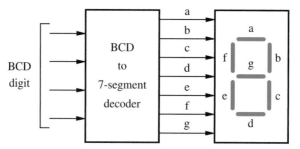

Figure P9.1　A 7-segment display with a BCD decoder.

Show the necessary connection to the microcontroller. Write a C-language program to perform the required task. Use polling to detect the arrival of each ASCII character.

9.10 Write an assembly language program to implement the task of Problem 9.9.

9.11 Solve Problem 9.9 by using interrupts to detect the arrival of each ASCII character.

9.12 Write an assembly language program to implement the task of Problem 9.11.

9.13 Repeat Problem 9.9, but assume that each 7-segment display unit has a 7-bit register associated with it, rather than a BCD-to-7-segment decoder. The register has a control input *Load*, such that the seven data bits are loaded into the register when *Load* = 1. Each bit in the register drives one segment of the associated display unit. Figure P9.2 shows the register-display arrangement. Arrange the microcontroller output connections such that the parallel port A provides the data for all four display units.

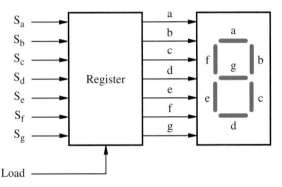

Figure P9.2 A 7-segment display with a register.

9.14 Repeat Problem 9.13, but write the program using assembly language.

9.15 Solve Problem 9.13 by using interrupts to detect the arrival of each ASCII character.

9.16 Write an assembly language program to implement the task of Problem 9.15.

9.17 In Section 9.5 we assumed that the source device generates characters in bursts of less than 80 characters. Would the programs in Figures 9.17 and 9.18 work properly if bursts of up to 80 characters are allowed? If not, show a modification to these programs.

9.18 In the program in Figure 9.17, the test for determining whether the circular buffer is empty is performed by checking if the *fin* and *fout* indexes have the same value. Instead, it is possible to introduce a counter variable, M, that indicates the current number of characters in the buffer. Modify the program using this approach.

9.19 Repeat Problem 9.18 for the program in Figure 9.18.

9.20 Modify the reaction timer presented in Section 9.6 assuming that the tested person will always respond in less than one second. Thus, the elapsed reaction time should be displayed as two digits representing the hundredths of a second. Connect the two 7-segment display units to Port A and modify the programs in Figures 9.20 and 9.21 to implement the desired operation.

9.21   In Figure 9.19, the 7-segment display unit for each digit incorporates a BCD-to-7-segment decoder; hence the microcontroller provides simultaneously a 4-bit BCD code for each digit that is to be displayed. Suppose that instead of using the decoder, each 7-segment unit has a 7-bit register with a control input *Load,* such that the seven data bits are loaded into the register when *Load* = 1. Each bit in the register drives one segment of the associated display unit. Figure P9.2 shows the register-display arrangement. Augment the programs in Figures 9.20 and 9.21 for use with this register-display circuit.

9.22   In Figure 9.21, a binary number representing the elapsed reaction time in hundredths of seconds is converted into an equivalent BCD number using successive divisions by 100 and 10. Another way of implementing this conversion is to perform successive divisions by 10, in which case the remainder obtained after each division is a desired BCD digit. What is the order of the digits produced this way? Modify the program in Figure 9.21 to perform the conversion in this way.

9.23   Use the microcontroller in Section 9.3 to generate a "time of day" clock. The time (in hours and minutes) is to be displayed on four 7-segment display units. Assume that each display unit has a BCD-to-7-segment decoder associated with it, as shown in Figure P9.1. Assume also that a 100-MHz clock is used. Show the required hardware connections and write a suitable program.

9.24   Repeat Problem 9.20 assuming that each 7-segment display unit has a register associated with it, as shown in Figure P9.2.

9.25   In a system implemented on a single chip, the processor and the main memory reside on the same chip. Is there a need for a cache in this system? Explain.

REFERENCES

1. *Test Access Port and Boundary-Scan Architecture,* IEEE Standard 1149.1, May 1990.

2. W. Wolf, *Computers as Components — Principles of Embedded Computing System Design,* Morgan Kaufmann Publishers, San Francisco, CA., 2001.

3. K. Hintz and D. Tabak, *Microcontrollers,* McGraw-Hill, New York, 1992.

4. J. B. Peatman, *Design with Microcontrollers,* McGraw-Hill, New York, 1988.

10

COMPUTER PERIPHERALS

CHAPTER OBJECTIVES

In this chapter you will learn about:

- How computer input and output devices work
- The operation of scanners and printers
- Graphics cards and processing of graphical images
- Synchronous and asynchronous serial data links
- High-speed Internet connections using ADSL and cable modems

In previous chapters, we discussed hardware and software features of processors, memories, disks, and CD ROMs. We also discussed the means by which a computer communicates with external devices, including the hardware and software facilities that support program-controlled I/O, interrupts, and direct memory access. This chapter presents the characteristics of some commonly used computer peripherals and how they are connected in a computer system.

The name *peripheral* refers to any external device connected to a computer. In this context, the computer consists only of the processor and its memory. Computer peripherals can be divided into two categories, according to function. The first category contains devices that perform input and output operations, such as the keyboard, mouse, trackball, printer, and video display. The second category contains devices intended primarily for secondary storage of data, with primary storage being provided by the main memory of the computer. Some mass storage devices, in particular magnetic disks, are used for *on-line storage* of data. In others, such as optical disks, floppy disks, and magnetic tapes, the storage medium can be removed from the drive unit for transferring data from one computer system to another. For example, the device most often used for distributing software is the optical disk, also know as a CD ROM. Secondary storage devices are discussed in Chapter 5.

Today, among the most important computer peripherals are devices that provide connection to the Internet. Much of the tremendous growth in the computer field in recent years is a result of the synergy between computers and communications, and the emergence of many innovative applications on the World Wide Web. These developments have touched every aspect of our lives, from business to entertainment and education.

In this chapter, we present an overview of the variety of input and output devices used in modern computer systems and give a brief description of the underlying technology. Devices that are outside the computer box often use a serial link, either wired or wireless, to communicate with the processor. We will present some of the basic ideas for serial communications.

10.1   INPUT DEVICES

Input devices include keyboards and devices used to move the cursor on the screen, such as the mouse, trackball, and joystick. Scanners and digital cameras are also extensively used to capture images and feed them into the computer in the form of digital data.

10.1.1   KEYBOARD

The most commonly encountered input device is a keyboard, usually complemented by a mouse or a trackball. Together with a video display as an output device, they are used for direct human interaction with the computer.

Keyboards are available in two types. One type consists of an array of mechanical switches mounted on a printed-circuit board. The switches are organized in rows and columns and connected to a microcontroller on the board. When a switch is pressed, the controller identifies the row and column, and thus determines which key is being pressed. After correcting for switch bounce (see Chapter 4), the controller generates a code representing that switch and sends it over a serial link to the computer.

The second type uses a flat structure consisting of three layers. The top layer is a plasticized material, with key positions marked on the top surface and conducting traces deposited on the underside. The middle layer is made of rubber, with holes at key positions. The bottom layer is metallic, with raised bumps at key positions. When pressure is applied to the top layer at a key position, the trace underneath comes in contact with the corresponding bump on the bottom layer, thus completing an electrical circuit in the same way as a mechanical switch. The current that flows in this circuit is sensed by the microcontroller. This arrangement provides a low-cost keyboard that also has the advantage of being robust and immune to problems caused by spilt food or drink. Such keyboards are commonly encountered in applications such as point-of-sale terminals.

10.1.2 MOUSE

The invention of the mouse in 1968 represented an important step in the development of new means for people to communicate with computers. Up to that point, text was the primary form of data entry. The mouse made it possible to enter graphic information directly, by drawing the desired objects, and opened the door to many new and powerful ideas, including windows and pull-down menus.

The mouse is a device shaped to fit comfortably in the operator's hand, such that it can be moved over a flat surface. An electronic circuit senses this movement and sends some measure of the distance traveled in the X and Y directions to the computer. Movement is monitored either mechanically or optically. A mechanical mouse is fitted with a ball mounted such that it can rotate freely as the mouse is moved. The rotation of the ball is sensed and used to advance two counters, one for each of the two axes of motion. The mouse is also fitted with two or three pushbuttons. The information from the counters and the buttons is collected by a microcontroller, encoded as a 3-byte packet, and sent to the computer over a serial link.

An optical mouse uses a light-emitting diode (LED) to illuminate the surface on which the mouse is placed, and a light-sensitive device senses the light reflected from the surface. In some models, the mouse must be placed on a special pad that has a pattern of vertical and horizontal lines. The reflected light changes as the mouse moves from light to dark areas on the surface underneath, and the mouse measures the distance traveled by counting these changes.

A much more sophisticated optical mouse, dubbed IntelliMouse, was introduced by Microsoft in 1999. It can be used with almost any surface. Instead of a simple light sensor, the image of a small area of the surface underneath is focused on a tiny digital camera, which converts the image into a digital representation. The camera takes 1500 such pictures every second. Unless the surface is perfectly uniform and smooth, such as a mirror, its image will contain features such as lines, changes in brightness, and so on. By comparing successive images, a processor inside the mouse is able to measure the distance traveled with considerable accuracy. The processor uses a signal-processing technique known as correlation to determine the distance traveled from one picture to the next. This is a computationally intensive task that must be repeated 1500 times each second. It is made possible only by the availability of powerful yet low-cost embedded processors. The processor used executes 18 million instructions per second.

Since the invention of the mouse, a number of devices have been introduced that perform the same function. These include the trackball, the joystick and the touchpad.

10.1.3 TRACKBALL, JOYSTICK, AND TOUCHPAD

The mouse enables an operator to move a cursor on a computer screen. A host of innovative input devices have been developed to perform a similar function, to suit various application environments and user preferences.

The operating principles of a *trackball* are very similar to those of a mechanical mouse. A ball is mounted in a shallow well on the keyboard. The user rotates the ball to indicate the desired movement of the cursor on the screen.

The *joystick* is a short, pivoted stick that can be moved by hand to point in any direction in the X-Y plane. When this information is sent to the computer, the software moves the cursor on the screen in the same direction.

The position of the stick can be sensed by a suitable linear or angular position transducer, such as the potentiometer arrangement shown in Figure 10.1. The voltage outputs of the X and Y potentiometers are fed to two analog-to-digital (A/D) converters, whose outputs determine the position of the joystick and, thus, the desired direction of motion.

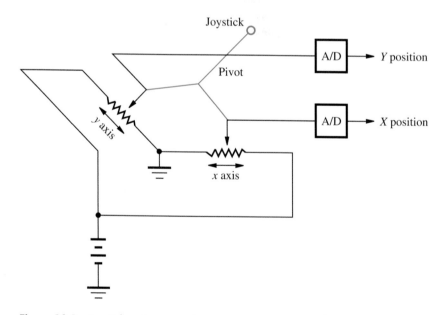

Figure 10.1   Joystick, using potentiometers as position transducers.

Joysticks are found in notebook computers and video games. In the case of a notebook computer, the joystick is mounted among the keys of the keyboard and sticks slightly above them. By virtue of its positioning, the joystick has the advantage of not requiring the operator's hand to be moved off the keyboard. It can be pushed with one finger to position the cursor on the screen. It is also mechanically robust and requires very little space. For use in video games, the joystick is shaped into a handle that suits the nature of the game. It is usually equipped with pushbuttons to be used for such purposes as shooting a ball or firing a gun.

Another very useful input device is the touchpad and its close relative, the touch screen. The touchpad is a small pad made of pressure-sensitive material. When the user's finger or the tip of a pen touches some point on the pad, the pressure causes a change in the electrical characteristics of the material at that spot. The location of the spot is detected and communicated to the computer. By moving a finger across the pad, the user can instruct the software to move the cursor on the screen in the same direction. This makes the touchpad a low-cost replacement for the mouse or the trackball, with a high degree of robustness and reliability because it contains no moving parts. Touchpads are well suited to notebook computers.

Many new materials have been developed for use as touchpads. Perhaps the most innovative is one that has a large number of tiny optical fibers embedded in it. The material can identify the location of an object touching it as well as the amount of pressure being applied. This material was developed for robotic applications in space. It is rapidly finding other applications, for example as an input device replacing and expanding the role of the piano keyboard.

A touchpad can be combined with a liquid-crystal display to produce a touch-sensitive screen that can be used for both input and output operations. This type of screen is commonly found in personal digital assistants (PDAs), such as the Palm Pilot. Another form of touch screen uses a cathode-ray tube (CRT). The change in capacitance caused by a finger touching the screen is sensed as the electron beam scans the screen to display an image. This arrangement is commonly found in cash registers and point-of-sale terminals.

10.1.4   SCANNERS

Scanners transform printed material and photographs into digital representations. In early scanners, the page to be scanned was mounted on a glass cylinder which rotates around the sensors. Most scanners today use a flat-bed arrangement, in which the page being scanned is placed over a flat glass surface. A source of light scans the page, and the reflected light is focused on a linear array of charge-coupled devices (CCDs). When a CCD device is exposed to light, an electrical charge is stored in a tiny capacitor associated with it such that the amount of charge is proportional to the intensity of the light. This charge is collected by appropriate circuitry and converted to a digital representation using an analog-to-digital converter. For color scanners, red, green, and blue filters are used to separate the primary colors and process them separately. As the light source moves across the page, the sensor array is read repeatedly, thus sampling successive lines of pixels of the image. It should be noted that these techniques are also used in digital copiers. A digital copier is, in effect, a combination of a scanner and a laser printer.

After scanning a printed page into a computer, the image is represented in the memory as an array of pixels. In its simplest form, each pixel is represented by one bit, indicating whether the corresponding spot on the image is light or dark. For higher quality images, more information is stored for each pixel to represent the color and intensity of light at that spot. Up to three bytes of information per pixel may be used, with one byte for each of the three primary colors.

Consider the case of a page of text. The dark areas of the image correspond to the printed characters. Many character recognition techniques have been developed that make it possible to analyze the pixel map stored in the memory and recognize the characters in the image. Thus, it becomes possible to create a text file that describes the contents of the printed page, with each character translated to a suitable binary code, such as ASCII. The resulting file may then be processed by a text-processing program such as Word.

10.2 OUTPUT DEVICES

Computer output may take a variety of forms, including alphanumeric text, graphical images, or sound. We describe below some of the commonly used output devices.

10.2.1 VIDEO DISPLAYS

Video displays are used whenever visual representation of computer output is needed. The most common display device uses a cathode-ray tube (CRT).

Let us start by describing how a picture is formed on a CRT. A focused beam of electrons strikes a fluorescent screen, causing emission of light that is seen as a bright spot against a dark background. The dot thus formed disappears when the beam is turned off or moved to another spot. Thus, in general, three independent variables need to be specified at all times, representing the position and intensity of the beam. The position of the beam corresponds to the X and Y coordinates of the spot on the screen. Its intensity, which is usually referred to as the Z-axis control, provides the *gray scale* or brightness information at that spot. The smallest addressable spot on the screen is called a pixel. It consists of a number of smaller dots of different sizes, arranged in some geometrical pattern. By illuminating these dots in various combinations, different levels of brightness can be obtained. This technique is known as *half-toning*. In color displays, each pixel has three different colors of fluorescent dots, red, green, and blue. Different colors are obtained by exciting these dots in different combinations.

The size of the spot formed on the screen by the electron beam determines the total number of pixels in an image. This is usually in the range of 700 to 2500 points along each of the X and Y coordinates. The Z-axis information is described in up to 24 bits, consisting of one byte for each color. This is judged to yield the highest color resolution that can be perceived by the human eye. The most common standard for computer video displays is VGA (Video Graphics Array) and its higher-quality variants. The basic VGA display has 640×480 pixels. Variations of this standard specify displays with higher resolution, such as 1024×768 (XVGA) and 1600×1200 (UXGA).

Both alphanumeric text and graphical pictures can be constructed using a technique called *raster scan*. The electron beam is swept successively across each row of pixels from left to right, until all rows have been scanned from the top to the bottom of the screen. Many video displays use *interlacing* to increase the perceived rate at which the screen is refreshed. The beam scans the screen in two passes, once for all odd-numbered rows and once for even-numbered rows. The image being displayed is stored in a *display buffer* memory that provides the Z-axis information during scanning. In the simplest representation, a *bit map* consisting of one bit for each pixel can be used to describe the image to be displayed on the screen. Hence, a screen with 1024×1024 pixels requires a 1M-bit display buffer memory. To refresh the display at the rate of 60 times per second, the data rate is 60 megabits/s. Today's high-quality displays use 32 bits per pixel, thus requiring much larger display buffers and communication bandwidth. Usually, only 24 of the 32 bits store color information. The fourth byte provides for compatibility with the word length of the host processor. It also provides room for future enhancements. Modern systems have the capability to overlap multiple distinct screen images, as in the case of window-based operating systems, and hence require several separate display buffers.

10.2.2 FLAT-PANEL DISPLAYS

Although cathode-ray tube technology has dominated display applications, flat-panel displays are becoming increasingly popular. They are thinner and lighter in weight. They provide better linearity and, in some cases, even higher resolution. Several types of flat-panel displays have been developed, including liquid-crystal panels, plasma panels, and electroluminescent panels. The availability of low-cost flat-panel displays has been instrumental in the development of notebook computers.

Liquid-crystal panels are constructed by sandwiching a thin layer of liquid crystal — a liquid that exhibits crystalline properties — between two transparent plates. The top plate has transparent electrodes deposited on it, and the back plate is a mirror. By applying appropriate electrical signals across the plates, various segments of the liquid crystal can be activated, causing changes in their light-diffusing or polarizing properties. Thus, these segments either transmit or block the light. An image is produced by passing light through selected segments of the liquid crystal and then reflecting it back from the mirror to the viewer. Liquid-crystal displays are found in watches, calculators, notebook computers, and many other devices.

Liquid-crystal displays come in two varieties. Static displays have a simple structure in which electrodes are deposited along one axis on the top plate and along an orthogonal axis on the lower plate, thus defining columns and rows. To illuminate a particular segment, a voltage is applied between one row electrode and one column electrode. This creates an electric field that causes the liquid crystal at their intersection point to turn on, and a bright spot is displayed. Displays that use this arrangement are simple to build and inexpensive, but the quality of the images they produce is low. The illuminated area is not well defined, so edges in the image are not sharp. Also, the long electrodes have a large capacitance, hence the speed with which a spot can be turned on or off is low. For example, if the cursor is moved across the screen quickly, the slow response causes a tail to be seen following the cursor.

A higher-quality display is produced by introducing a transistor at each intersection point. This provides faster response and better control over the area to be illuminated. The transistors are prepared on a thin film deposited on one of the plates. Hence this type of display is called a *thin-film transistor* (TFT) display. It is also known as an *active matrix* display. This is the type of display most commonly found in high-quality notebook computers.

Plasma panels consist of two glass plates separated by a thin gap filled with a gas such as neon. Each plate has several parallel electrodes running across it. The electrodes on the two plates run at right angles to each other. A voltage pulse applied between two electrodes, one on each plate, causes a small segment of gas at the intersection of the two electrodes to glow. The glow of gas segments is maintained by a lower voltage that is continuously applied to all electrodes. A similar pulsing arrangement is used to selectively turn points off. Plasma displays can provide high resolution but are rather expensive. They are found in applications where display quality is important and the bulky size of a cathode-ray tube is undesirable.

Electroluminescent panels use a thin layer of phosphor between two electrically conducting panels. The image is created by applying electrical signals to the plates, making the phosphor glow.

The viability of flat-panel displays for different applications is closely linked to developments in the competing cathode-ray tube display technology, which continues to provide a good combination of price and performance and permits easy implementation of color displays.

10.2.3 PRINTERS

Printers are used to produce hard copy of output data or text. They are usually classified as being either an impact or nonimpact type, depending on the nature of the printing mechanism used. Impact printers use mechanical printing mechanisms, and nonimpact printers rely on optical, ink-jet, or electrostatic techniques.

Nonimpact printers have few moving parts and can be operated at high speed. Laser printers use the same technology as photocopiers. A drum coated with positively charged photoconductive material is scanned by a laser beam. The positive charges that are illuminated by the beam are dissipated. Then a negatively charged toner powder is spread over the drum. It adheres to the positive charges, thus creating a page image that is then transferred to the paper. The drum is cleaned of any excess toner material to prepare it for printing the next page.

Other types of nonimpact printers use ink jets, in which droplets of different color inks are fired at the paper from tiny nozzles, to generate color output. A variety of techniques are used to fire the ink droplets. For example, in a *bubble ink-jet printer,* the nozzle is attached to a small chamber to which a heat pulse is applied. This causes the ink in the chamber to evaporate, forming a gas bubble that pushes a small amount of ink out of the nozzle. As the gas in the chamber cools down, it creates a vacuum that sucks in a new charge of ink. Ink-jet printers are generally more expensive than laser printers, and they produce higher-quality images.

Most printers form characters and graphic images in the same way that images are formed on a video screen, that is, by printing dots in matrices. This arrangement can easily accommodate a variety of fonts and can also be used for printing graphical images. However, because of the sensitivity of the human eye to regular patterns, a regular dot matrix is easily detected and interferes with the perceived quality of the image. High-quality printers use a technique called *dithering* to overcome this difficulty. Recall that a pixel consists of several dots, each having one of three colors. Dithering means that the geometrical arrangement of the dots in a pixel and the assignment of colors to each dot are varied. This breaks the monotony of a regular pattern and gives the appearance of having more color choices.

The highest quality printing is needed in applications such as graphic arts and photographic printing. Ink-jet printers that use a technique known as dye sublimation are suitable for these applications. They are also the most expensive. In this case, the temperature to which the ink is heated is controlled to change the amount of ink fired at the paper. Thus, the color intensity of each dot can be varied continuously. Also, special paper is used in which the ink diffuses, producing precisely controlled colors.

10.2.4 GRAPHICS ACCELERATORS

Many computer applications involve high-quality graphic images. Perhaps the most familiar use of graphics is in video games. Other applications include artistic work, medical imaging, and animated films. A high-quality image requires a large number of pixels to be displayed. Before an image is sent to a display screen, the color of each of these pixels has to be computed and stored in a memory buffer. From there, the information is sent to the screen at a rate of at least 30 times per second to keep the displayed image refreshed.

The task of computing pixel intensity and color can be done in software. The resulting image can be stored in a screen buffer in the computer's main memory, from where it can be sent to the display over the computer bus. However, the shear volume of data that need to be handled is such that this approach can easily swamp the processor and leave little computing power for other tasks. Also, using the computer bus to transfer the contents of the screen buffer to the display would consume a considerable portion of the bus bandwidth. With 32 bits per pixel, a 1024×1024-pixel image is represented by 4M bytes of data, which would create a minimum of 120 megabytes/s of traffic on the memory bus.

Most graphics applications require the ability to display three-dimensional (3D) objects. In computer games, for example, an artificial 3D world is created, with full-video images, entirely in software. The task of creating these images is computationally intensive. The most practical solution is to provide by a special-purpose processor, designed specifically to handle these intensive computations. Such a processor, known as a graphics-processing unit (GPU), is the basis of the popular graphics cards installed in most personal computers. The graphics card also includes a large high-speed memory, typically ranging from 8M to 64M bytes. This memory is used by the GPU while performing the computations, and it also stores the resulting image to be sent to the display screen. The display is connected directly to the graphics card, so that data transfers for refreshing the screen do not use the computer bus. A high-quality graphics card is capable of refreshing the screen between 75 and 200 times per second.

Graphics Port

The graphics card may be plugged into a computer bus such as PCI. More often, the computer motherboard includes a special connection slot known as the Accelerated Graphics Port (AGP), into which the graphics card is inserted. This is a 32-bit port that is capable of supporting higher data transfer rates than can be achieved on the PCI bus. It is usually described as AGP 1x, 2x, 4x, or 8x, where AGP 1x is the original standard which provides a data transfer rate of 264 megabytes/s. Later standards support multiples of this rate, with AGP 8x providing 2 gigabytes/s.

Graphics Processing

In computer graphics, a three-dimensional object is represented by dividing its surface into a large number of small polygons, usually triangles. The first task is to convert the 3D scene into a 2D representation that matches as closely as possible the image that would be seen by the human eye. *Projection* and *perspective* calculations determine the locations in the two-dimensional image of the vertices of the triangles representing various objects in the scene. Then, complex algorithms are used to determine appropriate color and shading for each of the triangles to create a realistic image. These computations take into account the lighting sources on the scene, reflections from various surfaces, shadows, and so on. An important step in this process is to give some texture to the surface, such as the appearance of wood grain or a brick wall. The texture is usually created using elements called *texels*. An array of texels is applied to individual image triangles to create the impression of a textured surface on the original three-dimensional object. Hidden parts of the scene are eliminated in a process known as *clipping* to save unnecessary computations. The final step is *sampling,* in which the image is sampled to determine the color and intensity of each image pixel. The entire computational process that reduces a 3D scene to a description of the pixels to be sent to the display is known as *rendering.*

For moving images, these computations must be repeated many times each second. To create the appearance of smooth motion on the screen, the image pixels must be recomputed at least 20 times per second, usually 30 to 40 times per second, to produce a high-quality video picture. This is called the *frame rate.* The ability of a video card to perform the required computations is often measured by its T&L (Transformations and Lighting) rating, which is the number of triangles per second for which the card can complete all the computations needed for projection, clipping, lighting, and sampling. Typical ratings are in the range 10 to 30 million triangles per second.

As an example, the salient characteristics of the RADEON VE graphics card manufactured by ATI Corp. are given in Table 10.1. The GeForce 2 MX graphics processor manufactured by *n*Vidia Corp. offers very similar capabilities. Both are popular for use in personal computers. Professional versions with enhanced capabilities are also available. Much more powerful processors can be expected in the near future in this rapidly expanding segment of the computer industry.

Table 10.1 RADEON VE graphics card

Feature	Description
GPU chip	RADEON VE
Bus	AGP 4x
Memory	Up to 64M bytes, DDR SDRAM
Color	32 bits, including 8 bits reserved for future use
Pixels	2048 × 1536
T&L rating	30M triangles per second
Screen refresh rate	75 to 200, where higher rates are for lower-resolution images
Additional capabilities	Provisions for use with TV, VCR, DVD, HDTV, and MPEG 2 compression

Graphics Software

Graphics cards offer a variety of sophisticated features. Making use of these features requires software designed specifically for the card. There are very few standards in this area, and the market is wide open for competition. Simply installing a better graphics card in a computer will not automatically improve the quality of the images produced. Specialized software for use with this card is needed. Some application programming interface (API) standards for graphics software are beginning to emerge. The objective of these standards is to enable hardware-independent software to be developed. Thus, the software for a computer game, for example, would work well with graphics cards manufactured by different companies and would be able to make use of the features that each provides. OpenGL (Open Graphics Language) is an example of such a standard. Increasingly, graphics cards are being designed for compatibility with this and a number of similar standards that relate to various aspects of graphics processing.

10.3 SERIAL COMMUNICATION LINKS

Devices such as the keyboard and mouse are connected directly to the computer with which they are used, typically through a serial communication link. Other devices, such as printers and scanners, may be connected to a computer either directly or via a communication network, so that they may be shared among several users. As the Internet plays an important role in many computer applications, a computer is often connected to the Internet either permanently or over dialed telephone links.

In the remainder of this chapter, we discuss some of the schemes that are commonly used in serial communication links. We start by presenting some basic ideas.

Modulation and Demodulation

In a digital circuit, we represent one bit by an electrical signal that has one of two voltage values, as we have seen elsewhere in this book. When the same representation is used over a communication link, the link is said to use *baseband*. An alternative scheme in which 0s and 1s are represented by modulating a sinusoidal *carrier signal* is also widely used. This is called *broadband* transmission. For example, the signal frequency may be changed between two values, f_1 to represent a 0 and f_2 to represent a 1. In this case, the link is said to use *frequency modulation* or *frequency shift keying* (FSK). Many other modulation schemes are in use. The phase of the carrier signal may be changed to provide *phase shift keying* (PSK) or its amplitude may be changed to provide *amplitude modulation* (AM). A scheme known as *quadrature amplitude modulation* (QAM) combines amplitude and phase modulation of the carrier signal. Since two parameters are being changed, there are four possible combinations. Hence, the transmitted signal can represent two bits of information.

The signal configuration transmitted in any clock period time is called a *symbol*. Thus, in the FSK scheme, there are two possible symbols, each consisting of a sinusoidal signal with a frequency f_1 or f_2. In QAM, four possible symbols are available, defined by their amplitude and phase. The term *baud* rate refers to the number of symbols transmitted per second. Equivalently, it is the number of times the state of a signal changes per second. This is the same as the rate of data transmission in bits per second only in the case of a binary modulation scheme, such as FSK. For QAM, the bit rate is twice the baud rate, because each symbol represents two bits of information. There exist modulation schemes that use 8, 16, or more symbols. In a system with 16 symbols, each symbol represents 4 bits. Hence, the bit rate is four times the baud rate.

A device called a *modem* (MOdulator-DEModulator) is installed at each end of a communications link to perform the desired signal transformations, as shown in Figure 10.2. The figure shows a computer connected to a network server. This could be a permanent connection or a dialed connection over a telephone line.

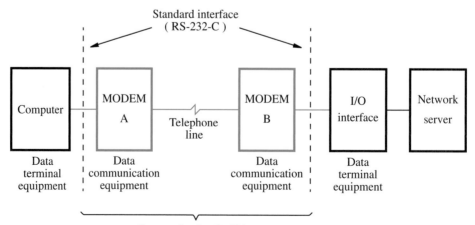

Figure 10.2 Remote connection to a network.

Synchronization

Serial communications means that data are sent one bit at a time. This requires that both the transmitting and the receiving devices use the same timing information for interpretation of individual bits. When the communicating devices are physically close to each other and multiple signal paths are available, a clock signal can be transmitted along with the data. However, this is not feasible over longer links, where only one signal path is available. More importantly, even if a second path is provided, the delays encountered by the data and the clock signals could be different. For these reasons, timing information and data are encoded on one transmission channel. A variety of encoding schemes have been developed that enable the receiver to decode the received signal and recover the timing and transmitted data correctly.

There are two basic ways of realizing serial transmission. For data transmission at speeds not exceeding a few tens of kilobits per second, a simple scheme can be used in which the sender and receiver use independent clock signals having the same nominal frequency. No attempt is made to guarantee that the two clocks have exactly the same phase or frequency. Hence, this scheme is called asynchronous transmission. The start-stop scheme to be described shortly is a common example of this approach.

Synchronous transmission is needed to transmit data at higher speed. In this case, the receiver recovers the clock timing used by the transmitter by continuously observing the positions of the transitions in the received signal and adjusting the phase of its local clock accordingly. As a result, the receiver's clock is synchronized with the transmitter's clock and can be used to recover the transmitted data correctly. There is a wide range of techniques used to encode timing information over synchronous links. They vary in their ability to make use of the bandwidth of the link and hence in the data rate they can achieve.

Full-Duplex and Half-Duplex Links

A communication link may be operated according to one of the following three schemes:

Simplex allows transmission in one direction only.

Half duplex (HDX) allows transmission in either direction, but not at the same time.

Full duplex (FDX) allows simultaneous transmission in both directions.

The simplex configuration is useful only if the remote location contains an input or an output device, but not both. Hence, it is seldom used. The choice between half and full duplex is a trade-off between economy and speed of operation.

Using the most straightforward electrical circuit arrangement, a pair of wires enables transmission in one direction only, that is, simplex operation. To obtain a half-duplex link, switches at both ends must be used to connect either the transmitter or the receiver, but not both, to the line. When transmission in one direction is completed, the switches are reversed to enable transmission in the reverse direction. Control of the position of the switches is a part of the function of the devices at each end of the line.

Full-duplex operation is possible on a four-wire link, with two wires dedicated to each direction of transmission. It is also possible on a two-wire link by using two nonoverlapping frequency bands. The two bands create two independent transmission channels, one for each direction of transmission. Alternatively, full-duplex operation can be achieved in a common frequency band using a device called a *hybrid* at each end of the line. The hybrid separates the signals traveling in opposite directions so that they do not interfere with each other. Dialed telephone connections use lines of this type.

In the case of synchronous half-duplex operation, a time delay occurs whenever the direction of transmission is reversed because the transmitting modem may have to transmit an initializing sequence of signals to allow the receiving end to adapt to the conditions of the channel. The amount of delay encountered depends on the modem and the transmission facilities, and may be anywhere from a few milliseconds to over a hundred milliseconds.

The discussion above relates directly to the characteristics of the transmission link and the modems. Other important factors that influence the choice between half- and full-duplex operation are the nature of the data traffic and the way the system reacts to errors during transmission. We discuss only the first of these factors here.

Many computer applications require the computer to receive input data, perform some processing, and then return output data. A half-duplex link satisfies the requirements for such an application. However, if the messages exchanged between the two ends are short and frequent, the delay encountered in reversing the direction of transmission becomes significant. For this reason, many applications use full-duplex transmission facilities, although actual data transmission never takes place in both directions at the same time.

In some situations, simultaneous transmission in both directions can be used to considerable advantage. For example, in the system in Figure 10.2, the user of the computer may wish to communicate directly with the network server, using the computer as a video terminal. Each character entered at the keyboard should be echoed back to be displayed on the computer screen. This may be done locally by the computer or remotely by the network server. The use of remote echo provides an automatic checking capability to ensure that no errors have been introduced during transmission. If a half-duplex link is used in such a case, transmission of the next character must be delayed until the first character has been echoed back. No such restriction is necessary with full-duplex operation. Links between nodes in a high-speed computer communication network is another example where full-duplex transmission is useful. Messages traveling in opposite directions on any given link often bear no relation to each other; hence, they can be transmitted simultaneously.

10.3.1 ASYNCHRONOUS TRANSMISSION

The simplest scheme for serial communications is asynchronous transmission using a technique called *start-stop*. To facilitate timing recovery, data are organized in small groups of 6 to 8 bits, with a well defined beginning and end. In a typical arrangement, alphanumeric characters encoded in 8 bits are transmitted as shown in Figure 10.3. The line connecting the transmitter and the receiver is in the 1 state when idle. Transmission of a character is preceded by a 0 bit, referred to as the Start bit, followed by eight data bits and one or two Stop bits. The Stop bits have a logic value of 1. The Start bit alerts the receiver that data transmission is about to begin. Its leading edge is used

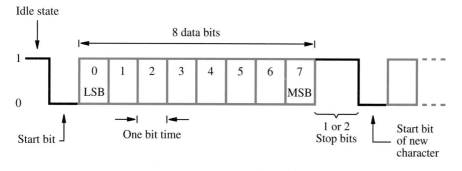

Figure 10.3 Asynchronous serial character transmission.

to synchronize the receiver clock with that of the transmitter. The Stop bits at the end delineate consecutive characters in the case of continuous transmission. When transmission stops, the line remains in the 1 state after the end of the Stop bits. It is the responsibility of the sender and receiver circuitry to insert and remove the Start and Stop bits.

To ensure proper synchronization at the receiving end, the receiver clock is derived from a local clock whose frequency is substantially higher than the transmission rate, typically 16 times higher. This means that 16 clock pulses occur during each data bit interval. This clock is used to increment a modulo-16 counter, which is reset to 0 when the leading edge of a Start bit is detected. When the count reaches 8, it indicates that the middle of the Start bit has been reached. The value of the Start bit is sampled to confirm that it is a valid Start bit, and the counter is again reset to 0. From this point onward, the incoming data signal is sampled whenever the count reaches 16, which should be close to the middle of each bit transmitted. Therefore, as long as the relative positioning of bits within a transmitted character is not in error by more than one half of a clock cycle, the receiver correctly interprets the bits of the encoded character.

A number of standard transmission rates are found in commercially available equipment, ranging from 300 to 56,000 bits per second. Start-stop transmission is used on short connections, such as the connection between the computer and the modem in Figure 10.2. For longer distances, such as for the connection between the two modems in the figure, start-stop can be used only at very low speeds. High-speed modems use the synchronous transmission schemes discussed in the next section.

When transmitting characters, they are represented by the 7-bit ASCII code (see Appendix E) occupying bits 0 through 6 in Figure 10.3. The MSB, bit 7 of the transmitted byte, is usually set to 0. Alternatively, it may be used as a parity bit, to aid in detecting transmission errors. Parity is the sum modulo 2 of a group of bits. Hence, it is equal to 1 if the transmitted data contains an odd number of 1s, and it is equal to 0 otherwise. When a parity bit is used, it is set by the transmitter such that the parity of the 8 bits transmitted is always the same, either odd or even. If a transmission error causes the value of one bit to change, the receiver will detect an incorrect parity and hence will be able to determine that an error has occurred.

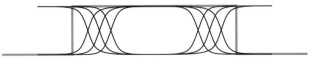

Figure 10.4   Overlapped transitions from successive bits showing the eye pattern.

The ASCII character set consists of letters, numbers, and special symbols such as $, +, and >. A number of nonprinting characters are also provided, for example, EOT (end of transmission) and CR (carriage return). These characters may be used to request specific actions, particularly when transmitting or receiving messages to or from a remote computer.

10.3.2 SYNCHRONOUS TRANSMISSION

In the start-stop scheme described above, the position of the 1-to-0 transition at the beginning of the start bit in Figure 10.3 is the key to obtaining correct timing. Hence, this scheme is useful only where the speed of transmission is sufficiently low and the conditions on the transmission link are such that the square waveforms shown in the figure maintain their shape. For higher speed and longer lines, much signal degradation takes place. Figure 10.4 shows a number of bits overlapped on top of each other to illustrate how the waveform may change from one bit position to another. Signal degradation is a result of such factors as signal distortion introduced by the line and the transmission equipment, by nearby sources of interference, jitter (random variations in the position of signal transitions), and so on. Because of the shape of the open area in the middle of a bit position, this figure is called the *eye pattern* of the transmission link. Sophisticated encoding and decoding schemes are used to help the receiver in determining the center point of the eye pattern, where 1s and 0s are farthest apart. This is the best point to sample the received signal.

In synchronous transmission, data are transmitted in blocks consisting of several hundreds or thousands of bits each. The beginning and end of each block are marked by appropriate codes, and data within a block are organized according to an agreed upon set of rules. Modems require a significant start-up time to complete such operations as transmitting and detecting carrier frequencies and establishing synchronization. In some modems, the start-up time is also used to adapt the modem circuits to the transmission properties of the link.

Network Connections — ADSL

In recent years, and particularly with the wide-spread use of the world-wide web, there has been an increasing demand for connecting computers at home and in the office via high-speed links to the Internet. Until recently, existing modems could not achieve the desired performance. A conventional modem converts digital signals to analog form using frequencies within the 4-kHz voice band of a telephone line. When a computer is using such a modem to communicate with another computer, the line is not available to make an ordinary telephone call. More importantly, the speed of transmission is limited to a few tens of kilobits per second. This is much less than the speeds needed to connect to a remote server or to the Internet.

Traditional telephone technology makes use of a small portion of the information carrying capacity of a telephone line. Depending on distance and the condition of the line, modern communication methods make it possible to transmit upwards of 50 megabits/s over the twisted-pair wire used in the telephone system. Many schemes have been developed to tap into this unused capacity by transmitting information in digital form directly between a subscriber's location at home or business and the central office of the telephone company. Telephone companies refer to the connection between a central office and a subscriber as the subscriber loop. Hence, when digital transmission is used, the scheme is called *digital subscriber loop* (DSL).

Computer communications is critically dependent on compatibility among equipment and services provided by several parties, including computer companies, modem manufacturers, and network service providers. Hence, agreement on a few standards that are accepted by all parties is essential. In the DSL domain, a few such standards have been developed. These include SDSL (Symmetric DSL), HDSL (High-speed DSL), and ADSL (Asymmetric DSL). Of these, ADSL is the most widely used for connecting home PCs to the Internet. We will discuss briefly the main features of this scheme.

The asymmetry in ADSL refers to the difference between transmission speeds in the upstream and downstream directions. Most of the time the information sent from a computer to a server on the Internet (the upstream direction) consists of input from the user. A low-speed connection is sufficient in this case. On the other hand, the information flowing to the user, such as an image to be displayed on the computer screen, requires transmission at high-speed to provide good response. For this reason, the speed of transmission in the downstream direction in ADSL is considerably higher than that used for upstream transmission.

The ADSL scheme uses different frequency bands and a technique called time-division multiplexing to create several channels of communication. One of these is allocated to regular telephone service. The others are allocated to the transmission of data in the upstream and downstream directions. A typical arrangement is shown in Figure 10.5. A single twisted pair wire carries information between the central office and the subscriber. At each end, a splitter separates data traffic from voice signals. At the subscriber end, data are directed to the computer over an appropriate data link, such as an Ethernet or a USB connection. Voice signals are sent to the telephone. At the central office, data are sent to a router device connected to the Internet, and voice signals are directed to the telephone switch. (A router is a switching device used to direct traffic in a data network.) This arrangement makes it possible to have the computer connected to the Internet all the time, without the need for dialing. At the same time, regular dialed telephone service continues to be available.

Cable Modems

Cable modems provide an alternative means for connecting a home computer to the Internet. They use the cable TV connection instead of the telephone connection.

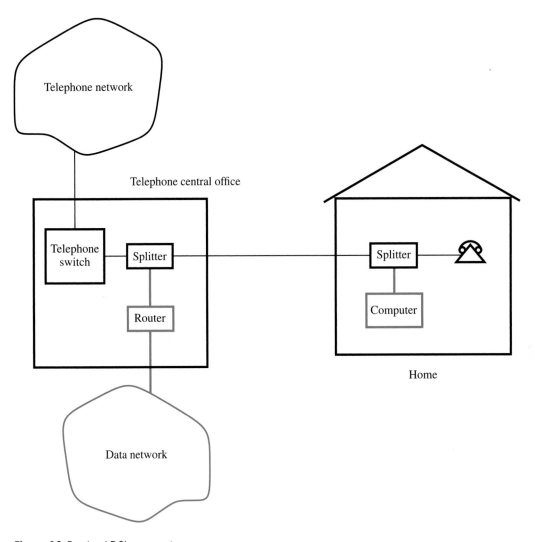

Figure 10.5 An ADSL connection.

The coaxial cable used in cable TV has a much higher bandwidth than a twisted pair wire. Hence the maximum speed possible with a cable modem is higher than what can be achieved with DSL schemes. However, cable TV uses a bus-like connection to all subscribers in a given neighborhood. Hence, the information carrying capacity of the cable is shared among all those connected to it. The full capacity is available to one user only when no other users on the same cable are active. A typical cable modem arrangement is shown in Figure 10.6.

The top speed available to any single user of a cable modem system is determined by the network service provider. It may vary from 600 kilobits/s to 10 megabits/s.

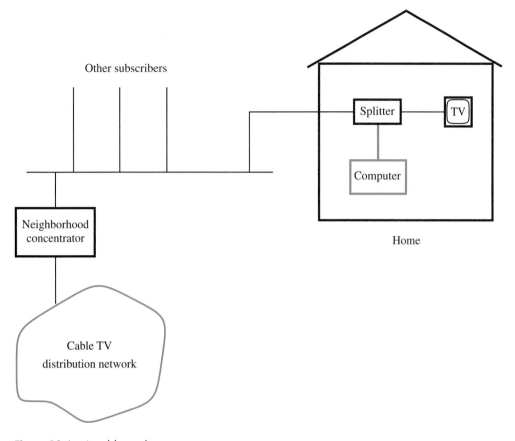

Figure 10.6 A cable-modem connection.

10.3.3 STANDARD COMMUNICATIONS INTERFACES

A standard interface refers to the collection of points at which two devices are connected together. One such standard that has gained wide acceptance is the EIA (Electronics Industry Association) Standard RS-232-C. Outside North America, this is known as CCITT (Comité Consultatif International Télégraphique et Téléphonique) Recommendation V24. This standard completely specifies the interface between data communication devices, such as modems, and data terminal equipment, such as computers. The RS-232-C interface consists of 25 connection points, which are described in Table 10.2.

Let us discuss a simple but common example. Consider the link in Figure 10.2, and assume that the connection is made over the dialed telephone network. The modems used are capable of going on- and off-hook, of sending dial tones, and of detecting an incoming ringing signal. They use the FSK transmission scheme described earlier and are capable of full-duplex operation. There are two transmission channels, one for each direction. One channel uses the frequencies 1275 and 1075 Hz, and the other uses frequencies 2225 and 2025 Hz to represent logic levels 1 and 0, respectively.

Table 10.2 Summary of the EIA Standard RS-232-C Signals (CCITT Recommendation V24).

Name			
EIA	**CCITT**	**Pin* no.**	**Function**
AA	101	1	Protective ground
AB	102	7	Signal ground-common return
BA	103	2	Transmitted data
BB	104	3	Received data
CA	105	4	Request to send
CB	106	5	Clear to send
CC	107	6	Data set ready
CD	108.2	20	Data terminal ready
CE	125	22	Ring indicator
CF	109	8	Received line signal detector
CG	110	21	Signal quality detector
CH	111	23§	Data signal rate selector (from DTE† to DCE‡)
CI	112	23§	Data signal rate selector (from DCE‡ to DTE†)
DA	113	24	Transmitter signal element timing (DTE†)
DB	114	15	Transmitter signal element timing (DCE‡)
DD	115	17	Receiver signal element timing (DCE‡)
SBA	118	14	Secondary transmitted data
SBB	119	16	Secondary received data
SCA	120	19	Secondary request to send
SCB	121	13	Secondary clear to send
SCF	122	12	Secondary received line signal detector

*Pins 9 and 10 are used for testing purposes, and pins 11, 18, and 25 are spare.
†Data terminal equipment.
‡Data communication equipment.
§The name of the signal on this pin depends on the signal's direction.

Figure 10.7 gives the sequence of logic signals needed to establish a connection, transmit data, and terminate the connection. The steps involved in this process are described briefly as follows:

1. When the network server is ready to accept a call, it sets the data-terminal-ready signal (CD) to 1.

2. Modem B monitors the telephone line, and when it detects the ringing current that indicates an incoming call, it signals the server by setting the ringing indicator (CE) to 1. If CD = 1 at the time the ringing current is detected, the modem

Step no.	Computer	Interface signals	Modem A	Modem B	Interface signals	Server
1				Enable automatic answering	CD	1 ←
2	Dialed digits →			1 → Goes off hook 1 →	CE CC	
3		CF	1 ←	← 2225 Hz 1 →	CA CB	1 ←
4	1 →	CA CB CC	1275 Hz → 1 ← 1 ←	1 →	CF	
5	Output data ← Input data →	BB BA	← Data 1275/1075 Hz →	← 2225/2025 Hz Data →	BA BB	← Output data → Input data
6		CF	← 0	Drop 2225 Hz and disconnect 0 → 0 → 0 →	CA CD CF CC CB	← 0 ← 0
7	(0 →) Terminate connection	CA CB CC	Drop 1275 ← 0 ← 0			
8					CD	1 ←

Figure 10.7 RS-232-C standard signalling sequence.

automatically answers the call by going off-hook. It then sets the modem-ready signal (CC) to 1.

3. The server instructs modem B to start transmitting the frequency representing a 1 (2225 Hz) by setting request-to-send (CA) to 1. When this is accomplished, modem B responds by setting clear-to-send (CB) to 1. The detection of this frequency at modem A causes it to set the received-line-signal detector (CF) to 1.

4. The computer sets CA to 1. Modem A transmits the 1275-Hz signal and sets CB and CC to 1. When modem B detects the 1275-Hz frequency, it sets CF to 1.

5. A full-duplex link is now established between the server and the computer, and it can be used for transmitting data in either direction. Interface pins BA (transmitted data) and BB (received data) are used for this purpose; all other signals in the interface remain unchanged.

6. When the user signs off, the server sets the request-to-send and data-terminal-ready signals, CA and CD, to 0, causing modem B to drop the 2225-Hz signal and disconnect from the line. Signals CB, CF, and CC are set to 0 by modem B. When modem A senses the disappearance of the signal on the line, it sets the received-line-signal detector (CF) to 0.

7. Modem A removes its 1275-Hz signal from the line, sets CB and CC to 0, and goes off-hook.

8. The server sets data-terminal-ready (CD) to 1 in preparation for a new call.

The initial connection procedure used with modems involves an exchange of messages in which the two sides agree on such parameters as the encoding scheme to be used, the speed of transmission, the size of data blocks, and so on. The RS-232-C interface can provide a serial connection between any two digital devices. The interpretation of individual signals such as CA and CD depends on the functional capabilities of the devices involved. When these signals are not needed, they are simply ignored by both devices. In most applications, no more than nine of the signals in Table 10.2 are used.

10.4 CONCLUDING REMARKS

This chapter presented an overview of input and output devices and their principles of operation. I/O devices are a fundamental part of a computer system because they constitute the link for feeding information into a computer and for receiving the results. Many new and innovative devices have been introduced in recent years. High-quality output devices are now available at affordable prices for personal computers. The range of input devices available also continues to expand, including digital cameras and hand-held devices of various kinds.

This chapter also presented some aspects of computer communications, in particular the basic technologies used over serial links. Such links are commonly used to connect computers to I/O devices and to each other. Examples of high-speed links to the Internet over common-carrier facilities (the telephone network) and the cable TV network have been briefly described. The connectivity that has resulted from the widespread use of such facilities has transformed the way we use computers and opened the door to a myriad of home and business applications. It is this synergy between the fields of computers and communications that has ushered in the modern era of information technology.

PROBLEMS

10.1 The display on a video screen must be refreshed at least 30 times per second to remain flicker-free. During each full scan of the screen, the total time required to illuminate each point is 1 μs. The beam is then turned off and moved to the next point to be illuminated. On average, moving the beam from one spot to the next takes 3 μs. Because of power-dissipation limitations, the beam cannot be turned on more than 10 percent of the time. Determine the maximum number of points that can be illuminated on the screen.

10.2 Consider a communication channel that uses eight-valued signals instead of the two-valued signals used in a binary channel. If the channel is rated at 9600 baud, what is its capacity in bits per second?

10.3 The following components are provided:

- A 6-bit binary counter, with Clock and Clear inputs and six outputs
- A 3-bit serial-input–parallel-output shift register
- A clock running at eight times the input data rate
- Logic gates and D flip-flops with Preset and Clear controls

Design a circuit using these components to load 3 bits of serial data from an input data line into the shift register. Assume the data to have the format of Figure 10.3, but with only 3 bits of data instead of 8. The circuit you design should have two outputs, A and B, both initially cleared to 0. Output A should be set to 1 if a Stop bit is detected following the data bits. Otherwise, output B should be set to 1. Give an explanation of the operation of your design.

10.4 An asynchronous link between two computers uses the start-stop scheme, with one start bit and one stop bit, and a transmission rate or 38.8 kilobits/s. What is the effective transmission rate as seen by the two computers?

10.5 A communication link uses odd parity for each character transmitted. Refer to Appendix E, and give the 8-bit pattern transmitted for the characters A, P, =, and 5.

10.6 Consider a communication line modem connected to a computer through an RS-232-C interface. The control signals associated with this interface are accessed by the computer through a 16-bit register, as shown in Figure P10.1. The status change bit, b_{15}, is set to 1 whenever there is a change in the state of bits b_{12} or b_{13}, or when b_{14} is set to 1. Bit b_{15} is cleared whenever this register is accessed by the processor. Write a program for one of the processors in Chapter 3 to implement the control sequence required to establish a telephone connection according to steps 1 through 4 of Figure 10.7.

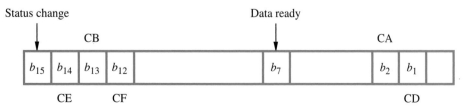

Figure P10.1 Organization of an I/O register for the modem interface in Problem 10.6.

PROCESSOR FAMILIES

CHAPTER OBJECTIVES

In this chapter you will learn about:

- The ARM, PowerPC, Sun SPARC, Compaq Alpha, and Intel IA-64 processor families which implement RISC ISAs
- The Motorola 680X0/ColdFire and Intel IA-32 processor families which implement CISC ISAs
- The Hewlett-Packard HP3000, whose instructions are designed to operate on a stack data structure

Chapter 2 showed how basic programming concepts are implemented at the assembly language level and illustrated the need for various machine instructions and addressing modes. In Chapter 3, the ARM, Motorola 68000, and Intel IA-32 instruction set architectures were used as examples. In this chapter, we continue the discussion of those three ISAs, elaborating on features found in the various members of the processor families that implement the ISAs, spanning a range of cost and performance levels. The ARM architecture exhibits RISC characteristics, and the Motorola and Intel IA-32 architectures have CISC features. The RISC-style PowerPC architecture, whose processor implementations compete in the same target market as IA-32 processors, is described. We also discuss the Sun SPARC, Compaq Alpha, and Intel IA-64 RISC architectures, which have 64-bit address and data lengths. These 64-bit processors are intended for use in high-performance workstations and servers. Finally, a very different approach, which is now mainly of historical interest, that of the Hewlett-Packard HP3000, shows how an instruction set can be organized for a machine that has computation facilities heavily influenced by the use of a stack data structure for holding operands.

Chapters 2, 3, 7, and 8 described various RISC and CISC approaches to processor design. We now briefly review some of the salient features of each approach before giving the family examples that exhibit these properties. CISC instruction sets provide many powerful instructions intended for more direct implementation of high-level language operations and program sequencing control structures. However, the execution of such instructions can become quite complex. The rationale of the CISC approach is that it leads to fewer machine language instructions for a given high-level language program, thus leading to shorter program execution times. This is true if complex instructions can be executed quickly and efficiently. In practice, however, the implementation of these instructions with the goal of meeting high instruction execution rates has proven to be very challenging, and has required relatively large chip area. In addition, CISC instruction sets are difficult targets for optimizing compilers.

The RISC approach of using relatively simple instructions may at first appear to be less effective than the CISC alternative because more RISC instructions are needed to perform a given computational task. However, RISC instructions are well-suited to pipelined execution that leads to high execution rates. A key advantage of RISC instruction sets is that they can be used effectively by optimizing compilers. Another advantage is related to *Very Large Scale Integration* (VLSI) fabrication technology. Because of the smaller chip area needed for instruction handling and sequencing control in RISC processors, more space is available for larger register sets and larger on-chip caches. Higher performance results because off-chip data and instruction accesses are reduced.

Taking all factors into account, the result is that although both approaches have led to very competitive commercial products, new machines developed since the early 1990s have predominantly featured RISC-style ISAs.

We also must emphasize, as explained in earlier chapters, that many factors other than the style of the instruction set are very important in the design of a processor that provides a high rate of instruction execution. Multiple, pipelined, functional units that enable superscalar execution of programs, as described in Chapter 8, are essential. Also, optimizing compilers that generate efficient machine language code from high-level language programs must be developed along with the hardware.

11.1 THE ARM FAMILY

In Part I of Chapter 3, we described the ARM instruction set architecture as an example of the RISC style of instruction set design. ARM processors are mainly intended for embedded system applications. Most implementations must therefore meet low-cost and low-power requirements. In many cases, such as mobile telephones, the target device is battery powered, and voltages in the range of 1 to 3 volts are used. Compared to the high-performance Intel Pentium processors that are targeted for the PC market, low-end ARM processors are significantly less complex, and require only a fraction of the transistors needed for Pentium chips. We will examine some of these issues in discussing various implementations of the ARM ISA. The book by Furber [1] contains a wealth of information on all aspects of ARM history, architecture, and implementation. The articles in [2] and the ARM web site [3] also provide detailed information.

From its original development in the mid-1980s, through to the year 2000, there have been five major versions of the ARM ISA, labeled v1 through v5. Version v3 is described in Chapter 3, and the ARM7 processor, developed in the mid-1990s, implements this version. A later section will describe processor implementations and their properties.

Relative to version v3, the other versions are briefly described as follows. Versions v1 and v2 supported only 26-bit memory addressing, and the 32-bit product multiply instructions were added in going from v1 to v2. Version v3 introduced full 32-bit addressing for byte and 32-bit word operands. Version v4 contains full 64-bit product multiply instructions, as well as the 32-bit product instructions. It also adds load and store instructions for 16-bit (half-word) data operands. Version v5, and an extension of it labeled v5E, add specialized instructions for: managing software breakpoints for debugging, normalizing numbers for the software implementation of floating-point arithmetic operations, and performing addition and multiplication operations on 16-bit operands to allow efficient execution of digital signal processing routines.

In addition to this evolution of the standard ARM ISA through five versions, in which all instructions are encoded into a 32-bit word format, a more compactly encoded subset coexists with versions v4 and v5. It is described in the next section.

11.1.1 THE THUMB INSTRUCTION SET

The ARM ISA specification includes a compact encoding of a subset of the v4 and v5 versions of the full set of instructions. The subset is called the *Thumb* instruction set, and the version names are extended to v4T and v5T to denote this inclusion. All Thumb instructions are encoded into a 16-bit half-word format.

The practical motivation for the Thumb instructions is that they lead to a reduction in memory space needed to store programs used in low-cost and low-power embedded system applications. The ARM7TDMI processor implements version v4T of the architecture. This processor, along with a small amount of RAM memory and digital signal processing hardware, fabricated on a single chip, is suitable for the mobile telephone application.

Programs consisting of Thumb instructions are executed as follows. The instructions are fetched from memory and dynamically (that is, as they are to be executed) "decompressed" from their highly encoded 16-bit format into corresponding standard 32-bit ARM instructions, and then executed. This is how they are handled in the main stream low-end processors. In some high-performance processors, the Thumb instructions are decoded directly for execution, avoiding the decompression step into standard ARM instructions. A bit in the Current Program Status Register (CPSR), labeled T, determines whether the incoming instruction stream consists of Thumb (T = 1) or standard 32-bit ARM instructions (T = 0). An application can contain a mix of Thumb and standard instruction routines.

Two of the main differences between Thumb and standard instructions are: A number of Thumb instructions use a 2-operand format in which the destination register is also one of the source operand registers; and Conditional execution, which applies to all standard ARM instructions, is used mainly for branches in the Thumb set. These changes clearly lead to savings in instruction encoding bit space.

11.1.2 PROCESSOR AND CPU CORES

The ARM company produces and licenses designs for ARM processors and closely associated components such as caches and memory management units. Companies that produce embedded systems and other application-specific computer products acquire these designs for incorporation into their products. In most cases, the ARM designs are integrated with application-specific hardware on the same chip. To capture this intended usage, the ARM designs are called *cores*. Designs are provided by ARM in two different forms: *hard macrocell* or *synthesizable*. The hard macrocell version is a detailed physical layout, targeted to a particular chip fabrication process. The synthesizable form is a high-level language software module that can be synthesized using a suitable cell library in the required target technology. This form allows a number of options on processor functionality to be easily included or omitted. The ARM7TDMI processor is a hard macrocell core, and the ARM7TDMI-S is its synthesizable version.

ARM designs are classified as either processor cores or CPU cores. A processor core contains only a processor and associated address and data bus connections. A CPU core contains cache and memory management components in addition to a processor. The name CPU is somewhat misleading, because traditionally it has meant Central Processing Unit, but we use the name here because it is an identifiable ARM term. We now give brief descriptions of some representative processor and CPU cores.

ARM7TDMI Processor Core

This core is commonly used for low-cost low-power applications. The processor has a simple 3-stage pipeline consisting of fetch, decode, and execute stages. It realizes version v4T of the architecture, supporting both the Thumb and standard instruction sets. Typical operational parameters are a 3.3 V power supply and a 66 MHz clock rate. But this core design can be synthesized for 0.9 V operation for low-power battery supply applications or for over 100-MHz clock rates to achieve higher performance.

ARM9TDMI and ARM10TDMI Processor Cores

These two processor cores are based on 5-stage and 6-stage pipelines, respectively. They have separate instruction and data ports to provide much higher performance levels than the ARM7TDMI can provide. At clock rates of 200 MHz and 300 MHz for these processors, performance levels of the 7, 9, and 10 versions of this processor core are in the ratios 1:2:4. The ARM10TDMI has a wider 64-bit path to each memory port, as compared to 32-bit paths for the other two processors. The ARM9TDMI and ARM10TDMI implement versions v4T and v5TE of the ISA, respectively. Both of them decode Thumb instructions directly for execution. Cache memories must be used with both of these cores to achieve the higher performance levels.

ARM720T CPU Core

This core consists of the ARM7TDMI processor core combined with an 8K-byte unified instruction and data cache, and virtual memory management hardware. The cache structure has 16-byte blocks and is 4-way set associative. The memory management unit uses a 64-entry associative translation lookaside buffer for holding recent translations. The clock rate for this integrated unit can be up to 60 MHz. The added cache and MMU circuitry increases the total silicon area required by a factor of about 5 over that required by the processor core alone, and power consumption triples.

ARM920T and ARM1020E CPU Cores

These CPU cores, based on the ARM9TDMI and ARM10TDMI processor cores, have separate instruction and data caches. Each of the caches in the ARM920T contains 16K bytes and has 32-byte blocks, with 64-way set associativity. There is an MMU for each memory port, and each of them has a 64-entry associative TLB. The ARM1020E has 32K bytes in each cache; otherwise, the caches and the MMUs are similar.

StrongARM SA-110 CPU Core

The StrongARM CPU core was developed by ARM in collaboration with Digital Equipment Corporation (now folded into the Compaq company), and the SA-110 version is manufactured by Intel. The processor component implements version v4 of the architecture. It does not support the Thumb instruction set. Otherwise, the processor is comparable to the ARM9TDMI processor core. The performance of the StrongARM SA-110 is comparable to that of the ARM920T, but it is implemented using an earlier technology and has higher power consumption at a 200-MHz clock rate.

The StrongARM processor has a 5-stage pipeline. There are separate 16K-byte instruction and data caches. Each cache has 32-byte blocks and 32-way set associativity. The translation lookaside buffers for each of the caches have 32 entries. The high-speed multiplier circuitry has a latency of three or fewer clock cycles, designed for good performance in digital signal processing applications.

11.2   THE MOTOROLA 680X0 AND COLDFIRE FAMILIES

In Part II of Chapter 3, we described the Motorola 68000 processor. Here, we discuss the key features of the follow-on processors in the 680X0 family and the closely associated ColdFire family. The book by Tabak [4] and the Motorola web site [5] describe these processors. Some general comments on Motorola processors are given first.

The 68000 processor was introduced in 1979. Through the 1980s and early 1990s, the 68000, 68020, 68030, and 68040 were targeted for the personal computer market, and were used in Apple computers. The latest member of the 680X0 family is the 68060, introduced in the mid-1990s. The 68060, and the closely related ColdFire family, are targeted for the embedded system market.

11.2.1   68020 PROCESSOR

The 68020 is much more powerful than the 68000, mainly because of some significant architectural enhancements. These advances were made possible by improved VLSI technology and larger packages that removed many constraints of pin limitations. The discussion here on the 68020 also applies to the 68030 and 68040. Later, we describe the additional enhancements found in the 68030 and 68040.

The 68020 has external connections for 32-bit addresses and 32-bit data. Although its data bus is 32 bits wide, the 68020 can deal efficiently with devices that transfer 8, 16, or 32 bits at a time. The processor can adjust dynamically to the data bus width requirements of a particular device in a manner that is transparent to the programmer. The 68020 bus includes control lines that are activated by the devices connected to the bus to indicate the required size of their data transfers. Thus, the processor can deal with devices of different data transfer sizes without knowing the actual size before a data transfer is initiated.

The 68000 restriction that word operands must be aligned on even address boundaries has been eliminated in the 68020; operands of any size may start at any address. This means that 16- and 32-bit operands can occupy parts of two adjacent 32-bit locations in the main memory. Two access cycles are therefore needed to reach such operands, and this affects performance. The processor automatically performs these two accesses. From the address, the processor knows which 32-bit locations must be accessed and in what pattern the individual bytes from these locations should be assembled to obtain the desired operand.

Register Set and Data Types

Like the 68000, the 68020 has user and supervisor modes of operation. In the user mode, the registers available are essentially the same as those given in Figure 3.18 for the 68000. In the supervisor mode, however, the 68020 has several additional control registers intended to simplify implementation of operating system software.

The 68000 addressable data units are bit, byte, word, long word, and packed binary-coded decimal (BCD). In addition to these, the 68020 allows quad word, unpacked BCD, and bit-field data types. A quad word consists of 64 bits, and unpacked BCD has one BCD digit per byte. A bit field consists of a variable number of bits in a 32-bit long word, and it is specified by the location of its leftmost bit and the number of bits in the field.

Addressing Modes

All 68000 addressing modes, shown in Table 3.2, are available in the 68020. Several extra versions of the indexed mode have been added to the 68020 to allow flexible and efficient access to data and address list structures.

The full indexed mode is more powerful because it allows a range of displacements, or offsets, and provides for a scaling factor. Recall that the 68000 syntax for the full indexed mode is

$$\text{disp}(An, Rk.\text{size})$$

where the displacement is a signed, 8-bit number and the size designation indicates whether 32 or 16 bits of the Rk register are to be used in computing the effective address. The 68020 version of this mode allows the displacement to be an 8-, 16-, or 32-bit value. It also introduces a scale factor by which the contents of Rk are multiplied. The value of the scale factor may be 1, 2, 4, or 8. The syntax for the mode is

$$(\text{disp}, An, Rk.\text{size}^*\text{scale})$$

Note that the displacement is given within the parentheses in this case. The effective address, EA, is computed as

$$\text{EA} = \text{disp} + [An] + ([Rk] \times \text{scale})$$

This mode is useful when dealing with lists of items that are 1, 2, 4, or 8 bytes long. If the scale factor is chosen so that it equals the size of the items, then successive items in the list can be accessed by incrementing the contents of Rk by 1.

Another powerful extension of indexed addressing is the memory indirect indexed modes, in which an address operand is obtained indirectly from the main memory. Two such modes exist. In *memory indirect postindexed* mode, an address is fetched from the memory before the normal indexing process takes place. Its syntax is

$$([\text{basedisp}, An], Rk.\text{size}^*\text{scale}, \text{outdisp})$$

and the effective address is computed as

$$\text{EA} = [\text{basedisp} + [An]] + ([Rk] \times \text{scale}) + \text{outdisp}$$

Note that two displacements are used. A base displacement of 16 or 32 bits is used to modify the address in An, which is then used to fetch the address operand from the memory. This allows an address to be selected from a list of addresses stored in memory starting at the location given by the contents of An. The second displacement is the normal displacement used in indexed addressing, called outer displacement to distinguish it from the base displacement.

The second version is the *memory indirect preindexed* mode, in which most of the indexing modification is done before the address operand is fetched. The syntax for this mode is

$$([\text{basedisp}, An, Rk.\text{size}^*\text{scale}], \text{outdisp})$$

and the effective address is determined as

$$EA = [\text{basedisp} + [An] + ([Rk] \times \text{scale})] + \text{outdisp}$$

In both of these modes, the values An, Rk, basedisp, and outdisp are optional and are not included in the computation of the effective address unless specified by the user. These addressing modes are useful for dealing with lists in which contiguous memory locations are used to store addresses of data items, rather than the data items themselves. The latter can be anywhere in memory.

A relative version of all indexed modes is available in which the program counter is used in place of the address register, An.

Instruction Set

All 68000 instructions are available in the 68020. Some have extra flexibility. For example, branch instructions can have 32-bit displacements, and several instructions have the option of using longer operands. Some new instructions are also provided, such as instructions that deal with bit-field operands.

On-Chip Cache

The 68020 chip includes a small instruction cache that has 256 bytes organized as 64 long-word blocks. A direct-mapping scheme is used when loading new words into the cache.

11.2.2 ENHANCEMENTS IN 68030 AND 68040 PROCESSORS

The 68030 differs from the 68020 in two significant ways. In addition to the instruction cache, the 68030 has another cache of the same size for data. The data cache organization has 16 blocks of 4 long words each. The 68030 also contains a memory management unit (MMU).

The execution unit in the 68030 generates virtual addresses. The cache access circuitry determines if the desired operand is in the cache, based on virtual addresses. The MMU translates the virtual address into a physical address in parallel with the cache access so that, in the case of a cache access miss, the physical address needed to access the operand in the main memory is immediately available.

The 68040 includes a floating-point unit that implements the IEEE floating-point standard described in Chapter 6. Instruction and data caches are included, as in the 68030. Memory management is improved over that in the 68030; the 68040 has two independent address translation caches that permit simultaneous translation of addresses for both instructions and data. The 68040 has a pipelined structure that permits fetching of instructions while previous instructions are still being processed. Two internal buses are used to transfer instructions and data from the respective caches. These buses, in conjunction with the two address translation circuits, allow simultaneous access to instruction and data caches.

Finally, the 68040 includes circuits that monitor activity on the external bus. This feature makes the 68040 suitable for use in multiprocessor systems. One of the key requirements in such systems is to maintain consistency of the common data that may temporarily reside in several caches of different processors. The bus-monitoring circuits detect bus transfers that change cached data, as we describe in Chapter 12.

11.2.3 68060 PROCESSOR

The latest member of the 680X0 family is the 68060 [6], introduced in the mid-1990s, with clock rates ranging from 50 to 75 MHz. This processor is intended for the embedded system market. New organizational and fabrication features result in performance that is 2.5 times that of a 40 MHz 68040.

The 68060 is a pipelined superscalar processor. The pipeline has four basic stages, with an additional two stages if a memory writeback operation is required. Up to three instructions can be initiated per clock cycle. Three function units — two integer units and a floating-point unit — comprise the main instruction processing hardware. There are separate, on-chip, 8K-byte instruction and data caches. Each cache is 4-way set associative and uses 16-byte blocks. Two 64-entry, 4-way, set associative, translation lookaside buffers to facilitate virtual to physical address translation are provided with the caches. Dynamic branch prediction is used to enhance smooth flow of instructions through the pipeline.

11.2.4 THE COLDFIRE FAMILY

Since the mid-1990s, Motorola has produced a series of processor components and small computer configurations, called the ColdFire family, that is targeted for the embedded system market. The processors are based on the 68060 processor core. A number of different products are configured with small amounts of memory and I/O port hardware for parallel and serial connections. These products meet a range of power and performance requirements for different applications. Both hardware chip products and synthesizable software designs are available in the ColdFire family.

11.3 THE INTEL IA-32 FAMILY

Intel processors [7] have attained strong commercial success as evidenced by their wide use in notebook and personal computers. In the 1980s, Intel produced the first series of processors used in the IBM PC. They were based on the 8086 processor, introduced in 1979, which generated 20-bit addresses externally and handled 16-bit data internally and externally. (It is interesting to note that an 8-bit version of the 8086, labeled the 8088, was actually used in the first IBM PC to keep cost as low as possible.) Because the 8086 was encapsulated in a 40-pin package, the address and data transfers were time-multiplexed on the same set of chip pins.

Progressively more powerful processors that implement an evolution of the same basic instruction set architecture have been introduced. These are the 80286, 80386, 80486 [4], and the current Pentium series. The 80286 was a 16-bit processor. The others all handle data and addresses both internally and externally in 32-bit sizes. The 80386 is the first processor in the IA-32 family. The 32-bit chips come in larger packages that obviate the need for address and data line multiplexing.

11.3.1 IA-32 MEMORY SEGMENTATION

In Section 3.16.1, we briefly discussed the use of segment registers (see Figure 3.37) in generating memory addresses in the IA-32 architecture. Here, we expand on that description. First, it is instructive to point out how the segment registers were originally used in the 8086. Current IA-32 processors can be put into a state that operates that way, called *real* mode. This allows current IA-32 processors to run 8086 machine code programs.

Real Mode

This address generation mode, used by the 8086 processor, views the memory as being organized in segments of 64K bytes each. A 64K-byte memory segment is spanned by the 16-bit effective addresses generated internally by the 8086 addressing modes. The processor uses the CS, SS, DS, and ES segment registers for accessing code, stack, and two data segments, respectively. The other two segment registers (FS and GS) were added in the 80386.

The 20-bit external memory addresses are generated as shown in Figure 11.1. The 16-bit value in a segment register is shifted left four bit positions to form a 20-bit address, which is the starting address of a segment. The 16-bit effective address generated by an 8086 addressing mode, labeled the offset in the figure, is added to the segment starting address to produce the desired 20-bit memory address.

Segments are located in different areas of the 20-bit address space by loading the high-order 16 bits of their starting address into the appropriate segment register. A total of sixteen, 64K-byte, nonoverlapping segments can be accommodated in the 1M-byte memory space spanned by 20-bit addresses. Note that segments can overlap. This is useful for sharing instruction and data space among different programs. The CS and SS segment usage is automatically determined for instruction and stack access references. The default for data access is to use the DS segment register. A prefix byte code can be added to an instruction to use the ES register for data accesses.

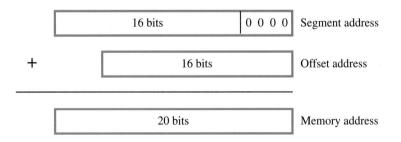

Figure 11.1 Generation of a memory address in the 8086 processor.

Protected Mode

IA-32 architecture processors normally use the *protected* mode for generating memory addresses. Figure 11.2 shows the most general way to generate a physical address using the contents of base and index registers along with a displacement value contained in the instruction. A 32-bit effective address is determined by multiplying the contents of the index register by a scale factor of 1, 2, 4, or 8 and then adding the result to the contents of the base register and the displacement. The high-order 14 bits of one of the six segment registers (shown in Figure 3.37) specifies a *selector,* which is then used as an index into a segment descriptor table from which a 32-bit base address is obtained. This address is added to the effective address in the segmentation unit to produce a 32-bit *linear address*. The paging unit translates the linear address into a 32-bit physical address using a page table.

The segment descriptor and page tables are large and are therefore kept in the main memory. In order to ensure fast address translation, a translation lookaside buffer, as described in Chapter 5, can be used. The segment descriptor tables contain access rights fields as well as segment limit fields to specify the maximum size of a segment. These parameters are managed by the operating system to ensure protection among different application programs that occupy the memory at the same time, giving rise to the name "protected mode."

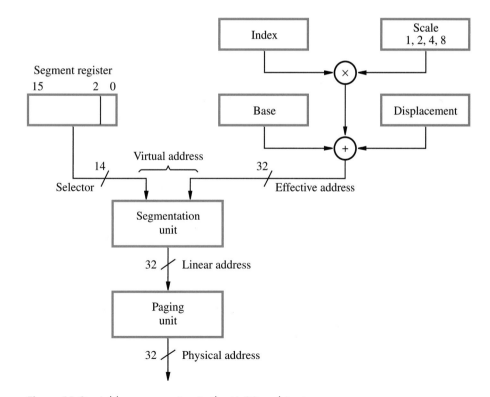

Figure 11.2 Address generation in the IA-32 architecture.

The segmentation and paging features can be used to organize the memory in any of the following ways:

- As a flat, 32-bit address space in which the effective address is used as the physical address
- As one or more variable-length segments (without paging)
- As a 32-bit space divided into one or more 4K-byte pages
- As a structure that combines segmentation and paging

11.3.2 SIXTEEN-BIT MODE

IA-32 processors can operate in a mode in which machine language programs for earlier 16-bit Intel processors (8086 and 80286) can be executed directly. In this mode, only the low-order halves of the processor registers shown in Figure 3.38, labeled AX, CX, . . . , are used. The internal address size is 16 bits, and the addressing modes available are a subset of those described in Table 3.3. For example, the value in the index register cannot be scaled in generating effective addresses.

The switch between 32-bit and 16-bit operation can actually be done on an instruction-by-instruction basis. It is also possible to independently choose address and data sizes. For example, full IA-32 addressing mode capability can be used in conjunction with 16-bit data manipulation. When program execution begins, a default mode is set. To switch to the other mode, a prefix byte, not shown in Figure 3.41, is added to an instruction.

11.3.3 80386 AND 80486 PROCESSORS

The 80386 was the first processor to implement the IA-32 architecture described in Chapter 3. It supported both memory segmentation and paging as described in Section 11.3.1.

The 80486 processor was one of the first chips to contain 1 million transistors, roughly the same number as in the Motorola 68040. This processor provides significantly improved performance over the 80386, an advance made possible by expanded circuitry. The 80486 includes both integer and floating-point processing units. The integer unit is fully compatible with the 80386 processor. The floating-point unit implements the IEEE floating-point standard presented in Chapter 6. In 80386-based computers, the same capability was achieved by using a coprocessor chip. Paging and memory management support in the 80486 is the same as in the 80386.

A 4-way, set-associative cache is included in the 80486 for instructions and data. The loading of new information into the cache is enhanced by a burst data transfer mechanism, which enables four 32-bit words to be read as a block and loaded into the cache. The cache has a write-through feature, whereby any data written into the cache are also automatically written into the main memory.

To achieve high performance, the 80486 exploits parallelism and pipelining to a considerable extent. Both the integer unit and the floating-point unit can execute instructions in parallel. When one instruction is being executed, subsequent instructions are fetched from the memory. Execution of frequently used instructions requires fewer clock cycles than in the 80386; those that load and store data or perform register-to-register operations require only one clock cycle.

11.3.4 PENTIUM PROCESSOR

The performance of the Pentium processor, introduced in 1993 [8], is a significant improvement over that of the 80486. The Pentium has 3 million transistors, compared to 1 million in the 80486, and its computational power is over twice that of the 80486 on integer-intensive benchmark programs and about five times that of the 80486 on floating-point-intensive benchmark programs.

The Pentium processor is a CISC architecture that achieves high performance by using many of the organizational features present in RISC processors, as is done in the 80486 to a lesser extent. In particular, separate on-chip caches of 8K bytes each are used for instructions and data. This superscalar processor, supported by multiple pipelined operation units, can issue two instructions per clock cycle. A 64-bit-wide external data bus allows caches to be rapidly loaded from main memory. The caches are 2-way set associative, with 32-byte blocks. Three independent, pipelined, operational units are included — two for integer operations and one for floating-point operations. Each integer pipeline is five stages deep, and each floating-point unit has eight stages.

The Pentium processor uses a simple form of dynamic branch prediction. It chooses the same direction that it chose the last time the branch was executed. This requires a table of last-branch address values to be kept for each branch instruction. The predicted direction is thus correct for all branches at the end of a program loop after the first branch, until the loop is exited.

11.3.5 PENTIUM PRO PROCESSOR

Introduced in 1995 with a clock rate of 133 MHz, the Pentium Pro [9], [10], provides about twice the performance of a 100-MHz Pentium. Most of the performance gain results from an increased superscalar factor and the capability to execute instructions out-of-order. The superscalar factor, or the maximum number of instructions that can be completed in a clock cycle, is three in the Pentium Pro, compared to two in the Pentium. Pipeline depth in the multiple execution units is twelve, compared to five in the Pentium, and datapath width inside the processor is 64 bits, double that of the Pentium. The Pentium Pro has separate on-chip first level (L1) instruction and data caches of 8K bytes each, the same size as in the Pentium. There is also a second level (L2) cache with a capacity of 256K bytes. It is in the same package as the processor chip, but it is on a separate chip, connected to the processor chip by a 64-bit bus.

Superscalar operation is supported by multiple execution units, including two for integer operations and two for floating-point operations. A major performance-enchancing feature of the Pentium Pro is its ability to execute instructions in an order different from that specified in the program fetched from memory. This feature allows more instructions to be executed in parallel. Of course, adequate control is provided to ensure that the resulting computations specified by the program are correct. Dynamic branch prediction is implemented in the Pentium Pro, as in the Pentium. This capability allows the processor to look far enough ahead in the instruction stream to take advantage of parallel execution.

External bus monitoring circuits enable the Pentium Pro to be used in multiprocessor systems. These monitoring circuits, and the control actions that they initiate, maintain coherence of common data that may temporarily reside in the caches of different processors. (See Chapter 12 for a discussion of cache coherence.)

11.3.6 PENTIUM II AND III PROCESSORS

The Pentium II processor added the MMX instructions that were briefly described in Section 3.23.2. These instructions facilitate parallel processing of short numbers in multimedia operations on pixels that describe graphical data. The data are operated on in the same eight 64-bit registers used to hold floating-point data. The L1 caches in the Pentium II are double the size of those in the Pentium Pro at 16K bytes each. The off-chip L2 cache holds 512K bytes.

The Pentium III processor introduced the vector (SIMD) instructions discussed in Section 3.23.3. These instructions, called streaming SIMD extension (SSE) instructions [11], are used to efficiently process vector operations on floating-point data. Four 32-bit floating-point operands are packed in each of eight new 128-bit registers, called the XMM registers. The caches are similar to those in the Pentium II, with one major additional option. A version of the Pentium III processor has a 256K-byte L2 cache on the same chip as the processor, providing a higher bandwidth path to the L1 caches.

When they were introduced in 1993, 1995, 1997, and 1999, the Pentium, Pentium Pro, Pentium II, and Pentium III processors had clock rates of 60, 200, 266, and 500 MHz, respectively. Improvements in circuit technology and VLSI fabrication techniques, which have allowed smaller transistor sizes and lower gate delays, have led to clock rates of up to 1 GHz for the current versions of the Pentium III processor.

11.3.7 PENTIUM 4 PROCESSOR

Introduced in 2000, the initial versions of the Pentium 4 have clock rates from 1.3 to 1.5 GHz [7]. The full IA-32 instruction set is supported, including the MMX and SSE instructions. The SSE instructions have been extended (SSE2) to handle two packed 64-bit floating-point numbers or two packed 64-bit integers in the 128-bit XMM registers. The longer integers are useful in implementing the encryption and decryption operations needed in secure data applications. Deeper pipelines — up to 20 stages, compared to 10 in the Pentium III — with shorter stages are one of the factors leading to the higher clock rates, along with improved circuit and fabrication technologies.

There are separate L1 data and instruction caches. The data cache has a capacity of 8K bytes and uses 4-way set associative access to 64-byte cache blocks. The instruction cache is organized to hold decoded instruction execution path segments, called *traces,* which can extend over more than one branch in the original program. If these paths are repeated, execution is faster. Of course, checks must be made to verify that the same branches are taken when traces are repeated. The term *trace cache* is used to describe this cacheing strategy. The decoded instructions are represented as microoperations. Up to four microoperations are needed to represent an IA-32 instruction. The trace cache can hold a number of execution path segments consisting of a total of 12K microoperations.

The 256K-byte, on-chip, L2 cache is organized into 128-byte blocks and is 8-way set associative. The transfer path between the L2 and L1 cache levels supports a transfer rate of 48 gigabytes/s compared to 16 gigabytes/s in the Pentium III.

The system bus on the Pentium 4 provides a much higher transfer rate than that supported by the Pentium III. The Pentium 4 system bus is 64 bits wide, and transfers can take place at 400 MHz. The transfer rate is therefore 3.2 gigabytes/s as compared to 1 gigabyte/s in the Pentium III.

11.3.8 ADVANCED MICRO DEVICES IA-32 PROCESSORS

Companies other than Intel make processors that implement the IA-32 architecture and compete with the corresponding Intel products for use in personal computers and workstations. Advanced Micro Devices (AMD) [12] has done this for some time. In 2000, AMD's Athlon processor was available with a clock rate of 1.2 GHz, providing performance comparable to the Intel Pentium 4.

The Athlon is a superscalar processor with two levels of cacheing on the processor chip. The L1 cache level has a total capacity of 128K bytes and the L2 cache contains 256K bytes. An interface for double data rate DRAM main memory (see Chapter 5) provides a peak transfer rate of 2.1 gigabytes/s. System I/O bus protocols running at 200 and 266 MHz are provided.

11.4 THE POWERPC FAMILY

In the early 1990s, IBM, Motorola, and Apple collaborated on the development of a RISC-style processor family, the PowerPC [13], [14], for the personal computer and workstation markets. PowerPC processors, produced by both IBM [15] and Motorola [5], have been used in IBM and Apple computers. In general, these processors have architectural features that have provided computing power similar to that of the Intel IA-32 processors over comparable time periods. The first processor implementing the PowerPC architecture, the 601, was produced in 1993. An overview of the instruction set architecture of this family is provided first, followed by a description of some of its processor implementations.

11.4.1 REGISTER SET

There are 32 general-purpose registers and 32 floating-point registers. The floating-point registers are 64 bits long. The IEEE standard is used for representation of floating-point numbers. The PowerPC architecture defines both 32-bit and 64-bit modes of operation.

The size of the general-purpose registers is determined by which of these modes is implemented by a particular processor.

11.4.2 MEMORY ADDRESSING MODES

Memory is byte addressable and is only accessed by Load and Store instructions that transfer data operands between the memory and the processor registers. In keeping with the RISC design style, only simple forms of indexed addressing are used. An effective address is generated by adding the contents of a base register to an index that is either an immediate value contained in the instruction or is the contents of an index register. As an option, the effective address can be loaded back into the base register. This facilitates loading or storing a sequence of operands in contiguous memory locations. Single instructions are available for transferring multiple operands. The Load and Store instructions have a number of versions that provide flexibility in transferring operands of different types and sizes.

11.4.3 INSTRUCTIONS

PowerPC instructions are 32 bits long and have a regular format. The arithmetic and logic instructions use a 3-register format that specifies two operand registers and a destination register for storing the result. A large number of conditional branch instructions are provided. The PowerPC has a MultiplyAdd instruction that performs the operation

$$RD \leftarrow ([RA] \times [RB]) \pm [RC]$$

on floating-point operands in registers RA, RB, and RC. A class of conditional branch instructions decrement a counter and then branch, based on whether or not the decremented value has reached 0. The MultiplyAdd, decrement-and-branch, and multiple operand move instructions, along with optional updating of the base register in indexed addressing, are examples of features that are not normally found in RISC ISAs. These four features are useful in performing multiple arithmetic operations required in signal-processing tasks, efficiently terminating loops, saving and restoring processor registers on procedure entry and exit, and processing lists of data items, respectively. PowerPC designers have incorporated these features without unduly compromising the efficient, streamlined flow of simple, pipelined instructions that is a basic property of RISC machines. We note that all of these features, except for decrement-and-branch, are also present in the ARM ISA in similar forms.

11.4.4 POWERPC PROCESSORS

In the IBM product line, the PowerPC architecture is a successor to the POWER architecture used in the processors of the IBM Risc System (RS)/6000 line of computers. The first implementation of the PowerPC architecture was the 601 processor, which is a transition processor between the two architectures; as such, it implements a superset of POWER and PowerPC instructions. This allows the 601 to run compiled POWER machine programs as well as PowerPC programs. Later processors in the family are purely PowerPC processors.

PowerPC 601 Processor

The 601 processor chip, containing 2.8 million transistors, was first used in IBM desktop machines. The 601 is a 32-bit processor, intended for notebook, desktop, and low-end multiprocessor systems. Different versions were available with processor clock rates of 50, 66, 80, and 100 MHz.

The PowerPC 601 has a 32K-byte cache on the processor chip for holding both instructions and data. The cache is organized in 8-way associative sets. Three independent execution units are provided: an integer unit, a floating-point unit, and a branch-processing unit. Up to three instructions can be issued for execution in a clock cycle for superscaler operation. The 601 has four pipeline stages for integer instructions and six for floating-point instructions.

PowerPC 603 Processor

The 603 processor also has a 32-bit processing width. Intended for notebook and desktop computers, it is a low-cost, low-power processor, consuming about 3 watts of electrical power at 80 MHz. The five execution units provided can operate in parallel, so the instruction issuing and control hardware, which can issue up to three instructions per clock cycle, is somewhat more complex than in the 601. The on-chip cache is divided into two 8K-byte sections for separate, temporary storage of instructions and data.

PowerPC 604 Processor

The 32-bit 604 processor was designed for higher performance than was available in either the 601 or the 603; both integer and floating-point speeds are approximately double those in the 601 and 603 processors. The 604 achieves this performance level with a 100-MHz clock rate and a superscaler capability for issuing up to four instructions per clock cycle. The processor has six independent execution units: three integer units, a floating-point unit, a memory load/store unit, and a branch-processing unit. Personal computers and midrange workstations were the intended market for this processor.

PowerPC 620 Processor

The 620 processor implements the full 64-bit PowerPC architecture and supports superscalar performance. It was targeted for high-end desktop computers, servers, transaction processing systems, and multiprocessor systems.

Like the 604, the 620 has six independent execution units, and up to four instructions can be completed in a clock cycle. The actual rate of processing instructions in a particular program is enhanced by the processor's ability to execute instructions out of order. Dynamic branch prediction is used, and the processor chip contains both instruction and data caches. Each cache holds 32K bytes and is organized in 8-way associative sets.

MPC7450 Processor

The 601, 603, 604, and 620 were the first implementations of the PowerPC by IBM. After this 6XX line, Motorola implemented the 7XX and 7XXX lines of PowerPC processors with their MPC prefix on the labeling. The latest processor in the MPC7XXX line is the MPC7450, introduced in early 2001 with clock rates up to 733 MHz. It is used in the Apple Power Mac G4 computer line.

The MPC7450 is a superscalar processor with a 7-stage pipeline. Up to four instructions per clock cycle can be issued into the function units. There are eleven such units: A load/store unit, a branch unit, four integer units, a floating-point unit, and four units that perform parallel arithmetic operations on packed vector data operands. Motorola uses the name AltiVec [16] for these latter units.

The AltiVec hardware performs parallel operations on vector data operands similar to the way that Intel Pentium processors perform MMX and SSE operations, as described in Sections 3.23.2 and 11.3.6. The packed data operated on by AltiVec instructions are located in thirty-two 128-bit vector registers, separate from the general-purpose and floating-point registers. A vector register can hold sixteen 8-bit integers, eight 16-bit integers, four 32-bit integers, or four single-precision (32-bit) floating-point numbers. Vector load and store instructions are used to transfer data between memory and the vector registers. AltiVec instructions speed up multimedia and signal-processing operations. One of the instructions is a Multiply-Accumulate instruction that multiplies corresponding elements in two vector registers and adds the products to corresponding elements of a third vector register. This operation is common in digital signal processing operations. Vector dot product instructions are also included.

The on-chip L1 cache level comprises separate 32K-byte instruction and data caches. These caches are 8-way set associative. An L2 cache is also included on the processor chip. It contains 256K bytes and is also 8-way set associative. Transfers between the L1 and L2 caches are done over a 256-bit path at the processor clock rate. An off-chip L3 cache is accessed over a 64-bit bus. It can be configured for 1M- or 2M-byte capacities.

11.5   THE SUN MICROSYSTEMS SPARC FAMILY

The SPARC architecture was developed by Sun Microsystems Corporation to be a scalable architecture. It is the basis for a series of processors that provide increasingly higher performance as implementation technology and organizational innovations develop. The basic instruction set architecture has remained the same. SPARC processors are intended for the high-performance workstation and server market. They are designed so that they can be used in multiple processor systems where the processors share a common main memory. Such systems are described in Chapter 12.

The SPARC architecture is a RISC-style architecture with a 3-register, 32-bit, fixed length instruction format. Two source operand registers and a destination register are specified in an instruction. All instructions that perform operations on data manipulate the operands in processor registers. There are 32 general-purpose registers for integers and addresses, and 32 registers for floating-point operands. The only instructions that access memory are the load and store instructions that transfer operands between the registers and the memory.

The first implementations of the SPARC architecture, in 1987, handled 32-bit addresses and 32-bit data. The latest version of the architecture, version 9, handles both addresses and data as 64-bit values, and is implemented by the UltraSPARC series of processors. Instructions continue to be 32 bits wide, and the programmer's model of all registers remains the same. Backward compatibility has been maintained, that is, the UltraSPARC processors can execute machine code from earlier versions of the architecture.

The SPARC architecture was introduced in Chapter 8. The UltraSPARC II processor was used there to illustrate how pipelining is implemented in a high-performance processor. The UltraSPARC family, which includes UltraSPARC I, II, and III, features multiple execution units and superscalar performance. In addition to the basic SPARC instruction set, a number of special instructions have been introduced to support graphics and multimedia applications. They are called the *visual instruction set* (VIS). VIS instructions provide parallel vector operations on graphics pixels or digital signal samples packed into 64-bit words. The VIS instructions are similar to the Intel MMX and SSE instructions (Part III of Chapter 3 and Section 11.3.6) and the Motorola AltiVec instructions (Section 11.4.4). Successive members of the UltraSPARC family offer increasingly higher performance, with higher clock speeds, faster memory and I/O interfaces, and larger and more sophisticated cache organizations. For example, the UltraSPARC I was manufactured using 0.5-micron CMOS technology and used a clock frequency of 167 MHz [17]. Its successor, the UltraSPARC II, has a very similar 9-stage pipeline organization, but achieves higher performance because of the faster 0.25-micron technology used [18]. It operates with clock frequencies in the range 250 to 480 MHz.

The most recent member of the family, the UltraSPARC III, uses a 14-stage pipeline [19]. There are four integer execution units and three floating-point units, including processing for the VIS instructions. The UltraSPARC III is manufactured in 0.18-micron technology. Clock frequencies are in the range 750 to 900 MHz, and future models are intended to run as high as 1.5 GHz. The on-chip L1 data cache contains 64K bytes and the instruction cache contains 32K bytes. They are both 4-way set associative and operate with 32-byte blocks. The external L2 cache is direct mapped and can be configured for 4M- or 8M-byte capacity. The UltraSPARC III provides extensive support for use in multiprocessor configurations that can potentially have hundreds of processors.

The microSPARC Family

Another family of processors based on the SPARC architecture is called microSPARC. Members of this family are 32-bit processors based on version 8 of the SPARC architecture specifications. They are intended for low-cost uniprocessor applications. Some of these processors, such as microSPARCIIep, include a PCI interface and memory controller on the processor chip, and are well suited for embedded applications. The fact that these microprocessors are fully compatible with the UltraSPARC processors offers considerable advantage to developers of embedded applications. The software intended for a given application can be developed and tested on powerful workstations and then downloaded to the target processor in the final stages of development.

11.6 THE COMPAQ ALPHA FAMILY

Digital Equipment Corporation introduced the Alpha architecture in 1992 as the successor to the 32-bit VAX family [20]. Digital Equipment was acquired by the Compaq company in 1998. Compaq [21] produces a line of high-end workstations and server systems that use Alpha processors, labeled with the numbering sequence 21X64, with $X = 0$, 1, and 2.

The Alpha architecture is a RISC design with 64-bit address and data sizes. There are 32 general-purpose and 32 floating-point registers. Multiple pipelined operation units are used in all 21X64 processors to achieve superscalar instruction execution rates, enhanced by both static and dynamic branch prediction. Separate on-chip data and instruction caches are used.

A basic goal of pipelined processor design is to keep logic depth short in each pipeline stage to minimize the stage delay for any given implementation technology, permitting a high clock rate. An important design characteristic of the Alpha architecture is that it uses only simple instruction formats and addressing modes to achieve short pipeline stage delays. Only 32-bit and 64-bit aligned loads and stores are permitted between the L1 cache and the processor, minimizing the delay in those transfers.

11.6.1 INSTRUCTION AND ADDRESSING MODE FORMATS

The Alpha ISA has only four instruction types, all 32 bits long:

Operate — Integer, floating-point, and byte-manipulation operations are included in this class. These instructions use a three-operand format, with operands contained in processor registers or in an immediate field of the instruction.

Memory — Load/store operations use register plus displacement indexed addressing as the only addressing mode.

Branch — Conditional branch instructions contain a displacement value that specifies the direction and distance of the branch target address relative to the program counter. There is no condition code register; condition codes are optionally written into a general-purpose register by operate instructions. This register is then named by branch instructions that need to test the codes. Unconditional branch instructions use the named register to hold the updated value of the program counter as the return address if the branch is a subroutine call.

Call-PAL — Privileged Architecture Library (PAL) instructions perform operating system functions not available in user mode. These privileged instructions can access hardware resources, that is, processor state registers, that are not accessible by the normal instruction set. PAL routines also contain instructions that do not exist in the defined Alpha instruction set. They service interrupts and manipulate memory management unit registers.

11.6.2 ALPHA 21064 PROCESSOR

The first implementation of the Alpha architecture, the 21064, is a 200-MHz chip with 1.7 million transistors that dissipates 30 watts of power [22]. It contains 8K-byte L1 instruction and data caches. Both caches are direct mapped and have 32-byte blocks. An external L2 cache can be configured with a capacity between 128K and 8M bytes. The memory management unit has separate translation lookaside buffers for instruction (12 entries) and data (32 entries) accesses.

A maximum of two instructions can be issued per clock cycle. Four independent processing units are used: an integer unit, a floating-point unit, a branching unit, and a memory load/store unit. The pipeline depths in these four units are seven, ten, six, and seven, respectively. The first four stages are common and can handle two instruction streams in parallel.

11.6.3 ALPHA 21164 PROCESSOR

The 21164 processor was introduced in 1994 [23]. It provides roughly double the performance of the first 21064 processors. The transistor count in the 21164 is 9.3 million, and 50 watts of power are dissipated at a clock rate of 300 MHz. An on-chip, unified, 96K-byte L2 cache is provided, in addition to the 8K-byte L1 instruction and data caches. The L2 cache is 3-way set associative and has 64-byte blocks. An off-chip L3 cache can be configured with a capacity between 1M and 64M bytes.

The maximum instruction issue rate is four instructions per clock cycle, double that of the 21064. There is one more functional unit than in the 21064. It is used to manage the L2 and L3 caches. Pipeline depths are similar. Memory management hardware includes a 48-entry translation lookaside buffer for accessing instructions, and the buffer for accessing data has 64 entries.

11.6.4 ALPHA 21264 PROCESSOR

The 21264 is the latest processor in the 21X64 line [24]. It was introduced in 1998 with a 500-MHz clock rate. In early 2001, versions running at up to 850 MHz were available. There are 15 million transistors in the processor chip.

The cache arrangement is significantly different from earlier Alpha processors. The L1 instruction and data caches are much larger at 64K bytes each. They are both 2-way set associative caches. The unified L2 cache is off-chip, and it can be configured with a capacity between 1M and 16M bytes. There is no L3 cache level. The increased hit rates in the larger L1 caches lead to an overall decrease in memory access latencies, even though the L2 cache is off-chip.

Another significant difference between the 21264 and earlier Alpha processors is the ability to issue instructions to the functional units in an out-of-order sequence, as discussed in Chapter 8. This increases the sustainable superscalar instruction execution rates achievable on typical programs. The maximum instruction issue rate is four per cycle, the same as in the 21164. But functional unit resources are increased by replicating sections of both the integer and floating-point units and adding a new functional unit for processing video data. This increase in instruction execution hardware, coupled with the higher clock rates and the out-of-order instruction issue capability, leads to a performance level about twice that of the 21164.

11.7 THE INTEL IA-64 FAMILY

Since the mid-1990s, Intel and Hewlett-Packard have been jointly developing a 64-bit microprocessor architecture called IA-64 [25]. The first processor that implements this architecture is called the Itanium (earlier code-named the Merced). The IA-64 architecture is completely different from the IA-32 architecture, which has been Intel's 32-bit architecture from the 80386 onward, through the continuing Pentium line of processors. Intel is expected to continue to produce processors for both the IA-32 and IA-64 architectures. Programming aspects of the IA-64 architecture are described in references [26] and [27].

The IA-64 architecture has a 64-bit address space and 64-bit integer and floating-point formats. The 3-register RISC-like instruction format occupies 41 bits. There are three 7-bit register fields for addressing the 128 general registers or the 128 floating-point registers. A 6-bit field specifies conditional execution of the instruction as described below. The remaining 14 bits of the instruction specify the OP code.

11.7.1 INSTRUCTION BUNDLES

A distinctive feature of the IA-64 architecture is that three 41-bit instructions are grouped into a 128-bit *bundle,* along with a 5-bit field called the *template* which specifies compiler-derived information about how instructions can be executed in parallel. For example, one of the template codes indicates the location of a *stop,* which marks the end of a group of instructions that can be executed in parallel. Such a group may extend over a number of bundles. Information in the templates is used by the processor to schedule the parallel execution of instructions on multiple functional units to achieve superscalar operation. This feature of the IA-64 architecture is called *Explicitly Parallel Instruction Computing* (EPIC). EPIC can be considered as an extension of the concept of *Very Long Instruction Word* (VLIW) instruction set design [28]. In VLIW architectures, each instruction specifies a number of possibly different operations that can be applied in parallel to independent data operands.

11.7.2 CONDITIONAL EXECUTION

A major aspect of the IA-64 architecture is the use of conditional execution of instructions, called *predication*. A 6-bit *predicate* field in each instruction selects one of 64 one-bit *predicate flags* contained in the processor. These flags effectively replace the condition code flags in conventional processors. If the named flag is equal to 1, the instruction is executed; otherwise, it is not. Actually, the instruction is processed through the instruction pipeline, but its results are written into the destination location only if the predicate flag is 1. This feature is similar to the conditional execution of instructions in the ARM architecture, described in Part I of Chapter 3.

Conditional execution of instructions increases the rate of executing program instructions by removing conditional branches in certain situations. For example, a short, forward, conditional branch can be eliminated by conditionally executing the code block between what would otherwise be the location of a conditional branch instruction and its target location. The predicate flag guarding execution of each instruction in the code block is set by a test or compare instruction ahead of the block.

A similar opportunity for performance enhancement occurs in generating IA-64 code for an *if-then-else* construct. Figure 11.3*a* shows conventional machine code for executing the Add instruction if the contents of registers R1 and R2 are equal, or executing the Subtract instruction if they are not. The corresponding IA-64 code is shown in Figure 11.3*b*. The IA-64 CompareEqual instruction operates as follows. Predicate flag P1 is set to 1 if the contents of R1 and R2 are equal; otherwise, it is set to 0. Flag P2 is set to the complement of P1. The Add instruction is executed if P1 = 1, and the Subtract instruction is executed if P2 = 1. Double semicolons indicate the positions of stops. In this example, the Add and Subtract instructions between the two double semicolons can be scheduled for parallel execution. Only one of them will have its result actually written into the destination register specified, as determined by the values of P1 and P2. The instruction execution pipelines will not be stalled if the values of P1 and P2 are determined before the write stages of the Add and Subtract instructions are reached. In

```
                Compare       R1,R2
                Branch≠0      ELSE
        THEN:   Add           R3,R4,R5
                Branch        NEXT
        ELSE:   Subtract      R6,R7,R8
        NEXT:   ...
```

(a) Conventional code

```
                CompareEqual  P2,P1 = R1,R2 ;;
                (P1) Add      R3,R4,R5
                (P2) Subtract R6,R7,R8 ;;
        NEXT:   ...
```

(b) IA-64 code

Figure 11.3 Implementing *if-then-else* code in the IA-64 architecture.

addition to these types of performance enhancing features, the IA-64 also uses branch prediction and speculative execution as discussed in Chapter 8.

11.7.3 SPECULATIVE LOADS

In order to mitigate against the delays introduced by register load instructions that may need to access main memory, a special form of load, called a *speculative load,* can be generated by the compiler. This load is placed ahead of where it would normally appear in a conventionally compiled program. This increases the chance that it will be in the register when it is needed, avoiding any memory access delay. A check must be made that it actually is there when it is about to be used. Special care must be taken in handling speculative loads that are moved ahead of predicted branches.

11.7.4 REGISTERS AND THE REGISTER STACK

The IA-64 architecture specifies 128 general registers that can be used to hold 64-bit integers or 64-bit addresses. There are also 128 registers for holding double-precision (64-bit) floating-point numbers. Two single-precision numbers can be packed into one register. In addition, there are eight 64-bit registers for holding subroutine call/return linkage addresses.

The first 32 of the 128 general registers, R0 through R31, are used as normal data or address registers. The remaining 96 registers, R32 through R127, are handled as a *register stack* for holding the local variables of subroutines and the parameters passed between calling and called routines. This register stack effectively replaces the processor stack, implemented in memory, as described in Section 2.9.1. The register stack is managed in such a way that registers need not be saved/restored to/from the memory as a sequence of nested subroutines is called, as described below. This assumes that the total local and parameter variable register space required by all of the subroutines does not exceed 96. If that happens, the processor control hardware automatically "spills" a portion of the register stack into the memory to create the needed excess register space, and it automatically loads that portion back into the register stack as returns are executed.

Register renaming is also managed automatically by the processor so that all routines — the main routine and called subroutines — always refer to their local registers from R32 upward, even though the actual physical registers may be different. (Another version of register renaming was discussed in Chapter 8.) An overlap region of the high end of a caller's local registers with the low end of the called routine's local registers is used to implement parameter passing.

Figure 11.4 shows an example of how the register stack is managed when the main program calls a subroutine. The register ordering in this figure shows a stack that grows upward. This is done for easy comparison with stack illustrations in Chapter 2, where stacks grow toward lower memory addresses. Registers R0 through R31 are available to all routines and can be considered as holding global variables. They are not shown in the figure. The main program is assumed to use the eight registers R32 through R39 for its local variables, and the four registers R40 through R43 to pass parameters to a

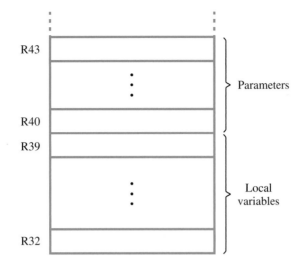

(a) Active register area in the main program after execution of Alloc 8,4

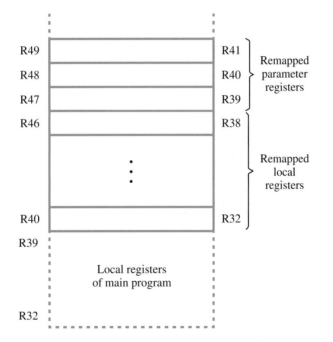

(b) Active register area in the subroutine after execution of Alloc 7,3

Figure 11.4 Register stack allocations for local variables and parameter passing in IA-64.

subroutine. This use of registers is declared to the processor hardware by executing the instruction

Alloc   8,4

in the main program. Figure 11.4a shows this situation. After the main program calls the subroutine, the subroutine executes the instruction

Alloc   7,3

to declare that it requires seven local registers, including the four used to receive parameters passed from the calling routine, as well as three registers to pass parameters to a second subroutine. The ten (physical) registers R40 through R49 are remapped by the processor hardware so that they can be referenced as (logical) registers R32 through R41 by the subroutine. The part of the register stack that is active during execution of the subroutine is shown in Figure 11.4b. The information needed to do this dynamic remapping at execution time is derived from the values in the Alloc instruction executed by the main program. When the subroutine performs the return to the main program, the active portion of the register stack returns to the state shown in Figure 11.4a. The register stack implements a version of multiple *register windows,* as employed in the Berkeley RISC designs [29], [30], and in the UltraSPARC II processor (see Chapter 8).

Another form of register renaming, called *register rotation,* is also used in the IA-64. It is used to overlap the execution of successive iterations of a loop, assuming that there are no iteration-to-iteration data dependency restrictions. Normally, successive iterations of a loop use the same registers, those named in the loop body. In the IA-64 architecture, the compiler generates code for a single copy of the loop body in a form that allows the hardware to automatically rename the registers so that different physical registers are used on successive iterations of the loop. This permits the instruction scheduling and issuing hardware to start successive iterations before previous iterations have completed. This technique for reducing total loop execution time is called *software pipelining*. It differs from loop unrolling, in which replicated copies of the loop body are placed in the machine instruction code.

11.7.5 ITANIUM PROCESSOR

The Itanium processor is the first implementation of the IA-64 architecture [31]. It has a relatively large number of replicated functional units for the different types of operations: integer, floating-point, and multimedia (like the MMX operations of the IA-32 architecture, described in Part III of Chapter 3). Superscalar execution is achieved by the ability to issue up to six instructions (two 3-instruction bundles) on each 800-MHz clock cycle into the 10-stage pipeline. The functional units are: 4 integer units, 4 floating-point units, 4 multimedia (MMX) units, 2 load/store units, and 3 branch units. The integer register bank has 8 read ports and 6 write ports in order to exchange data simultaneously with the multiple function units.

There are three levels of cache units. Both L1 and L2 caches are on the same chip as the processor, and L3 is implemented on separate chips in the same cartridge package with the processor. The L1 cache level consists of separate instruction and data caches, each containing 16K bytes. These caches are 4-way set associative, and they have 32-byte blocks. The instruction cache can deliver two 3-instruction bundles (256 bits) to the processor per clock cycle. The L2 cache contains 96K bytes. It is 6-way set associative and has 64-byte blocks. The L3 cache contains a total of 4M bytes, with 64-byte blocks. It is 4-way set associative and communicates with the L2 cache over a 128-bit internal bus connection at the processor clock rate, providing a transfer rate of 12.8 gigabytes/s.

Interactions between the caches and between the L1 cache and the processor are organized in a way that minimizes the effect of processor pipeline stalls and cache misses on the average instruction execution rate. Some aspects of these interactions are worth noting. There is a decoupling buffer between the L1 instruction cache and the processor. It can contain up to eight 3-instruction bundles. This allows prefetching of instructions from the L1 cache into the buffer to continue when the processor stalls in issuing instructions. Conversely, the processor can continue to fetch and issue instructions from the buffer when a cache miss occurs in the prefetching process. There is also a buffer between the L1 and L2 caches to allow the prefetching of instructions from L2 into L1. It is twice the size of the buffer between the L1 cache and the processor instruction issue hardware. The L1 cache only feeds the integer register bank. Floating-point operands are loaded into the floating-point registers directly from the L2 cache.

There is a 64-bit system bus connecting the package containing the processor and the caches to other system components such as main memory and I/O devices. It can support a 266-MHz transfer rate, which is 2.1 gigabytes/s.

The external bus controller can accommodate the direct connection of up to four Itanium processors in a multiprocessor configuration. The controller handles the cache coherence operations required when the multiple processors share common external memory units, as described in Chapter 12.

11.8 A STACK PROCESSOR

All processors discussed in this book use general-purpose registers to hold data operands. Instructions can access them in any desired order. Some years ago, the Hewlett-Packard Company designed and manufactured a computer called the HP3000, whose main architectural feature is an instruction set that is keyed to processing operands held in a stack data structure. Access to operands in a stack is restricted to only those operands residing at the top of the stack, and results are always returned to the top of the stack. This type of organization is not appropriate for current RISC and CISC processor designs that are highly parallel. In these processors, simultaneous access to several operands in a large register set is required for high performance. Nevertheless, the HP3000, and the earlier series of B5500, B6500, and B6700 computers produced by the Burroughs Corporation, which also featured stack-oriented processing, are historically important as commercial implementations of stack computing. The way these machines process arithmetic expressions is both interesting and elegant. We illustrate the main ideas by describing the HP3000 instruction set and addressing modes. Our discussion concentrates on only the features that characterize the stack organization of this computer.

11.8.1 STACK STRUCTURE

The HP3000 is a 16-bit computer. Its memory contains program instructions and data in separate domains; instructions and data cannot be intermixed except for immediate data that can be used in programs. Hardware registers are used as pointers to the program and data segments, as shown in Figure 11.5.

Three registers specify the program segment. The program base (PB) and the program limit (PL) registers indicate the memory area occupied by the program, and the program counter (PC) points to the current instruction. Each of these registers contains the appropriate 16-bit address.

The data segment is divided into two parts — the stack and the data area. Five 16-bit pointers are used to delineate and access these memory locations. The contents of the data base (DB) register denote the starting location of the stack. The stack grows in the higher-address direction. If the top element of the stack is at location i, then the next element pushed onto the stack will be at location $i + 1$. This contrasts with other stacks discussed in the book, where it has been assumed that they grow in the direction of decreasing addresses. The address of the top element in the stack, also called the

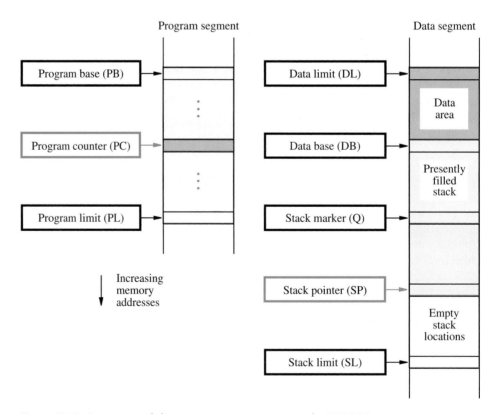

Figure 11.5 Program and data segment organization in the HP3000.

top of stack (TOS), is stored in the 16-bit stack pointer (SP). The SP is not actually a single hardware register, as we explain shortly, but it can be thought of that way. It is incremented or decremented when data elements are pushed onto or popped off the stack. From the user's point of view, it functions as any other 16-bit pointer register. The upper limit of the stack is defined by the contents of the stack limit (SL) register. Therefore, the stack is allowed to grow until [SP] = [SL]. Any attempt to extend the stack past the limits defined by DB and SL is prevented by the hardware. The data area extends from the location immediately preceding the location pointed to by the DB register to the limit specified in the data limit (DL) register.

The pointer registers specify the stack's current size, maximum size, and location in memory. The stack is thus a dynamic structure that can be easily changed. Figure 11.5 shows one other pointer, the stack marker (Q) register. This register denotes the starting point for the data stack of the current procedure. Actually, Q points to the fourth word of a four-word entry in the stack, called the *stack marker,* that facilitates passing control between procedures. The Q register serves a role similar to the frame pointer register described in Chapter 2. When a procedure must be suspended, for example, as a result of an interrupt, the information needed to allow proper return to the suspended procedure is placed onto the stack in the form of a stack marker.

The first word of the stack marker stores the current contents of an index register, and the second word contains the return address. The return address information is actually stored as the difference between the value in the PC, which points to the next instruction to be executed in the current procedure, and the contents of the PB register. By storing the difference, instead of the absolute value, programs can be moved out of the memory and later returned to a different place in the memory. The new area in memory is pointed to by loading a new value in the PB register. The third word saves the status information contained in the status register, and the fourth word stores the distance between this stack marker and the one immediately preceding it.

Figure 11.6 shows one stack marker, denoted k, that was placed on the stack at the time Procedure$_k$ was initiated, and another stack marker, denoted $k + 1$, that is placed onto the stack when a new procedure, Procedure$_{k+1}$, is initiated. When the new procedure is completed, the machine transfers control to the previous procedure using the data in the stack marker $k + 1$. At that time, the Q register must be set to point to the fourth word of stack marker k. This is readily accomplished because the distance between the stack markers is stored as a part of each marker. Also, the SP is set to point to the location immediately preceding stack marker $k + 1$. As a result, SP points to the top of the stack used by Procedure$_k$, thus restoring the situation that existed at the time Procedure$_{k+1}$ was invoked. This technique can be used to nest any number of procedures. Parameter passing between procedures also uses the stack.

In addition to the pointer registers, HP3000 computers have other hardware registers used in the internal organization of the machine. The only two of these that are visible to the programmer are the index and status registers, which function in essentially the same ways as similarly named registers in most other computers. Note, however, that there are no general-purpose registers available to the programmer. Instead, data are manipulated using the stack as temporary storage, as we show in an example in the next section.

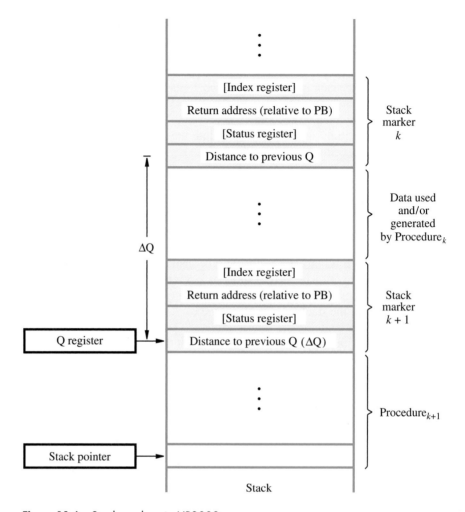

Figure 11.6   Stack markers in HP3000.

11.8.2 STACK INSTRUCTIONS

As a basic strategy, stack computers perform operations on data that occupy the top few locations of the stack. Furthermore, the results generated are left on the stack. This assumes that there are instructions that can move data between the stack and the memory.

The HP3000 has a variety of instructions that are all 16 bits long. Most of the instructions involve the stack in some way, and typically either the operands, operand addresses, or other relevant parameters reside in the stack. This allows great flexibility in using the 16-bit code space of the instructions. There are 13 major classes of instructions. Instead of describing the full HP3000 instruction set, we restrict our attention to the classes that illustrate the stack organization of the machine. Let us first consider the Memory Address instructions, whose format is shown in Figure 11.7. Eleven valuations

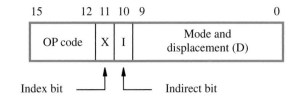

Figure 11.7 Memory Address instruction format in HP3000.

Mode		Bit pattern $b_9\ b_8\ b_7\ b_6\ b_5\ b_4\ b_3\ b_2\ b_1\ b_0$	Effective memory address
PC +	relative	0 0 ←—— D ——→	$[PC]+D$
PC −	relative	0 1 ←—— D ——→	$[PC]-D$
DB +	relative	1 0 ←—— D ——→	$[DB]+D$
Q +	relative	1 1 0 ←—— D ——→	$[Q]-D$
Q −	relative	1 1 1 0 ←— D ——→	$[Q]-D$
SP −	relative	1 1 1 1 ←— D ——→	$[SP]-D$

of the 5-bit OP-code field are used to specify instructions in this class. The Memory Address instructions include:

LOAD Push a specific memory word onto the stack.

STOR Pop the top word of the stack (TOS) into a specified memory location.

ADDM Add a specified memory word to TOS, and replace the TOS operand with the resultant sum.

MPYM Multiply a specified memory word with TOS, and replace the TOS operand with the least significant word of the product.

INCM Increment a specified memory word.

These instructions specify the memory operand in the relative address mode, in which addresses are given relative to the contents of the PC, DB, Q, or SP registers. The 10-bit mode and displacement field indicates the mode and the magnitude of the displacement, as the figure shows. The displacement is not the same in all modes because the displacement field varies from 6 to 8 bits. Index and indirect bits specify whether indexed or indirect addressing or both are to be performed. These are the only addressing modes that can be used to address operands in the data area of Figure 11.5.

The second class of instructions is the Move instructions, which reference either one or two memory operands. These instructions can move words or bytes from one memory location to another, compare two strings of bytes in the memory, or scan a byte string until a particular byte value is found. Memory addresses are again computed in the relative mode. The displacement is not given explicitly within the instruction,

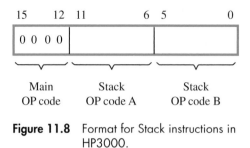

Figure 11.8 Format for Stack instructions in HP3000.

however, but is included as data in the stack. Moreover, addresses can only be specified relative to the program or data bases, that is, the contents of the PB or DB registers. A good example of this class of instructions is the basic MOVE instruction. It transfers k words from one memory location to another, where

- The first stack element, TOS, specifies k.
- The contents of the second stack element give the address of the first source memory location relative to either PB or DB.
- The contents of the third stack element give the address of the first destination memory location relative to DB.

This instruction can be represented within a 16-bit code space because most of the addressing data and the length parameter are given in implicitly specified stack locations. These data must be loaded onto the stack before the instruction can be executed.

Next, we consider the Stack instructions, whose format is shown in Figure 11.8. This class of instructions is identified by four zeros in the high-order bit positions. The remaining 12 bits are available to specify particular instructions and are split into two 6-bit fields, each of which can be used to specify a distinct operation. The 6 bits allow as many as 64 distinct stack operations to be defined. This number is large enough to accommodate a variety of stack operations. An instruction specifying one stack operation uses 10 bits (the main OP code plus stack OP code A) and disregards the remaining 6 bits. When the remaining bits specify a second stack operation (using stack OP code B), that operation is performed after the first operation is completed. In this way, two stack operations can be packed within a single instruction. Such efficient utilization of the instruction code space is possible only because addressing data and operands are not included explicitly as part of an instruction.

Some examples of Stack instructions are

ADD Add the contents of the top two words on the stack, delete them from the stack, and push the sum onto the stack.

CMP Compare the contents of the top two words on the stack, set the condition codes accordingly, and delete both words from the stack.

DIV Divide the integer in the second word of the stack by the integer in TOS. Replace the second word with the quotient and the word in TOS with the remainder.

DEL Delete the top word of the stack.

Many instructions of this type are provided, although some are more complicated. A Divide Long (DIVL) instruction, for example, divides a double-word integer in the second and third elements of the stack by the integer in the first element. Then these three words are deleted, and the remainder and quotient are pushed onto the stack to become the first and second elements, respectively. We use the term "instruction" somewhat loosely in this discussion of stack instructions. It would be more accurate to refer to Add and Divide operations, for example, since these two operations can be specified within a single instruction. However, it is more customary to speak in terms of instructions when describing such actions, and it is appropriate to describe the preceding technique as packing two instructions into one. Such packing is possible only when two consecutive stack operations are to be performed. In other cases, OP code B is left unused.

So far, we have emphasized only one advantage of compressing instructions, that of the low code-space requirements. Another advantage stems from the reduced number of memory accesses because two instructions are effectively fetched as part of one 16-bit word. We must remember that, during execution of a stack instruction, operands in the stack must be accessed, and this requires memory accesses if the stack resides in the memory.

To illustrate the role of the stack as temporary storage for intermediate results in arithmetic processing, we consider a simple example. Figure 11.9 shows how the arithmetic expression

$$w = \frac{(a + b)}{c/d + (e \times f)/(g + h)}$$

is evaluated. We assume that the values of the variables $a, b, \ldots, h$ are not available at the top of the stack. They are stored in memory locations with addresses A, B, $\ldots$, H, and can be accessed with the addressing mechanism given in Figure 11.7. Furthermore, assume all operands are integers whose sizes are such that only single-length products need to be considered. The figure shows 13 processing steps that must be performed. The required operations follow the order obtained by scanning the numerator and denominator of the expression from left to right. In our notation, the top element of the stack (TOS) is denoted as S. Thus, the operation S ← [S] + [B] means that the contents of TOS and operand B are added, and the sum replaces the value in TOS. The operation S ← [S − 1]/[S] indicates that the contents of the second element in the stack are divided by the contents of TOS. The two operands are deleted from the stack and the quotient and remainder are pushed onto the stack.

The HP3000 machine instructions needed to perform the necessary computation are shown in the figure. Their function is described earlier in this section. Most steps can be implemented with a single instruction, except for the division operation. The DIV instruction replaces the dividend and the divisor with the quotient and the remainder, respectively. Because we are only interested in the quotient, we use the DEL instruction to delete the remainder from the stack. Whenever two consecutive Stack instructions are encountered, they can be combined into one 16-bit instruction, as we explain earlier. All intermediate results are stored on the stack. Figure 11.9*b* shows the top elements of the stack after step 9 is completed.

Step	Operation performed	Machine instruction	
1	$S \leftarrow [A]$	LOAD	A
2	$S \leftarrow [S] + [B]$	ADDM	B
3	$S \leftarrow [C]$	LOAD	C
4	$S \leftarrow [D]$	LOAD	D
5	$S \leftarrow [S - 1]/[S]$	DIV DEL	} combined
6	$S \leftarrow [E]$	LOAD	E
7	$S \leftarrow [S] \times [F]$	MPYM	F
8	$S \leftarrow [G]$	LOAD	G
9	$S \leftarrow [S] + [H]$	ADDM	H
10	$S \leftarrow [S - 1]/[S]$	DIV DEL	} combined
11	$S \leftarrow [S - 1] + [S]$	ADD	
12	$S \leftarrow [S - 1]/[S]$	DIV DEL	} combined
13	$W \leftarrow [S]$	STOR	W

(a) Operations to be performed and the necessary machine instructions

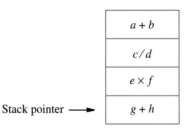

(b) Temporary results stored in the stack after step 9

Figure 11.9   Stack usage in processing the expression
$w = (a + b)/[c/d + (ef)/(g + h)]$.

11.8.3 HARDWARE REGISTERS IN THE STACK

Accessing memory locations is one of the most critical time constraints in a computer. The time needed to read an operand from the memory is longer than the time required to perform operations in processor registers. This is the main reason for including general-purpose registers and caches in the processor. In the case of stack computers, the temporary storage function of the general-purpose registers is provided through the stack mechanism. If the stack is implemented entirely in the memory, the processor must make frequent memory accesses because all temporary storage locations are part of the stack.

The possibility of implementing the entire stack with hardware registers could be expensive and somewhat inflexible. A compromise between an all-register or an all-memory implementation of the stack is possible, however, if most of the stack is located in the memory and its top few elements are held in hardware registers in the processor. The time to access the stack is then reduced because most accesses involve only the top few elements and therefore only require register transfers within the processor. In the HP3000 computer, four registers contain the top four elements of the stack.

Including hardware registers in the stack implies that the true top of the stack (TOS) is often one of the registers. This means that the SP does not necessarily point to a memory location. To keep track of where the top elements of the stack are at any given time, the SP function is implemented by two registers. A 16-bit stack in memory (SM) register contains the address of the highest memory location presently occupied by the stack, and a 3-bit register (SR) indicates whether zero, one, two, three, or four top elements of the stack are presently contained in the hardware registers. Thus, the value [SP] is

$$[SP] = [SM] + [SR]$$

This value is equal to the address in the memory where the top element of the stack would be if all elements of the stack were in the memory. This structure is illustrated in Figure 11.10. The programmer does not have to be aware of the inclusion of hardware registers in the stack. For the programmer's purpose, only one pointer exists — the stack pointer, SP.

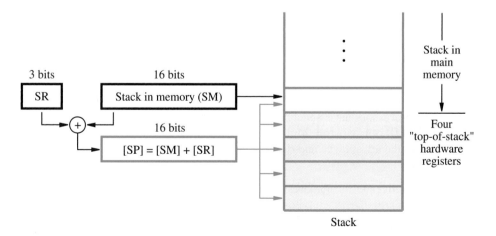

Figure 11.10 Top-of-stack structure in the HP3000.

11.9 CONCLUDING REMARKS

High-performance processors all employ on-chip caches for instructions, data, and address translation operations. They have multiple, independent, pipelined processing units and they have the capability to issue more than one instruction per processor clock cycle to these units, possibly in out-of-order sequence. Sophisticated methods for dynamic branch prediction and speculative execution of alternate program paths, made possible by predicated execution of instructions, increases overall performance. These design features are fundamental to achieving high execution rates for programs, independent of whether the instruction sets and addressing modes follow the RISC or CISC design approaches. Optimizing compilers that translate high-level language programs into efficient machine language code are also critical to achieving high performance. Many factors must be considered when evaluating the performance of a computer, and standardized benchmark programs are commonly used for this purpose, as discussed in Chapter 1.

PROBLEMS

11.1 How is conditional execution of ARM instructions (see Part I of Chapter 3) related to predicated execution of IA-64 instructions? Comment on similarities and differences.

11.2 The 16-bit Thumb instruction subset of ARM instructions is intended for compact program encoding. Estimate the number of Thumb instructions needed to program the evaluation of the arithmetic expression shown in Figure 11.9. Assume that the Thumb subset has an appropriate divide instruction (which it does not) for the purposes of this question. How does the estimated Thumb instruction count compare to the HP3000 program instruction count in Figure 11.9a?

11.3 Discuss the similarities and differences between the Motorola 680X0 family and the Intel 80X86 family of processors, up to the 68040 and the 80486 versions.

11.4 The 68030 microprocessor has a 256-byte instruction cache and a 256-byte data cache. Is this better than having a 512-byte instruction cache and no data cache? What are the advantages and disadvantages of these two alternatives? Answer the same two questions for a unified 512-byte instruction and data cache.

11.5 Intel IA-32 processors have special instructions for dedicated I/O operations, as described in Part III of Chapter 3. Motorola 680X0 processors use only memory-mapped I/O. What are the advantages and disadvantages of memory-mapped I/O compared to dedicated I/O?

11.6 Discuss the relative merits of addressing modes in the Motorola 680X0 and Intel 80X86 processors. In particular, discuss how the addressing modes in each processor facilitate program relocation, implementation of a stack, accessing an operand list, and manipulating character strings.

11.7 Section 11.3.1 explains that an IA-32 processor can view the memory as being organized in four different ways, depending on how segmentation and paging are used. Give some examples of situations in which each of the four possibilities is beneficial.

11.8 Write an ARM, 68000, or IA-32 program to evaluate the arithmetic expression in Figure 11.9. How does your program compare to the one in the figure with respect to the number of machine instructions required? Assume that the standard ARM instruction set has an appropriate divide instruction (which it does not) for the purposes of this question.

11.9 In Alpha processors, only 32-bit and 64-bit aligned loads and stores are directly handled in the datapath between the cache and the processor. Sketch the combinational logic network that would be required in a 32-bit-wide datapath to permit loading any one of the four bytes of a 32-bit quantity into the low-order byte position at the destination side of the path.

11.10 Compare the handling of the register stack in the IA-64 processors to that of the processor (memory) stack in Chapter 2. In particular, what are the counterparts of the Chapter 2 stack pointer, SP, and frame pointer, FP, in the IA-64 scheme?

11.11 Give a general description of the hardware needed to support execution of the Alloc X,Y instruction used for managing the IA-64 register stack. Assume that small registers and adders are available. How are they used?

11.12 The Alpha 21264 processor has a much different arrangement of caches than the 21164. Why is the arrangement in the 21264 better? That is, under what circumstances do programs execute more quickly on the 21264, based only on the effects of cacheing? Include more than an observation on hit rates in your answer.

11.13 Show how the expression

$$w = a\left[(b \times c) + (d \times e) + \frac{f \times g}{h \times i}\right]$$

can be evaluated in an HP3000 computer.

11.14 In an HP3000 computer, Procedure$_i$ generates eight words of data, $DI_1, \ldots, DI_8$, which are stored in the stack. After these words are placed in the stack, but before the completion of Procedure$_i$, a new procedure, Procedure$_j$, is called. It generates 10 words of data, $DJ_1, \ldots, DJ_{10}$, which are also stored in the stack. Then another procedure, Procedure$_k$, is called, which places three words of data in the stack. Show the contents of the top words of the stack at this time.

11.15 Show how the expression

$$w = (a + b)(c + d) + (d \times e)$$

can best be evaluated by the HP3000, ARM, Motorola 68000, and IA-32 computers. The values of variables w, a, b, c, d, and e are stored in memory locations. The following assumptions are made. The addresses do not reference successive locations. Direct memory addressing in the DB+ relative mode is used in the HP3000. Absolute/Direct memory addressing is used in the 68000 and IA-32 computers, and Relative addressing is used in the ARM computer. All products are single length.

11.16   What is the largest number of stack locations occupied during execution of the program in Figure 11.9?

11.17   Repeat Problem 11.16 for the HP3000 programs in Problems 11.13 and 11.15.

REFERENCES

1. S. Furber, *ARM System-on-Chip Architecture,* 2nd ed., Addison-Wesley, Great Britain, 2000.

2. *IEEE Micro,* vol. 17, no. 4, eight articles on ARM, July/August 1997.

3. ARM web site: arm.com

4. D. Tabak, *Advanced Microprocessors,* McGraw-Hill, New York, 1991.

5. Motorola web site: motorola.com

6. J. Circello, et al., "The Superscalar Architecture of the MC68060," *IEEE Micro,* vol. 15, no. 2, April 1995, pp. 10–21.

7. Intel web site: intel.com

8. D. Alpert and D. Avnon, "Architecture of the Pentium Microprocessor," *IEEE Micro,* vol. 13, no. 3, June 1993, pp. 11–21.

9. R.P. Colwell and R.L. Steck, "A 0.6-Micron BiCMOS Processor with Dynamic Execution," *Proceedings of the International Solid State Circuits Conference,* February 1995.

10. "A Tour of the P6 (Pentium Pro) Microarchitecture," Intel Corporation, 1995.

11. S.K. Raman, V. Pentkovski, and J. Keshava, "Implementing Streaming SIMD Extensions on the Pentium III Processor," *IEEE Micro,* vol. 20, no. 4, July/August 2000, pp. 47–57.

12. Advanced Micro Devices web site: amd.com

13. *Communications of the ACM,* vol. 37, no. 6, eight articles on the PowerPC, June 1994.

14. *IEEE Micro,* vol. 14, no. 5, five articles on the PowerPC, October 1994.

15. IBM web site: ibm.com

16. K. Diefendorff, et al., "AltiVec Extensions to PowerPC Accelerates Media Processing," *IEEE Micro,* vol. 20, no. 2, March/April 2000, pp. 85–95.

17. M. Tremblay and J.M. O'Connor, "UltraSparc I: A Four-Issue Processor Supporting Multimedia," *IEEE Micro,* vol. 16, no. 2, April 1996, pp. 42–50.

18. Sun Microsystems web site: sun.com

19. T. Horel and G. Lauterbach, "UltraSPARC III: Designing Third Generation 64-bit Performance," *IEEE Micro,* vol. 19, no. 3, May/June 1999, pp. 73–85.

20. *Digital Technical Journal,* vol. 4, no. 4, issue on Alpha, 1992.

21. Compaq web site: compaq.com

22. E. McLellan, "The Alpha AXP Architecture and 21064 Processor," *IEEE Micro,* vol. 13, no. 3, June 1993, pp. 36–47.

23. J.H. Edmondson, et al., "Superscalar Execution in the 21164 Alpha Microprocessor," *IEEE Micro,* vol. 15, no. 2, April 1995, pp. 33–43.

24. R.E. Kessler, "The Alpha 21264 Microprocessor," *IEEE Micro,* vol. 19, no. 2, March/April 1999, pp. 24–36.

25. *IEEE Micro,* vol. 20, no. 5, six articles on the IA-64 architecture and the Itanium processor, September/October 2000.

26. C. Dulong, "The IA-64 Architecture at Work," *COMPUTER,* vol. 31, no. 7, July 1998, pp. 24–32.

27. R. Krishnaiyer, et al., "An Advanced Optimizer for the IA-64 Architecture," *IEEE Micro,* vol. 20, no. 6, November/December 2000, pp. 60–68.

28. R.P. Colwell, et al., "A VLIW Architecture for a Trace Scheduling Compiler," *IEEE Transactions on Computers,* vol. 37, no. 8, August 1988, pp. 967–979.

29. D. Patterson and D. Ditzel, "The Case for the Reduced Instruction Set Computer," ACM SIGARCH *Computer Architecture News,* vol. 8, no. 6, October 1980, pp. 25–33.

30. M. Katevenis, *Reduced Instruction Set Computer Architectures for VLSI,* MIT Press, Cambridge, MA, 1985.

31. W.A. Samaras, N. Cherukuri, and S. Venkataraman, "The IA-64 Itanium Processor Cartridge," *IEEE Micro,* vol. 21, no. 1, January/February 2001, pp. 82–89.

CHAPTER 12

LARGE COMPUTER SYSTEMS

CHAPTER OBJECTIVES

In this chapter you will learn about:

- Large computer systems that consist of multiple processors, or multiple computers
- Different structures for implementing multiprocessors
- Interconnection networks and LANs
- Memory organization in multiprocessors
- Cache coherence for shared data
- Shared-memory and message-passing paradigms
- Performance issues in multiprocessor systems

When a computer application requires a very large amount of computation to be completed in a reasonable amount of time, we must use machines with correspondingly large computing capacity. Such machines are often called *supercomputers*. Typical applications that require supercomputers include weather forecasting, finite element analysis in structural design, fluid flow analysis, simulation of large complex physical systems, and computer-aided design (CAD). None of the machines discussed in previous chapters are in the supercomputer class.

A high-performance processor can be designed using fast circuit technology and architectural features such as multiple functional units, pipelining, large caches, interleaved main memory, and separate buses for instructions and data. All these possibilities are exploited in ongoing research and development efforts by many manufacturers to produce processors intended primarily for use in workstations. Their quest is to increase performance without substantially increasing cost, and the results have been spectacular — we now have workstations that outperform machines that were considered to be in the supercomputer class only a decade ago.

However, many applications still demand computing power that greatly exceeds the capability of workstations. Thus, the need for supercomputing power remains strong. One approach is to build a supercomputer that has only a few very powerful processing units. This is typically done by using the fastest possible circuits, wide paths for accessing a large main memory, and extensive I/O capability. Such computers dissipate considerable power and require expensive cooling arrangements. In computationally demanding applications, supercomputers are needed to handle vectors of data, where a *vector* is a linear array of numbers (elements), as efficiently as possible. Single operations are often performed on entire vectors. For example, an add operation may generate a vector that is the element-by-element sum of two 64-element vectors. Also, a single memory access operation can cause an entire vector to be transferred between the main memory and processor registers. If an application is conducive to vector processing, then computers that feature a vector architecture provide excellent performance. Supercomputers of this class have been marketed by companies such as Cray (Cray-1, Y-MP, and SV1), Fujitsu (VP5000), Hitachi (SR8000), and NEC (SX-5). The main drawback of such machines has been their high cost — both the purchase price and the operating and maintenance cost.

An attractive alternative for providing supercomputing power is to use a large number of processors designed for the workstation market. This can be done in two basic ways. The first possibility is to build a machine that includes an efficient high-bandwidth medium for communication among the multiple processors, memory modules, and I/O devices. Such machines are usually referred to as *multiprocessors*. The second possibility is to implement a system using many workstations connected by a local area communication network. Systems of this type are often called *distributed computer systems*. Multiprocessors and distributed computer systems have many similarities. The former offer superior performance but at a higher price. The latter are naturally available in a modern computing environment at low cost. In the remainder of this chapter, we discuss the salient characteristics of each of these types. They provide large computing capabilities at a reasonable cost.

A system that uses many processors derives its high performance from the fact that many computations can proceed in parallel. The difficulty in using such a system efficiently is that it may not be easy to break an application down into small tasks that can be assigned to individual processors for simultaneous execution. Determining these tasks and then scheduling and coordinating their execution in multiple processors requires sophisticated software and hardware techniques. We consider these issues later in the chapter.

12.1   FORMS OF PARALLEL PROCESSING

Many opportunities are available for parts of a given computational task to be executed in parallel. We have already seen several of them in earlier chapters. For example, in handling I/O operations, most computer systems have hardware that performs direct memory access (DMA) between an I/O device and main memory. The transfer of data in either direction between the main memory and a magnetic disk can be accomplished under the direction of a DMA controller that operates in parallel with the processor.

When a block of data is to be transferred from disk to main memory, the processor initiates the transfer by sending instructions to the DMA controller. While the controller transfers the required data using cycle stealing, the processor continues to perform some computation that is unrelated to the data transfer. When the controller completes the transfer, it sends an interrupt request to the processor to signal that the requested data are available in the main memory. In response, the processor switches to a computation that uses the data.

This simple example illustrates two fundamental aspects of parallel processing. First, the overall task has the property that some of its subtasks can be done in parallel by different hardware components. In this example, a processor computation and an I/O transfer are performed in parallel by the processor and the DMA controller. Second, some means must exist for initiating and coordinating the parallel activity. Initiation occurs when the processor sets up the DMA transfer and then continues with another computation. When the transfer is completed, the coordination is achieved by the interrupt signal sent from the DMA controller to the processor. This allows the processor to begin the computation that operates on the transferred data.

The preceding example illustrates a simple case of parallelism involving only two tasks. In general, large computations can be divided into many parts that can be performed in parallel. Several hardware structures can be used to support such parallel computations.

12.1.1   CLASSIFICATION OF PARALLEL STRUCTURES

A general classification of parallel processing has been proposed by Flynn [1]. In this classification, a single-processor computer system is called a *Single Instruction stream, Single Data stream* (SISD) system. A program executed by the processor constitutes the single instruction stream, and the sequence of data items that it operates on constitutes the single data stream. In the second scheme, a single stream of instructions is broadcast to a number of processors. Each processor operates on its own data. This scheme, in which all processors execute the same program but operate on different data, is called a *Single Instruction stream, Multiple Data stream* (SIMD) system. The multiple data streams are the sequences of data items accessed by the individual processors in their own memories. The third scheme involves a number of independent processors, each executing a different program and accessing its own sequence of data items. Such machines are called *Multiple Instruction stream, Multiple Data stream* (MIMD) systems. The fourth possibility is a *Multiple Instruction stream, Single Data stream* (MISD) system. In such a system, a common data structure is manipulated by separate processors, each executing a different program. This form of computation does not occur often in practice, so it is not pursued here.

This chapter concentrates on MIMD structures because they are most useful for general purposes. However, we first briefly consider the SIMD structure to illustrate the kind of applications for which it is well-suited.

12.2 ARRAY PROCESSORS

The SIMD form of parallel processing, also called *array processing,* was the first form of parallel processing to be studied and implemented. In the early 1970s, a system named ILLIAC-IV [2] was designed at the University of Illinois using this approach and was later built by Burroughs Corporation. Figure 12.1 illustrates the structure of an array processor. A two-dimensional grid of processing elements executes an instruction stream that is *broadcast* from a central control processor. As each instruction is broadcast, all elements execute it simultaneously. Each processing element is connected to

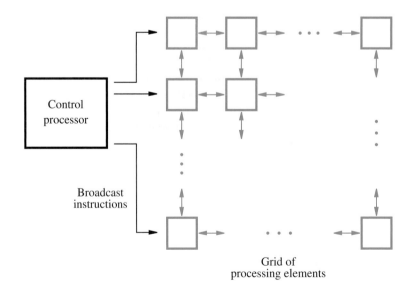

Figure 12.1 An array processor.

its four nearest neighbors for purposes of exchanging data. End-around connections may be provided in both rows and columns, but they are not shown in the figure.

Let us consider a specific computation in order to understand the capabilities of the SIMD architecture. The grid of processing elements can be used to solve two-dimensional problems. For example, if each element of the grid represents a point in space, the array can be used to compute the temperature at points in the interior of a conducting plane. Assume that the edges of the plane are held at some fixed temperatures. An approximate solution at the discrete points represented by the processing elements is derived as follows. The outer edges are initialized to the specified temperatures. All interior points are initialized to arbitrary values, not necessarily the same. Iterations are then executed in parallel at each element. Each iteration consists of calculating an improved estimate of the temperature at a point by averaging the current values of its four nearest neighbors. The process stops when changes in the estimates during successive iterations are less than some predefined small quantity.

The capability needed in the array processor to perform such calculations is quite simple. Each element must be able to exchange values with each of its neighbors over the paths shown in the figure. Each processing element has a few registers and some local memory to store data. It also has a register, which we can call the network register, that facilitates movement of values to and from its neighbors. The central processor can broadcast an instruction to shift the values in the network registers one step up, down, left, or right. Each processing element also contains an ALU to execute arithmetic instructions broadcast by the control processor. Using these basic facilities, a sequence of instructions can be broadcast repeatedly to implement the iterative loop. The control processor must be able to determine when each of the processing elements has developed its component of the temperature to the required accuracy. To do this, each element sets an internal status bit to 1 to indicate this condition. The grid interconnections include a facility that allows the controller to detect when all status bits are set at the end of an iteration.

An interesting question with respect to array processors is whether it is better to use a relatively small number of powerful processors or a large number of very simple processors. ILLIAC-IV is an example of the former choice. Its 64 processors had a 64-bit internal structure. Array processors introduced in the late 1980s are examples of the latter choice. The CM-2 machine produced by the Thinking Machines Corporation could accommodate up to 65,536 processors, but each processor is only one bit wide. Maspar's MP-1216 has a maximum of 16,384 processors that are 4 bits wide. The Cambridge Parallel Processing Gamma II Plus machines can have up to 4096 processors that can operate on either byte-sized or bit-sized operands. These choices reflect the belief that, in the SIMD environment, it is more useful to have a high degree of parallelism rather than to have fewer but more powerful processors.

Array processors are highly specialized machines. They are well-suited to numerical problems that can be expressed in matrix or vector format. Recall that supercomputers with a vector architecture are also suitable for solving such problems. A key difference between vector-based machines and array processors is that the former achieve high performance through heavy use of pipelining, whereas the latter provide extensive parallelism by replication of computing modules. Neither array processors nor vector-based machines are particularly useful in speeding up general computations, and they do not have a large commercial market.

12.3   THE STRUCTURE OF GENERAL-PURPOSE MULTIPROCESSORS

The array processor architecture described in the preceding section is a design for a computer system that corresponds directly to a class of computational problems that exhibit an obvious form of data parallelism. In more general cases in which parallelism is not so obvious, it is useful to have an MIMD architecture, which involves a number of processors capable of independently executing different routines in parallel.

Figures 12.2, 12.3, and 12.4 show three possible ways of implementing a multiprocessor system. The most obvious scheme is given in Figure 12.2. An *interconnection network* permits *n* processors to access *k* memories so that any of the processors can access any of the memories. The interconnection network may introduce considerable delay between a processor and a memory. If this delay is the same for all accesses to memory, which is common for this organization, then such a machine is called

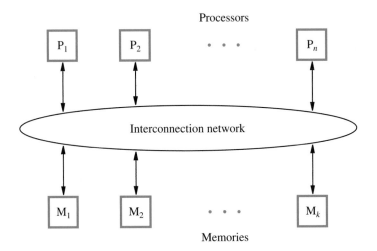

Figure 12.2   A UMA multiprocessor.

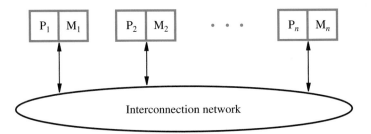

Figure 12.3   A NUMA multiprocessor.

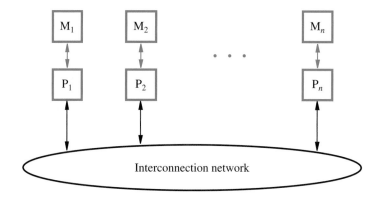

Figure 12.4 A distributed memory system.

a Uniform Memory Access (UMA) multiprocessor. Because of the extremely short instruction execution times achievable by processors, the network delay in fetching instructions and data from the memories is unacceptable if it is too long. Unfortunately, interconnection networks with very short delays are costly and complex to implement.

An attractive alternative, which allows a high computation rate to be sustained in all processors, is to attach the memory modules directly to the processors. This organization is shown in Figure 12.3. In addition to accessing its local memory, each processor can also access other memories over the network. Since the remote accesses pass through the network, these accesses take considerably longer than accesses to the local memory. Because of this difference in access times, such multiprocessors are called Non-Uniform Memory Access (NUMA) multiprocessors.

The organizations of Figures 12.2 and 12.3 provide a *global memory,* where any processor can access any memory module without intervention by another processor. A different way of organizing the system is shown in Figure 12.4. Here, all memory modules serve as private memories for the processors that are directly connected to them. A processor cannot access a remote memory without the cooperation of the remote processor. This cooperation takes place in the form of messages exchanged by the processors. Such systems are often called *distributed-memory* systems with a *message-passing protocol.*

The preceding discussion uses processors and memory modules as the main functional units in a multiprocessor system. Although we have not discussed I/O modules explicitly, any multiprocessor must provide extensive I/O capability. This capability can be provided in different ways. Separate I/O modules can be connected directly to the network, providing standard I/O interfaces, as discussed in Chapter 4. Some I/O functions can also be incorporated into the processor modules.

Figures 12.2, 12.3, and 12.4 depict a high-level view of possible multiprocessor organizations. The performance and cost of these machines depend greatly on implementation details. In the next two sections, we consider the most popular schemes for realizing the communication network and the structure of the memory hierarchy.

12.4 INTERCONNECTION NETWORKS

In this section, we examine some of the possibilities for implementing the interconnection network in multiprocessor systems. In general, the network must allow information transfer between any pair of modules in the system. The network may also be used to broadcast information from one module to many other modules. The traffic in the network consists of requests (such as read and write), data transfers, and various commands.

The suitability of a particular network is judged in terms of cost, bandwidth, effective throughput, and ease of implementation. The term *bandwidth* refers to the capacity of a transmission link to transfer data and is expressed in bits or bytes per second. The *effective throughput* is the actual rate of data transfer. This rate is less than the available bandwidth because a given link usually does not carry data all of the time.

Information transfer through the network usually takes place in the form of *packets* of fixed length and specified format. For example, a read request is likely to be a single packet that contains the addresses of the source (the processor module) and destination (the memory module) and a command field that indicates what type of read operation is required. A write request that writes one word in a memory module is also likely to be a single packet that includes the data to be written. On the other hand, a read response that involves an entire cache block requires several packets. Longer messages may require many packets.

Ideally, a complete packet would be handled in parallel in one clock cycle at any node or switch in the network. This implies having wide links, comprising many wires. However, to reduce cost and complexity, the links are often considerably narrower. In such cases, a packet must be divided into smaller pieces, each of which can be transmitted in one clock cycle.

12.4.1 SINGLE BUS

The simplest and most economical means for interconnecting a number of modules is to use a single bus. The detailed aspects of bus design, as discussed in Chapter 4, apply here as well. Since several modules are connected to the bus and any module can request a data transfer at any time, it is essential to have an efficient bus arbitration scheme. Examples of such schemes are given in Chapter 4.

In a simple mode of operation, the bus is dedicated to a particular source-destination pair for the full duration of the requested transfer. For example, when a processor issues a read request on the bus, it holds the bus until it receives the desired data from the memory module. Since the memory module needs a certain amount of time to access the data (as discussed in Chapter 5), the bus will be idle until the memory is ready to respond with the data. Then the data are transferred to the processor. When this transfer is completed, the bus can be assigned to handle another request.

Suppose that a bus transfer takes T time units, and the memory access time is $4T$ units. It then takes $6T$ units to complete a read request. Thus, the bus is idle for two-thirds of the time. A scheme known as the *split-transaction protocol* makes it possible to use the bus during the idle period to serve another request. Consider the following method of handling a series of read requests, possibly from different processors. After transferring the address involved in the first request, the bus may be reassigned to transfer the address for the second request. Assuming that this request is to a different memory module, we now have two modules proceeding with read access cycles in parallel. If neither module has finished with its access, the bus may be reassigned to a third request, and so on. Eventually, the first memory module completes its access cycle and uses the bus to transfer the word to the source that requested it. As other modules complete their cycles, the bus is used to transfer their data to the corresponding sources. Note that the actual length of time between address transfer and word return is not critical. Address and data transfers for different requests represent independent uses of the bus that can be interleaved in any order.

The split-transaction protocol allows the bus and the available bandwidth to be used more efficiently. The performance improvement achieved with this protocol depends on the relationship between the bus transfer time and the memory access time. Performance is improved at the cost of increased bus complexity. There are two reasons why complexity increases. Since a memory module needs to know which source initiated a given read request, a source identification tag must be attached to the request. This tag is later used to send the requested data to the source. Complexity also increases because all modules, not just the processors, must be able to act as bus masters.

Multiprocessors that use the split-transaction bus vary in size from 4 to 32 processors. In larger sizes, the bandwidth of the bus can become a problem. The bandwidth can be increased if a wider bus, that is, a bus that has more wires, is used. Most of the data transferred between processors and memory modules consist of cache blocks, where a block consists of a number of words. If the bus is wide enough to transfer several words at a time, then a complete block can be transferred more quickly than if the words are transferred one at a time. The Challenge multiprocessor from Silicon Graphics Corporation uses a bus that allows parallel transfer of 256 bits of data.

The main limitation of a single bus is that the number of modules that can be connected to the bus is not large. An ordinary bus functions well if no more than 10 to 15 modules are connected to it. Using a wider bus to increase the bandwidth allows the number of modules to be doubled. The bandwidth of a single bus is limited by contention for the use of the bus and by the increased propagation delays caused by electrical loading when many modules are connected. Networks that allow multiple independent transfer operations to proceed in parallel can provide significantly increased data transfer rates.

12.4.2 CROSSBAR NETWORKS

A versatile switching arrangement is shown in Figure 12.5. It is known as the *crossbar switch,* which was originally developed for use in telephone networks. For clarity of illustration, the switches in the figure are depicted as mechanical switches, although in practice these are electronic switches. Any module, Q_i, can be connected to any other module, Q_j, by closing an appropriate switch. Such networks, where there is a direct link between all pairs of nodes, are called *fully connected* networks. Many simultaneous transfers are possible. If n sources need to send data to n distinct destinations, then all

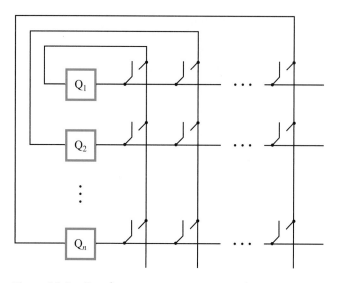

Figure 12.5   Crossbar interconnection network.

of these transfers can take place concurrently. Since no transfer is prevented by the lack of a communication path, the crossbar is called a *nonblocking switch.*

In Figure 12.5, we show just a single switch at each crosspoint. In an actual multi-processor, however, the paths through the crossbar network are much wider. This means that many switches are needed at each crosspoint. Since the number of crosspoints is n^2 in a network used to interconnect n modules, the total number of switches becomes large as n increases. This results in high cost and cumbersome implementation. Crossbars are attractive as interconnection networks when the number of interconnected nodes is not large.

One of the larger crossbar switches is found in Sun's E10000 system, in which 16 four-processor nodes are connected by a 16×16 crossbar switch. It is also possible to use a multilevel crossbar switch, where a crossbar switch at level 1 connects to a crossbar switch at level 2, and so on. In this way it is possible to connect a larger number of processors. Such schemes are found in Fujitsu's VPP5000, Hitachi's SR8000, and NEC's SX-5 machines. A multilevel crossbar has become a popular choice for a high-performance interconnection medium.

12.4.3 MULTISTAGE NETWORKS

The bus and crossbar systems just described use a single stage of switching to provide a path from a source to a destination. It is also possible to implement interconnection networks that use multiple stages of switches to set up paths between sources and destinations. Such networks are less costly than the crossbar structure, yet they provide a reasonably large number of parallel paths between sources and destinations. Multistage switching is best illustrated by an example. Figure 12.6 shows a three-stage

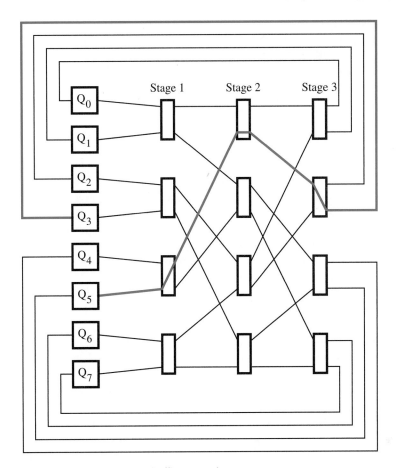

Figure 12.6 Multistage shuffle network.

network called a *shuffle network* that interconnects eight modules. The term "shuffle" describes the pattern of connections from the outputs of one stage to the inputs of the next stage. This pattern is identical to the repositioning of playing cards in a deck that is shuffled by splitting the deck into two halves and interleaving the cards in each half.

Each switchbox in the figure is a 2×2 switch that can route either input to either output. If the inputs request distinct outputs, then they can both be routed simultaneously in the straight-through or crossed pattern. If both inputs request the same output, only one request can be satisfied. The other one is blocked until the first request finishes using the switch. It can be shown that a network consisting of s stages can be used to interconnect 2^s modules. In this case, there is exactly one path through the network from any module Q_i to any other module Q_j. Therefore, this network provides full connectivity between sources and destinations. Many request patterns, however, cannot be satisfied simultaneously. For example, the connection from Q_0 to Q_4 cannot be provided at the same time as the connection from Q_1 to Q_5.

A multistage network is less expensive to implement than a crossbar network. If n nodes are to be interconnected using the scheme in Figure 12.6, then we must use $s = \log_2 n$ stages with $n/2$ switchboxes per stage. Since each switchbox contains four switches, the total number of switches is

$$4 \times \frac{n}{2} \times \log_2 n = 2n \times \log_2 n$$

which, for large networks, is considerably less than the n^2 switches needed in a crossbar network.

A particular request can be routed through the network using the following scheme. The source sends a binary pattern representing the destination number into the network. As the pattern moves through the network, each stage examines a different bit to determine switch settings. Stage 1 uses the most significant bit, stage 2 the middle bit, and stage 3 the least significant bit. When a request arrives on either input of a switch, it is routed to the upper output if the controlling bit is a 0 and to the lower output if the controlling bit is a 1. For example, a request from source Q_5 for destination Q_3 moves through the network as shown by the blue lines in Figure 12.6. Its route is controlled by the bit pattern 011, which is the destination address.

A good example of a multiprocessor based on a multistage network was the BBN Butterfly manufactured by BBN Advanced Computers. A 64-processor model of this system contained a three-stage network built with 4×4 switches. The routing through each stage of these switches was determined by successive 2-bit fields of the destination address. A current example is the IBM RS/6000 SP multiprocessor, which can use a multistage network as one of several options for interconnecting clusters of processors.

Multistage networks are less capable of providing concurrent connections than crossbar switches, but they are also less costly to implement. Interest in these networks peaked in the 1980s and has diminished greatly in the past few years. Other schemes, which we discuss in the remainder of this section, have become more attractive.

12.4.4 HYPERCUBE NETWORKS

In the three schemes discussed previously, the interconnection network imposes the same delay for paths connecting any two modules. Such schemes can be used to implement UMA multiprocessors. We now discuss network topologies that are suitable only for NUMA multiprocessors. The first such scheme that gained popularity uses the topology of an n-dimensional cube, called a *hypercube,* to implement a network that interconnects 2^n nodes. In addition to the communication circuits, each node usually includes a processor and a memory module as well as some I/O capability.

Figure 12.7 shows a three-dimensional hypercube. The small circles represent the communication circuits in the nodes. The functional units attached to each node are not shown in the figure. The edges of the cube represent bidirectional communication links between neighboring nodes. In an n-dimensional hypercube, each node is directly connected to n neighbors. A useful way to label the nodes is to assign binary addresses

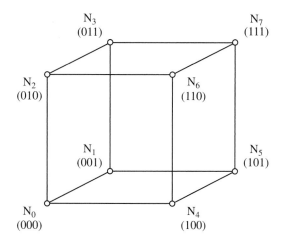

Figure 12.7 A 3-dimensional hypercube network.

to them in such a way that the addresses of any two neighbors differ in exactly one bit position, as shown in the figure.

Routing messages through the hypercube is particularly easy. If the processor at node N_i wishes to send a message to node N_j, it proceeds as follows. The binary addresses of the source, i, and the destination, j, are compared from least to most significant bits. Suppose that they differ first in position p. Node N_i then sends the message to its neighbor whose address, k, differs from i in bit position p. Node N_k forwards the message to the appropriate neighbor using the same address comparison scheme. The message gets closer to destination node N_j with each of these hops from one node to another. For example, a message from node N_2 to node N_5 requires 3 hops, passing through nodes N_3 and N_1. The maximum distance that any message needs to travel in an n-dimensional hypercube is n hops.

Scanning address patterns from right to left is only one of the methods that can be used to determine message routing. Any other scheme that moves a message closer to its destination on each hop is equally acceptable, as long as the routing decision can be made at each node on the path using only local information. This feature of the hypercube is attractive from the reliability viewpoint. The existence of multiple paths between two nodes means that when faulty links are encountered, they can usually be avoided by simple, local routing decisions. If one of the shortest routes is not available, a message may be sent over a longer path. When this is done, care must be taken to avoid looping, which is the situation in which the message circulates in a closed loop and never reaches its destination.

Hypercube interconnection networks have been used in a number of machines. The better known examples include Intel's iPSC, which used a 7-dimensional cube to connect up to 128 nodes, and NCUBE's NCUBE/ten, which had up to 1024 nodes in a 10-dimensional cube. The hypercube networks lost much of their popularity in the early 1990s when mesh-based structures emerged as a more attractive alternative.

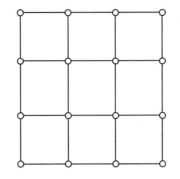

Figure 12.8 A 2-dimensional mesh network.

12.4.5 Mesh Networks

One of the most natural ways of interconnecting a large number of nodes is by means of a *mesh*. An example of a mesh with 16 nodes is given in Figure 12.8. Again, the links between the nodes are bidirectional. Meshes gained popularity in the early 1990s and essentially displaced hypercubes as a choice for interconnection networks in large multiprocessors.

Routing in a mesh network can be done in several different ways. One of the simplest and most effective possibilities is to choose the path between a source node N_i and a destination node N_j such that the transfer first takes place in the horizontal direction from N_i toward N_j. When the column in which N_j resides is reached, the transfer proceeds in the vertical direction along this column. Well-known examples of mesh-based multiprocessors are Intel's Paragon and the experimental machines Dash [3] and Flash [4] at Stanford University and Alewife [5] at MIT.

If a wraparound connection is made between the nodes at the opposite edges in Figure 12.8, the result is a network that consists of a set of bidirectional rings in the X direction connected by a similar set of rings in the Y direction. In this network, called a *torus*, the average latency of information transfer is reduced, but at the cost of greater complexity. Such an interconnection network is used in Fujitsu's AP3000 machines.

Both the regular mesh and the torus schemes can also be implemented as three-dimensional networks, in which the links are between neighbors in the X, Y, and Z directions. An example of a three-dimensional torus is found in Cray's T3E multiprocessor.

12.4.6 Tree Networks

A hierarchically structured network implemented in the form of a tree is another interconnection topology. Figure 12.9a depicts a four-way tree that interconnects 16 modules. In this tree, each parent node allows communication between two of its children at a time. An intermediate-level node, for example node A in the figure, can provide a connection from one of its child nodes to its parent. This enables two leaf nodes that are

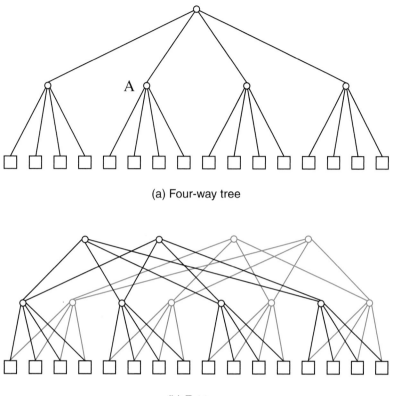

(a) Four-way tree

(b) Fat tree

Figure 12.9 Tree-based networks.

any distance apart to communicate. Only one path at a time can be established through a given node in the tree.

A tree network performs well if there is a large amount of locality in communication, that is, if only a small portion of network traffic goes through the single root node. If this is not the case, performance deteriorates rapidly because the root node becomes a bottleneck.

To reduce the possibility of a bottleneck, the number of links in the upper levels of a tree hierarchy can be increased. This is done in a *fat tree* network, in which each node in the tree (except at the top level) has more than one parent. An example of a fat tree is given in Figure 12.9*b*. In this case, each node has two parent nodes. A fat tree structure was used in the CM-5 machine by Thinking Machines Corporation.

12.4.7 RING NETWORKS

One of the simplest network topologies uses a ring to interconnect the nodes in the system, as shown in Figure 12.10*a*. The main advantage of this arrangement is that the ring is easy to implement. Links in the ring can be wide, usually accommodating

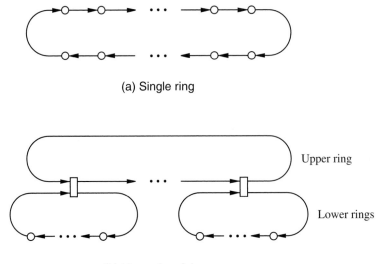

(a) Single ring

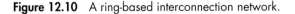

(b) Hierarchy of rings

Figure 12.10   A ring-based interconnection network.

a complete packet in parallel, because each node is connected to only two neighbors. However, it is not useful to construct a very long ring to connect many nodes because the latency of information transfer would be unacceptably large.

Rings can be used as building blocks for the topologies discussed in previous sections, such as meshes, hypercubes, trees, and fat trees. We consider the simple possibility of using rings in a tree structure; this results in a hierarchy of rings as shown in Figure 12.10b. A two-level hierarchy is depicted in the figure, but more levels can be used. Having short rings reduces substantially the latency of transfers that involve nodes on the same ring. Moreover, the latency of transfers between two nodes on different rings is shorter than if a single ring were used. The drawback of this scheme is that the highest-level ring may become a bottleneck for traffic.

Commercial machines that feature ring networks include Exemplar V2600 by Hewlett-Packard and KSR-2 by Kendal Square Research. Rings have also been used in the experimental machines Hector [6] and NUMAchine [7] at the University of Toronto.

12.4.8   PRACTICAL CONSIDERATIONS

We have seen that several different topologies can be used to implement the interconnection network in a multiprocessor system. It would be difficult to argue that any topology is clearly superior to others. Each has certain advantages and disadvantages. When comparing different approaches, we must take into account several practical considerations.

The most fundamental requirement is that the communication network be fast enough and have sufficient throughput to satisfy the traffic demand in a multiprocessor system. This implies high speed of transfer along the communication path and a simple routing mechanism to allow routing decisions to be made quickly. The network should be easy to implement; the wiring complexity must be reasonable and conducive to simple packaging. Complexity is inevitably reflected in the cost of the network, which is another major consideration.

Multiprocessors of different sizes are needed. The ideal network would be suitable for all sizes, ranging from just a few processors to possibly thousands of processors. The term *scalability* is often used to describe the ability of a multiprocessor architecture (which includes the interconnection network) to provide increased performance as the size of the system increases, while the increase in cost is proportional to the increase in size. It is particularly advantageous if a relatively small multiprocessor system can be acquired at a low cost but can be easily expanded to a large system with a linear increase in cost and performance. Unfortunately, this is not true for many commercial products. Often, the up-front cost for even a small system is large because much of the communication hardware needed to accommodate a larger system must be provided in one piece.

In addition to providing the basic communication between sources and destinations, it is useful to have *broadcasting* capability where a message traverses the entire network and is received by all nodes. The ability to send a message to only a subset of the network nodes is also beneficial. Such transfers are called *multicasting*.

The choice of the interconnection network affects the implementation of schemes used to ensure that any multiple copies of data that may exist in caches of different processors acquire the updates made so that all copies always have the same values. Such schemes are discussed in Section 12.6.2.

Reliability is another important factor. The more complex the network, the more likely it is to fail. Ideally, the machine could continue to function even if some link in the network fails. This is possible in networks that provide at least two different paths between each pair of communicating nodes. In general, simple networks tend to be robust, and they do not fail any more often than the processing and memory modules in the system. Highly reliable networks that include additional hardware can be built at considerable cost. This topic is beyond the scope of this book.

To demonstrate how all these characteristics can be evaluated, let us make a brief qualitative comparison of networks based on meshes and rings.

Meshes and Rings

Both mesh and ring networks are characterized by point-to-point links (connecting adjacent nodes), which can be driven at high clock rates. Both are viable in small configurations and can be expanded without difficulty. Incremental expansion is simpler in a ring network than in a mesh network.

In Figures 12.8 and 12.10, we indicate the nodes in the network as small circles and the links as single lines. Consider a more detailed picture; Figure 12.11 shows the communication paths associated with one node that has a processing module attached to it. The switch block includes both the circuitry that selects the path for a transfer and the buffers needed to hold the data being transferred. Data are transferred from the buffer in one node to the buffer in the next node in one clock cycle. Figure 12.11*a* depicts a node in a two-dimensional mesh network. Since bidirectional communication is needed

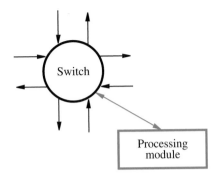

(a) Node in a mesh

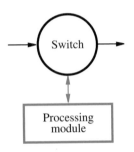

(b) Node in a ring

Figure 12.11   Nodes in mesh and
ring networks.

in both the X and Y directions, eight distinct network links must be connected to the node. The width of these links is limited by the total number of wires that can be used, taking into account the cost and packaging. Thus, it is unlikely that an individual link could be wide enough to carry an entire packet in parallel. To deal with this constraint, a packet can be divided into smaller portions to correspond to the width of the link. The term *flit* (FLow control digIT) is often used to refer to a portion of the packet that can be accepted by the switching circuitry in the node for forwarding, or buffering in case the forward path is blocked by another transfer. In practice, it is convenient if the flit corresponds to the width of the link.

   If a packet must be divided into flits, how should it be routed through the network? A straightforward scheme, known as the *store-and-forward* method, is to provide a large enough buffer in each node to hold all flits of a packet. Thus, an entire packet is transferred from one node to another, where it is stored until it can be forwarded to the next node. (The number of clock cycles required for the transfer depends on the number of flits.) The negative aspects of this scheme are the size of the buffers needed and the increased latency in passing through a node. An attractive alternative is the *wormhole* routing scheme (which has also been referred to as *pipelining*), in which the sequence of flits that constitute a packet can be viewed as a *worm* that moves through the network. The first flit in a worm contains a *header* that includes the address of the destination node. As this flit moves through the network, it establishes a path along which the remaining flits will pass. The tail of the worm closes the established path. The head of the worm may be temporarily blocked at any node, because another worm may be passing through this node. However, once the head moves, the rest of the worm moves along in subsequent clock cycles. Some control mechanism must stop the transmission of flits from preceding nodes when the head of the worm is blocked; a simple scheme using two buffers per node for each direction of transfer has been developed for this purpose [8]. Wormhole routing has lower latency than store-and-forward routing because the head flit is sent on its way without waiting for the remaining flits of the packet.

Wormhole routing is an application of a strategy known as *circuit switching*, which is a familiar concept from telephone networks, where a path through the network is established when a number is dialed. The conversation takes place along this path, called a *circuit*. The circuit is deactivated when the calling party hangs up. In the case of wormhole routing, it is the head flit that establishes the path. The progression of this flit may be temporarily blocked as explained above. Once a circuit is established, however, the remaining flits of the packet move toward the destination without experiencing any contention. In contrast, strategies in which an entire packet is buffered at each node, as in the store-and-forward method, are called *packet switching*. In this case, no circuit is set up, and the packet moves through the network as the buffer in each node becomes available.

Connections to a node in a ring network are shown in Figure 12.11*b*. Here, transfer occurs in only one direction, in addition to the connection to the processing module. Thus, the width of the link can be four times that in a mesh network for the same wire count. This means that it is feasible for an entire packet to be transferred in parallel from one node to another in one clock cycle. Figure 12.11*b* shows a node in the lowest level ring, to which a processing module is attached. If a ring hierarchy such as that in Figure 12.10*b* is used, then the inter-ring interfaces between lower and upper rings will have two input and two output links, one of each belonging to the upper- and lower-level rings.

Routing in a hierarchical ring network is very simple. A packet is never blocked, except possibly at an inter-ring interface when incoming packets on both upper- and lower-level rings are destined to continue along just one of the rings. To handle this situation, buffers (queues) must be provided in the interface, one from the lower- to the upper-level ring and another in the opposite direction. A processing module may inject a new packet onto the ring whenever no packet is arriving to the node from its upstream neighbor.

Next we consider the ability of networks to broadcast or multicast data. This ability is naturally available in ring networks. For example, a packet can be broadcast to all nodes by sending it to the top-level ring. As the packet traverses this ring, a copy is made at each inter-ring interface and sent along to the next lower-level ring. This process is repeated at all levels so that the copies of the original packet visit all nodes in the lowest-level rings. Broadcasting in a mesh network is more difficult, because the broadcast packet has to be broken up into flits and the progress of the broadcast worm may be blocked at various nodes by other traffic. Moreover, the completion of a broadcast is not easy to detect.

The main disadvantage of a hierarchical ring network is that the ring at the top of the hierarchy may become a bottleneck if too many packets need to be transferred over it. This will occur if the locality in communication is low. The limited bandwidth of the top-level ring restricts the scalability of systems based on such networks to hundreds of processors. In contrast, mesh-based systems scale well to thousands of processors.

The preceding discussion shows that both meshes and rings are good choices for interconnection networks. Ring-based systems are easier to implement, but do not scale as well as mesh-based systems. Thus, rings merit serious consideration if the maximum size of the system is a few hundred processors. Mesh systems are suitable for use in both small and very large systems. For very small systems, say, up to 16 processors, the most effective choices are a single bus or a crossbar switch.

Since the size of a multiprocessor system has important implications, the reader may wonder what range of systems are in practical use. Most multiprocessor systems are relatively small. Many machines are in the range of 4 to 128 processors. Some very large machines with thousands of processors exist. However, the market for such large machines is small.

12.4.9 MIXED TOPOLOGY NETWORKS

We have considered several possible network topologies and showed that all existing topologies have certain advantages and disadvantages. Designers of multiprocessor systems strive to achieve superior performance at a reasonable cost. In an effort to exploit the most advantageous characteristics of different topologies, many successful machines feature mixed topologies. Bus and crossbar are excellent choices for connecting a few processors together. So, we often see a cluster of processors, typically from 2 to 8, connected using a bus or a crossbar. Such clusters, usually referred to as nodes, are then interconnected using a suitable topology to form a larger system.

Data General's AV25000 system uses nodes where processors are connected by a bus. These nodes are then interconnected using a ring network. Hewlett-Packard's Exemplar V2600 also uses a ring network to interconnect nodes, where each node has a crossbar switch connecting the processors. Compaq's AlphaServer SC uses a fat tree to interconnect the nodes that comprise processors connected by a crossbar switch.

12.4.10 SYMMETRIC MULTIPROCESSORS

Consider a multiprocessor system in which all processors have identical access to all memory modules and all I/O devices, so that the operating system software can treat any processor as interchangeable with any other processor. Then, if any processor can execute either the operating system kernel or user programs, the machine is called a *symmetric multiprocessor* (SMP). This also implies that any processor can initiate an I/O operation on any I/O device, and it can handle any external interrupt.

SMPs are usually implemented using either a bus or a crossbar network. Often, an SMP is used as a node in a much larger multiprocessor system. For example, SMP nodes are used in the Exemplar V2600 and AlphaServer SC multiprocessors mentioned above.

12.5 MEMORY ORGANIZATION IN MULTIPROCESSORS

In Chapter 5 we saw that the organization of the memory in a uniprocessor system has a large impact on performance. The same is true in multiprocessor systems. To exploit the locality of reference phenomenon, each processor usually includes a primary cache and a secondary cache. If the organization in Figure 12.2 is used, then each processor module can be connected to the communication network as shown in Figure 12.12. Only the secondary cache is shown in the figure since the primary cache is assumed to be a part of the processor chip. The memory modules are accessed using a single *global address space,* where a range of physical addresses is assigned to each memory module. In such a *shared memory* system, the processors access all memory modules in the same way. From the software standpoint, this is the simplest use of the address space.

In NUMA-organized multiprocessors, shown in Figure 12.3, each node contains a processor and a portion of the memory. A natural way of implementing the node is illustrated in Figure 12.13. In this case, it is also convenient to use a single global address space. Again, the processor accesses all memory modules in the same way, but

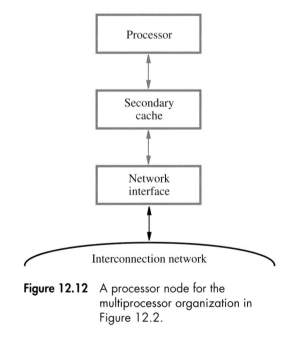

Figure 12.12 A processor node for the multiprocessor organization in Figure 12.2.

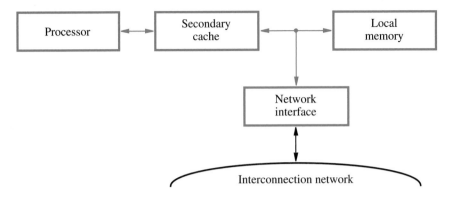

Figure 12.13   Node structure for the multiprocessor organization in Figure 12.3.

the accesses to the local memory component of the global address space take less time to complete than accesses to remote memory modules.

In the organization of Figure 12.4, each processor accesses directly only its own local memory. Thus, each memory module constitutes the *private address space* of one processor; there is no global address space. Any interaction among programs or processes running on different processors is implemented by sending *messages* from one processor to another. In this form of communication, each processor views the interconnection network as an I/O device. In effect, each node in such a system behaves as a computer in the same manner as discussed in previous chapters for uniprocessor machines. For this reason, systems of this type are referred to also as *multicomputers*. This organization provides the easiest way to connect a number of computers into a large system. Communication between tasks running on different computers is relatively slow because the exchange of messages requires software intervention. We consider this type of system in Section 12.7.

When data are shared among many processors, we must ensure that the processors observe the same value for a given data item. The presence of many caches in a shared-memory system creates a problem in this respect. Multiple copies of some data items may exist in various caches. Whenever a processor changes (writes) a data item in its own cache, the same change must be made in all caches that have a copy. Alternatively, the other copies must be invalidated. In other words, shared data must be *coherent* in all caches in the system. The problem of maintaining cache coherence can be solved in several different ways. We examine the most popular solutions in Section 12.6.2.

12.6 PROGRAM PARALLELISM AND SHARED VARIABLES

The introduction to this chapter states that it is difficult to break large tasks down into subtasks that can be executed in parallel on a multiprocessor. In some special cases, however, this division is easy. If a large task originates as a set of independent programs, then these programs can simply be executed on different processors. Unless

$\vdots$

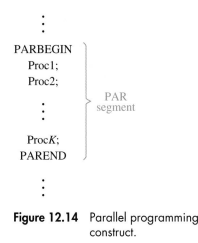

PARBEGIN
    Proc1;
    Proc2;

    $\vdots$ PAR
               segment

    Proc*K*;
  PAREND

$\vdots$

Figure 12.14 Parallel programming construct.

these programs block each other in competing for shared I/O devices, the multiprocessor is fully used by such a workload.

Another easy case occurs when a high-level source programming language has constructs that allow an application programmer to explicitly declare that certain subtasks of a program can be executed in parallel. Figure 12.14 shows such a construct, often called a PAR segment. The PARBEGIN and PAREND control statements bracket a list of procedures, named Proc1 through Proc*K,* that can be executed in parallel. The order of execution of this program is as follows. When the segment of the program preceding the PARBEGIN statement is completed, any or all of the K parallel procedures can be started immediately, depending on the number of idle processors available. They can be started in any order. Execution of the part of the program following PAREND is allowed to begin only after all of the K procedures have completed execution.

If this program is the only one being executed on the multiprocessor, then the burden of using the processors efficiently is placed on the application programmer. The degree of parallelism, K, of the PAR segments and their total size relative to the sequential segments determine the level of utilization achievable by the multiprocessor.

The most challenging task in achieving high utilization of multiprocessor systems is to develop compilers that can automatically detect parallelism in a user program. The usefulness of automatic detection of parallelism is based on the following reasoning. An application programmer naturally visualizes a program as a set of serially performed operations. However, even though the programmer specifies the operations as a serial list of instructions in some high-level language, many opportunities may exist for executing various groups of instructions in parallel. A simple example is that of successive passes through a loop. If no data dependency is involved between different iterations of the loop, then successive passes can be executed in parallel. On the other hand, if the first pass through the loop generates data that are needed in the second pass, and so on, then parallel execution is not possible. Data dependencies must be detected by the compiler to determine which operations can be performed in parallel and which cannot. The design of compilers that can detect parallelism is complex. Even after the parallel parts of a program are identified, their subsequent scheduling for execution on a multiprocessor with a limited number of processors is a nontrivial task. Scheduling may be done either by the compiler or at runtime by the operating system. We do not pursue this topic of determining and scheduling tasks that can be executed in parallel. Instead, we turn to the issue of accessing shared variables that are modified by programs running in parallel on different processors of a multiprocessor system.

12.6.1 ACCESSING SHARED VARIABLES

Assume that we have identified two tasks that can run in parallel on a multiprocessor. The tasks are largely independent, but from time to time they access and modify some common, shared variable in the global memory. For example, let a shared variable SUM represent the balance in an account. Moreover, assume that several tasks running on different processors need to update this account. Each task manipulates SUM in the following way: The task reads the current value from SUM, performs an operation that depends on this value, and writes the result back into SUM. It is easy to see how errors can occur if such *read-modify-write* accesses to SUM are performed by tasks T1 and T2 running in parallel on processors P1 and P2. Suppose that both T1 and T2 read the current value from SUM, say 17, and then proceed to modify it locally. T1 adds 5 for a result of 22, and T2 subtracts 7 for a result of 10. They then proceed to write their individual results back into SUM, with T2 writing first followed by T1. The variable SUM now has the value 22, which is wrong. SUM should contain the value 15 (= 17 + 5 − 7), which is the intended result after applying the modifications strictly one after the other, in either order.

To guarantee correct manipulation of the shared variable SUM, each task must have exclusive access to it during the complete read-modify-write sequence. This can be provided by using a global *lock* variable, LOCK, and a machine instruction called Test-and-Set. The variable LOCK has two possible values, 0 or 1. It serves as a guard to ensure that only one task at a time is allowed access to SUM during the time needed to execute the instructions that update the value of this shared variable. Such a sequence of instructions is called a *critical section*. LOCK is manipulated as follows. It is equal to 0 when neither task is in its critical section that operates on SUM. When either task wishes to modify SUM, it first checks the value of LOCK and then sets it to 1, regardless of its original value. If the original value was 0, then the task can safely proceed to work on SUM because no other task is currently doing so. On the other hand, if the original value of LOCK was 1, then the task knows that some other task is operating on SUM. It must wait until that task resets LOCK to 0 before it can proceed. This desired mode of operation on LOCK is made foolproof by the Test-and-Set instruction. As its name implies, this instruction performs the critical steps of testing and setting LOCK in an indivisible sequence of operations executed as a single machine instruction. While this instruction is executing, the memory module involved must not respond to access requests from any other processor.

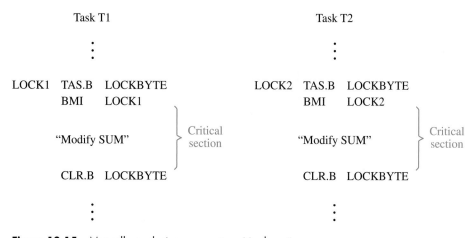

Task T1   Task T2

Figure 12.15 Mutually exclusive access to critical sections.

As a specific example, consider the Test-and-Set instruction denoted as TAS in the Motorola 68000 microprocessor. This instruction has one operand that is always a byte. Assume that it is stored in the memory at location LOCKBYTE. Bit b_7, the most significant bit of this operand, serves as the variable LOCK just discussed. The TAS instruction performs the uninterruptible test and set operations on bit b_7. Condition code flag N (Negative) is set to the original value of b_7. Thus, after the execution of TAS is completed, the program can continue into its critical section if N equals 0, but it must wait if N equals 1. Figure 12.15 shows how two tasks, T1 and T2, can manipulate LOCKBYTE to enter critical sections of code in which they update the shared variable SUM. The TAS instruction is followed by a conditional branch instruction. This instruction causes a branch back to TAS if N = 1, resulting in a wait loop that continues to execute TAS on the operand in location LOCKBYTE until it finds b_7 equal to 0. The branch instruction fails if TAS is executed when b_7 is 0, allowing the program to continue into its critical section. When execution of the critical section is completed, LOCKBYTE is cleared. As a result, bit b_7 is reset to 0, allowing any waiting program to proceed into its critical section.

The TAS instruction is an example of a simple machine instruction that can be used to implement a lock. Most computers include an instruction of this type. These instructions may provide additional capabilities, such as incorporating a conditional branch based on the result of the test.

12.6.2 CACHE COHERENCE

Shared data leads to another problem in a multiprocessor machine; the presence of multiple caches means that copies of shared data may reside in several caches. When any processor writes to a shared variable in its own cache, all other caches that contain a copy of that variable will then have the old, incorrect value. They must be informed of the change so that they can either update their copy to the new value or invalidate it.

Cache coherence is defined as the situation in which all cached copies of shared data have the same value at all times.

In Chapter 5 we discussed two basic approaches for performing write operations on data in a cache. The write-through approach changes the data in both the cache and the main memory. The write-back approach changes the data only in the cache; the main memory copy is updated when a dirty data block in the cache has to be replaced. Similar approaches can also be used in a multiprocessor system.

Write-Through Protocol

A write-through protocol can be implemented in two fundamental versions. One version is based on updating the values in other caches, while the second relies on invalidating the copies in other caches.

Let us consider the *write-through with update* protocol first. When a processor writes a new value into its cache, the new value is also written into the memory module that holds the cache block being changed. Since copies of this block may exist in other caches, these copies must be updated to reflect the change caused by the write operation. Conceptually, the simplest way of doing this is to broadcast the written data to all processor modules in the system. As each processor module receives the broadcast data, it updates the contents of the affected cache block if this block is present in its cache (primary or secondary).

The second version of write-through protocol is based on *invalidation* of copies. When a processor writes a new value into its cache, this value is written into the memory module, and all copies in other caches are invalidated. Again, broadcasting can be used to send the invalidation requests throughout the system.

Write-Back Protocol

In the write-back protocol, multiple copies of a cache block may exist if different processors have loaded (read) the block into their caches. If some processor wants to change this block, it must first become an exclusive owner of this block. When the ownership is granted to this processor by the memory module that is the home location of the block, all other copies, including the one in the memory module, are invalidated. Now the owner of the block may change the contents at will without having to take any other action. When another processor wishes to read this block, the data are sent to this processor by the current owner. The data are also sent to the home memory module, which reacquires ownership and updates the block to contain the latest value.

The write-back protocol causes less traffic than the write-through protocol, because a processor is likely to perform several writes to a cache block before this block is needed by another processor.

So far, we have assumed that update and invalidate requests in these protocols are broadcast through the interconnection network. Whether it is practical to implement such broadcasts depends largely on the structure of the interconnection network. The most natural network for supporting broadcasting is the single bus, discussed in Section 12.4.1. In small multiprocessors that use a single bus, cache coherence can be realized using a scheme known as snooping.

Snoopy Caches

In a single-bus system, all transactions between processors and memory modules occur via the bus. In effect, they are broadcast to all units connected to the bus. Suppose that each cache associated with a processor has a controller circuit that observes the transactions on the bus that involve other processors. Suppose also that the write-back protocol just described is used.

Whenever a processor writes to its cache block for the first time, the cache block is marked as dirty, and the write is broadcast on the bus. The memory module and all other caches invalidate their copies. The processor that performed the write is now the owner of the cache block. It can do further writes in the same block without broadcasting them. If another processor issues a read request for the same block, the memory module cannot respond because it does not have a valid copy. But the present owner also sees this request when it appears on the bus, and it must supply the correct value to the requesting processor. The memory module is informed that an owner is supplying the correct value by a broadcast signal from the owner (which includes the data that the owner places on the bus), and the memory updates its value. Finally, the owner marks its copy as clean. Operation now proceeds with multiple caches and the memory module all having the correct value of the block. In the case in which a dirty value must be replaced to make room in the cache for a new block, a write-back operation to the memory module must be performed.

If two processors want to write to the same cache block at the same time, one of the processors will be granted the use of the bus first and will become the owner. As a result, the other processor's copy of the cache block will be invalidated. The second processor can then repeat its write request. This sequential handling of write requests ensures that the two processors can correctly change different words in a given cache block.

The scheme just described is based on the ability of cache controllers to observe the activity on the bus and take appropriate actions. We refer to such schemes as *snoopy-cache* techniques.

For performance reasons, it is important that the snooping function not interfere with the normal operation of a processor and its cache. Such interference would occur if, for each request on the bus, the cache controller had to access the tags of its cache to see if the block in question is present in the cache. In most cases, the answer would be negative. To eliminate unnecessary interference, each cache can be provided with a set of duplicate tags, which maintain the same status information about the blocks in the cache but can be accessed separately by the snooping circuitry.

While the concept of snoopy caches is effective and simple to implement, it is suitable only for single-bus systems. In larger multiprocessors, more complex arrangements must be used.

Directory-Based Schemes

Enforcing cache coherence using a broadcast mechanism for distribution of invalidation or update requests becomes less attractive as the multiprocessor system grows in size. The main reason is that a large amount of unnecessary traffic may be generated by a full broadcast because, in practical applications, copies of a given block are usually present in only a few caches.

A useful alternative is to keep a *directory* of the locations, that is, the caches where copies exist at any given time. One way to implement a directory scheme is to include additional status bits for each block in a particular memory module, which indicate the caches where copies of this block may be found. Then, instead of broadcasting to all caches, the memory module can send individual messages, or a multicast such as an invalidate request in the write-back protocol, to only those caches that have a copy. Of course, the additional bits in the memory modules increase the cost of these modules. Different versions of directory schemes have been proposed and some have been implemented in existing multiprocessor systems.

SCI Standard

A specific approach to cache coherence has been standardized by the Institute of Electrical and Electronics Engineers (IEEE). It is a part of the SCI (Scalable Coherent Interface) standard [9], which defines a multiprocessor backplane that is intended to provide fast signaling, scalable architecture, cache coherence, and simple implementation. The interconnection network uses point-to-point links, and the communication protocol is based on a single-requester single-responder principle. A packet originates at a source node and is addressed to a single target. If a packet sent by the source is accepted by the target, the latter returns a positive acknowledgement packet. If the packet is not accepted, then a negative acknowledgment is returned, which causes a retry.

Cache coherence is achieved using a distributed directory-based protocol. A doubly-linked list is established for each cache block that contains shared data. Each processor node that caches a given block of shared data includes pointers to the previous and to the next nodes that share the block. These pointers are part of the cache-block tag. The head of this doubly-linked list has a pointer to the memory module that holds the block. When a new node accesses the memory module to read this block, the node becomes the new head of the list and the memory directory is updated by replacing the pointer to the previous head with the address of the new head. A write access to the memory can be performed only by the head of the list. If another node wishes to perform a write, it can do so by inserting itself at the head of the list and purging the rest of the entries in the list.

The SCI cache coherence scheme scales well because the memory directory and the processor cache-tag storage requirements do not increase as the size of the linked list increases. The disadvantage of this scheme is that this additional storage presents a costly fixed overhead that is incurred in all cases.

Although the SCI standard does not specify a particular topology for the interconnection network, the ring topology is one of the natural choices. Hewlett-Packard's Exemplar V2600 and Data General's AV25000 multiprocessors use a ring topology and implement the coherence protocol described above.

CC-NUMA Multiprocessors

Cache coherence is an important issue in multiprocessor systems. It has been the topic of extensive research. We have briefly described some key implementation schemes. Many subtle details are beyond the scope of this book.

A multiprocessor may have the cache coherence implemented either in hardware or in software. From the performance point of view, it is advantageous to have hardware-controlled cache coherence. Most of the current NUMA multiprocessors have cache coherence implemented in hardware. They are often referred to as *cache-coherent NUMA* (CC-NUMA) systems.

12.6.3 NEED FOR LOCKING AND CACHE COHERENCE

We should note that the requirement for lock guard controls on access to shared variables is independent of the need for cache coherence controls — both types of controls are needed. Consider a situation in which cache coherence is maintained by using the write-through policy accompanied by cache updating of writes to shared variables. Suppose that the contents of SUM in the example in Section 12.6.1 have been read into the caches of the two processors that execute tasks T1 and T2. If the read operations are part of an update sequence and are not made mutually exclusive by the use of a lock guard control, then the original error can still occur. If task T1 writes its new value last, as before, then SUM will contain the value 22, which is wrong. Cache coherence is maintained throughout this sequence of events. However, incorrect results are obtained because lock guard controls are not used.

12.7 MULTICOMPUTERS

In Section 12.5 we introduced the concept of multicomputers. We now examine the salient features of such systems in more detail.

A multicomputer system is structured as shown in Figure 12.4. Each processing node in the system is a self-contained computer that communicates with other processing nodes by sending messages over the network. Systems of this type are often called *message-passing systems,* in contrast to the shared-memory multiprocessors discussed previously.

In multicomputer systems, the demands on the interconnection network are less stringent than in shared-memory multiprocessor systems. A shared-memory machine must have a fast network with high bandwidth because processor modules frequently access the remote memory modules that constitute the shared memory. A slow network would quickly become a bottleneck, and performance would severely degrade.

In a multicomputer, messages are sent much less frequently, resulting in much less traffic than in the shared-memory systems. Therefore, a simpler and less expensive network can be used. In view of this disparity in the intensity of communication, the terms *tightly coupled* and *loosely coupled* have also been associated with shared-memory and message-passing systems, respectively.

Any network described in Section 12.4 can be used in a multicomputer system. Since the traffic demands are relatively modest, the physical implementation of the interconnection network is likely to be inexpensive. The links in the network often involve bit-serial lines driven by I/O device interfaces. An interface circuit reads a message from the memory of the source computer using the DMA technique, converts it into a bit-serial format, and transmits it over the network to the destination computer. Source and destination addresses are included in a header of the message for routing purposes. The message is routed to the destination computer where it is written into a memory buffer by the I/O interface of that computer.

In the 1980s, hypercube-based interconnection networks were very popular. Such networks were used in several message-passing multiprocessor systems, typically using bit-serial transmission. Examples of such machines are Intel's iPSC, NCUBE's NCUBE/ten, and Thinking Machines' CM-2. Then in the early 1990s, other topologies gained popularity for both message-passing and shared-memory machines. Thinking Machines' CM-5 is an example of a message-passing machine that uses a fat tree network with a link width of four. Intel's Paragon uses a mesh network with a link width of 16. To facilitate message passing, it is useful to include a special communications unit at each node in the network. For example, the Paragon machine has a message processor that essentially frees the application processor from having to be involved in the details of message handling.

12.7.1 LOCAL AREA NETWORKS

Because the communication demands in a multicomputer system are relatively low, we can consider replacing the specialized interconnection network with some readily available standard network that was developed for more general communication purposes. Many networks exist for interconnecting various types of computing equipment. Networks that span a small geographic area with distances not exceeding a few kilometers are called *local area networks* (LANs). Networks that cover larger areas that involve distances up to thousands of kilometers are referred to as *long-haul networks,* or *wide area networks*.

The most popular LANs use either the bus or the ring topology. The transmission media for either bus or ring LANs can be twisted wire pair, coaxial cable, or optical fiber. Bit-serial transmission is used, and rates range from ten to hundreds of megabits per second. Only one message packet at a time can be successfully transmitted on the single shared path. Source and destination device addresses precede the data field of a packet, and appropriate delimiters indicate the start and end of the packet. In general, packets have variable lengths ranging from tens of bytes to over 1000 bytes.

A protocol that implements distributed access control is needed to ensure orderly transfer of packets between arbitrary pairs of communicating devices. We will sketch the basic ideas involved in two widely used protocols — the Ethernet bus and the token ring. These protocols are specified in detail in IEEE standards [10].

12.7.2 ETHERNET (CSMA/CD) BUS

The Ethernet bus access protocol, also called the Carrier Sense Multiple Access with Collision Detection (CSMA/CD) protocol, is conceptually one of the simplest protocols. Whenever an attached device has a message to transmit, it waits until it senses that the bus is idle and then begins transmission. The device then monitors the bus for 2τ seconds as it transmits its message, where τ is the end-to-end bus propagation delay. If the device does not observe any distortion of its transmitted signal during the 2τ interval, then it assumes that no other station has started transmission and continues its transmission to completion. On the other hand, if distortion is observed, caused by the beginning of a transmission from some other device, then both devices must stop transmitting. The mutually destructive distortion of the two transmitted signals is called a *collision,* and the time interval 2τ is called the *collision window.*

Messages that have been destroyed by collision must be retransmitted. If the devices involved in the collision attempt to retry immediately, their packets will almost certainly collide again. A basic strategy used to prevent collision of the retries is as follows. Each device independently waits for a random amount of time, then waits until the bus is idle and begins retransmission. If the random waits are a few multiples of 2τ, the probability of repeated collisions is reduced.

12.7.3 TOKEN RING

The token-ring protocol is used for ring networks. A single, appropriately encoded short message, called a *token,* circulates continuously around the ring. The arrival of the token at a ring node represents permission to transmit. If the node has nothing to transmit, it forwards the token to the next node downstream with as little delay as possible. If the node has data ready for transmission, it inhibits propagation of the token. Instead it transmits a packet of information preceded by an appropriately encoded header flag. As the packet is transmitted around the ring, its contents are read and copied as it travels past the destination node. The packet continues to travel around the ring until it reaches the source node, where it is discarded. When the source node completes transmitting a packet, it releases the token, which again starts to circulate around the ring. The packet size on a token ring is variable and is limited only by the amount of buffer memory available in each node because the destination node must be able to store complete packets.

The main reason for considering the standard LANs in the context of multicomputer systems is not because they can be used in self-contained systems that we have been discussing, but because they can be used in conjunction with standard workstations to conveniently form a multicomputer system.

12.7.4 NETWORK OF WORKSTATIONS

Today, most commercial, educational, and government organizations have a collection of workstations to meet their computing needs. These workstations are usually connected to a LAN that allows access to fileservers, printers, and specialized computing resources. (See Figure 12.16.)

Although each workstation is normally used as a separate computer, many workstations can be viewed as a multicomputer system. All that is needed is the software to allow parallel processing. Of course, some significant differences exist between such a system and a commercial message-passing multiprocessor machine. In particular,

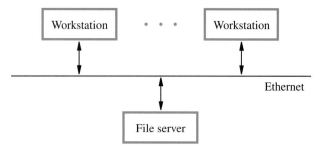

Figure 12.16   A typical network of workstations.

communication over the LAN is slower, largely because the operating system must intervene when messages have to be exchanged between programs running on different computers. This means that a network of workstations does not perform as well as a self-contained system with a specialized interconnection network. But the great advantage is that the network of workstations is usually readily available. It is certainly useful to be able to run very large applications on such systems when the workstations are not used for their normal purposes, which is typically the case at night.

12.8   PROGRAMMER'S VIEW OF SHARED MEMORY AND MESSAGE PASSING

In previous sections, we considered the hardware implications of multiprocessor systems that feature shared-memory and message-passing paradigms. Now we briefly examine how these paradigms affect the user, namely, the programmer who is implementing a parallel application. We consider a small example that involves only two processors. This keeps the discussion simple yet allows us to elaborate the key ideas.

Assume we want to compute the dot product of two N-element vectors. A sequential program for this task is outlined in Figure 12.17. It is suitable for execution on a single processor. The program is mostly self-explanatory. The **read** statements load the values of the two vectors from a disk (or some other I/O device) into the main memory. This task is done by the operating system. Let us attempt to parallelize this program to run on two processors. Evidently, the potential for parallelization lies in the loop that computes the dot product by generating the product of a pair of elements and adding the result to the previously accumulated partial dot product.

12.8.1   SHARED MEMORY CASE

Our first attempt to write a program for two processors is shown in Figure 12.18. As the program starts executing on one processor, it loads the vectors into memory and initializes the *dot_product* variable to 0. We achieve parallelism by having a second

```
integer array a[1..N], b[1..N]
integer dot_product
.
.
read a[1..N] from vector_a
read b[1..N] from vector_b
dot_product := 0
do_dot (a, b)
print dot_product
.
.
do_dot (integer array x[1..N], integer array y[1..N])
        for k:= 1 to N
                dot_product := dot_product + x[k] * y[k]
        end
end
```

Figure 12.17 A sequential program to compute the dot product.

```
shared integer array a[1..N], b[1..N]
shared integer dot_product
shared lock dot_product_lock
shared barrier done
.
.
read a[1..N] from vector_a
read b[1..N] from vector_b
dot_product := 0
create_thread (do_dot, a, b)
do_dot (a, b)
print dot_product
.
.
do_dot (integer array x[1..N], integer array y[1..N])
        private integer id
        id := mypid()
        for k:= (id*N/2) + 1 to (id + 1)*N/2
                lock (dot_product_lock)
                        dot_product := dot_product + x[k] * y[k]
                unlock (dot_product_lock)
        end
        barrier (done)
end
```

Figure 12.18 A first attempt at a program to compute the dot product on two processors in a shared memory machine.

processor perform half of the computations needed to obtain the dot product. This is done by creating a separate thread to be executed on the second processor.

A thread is an independent path of execution within a program. Actually, the term *thread* is used to refer to a thread of control, where multiple threads execute portions of the program and can run in parallel as if they were separate programs. Thus, two or more threads can be running on different processors, executing either the same or different code. The key point is that all threads are part of a single program and run in the same address space. We should note that in the commonly used uniprocessor environment, each program has a single thread of control.

In the program in Figure 12.18, a new thread is created by the *create_thread* statement. This thread will execute the *do_dot* routine and terminate. The operating system will assign the identification number of 1 to the new thread. The first processor continues by executing the *do_dot (a,b)* statement as thread 0. The statement *id := mypid()* sets the variable *id* to the assigned identification number of the thread. Using the *id* value in the **for** loop allows simple specification of which halves of the vectors *a* and *b* should be handled by a particular thread.

Changing the accumulated value of the *dot_product* variable is the critical section in the *do_dot* routine; hence, each thread must have exclusive access to this variable. This is achieved by the locking mechanism, as discussed in Section 12.6.1. Thread 0 does not proceed past the barrier statement in the *do_dot* routine until the other thread has reached the same synchronization point. This ensures that both threads have completed their updates of the *dot_product* variable before thread 0 is allowed to print the final result. The *barrier* concept can be realized in different ways. A simple approach is to use a shared variable, such as *done* in Figure 12.18. This variable is initialized to the number of threads (two in our example) and then decremented as each thread arrives at the barrier.

The program in Figure 12.18 has one major flaw. The locking arrangement used does not allow the expected parallelism to be achieved because both threads continuously write the same shared variable, *dot_product*. Thus, the potentially parallel part of the required computation will in fact be done serially.

To achieve the desired parallelism, we can modify the program as shown in Figure 12.19. Instead of using the shared variable, *dot_product,* in the **for** loop, a private variable, *local_dot_product,* is introduced to accumulate the partial dot product as it is being computed by each thread. Thus, only upon completion of the loop is it necessary to enter a critical section where each thread updates the shared variable, *dot_product*. This modification allows both threads to execute the **for** loop in parallel.

This example can be easily extended to a larger number of processors. All that needs to be done is to create more threads. The loop bound expressions in the **for** loop will determine the range of elements that each thread uses in the computation based on the value of the assigned *id*.

The effectiveness of the program in Figure 12.19 depends on the size of the data vectors. The larger the vectors, the more effective this approach is. For small vectors, the overhead of creating threads and providing synchronization outweighs any benefit that parallelism may provide.

```
shared integer array a[1..N], b[1..N]
shared integer dot_product
shared lock dot_product_lock
shared barrier done
.
.

read a[1..N] from vector_a
read b[1..N] from vector_b
dot_product := 0
create_thread (do_dot, a, b)
do_dot (a, b)
print dot_product
.
.

do_dot (integer array x[1..N], integer array y[1..N])
        private integer local_dot_product
        private integer id
        id := mypid()
        local_dot_product := 0
        for k:= (id*N/2) + 1 to (id + 1)*N/2
                local_dot_product := local_dot_product + x[k] * y[k]
        end
        lock (dot_product_lock)
                dot_product := dot_product + local_dot_product
        unlock (dot_product_lock)
        barrier (done)
end
```

Figure 12.19   An efficient program to compute the dot product on two
processors in a shared memory machine.

12.8.2 MESSAGE-PASSING CASE

In this case the memory is distributed, and each processor can access directly only its own memory. The desired program will run on two processors and the arrays will have to be explicitly divided into halves, with each half being stored in the memory of one processor. Each copy of the program will have access only to its portion of the data. Applications of this type are called *Single Program Multiple Data* (SPMD). The reader should note the difference between this type of application and the SIMD type introduced in Section 12.1.1. In the SIMD type, all processors execute the same instruction at any given time.

A possible program is given in Figure 12.20. The vector data must first be loaded into the private memories of the two processors. The program that is assigned the *id* value of 0 reads the first half of vector *a* from the disk, with the help of the operating

```
integer array a[1..N/2], b[1..N/2], temparray[1..N/2]
integer dot_product
integer id
integer temp
    .
    .
    .
id := mypid()
if (id = 0) then
                read a[1..N/2] from vector_a
                read temparray[1..N/2] from vector_a
                send (temparray[1..N/2], 1)
                read b[1..N/2] from vector_b
                read temparray[1..N/2] from vector_b
                send (temparray[1..N/2], 1)
        else    receive (a[1..N/2], 0)
                receive (b[1..N/2], 0)
end
dot_product := 0
do_dot (a, b)
if (id = 1)    send (dot_product, 0)
        else   receive (temp, 1)
               dot_product := dot_product + temp
               print dot_product
end
    .
    .
    .
do_dot (integer array x[1..N/2], integer array y[1..N/2])
        for k:= 1 to N/2
                dot_product := dot_product + x[k] * y[k]
        end
end
```

Figure 12.20 A message-passing program to compute the dot product on two processors.

system, and it stores the data in its memory under this name. It then reads the remaining second half of vector *a* and places the data in a memory buffer called *temparray*. Next, it sends a message containing the data from this buffer to the processor that executes the program that is assigned the *id* value of 1. The same operations are then repeated for the data that constitute vector *b*. The program with the *id* value of 1 receives the second halves of vectors *a* and *b* and stores them in its memory under the same names.

The *do_dot* routine now simply computes the dot product for the N/2 elements. Note that the loop bounds are the same for both processors because each uses the data stored in its own memory. The message-passing feature is also illustrated by the action taken when the processors complete execution of the *do_dot* routine: The program that has the *id* value of 0 will compute and print the final dot product. It will do so when it receives the message with the value of the partial dot product that was computed and sent by program 1. This value is received in a temporary buffer called *temp*.

Again, it is easy to see how this example could be extended to many processors. The vectors would have to be partitioned into portions that would be assigned to each processor for computation. One of the processors, for example, the one that executes the program with $id = 0$, would be designated to compute the final result using the data received in messages from other processors.

The overhead of establishing parallel execution on multiple processors consists of the time needed to load the copies of the program into different processors, the time used to set up the partitioned arrays in the memories associated with different processors, and the time needed to send other messages among processors. Performance benefits depend on the size of the vectors and the number of processors used.

Shared-memory and message-passing paradigms have certain strengths and weaknesses. The shared-memory environment is more natural to use because it is an extension of the uniprocessor programming model. Hence, it is easier to write parallel programs that are reasonably efficient. Since the memory access latency may be high if data reside in remote memory modules, it is important to minimize the number of write accesses to global variables. The amount of traffic in the network may be large, causing the network to become a bottleneck. Synchronization of processes is the responsibility of the programmer and influences the performance of an application significantly.

Message passing gives a less natural programming environment because of multiple address spaces in private memories. The time overhead of message passing is very significant; hence, the programmer must try to structure programs to minimize its effect. Since messages are relatively infrequent, the interconnection network is not likely to be a problem. Synchronization is implicit in the messages passed between processes. Perhaps the biggest advantage of message passing is that it can be supported by less expensive and more commonly available hardware.

12.9 PERFORMANCE CONSIDERATIONS

This chapter has concentrated on the design of systems that use multiple processors to reduce the time needed to run a large application. The most important performance measure is the speedup achieved on a multiprocessor system in comparison with the time it would take to run the same application on a single processor. The *speedup* is defined as

$$S_P = \frac{T_1}{T_P}$$

where T_1 and T_P are the times needed if one or P processors are used, respectively. Figure 12.21 shows three types of speedup that may occur as a function of the number of processors in the system. Intuitively, we would expect that, as the number of processors is increased, the time needed to run an application that is parallelizable should decrease proportionately. This would give a linear speedup, where $S = P$, which is the goal in scalable systems. Unfortunately, this goal is not easy to achieve.

As the previous section shows, it is not possible to parallelize all parts of an application program. The sequential parts will take the same amount of time regardless

Speedup (*S*)

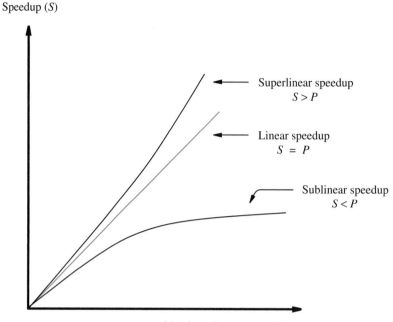

Figure 12.21 Speedup curves in multiprocessor systems.

of the number of processors used. It is the relative proportion of sequential parts that limits the achievable speedup.

Another reason why linear speedup is difficult to achieve is the overhead caused by initialization, synchronization, communication, cache coherence control, and load imbalance. Overhead tends to increase with the size of the system. We have encountered examples of such overhead in previous sections, except for load imbalance. It is usually necessary to wait for the last processor to complete a parallel task before proceeding with the next set of tasks. Hence, when a parallel task is spread over a number of processors, it is most efficient if all processors reach a given synchronization point at about the same time, in which case the load is balanced.

In practical systems the speedup achievable with most applications is sublinear, and a point is reached where adding processors no longer improves performance. Curiously, there exist some applications for which even superlinear speedup is possible, but these are not common. We give an example of such an application in the next subsection.

12.9.1 AMDAHL'S LAW

Let us consider the improvement in performance from a quantitative point of view. An enhancement in a computer system inevitably improves some part of the system but not the entire system. The improved performance depends on the impact of the enhanced part. This reasoning was formalized by Gene Amdahl in a well known "law" [11].

It can be stated as

$$S_{\text{new}} = \frac{Old\ time}{New\ time} = \frac{1}{1 - f_{\text{enhanced}} + f_{\text{enhanced}}/S_{\text{enhanced}}}$$

where

- S_{new} is the speedup in the new system, which includes the enhancement.
- S_{enhanced} is the speedup achievable if only the enhanced part of the system is used.
- f_{enhanced} is the fraction of the computation time in the old system that can be improved with the enhancement made.

In terms of a multiprocessor system, this law can be restated as follows. Let f be the fraction of a computation (in terms of time) that is parallelizable, P be the number of processors in the system, and S_P be the speedup achievable in comparison with sequential execution. Then we have

$$S_P = \frac{1}{1 - f + f/P} = \frac{P}{P - f(P - 1)}$$

This formula assumes that the parallelizable part is performed by all processors using perfect load balance.

Suppose that a given application is run on a 64-processor machine and that 70 percent of the application is parallelizable. Then the expected improvement is

$$S_{64} = \frac{64}{64 - 0.7 \times 63} = 3.22$$

If the same application is run on a 16-processor machine, the expected speedup would be 2.91. This indicates that the speedup is much less than the number of processors in the machine. Moreover, the difference in speedup achieved by increasing from 16 to 64 processors is minimal. Clearly, it makes little sense to use large multiprocessors for applications that have significant sequential (nonparallelizable) parts. For good speedup, the sequential parts must be very short. For an application with $f = 0.95$, the speedup in the preceding machines would be 15.42 and 9.14, respectively. Amdahl's law, in fact, states that linear speedup cannot be achieved because almost all applications have some sections that cannot be parallelized.

This discussion assumes that each processor performs an equal amount of parallel computation. Such equal load balancing may not necessarily occur. If it is necessary to wait for the slowest processor to complete its parallel assignment before continuing with the next step, then the results will be worse than predicted by the preceding formula. However, there exist applications where the opposite may occur, namely, where the tasks performed by all processors may be terminated as soon as one processor completes its task. For example, such unusual behavior occurs in applications based on a technique known as simulated annealing. To illustrate this technique, suppose that in the design of a VLSI chip, it is desired to place the logic gates such that the total length of wires in the resulting circuit is minimized. This requires trying a large number of different placements, which can be done by assigning the best placement known at a given time to all processors as a starting point for the next iteration. Then each processor can use a different randomized approach to change the positions of the gates in search for a better placement. As soon as one processor finds a placement that is superior to the starting placement by some predetermined amount, this processor's solution can be used as the new starting point for all the processors, without waiting for the other processors to also find acceptable solutions. An application of this type may exhibit superlinear speedup, because if it is performed by a single processor, this processor may spend a lot of time investigating unpromising possibilities before it reaches a good one.

12.9.2   PERFORMANCE INDICATORS

From a user's point of view, the most important characteristics of a computer system are its cost, ease of use, reliability, and performance. Several indicators of performance are used to depict the processing capability of computers. The discussion of this issue in Section 8.8 applies equally to multiprocessor systems.

The raw power of a processor can be indicated in terms of the number of operations it can perform in one second. Two popular measures are MIPS, the number of millions of instructions executed per second, and MFLOPS (pronounced megaFLOPS), the number of millions of floating-point operations performed per second. When a manufacturer gives the MIPS and MFLOPS numbers for a given processor, these numbers indicate the processor's maximum capability. This maximum is not always achievable in practical applications. In a multiprocessor system, the total MIPS and MFLOPS are simply the sums of the values for all the processors.

Another common performance indicator is the communications capability of the interconnection network, usually given as the total bandwidth in bytes per second. This assumes an optimal situation in which sufficient data are available for transfer to keep the largest possible number of network links busy, thus maximizing the amount of data that can be transferred at one time.

While indicators such as MIPS, MFLOPS, and network bandwidth give a useful impression of what the system is capable of doing, they are not a measure of the actual performance we expect to observe when application programs are executed. Practical applications can use only a fraction of the total resources available at any given time. This fraction varies from one system to another and from one application to another. A proper comparison of two different systems is possible only if a desired set of applications is run on both systems and their performance is observed. To facilitate such comparisons, a number of *benchmark* programs have been developed. These programs are indicative of the behavior found in a variety of common applications. Comparing different systems based on benchmark programs has become widely accepted.

12.10   CONCLUDING REMARKS

Multiprocessors provide a way to realize supercomputing capability at a reasonable cost. They are most cost-effective in the range of tens to hundreds of processors. Very large systems comprising thousands of processors are difficult to use fully, and their cost curtails the market demand significantly.

A particularly cost-effective possibility is to implement a multicomputer system using workstations interconnected by a local area network. This possibility will become even more attractive as local area network speeds increase.

Successful use of multiprocessors depends heavily on the availability of system software that makes good use of the available resources. An application program will not show good performance if the locality and parallelism inherent in the application are not properly exploited. The compiler must detect the opportunities for parallel execution. The operating system must schedule the execution to make good use of locality, by assigning tasks that involve a large amount of interaction to processors that are close to each other. The application programmer may provide useful hints in this respect, but it is best if the system software can do this on its own.

This chapter provides an overview of the most important aspects of multiprocessor and multicomputer systems. Many details should be studied to understand fully the capabilities of these systems and the design issues involved. For detailed study, the reader should consult books that focus on this subject [12–16].

PROBLEMS

12.1   Write a program loop whose instructions can be broadcast from the control processor in Figure 12.1 that will enable an array processor to iteratively compute temperatures in a plane, as discussed in Section 12.2. In addition to instructions that shift the network register contents between adjacent processing elements (PEs), assume that there are two-operand instructions for moves between PE registers and local memory and for arithmetic operations. Assume also that each PE stores the current estimate of its grid point temperature in a local memory location named CURRENT and that a few registers, R0, R1, and so on, are available for processing. Each boundary PE maintains a fixed boundary temperature value in its network register and does not execute the broadcast program. A small value stored in location EPSILON in each PE is used to determine when the local temperature has reached the required level of accuracy. At the end of each iteration of the loop, each PE must set its status bit, STATUS, to 1 if its new temperature satisfies the following condition:

$$|\text{New temperature} - [\text{CURRENT}]| < [\text{EPSILON}]$$

Otherwise, STATUS is set to 0.

12.2   Assume that a bus transfer takes T seconds and memory access time is $4T$ seconds. A read request over a conventional bus then requires $6T$ seconds to complete. How many conventional buses are needed to equal or exceed the bandwidth of a split-transaction bus that operates with the same time delays? Consider only read requests, ignore memory conflicts, and assume that all memory modules are connected to all buses in the multiple bus case. Does your answer increase or decrease if memory access time increases?

12.3   In a bus-based multiprocessor, the system bus can become a bottleneck if it does not support a high enough transfer rate. Suppose that a split-transaction bus is designed to be four times as wide as the word length of the processors used in the system. Will this increase the effective transfer rate to four times the rate of a similar bus that is only as wide as the processor word length? Explain your answer.

12.4   Assume that the cost of a 2×2 switch in a shuffle network is twice the cost of a crosspoint in a crossbar switch. There are n^2 crosspoints in an $n \times n$ crossbar switch. As n increases, the crossbar becomes more costly than the shuffle network. What is the smallest value of n for which crossbar cost is five times more costly than the shuffle network?

12.5   Shuffle networks can be built from 4×4 and 8×8 switches, for example, instead of from 2×2 switches. Draw a 16×16 ($n = 16$) shuffle network built from 4×4 switches. If the cost of a 4×4 switch is four times the cost of a 2×2 switch, compare the cost of shuffle networks built from 4×4 switches with those built from 2×2 switches for n values in the sequence $4, 4^2, 4^3$, and so on. Qualitatively compare the blocking probability of these two different ways of building shuffle networks.

12.6   Suppose that each procedure of a PAR segment (see Figure 12.14) requires 1 unit of time to execute. A program consists of three sequential segments. Each segment requires k time units and must be executed on a single processor. The three sequential segments are separated by two PAR segments, each of which consists of k procedures that can be executed on independent processors. Derive an expression for speedup for this program when it is run on a multiprocessor with n processors. Assume $n \leq k$. What is the limiting value of the speedup when k is large and $n = k$? What does this result tell you about the effect of sequential segments in programs that have some segments with substantial parallelism?

12.7   The shortest distance a message travels in an n-dimensional hypercube is 1 hop, and the longest distance a message needs to travel is n hops. Assuming that all possible source/destination pairs are equally likely, is the average distance a message needs to travel larger or smaller than $(1 + n)/2$? Justify your answer.

12.8   A task that "busy-waits" on a lock variable by using a Test-and-Set instruction in a two-instruction loop, as in Figure 12.15, wastes bus cycles that could otherwise be used for computation. Suggest a way around this problem that involves a centralized queue of waiting tasks that is maintained by the operating system. Assume that the operating system can be called by a user task and that the operating system chooses which task is to be executed on a processor from among those ready for execution.

12.9   What are the arguments for and against invalidation and updating as strategies for maintaining cache coherence?

12.10   Section 12.6.3 argues that cache coherence controls cannot replace the need for lock variables. Can the use of lock variables replace the need for explicit cache coherence controls?

12.11   Estimate the improvement in performance that can be achieved if the program in Figure 12.19 is used rather than the program in Figure 12.18. Make some appropriate assumptions about the amount of time it takes to perform each step in the program.

12.12 Modify the program in Figure 12.19 to make it suitable for execution in a four-processor machine.

12.13 Modify the program in Figure 12.20 to make it suitable for execution in a four-processor system.

12.14 For small vectors, the approach in Figure 12.19 will be worse than if the dot product is computed using a single processor. Estimate the minimum size of the vectors for which this approach leads to better performance. Make some appropriate assumptions about the amount of time it takes to perform each step in the program.

12.15 Repeat Problem 12.14 for the approach in Figure 12.20.

12.16 Shared-memory multiprocessors and message-passing multicomputers are architectures that support simultaneous execution of tasks that interact with each other. Which of these two architectures can emulate the action of the other more easily? Briefly justify your answer.

12.17 The Ethernet bus LAN protocol is really only suitable when message transmission time is significantly larger than 2τ, where τ is the end-to-end bus propagation delay. Consider the case in which transmission time is less than τ. Is it possible for a destination station to correctly receive an undistorted message, even though the source station observes a collision inside the 2τ collision window period? If not, justify your answer. If you think it is possible, give the relative locations of the source, destination, and interfering stations on the bus and describe the relevant event times.

12.18 A *mailbox memory* is a RAM memory with the following feature. A full/empty bit, F/E, is associated with each memory word location. The instruction

$$\text{PUT} \quad \text{R0,BOXLOC,WAITSEND}$$

is executed indivisibly as follows. The F/E bit associated with mailbox memory location BOXLOC is tested. If it is 0, denoting empty, then the contents of register R0 are written into BOXLOC, F/E is set to 1, denoting full, and execution continues with the next sequential instruction. Otherwise (that is, for F/E = 1), no operations are performed and execution control is passed to the instruction at location WAITSEND in program memory.

(*a*) Give an appropriate definition for the instruction

$$\text{GET} \quad \text{R0,BOXLOC,WAITREC}$$

that is complementary to the PUT instruction.

(*b*) Suppose two tasks, T_1 and T_2, running on different processors in a multiprocessor system, pass a stream of one-word messages from T_1 to T_2 using PUT and GET instructions on a shared mailbox memory unit. Write program segments for T_1 and T_2 in assembly-language style that accomplish the same thing on a shared-memory multiprocessor system that does not have a mailbox memory unit but does have a TAS instruction as described in Section 12.6.1.

REFERENCES

1. M.J. Flynn, "Very High-Speed Computing Systems," *Proceedings of the IEEE,* vol. 54, December 1966, pp. 1901–1909.

2. D.L. Slotnick, "The Fastest Computer," *Scientific American,* vol. 224, February 1971, pp. 76–88.

3. D. Lenoski, et al., "The Stanford DASH Multiprocessor," *Computer,* vol. 25, March 1992, pp. 63–79.

4. J. Kuskin, et al., "The Stanford FLASH Multiprocessor," *Proceedings of the 21st Annual International Symposium on Computer Architecture,* Chicago, April 1994, pp. 302–313.

5. A. Agarwal, et al., "The MIT Alewife Machine: Architecture and Performance," *Proceedings of the 22nd Annual International Symposium on Computer Architecture,* Santa Margherita Ligure, Italy, June 1995, pp. 2–13.

6. Z.G. Vranesic, M. Stumm, D.M. Lewis, and R. White, "Hector: A Hierarchically Structured Shared-Memory Multiprocessor," *Computer,* vol. 24, January 1991, pp. 72–79.

7. R. Grindley, et al., "The NUMAchine Multiprocessor," *Proceedings of the 2000 International Conference on Parallel Processing,* Toronto, Ont., August 2000, pp. 487–496.

8. W.J. Dally and P. Song, "Design of a Self-Timed Multicomputer Communication Controller," *Proceedings of the 1987 International Conference on Computer Design,* October 1987, pp. 230–234.

9. D. Gustavson, "The Scalable Coherent Interface and Related Standards Projects," *IEEE Micro,* vol. 12, January 1992, pp. 10–22.

10. *IEEE Local Area Standard 802,* IEEE, 1985.

11. G.M. Amdahl, "Validity of the Single Processor Approach to Achieving Large-Scale Computing Capabilities," *Proceedings of AFIPS Spring Joint Computer Conference,* Atlantic City, NJ, April 1967, pp. 483–485.

12. D. Culler, J.P. Singh, and A. Gupta, *Parallel Computer Architecture — A Hardware/Software Approach,* Morgan Kaufmann, San Francisco, CA, 1998.

13. G.S. Almasi and A. Gottlieb, *Highly Parallel Computing,* 2nd ed., Benjamin-Cummings, Redwood City, CA, 1994.

14. K. Hwang, *Advanced Computer Architecture,* McGraw-Hill, New York, 1993.

15. H.S. Stone, *High-Performance Computer Architecture,* 3rd ed., Addison-Wesley, Reading, MA, 1993.

16. D. Tabak, *Multiprocessors,* Prentice-Hall, Englewood Cliffs, NJ, 1990.

APPENDIX

A

LOGIC CIRCUITS

Information in digital computers is represented and processed by electronic networks called *logic circuits*. These circuits operate on *binary variables* that assume one of two distinct values, usually called 0 and 1. In this appendix we will give a concise presentation of logic functions and circuits for their implementation, including a brief review of integrated circuit technology.

A.1   BASIC LOGIC FUNCTIONS

It is helpful to introduce the topic of binary logic by examining a practical problem that arises in all homes. Consider a lightbulb whose on/off status is controlled by two switches, x_1 and x_2. Each switch can be in one of two possible positions, 0 or 1, as shown in Figure A.1*a*. It can thus be represented by a binary variable. We will let the switch names serve as the names of the associated binary variables. The figure also shows an electrical power supply and a lightbulb. The way the switch terminals are interconnected determines how the switches control the light. The light will be on only if a closed path exists from the power supply through the switch network to the lightbulb. Let a binary variable f represent the condition of the light. If the light is on, $f = 1$, and if the light is off, $f = 0$. Thus, $f = 1$ means that there is at least one closed path through the network, and $f = 0$ means that there is no closed path. Clearly, f is a function of the two variables x_1 and x_2.

Let us consider some possibilities for controlling the light. First, suppose that the light is to be on if either switch is in the 1 position, that is, $f = 1$ if

$$x_1 = 1 \quad \text{and} \quad x_2 = 0$$

or

$$x_1 = 0 \quad \text{and} \quad x_2 = 1$$

or

$$x_1 = 1 \quad \text{and} \quad x_2 = 1$$

The connections that implement this type of control are shown in Figure A.1*b*. A logic *truth table* that represents this situation is shown beside the wiring diagram. The table lists all possible switch settings along with the value of f for each setting. In logic terms, this table represents the OR function of the two variables x_1 and x_2. The operation is represented algebraically by a "+" sign or a "∨" sign, so that

$$f = x_1 + x_2 = x_1 \vee x_2$$

We say that x_1 and x_2 are the *input* variables and f is the *output* function.

We should point out some basic properties of the OR operation. It is commutative, that is,

$$x_1 + x_2 = x_2 + x_1$$

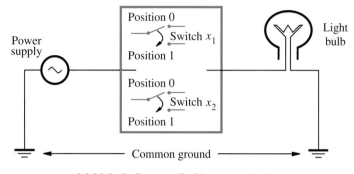

(a) Light bulb controlled by two switches

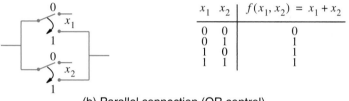

x_1	x_2	$f(x_1, x_2) = x_1 + x_2$
0	0	0
0	1	1
1	0	1
1	1	1

(b) Parallel connection (OR control)

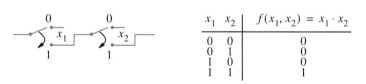

x_1	x_2	$f(x_1, x_2) = x_1 \cdot x_2$
0	0	0
0	1	0
1	0	0
1	1	1

(c) Series connection (AND control)

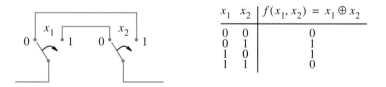

x_1	x_2	$f(x_1, x_2) = x_1 \oplus x_2$
0	0	0
0	1	1
1	0	1
1	1	0

(d) EXCLUSIVE-OR connection (XOR control)

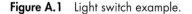

Figure A.1   Light switch example.

It can be extended to n variables, so that

$$f = x_1 + x_2 + \cdots + x_n$$

has the value 1 if any variable x_i has the value 1. This represents the effect of connecting more switches in parallel with the two switches in Figure A.1b. Also, inspection of the truth table shows that

$$1 + x = 1$$

and

$$0 + x = x$$

Now, suppose that the light is to be on only when both switches are in the 1 position. The connections for this, along with the corresponding truth-table representation, are shown in Figure A.1c. This is the AND function, which uses the symbol "·" or "∧" and is denoted as

$$f = x_1 \cdot x_2 = x_1 \wedge x_2$$

Some basic properties of the AND operation are

$$x_1 \cdot x_2 = x_2 \cdot x_1$$

$$1 \cdot x = x$$

and

$$0 \cdot x = 0$$

The AND function also extends to n variables, with

$$f = x_1 \cdot x_2 \cdot \cdots \cdot x_n$$

having the value 1 only if all the x_i variables have the value 1. This represents the case in which more switches are connected in series with the two switches in Figure A.1c.

The final possibility that we will discuss for the way the switches determine the light status is another common situation. If we assume that the switches are at the two ends of a stairway, it should be possible to turn the light on or off from either switch. That is, if the light is on, changing either switch position should turn it off; and if it is off, changing either switch position should turn it on. Assume that the light is off when both switches are in the 0 position. Then changing either switch to the 1 position should turn the light on. Now suppose that the light is on with $x_1 = 1$ and $x_2 = 0$. Switching x_1 back to 0 will obviously turn the light off. Furthermore, it must be possible to turn the light off by changing x_2 to 1, that is, $f = 0$ if $x_1 = x_2 = 1$. The connections to implement this type of control are shown in Figure A.1d. The corresponding logic operation is called the EXCLUSIVE-OR (XOR) function, which is represented by the symbol "⊕". Some of its properties are

$$x_1 \oplus x_2 = x_2 \oplus x_1$$

$$1 \oplus x = \overline{x}$$

and

$$0 \oplus x = x$$

where $\bar{x}$ denotes the NOT function of the variable x. This single-variable function, $f = \bar{x}$, has the value 1 if $x = 0$ and the value 0 if $x = 1$. We say that the input x is being *inverted* or *complemented*.

A.1.1 ELECTRONIC LOGIC GATES

The use of switches, closed or open electrical paths, and lightbulbs to illustrate the idea of logic variables and functions is convenient because of their familiarity and simplicity. The logic concepts that have been introduced are equally applicable to the electronic circuits used to process information in digital computers. The physical variables are electrical voltages and currents instead of switch positions and closed or open paths. For example, consider a circuit that is designed to operate on inputs that are at either +5 or 0 volts. The circuit outputs are also at either +5 or 0 V. Now, if we say that +5 V represents logic 1 and 0 V represents logic 0, then we can describe what the circuit does by specifying the truth table for the logic operation that it performs.

With the help of transistors, it is possible to design simple electronic circuits that perform logic operations such as AND, OR, XOR, and NOT. It is customary to use the name *gates* for these basic logic circuits. Standard symbols for these gates are shown in Figure A.2. A somewhat more compact graphical notation for the NOT operation

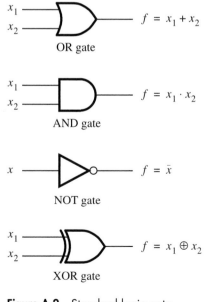

Figure A.2 Standard logic gate symbols.

is used when inversion is applied to a logic gate input or output. In such cases, the inversion is denoted by a small circle.

The electronic implementation of logic gates will be discussed in Section A.5. We will now proceed to discuss how basic gates can be used to construct logic networks that implement more complex logic functions.

A.2 SYNTHESIS OF LOGIC FUNCTIONS

Consider the network composed of two AND gates and one OR gate that is shown in Figure A.3a. It can be represented by the expression

$$f = \overline{x}_1 \cdot x_2 + x_1 \cdot \overline{x}_2$$

The construction of the truth table for this expression is shown in Figure A.3b. First, the values of the AND terms are determined for each input valuation. Then the values of the function f are determined using the OR operation. The truth table for f is identical

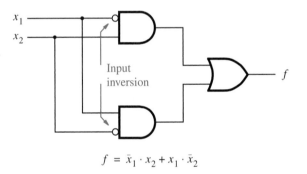

$$f = \overline{x}_1 \cdot x_2 + x_1 \cdot \overline{x}_2$$

(a) Network for the XOR function

x_1 x_2	$\overline{x}_1 \cdot x_2$	$x_1 \cdot \overline{x}_2$	$f = \overline{x}_1 \cdot x_2 + x_1 \cdot \overline{x}_2$ $= x_1 \oplus x_2$
0 0	0	0	0
0 1	1	0	1
1 0	0	1	1
1 1	0	0	0

(b) Truth table construction of $\overline{x}_1 \cdot x_2 + x_1 \cdot \overline{x}_2$

Figure A.3   Implementation of the XOR function using AND, OR, and NOT gates.

Table A.1 Two 3-variable functions

x_1	x_2	x_3	f_1	f_2
0	0	0	1	1
0	0	1	1	1
0	1	0	0	1
0	1	1	1	0
1	0	0	0	1
1	0	1	0	1
1	1	0	0	0
1	1	1	1	0

to the truth table for the XOR function, so the three-gate network in Figure A.3a is an implementation of the XOR function using AND, OR, and NOT gates. The logic expression $\overline{x}_1 \cdot x_2 + x_1 \cdot \overline{x}_2$ is called a *sum-of-products* form because the OR operation is sometimes called the "sum" function and the AND operation the "product" function.

We should note that it would be more proper to write

$$f = ((\overline{x}_1) \cdot x_2) + (x_1 \cdot (\overline{x}_2))$$

to indicate the order of applying the operations in the expression. To simplify the appearance of such expressions, we define a hierarchy among the three operations AND, OR, and NOT. In the absence of parentheses, operations in a logic expression should be performed in the following order: NOT, AND, and then OR. Furthermore, it is customary to omit the "·" operator when there is no ambiguity.

Returning to the sum-of-products form, we will now explain how any logic function can be synthesized in this form directly from its truth table. Consider the truth table of Table A.1 and suppose we wish to synthesize the function f_1 using AND, OR, and NOT gates. For each row of the table in which $f_1 = 1$, we include a product (AND) term in the sum-of-products form. The product term includes all three input variables. The NOT operator is applied to these variables individually so that the term is 1 only when the variables have the particular valuation that corresponds to that row of the truth table. This means that if $x_i = 0$, then $\overline{x}_i$ is entered in the product term, and if $x_i = 1$, then x_i is entered. For example, the fourth row of the table has the function entry 1 for the input valuation

$$(x_1, x_2, x_3) = (0, 1, 1)$$

The product term corresponding to this is $\overline{x}_1 x_2 x_3$. Doing this for all rows in which the function f_1 has the value 1 leads to

$$f_1 = \overline{x}_1 \overline{x}_2 \overline{x}_3 + \overline{x}_1 \overline{x}_2 x_3 + \overline{x}_1 x_2 x_3 + x_1 x_2 x_3$$

The logic network corresponding to this expression is shown on the left side in Figure A.4. As another example, the sum-of-products expression for the XOR function

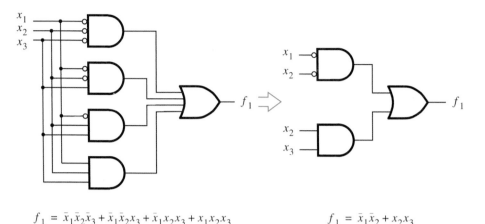

$$f_1 = \bar{x}_1\bar{x}_2\bar{x}_3 + \bar{x}_1\bar{x}_2x_3 + \bar{x}_1x_2x_3 + x_1x_2x_3 \qquad\qquad f_1 = \bar{x}_1\bar{x}_2 + x_2x_3$$

Figure A.4 A logic network for f_1 of Table A.1 and an equivalent minimal network.

can be derived from its truth table using this technique. This approach can be used to derive sum-of-products expressions and the corresponding logic networks for truth tables of any size.

A.3 MINIMIZATION OF LOGIC EXPRESSIONS

We have shown how to derive one sum-of-products expression for each truth table. In fact, there are many equivalent expressions and logic networks for any particular truth table. Two logic expressions or logic gate networks are equivalent if they have identical truth tables. An expression that is equivalent to the sum-of-products expression we derived for f_1 in the previous section is

$$\bar{x}_1\bar{x}_2 + x_2x_3$$

To prove this, we construct the truth table for the simpler expression and show that it is identical to the truth table for f_1 in Table A.1. This is done in Table A.2. The construction of the table for $\bar{x}_1\bar{x}_2 + x_2x_3$ is done in three steps. First, the value of the product term $\bar{x}_1\bar{x}_2$ is computed for each valuation of the inputs. Then x_2x_3 is evaluated. Finally, these two columns are ORed together to obtain the truth table for the expression. This truth table is identical to the truth table for f_1 given in Table A.1.

　　To simplify logic expressions we will perform a series of algebraic manipulations. The new logic rules that we will use in these manipulations are the distributive rule

$$w(y + z) = wy + wz$$

and the identity

$$w + \bar{w} = 1$$

Table A.2 Evaluation of the expression $\overline{x}_1\overline{x}_2 + x_2x_3$

x_1	x_2	x_3	$\overline{x}_1\overline{x}_2$	x_2x_3	$\overline{x}_1\overline{x}_2 + x_2x_3 = f_1$
0	0	0	1	0	1
0	0	1	1	0	1
0	1	0	0	0	0
0	1	1	0	1	1
1	0	0	0	0	0
1	0	1	0	0	0
1	1	0	0	0	0
1	1	1	0	1	1

Table A.3 Truth-table technique for proving equivalence of expressions

w	y	z	$y + z$	Left-hand side $w(y + z)$	wy	wz	Right-hand side $wy + wz$
0	0	0	0	0	0	0	0
0	0	1	1	0	0	0	0
0	1	0	1	0	0	0	0
0	1	1	1	0	0	0	0
1	0	0	0	0	0	0	0
1	0	1	1	1	0	1	1
1	1	0	1	1	1	0	1
1	1	1	1	1	1	1	1

Table A.3 shows the truth-table proof of the distributive rule. It should now be clear that rules such as this can always be proved by constructing the truth tables for the left-hand side and the right-hand side to show that they are identical. Logic rules, such as the distributive rule, are sometimes called *identities*. Although we will not need to use it here, another form of distributive rule that we should include for completeness is

$$w + yz = (w + y)(w + z)$$

The objective in logic minimization is to reduce the cost of implementation of a given logic function according to some criterion. More particularly, we wish to start with a sum-of-products expression derived from a truth table and simplify it to an equivalent *minimal sum-of-products* expression. To define the criterion for minimization, it is necessary to introduce a size or cost measure for a sum-of-products expression. The usual cost measure is a count of the total number of gates and gate inputs required in implementing the expression in the form shown in Figure A.4. For example, the larger expression in this figure has a cost of 21, composed of a total of 5 gates and 16 gate inputs. Input inversions are ignored in this counting process. The cost of the simpler expression is 9, composed of 3 gates and 6 inputs. We are now in a position to state that a sum-of-products expression is minimal if there is no other equivalent sum-of-products expression with a lower cost. In the simple examples that we will introduce, it is usually reasonably clear when we have arrived at a minimal expression. Thus, we will not give rigorous proofs of minimality.

The general strategy in performing algebraic manipulations to simplify a given expression is as follows. First, group product terms in pairs that differ only in that some variable appears complemented $(\overline{x})$ in one term and true (x) in the other. When the common subproduct consisting of the other variables is factored out of the pair by the distributive rule, we are left with the term $x + \overline{x}$, which has the value 1. Applying this procedure to the first expression for f_1, we obtain

$$f_1 = \overline{x}_1\overline{x}_2\overline{x}_3 + \overline{x}_1\overline{x}_2 x_3 + \overline{x}_1 x_2 x_3 + x_1 x_2 x_3$$
$$= \overline{x}_1\overline{x}_2(\overline{x}_3 + x_3) + (\overline{x}_1 + x_1)x_2 x_3$$
$$= \overline{x}_1\overline{x}_2 \cdot 1 + 1 \cdot x_2 x_3$$
$$= \overline{x}_1\overline{x}_2 + x_2 x_3$$

This expression is minimal. The network corresponding to it is shown in Figure A.4.

The grouping of terms in pairs so that minimization can lead to the simplest expression is not always as obvious as it is in the preceding example. A rule that is often helpful is

$$w + w = w$$

This allows us to repeat product terms so that a particular term can be combined with

Table A.4 Rules of binary logic

Name	Algebraic identity	
Commutative	$w + y = y + w$	$wy = yw$
Associative	$(w + y) + z = w + (y + z)$	$(wy)z = w(yz)$
Distributive	$w + yz = (w + y)(w + z)$	$w(y + z) = wy + wz$
Idempotent	$w + w = w$	$ww = w$
Involution	$\overline{\overline{w}} = w$	
Complement	$w + \overline{w} = 1$	$w\overline{w} = 0$
de Morgan	$\overline{w + y} = \overline{w}\,\overline{y}$	$\overline{wy} = \overline{w} + \overline{y}$
	$1 + w = 1$	$0 \cdot w = 0$
	$0 + w = w$	$1 \cdot w = w$

more than one other term in the factoring process. As an example of this, consider the function f_2 in Table A.1. The sum-of-products expression that can be derived for it directly from the truth table is

$$f_2 = \overline{x}_1\overline{x}_2\overline{x}_3 + \overline{x}_1\overline{x}_2 x_3 + \overline{x}_1 x_2\overline{x}_3 + x_1\overline{x}_2\overline{x}_3 + x_1\overline{x}_2 x_3$$

By repeating the first product term $\overline{x}_1\overline{x}_2\overline{x}_3$ and interchanging the order of terms (by the commutative rule), we obtain

$$f_2 = \overline{x}_1\overline{x}_2\overline{x}_3 + \overline{x}_1\overline{x}_2 x_3 + x_1\overline{x}_2\overline{x}_3 + x_1\overline{x}_2 x_3 + \overline{x}_1\overline{x}_2\overline{x}_3 + \overline{x}_1 x_2\overline{x}_3$$

Grouping the terms in pairs and factoring yields

$$f_2 = \overline{x}_1\overline{x}_2(\overline{x}_3 + x_3) + x_1\overline{x}_2(\overline{x}_3 + x_3) + \overline{x}_1(\overline{x}_2 + x_2)\overline{x}_3$$
$$= \overline{x}_1\overline{x}_2 + x_1\overline{x}_2 + \overline{x}_1\overline{x}_3$$

The first pair of terms is again reduced by factoring, and we obtain the minimal expression

$$f_2 = \overline{x}_2 + \overline{x}_1\overline{x}_3$$

This completes our discussion of algebraic simplification of logic expressions. The obvious practical application of this mathematical exercise stems from the fact that networks with fewer gates and inputs are cheaper and easier to implement. Therefore, it is of economic interest to be able to determine the minimal expression that is equivalent to a given expression. The rules that we have used in manipulating logic expressions are summarized in Table A.4. They are arranged in pairs to show their symmetry as they apply to both the AND and OR functions. So far, we have not had occasion to use either involution or de Morgan's rules, but they will be found to be useful in the next section.

A.3.1 MINIMIZATION USING KARNAUGH MAPS

In our algebraic minimization of the functions f_1 and f_2 of Table A.1, it was necessary to guess the best way to proceed at certain points. For instance, the decision to repeat the term $\overline{x}_1\overline{x}_2\overline{x}_3$ as the first step in minimizing f_2 is not obvious. There is a geometric technique that can be used to quickly derive the minimal expression for a logic function of a few variables. The technique depends on a different form for presentation of the truth table, a form called the *Karnaugh map*. For a three-variable function, the map is a rectangle composed of eight squares arranged in two rows of four squares each, as shown in Figure A.5a. Each square of the map corresponds to a particular valuation of the input variables. For example, the third square of the top row represents the valuation $(x_1, x_2, x_3) = (1, 1, 0)$. Because there are eight rows in a three-variable truth table, the map obviously requires eight squares. The entries in the squares are the function values for the corresponding input valuations.

The key idea in the formation of the map is that horizontally and vertically adjacent squares correspond to input valuations that differ in only one variable. When two adjacent squares contain 1s, they indicate the possibility of an algebraic simplification.

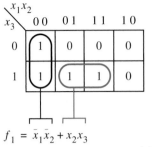
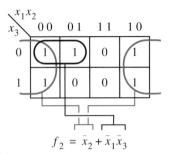

$$f_1 = \bar{x}_1\bar{x}_2 + x_2x_3 \qquad f_2 = \bar{x}_2 + \bar{x}_1x_3$$

(a) Three-variable maps

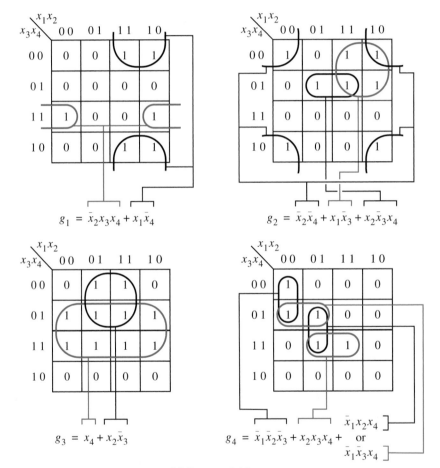

$$g_1 = \bar{x}_2x_3x_4 + x_1\bar{x}_4$$

$$g_2 = \bar{x}_2\bar{x}_4 + x_1\bar{x}_3 + x_2\bar{x}_3x_4$$

$$g_3 = x_4 + x_2\bar{x}_3$$

$$g_4 = \bar{x}_1\bar{x}_2\bar{x}_3 + x_2x_3x_4 + \begin{array}{l} \bar{x}_1x_2x_4 \\ \text{or} \\ \bar{x}_1\bar{x}_3x_4 \end{array}$$

(b) Four-variable maps

Figure A.5   Minimization using Karnaugh maps.

In the map for f_2 in Figure A.5a, the 1 values in the leftmost two squares of the top row correspond to the product terms $\overline{x}_1\overline{x}_2\overline{x}_3$ and $\overline{x}_1 x_2\overline{x}_3$. The simplification

$$\overline{x}_1\overline{x}_2\overline{x}_3 + \overline{x}_1 x_2\overline{x}_3 = \overline{x}_1\overline{x}_3$$

was performed earlier in minimizing the algebraic expression for f_2. This simplification can be obtained directly from the map by grouping the two 1s as shown. The product term that corresponds to a group of squares is the product of the input variables whose values are constant on these squares. If the value of input variable x_i is 0 for all 1s of a group, then $\overline{x}_i$ is entered in the product, but if x_i has the value 1 for all 1s of the group, then x_i is entered in the product. Adjacency of two squares includes the property that the left-end squares are adjacent to the right-end squares. Continuing with our discussion of f_2, the group of four 1s consisting of the left-end column and the right-end column simplifies to the single-variable term $\overline{x}_2$ because x_2 is the only variable whose value remains constant over the group. All four possible combinations of values of the other two variables occur in the group.

Karnaugh maps can be used for more than three variables. A Karnaugh map for four variables can be obtained from two 3-variable maps. Examples of four-variable maps are shown in Figure A.5b, along with minimal expressions for the functions represented by the maps. In addition to two- and four-square groupings, it is now possible to form eight-square groupings. Such a grouping is illustrated in the map for g_3. Note that the four corner squares constitute a valid group of four and are represented by the product term $\overline{x}_2\overline{x}_4$ in g_2. As in the case of three-variable maps, the term that corresponds to a group of squares is the product of the variables whose values do not change over the group. For example, the grouping of four 1s in the upper right-hand corner of the map for g_2 is represented by the product term $x_1\overline{x}_3$ because $x_1 = 1$ and $x_3 = 0$ over the group. The variables x_2 and x_4 have all the possible combinations of values over this group. It is also possible to use Karnaugh maps for five-variable functions. In this case, two 4-variable maps are used, one of them corresponding to the 0 value for the fifth variable and the other corresponding to the 1 value.

The general procedure for forming groups of two, four, eight, and so on in Karnaugh maps is readily derived. Two adjacent pairs of 1s can be combined to form a group of four. Similarly, two adjacent groups of four can be combined to form a group of eight. In general, the number of squares in any valid group must be equal to 2^k, where k is an integer.

We will now consider a procedure for using Karnaugh maps to obtain minimal sum-of-products expressions. As can be seen in the maps of Figure A.5, a large group of 1s corresponds to a small product term. Thus, a simple gate implementation results from covering all the 1s in the map with as few groups as possible. In general, we should choose the smallest set of groups, picking large ones wherever possible, that cover all the 1s in the map. Consider, for example, the function g_2 in Figure A.5b. As we have already seen, the 1s in the four corners constitute a group of four that is represented by the product term $\overline{x}_2\overline{x}_4$. Another group of four exists in the upper right-hand corner and is represented by the term $x_1\overline{x}_3$. This covers all the 1s in the map except for the 1 in the square where $(x_1, x_2, x_3, x_4) = (0, 1, 0, 1)$. The largest group of 1s that includes this square is the two-square group represented by the term $x_2\overline{x}_3 x_4$. Therefore, the minimal expression for g_2 is

$$g_2 = \overline{x}_2\overline{x}_4 + x_1\overline{x}_3 + x_2\overline{x}_3x_4$$

Minimal expressions for the other functions shown in the figure can be derived in a similar manner. Note that in the case of g_4 there are two possible minimal expressions, one including the term $\overline{x}_1x_2x_4$ and the other including the term $\overline{x}_1\overline{x}_3x_4$. It is often the case that a given function has more than one minimal expression.

In all our examples, it is relatively easy to derive minimal expressions. In general, there are formal algorithms for this process, but we will not consider them here.

A.3.2 DON'T-CARE CONDITIONS

In many situations, some valuations of the inputs to a digital circuit never occur. For example, consider the binary-coded decimal (BCD) number representation. Four binary variables b_3, b_2, b_1, and b_0 represent the decimal digits 0 through 9, as shown in Figure A.6. These four variables have a total of 16 distinct valuations, only 10 of which are used for representing the decimal digits. The remaining valuations are not used. Therefore, any logic circuit that processes BCD data will never encounter any of these six valuations at its inputs.

Figure A.6 gives the truth table for a particular function that may be performed on a BCD digit. We do not care what the function values are for the unused input valuations; hence, they are called *don't-cares* and are denoted as such by the letter "d" in the truth table. To obtain a circuit implementation, the function values corresponding to don't-care conditions can be arbitrarily assigned to be either 0 or 1. The best way to assign them is in a manner that will lead to a minimal logic gate implementation. We should interpret don't-cares as 1s whenever they can be used to enlarge a group of 1s. Because larger groups correspond to smaller product terms, minimization is enhanced by the judicious inclusion of don't-care entries.

The function in Figure A.6 represents the following processing on a decimal digit input: The output f is to have the value 1 whenever the inputs represent a nonzero digit that is evenly divisible by 3. Three groups are necessary to cover the three 1s of the map, and don't-cares have been used to enlarge these groups as much as possible.

A.4 SYNTHESIS WITH NAND AND NOR GATES

We will now consider two other basic logic gates called NAND and NOR, which are extensively used in practice because of their simple electronic realizations. The truth table for these gates is shown in Figure A.7. They implement the equivalent of the AND and OR functions followed by the NOT function, which is the motivation for the names and standard logic symbols for these gates. Letting the arrows "↑" and "↓" denote the NAND and NOR operators, respectively, and using de Morgan's rule in Table A.4,

Decimal digit represented	Binary coding $b_3\ b_2\ b_1\ b_0$	f
0	0 0 0 0	0
1	0 0 0 1	0
2	0 0 1 0	0
3	0 0 1 1	1
4	0 1 0 0	0
5	0 1 0 1	0
6	0 1 1 0	1
7	0 1 1 1	0
8	1 0 0 0	0
9	1 0 0 1	1
	1 0 1 0	d
	1 0 1 1	d
unused	1 1 0 0	d
	1 1 0 1	d
	1 1 1 0	d
	1 1 1 1	d

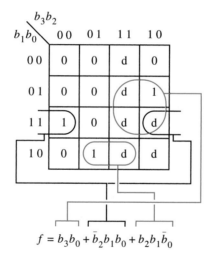

$$f = b_3 b_0 + \bar{b}_2 b_1 b_0 + b_2 b_1 \bar{b}_0$$

Figure A.6 Four-variable Karnaugh map illustrating don't cares.

we have

$$x_1 \uparrow x_2 = \overline{x_1 x_2} = \bar{x}_1 + \bar{x}_2$$

and

$$x_1 \downarrow x_2 = \overline{x_1 + x_2} = \bar{x}_1 \bar{x}_2$$

NAND and NOR gates with more than two input variables are available, and they

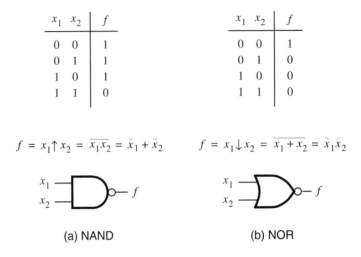

x_1 x_2	f
0 0	1
0 1	1
1 0	1
1 1	0

x_1 x_2	f
0 0	1
0 1	0
1 0	0
1 1	0

$$f = x_1 \uparrow x_2 = \overline{x_1 x_2} = \bar{x}_1 + \bar{x}_2$$

$$f = x_1 \downarrow x_2 = \overline{x_1 + x_2} = \bar{x}_1 \bar{x}_2$$

(a) NAND   (b) NOR

Figure A.7   NAND and NOR gates.

operate according to the obvious generalization of de Morgan's law as

$$x_1 \uparrow x_2 \uparrow \cdots \uparrow x_n = \overline{x_1 x_2 \cdots x_n} = \bar{x}_1 + \bar{x}_2 + \cdots + \bar{x}_n$$

and

$$x_1 \downarrow x_2 \downarrow \cdots \downarrow x_n = \overline{x_1 + x_2 + \cdots + x_n} = \bar{x}_1 \bar{x}_2 \cdots \bar{x}_n$$

Logic design with NAND and NOR gates is not as straightforward as with AND, OR, and NOT gates. One of the main difficulties in the design process is that the associative rule is not valid for NAND and NOR operations. We will expand on this problem later. First, however, let us describe a simple, general procedure for synthesizing any logic function using only NAND gates. There is a direct way to translate a logic network expressed in sum-of-products form into an equivalent network composed only of NAND gates. The procedure is easily illustrated with the aid of an example. Consider the following algebraic manipulation of a logic expression corresponding to a four-input network composed of three 2-input NAND gates:

$$(x_1 \uparrow x_2) \uparrow (x_3 \uparrow x_4) = \overline{(\overline{x_1 x_2})(\overline{x_3 x_4})}$$
$$= \overline{\overline{x_1 x_2}} + \overline{\overline{x_3 x_4}}$$
$$= x_1 x_2 + x_3 x_4$$

We have used de Morgan's rule and the involution rule in this derivation. Figure A.8 shows the logic network equivalent of this derivation. Since any logic function can be synthesized in a sum-of-products (AND-OR) form and because the preceding derivation is obviously reversible, we have the result that any logic function can be synthesized in NAND-NAND form. We can see that this result is true for functions of any number of variables. The required number of inputs to the NAND gates is obviously the same as the number of inputs to the corresponding AND and OR gates.

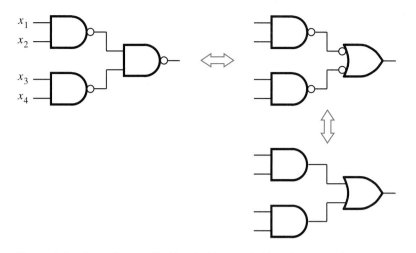

Figure A.8 Equivalence of NAND-NAND and AND-OR networks.

Let us return to the comment that the nonassociativity of the NAND operator can be an annoyance. In designing logic networks with NAND gates using the procedure illustrated in Figure A.8, a requirement for a NAND gate with more inputs than can be found on standard commercially available gates may arise. If this happens when one is using AND and OR gates, there is no problem because the AND and OR operators are associative, and a straightforward cascade of limited fan-in gates can be used. The case of implementing three-input AND and OR functions with two-input gates is shown in Figure A.9a. The solution is not as simple in the case of NAND gates. For example, a three-input NAND function cannot be implemented by a cascade of 2 two-input NAND gates. Three gates are needed, as shown in Figure A.9b.

A discussion of the implementation of logic functions using only NOR gates proceeds in a similar manner. Any logic function can be synthesized in a product-of-sums (OR-AND) form. Such networks can be implemented by equivalent NOR-NOR networks.

The preceding discussion introduced some basic concepts in logic design. Detailed discussion of the subject can be found in any of a number of textbooks (see References 1, 3, 7–11).

It is important for the reader to appreciate that many different realizations of a given logic function are possible. For practical reasons, it is useful to find realizations that minimize the cost of implementation. It is also often necessary to minimize the propagation delay through a logic network. We introduced the concept of minimization in the previous sections to give an indication of the nature of logic synthesis and the reductions in cost that may be achieved. For example, Karnaugh maps graphically show the manipulation possibilities that lead to optimal solutions. Although it is important to understand the principles of optimization of logic networks, it is not necessary to do the optimization by hand. Sophisticated *computer-aided design* (CAD) programs exist for such synthesis. The designer needs to specify only the desired functional behavior, and the CAD software generates a cost-effective network that implements the required functionality.

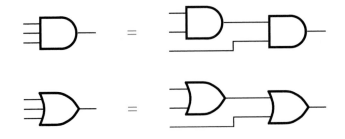

(a) Implementing three-input AND and OR functions with two-input gates

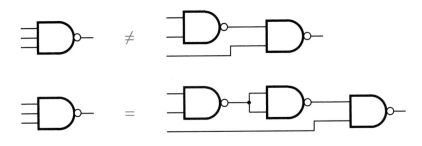

(b) Implementing a three-input NAND function with two-input gates

Figure A.9 Cascading of gates.

A.5 PRACTICAL IMPLEMENTATION OF LOGIC GATES

Let us now turn our attention to the means by which logic variables can be represented and logic functions can be implemented in practice. The choice of a physical parameter to represent logic variables is obviously technology-dependent. In electronic circuits, either voltage or current levels can be used for this purpose.

To establish a correspondence between voltage levels and logic values or states, the concept of a *threshold* is used. Voltages above a given threshold are taken to represent one logic value, with voltages below that threshold representing the other. In practical situations, the voltage at any point in an electronic circuit undergoes small random variations for a variety of reasons. Because of this "noise," the logic state corresponding to a voltage level near the threshold cannot be reliably determined. To avoid such ambiguity, a "forbidden range" should be established, as shown in Figure A.10. In this case, voltages below $V_{0,max}$ represent the 0 value, and voltages above $V_{1,min}$ represent the 1 value. In subsequent discussion, we will often use the terms "low" and "high" to represent the voltage levels corresponding to logic values 0 and 1, respectively.

We will begin our discussion of electronic circuits that implement basic logic functions by considering simple circuits consisting of resistors and transistors that act as switches. Consider the circuits in Figure A.11. When switch S in Figure A.11a is closed, the output voltage V_{out} is equal to 0 (ground). When S is open, the output

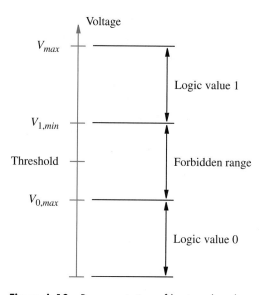

Figure A.10 Representation of logic values by voltage levels.

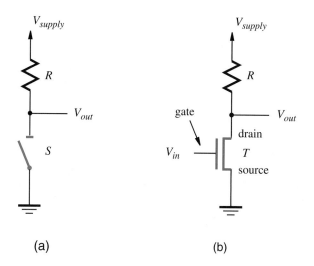

Figure A.11 An inverter circuit.

voltage V_{out} is equal to the supply voltage, V_{supply}. The same effect can be obtained in Figure A.11b, in which a transistor T is used to replace the switch S. When the input voltage applied to the gate of the transistor is 0 (that is, when $V_{in} = 0$), the transistor is equivalent to an open switch, and $V_{out} = V_{supply}$. When V_{in} changes to V_{supply}, the transistor acts as a closed switch and the output voltage V_{out} is very close to 0. Thus, the circuit performs the function of a logic NOT gate.

We can now discuss the implementation of more complex logic functions. Figure A.12 shows a circuit realization for a NOR gate. In this case, V_{out} in Figure A.12a is high only when both switches S_a and S_b are open. Similarly, V_{out} in Figure A.12b is high only when both inputs V_a and V_b are low. Thus, the circuit is equivalent to a NOR gate in which V_a and V_b correspond to two logic variables x_1 and x_2. We can easily verify that a NAND gate can be obtained by connecting the transistors in series as shown in Figure A.13. The logic functions AND and OR can be implemented using NAND and NOR gates, respectively, followed by the inverter of Figure A.11.

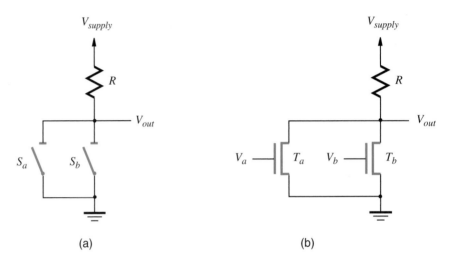

Figure A.12 A transistor circuit implementation of a NOR gate.

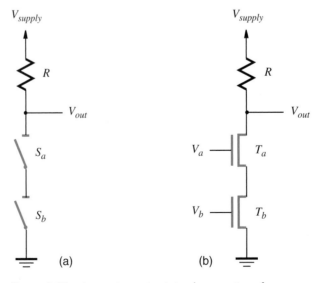

Figure A.13 A transistor circuit implementation of a NAND gate.

Note that NAND and NOR gates are simpler in their circuit implementations than AND and OR gates. Hence, it is not surprising to find that practical realizations of logic functions use NAND and NOR gates extensively. Many of the examples given in this book show circuits consisting of AND, OR, and NOT gates for ease of understanding. In practice, logic circuits contain all five types of gates.

A.5.1 CMOS CIRCUITS

Figures A.11 through A.13 illustrate the general structure of circuits implemented using *NMOS technology*. The name derives from the fact that the transistors used to realize the logic functions are of NMOS type. Two types of *metal-oxide semiconductor* (MOS) transistors are available for use as switches. An n-channel transistor is said to be of NMOS-type, and it behaves as a closed switch when its gate input is raised to the positive power supply voltage, V_{supply}, as indicated in Figure A.14a. The opposite behavior is achieved with a p-channel transistor, which is said to be of PMOS type. It acts as an open switch when the gate voltage, V_G, is equal to V_{supply}, and as a closed switch

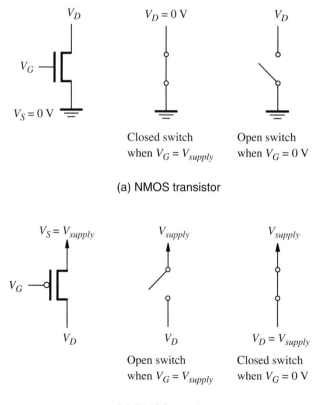

(a) NMOS transistor

(b) PMOS transistor

Figure A.14 NMOS and PMOS transistors in logic circuits.

when $V_G = 0$, as indicated in Figure A.14b. Note that the graphical symbol for a PMOS transistor has a bubble on the gate input to indicate that its behavior is complementary to that of an NMOS transistor. Note also that the names source and drain are associated with the opposite terminals of PMOS transistors in comparison with NMOS transistors. The source of an NMOS transistor is connected to ground, while the source of a PMOS transistor is connected to V_{supply}. This naming convention is due to the nature of the current that flows through these transistors.

A drawback of the circuits in Figures A.11 through A.13 is their power consumption. In the state in which the switches are closed to provide a path between ground and the pull-up resistor R, there is current flowing from V_{supply} to ground. In the opposite state, in which switches are open, there is no path to ground and there is no current flowing. (In MOS transistors no current flows through the gate terminal.) Thus, depending on the states of its gates, there may be significant power consumption in a logic circuit.

An effective solution to the power consumption problem lies in using both NMOS and PMOS transistors to implement circuits that do not dissipate power when in a steady state. This approach leads to the CMOS (complementary metal-oxide semiconductor) technology. The basic idea of CMOS circuits is illustrated by the inverter circuit in Figure A.15. When $V_x = V_{supply}$, which corresponds to the input x having the logic value 1, transistor T_1 is turned off and T_2 is turned on. Thus, T_2 pulls the output voltage V_f down to 0. When V_x changes to 0, transistor T_1 turns on and T_2 turns off. Thus, T_1 pulls the output voltage V_f up to V_{supply}. Therefore, the logic values of x and f are complements of each other, and the circuit implements a NOT gate.

A key feature of this circuit is that transistors T_1 and T_2 operate in a complementary fashion; when one is on, the other is off. Hence, there is always a closed path from the output point f to either V_{supply} or ground. There is no closed path between V_{supply} and ground at any time except during a very short transition period when the transistors are changing their states. This means that the circuit does not dissipate appreciable power when it is in a steady state. It dissipates power only when it is switching from one logic

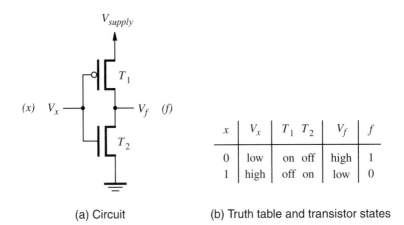

x	V_x	T_1 T_2	V_f	f
0	low	on off	high	1
1	high	off on	low	0

(a) Circuit   (b) Truth table and transistor states

Figure A.15   CMOS realization of a NOT gate.

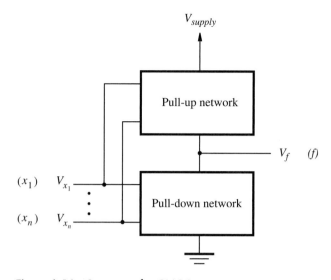

Figure A.16   Structure of a CMOS circuit.

state to another. Therefore, power dissipation in this circuit is dependent on the rate at which state changes take place.

We can now extend the CMOS concept to circuits that have n inputs, as shown in Figure A.16. NMOS transistors are used to implement the pull-down network, such that a closed path is established between the output point f and ground when a desired function $F(x_1, \ldots, x_n)$ is equal to 0. The pull-up network is built with PMOS transistors, such that a closed path is established between the output f and V_{supply} when $F(x_1, \ldots, x_n)$ is equal to 1. The pull-up and pull-down networks are functional complements of each other, so that in steady state there exists a closed path only between the output f and either V_{supply} or ground, but not both.

The pull-down network is implemented in the same way as shown in Figures A.11 through A.13. Figure A.17 gives the implementation of a NAND gate, and Figure A.18 gives a NOR gate. Figure A.19 shows how an AND gate is realized by inverting the output of a NAND gate.

In addition to low power dissipation, CMOS circuits have the advantage that MOS transistors can be implemented in very small sizes and thus occupy a very small area on an integrated circuit chip. This results in two significant benefits. First, it is possible to fabricate chips containing millions of transistors, which has led to the realization of modern microprocessors and large memory chips. Second, the smaller the transistor, the faster it can be switched from one state to another. Thus, CMOS circuits can now be operated at speeds in the gigahertz range.

Different CMOS circuits have been developed to operate with power supply voltages in the range from 1.5 to 15 V. The most commonly used power supplies are 5 V and 3.3 V. Circuits that use lower power supply voltages dissipate much less power (power dissipation is proportional to V_{supply}^2), which means that more transistors can be placed on a chip without causing overheating. A drawback of lower power supply voltage is reduced noise immunity.

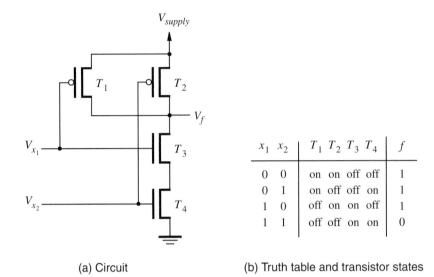

(a) Circuit

(b) Truth table and transistor states

x_1	x_2	T_1	T_2	T_3	T_4	f
0	0	on	on	off	off	1
0	1	on	off	off	on	1
1	0	off	on	on	off	1
1	1	off	off	on	on	0

Figure A.17   CMOS realization of a NAND gate.

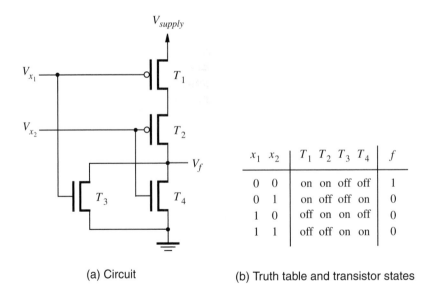

(a) Circuit

(b) Truth table and transistor states

x_1	x_2	T_1	T_2	T_3	T_4	f
0	0	on	on	off	off	1
0	1	on	off	off	on	0
1	0	off	on	on	off	0
1	1	off	off	on	on	0

Figure A.18   CMOS realization of a NOR gate.

Transitions between low and high signal levels in a CMOS inverter are illustrated in more detail in Figure A.20. The blue curve, known as the *transfer characteristic,* shows the output voltage as a function of the input voltage. The curve indicates that a rather sharp transition in output voltage takes place when the input voltage passes through the value of about $V_{supply}/2$. There is a *threshold* voltage, V_t, and a small value δ such that

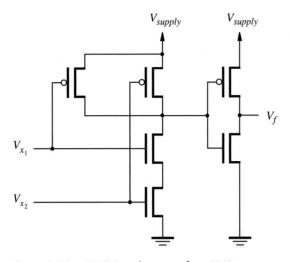

Figure A.19 CMOS realization of an AND gate.

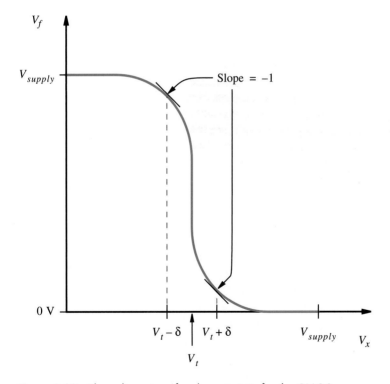

Figure A.20 The voltage transfer characteristic for the CMOS inverter.

$V_{out} \approx V_{supply}$ if $V_{in} < V_t - \delta$ and $V_{out} \approx 0$ if $V_{in} > V_t + \delta$. This means that the input signal need not be exactly equal to the nominal value of either 0 or V_{supply} to produce the correct output signal. There is room for some error, called *noise,* in the input signal that will not cause adverse effects. The amount of noise that can be tolerated is called the *noise margin.* This margin is $V_{supply} - (V_t + \delta)$ volts when the logic value of the input is 1, and it is $V_t - \delta$ when the logic value of the input is 0. CMOS circuits have excellent noise margins.

In this section, we have introduced the basic features of CMOS circuits. For a more detailed discussion of this technology the reader may consult References [1] and [8].

A.5.2 PROPAGATION DELAY

Logic circuits do not switch instantaneously from one state to another. Speed is measured by the rate at which state changes can take place. A related parameter is *propagation delay,* which is defined in Figure A.21. When a state change takes place at the input, a delay is encountered before the corresponding change at the output is observed. This propagation delay is usually measured between the 50-percent points of the transitions, as shown in the figure. Another important parameter is the *transition time,* which is normally measured between the 10- and 90-percent points of the signal swing, as shown. The maximum speed at which a logic circuit can be operated decreases as the

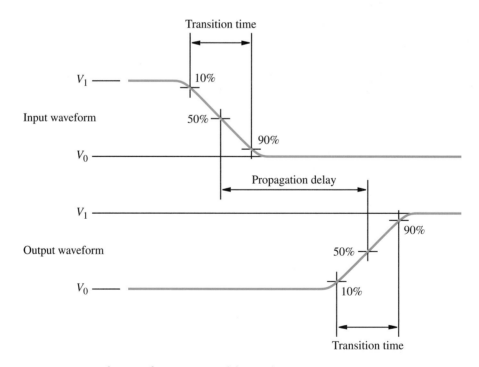

Figure A.21   Definition of propagation delay and transition time.

propagation delay through different paths within that circuit increases. The delay along any path in a logic circuit is the sum of individual gate delays along this path.

A.5.3 FAN-IN AND FAN-OUT CONSTRAINTS

The number of inputs to a logic gate is called its *fan-in*. The number of gate inputs that the output of a logic gate drives is called its *fan-out*. Practical circuits do not allow large fan-in and fan-out because they both have an adverse effect on the propagation delay and hence the speed of the circuit.

Each transistor in a CMOS gate contributes a certain amount of capacitance. As the capacitance increases, the circuit becomes slower and its signal levels and noise margins become worse. Therefore, it is necessary to limit the fan-in and fan-out, typically to a number less than ten. If the number of desired inputs exceeds the maximum fan-in, it is necessary to use an additional gate of the same type. Figure A.9a shows how two gates of the same type can be cascaded. If the number of outputs that have to be driven by a particular gate exceeds the acceptable fan-out, it is possible to use two copies of that gate.

A.5.4 TRI-STATE BUFFERS

In the logic gates discussed so far, it is not possible to connect the outputs of two gates together. This would make no sense from the logic point of view because if one gate generated an output value of 1 and the other an output of 0, it would be uncertain what the combined output signal would be. More importantly, in CMOS circuits, the gate that generates the output of 1 establishes a direct path from the output terminal to V_{supply}, while the gate that generates 0 establishes a path to ground. Thus, the two gates would provide a short circuit across the power supply, which would damage the gates.

Yet, in the design of computer systems, there are many cases where an input signal to a circuit may be derived from one of a number of different sources. This can be done using multiplexer logic circuits, which are discussed in Section A.10. It can also be done using special gates called *tri-state buffers*. A tri-state buffer has three states. Two of the states produce the normal 0 and 1 signals. The third state places the output terminal of the buffer into a high-impedance state in which the output is electrically disconnected from the input it is supposed to drive.

Figure A.22 depicts a tri-state buffer. The buffer has two inputs and one output. The *enable* input, e, controls the operation of the buffer. When $e = 1$, the output f has the same logic value as the input x. When $e = 0$, the output is placed in the high-impedance state, Z. An equivalent circuit is shown in Figure A.22b. The triangular symbol in this figure represents a noninverting driver. This is a circuit that performs no logic operation because its output merely replicates the input signal. Its purpose is to provide additional electrical driving capability. When combined with the output switch shown in the figure, it behaves according to the truth table given in Figure A.22c. This table describes the required tri-state behavior. Figure A.22d shows a circuit implementation of the tri-state buffer. One NMOS and one PMOS transistor are connected in parallel to implement the switch, which is connected to the output of the driver. Because the two transistor

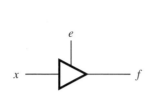

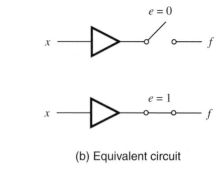

(a) Symbol   (b) Equivalent circuit

e	x	f
0	0	Z
0	1	Z
1	0	0
1	1	1

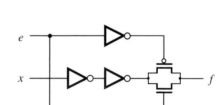

(c) Truth table   (d) Implementation

Figure A.22   Tri-state buffer.

types require complementary control signals at their gate inputs, an inverter is used as shown. When $e = 0$, both transistors are turned off, resulting in an open switch. When $e = 1$, both transistors are turned on, resulting in a closed switch.

The driver circuit has to be able to drive a number of inputs of other gates whose combined capacitance may exceed the drive capability of an ordinary logic gate circuit. To provide a sufficient drive capability, the driver circuit needs larger transistors. Hence, the two cascaded NOT gates that realize the driver are implemented with transistors of larger size than in regular logic gates.

The reader may wonder why is it necessary to use the PMOS transistor in the output switch because from the logic function point of view the same behavior could be achieved using just the NMOS transistor. The reason is that these transistors have to "pass" the logic value generated by the driver circuit to the output f, and it turns out that NMOS transistors pass the logic value 0 well but the logic value 1 poorly, while PMOS transistors pass 1 well and 0 poorly. The parallel arrangement of NMOS and PMOS transistors passes both 1s and 0s well. For a more detailed discussion of this issue and tri-state buffers in general, the reader may consult Reference [1].

A.5.5 INTEGRATED CIRCUIT PACKAGES

The main features of electronic circuits used to implement logic functions were discussed in previous sections. In practical design, it is necessary to use integrated circuits (ICs) that are commercially available. When ICs became available in the 1960s, there

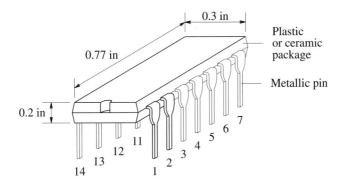

(a) Physical appearance

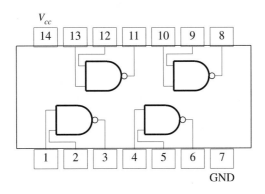

(b) Schematic of an integrated circuit providing four 2-input NAND gates

Figure A.23 A 14-pin integrated circuit package.

quickly developed a trend to provide logic gates in the form of standardized IC chips. An IC chip is mounted inside a sealed protective package with a number of metallic pins for external connections. Standard IC packages are available with different numbers of pins. A simple package containing four NAND gates is shown in Figure A.23. The four gates utilize common power supply and ground pins. Such ICs comprising only a few logic gates are referred to as *small-scale integrated* (SSI) *circuits.*

The SSI circuits provide too little functionality for the physical space that they require. Moreover, their performance is inferior because of the electrical characteristics of the pins on an IC package. In general, it is necessary to use larger transistors to provide the signals needed to drive external wires connected to pins. This increases both propagation delay and power dissipation.

A CMOS NAND gate provided as part of an IC package like the one illustrated in Figure A.23 may have a propagation delay of 5 nanoseconds. However, the delay of a NAND circuit inside a large CMOS network implemented on a single chip may be 0.2 ns or less, depending on the manufacturing technology used.

Much larger ICs are available today, and almost all logic circuits are realized with such chips. A chip may implement a useful functional block such as an adder, multiplier, register, encoder, or decoder. But it may also provide just an assortment of gates and programmable interconnection switches that can be configured by the designer to realize a variety of arbitrary functions. In subsequent sections, we will discuss some commonly used functional blocks as well as general user-programmable logic devices.

A.6   FLIP-FLOPS

The majority of applications of digital logic require the storage of information. For example, a circuit that controls a combination lock must remember the sequence in which the digits are dialed in order to determine whether to open the lock. Another important example is the storage of programs and data in the memory of a digital computer.

The basic electronic element for storing binary information is termed a *latch*. Consider the two cross-coupled NOR gates in Figure A.24a. Let us examine this circuit, starting with the situation in which R = 1 and S = 0. Simple analysis shows that $Q_a = 0$ and $Q_b = 1$. Under this condition, both inputs to gate G_a are equal to 1. Thus, if R is changed to 0, no change will take place at the outputs Q_a and Q_b. If S is set to 1 with R equal to 0, Q_a and Q_b will become 1 and 0, respectively, and will remain in this state after S is returned to 0. Hence, this logic circuit constitutes a memory element, or a latch, that remembers which of the two inputs S and R was most recently equal to 1. A truth table for this latch is given in Figure A.24b. Some typical waveforms that characterize the latch are shown in Figure A.24c. The arrows in Figure A.24c indicate the cause-effect relationships among the signals. Note that when the R and S inputs change from 1 to 0 at the same time, the resulting state is undefined. In practice, the latch will assume one of its two stable states at random. The input valuation R = S = 1 is not used in most applications of such latches.

Because of the nature of the operation of the preceding circuit, the S and R lines are referred to as the *set* and *reset* inputs. Since the valuation R = S = 1 is normally not used, the Q_a and Q_b are usually represented by Q and $\overline{Q}$, respectively. However, $\overline{Q}$ should be regarded merely as a symbol representing the second output of the latch rather than as the complement of Q, because the input valuation R = S = 1 yields $Q = \overline{Q} = 0$.

A.6.1   GATED LATCHES

Many applications require that the time at which a latch is set or reset be controlled from an input other than R and S, termed a *clock* input. The resulting configuration is called a *gated SR latch*. A logic circuit, truth table, characteristic waveforms, and a graphical symbol for such a latch are given in Figure A.25. When the clock, *Clk,* is equal to 1, points S' and R' follow the inputs S and R, respectively. On the other hand, when *Clk* = 0, the S' and R' points are equal to 0, and no change in the state of the latch can take place.

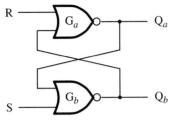

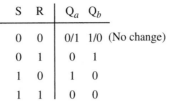

S	R	Q_a	Q_b	
0	0	0/1	1/0	(No change)
0	1	0	1	
1	0	1	0	
1	1	0	0	

(a) Network   (b) Truth table

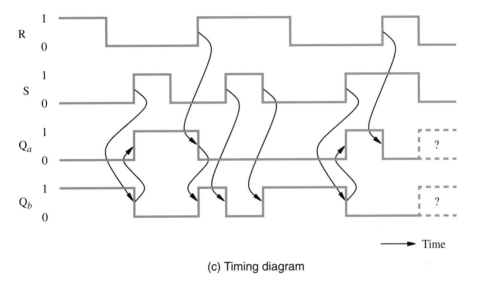

(c) Timing diagram

Figure A.24 A basic latch implemented with NOR gates.

So far we have used truth tables to describe the behavior of logic circuits. A truth table gives the output of a network for various input valuations. Logic circuits whose outputs are uniquely defined for each input valuation are referred to as *combinational circuits*. This is the class of circuits discussed in Sections A.1 to A.4. When memory elements are present, a different class of circuits is obtained. The output of such circuits is a function not only of the present valuation of the input variables but also of their previous behavior. An example of this is shown in Figure A.24. Circuits of this type are called *sequential circuits*.

Because of the memory property, the truth table for the latch has to be modified to show the effect of its present state. Figure A.25*b* describes the behavior of the gated SR latch, where $Q(t)$ denotes its present state. The transition to the next state, $Q(t + 1)$, occurs following a clock pulse. Note that for the input valuation $S = R = 1$, $Q(t + 1)$ is undefined for reasons discussed earlier.

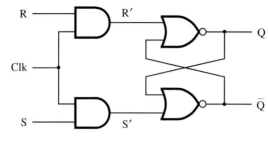

Clk	S	R	Q(t + 1)
0	x	x	Q(t) (no change)
1	0	0	Q(t) (no change)
1	0	1	0
1	1	0	1
1	1	1	x

(a) Circuit

(b) Truth table

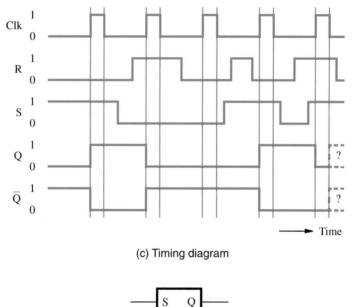

(c) Timing diagram

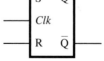

(d) Graphical symbol

Figure A.25 Gated SR latch.

The gated SR latch can be implemented using NAND gates as shown in Figure A.26. It is a useful exercise to show that this circuit is functionally equivalent to the circuit in Figure A.25a (see Problem A.20).

A second type of gated latch, called the *gated D latch,* is shown in Figure A.27. In this case, the two signals S and R are derived from a single input D. At a clock pulse,

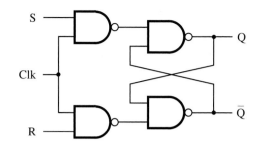

Figure A.26   Gated SR latch implemented with NAND gates.

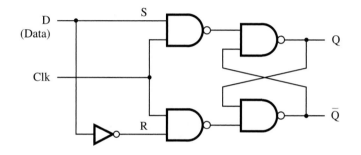

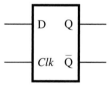

(a) Circuit

Clk	D	Q(t + 1)
0	x	Q(t)
1	0	0
1	1	1

(b) Truth table

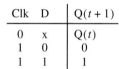

(c) Graphical symbol

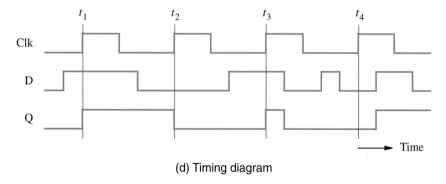

(d) Timing diagram

Figure A.27   Gated D latch.

the Q output is set to 1 if D = 1 or is reset to 0 if D = 0. This means that the D flip-flop samples the D input at the time the clock is high and stores that information until a subsequent clock pulse arrives.

A.6.2 MASTER-SLAVE FLIP-FLOP

In the circuit of Figure A.25, we assumed that while *Clk* = 1, the inputs S and R do not change. Inspection of the circuit reveals that the outputs will respond immediately to any change in the S or R input during this time. Similarly, for the circuit of Figure A.27, Q = D while *Clk* = 1. This is undesirable in many cases, particularly in circuits involving counters and shift registers, which will be discussed later. In such circuits, immediate propagation of logic conditions from the data inputs (R, S, and D) to the latch outputs may lead to incorrect operation. The concept of a *master-slave* organization eliminates this problem. Two gated D latches can be connected to form a *master-slave D flip-flop,* as shown in Figure A.28a. The first, referred to as the master, is connected to the input line D when Clock = 1. A 1-to-0 transition of the clock isolates the master from the input and transfers the contents of the master stage to the slave stage. We can see that no direct path ever exists from the input D to the output Q.

It should be noted that while Clock = 1, the state of the master stage is immediately affected by changes in the input D. The function of the slave stage is to hold the value at the output of the flip-flop while the master stage is being set up to the next-state value determined by the D input. The new state is transferred from the master to the slave after the 1-to-0 transition on Clock. At this point, the master stage is isolated from the inputs so that further changes in the D input will not affect this transfer. Examples of state transitions are shown in the form of a timing diagram in Figure A.28b.

The term *flip-flop* refers to a storage element that changes its output state at the edge of a controlling clock signal. In the above master-slave D flip-flop, the observable change takes place at the negative (1-to-0) edge of the clock. The change is observable when it reaches the Q terminal of the slave stage. Note that in the circuit in Figure A.28 we could have used the complement of Clock signal to control the master stage and the uncomplemented Clock to control the slave stage. In that case, the changes in the flip-flop output Q would occur at the positive edge of the clock.

A graphical symbol for a flip-flop is given in Figure A.28c. We have used an arrowhead, instead of the label *Clk,* to denote the clock input to the flip-flop. This is a standard way of denoting that the positive edge of the clock causes changes in the state of the flip-flop. In our figure it is the negative edge which causes changes, so a small circle is used (in addition to the arrowhead) on the clock input.

A.6.3 EDGE TRIGGERING

A flip-flop is said to be *edge triggered* if data present at the input are transferred to the output only at a transition in the clock signal. The input and output are isolated from each other at all other times. The terms *positive (leading) edge triggered* and *negative (trailing) edge triggered* describe flip-flops in which data transfer takes place at the

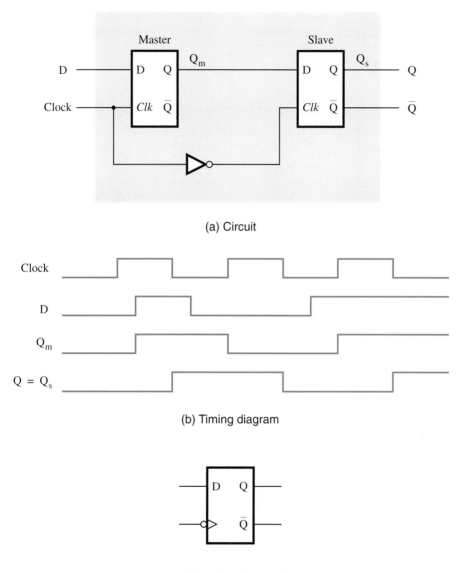

(a) Circuit

(b) Timing diagram

(c) Graphical symbol

Figure A.28   Master-slave D flip-flop.

0-to-1 and the 1-to-0 clock transitions, respectively. For proper operation, edge-triggered flip-flops require the triggering edge of the clock pulse to be well defined and to have a very short transition time. The master-slave flip-flop in Figure A.28 is negative-edge triggered.

   A different implementation for a negative edge-triggered D flip-flop is given in Figure A.29a. Let us consider the operation of this flip-flop. If $Clk = 1$, the outputs

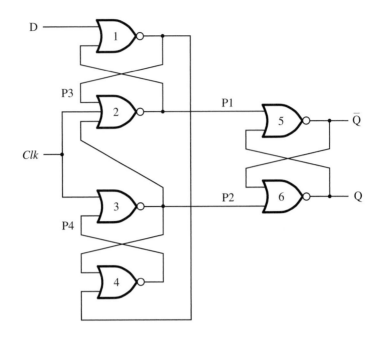

(a) Network

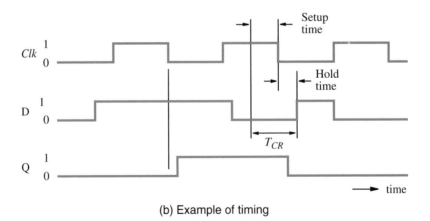

(b) Example of timing

Figure A.29   A negative edge-triggered D flip-flop.

of gates 2 and 3 are both 0. Therefore, the flip-flop outputs Q and $\overline{Q}$ maintain the current state of the flip-flop. It is easy to verify that during this period, points P3 and P4 immediately respond to changes at D. Point P3 is kept equal to $\overline{D}$, and P4 is maintained equal to D. When *Clk* drops to 0, these values are transmitted to P1 and P2 by gates 2 and 3, respectively. Thus, the output latch, consisting of gates 5 and 6, acquires the new state to be stored.

We now verify that while $Clk = 0$, further changes at D do not change points P1 and P2. Consider two cases. First, suppose $D = 0$ at the negative edge of Clk. The 1 at P2 maintains an input of 1 at each of the gates 2 and 4, holding P1 and P2 at 0 and 1, respectively, independent of further changes in D. Second, suppose $D = 1$ at the negative edge of Clk. The 1 at P1 means that further changes at D cannot affect the output of gate 1, which is maintained at 0.

When Clk goes to 1 at the start of the next clock pulse, points P1 and P2 are again forced to 0, isolating the output from the remainder of the circuit. Points P3 and P4 then follow changes at D, as we have previously described.

An example of the operation of this type of D flip-flop is shown in Figure A.29*b*. The state acquired by the flip-flop upon the 1 to 0 transition of Clk is equal to the value on the D input immediately preceding this transition. However, there is a critical time period T_{CR} around the negative edge of Clk during which the value on D should not change. This region is split into two parts, the *setup time* before the clock edge and the *hold time* after the clock edge, as shown in the figure. The timing diagram shows that the output Q changes slightly after the negative edge of the clock. This is the effect of the propagation delay through the NOR gates.

A.6.4 T FLIP-FLOP

The most commonly used flip-flops are the D flip-flops because they are useful for temporary storage of data. However, there are applications for which other types of flip-flops are convenient. Counter circuits, discussed in Section A.8, are implemented efficiently using T flip-flops. A *T flip-flop* changes its state every clock cycle if its input T is equal to 1. We say that it "toggles" its state.

Figure A.30 presents the T flip-flop. Its circuit is derived from a D flip-flop as shown in Figure A.30*a*. Its truth table, graphical symbol, and a timing diagram example are also given in the figure. Note that we have assumed a positive edge-triggered flip-flop.

A.6.5 JK FLIP-FLOP

Another flip-flop that is sometimes encountered in practice is the *JK flip-flop,* which combines the behaviors of SR and T flip-flops. It is presented in Figure A.31. Its operation is defined by the truth table in Figure A.31*b*. The first three entries in this table define the same behavior as those in Figure A.25*b* (when $Clk = 1$), so that J and K correspond to S and R. For the input valuation $J = K = 1$, the next state is defined as the complement of the present state of the flip-flop. That is, when $J = K = 1$, the flip-flop functions as a *toggle,* reversing its present state.

A JK flip-flop can be implemented using a D flip-flop connected such that

$$D = J\overline{Q} + \overline{K}Q$$

The corresponding circuit is shown in Figure A.31*a*.

The JK flip-flop is versatile. It can be used to store data, just like the D flip-flop. It can also be used to build counters, because it behaves like the T flip-flop if its J and K input terminals are connected together.

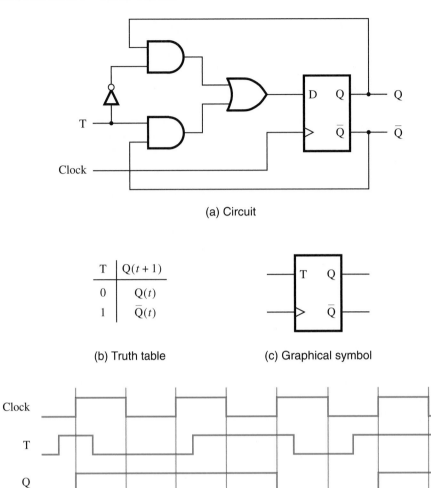

(a) Circuit

T	$Q(t+1)$
0	$Q(t)$
1	$\bar{Q}(t)$

(b) Truth table

(c) Graphical symbol

(d) Timing diagram

Figure A.30   T flip-flop.

A.6.6 FLIP-FLOPS WITH PRESET AND CLEAR

The state of a flip-flop is determined by its present state and the logic values on its input terminals. Sometimes it is desirable to force a flip-flop into a particular state, either 0 or 1, regardless of its present state and the values of the normal inputs. For example, when a computer is powered on, it is necessary to place all flip-flops into a known state. Usually, this means resetting their outputs to state 0. In some cases it is desirable to preset some flip-flops into state 1.

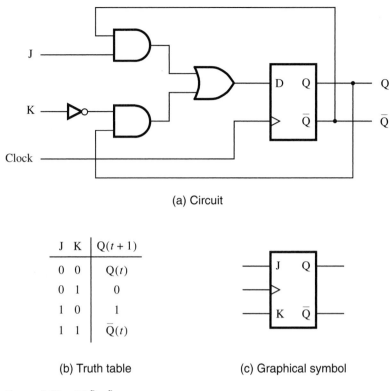

(a) Circuit

J	K	Q(t + 1)
0	0	Q(t)
0	1	0
1	0	1
1	1	$\overline{Q}(t)$

(b) Truth table   (c) Graphical symbol

Figure A.31 JK flip-flop.

Figure A.32 illustrates how preset and clear control inputs can be added to a master-slave D flip-flop, to force the flip-flop into state 1 or 0 independent of the D input and the clock. These inputs are active low, as indicated by the overbars and bubbles in the figure. When both the $\overline{\text{Preset}}$ and $\overline{\text{Clear}}$ inputs are equal to 1, the flip-flop is controlled by the clock and D input in the normal way. When $\overline{\text{Preset}} = 0$, the flip-flop is forced to the 1 state, and when $\overline{\text{Clear}} = 0$, the flip-flop is forced to the 0 state. The preset and clear controls are also often incorporated in the other flip-flop types.

A.7 REGISTERS AND SHIFT REGISTERS

An individual flip-flop can be used to store one bit. However, in machines in which data are handled in words consisting of many bits (perhaps as many as 64), it is convenient to arrange a number of flip-flops into a common structure called a *register*. The operation of all flip-flops in a register is synchronized by a common clock. Thus, data are written (loaded) into or read from all flip-flops at the same time.

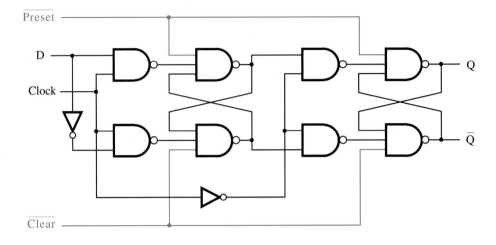

(a) Circuit

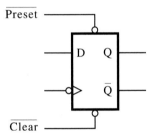

(b) Graphical symbol

Figure A.32   Master-slave D flip-flop with Preset and Clear.

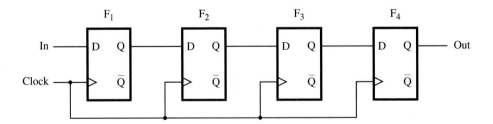

Figure A.33   A simple shift register.

Processing of digital data often requires the capability to shift and rotate the data, so it is necessary to provide the hardware with this facility. A simple mechanism for realizing both operations is a register whose contents may be shifted to the right or left one bit position at a time. As an example, consider the 4-bit shift register in Figure A.33. It consists of D flip-flops connected so that each clock pulse will cause the transfer of the contents (state) of F_i to F_{i+1}, effecting a "right shift." Data are shifted serially into and out of the register. A rotation of the data can be implemented by connecting Out to In.

Proper operation of a shift register requires that its contents be shifted exactly one position for each clock pulse. This places a constraint on the type of storage elements that can be used. Gated latches, depicted in Figure A.27, are not suitable for this purpose. While the clock is high, the value on D input quickly propagates to the output. From there, the value propagates through the next gated latch in the same manner. Hence, there is no control over the number of shifts that will take place during a single clock pulse. This number depends on the propagation delays of the gated latches and the duration of the clock pulse. The solution to the problem is to use either the master-slave or the edge-triggered flip-flops.

A particularly useful form of a shift register is one that can be loaded and read in parallel. This can be accomplished with some additional gating as illustrated in Figure A.34, which shows a 4-bit register constructed with D flip-flops. The register can be loaded either serially or in parallel. When the register is clocked, a shift takes place if $\overline{\text{Shift}}/\text{Load} = 0$; otherwise, a parallel load is performed.

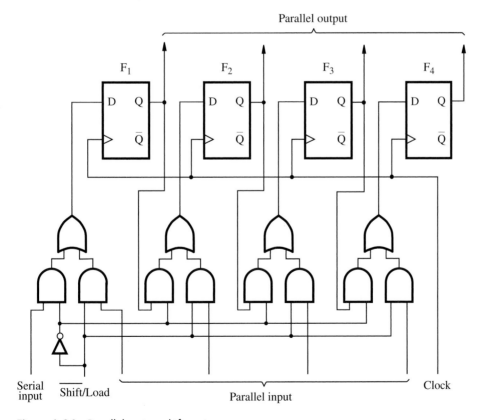

Figure A.34 Parallel-access shift register.

A.8   COUNTERS

In the preceding section, we discussed the applicability of flip-flops in the construction of shift registers. They are equally useful in the implementation of *counter* circuits. It is hardly necessary to justify the need for counters in digital machines. In addition to being hardware mechanisms for realizing ordinary counting functions, counters are also used to generate control and timing signals. A counter driven by a high-frequency clock can be used to produce signals whose frequencies are submultiples of the original clock frequency. In such applications a counter is said to be functioning as a *scaler*.

A simple three-stage (or 3-bit) counter constructed with T flip-flops is shown in Figure A.35. Recall that when the T input is equal to 1, the flip-flop acts as a toggle, that is, its state changes with each successive clock pulse. Thus, two clock pulses will cause Q_0 to change from the 1 state to the 0 state and back to the 1 state or from 0 to 1 to 0. This means that the output waveform of Q_0 has half the frequency of the clock. Similarly, because the second flip-flop is driven by Q_0, the waveform at Q_1 has half the frequency of Q_0, or one-fourth the frequency of the clock. Note that we have assumed that the positive edge of the clock input to each flip-flop triggers the change of its state.

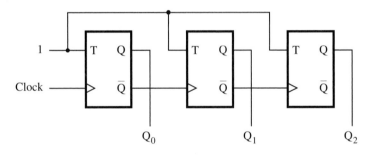

(a) Circuit

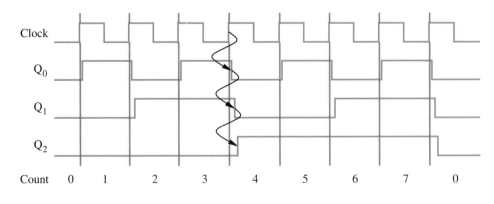

(b) Timing diagram

Figure A.35   A 3-bit up-counter.

Such a counter is often called a *ripple counter* because the effect of an input clock pulse ripples through the counter. For example, the positive edge of pulse 4 will change the state of Q_0 from 1 to 0. This change in Q_0 will then force Q_1 from 1 to 0, which in turn forces Q_2 from 0 to 1. If each flip-flop introduces some delay Δ, then the delay in setting Q_2 is 3Δ. Such delays can be a problem when very fast operation of counter circuits is required. In many applications, however, these delays are small in comparison with the clock period and can be neglected.

With the addition of some extra logic gates, it is possible to construct a "synchronous" counter in which each stage is under the control of the common clock so that all flip-flops can change their states simultaneously. Such counters are capable of operation at higher speed because the total propagation delay is reduced considerably. In contrast, the counter in Figure A.35 is said to be "asynchronous."

A.9 DECODERS

Much of the information in computers is handled in a highly encoded form. In an instruction, an *n*-bit field may be used to denote 1 out of 2^n possible choices for the action to be taken. To perform the desired action, the encoded instruction must first be decoded. A circuit capable of accepting an *n*-variable input and generating the corresponding output signal on one out of 2^n output lines is called a *decoder*. A simple example of a two-input to four-output decoder is given in Figure A.36. One of the four output lines is selected by the inputs x_1 and x_2, as indicated in the figure. The selected output has the logic value 1, and the remaining outputs have the value 0.

Other useful types of decoders exist. For example, using information in BCD form often requires decoding circuits in which a four-variable BCD input is used to select

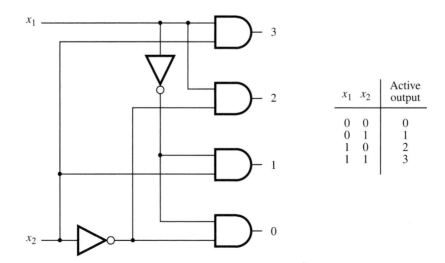

x_1	x_2	Active output
0	0	0
0	1	1
1	0	2
1	1	3

Figure A.36 A two-input to four-output decoder.

No.	x_1 x_2 x_3 x_4	a b c d e f g
0	0 0 0 0	1 1 1 1 1 1 0
1	0 0 0 1	0 1 1 0 0 0 0
2	0 0 1 0	1 1 0 1 1 0 1
3	0 0 1 1	1 1 1 1 0 0 1
4	0 1 0 0	0 1 1 0 0 1 1
5	0 1 0 1	1 0 1 1 0 1 1
6	0 1 1 0	1 0 1 1 1 1 1
7	0 1 1 1	1 1 1 0 0 0 0
8	1 0 0 0	1 1 1 1 1 1 1
9	1 0 0 1	1 1 1 1 0 1 1

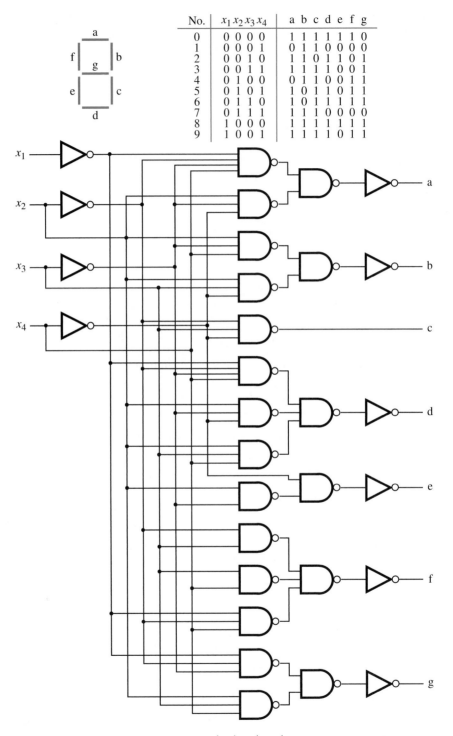

Figure A.37   A BCD to seven-segment display decoder.

1 out of 10 possible outputs. As another specific example, let us consider a decoder suitable for driving a seven-segment display. Figure A.37 shows the structure of a seven-segment element used for display purposes. We can easily see that any decimal number from zero to nine can be displayed with this element simply by turning some segments on (light) while leaving others off (dark). The necessary functions are indicated in the table. They can be realized using the decoding circuit shown in the figure. Note that the circuit is constructed with NAND gates. We encourage the reader to verify that the circuit implements the required functions.

A.10 MULTIPLEXERS

In the preceding section, we saw that decoders select one output line on the basis of input signals. The selected output line has logic value 1, while the other outputs have the value 0. Another class of very useful selector circuits exists in which any one of n data inputs can be selected to appear as the output. The choice is governed by a set of "select" inputs. Such circuits are called *multiplexers*. An example of a multiplexer circuit is shown in Figure A.38. It has two select inputs, w_1 and w_2. Their four possible valuations are used to select one of four inputs, x_1, x_2, x_3, or x_4, to appear as the output z. A simple logic circuit that can implement the required operation is also given. Obviously, the same structure can be used to realize larger multiplexers, in which k select inputs are used to connect one of the 2^k data inputs to the output.

The obvious application of multiplexers is in the gating of data that may come from a number of different sources. For example, loading a 16-bit data register from one of four distinct sources can be accomplished with sixteen 4-input multiplexers.

Multiplexers are also very useful as basic elements for implementing logic functions. Consider a function f defined by the truth table of Figure A.39. It can be represented as shown in the figure by factoring out the variables x_1 and x_2. Note that for each valuation of x_1 and x_2, the function f corresponds to one of four terms: 0, 1, x_3, or $\overline{x}_3$. This suggests the possibility of using a four-input multiplexer circuit, in which x_1 and x_2 are the two select inputs that choose one of the four data inputs. Then, if the data inputs are connected to 0, 1, x_3, or $\overline{x}_3$ as required by the truth table, the output of the multiplexer will correspond to the function f. The approach is completely general. Any function of three variables can be realized with a single four-input multiplexer. Similarly, any function of four variables can be implemented with an eight-input multiplexer, and so on.

A.11 PROGRAMMABLE LOGIC DEVICES (PLDS)

Sections A.2 and A.3 showed how a given switching function can be represented in terms of sum-of-products expressions and implemented by corresponding AND-OR gate networks. Section A.10 showed how multiplexers can be used to realize switching functions. In this section we will consider another class of circuits that can be used for

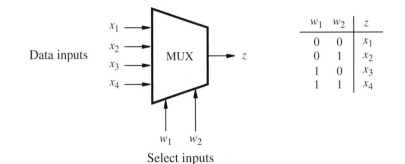

w_1	w_2	z
0	0	x_1
0	1	x_2
1	0	x_3
1	1	x_4

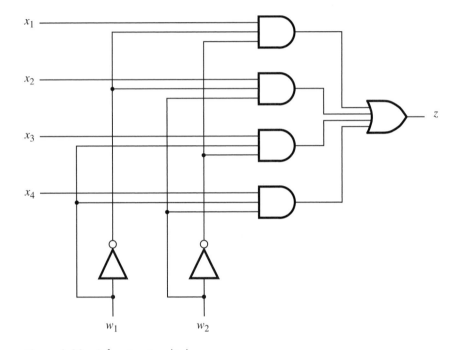

Figure A.38 A four-input multiplexer.

the same purpose. These circuits consist of arrays of switching elements that can be programmed to allow implementation of sum-of-products expressions. They are called *programmable logic devices* (PLDs).

Figure A.40 shows the block diagram of a PLD. It has n input variables $(x_1, \ldots, x_n)$ and m output functions $(f_1, \ldots, f_m)$. Each function f_i is realized as a sum of product terms that involve the input variables. The variables $x_1, \ldots, x_n$ are presented in true and complemented form to the AND array, where up to k product terms are formed. These are then gated into the OR array, where the output functions are formed. Two commonly used types of PLDs are described in the remainder of this section.

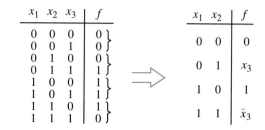

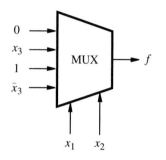

Figure A.39 Multiplexer implementation of a logic function.

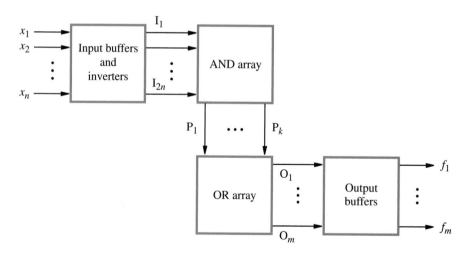

Figure A.40 A block diagram for a PLD.

A.11.1 PROGRAMMABLE LOGIC ARRAY (PLA)

A circuit in which connections to both the AND and the OR arrays can be programmed is called a *programmable logic array* (PLA). Figure A.41 illustrates the functional structure of a PLA using a simple example. The programmable connections must be

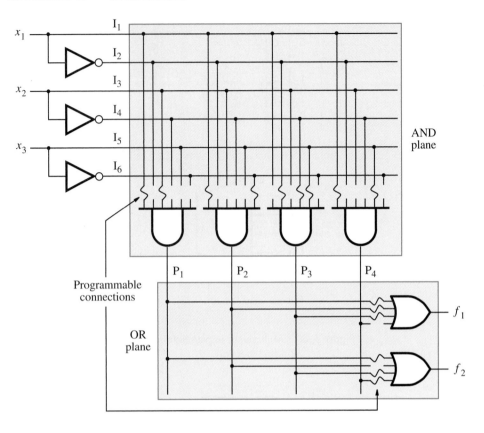

$$f_1 = x_1x_2 + x_1\bar{x}_3 + \bar{x}_1\bar{x}_2x_3$$

$$f_2 = x_1x_2 + \bar{x}_1\bar{x}_2x_3 + x_1x_3$$

Figure A.41   Functional structure of a PLA.

such that if no connection is made to a given input of an AND gate, the input behaves as if a logic value of 1 is driving it (that is, this input does not contribute to the product term realized by this gate). Similarly, if no connection is made to a given input of an OR gate, this input must have no effect on the output of the gate (that is, the input must behave as if a logic value of 0 is driving it).

Programmed connections may be realized in different ways. In one method, programming consists of blowing fuses in positions where connections are not required. This is done by applying higher-than-normal current. Another possibility is to use transistor switches controlled by erasable memory elements (see Section 5.3 on EPROM memory circuits) to provide the connections as desired. This allows the PLA to be reprogrammable.

The simple PLA in Figure A.41 can generate up to four product terms from three input variables. Two output functions may be implemented using these product terms. Some of the product terms may be used in more than one output function. The PLA is

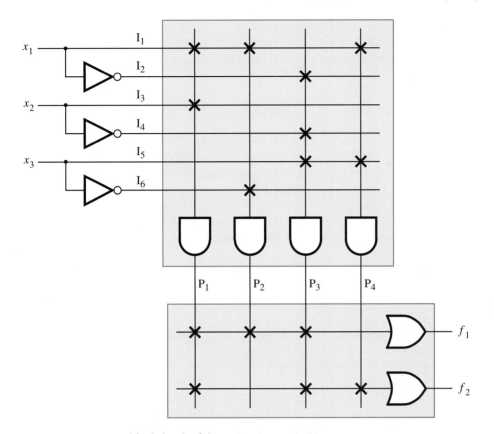

Figure A.42 A simplified sketch of the PLA in Figure A.41.

configured to realize the following two functions:

$$f_1 = x_1 x_2 + x_1 \overline{x}_3 + \overline{x}_1 \overline{x}_2 x_3$$
$$f_2 = x_1 x_2 + x_1 x_3 + \overline{x}_1 \overline{x}_2 x_3$$

Only four product terms are needed, because two terms can be shared by both functions. Practical PLAs come in much larger sizes.

Although Figure A.41 depicts clearly the basic functionality of a PLA, this style of presentation is awkward for describing a larger PLA. It has become customary in technical literature to represent the product and sum terms by means of corresponding gate symbols that have only one symbolic input line. An $\times$ is placed on this line to represent each programmed connection. This drawing convention is used in Figure A.42 to represent the PLA example from Figure A.41. In general, a programmable connection can be made at any crossing of a vertical line and a horizontal line in the diagram, to implement arbitrary functions of input variables.

The PLA structure is very efficient in terms of the area needed for its implementation on an integrated circuit chip. For this reason, such structures are often used for implementing control circuits in processor chips. In this case, the desired connections are put in place as the last step in the manufacturing process, rather than making them programmable after the chip has been fabricated.

A.11.2 PROGRAMMABLE ARRAY LOGIC (PAL)

In a PLA, the inputs to both the AND array and the OR array are programmable. A similar device, in which the inputs to the AND array are programmable but the connections to the OR gates are fixed, has found great popularity in practical applications. Such devices are known as *programmable array logic* (PAL) chips.

Figure A.43 shows a simple example of a PAL that can implement two functions. The number of AND gates connected to each OR gate in a PAL determines the maximum number of product terms that can be realized in a sum-of-products representation of a

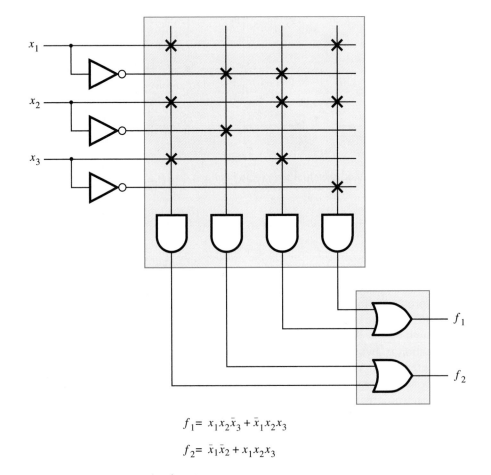

$$f_1 = x_1 x_2 \bar{x}_3 + \bar{x}_1 x_2 x_3$$

$$f_2 = \bar{x}_1 \bar{x}_2 + x_1 x_2 x_3$$

Figure A.43   An example of a PAL.

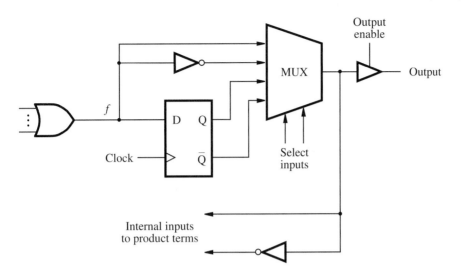

Figure A.44 An example of the output of a PAL element.

given function. The AND gates are permanently connected to specific OR gates, which means that a particular product term cannot be shared among output functions.

PAL chips are available in various configurations. A substantial number of input variables and output functions can be provided, allowing large functions to be realized. The versatility of a PAL may be enhanced further by including flip-flops in the outputs from the OR gates. Such PAL chips enable the designer of a digital system to implement a relatively complex logic network using a single chip.

Figure A.44 indicates the kind of flexibility that can be provided. A multiplexer is used to choose whether a true, complemented, or stored (from the previous clock cycle) value of f is to be presented at the output pin of the PAL chip. The select inputs to the multiplexer can be set as programmable connections. The output pin is driven by a tri-state driver under control of the Output-enable signal. Note that the signal from the output of the multiplexer is also made available as an internal input that can be used in product terms that feed other OR gates in the PAL. This facilitates the realization of circuits that have several levels (stages) of logic gates.

A.11.3 COMPLEX PROGRAMMABLE LOGIC DEVICES (CPLDS)

PALs are useful devices, but their relatively small size means that many such chips may be needed to implement a typical digital system. Larger devices of a similar type have been developed to deal with this issue. They are known as *complex programmable logic devices* (CPLDs). They comprise two or more PAL-like blocks and programmable interconnection wires. Figure A.45 indicates the structure of a CPLD chip. Each PAL-like block is connected to a number of input/output pins. Connections between PAL-like blocks are established by programming the switches associated with the interconnection wires.

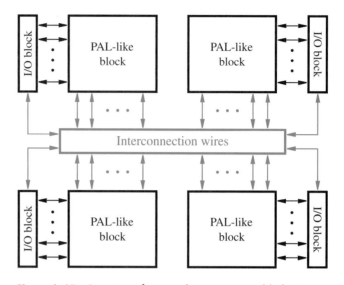

Figure A.45   Structure of a complex programmable logic device (CPLD).

The interconnection resource consists of horizontal and vertical wires. Each horizontal wire can be connected to some of the vertical wires by programming the corresponding switches. It is impractical to provide full connectivity, where each horizontal wire can be connected to any of the vertical wires, because the number of required switches would be large. Satisfactory connectivity can be achieved with a much smaller number of switches.

Commercial CPLDs come in different sizes, ranging from 2 to more than 100 PAL-like blocks. A CPLD chip is programmed by loading the programming information into it via a *JTAG port*. This is a 4-pin port that conforms to an IEEE standard developed by the Joint Test Action Group.

A.12   Field-Programmable Gate Arrays

PAL chips provide general functionality but are somewhat limited in size because an output pin is provided for each sum-of-products circuit. A more powerful class of programmable devices has been developed to overcome these size limitations. They are known as *field-programmable gate arrays* (FPGAs). Figure A.46 shows a conceptual block diagram of an FPGA. It consists of an array of logic blocks (indicated as black boxes) that can be connected by general interconnection resources. The *interconnect,* shown in blue, consists of segments of wire and programmable switches. The switches are used to connect the logic blocks to the wire segments and to establish connections between different wire segments as desired. This allows a large degree of routing flexibility on the chip. Input and output buffers are provided for access to the pins of the chip.

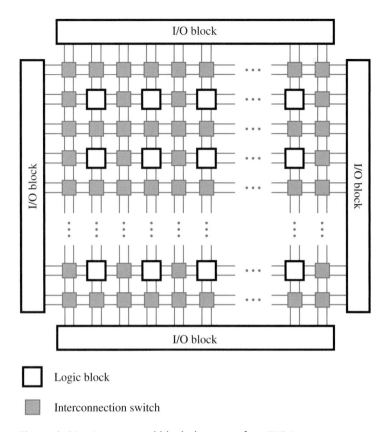

Logic block

Interconnection switch

Figure A.46   A conceptual block diagram of an FPGA.

There are a variety of designs for the logic blocks and the interconnect structure. A logic block may be just a simple multiplexer-based circuit capable of implementing logic functions as discussed in Section A.10. Another popular design uses a simple lookup table as a logic block. For example, a four-input lookup table can be implemented in the form of a 16-bit memory circuit in which the truth table of a logic function is stored. Each memory bit corresponds to one combination of the input variables. Such a lookup table can be programmed to implement any function of four variables. The logic blocks may contain flip-flops to provide additional flexibility of the type encountered in Figure A.44.

In addition to the logic blocks, many FPGA chips include a substantial number of memory cells (not shown in Figure A.46), which may be used to implement structures such as first-in first-out (FIFO) queues or RAM and ROM components in system-on-a-chip applications, which are discussed in Chapter 9.

From the user's point of view, there are two major differences between FPGAs and CPLDs. The FPGA chips have much greater functionality and can be used to implement rather large logic networks. An FPGA chip may implement a circuit that requires over a million logic gates. The second important consideration is the speed of these devices.

Since programmable switches are used to establish all connections in the interconnect, an FPGA will inevitably have significantly longer propagation delays compared with a less flexible device such as a PAL or a CPLD.

The growing popularity of FPGAs is due to the fact that they allow a designer to implement very complex logic networks on a single chip without having to design and fabricate a custom VLSI chip, which is both expensive and time-consuming. Using CAD tools, it is possible to generate an FPGA design in a matter of days, rather than the months needed to produce a custom-designed VLSI chip. The FPGA implementations are also attractive in terms of cost. Even the largest FPGAs cost only a few hundred dollars, and the cost associated with the design time is very small compared to the cost of designing a custom chip.

An introductory discussion of programmable logic devices can be found in many modern books on logic design. For a more extensive treatment of these devices, the reader may consult other books [1, 3–6] and manufacturers' literature.

A.13 Sequential Circuits

A combinational circuit is one whose output is determined entirely by its present inputs. Examples of such circuits are the decoders and multiplexers presented in Sections A.9 and A.10. A different class of circuits are those whose outputs depend on both the present inputs and on the sequence of previous inputs. They are called *sequential circuits*. Such circuits can be in different *states,* depending on what the sequence of inputs has been up to a given time. The state of a circuit determines the behavior when various input patterns are applied to the circuit. We encountered two specific forms of such circuits in Sections A.7 and A.8, called shift registers and counters. In this section, we will introduce more examples of sequential circuits, provide a general form for them, and give a brief introduction to the design of these circuits.

A.13.1 An Example of an Up/Down Counter

Figure A.35 shows the configuration of an up counter, implemented with three T flip-flops, which counts in the sequence 0, 1, 2, . . . , 7, 0, ... A similar circuit can be used to count in the down direction, that is, 0, 7, 6, . . . , 1, 0, . . . (see Problem A.26). These simple circuits are made possible by the toggle feature of T flip-flops.

We now consider the possibility of implementing such counters with D flip-flops. As a specific example, we will design a counter that counts either up or down, depending on the value of an external control input. To keep the example small, let us restrict the size to a mod-4 counter, which requires only two state bits to represent the four possible count values. We will show how this counter can be designed using general techniques for the synthesis of sequential circuits. The desired circuit will count up if an input signal x is equal to 0 and down if x is 1. The count will change on the negative edge of the clock signal. Let us assume that we are particularly interested in the state when the count is equal to 2. Thus, an output signal, z, should be asserted when the count is equal to 2; otherwise $z = 0$.

The desired counter can be implemented as a sequential circuit. In order to determine what the new count will be when a clock pulse is applied, it is sufficient to know the value of x and the present count. It is not necessary to know what the actual sequence of previous input values has been, as long as we know the present count that has been reached. This count value is said to determine the *present state* of the circuit, which is all that the circuit remembers about previous input values. If the present count is 2 and $x = 0$, the next count will be 3. It makes no difference whether the count of 2 was reached counting down from 3 or up from 1.

Before we show a circuit implementation, let us depict the desired behavior of the counter by means of a state diagram. The counter has four distinct states: S0, S1, S2, and S3. A *state diagram* is a graph in which states are represented as circles (sometimes called nodes). Transitions between states are indicated by labeled arrows. The label associated with an arrow specifies the value of the input x that will cause this particular transition to occur and the value of the output produced as a result. Figure A.47 shows the state diagram of our up/down counter. For example, the arrow emanating from state S1 (count $= 1$) for an input $x = 0$ points to state S2, thus specifying the transition to state S2. It also indicates that the output z must be equal to 0 while the circuit is in state S1 and the value of x is 0. An arrow from S2 to S3 specifies that when $x = 0$ the next clock pulse will cause a transition from S2 to S3, and that the output z should be 1 while the circuit is in state S2.

Note that the state diagram describes the functional behavior of the counter without any reference to how it is implemented. Figure A.47 can be used to describe an electronic digital circuit, a mechanical counter, or a computer program that behaves in this way. Such diagrams are a powerful means of describing any system that exhibits sequential behavior.

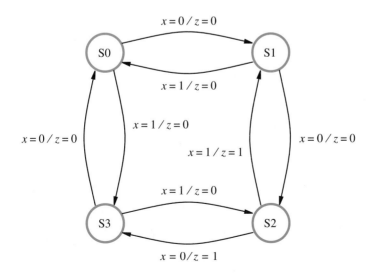

Figure A.47   State diagram of a mod-4 up/down counter that detects the count of 2.

Present state	Next state		Output z	
	$x = 0$	$x = 1$	$x = 0$	$x = 1$
S0	S1	S3	0	0
S1	S2	S0	0	0
S2	S3	S1	1	1
S3	S0	S2	0	0

Figure A.48   State table for the example of the up/down counter.

A different way of presenting the information in a state diagram is to use a *state table.* Figure A.48 gives the state table for the example in Figure A.47. The table indicates transitions from all present states to the *next states,* as required by the applied input x. The output signal, z, is determined by the present state of the circuit and the value of the applied input, x.

Having specified the desired up/down counter in general terms, we will now consider its physical realization. Two bits are needed to encode the four states that indicate the count. Let these bits be y_2 (high-order) and y_1 (low-order). The states of the counter are determined by the values of y_2 and y_1, which we will write in the form y_2y_1. We will assign values to y_2y_1 for each of the four states as follows: $S0 = 00$, $S1 = 01$, $S2 = 10$, and $S3 = 11$. We have chosen the assignment such that the binary number y_2y_1 represents the count in an obvious way. The variables y_2 and y_1 are called the *state variables* of the sequential circuit. Using this *state assignment,* the state table for our example is as shown in Figure A.49. Note that we are using the variables Y_1 and Y_2 to denote the next state in the same manner as y_1 and y_2.

It is important to note that we could have chosen a different assignment of y_2y_1 values to the various states. For example, a possible state assignment is: $S0 = 10$, $S1 = 11$, $S2 = 01$, and $S3 = 00$. For a counter circuit, this assignment is less intuitive than the one in Figure A.49, but the resultant circuit will work properly. Different state assignments usually lead to different costs in implementing the circuit (see Problem A.32).

Our intention in this example is to use D flip-flops to store the values of the two state variables between successive clock pulses. The output, Q, of a flip-flop is the present-state variable y_i, and the input, D, is the next-state variable Y_i. Note that Y_i is a function of y_2, y_1, and x, as indicated in Figure A.49. From the figure, we see that

$$Y_2 = \overline{y}_2 y_1 \overline{x} + y_2 \overline{y}_1 \overline{x} + \overline{y}_2 \overline{y}_1 x + y_2 y_1 x$$

$$= y_2 \oplus y_1 \oplus x$$

$$Y_1 = \overline{y}_2 \overline{y}_1 \overline{x} + y_2 \overline{y}_1 \overline{x} + \overline{y}_2 \overline{y}_1 x + y_2 \overline{y}_1 x$$

$$= \overline{y}_1$$

Present state	Next state		Output z	
	$x = 0$	$x = 1$	$x = 0$	$x = 1$
$y_2 y_1$	$Y_2\ Y_1$	$Y_2\ Y_1$		
0 0	0 1	1 1	0	0
0 1	1 0	0 0	0	0
1 0	1 1	0 1	1	1
1 1	0 0	1 0	0	0

Figure A.49 State assignment for the example in Figure A.48.

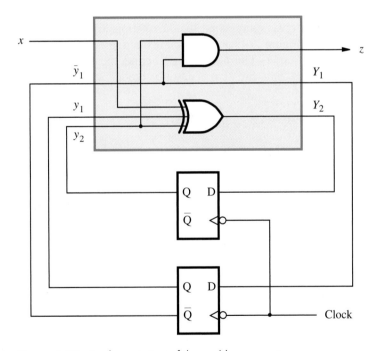

Figure A.50 Implementation of the up/down counter.

The output z is determined as

$$z = y_2 \bar{y}_1$$

These expressions lead to the circuit shown in Figure A.50.

A.13.2 TIMING DIAGRAMS

To fully understand the operation of the counter circuit, it is useful to consider its timing diagram. Figure A.51 gives an example of a possible sequence of events. It assumes that state transitions (changes in flip-flop values) occur on the negative edge of the clock and that the counter starts in state S0. Since $x = 0$, the counter advances to state S1 at t_0, then to S2 at t_1, and to S3 at t_2. The output changes from 0 to 1 when the counter enters state S2. It goes back to 0 when state S3 is reached. At the end of S3, at t_3, the counter goes to S0. We have assumed that at this time the input x changes to 1, causing the counter to count in the down sequence. When the count again reaches S2, at t_5, the output z goes to 1.

Note that all signal changes occur just after the negative edge of the clock, and signals do not change again until the negative edge of the next clock pulse. The delay from the clock edge to the time at which variables y_i change is the propagation delay of the flip-flops used to implement the counter circuit. It is important to note that the input x is also assumed to be controlled by the same clock, and it changes only near the beginning of a clock period. These are essential features of circuits where all changes are controlled by a clock. Such circuits are called *synchronous sequential circuits*.

Another important observation concerns the relationship between the labels used in the state diagram in Figure A.47 and the timing diagram. For example, consider the clock period between t_1 and t_2. During this clock period, the machine is in state S2 and the input value is $x = 0$. This situation is described in the state diagram by the arrow

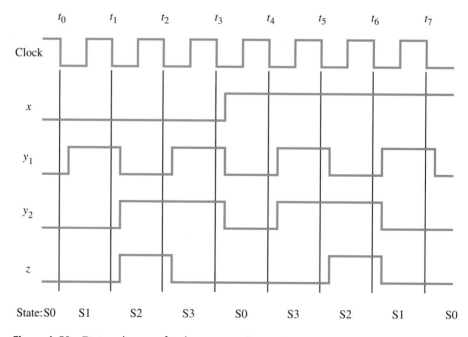

Figure A.51   Timing diagram for the circuit in Figure A.50.

emanating from state S2 labeled $x = 0$. Since this arrow points to state S3, the timing diagram shows y_2 and y_1 changing to the values corresponding to state S3 at the next clock edge, t_2. The output value associated with the arrow gives the value of z while the counter is in state S2.

A.13.3   THE FINITE STATE MACHINE MODEL

The specific example of the up/down counter implemented as a synchronous sequential circuit with flip-flops and combinational logic gates, as shown in Figure A.50, is easily generalized to the formal *finite state machine* model given in Figure A.52. In this model, the time delay through the delay elements is equal to the duration of the clock cycle. This is the time that elapses between changes in Y_i and the corresponding changes in y_i. The model assumes that the combinational logic block has no delay; hence, the outputs z, Y_1, and Y_2 are instantaneous functions of the inputs x, y_1, and y_2. In an actual circuit, some delay will be introduced by the circuit elements, as shown in Figure A.51. The circuit will work properly if the delay through the combinational logic block is short with respect to the clock cycle. The next-state outputs Y_i must be available in time to cause the flip-flops to change to the desired next state at the end of the clock cycle. Also, while the output z may not be at the desired value during all of the clock cycle, it must reach this value well before the end of the cycle.

Inputs to the combinational logic block consist of the flip-flop outputs, y_i, which represent the present state, and the external input, x. The outputs of the block are the

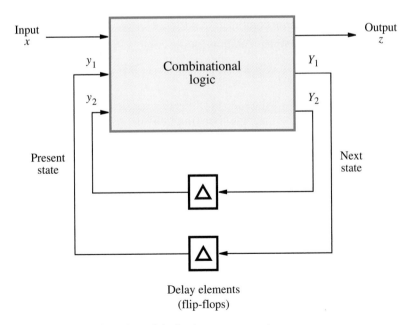

Figure A.52   A formal model of a finite state machine.

inputs to the flip-flops, which we have called Y_i, and the external output, z. When the active clock edge arrives marking the end of the present clock cycle, the values on the Y_i lines are loaded into the flip-flops. They become the next set of values of the state variables, y_i. Since these signals are connected to the input of the combinational block, they, along with the next value of the external input x, will produce new z and Y_i values. A clock cycle later, the new Y_i values are transferred to y_i, and the process repeats. In other words, the flip-flops constitute a feedback path from the output to the input of the combinational block, introducing a delay of one clock period.

Although we have shown only one external input, one external output, and two state variables in Figure A.52, it is clear that multiple versions are possible for any of the three types of variables.

A.13.4 SYNTHESIS OF FINITE STATE MACHINES

Let us summarize how to design a synchronous sequential circuit having the general organization in Figure A.52, based on a state diagram like that in Figure A.47. The design, or synthesis, process involves the following steps:

1. Develop an appropriate state diagram or state table.
2. Determine the number of flip-flops needed, and choose a suitable type of flip-flop.
3. Determine the values to be stored in these flip-flops for each state in the state diagram. This is referred to as state assignment.
4. Develop the state-assigned state table.
5. Derive a truth table for the combinational logic block.
6. Find a suitable circuit implementation for the combinational logic block.

Example

As a further example of a finite state machine that has both inputs and outputs, consider a coin-operated vending machine. For simplicity, let us assume that the machine accepts only quarters and dimes. The quarters or dimes are applied as inputs until a total of 30 cents or more is deposited. When this total is reached, an output (merchandise) is provided. No change is provided if more than 30 cents is deposited. Let binary inputs x_1 and x_2 represent coins being deposited, such that $x_1 = 1$ or $x_2 = 1$ if a quarter or a dime is deposited, respectively. Otherwise, these inputs are equal to 0. Only one coin is deposited at a time, so that input combination $x_1x_2 = 11$ never occurs. Also, let a binary output z represent merchandise provided by the machine, such that $z = 0$ for no merchandise and $z = 1$ for merchandise provided.

The first task in designing a logic circuit for the vending machine is to draw a state diagram or a state table. It is best to give a word description of each state needed and then decide later how many flip-flops will be needed to represent the required number of states. The states represent the total amount of money deposited at any point in the process. Based on the fact that dimes or quarters can be deposited in any order until the

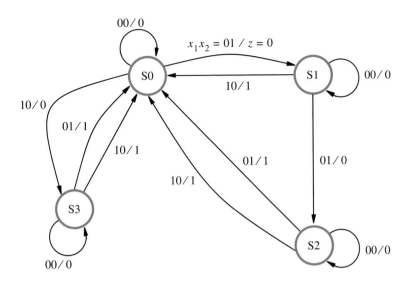

$x_1 = 1 \sim$ quarter deposited

$x_2 = 1 \sim$ dime deposited

$z = 1 \sim$ dispense merchandise
(i.e., a total of 30 cents deposited)

Input combination $x_1x_2 = 11$ cannot occur

Figure A.53 State diagram for the vending machine example.

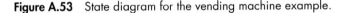

total is equal to or greater than 30 cents, the states needed are:

S0 = nothing deposited (the "start" state)
S1 = 10 cents
S2 = 20 cents
S3 = 25 cents

We do not need any more states because when the present state is either S2 or S3, either a dime or a quarter will suffice as the present input to generate the $z = 1$ output and move to state S0 to start again.

A state diagram description of the desired behavior for the vending machine is given in Figure A.53. Note that the input $x_1x_2 = 11$ does not appear because both a quarter and a dime cannot be deposited at the same time. Also notice that each state has an arrow looping back to itself labeled 00/0. This indicates that if no coins are being deposited during a clock cycle, the circuit stays in its present state.

Only four states are needed for this machine. This will require two flip-flops. If we label them y_2 and y_1, and assign their values to represent the states as S0 = 00, S1 = 01, S2 = 10, and S3 = 11, Figure A.54 shows the resultant assigned state table.

Present state	Next state				Output z			
	$x_1 x_2 = 00$	$x_1 x_2 = 01$	$x_1 x_2 = 10$	$x_1 x_2 = 11$	$x_1 x_2 = 00$	$x_1 x_2 = 01$	$x_1 x_2 = 10$	$x_1 x_2 = 11$
$y_2 y_1$	$Y_2 Y_1$	$Y_2 Y_1$	$Y_2 Y_1$	$Y_2 Y_1$				
S0 0 0	0 0	0 1	1 1	-	0	0	0	-
S1 0 1	0 1	1 0	0 0	-	0	0	1	-
S2 1 0	1 0	0 0	0 0	-	0	1	1	-
S3 1 1	1 1	0 0	0 0	-	0	1	1	-

Figure A.54   Assigned state table for the vending machine example.

We have used dashes in the table to indicate that the input combination of $x_1 x_2 = 11$ does not appear. These entries are don't-care conditions, which we can take advantage of in the design of the combinational logic block, which will be discussed next.

This completes the first four steps in the synthesis procedure. We now go to step 5. The assigned state table in Figure A.54 leads directly to the truth table in Figure A.55, which specifies the functions of the combinational logic block. From the table, it is easy to derive the following expressions that give the implementation of the logic block:

$$Y_2 = \overline{x}_1 \overline{x}_2 y_2 + x_2 \overline{y}_2 y_1 + x_1 \overline{y}_2 \overline{y}_1$$
$$Y_1 = \overline{x}_1 \overline{x}_2 y_1 + \overline{y}_2 \overline{y}_1 (x_1 + x_2)$$
$$z = y_2 (x_1 + x_2) + x_1 y_1$$

Observe that the logic terms $\overline{x}_1 \overline{x}_2$, $\overline{y}_1 \overline{y}_2$, and $(x_1 + x_2)$ appear in more than one of the expressions. This leads to a cost saving in the implementation of the block.

Sequential circuits can easily be implemented with PALs, CPLDs and FPGAs because these devices contain flip-flops as well as combinational logic gates. Modern computer-aided design tools can be used to synthesize sequential circuits directly from a specification given in terms of a state diagram.

Note that the next-state and output entries in Figure A.54 are the same for states S2 and S3 for all input combinations where a change of state occurs. This implies that two different states are not really needed to represent the totals 20 cents and 25 cents. One state would be sufficient, because from either of these total deposits, the next coin deposited will cause merchandise to be provided ($z = 1$) and will cause a return to the starting state S0. Thus, states S2 and S3 are *equivalent* and can be replaced by a single state. This means that only three states are needed to implement the machine. Two flip-flops are still required. However, in more general situations, a reduction in the number of states through state equivalences often leads to fewer flip-flops and simpler circuits.

Another economy that can be achieved in implementing sequential circuits is in the combinational logic required. Different state assignments will lead to different logic

3-bit Gray code inputs			Binary code outputs		
a	b	c	f_1	f_2	f_3
0	0	0	0	0	0
0	0	1	0	0	1
0	1	1	0	1	0
0	1	0	0	1	1
1	1	0	1	0	0
1	1	1	1	0	1
1	0	1	1	1	0
1	0	0	1	1	1

(a) Three-bit Gray code to binary code conversion

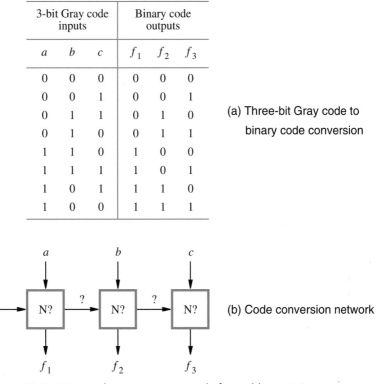

(b) Code conversion network

Figure PA.2 Gray code conversion example for Problem A.14.

A.15 Implement the XOR function using only 4 two-input NAND gates.

A.16 Figure A.37 defines a BCD to seven-segment display decoder. Give an implementation for this truth table using AND, OR, and NOT gates. Verify that the same functions are correctly implemented by the NAND gate circuits shown in the figure.

A.17 In the logic network shown in Figure PA.3, gate 3 fails and produces the logic value 1 at its output F1 regardless of the inputs. Redraw the network, making simplifications

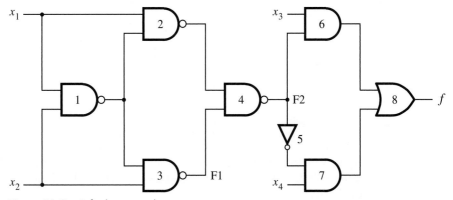

Figure PA.3 A faulty network.

wherever possible, to obtain a new network that is equivalent to the given faulty network and that contains as few gates as possible. Repeat this problem, assuming that the fault is at position F2, which is stuck at a logic value 0.

A.18   Figure A.16 shows the structure of a general CMOS circuit. Derive a CMOS circuit that implements the function

$$f(x_1, \ldots, x_4) = \overline{x}_1\overline{x}_2 + \overline{x}_3\overline{x}_4$$

Use as few transistors as possible. (Hint: Consider series/parallel networks of transistors. Note the complementary series and parallel structure of the pull-up and pull-down networks in Figures A.17 and A.18.)

A.19   Draw the waveform for the output Q in the JK circuit of Figure A.31, using the input waveforms shown in Figure PA.4 and assuming that the flip-flop is initially in the 0 state.

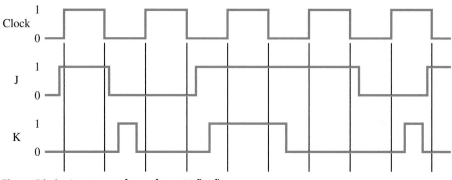

Figure PA.4   Input waveforms for a JK flip-flop.

A.20   Derive the truth table for the NAND gate circuit in Figure PA.5. Compare it to the truth table in Figure A.24b and then verify that the circuit in Figure A.26 is equivalent to the circuit in Figure A.25a.

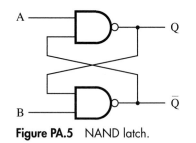

Figure PA.5   NAND latch.

A.21   Compute both the setup time and the hold time in terms of NOR gate delays for the negative edge-triggered D flip-flop shown in Figure A.29.

A.22   In the circuit of Figure A.27a, replace all NAND gates with NOR gates. Derive a truth table for the resulting circuit. How does this circuit compare with the circuit in Figure A.27a?

A.23 Figure A.33 shows a shift register network that shifts the data to the right one place at a time under the control of a clock signal. Modify this shift register to make it capable of shifting data either one or two places at a time under the control of the clock and an additional control input ONE/TWO.

A.24 A 4-bit shift register that has two control inputs — INITIALIZE and RIGHT/LEFT — is required. When INITIALIZE is set to 1, the binary number 1000 should be loaded into the register independently of the clock input. When INITIALIZE $= 0$, pulses at the clock input should rotate this pattern. The pattern rotates right or left when the RIGHT/LEFT input is equal to 1 or 0, respectively. Give a suitable design for this register using D flip-flops that have preset and clear inputs as shown in Figure A.32.

A.25 Derive a three-input to eight-output decoder network, with the restriction that the gates to be used cannot have more than two inputs.

A.26 Figure A.35 shows a 3-bit up counter. A counter that counts in the opposite direction (that is, $7, 6, \ldots, 1, 0, 7, \ldots$) is called a down counter. A counter capable of counting in both directions under the control of an UP/DOWN signal is called an up/down counter. Show a logic diagram for a 3-bit up/down counter that can also be preset to any state through parallel loading of its flip-flops from an external source. A LOAD/COUNT control is used to determine whether the counter is being loaded or is operating as a counter.

A.27 Figure A.35 shows an asynchronous 3-bit up-counter. Design a 4-bit synchronous up-counter, which counts in the sequence $0, 1, 2, \ldots, 15, 0 \ldots$. Use T flip-flops in your circuit. In the synchronous counter all flip-flops have to be able to change their states at the same time. Hence, the primary clock input has to be connected directly to the clock inputs of all flip-flops.

A.28 A switching function to be implemented is described by the expression

$$f(x_1, x_2, x_3, x_4) = x_1 x_3 \overline{x}_4 + \overline{x}_1 \overline{x}_3 x_4 + \overline{x}_2 \overline{x}_3 \overline{x}_4$$

(*a*) Show an implementation of f in terms of an eight-input multiplexer circuit.

(*b*) Can f be realized with a four-input multiplexer circuit? If so, show how.

A.29 Repeat Problem A.28 for

$$f(x_1, x_2, x_3, x_4) = x_1 \overline{x}_2 x_3 + x_2 x_3 x_4 + \overline{x}_1 \overline{x}_4$$

A.30 (*a*) What is the total number of distinct functions, $f(x_1, x_2, x_3)$, of three binary variables?

(*b*) How many of these functions are implementable with one PAL circuit of the type shown in Figure A.43?

(*c*) What is the smallest change in the circuit in Figure A.43 that should be made to allow any three-variable function to be implemented with a single PAL circuit?

A.31 Consider the PAL circuit in Figure A.43. Suppose that the circuit is modified by adding a fourth input variable, x_4, whose uncomplemented and complemented forms can be connected to all four AND gates in the same way as the variables x_1, x_2, and x_3.

(*a*) Can this modified PAL be used to implement the function

$$f = x_1\overline{x}_2\overline{x}_3 + \overline{x}_1 x_2 \overline{x}_3 + \overline{x}_1 \overline{x}_2 x_3$$

If so, show how.

(*b*) How many functions of three variables cannot be implemented with this PAL?

A.32   Complete the design of the up/down counter in Figure A.47 by using the state assignment $S0 = 10$, $S1 = 11$, $S2 = 01$, and $S3 = 00$. How does this design compare with the one given in Section A.13.1?

A.33   Design a 2-bit synchronous counter of the general form shown in Figure A.50 that counts in the sequence $\ldots, 0, 3, 1, 2, 0, \ldots$, using D flip-flops. This circuit has no external inputs, and the outputs are the flip-flop values themselves.

A.34   Repeat Problem A.33 for a 3-bit counter that counts in the sequence $\ldots, 0, 1, 2, 3, 4,$ $5, 0, \ldots$, taking advantage of the unused count values 6 and 7 as don't-care conditions in designing the combinational logic.

A.35   In Section A.13, D flip-flops were used in the design of synchronous sequential circuits. This is the simplest choice in the sense that the logic function values for a D input are directly determined by the desired next-state values in the state table. Suppose that JK flip-flops are to be used instead of D flip-flops. Describe, by the construction of a table, how to determine the binary value for each of the J and K inputs for a flip-flop as a function of each possible required transition from present state to next state for that flip-flop. (*Hint:* The table should have four rows, one for each of the transitions $0 \rightarrow 0$, $0 \rightarrow 1$, $1 \rightarrow 0$, and $1 \rightarrow 1$; and each J and K entry is to be 0, 1, or "don't care," as required.) Apply the information in your table to the design of individual combinational logic functions for each J and K input for each of the two flip-flops of the 2-bit binary counter of Problem A.33. How does the simplicity of the logic required compare to that needed for the design of the counter using D flip-flops?

A.36   Repeat Problem A.34 using JK flip-flops instead of D flip-flops. The general procedure for doing this is provided by the answer to Problem A.35.

A.37   In the vending machine example used in Section A.13.4 to illustrate the finite state machine model, a single binary output, z, was used to indicate the dispensing of merchandise. Change was not provided as an output. The purpose of this problem is to expand the output to include providing proper change. Assume that the only input sequences of dimes and quarters are: 10-10-10, 10-25, 25-10, and 25-25. Coincident with the last coin input, the outputs to be provided for these sequences are 0, 5, 5, and 20, respectively. Use two new binary outputs, z_2 and z_3, to represent the three distinct outputs. (This does not correspond directly to coins in use, but it keeps the problem simple.)

(*a*) Specify the new state table that incorporates the new outputs.

(*b*) Develop the logic expressions for the new outputs z_2 and z_3.

(*c*) Are there any equivalent states in the new state table?

A.38 Finite state machines can be used to detect the occurrence of certain subsequences in the sequence of binary inputs applied to the machine. Such machines are called *finite state recognizers*. Suppose that a machine is to produce a 1 as its output coincident with the second 1 in the pattern 011 whenever that subsequence occurs in the input sequence applied to the machine.

(*a*) Draw the state diagram for this machine.

(*b*) Make a state assignment for the required number of flip-flops and construct the assigned state table, assuming that D flip-flops are to be used.

(*c*) Derive the logic expressions for the output and the next-state variables.

A.39 Repeat Part *a* only of Problem A.38 for a machine that is to recognize the occurrence of either of the subsequences 011 and 010 in the input sequence, including the cases where overlap occurs. For example, the input sequence 110101011... is to produce the output sequence 000010101....

REFERENCES

1. S. Brown and Z. Vranesic, *Fundamentals of Digital Logic with VHDL Design,* McGraw-Hill, Burr Ridge, IL, 2000.

2. A.S. Sedra and K.C. Smith, *Microelectronic Circuits,* 4th ed., Oxford, New York, 1998.

3. J.F. Wakerley, *Digital Design Principles and Practices,* Prentice Hall, Upper Saddle River, NJ, 2000.

4. J.H. Jenkins, *Designing with FPGAs and CPLDs,* Prentice-Hall, Englewood Cliffs, N.J., 1994.

5. S.M. Trimberger, *Field-Programmable Gate Array Technology,* Kluwer, Boston, 1994.

6. S.D. Brown, R.J. Francis, J. Rose, and Z.G. Vranesic, *Field-Programmable Gate Arrays,* Kluwer, Boston, 1992.

7. R.H. Katz, *Contemporary Logic Design,* Benjamin Cummings, Redwood City, Calif., 1994.

8. J.P. Hayes, *Digital Logic Design,* Addison-Wesley, Reading, Mass., 1993.

9. F.H. Hill and G.R. Peterson, *Computer Aided Logical Design with Emphasis on VLSI,* 4th ed., Wiley, New York, 1993.

10. C.H. Roth, *Fundamentals of Logic Design,* 4th ed., West, St. Paul, Minn., 1992.

11. M.M. Mano and C.R. Kime, *Logic and Computer Design Fundamentals,* Prentice-Hall, Upper Saddle River, N.J., 1997.

12. M. Abramovici, M.A. Breuer, and A.D. Friedman, *Digital Systems Testing and Testable Design,* revised edition, IEEE Press, New York, 1995.

13. V.N. Yarmolik, *Fault Diagnosis of Digital Circuits,* Wiley, Chichester, England, 1994.

14. P.K. Lala, *Digital System Design Using Programmable Logic Devices,* Prentice-Hall, Englewood Cliffs, N.J., 1990.

15. B.W. Johnson, *Design and Analysis of Fault-Tolerant Digital Systems,* Addison-Wesley, Reading, Mass., 1989.

16. A.J. Miczo, *Digital Logic Testing and Simulation,* Wiley, New York, 1986.

17. D.K. Pradhan, *Fault-Tolerant Computing,* Prentice-Hall, Englewood Cliffs, N.J., 1986.

APPENDIX

B

ARM INSTRUCTION SET

This appendix contains a summary of version v3 of the ARM instruction set architecture (ISA), which was described in Part I of Chapter 3. A brief discussion of enhancements introduced in later versions of the ISA is also included. The ARM register structure is shown in Figure 3.1. Figure 3.2 shows the general format of an instruction. Here, we give the details for the different types of instructions. All instructions are encoded into a 32-bit word. The memory is byte addressable and addresses are 32 bits long. There are two operand sizes: word (32 bits) and byte (8 bits). A byte operand occupies the lower 8 bits of a processor register. When a byte operand is loaded into a register, the high-order three bytes are cleared to zero.

B.1 INSTRUCTION ENCODING

The encodings for five types of instructions are shown in Figure B.1. Instruction types are distinguished by the bit patterns starting at bit position b_{27}. The multiply instructions in Figure B.1b are detected to be different from the group containing the other arithmetic and logic instructions, shown in Figure B.1a, as follows. When I $= 0$ in the latter group, either bit b_7 or bit b_4 is 0, whereas both of these bits are 1 in the multiply instructions. Note that the Rn and Rd fields are reversed in the multiply instructions.

The sections that follow give the encoding details, with examples, for each of the five types of instructions. The full ARM architecture has additional instructions associated with coprocessor operations. We provide a brief discussion of them.

Conditional Execution of Instructions

The conditions for conditional execution of instructions are listed in Table B.1. The mnemonic for a desired condition is added to an instruction OP-code mnemonic as a suffix. The AL condition specifies that the instruction is executed irrespective of the state of the condition code flags. This is the default condition if the suffix is omitted in assembly language programs. For example, ADD (Add) and B (Branch) are always executed, but ADDEQ and BEQ are executed only if Z $= 1$. Conditional execution of an instruction often follows a Compare instruction. The Name column in Table B.1 is written with this in mind.

B.1.1 ARITHMETIC AND LOGIC INSTRUCTIONS

Arithmetic and logic operations, as well as compare, test, and move operations, are performed by instructions with the format shown in Figure B.2. The first operand is contained in register Rn. The second operand is contained in register Rm or is an unsigned 8-bit immediate operand, as indicated by the I bit. The result of the operation specified by the 4-bit OP code is placed in register Rd. If the S bit is equal to 1, condition code flags are affected by the result; otherwise (S $= 0$), they are not.

The general assembly language form for these instructions is

$$\text{OP\{Cond\}\{S\}} \quad \text{R}d,\text{R}n,\text{Operand 2}$$

31	28 27		24	21	19	16 15	12 11	0
Condition	0 0	I	OP code	S	Rn	Rd	Operand 2	

(a) Arithmetic, logic, compare, test, and move

31	28 27		19	16 15	12 11	8 7	4 3	0
Condition	0 0 0 0 0 0	A S	Rd	Rn	Rs	1 0 0 1	Rm	

(b) Multiply and Multiply Accumulate

31	28 27		19	16 15	12 11	0
Condition	0 1	I P U B W L	Rn	Rd	Offset	

(c) Single word or byte transfer from/to memory

31	28 27		19	16 15	0
Condition	1 0 0	P U - W L	Rn	Register list	

(d) Multiple word transfer from/to memory

31	28 27	23		0
Condition	1 0 1	K	Offset	

(e) Branch and Branch with Link

I Immediate	P Pre/Post-index	W Writeback
S Set	U Up/Down	L Load/Store
A Accumulate	B Byte/Word	K Link

Figure B.1   ARM instruction encoding formats.

Table B.1 Condition field encoding in ARM instructions

Condition field $b_{31} \ldots b_{28}$	Condition suffix	Name	Condition code test
0 0 0 0	EQ	Equal (zero)	$Z = 1$
0 0 0 1	NE	Not equal (nonzero)	$Z = 0$
0 0 1 0	CS/HS	Carry set/Unsigned higher or same	$C = 1$
0 0 1 1	CC/LO	Carry clear/Unsigned lower	$C = 0$
0 1 0 0	MI	Minus (negative)	$N = 1$
0 1 0 1	PL	Plus (positive or zero)	$N = 0$
0 1 1 0	VS	Overflow	$V = 1$
0 1 1 1	VC	No overflow	$V = 0$
1 0 0 0	HI	Unsigned higher	$\overline{C} \vee Z = 0$
1 0 0 1	LS	Unsigned lower or same	$\overline{C} \vee Z = 1$
1 0 1 0	GE	Signed greater than or equal	$N \oplus V = 0$
1 0 1 1	LT	Signed less than	$N \oplus V = 1$
1 1 0 0	GT	Signed greater than	$Z \vee (N \oplus V) = 0$
1 1 0 1	LE	Signed less than or equal	$Z \vee (N \oplus V) = 1$
1 1 1 0	AL	Always	
1 1 1 1		Not used	

For example, if the second operand is contained in a register ($I = 0$), the instruction

$$\text{ADD} \quad \text{R0,R1,R2}$$

is executed unconditionally and performs the operation

$$\text{R0} \leftarrow [\text{R1}] + [\text{R2}]$$

without affecting the condition code flags. If the OP code is changed to ADDS, the flags are affected by the result of the operation. If the latter instruction is to be executed conditionally, on the equal condition (EQ), the OP code is written as ADDEQS.

If the second operand is an immediate value ($I = 1$), it is given by the expression #constant. For example,

$$\text{ADD} \quad \text{R0,R1,\#17}$$

performs the operation

$$\text{R0} \leftarrow [\text{R1}] + 17$$

The immediate value is zero-extended to 32 bits before being used in the operation.

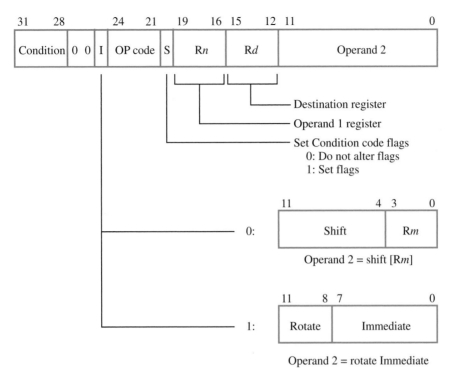

Figure B.2 ARM arithmetic, logic, compare, test, and move instructions.

Shifting of Operand 2

- If Operand 2 is contained in a register ($I = 0$), it can be shifted before being used, as shown in Figure B.3. The shift is specified in bits b_{11-4}. If $b_4 = 0$, a shift amount in the range 0 through 31 is given by the 5-bit unsigned number in bits b_{11-7}. The type of shift is specified in bits b_6 and b_5. The condition code flag C is involved in the four shifts as shown in Figures 2.30 and 2.32. The rotate right operation (ROR) is done without the C bit when the shift amount is nonzero. However, when the shift amount is zero, the meaning is: rotate right one bit position including the C bit, as shown in Figure 2.32d. This operation can be indicated in the assembly language by using the mnemonic RRX (rotate right extended) with no shift amount specified. An example of the instruction syntax when the shift amount is specified directly in the instruction, as just described, is

$$\text{ADD} \quad \text{R0,R1,R2, LSL \#4}$$

which shifts the operand in R2 left 4 bit positions (thus multiplying it by 16) before adding it to the contents of R1. If $b_4 = 1$, the shift amount is specified in the low-order 5 bits of register Rs, as shown in Figure B.3. For example, the instruction

$$\text{ADD} \quad \text{R0,R1,R2, LSR R3}$$

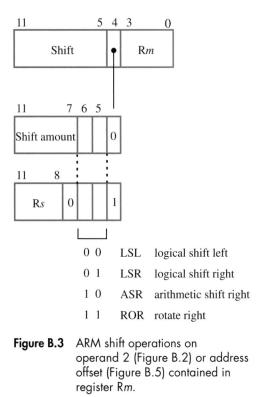

Figure B.3   ARM shift operations on operand 2 (Figure B.2) or address offset (Figure B.5) contained in register R*m*.

shifts the contents of the operand in R2 to the right a number of positions specified by the contents of R3.

- If Operand 2 is an immediate operand ($I = 1$), it can be rotated to the right as indicated in Figure B.2. This option permits a large number of 32-bit values to be generated by rotating the unsigned 8-bit immediate value. The number of rotation positions is $2n$, where n is the 4-bit number contained in bits b_{11-8}. Therefore, the range of rotations is an even number of bits from 0 through 30. This feature of the ARM instruction set partly compensates for the lack of 32-bit immediate operands in instructions. It is clear, however, that not all 32-bit values can be generated this way. A short sequence of instructions, including rotations and OR operations, can be used to synthesize 32-bit values that cannot be specified by rotation of a single 8-bit value.

The full set of 16 arithmetic and logic instructions is shown in Tables B.2 and B.3, along with the two multiply instructions discussed in the next subsection. There are six Add and Subtract instructions. The Add-with-carry and Subtract-with-carry instructions are needed to provide the capability to operate with multiple-word operands. Since only Operand 2 can be shifted, the two Reverse Subtract instructions are provided to allow the shifted operand to be the first operand of the subtract operation.

Table B.2   ARM arithmetic instructions

Mnemonic (Name)	OP code $b_{24} \ldots b_{21}$	Operation performed	CC flags affected if S = 1			
			N	Z	V	C
ADD (Add)	0 1 0 0	$Rd \leftarrow [Rn] + \text{Oper2}$	x	x	x	x
ADC (Add with carry)	0 1 0 1	$Rd \leftarrow [Rn] + \text{Oper2} + [C]$	x	x	x	x
SUB (Subtract)	0 0 1 0	$Rd \leftarrow [Rn] - \text{Oper2}$	x	x	x	x
SBC (Subtract with carry)	0 1 1 0	$Rd \leftarrow [Rn] - \text{Oper2} + [C] - 1$	x	x	x	x
RSB (Reverse subtract)	0 0 1 1	$Rd \leftarrow \text{Oper2} - [Rn]$	x	x	x	x
RSC (Reverse subtract with carry)	0 1 1 1	$Rd \leftarrow \text{Oper2} - [Rn] + [C] - 1$	x	x	x	x
MUL (Multiply)	(See Figure B.4)	$Rd \leftarrow [Rm] \times [Rs]$	x	x		
MLA (Multiply accumulate)	(See Figure B.4)	$Rd \leftarrow [Rm] \times [Rs] + [Rn]$	x	x		

Table B.3 ARM logic, compare, test, and move instructions

Mnemonic (Name)	OP code $b_{24} \ldots b_{21}$	Operation performed	CC flags affected if S = 1			
			N	Z	V	C
AND (Logical AND)	0 0 0 0	$Rd \leftarrow [Rn] \wedge Oper2$	x	x		x
ORR (Logical OR)	1 1 0 0	$Rd \leftarrow [Rn] \vee Oper2$	x	x		x
EOR (Exclusive-OR)	0 0 0 1	$Rd \leftarrow [Rn] \oplus Oper2$	x	x		x
BIC (Bit clear)	1 1 1 0	$Rd \leftarrow [Rn] \wedge \neg Oper2$	x	x		x
CMP (Compare)	1 0 1 0	$[Rn] - Oper2$	x	x	x	x
CMN (Compare negative)	1 0 1 1	$[Rn] + Oper2$	x	x	x	x
TST (Bit test)	1 0 0 0	$[Rn] \wedge Oper2$	x	x		x
TEQ (Test equal)	1 0 0 1	$[Rn] \oplus Oper2$	x	x		x
MOV (Move)	1 1 0 1	$Rd \leftarrow Oper2$	x	x		x
MVN (Move complement)	1 1 1 1	$Rd \leftarrow \neg Oper2$	x	x		x

When an immediate value is used as Operand 2 in an Add or Subtract instruction, it can only be a positive value. But the assembly language allows the instructions

ADD   R0,R1,#−5

and

SUB   R0,R1,#−7

to be used, assembling them as

SUB   R0,R1,#5

and

ADD   R0,R1,#7

respectively.

In addition to the four logic instructions, AND, ORR, EOR, and BIC, the Move complement (MVN) instruction performs the logical NOT operation. The compare and test instructions always affect the condition code flags.

The two Move instructions are used to transfer Operand 2 or its bit complement into the destination register. Operand 2 can be contained in a register or it can be an immediate operand. Thus, in addition to performing register transfers, these two instructions are used to load constants into registers. The MVN instruction can be used to load negative numbers in the 2's-complement representation as follows. The instruction

MOV   R0,#−10

is assembled as

MVN   R0,#9

The bit-complement of $9 = 0 \ldots 01001$ is $1 \ldots 10110$, which is the 2's-complement representation for -10.

Multiply Instructions

The format and operation for the two multiply instructions are shown in Figure B.4 and Table B.2. None of the operands can be shifted. The product generated is a single-precision 32-bit value.

B.1.2 MEMORY LOAD AND STORE INSTRUCTIONS

The format for the two instructions used to access memory is shown in Figure B.5, and their operation is shown in Table B.4. The L bit, b_{20}, is 1 for a Load (LDR) instruction and 0 for a Store (STR) instruction. The B bit, b_{22}, is 1 for a byte operand and is 0 for a 32-bit word operand. A byte operand is located in the low-order byte position of Rd. The effective address of the memory operand is determined by adding (U = 1) or subtracting (U = 0) the offset specified by the Offset field with the contents of register Rn. The P and W bits determine the pre- or post-indexing and writeback operations as

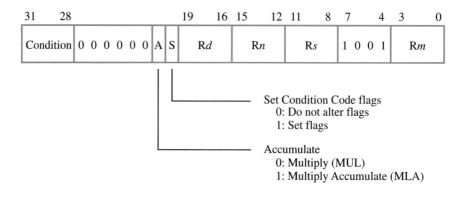

MUL: $Rd \leftarrow [Rm] \times [Rs]$

MLA: $Rd \leftarrow [Rm] \times [Rs] + [Rn]$

Figure B.4   ARM Multiply and Multiply Accumulate instructions.

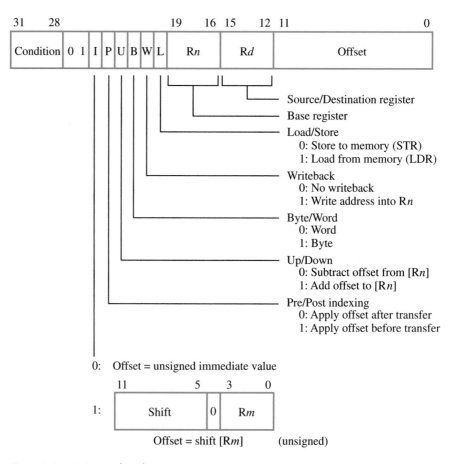

Figure B.5   ARM Load and Store instructions.

Table B.4 ARM instructions for single word or byte transfer from/to memory

Mnemonic (Name)	Instruction bits B L	Operation performed
LDR (Load word)	0 1	$Rd \leftarrow [EA]$
LDRB (Load byte)	1 1	$Rd \leftarrow [EA]$
STR (Store word)	0 0	$EA \leftarrow [Rd]$
STRB (Store byte)	1 0	$EA \leftarrow [Rd]$

indicated in Figure B.5 and described in Table 3.1. The I bit determines how the Offset field is interpreted, as specified in Figures B.5 and B.3. Note that only one of the two shifting methods can be used on the contents of register R*m*.

Examples of memory access operations are as follows. For the instruction

$$\text{LDR} \quad \text{R0,[R1,\#100]}$$

the operation performed is

$$R0 \leftarrow [[R1] + 100]$$

and the bit settings are $I = 0$, $P = 1$, $U = 1$, $B = 0$, $W = 0$, and $L = 1$. The range of offsets is ± 4095. For the instruction

$$\text{LDR} \quad \text{R0,[R1,R2]}$$

the operation performed is

$$R0 \leftarrow [[R1] + [R2]]$$

with the I bit changed to 1 and all the other settings left the same.

When the offset is contained in a register, it can be shifted before being added to or subtracted from the base register R*n*. The shift can only be specified by the 5-bit immediate method shown in Figure B.3. For example, the instruction

$$\text{LDR} \quad \text{R0,[R1,}-\text{R2, LSL \#4]!}$$

performs the operation

$$R0 \leftarrow [[R1] - 16 \times [R2]]$$

and the effective address is written back into R1. The bit settings for this instruction are I = 1, P = 1, U = 0, B = 0, W = 1, and L = 1.

If the program counter, R15, is specified as the base register, the Relative addressing mode is implemented as indicated in Table 3.1. In this case, pre-indexing without writeback, along with an immediate offset, is used to generate the effective address of the operand. The assembly language allows the absolute address of the operand to be named. The assembler computes the offset value relative to the updated contents of the program counter at the time the instruction is executed. For example, if the instruction

LDR   R0,PARAMETER

is to be placed at address 1000 and the label PARAMETER represents the address 1100, the assembler will generate the instruction

LDR   R0,[R15,#92]

At the time the offset is added to the contents of the program counter, the counter has been updated to contain 1008, so the offset must be 92 to generate the correct effective address of $1100 = 1008 + 92$.

B.1.3   BLOCK LOAD AND STORE INSTRUCTIONS

Figure B.6 shows the encoding for the instructions used to transfer data between a block of consecutive memory words and a specified subset of the 16 processor registers. The

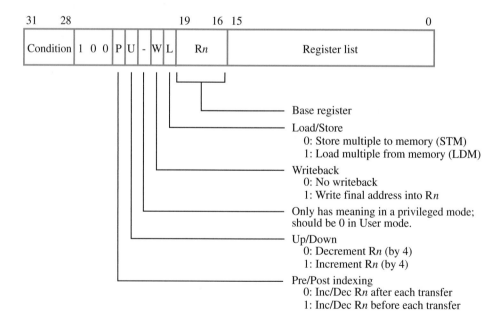

Figure B.6   ARM block transfer instructions.

OP code LDM (Load multiple) is used for loading memory operands into the registers, and STM (Store multiple) is used for the store operation. The L bit is 1 for the load operation and 0 for the store operation. The registers involved are specified by the locations of 1s in the 16-bit Register-list field in bits b_{15-0}. The location of the beginning of the block of words in memory is specified by the contents of the base register Rn. The block runs toward higher addresses if the U bit is 1 and toward lower addresses if the U bit is 0. Pre- or post-indexing of Rn is specified by the P bit. The index value is always 4 because the operands are consecutive 4-byte words. The final address generated in performing the block transfer is written back into Rn if the W bit is 1; otherwise (W = 0), Rn is left containing the initial address. Irrespective of whether or not the block runs toward higher or lower addresses, the lowest number register is always associated with the lowest address value in the block. Table B.5 shows the OP-code mnemonics for all possible settings of the P, U, and L bits. Suffixes on the LDM and STM OP codes indicate the settings of the P and U bits. For example, the P = 0 and U = 1 settings in the first entry in Table B.5 are indicated by the suffix IA, standing for "increment after," meaning that the contents of the base register Rn are incremented by 4 after each transfer is performed, that is, Rn is post-indexed. The alternate mnemonics and names shown in Table B.5 are explained next.

The main use for block transfers is in saving and restoring registers on a stack on entry to and return from subroutines. If we assume that R13 is used as the stack pointer and R14 (the link register) holds the return address, then the instruction

$$\text{STMDB} \quad \text{R13!,\{R0−R3,R14\}}$$

which is the last entry in Table B.5, pushes the contents of registers R0 through R3 and R14 onto the stack. The stack grows toward lower memory addresses and the contents of R0 are transferred last into the lowest address. The corresponding instruction

$$\text{LDMIA} \quad \text{R13!,\{R0−R3,R15\}}$$

which is the first entry in Table B.5, pops the saved contents of R0 through R3 back into those registers, and pops the saved value from R14 (the return address) into R15, the program counter, implementing the return operation. The contents of the highest address are transferred last into R15. The suffixes DB and IA on these two OP codes stand for "decrement before" (DB) and "increment after" (IA), describing how the base register contents are manipulated. The alternate OP-code mnemonics (shown in Table B.5) that can be used for the same instructions are STMFD and LDMFD. The suffix FD stands for "full descending." This is meant to describe the fact that the stack grows toward lower memory addresses (descending) and the initial contents of the base register, R13, are the address of the current top element of the stack (full). For a stack that grows toward higher addresses and uses a stack pointer that points to the empty location beyond the current top element, the descriptor name is "empty ascending," and the suffix is EA. The use of LDM and STM instructions in entering and returning from interrupt service routines is discussed in Chapter 4.

Table B.5 ARM instructions for multiple word transfers from/to memory

Mnemonic (Name)	Instruction bits			Operation performed
	P	**U**	**L**	
LDMIA/LDMFD (Increment after/ Full descending)	0	1	1	$R_{low}, \ldots, R_{high} \leftarrow [[Rn]], [[Rn] + 4], \ldots$
LDMIB/LDMED (Increment before/ Empty descending)	1	1	1	$R_{low}, \ldots, R_{high} \leftarrow [[Rn] + 4], [[Rn] + 8], \ldots$
LDMDA/LDMFA (Decrement after/ Full ascending)	0	0	1	$R_{high}, \ldots, R_{low} \leftarrow [[Rn]], [[Rn] - 4], \ldots$
LDMDB/LDMEA (Decrement before/ Empty ascending)	1	0	1	$R_{high}, \ldots, R_{low} \leftarrow [[Rn] - 4], [[Rn] - 8], \ldots$
STMIA/STMEA (Increment after/ Empty ascending)	0	1	0	$[Rn], [Rn] + 4, \ldots \leftarrow [R_{low}], \ldots, [R_{high}]$
STMIB/STMFA (Increment before/ Full ascending)	1	1	0	$[Rn] + 4, [Rn] + 8, \ldots \leftarrow [R_{low}], \ldots, [R_{high}]$
STMDA/STMED (Decrement after/ Empty descending)	0	0	0	$[Rn], [Rn] - 4, \ldots \leftarrow [R_{high}], \ldots, [R_{low}]$
STMDB/STMFD (Decrement before/ Full descending)	1	0	0	$[Rn] - 4, [Rn] - 8, \ldots \leftarrow [R_{high}], \ldots, [R_{low}]$

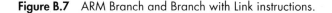

31 28		23		0
Condition	1 0 1	K	Offset	

K=0 :Branch (B)
K=1 :Branch with Link (BL); store return address in register R14

Figure B.7 ARM Branch and Branch with Link instructions.

B.1.4 BRANCH AND BRANCH WITH LINK INSTRUCTIONS

Figure B.7 shows the encoding of the Branch (B) and Branch with Link (BL) instructions. Offset is a signed 24-bit number. It is shifted left two bit positions (all branch targets are aligned word addresses), sign extended to 32 bits, and added to the updated PC to generate the branch target address. The updated PC points to the instruction that is two words (8 bytes) forward from the branch instruction.

The assembly language permits the absolute address of the branch target to be used. For example, the instruction

BEQ   ROUTINE

is a conditional branch on the condition $Z = 1$ to the location ROUTINE. If the Branch instruction is at address 2000 and ROUTINE is the address 3000, the assembler will compute the offset value to be inserted into the instruction as 248. The actual distance to the target address from the updated contents, 2008, of the program counter is 992. This value is 248 shifted left 2 bit positions (multiplied by 4). Thus, the branch target address is computed as $2008 + 992 = 3000$.

The Branch with Link (BL) instruction is used to call a subroutine. Before branching to the subroutine, the address of the instruction that immediately follows the BL instruction (the return address) is stored in register R14, which is used as a link register. The return from a subroutine is handled as described in Section 3.6.

B.1.5 MACHINE CONTROL INSTRUCTIONS

Software Interrupt

When execution of a user program is completed, control is transferred to a supervisor program (part of the operating system) by a software interrupt instruction (SWI). We did not show the SWI instruction in the example programs in Part I of Chapter 3. An example of where it needs to be placed is immediately after the STR instruction in the program in Figure 3.8. An SWI instruction is also used in transferring control to operating system routines that run in supervisor mode while executing input/output operations for a user program, as described in Chapter 4.

The assembly language instruction format for the SWI instruction is shown in Table B.6, along with the operations performed. The OP code SWI is encoded by the

Table B.6 ARM instructions for status register transfers, software interrupt, and data swap

Mnemonic (Name)	Instruction formats	Operation performed
MRS (Copy status register)	User mode: MRS Rd,CPSR	R$d \leftarrow$ [CPSR]
	Privileged mode: MRS Rd,CPSR MRS Rd,SPSR	R$d \leftarrow$ [CPSR] R$d \leftarrow$ [SPSR_$mode$]
MSR (Write to status register)	User mode: MSR CPSR,Rm MSR CPSR,imm32	CPSR$_{31-28} \leftarrow$ [Rm]$_{31-28}$ CPSR$_{31-28} \leftarrow$ imm32$_{31-28}$
	Privileged mode: MSR CPSR,Rm MSR CPSR_flg,Rm MSR CPSR_flg,imm32 MSR SPSR,Rm MSR SPSR_flg,Rm MSR SPSR_flg,imm32	CPSR $\leftarrow$ [Rm] CPSR$_{31-28} \leftarrow$ [Rm]$_{31-28}$ CPSR$_{31-28} \leftarrow$ imm32$_{31-28}$ SPSR_$mode \leftarrow$ [Rm] SPSR_$mode_{31-28} \leftarrow$ [Rm]$_{31-28}$ SPSR_$mode_{31-28} \leftarrow$ imm32$_{31-28}$
SWI (Software interrupt)	SWI imm24	R14_svc $\leftarrow$ updated[PC]; SPSR_svc $\leftarrow$ [CPSR]; PC $\leftarrow$ 0x08
SWP (Swap)	SWP Rd,Rm,[Rn]	R$d \leftarrow$ [[Rn]]; [Rn] $\leftarrow$ [Rm]

pattern 1111 in the instruction bit field b_{27-24}. As with all other ARM instructions, it can be executed conditionally. The low-order 24 bits of the instruction contain an immediate operand that is ignored during execution of the instruction. The user program can use this field to pass a parameter to the operating system to declare the service being requested, such as an I/O operation.

Processor Status Register Transfers

Instructions that handle the current processor status register, CPSR, and the saved processor status registers, SPSR_mode (see Figures 3.1 and 4.12) are provided, mainly for use by privileged mode programs. Limited use of these instructions in user programs is also permitted. When an external interrupt suspends execution of a user program, the current CPSR contents are automatically saved in an SPSR_mode register while a privileged mode routine handles the interrupt. Such routines have to manipulate status register contents. These issues are discussed in Chapter 4. The MRS and MSR instructions, shown in Table B.6, are used for reading and writing the contents of the CPSR and SPSR_mode registers. Both user mode and privileged mode programs can read the status registers. User mode programs can write only to the N, Z, V, and C condition code flags in bit field b_{31-28} of the CPSR register. Privileged mode programs can write to all 32 bits of the CPSR and SPSR_mode registers, and can also write selectively to just the condition code flag field. The source operand for write operations is either the contents of a general-purpose register or a 32-bit immediate value denoted imm32 in Table B.6. Only the high-order 4 bits of an immediate operand are used, so the operand can always be generated by a rotation of the short 8-bit immediate field value in an instruction.

The MRS and MSR instructions are encoded in the machine instruction format normally used for arithmetic and logic instructions (see Figure B.1). The CMP, CMN, TST, and TEQ instructions in this group, shown in Table B.3, always set the condition code flags. Therefore, the S bit is always set to 1 in these instructions. When the S bit is set to 0, the four OP codes for these instructions represent the MRS and MSR instructions operating on either the CPSR or the SPSR_mode registers. Other instruction bit positions are used to distinguish between full or partial writes and register or immediate source operands for the MSR instruction.

Register/Memory Swap

An instruction is provided that reads the contents of a memory location into one register and writes the contents of another register into the same memory location in an uninterruptible pair of operations. This Swap instruction (with the mnemonic SWP), shown in Table B.6, can be executed in either user or privileged modes. Its main use is in implementing operations on lock variables to coordinate correct operations on memory data that are shared between programs in multiprocessor configurations (see Chapter 12). Being "uninterruptible" means that no access to memory by a different processor is permitted between the read and write operations performed by the Swap instruction. The registers Rm and Rd can be the same, effecting an exchange operation between the register and the memory operand.

B.2   OTHER ARM INSTRUCTIONS

In this section, we briefly describe coprocessor instructions and instructions introduced in versions v4 and v5 of the architecture.

B.2.1   COPROCESSOR INSTRUCTIONS

Hardware units for executing operations not performed by the defined ARM instruction set are called coprocessors. An example is a hardware unit for executing operations on floating-point numbers. Other examples include application-specific processing on digital signals or video data that may be required in an embedded system. If an ARM processor design is provided in a software-synthesizable form, as described in Chapters 9 and 11, a software module that specifies a coprocessor can be integrated with the software description of the processor and used to generate a single-chip implementation. Programming of the combined units is facilitated by including instruction templates in the ARM instruction set for directing the coprocessor to perform its operations, transferring data between coprocessor registers and memory, and transferring data between coprocessor registers and ARM registers.

B.2.2   VERSIONS V4 AND V5 INSTRUCTIONS

An extended set of memory access and multiply instructions have been included in the two versions of the instruction set architecture that follow version v3. Versions v4 and v5 have Load and Store instructions that transfer signed bytes and signed/unsigned 16-bit half words between memory and the processor registers. Internally, ARM processors perform operations only on 32-bit operands. When signed bytes or signed half words are loaded into processor registers by v4 and v5 instructions, they are sign-extended to the 32-bit length.

Versions v4 and v5 also provide additional forms of the MUL and MULA instructions found in version v3 (see Figure B.4). Signed and unsigned versions of these two instructions that produce 64-bit products are provided.

B.3   PROGRAMMING EXPERIMENTS

The ARM web site URL: www.arm.com/hr.ns4/html/SDT202u contains software development tools that can be used to enter, edit, assemble, and run (simulated) ARM assembly language programs. For the program in Figure 3.8, the AREA directives should be changed to

```
AREA    addloop,    CODE
AREA    addloopdata,    DATA
```

to enable assembly. Also, as described in Section B.1.5, a software interrupt instruction in the form

```
SWI    0x123456
```

is needed after the SRT instruction.

C

MOTOROLA 68000 INSTRUCTION SET

This appendix contains a summary of the Motorola 68000 instruction set. Part II of Chapter 3 gives an introductory discussion of the main characteristics of this processor, including a description of the register structure and the addressing modes, summarized in Figure 3.18 and Table 3.2, respectively. Note that Table 3.2 includes the assembler syntax for the addressing modes.

The general format for encoding the address field for an operand is shown in Table C.1. A 6-bit field specifies the addressing mode and the register involved. For the modes in which it is not necessary to specify a particular register, all 6 bits are used to specify the addressing mode.

The names of addressing modes in Table C.1 are consistent with those used in this book. Some of these names differ from those used in Motorola literature. Because the reader will find it useful to consult the manufacturer's data sheets and user manuals, we summarize the differences in the terminology in Table C.2. The Motorola terminology is highly descriptive but somewhat awkward to use for discussion.

The 68000 instructions are presented in this appendix in the form of a table. To keep the table reasonably small, extensive notational abbreviations are used. Table C.3 gives the notational symbols and their meanings. Note that symbols that correspond to bit patterns in the OP-code field have one letter for each bit position involved.

Table C.4 provides a complete list of the available instructions. The addressing modes allowed for each instruction are indicated in a matrix format. For each source

(Continued on page 766.)

Table C.1 Address field encoding for 68000

Address field

Mode	Register

5   4   3   2   1   0

Addressing mode	Mode field	Register field
Data register direct	000	Register number
Address register direct	001	Register number
Address register indirect	010	Register number
Autoincrement	011	Register number
Autodecrement	100	Register number
Indexed basic	101	Register number
Indexed full	110	Register number
Absolute short	111	000
Absolute long	111	001
Relative basic	111	010
Relative full	111	011
Immediate or status register	111	100

Table C.2 Differences from Motorola terminology

Terminology used in this book	Motorola terminology
Autoincrement	Address register indirect with postincrement
Autodecrement	Address register indirect with predecrement
Indexed basic	Address register indirect with displacement
Indexed full	Address register indirect with index
Relative basic	Program counter with displacement
Relative full	Program counter with index

Table C.3 Notation for Table C.4

Symbol	Meaning
s	Source operand
d	Destination operand
An	Address register n
Dn	Data register n
Xn	An address or data register, used as an index register
PC	Program counter
SP	Stack pointer
SR	Status register
CCR	Condition-code flags in SR
AAA	Address register number
DDD	Data register number
rrr	Source register number
RRR	Destination register number
eeeeee	Effective address of the source operand
EEEEEE	Effective address of the destination operand
MMM	Effective address mode of destination
CCCC	Specification for a condition code test
P...P	Displacement
Q...Q	Quick immediate data
SS	Size: 00 ≡ byte, 01 ≡ word, 10 ≡ long word (for most instructions); 01 ≡ byte, 11 ≡ word, 10 ≡ long word (for MOVE and MOVEA instructions)
VVVV	Trap vector number
u	Condition code flag state is undefined (meaningless)
d(An)	Indexed basic addressing mode
d(An,Xi)	Indexed full addressing mode
d(PC)	Relative basic addressing mode
d(PC,Xi)	Relative full addressing mode

Table C.4 68000 instruction set

Mnemonic (Name)	Size	Addressing mode		Dn	An	(An)	(An)+	-(An)	d(An)	d(An,Xi)	Abs.W	Abs.L	d(PC)	d(PC,Xi)	Immed	SR or CCR
ABCD (Add BCD)	B	s = Dn s = -(An)	d = d =	x				x								
ADD (Add)	B,W,L	s = Dn d = Dn	d = s =	x x	 x	x x	x x	x x	x x	x x	x x	x x	 x	 x	 x	
ADDA (Add address)	W L	d = An d = An	s = s =	x x	x x	x x	x x	x x	x x	x x	x x	x x	x x	x x	x x	
ADDI (Add immediate)	B,W,L	s = Immed	d =	x		x	x	x	x	x	x	x				
ADDQ (Add quick)	B,W,L	s = Immed3	d =	x	x	x	x	x	x	x	x	x				
ADDX (Add extended)	B,W,L	s = Dn s = -(An)	d = d =	x				x								
AND (Logical AND)	B,W,L	s = Dn d = Dn	d = s =	x x		x x	x x	x x	x x	x x	x x	x x	 x	 x	 x	
ANDI (AND immediate)	B,W,L	s = Immed	d =	x		x	x	x	x	x	x	x				x
ASL (Arithmetic shift left)	B,W,L	count = [Dn] count = QQQ count = 1	d = d = d =	x x		 x	 x	 x	 x	 x	 x	 x				
ASR (Arithmetic shift right)	B,W,L	count = [Dn] count = QQQ count = 1	d = d = d =	x x		 x	 x	 x	 x	 x	 x	 x				
BCHG* (Test a bit and change it)	B L	bit# = [Dn] bit# = Immed bit# = [Dn] bit# = Immed	d = d = d = d =	 x x		x x	x x	x x	x x	x x	x x	x x				
BCLR* (Test a bit and clear it)	B L	bit# = [Dn] bit# = Immed bit# = [Dn] bit# = Immed	d = d = d = d =	 x x		x x	x x	x x	x x	x x	x x	x x				

OP code $b_{15} \ldots b_0$	Operation performed	X	N	Z	V	C
1100 RRR1 0000 0rrr 1100 RRR1 0000 1rrr	$d \leftarrow [s]+[d]+[X]$ Binary-coded decimal addition	x	u	x	u	x
1101 DDD1 SSEE EEEE 1101 DDD0 SSee eeee	$d \leftarrow [Dn]+[d]$ $Dn \leftarrow [s]+[Dn]$	x x	x x	x x	x x	x x
1101 AAA0 11ee eeee 1101 AAA1 11ee eeee	$An \leftarrow [s]+[An]$					
0000 0110 SSEE EEEE	$d \leftarrow s+[d]$	x	x	x	x	x
0101 QQQ0 SSEE EEEE	$d \leftarrow QQQ+[d]$	x	x	x	x	x
1101 RRR1 SS00 0rrr 1101 RRR1 SS00 1rrr	$d \leftarrow [s]+[d]+[X]$ Multiprecision addition	x	x	x	x	x
1100 DDD1 SSEE EEEE 1100 DDD0 SSee eeee	$d \leftarrow [Dn] \wedge [d]$		x	x	0	0
0000 0010 SSEE EEEE	$d \leftarrow s \wedge [d]$		x	x	0	0
1110 rrr1 SS10 0DDD 1110 QQQ1 SS00 0DDD 1110 0001 11EE EEEE		x	x	x	x	x
1110 rrr0 SS10 0DDD 1110 QQQ0 SS00 0DDD 1110 0000 11EE EEEE		x	x	x	x	x
0000 rrr1 01EE EEEE 0000 1000 01EE EEEE 0000 rrr1 01EE EEEE 0000 1000 01EE EEEE	$Z \leftarrow \overline{(\text{bit\# of d})}$; then complement the tested bit in d.				x	
0000 rrr1 10EE EEEE 0000 1000 10EE EEEE 0000 rrr1 10EE EEEE 0000 1000 10EE EEEE	$Z \leftarrow \overline{(\text{bit\# of d})}$; then clear the tested bit in d.				x	

(Continued)

Mnemonic (Name)	Size	Addressing mode		Dn	An	(An)	(An)+	-(An)	d(An)	d(An,Xi)	Abs.W	Abs.L	d(PC)	d(PC,Xi)	Immed	SR or CCR
BSET* (Test a bit and set it)	B	bit# = [Dn]	d =			x	x	x	x	x	x	x				
		bit# = Immed	d =			x	x	x	x	x	x	x				
	L	bit# = [Dn]	d =	x												
		bit# = Immed	d =	x												
BTST* (Test a bit)	B	bit# = [Dn]	d =			x	x	x	x	x	x	x				
		bit# = Immed	d =			x	x	x	x	x	x	x				
	L	bit# = [Dn]	d =	x												
		bit# = Immed	d =	x												
CHK (Check register)	W	d = Dn	s =	x		x	x	x	x	x	x	x	x	x	x	
CLR (Clear)	B,W,L		d =	x		x	x	x	x	x	x	x				
CMP (Compare)	B,W,L	d = Dn	s =	x	x	x	x	x	x	x	x	x	x	x	x	
CMPA (Compare address)	W	d = An	s =	x	x	x	x	x	x	x	x	x	x	x	x	
	L	d = An	s =	x	x	x	x	x	x	x	x	x	x	x	x	
CMPI (Compare immed)	B,W,L	s = Immed	d =	x		x	x	x	x	x	x	x				
CMPM (Compare memory)	B,W,L	s = (An)+	d =				x									
DIVS (Divide signed)	W	d = Dn	s =	x		x	x	x	x	x	x	x	x	x	x	
DIVU (Divide unsigned)	W	d = Dn	s =	x		x	x	x	x	x	x	x	x	x	x	
EOR (Logical XOR)	B,W,L	s = Dn	d =	x		x	x	x	x	x	x	x				
EORI (XOR immediate)	B,W,L	s = Immed	d =	x		x	x	x	x	x	x	x				x
EXG (Exchange)	L	s = Dn	d =	x	x											
		s = An	d =	x	x											
EXT (Sign extend)	W		d =	x												
	L		d =	x												

Condition flags columns: **X N Z V C**

OP code $b_{15}\ldots b_0$	Operation performed	X	N	Z	V	C
0000 rrr1 11EE EEEE 0000 1000 11EE EEEE 0000 rrr1 11EE EEEE 0000 1000 11EE EEEE	$Z \leftarrow \overline{(\text{bit\# of d})}$; then set to 1 the tested bit in d.			x		
0000 rrr1 00EE EEEE 0000 1000 00EE EEEE 0000 rrr1 00EE EEEE 0000 1000 00EE EEEE	$Z \leftarrow \overline{(\text{bit\# of d})}$;			x		
0100 DDD1 10ee eeee	If [Dn] < 0 or [Dn] > [s], then raise an interrupt.		x	u	u	u
0100 0010 SSEE EEEE	d ← 0		0	1	0	0
1011 DDD0 SSee eeee	[d] − [s]		x	x	x	x
1011 AAA0 11ee eeee 1011 AAA1 11ee eeee	[An] − [s]		x	x	x	x
0000 1100 SSEE EEEE	[d] − [s]		x	x	x	x
1011 RRR1 SS00 1rrr	[d] − [s]		x	x	x	x
1000 DDD1 11ee eeee	d ← [d] ÷ [s], using 32 bits of d and 16 bits of s.		x	x	x	0
1000 DDD0 11ee eeee	d ← [d] ÷ [s], using 32 bits of d and 16 bits of s.		x	x	x	0
1011 rrr1 SSEE EEEE	d ← [Dn] ⊕ [d]		x	x	0	0
0000 1010 SSEE EEEE	d ← s ⊕ [d]		x	x	0	0
1100 DDD1 0100 0DDD 1100 AAA1 0100 1AAA 1100 DDD1 1000 1AAA	[s] ↔ [d]					
0100 1000 1000 0DDD 0100 1000 1100 0DDD	(bits 15−8 of d) ← (bit 7 of d) (bits 31−16 of d) ← (bit 15 of d)		x x	x x	0 0	0 0

(*Continued*)

Mnemonic (Name)	Size	Addressing mode		Dn	An	(An)	(An)+	-(An)	d(An)	d(An,Xi)	Abs.W	Abs.L	d(PC)	d(PC,Xi)	Immed	SR or CCR
JMP (Jump)		d=				x			x	x	x	x	x	x		
JSR (Jump to subroutine)		d =				x			x	x	x	x	x	x		
LEA (Load effective address)	L	d = An	s =			x			x	x	x	x	x	x		
LINK (Link and allocate)		disp = Immed	s =		x											
LSL (Logical shift left)	B,W,L	count = [Dn]	d =	x												
		count = QQQ	d =	x												
	W	count = I	d =			x	x	x	x	x	x	x				
LSR (Logical shift right)	B,W,L	count = [Dn]	d =	x												
		count = QQQ	d =	x												
	W	count = I	d =			x	x	x	x	x	x	x				
MOVE (Move)	B,W,L	s =Dn	d =	x		x	x	x	x	x	x	x				
		s = An	d =	x		x	x	x	x	x	x	x				
		s = (An)	d =	x		x	x	x	x	x	x	x				
		s = (An)+	d =	x		x	x	x	x	x	x	x				
		s = −(An)	d =	x		x	x	x	x	x	x	x				
		s = d(An)	d =	x		x	x	x	x	x	x	x				
		s = d(An,Xi)	d =	x		x	x	x	x	x	x	x				
		s = Abs.W	d =	x		x	x	x	x	x	x	x				
		s = Abs.L	d =	x		x	x	x	x	x	x	x				
		s = d(PC)	d =	x		x	x	x	x	x	x	x				
		s = d(PC,Xi)	d =	x		x	x	x	x	x	x	x				
		s = Immed	d =	x		x	x	x	x	x	x	x				
	W	d = CCR	s =	x		x	x	x	x	x	x	x	x	x	x	
		d = SR	s =	x		x	x	x	x	x	x	x	x	x	x	
		s = SR	d =	x		x	x	x	x	x	x	x				
	L	s = SP	d =				x									
		d = SP	s =				x									
MOVEA (Move address)	W,L	d = An	s =	x	x	x	x	x	x	x	x	x	x	x	x	

758

OP code $b_{15} \ldots b_0$	Operation performed	Condition flags X	N	Z	V	C
0100 1110 11EE EEEE	PC ← effective address of d					
0100 1110 10EE EEEE	SP ← [SP]−4; [SP] ← [PC]; PC ← effective address of d					
0100 AAA1 11ee eeee	An ← effective address of s					
0100 1110 0101 0AAA	SP ← [SP]−4; [SP] ← [An]; An ← [SP]; SP ← [SP] + disp					
1110 rrr1 SS10 1DDD 1110 QQQ1 SS00 1DDD 1110 0011 11EE EEEE	$\boxed{C} \leftarrow \boxed{\text{operand}} \leftarrow 0$; $\boxed{X}$	x	x	x	0	x
1110 rrr0 SS10 1DDD 1110 QQQ0 SS00 1DDD 1110 0010 11EE EEEE	$0 \rightarrow \boxed{\text{operand}} \rightarrow \boxed{C}$; $\boxed{X}$	x	x	x	0	x
00SS RRRM MMee eeee	d ← [s]		x	x	0	0
0100 0100 11ee eeee	CCR ← [bits 7−0 of s]	x	x	x	x	x
0100 0110 11ee eeee	SR ← [s]	x	x	x	x	x
0100 0000 11EE EEEE	d ← [SR]					
0100 1110 0110 1AAA	d ← [SP]					
0100 1110 0110 0AAA	SP ← [d]					
00SS AAA0 01ee eeee	An ← [s]					

(*Continued*)

Mnemonic (Name)	Size	Addressing mode		Dn	An	(An)	(An)+	-(An)	d(An)	d(An,Xi)	Abs.W	Abs.L	d(PC)	d(PC,Xi)	Immed	SR or CCR
MOVEM* (Move multiple registers)	W	s = Xn	d =			x		x	x	x	x	x				
		d = Xn	s =			x	x		x	x	x	x	x	x		
	L	s = Xn	d =			x		x	x	x	x	x				
		d = Xn	s =			x	x		x	x	x	x	x	x		
MOVEP* (Move peripheral data)	W	s = Dn	d =						x							
	L	s = Dn	d =						x							
	W	s = d(An)	d =	x												
	L	s = d(An)	d =	x												
MOVEQ (Move quick)	L	s = Immed8	d =	x												
MULS (Multiply signed)	W	d = Dn	s =	x		x	x	x	x	x	x	x	x	x	x	
MULU (Multiply unsigned)	W	d = Dn	s =	x		x	x	x	x	x	x	x	x	x	x	
NBCD (Negate BCD)	B		d =	x		x	x	x	x	x	x	x				
NEG (Negate)	B,W,L		d =	x		x	x	x	x	x	x	x				
NEGX (Negate extended)	B,W,L		d =	x		x	x	x	x	x	x	x				
NOP (No operation)																
NOT (Complement)	B,W,L		d =	x		x	x	x	x	x	x	x				
OR (Logical OR)	B,W,L	s = Dn	d =			x	x	x	x	x	x	x				
		d = Dn	s =	x		x	x	x	x	x	x	x	x	x	x	
ORI (OR immediate)	B,W,L	s = Immed	d =	x		x	x	x	x	x	x	x				x
PEA (Push effective address)	L		s =			x			x	x	x	x	x	x		

		Condition flags			
OP code $b_{15} \ldots b_0$	Operation performed	X	N	Z	V	C
0100 1000 10EE EEEE 0100 1100 10ee eeee 0100 1000 11EE EEEE 0100 1100 11ee eeee	$d \leftarrow [Xn]$ ⎫ A second word is $Xn \leftarrow [s]$ ⎪ used to specify $d \leftarrow [Xn]$ ⎬ the registers $Xn \leftarrow [s]$ ⎭ involved.					
0000 DDD1 1000 1AAA 0000 DDD1 1100 1AAA 0000 DDD1 0000 1AAA 0000 DDD1 0100 1AAA	Alternate bytes of d $\leftarrow$ [Dn] Dn $\leftarrow$ alternate bytes of d					
0111 DDD0 QQQQ QQQQ	$Dn \leftarrow QQQQQQQQ$		x	x	0	0
1100 DDD1 11ee eeee	$Dn \leftarrow [s] \times [Dn]$		x	x	0	0
1100 DDD0 11ee eeee	$Dn \leftarrow [s] \times [Dn]$		x	x	0	0
0100 1000 00EE EEEE	$d \leftarrow 0 - [d] - [X]$ using BCD arithmetic	x	u	x	u	x
0100 0100 SSEE EEEE	$d \leftarrow 0 - [d]$	x	x	x	x	x
0100 0000 SSEE EEEE	$d \leftarrow 0 - [d] - [X]$	x	x	x	x	x
0100 1110 0111 0001	none					
0100 0110 SSEE EEEE	$d \leftarrow \overline{[d]}$		x	x	0	0
1000 DDD1 SSEE EEEE 1000 DDD0 SSee eeee	$d \leftarrow [s] \vee [d]$		x	x	0	0
0000 0000 SSEE EEEE	$d \leftarrow s \vee [d]$		x	x	0	0
0100 1000 01ee eeee	$SP \leftarrow [SP] - 4;$ $[SP] \leftarrow$ effective address of s					

(Continued)

Mnemonic (Name)	Size	Addressing mode	Dn	An	(An)	(An)+	-(An)	d(An)	d(An,Xi)	Abs.W	Abs.L	d(PC)	d(PC,Xi)	Immed	SR or CCR
RESET															
ROL (Rotate left without X)	B,W,L W	count = [Dn] d = count = QQQ d = count = 1 d =	x x		x	x	x	x	x	x	x				
ROR (Rotate right without X)	B,W,L W	count = [Dn] d = count = QQQ d = count = 1	x x		x	x	x	x	x	x	x				
ROXL (Rotate left with X)	B,W,L W	count = [Dn] d = count = QQQ d = count = 1 d =	x x		x	x	x	x	x	x	x				
ROXR (Rotate right with X)	B,W,L W	count = [Dn] d = count = QQQ d = count = 1 d =	x x		x	x	x	x	x	x	x				
RTE (Return from exception)															
RTR (Return and restore CCR)															
RTS (Return from subroutine)															
SBCD (Subtract BCD)	B	s = Dn d = s = − (An) d =	x				x								
Scc (Set on condition)	B	d=	x		x	x	x	x	x	x	x				
STOP (Load SR and stop)		s =												x	

OP code $b_{15} \ldots b_0$	Operation performed	Condition flags				
		X	**N**	**Z**	**V**	**C**
0100 1110 0111 0000	Assert RESET output line.					
1110 rrr1 SS11 1DDD 1110 QQQ1 SS01 1DDD 1110 0111 11EE EEEE	[C] ← [operand] ← (rotate left into C)		x	x	0	x
1100 rrr1 SS11 1DDD 1110 QQQ0 SS01 1DDD 1110 0111 11EE EEEE	→ [operand] → [C] (rotate right into C)		x	x	0	x
1110 rrr1 SS11 0DDD 1110 QQQ1 SS01 0DDD 1110 0101 11EE EEEE	[C] ← [operand] ← [X] (rotate left through X)	x	x	x	0	x
1110 rrr0 SS11 0DDD 1110 QQQ0 SS01 0DDD 1110 0100 11EE EEEE	[X] → [operand] → [C] (rotate right through X)	x	x	x	0	x
0100 1110 0111 0011	SR ← [[SP]]; SP ← [SP] + 2; PC ← [[SP]]; SP ← [SP] + 4;	x	x	x	x	x
0100 1110 0111 0111	CCR ← [[SP]]; SP ← [SP] + 2; PC ← [[SP]]; SP ← [SP] + 4;	x	x	x	x	x
0100 1110 0111 0101	PC ← [[SP]]; SP ← [SP] + 4					
1000 RRR1 0000 0rrr 1000 RRR1 0000 1rrr	d ← [d] − [s] − [X] Binary-coded decimal subtraction	x	u	x	u	x
0101 CCCC 11EE EEEE	Set all 8 bits of d to 1 if cc is true, otherwise clear them to 0.					
0100 1110 0111 0010	SR ← s; wait for interrupt.	x	x	x	x	x

(Continued)

Mnemonic (Name)	Size	Addressing mode		Addressing mode												
				Dn	An	(An)	(An)+	-(An)	d(An)	d(An,Xi)	Abs.W	Abs.L	d(PC)	d(PC,Xi)	Immed	SR or CCR
SUB (Subtract)	B,W,L	s = Dn	d =	x		x	x	x	x	x	x	x				
		d = Dn	s =	x	x	x	x	x	x	x	x	x	x	x	x	
SUBA (Subtract address)	W	d = An	s =	x	x	x	x	x	x	x	x	x	x	x	x	
	L	d = An	s =	x	x	x	x	x	x	x	x	x	x	x	x	
SUBI (Subtract immed)	B,W,L	s = Immed	d =	x		x	x	x	x	x	x	x				
SUBQ (Subtract quick)	B,W,L	s = Immed3	d =	x	x	x	x	x	x	x	x	x				
SUBX (Subtract extended)	B,W,L	s = Dn	d =	x												
		s = -(An)	d =					x								
SWAP (Swap register halves)	W		d =	x												
TAS (Test and set)	B		d =	x		x	x	x	x	x	x	x				
TRAP (Trap)		s = Immed4														
TRAPV (Trap on overflow)																
TST (Test)	B,W,L		d =	x		x	x	x	x	x	x	x				
UNLK (Unlink)						x										

OP code $b_{15}\ldots b_0$	Operation performed	Condition flags				
		X	N	Z	V	C
1001 DDD1 SSEE EEEE 1001 DDD0 SSee eeee	$d \leftarrow [d] - [s]$	x	x	x	x	x
1001 AAA0 11ee eeee 1001 AAA1 11ee eeee	$An \leftarrow [An] - [s]$					
0000 0100 SSEE EEEE	$d \leftarrow [d] - s$	x	x	x	x	x
0101 QQQ1 SSEE EEEE	$d \leftarrow [d] - QQQ$	x	x	x	x	x
1001 RRR1 SS00 0rrr 1001 RRR1 SS00 1rrr	$d \leftarrow [d] - [s] - [X]$	x	x	x	x	x
0100 1000 0100 0DDD	$[Dn]_{31-16} \leftrightarrow [Dn]_{15-0}$		x	x	0	0
0100 1010 11EE EEEE	Test d and set N and Z flags; set bit 7 of d to 1.		x	x	0	0
0100 1110 0100 VVVV	$SP \leftarrow [SP] - 4;$ $[SP] \leftarrow [PC];$ $SP \leftarrow [SP] - 2;$ $[SP] \leftarrow [SR];$ $PC \leftarrow$ vector					
0100 1110 0111 0110	If V = 1, then $SP \leftarrow [SP] - 4;$ $[SP] \leftarrow [PC];$ $SP \leftarrow [SP] - 2;$ $[SP] \leftarrow [SR];$ $PC \leftarrow$ TRAPV vector					
0100 1010 SSEE EEEE	Test d and set N and Z flags.		x	x	0	0
0100 1110 0101 1AAA	$SP \leftarrow [An];$ $An \leftarrow [[SP]];$ $SP \leftarrow [SP] + 4$					

(Concluded)

(destination) addressing mode provided, all destination (source) addressing modes permitted are denoted with an x. For example, for the AND instruction, if the source is a data register, the destination mode may be (An), (An)+, −(An), d(An), d(An,Xi), Abs.W, or Abs.L. Moreover, if the destination is a data register, the source can be specified in any of the 11 modes shown in the table.

The OP-code column shows the actual bit pattern of the first 16-bit word of an instruction. Instructions that have immediate source data use a second word for 8- and 16-bit operands, and a second and third word for 32-bit operands. For the indexed and relative addressing modes, the required index value (that is, the displacement) is given in the word that follows the OP code.

Shift and Rotate instructions can specify a count of the number of bit positions by which the operand is to be shifted or rotated. The count can be given as the contents of a data register or as an immediate 3-bit value within the OP code. If a memory operand is involved, the count is always equal to 1.

Branch instructions are listed in Table C.5. The branch offset (the displacement) is a signed 2's-complement number that specifies the relative distance in bytes. For conditional branch instructions, as well as for Scc (Set on condition) instructions, the condition code suffix possibilities (cc) are shown in Table C.6. This table also indicates the condition that is tested to determine if a branch is to be taken.

The operation performed for a given instruction is indicated in Tables C.4 and C.5. For most instructions, the action taken is obvious. However, for a few instructions, additional comments are in order. The instructions labeled with an asterisk in the mnemonic column are discussed further in the following paragraphs.

BCHG, BCLR, BSET, and BTST

All of these instructions test a specified bit of the destination operand. The number of the bit position to be tested (bit#) is indicated either as the contents of a data register or as an immediate value within the instruction. The test is made by loading the complement of the tested bit into the condition flag Z.

MOVEM

This instruction moves the contents of one or more registers to or from consecutive memory locations. The registers involved in the transfer are specified in the second word of the instruction. Bits 0 through 7 correspond to D0 through D7, and bits 8 through 15 correspond to A0 through A7. This arrangement is valid for all addressing modes except the autodecrement mode, in which case the order of registers is reversed.

MOVEP

This instruction is useful for data transfers between the 68000 and 8-bit peripheral devices. The data are transferred in bytes, with the memory address incremented by 2 after each byte. Thus, if the starting address is even, all bytes are transferred to or from even-numbered address locations by means of the high-order eight lines of the data bus. Similarly, if the starting address is odd, then all transfers are done via the low-order eight lines of the data bus. The high-order byte of a data register is transferred first and the low-order byte is transferred second.

Table C.5 68000 branch instructions

Mnemonic (Name)	Displacement size	OP code	Operation performed
BRA (Branch always)	8 16	0100 0000 PPPP PPPP 0110 0000 0000 0000 PPPP PPPP PPPP PPPP	PC ← [PC] + disp
Bcc (Branch conditionally)	8 16	0110 CCCC PPPP PPPP 0110 CCCC 0000 0000 PPPP PPPP PPPP PPPP	If cc is true, then PC ← [PC] + disp
BSR (Branch to subroutine)	8 16	0110 0001 PPPP PPPP 0110 0001 0000 0000 PPPP PPPP PPPP PPPP	SP ← [SP] − 4; [SP] ← [PC]; PC ← [PC] + disp

DBcc (Decrement and branch conditionally)	16	0101 CCCC 1100 1DDD
		PPPP PPPP PPPP PPPP
			If cc is false, then
			Dn ← [Dn] − 1;
			If [Dn] ≠ − 1, then
			PC ← [PC] + disp

DBRA (Decrement and branch)	The assembler interprets this instruction as DBF (see the DBcc entry).		

The 68000 has two basic modes of operation. In the supervisor mode, all instructions can be used. In the user mode, some instructions cannot be executed. Instructions that can only be used in the supervisor mode are called privileged instructions. These are

- ANDI, EORI, ORI, and MOVE instructions when the destination is the status register SR
- MOVE instruction, which moves the contents of the user stack pointer to or from an address register
- RESET, RTE, and STOP instructions

The information presented in this appendix should enable the reader to write and debug assembly-language programs for the 68000. The size and structure of assembled

Table C.6 Condition codes for Bcc, DBcc, and Scc instructions

Machine code CCCC	Condition suffix cc	Name	Test condition
0000	T	True	Always true
0001	F	False	Always false
0010	HI	High	$C \vee Z = 0$
0011	LS	Low or same	$C \vee Z = 1$
0100	CC	Carry clear	$C = 0$
0101	CS	Carry set	$C = 1$
0110	NE	Not equal	$Z = 0$
0111	EQ	Equal	$Z = 1$
1000	VC	Overflow clear	$V = 0$
1001	VS	Overflow set	$V = 1$
1010	PL	Plus	$N = 0$
1011	MI	Minus	$N = 1$
1100	GE	Greater or equal	$N \oplus V = 0$
1101	LT	Less than	$N \oplus V = 1$
1110	GT	Greater than	$Z \vee (N \oplus V) = 0$
1111	LE	Less or equal	$Z \vee (N \oplus V) = 1$

| T and F suffixes cannot be used in the Bcc instruction

instructions can be determined on the basis of the OP codes given and the addressing modes employed. Lack of space has prevented the inclusion of timing information, such as the number of machine cycles needed to execute a given instruction. This information, as well as further details about the instruction set, can be found in the manufacturer's literature.

INTEL IA-32 INSTRUCTION SET

This appendix contains a summary of the Intel IA-32 instruction set which was introduced in Part III of Chapter 3. This instruction set is very extensive. We only describe a small part of it, about 50 instructions, including all of those used in Chapter 3. Some general aspects of other instruction types are also covered.

The IA-32 register structure is shown in Figures 3.37 and 3.38 and described in Section 3.16.1. The general format of an instruction is shown in Figure 3.41. Memory is byte addressable and addresses are 32 bits long. There are two operand sizes: doubleword (32 bits) and byte (8 bits). Word operands (16 bits) were used in earlier 16-bit Intel processors. IA-32 processors can operate in a 16-bit mode to execute machine programs prepared for the earlier 16-bit processors.

D.1 INSTRUCTION ENCODING

Figure D.1a shows the general format for encoding IA-32 instructions. The OP code is either one or two bytes long. For some instructions, the OP code is extended into the 3-bit Reg/OPcode field of the ModR/M byte shown in Figure D.1b. Since the encoding

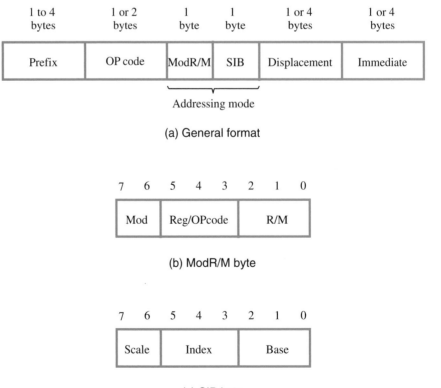

Figure D.1   IA-32 instruction format.

of the OP codes is very irregular, we will not give any details. Prefix bytes, which are not needed in encoding most of the common instructions discussed here, are discussed in Section D.3.

The length of an instruction can range from one byte (an OP code) to 11 or more bytes when both a 4-byte displacement and a 4-byte immediate operand are specified, along with two addressing mode bytes and the OP code. For example, the Increment (INC) and Decrement (DEC) instructions on a register operand require only a 1-byte OP code that includes a 3-bit field to name the register. As an example of a long instruction, 11 bytes are needed to encode the instruction

$$MOV \quad DWORD\ PTR\ [EBP + ESI*4 + DISP],10$$

as discussed in Section 3.17.1. Other instruction examples are also discussed in that section.

The operand data size (8 bits or 32 bits) is indicated in the OP code. The OP code also indicates whether or not one of the operands is an immediate value contained in the last field of the instruction.

At least one of the operands in a two-operand instruction must be in a register. It is named in the Reg/OPcode field of the ModR/M byte. The 3-bit codes for the registers are shown in Table D.1. If the other operand is in a register, it is named in the R/M field of the same byte. If the other operand is not in a register, it may be an immediate value or it may be the contents of a memory location. The address of a memory operand is specified by the two addressing mode bytes and the displacement field as described in the next section. The specification of which operand is the source in the encoding of a two-operand instruction is determined by a bit in the OP code, called the *direction* bit, as described in Section 3.17.1.

Table D.1 Register field encoding in IA-32 instructions

Reg/Base/Index* field	Register
0 0 0	EAX
0 0 1	ECX
0 1 0	EDX
0 1 1	EBX
1 0 0	ESP
1 0 1	EBP
1 1 0	ESI
1 1 1	EDI

*ESP (100) cannot be used as an index register.

D.1.1 ADDRESSING MODES

Table 3.3 lists the IA-32 addressing modes, the assembler syntax used to specify them, and the way that the effective address EA is generated. We have already discussed the Immediate mode and the use of the Reg/OPcode field of the ModR/M byte to specify a register as the location of one operand. The other operand is specified as shown in Table D.2. The Register indirect, Base with displacement, and Register addressing

Table D.2 IA-32 addressing modes selected by the ModR/M and SIB bytes

Mod field $b_7\ b_6$	R/M field $b_2\ b_1\ b_0$	Addressing mode
0 0	Reg	Register indirect $\quad$ EA = [Reg]
0 1	Reg	Base with 8-bit displacement $\quad$ EA = [Reg] + Disp8
1 0	Reg	Base with 32-bit displacement $\quad$ EA = [Reg] + Disp32
1 1	Reg	Register $\quad$ EA = Reg

Exceptions

Mod field $b_7\ b_6$	R/M field $b_2\ b_1\ b_0$	Addressing mode
0 0	1 0 1	Direct $\quad$ EA = Disp32
0 0	1 0 0	Base with index (uses SIB byte) $\quad$ EA = [Base] + [Index] × Scale When Base = EBP the addressing mode is: Index with 32-bit displacement $\quad$ EA = [Index] × Scale + Disp32
0 1	1 0 0	Base with index and 8-bit displacement (uses SIB byte) $\quad$ EA = [Base] + [Index] × Scale + Disp8
1 0	1 0 0	Base with index and 32-bit displacement (uses SIB byte) $\quad$ EA = [Base] + [Index] × Scale + Disp32

Table D.3 Scale field encoding in IA-32 SIB byte

Scale field	Scale
0 0	1
0 1	2
1 0	4
1 1	8

modes are determined by the 2-bit Mod field of the ModR/M byte as shown in the first four rows of the table. The 3-bit R/M field normally specifies the register (Reg) involved in these modes. Exceptions to this are used to generate the addressing modes listed in the remainder of the table. All of these modes use the SIB byte, shown in Figure D.1c, except for the Direct mode. The SIB byte encodes the base and index registers as shown in Table D.1. The scale factors of 1, 2, 4, and 8, are encoded as shown in Table D.3.

As noted in Table 3.3, the ESP register (encoding 100) cannot be used as an index register. This is not actually a programming restriction because ESP is used as the processor stack pointer. When the bit pattern 100 is placed in the Index field of the SIB byte, no scaled index is used, but the other components of the addressing mode operate normally in generating the effective address of the operand. This has the following useful effect. From Table D.2, it would appear that ESP cannot be used in the first three modes listed because the ESP encoding (100) is used to signify exceptions that generate the last three modes in the table. But if 100 is placed in both the Base and Index fields of the SIB byte, the addressing modes generated are effectively the first three in the table with ESP as the base register because no index is used.

Note that the base register encoding of 101 (EBP) is used as an exception in the Base with index addressing mode in order to generate the Index with 32-bit displacement mode. The EBP register can still be used effectively as the base register in a Base with index mode by using it in the Base with index and displacement mode with a displacement value of zero.

D.2 BASIC INSTRUCTIONS

A set of commonly used IA-32 instructions is listed alphabetically in Table D.4. All of the instructions used in Chapter 3 are included except for the jump instructions and the specialized string instructions with the repeat option that were used in Section 3.21.3 for I/O block transfers. The conditional and unconditional jump instructions are described in the next two subsections. String instructions are described in Section D.4. In Table D.4, the OP-code mnemonic and name of the instruction are shown in the

(Continued on page 782.)

Table D.4 IA-32 instructions

Mnemonic (Name)	Size	Operands		Operation performed	CC flags affected			
		dst	src		S	Z	O	C
ADC (Add with carry)	B,D	reg reg mem reg mem	reg mem reg imm imm	dst ← [dst] + [src] + [CF]	x	x	x	x
ADD (Add)	B,D	reg reg mem reg mem	reg mem reg imm imm	dst ← [dst] + [src]	x	x	x	x
AND (Logical AND)	B,D	reg reg mem reg mem	reg mem reg imm imm	dst ← [dst] ∧ [src]	x	x	0	0
BT (Bit test)	D	reg reg mem mem	reg imm8 reg imm8	bit# = [src]; CF ← bit# of [dst]				x
BTC (Bit test and complement)	D	reg reg mem mem	reg imm8 reg imm8	bit# = [src]; CF ← bit# of [dst]; complement bit# of [dst]				x
BTR (Bit test and reset)	D	reg reg mem mem	reg imm8 reg imm8	bit# = [src]; CF ← bit# of [dst]; clear bit# of [dst] to 0				x

Mnemonic (Name)	Size	Operands		Operation performed	CC flags affected			
		dst	src		S	Z	O	C
BTS (Bit test and set)	D	reg reg mem mem	reg imm8 reg imm8	bit# = [src]; CF ← bit# of [dst]; set bit# of [dst] to 1				x
CALL (Subroutine call)	D	reg mem		ESP ← [ESP] − 4; [ESP] ← [EIP]; EIP ← EA of dst				
CLC (Clear carry)				CF ← 0				0
CLI (Clear int. flag)				IF ← 0				
CMC (Compl. carry)				CF ← $\overline{\text{CF}}$				x
CMP (Compare)	B,D	reg reg mem reg mem	reg mem reg imm imm	[dst] − [src]	x	x	x	x
DEC (Decrement)	B,D	reg mem		dst ← [dst] − 1	x	x	x	
DIV (Unsigned divide)	B,D		reg mem	for B: [AL]/[src]; AL ← quotient; AH ← remainder for D: [EAX]/[src]; EAX ← quotient; EDX ← remainder	?	?	?	?

(Continued)

Mnemonic (Name)	Size	Operands		Operation performed	CC flags affected			
		dst	src		S	Z	O	C
HLT (Halt)				Halts execution until reset or external interrupt occurs				
IDIV (Signed divide)	B,D		reg mem	for B: [AL]/[src]; AL ← quotient; AH ← remainder for D: [EAX]/[src]; EAX ← quotient; EDX ← remainder	?	?	?	?
IMUL (Signed multiplication)	B,D		reg mem	(double-length product) for B: AX ← [AL] × [src] for D: EDX,EAX ← [EAX] × [src]	?	?	x	x
	D	reg reg	reg mem	(single-length product) reg ← [reg] × [src]	?	?	x	x
IN (Isolated input)	B,D	dst = AL or EAX src = imm8 or [DX]		AL or EAX ← [src]				
INC (Increment)	B,D	reg mem		dst ← [dst] + 1	x	x	x	
INT (Software interrupt)	D		imm8	Push EFLAGS; Push EIP; EIP ← address (determined by imm8)				

Mnemonic (Name)	Size	Operands		Operation performed	CC flags affected			
		dst	src		S	Z	O	C
IRET (Return from interrupt)	D			Pop EIP; Pop EFLAGS	x	x	x	x
LEA (Load effective address)	D	reg	mem	reg ← EA of src				
LOOP (Loop)	D	target		ECX ← [ECX] − 1; If ([ECX] ≠ 0) EIP ← target				
LOOPE (Loop on equal/zero)	D	target		ECX ← [ECX] − 1; If ([ECX] ≠ 0 ∧ [Z] = 1) EIP ← target				
LOOPNE (Loop on not equal/ not zero)	D	target		ECX ← [ECX] − 1; If ([ECX] ≠ 0 ∧ [Z] ≠ 1) EIP ← target				
MOV (Move)	B,D	reg reg mem reg mem	reg mem reg imm imm	dst ← [src]				
MOVSX (Sign extend byte into register)	B	reg reg	reg mem	reg ← sign extend [src]				

(Continued)

Mnemonic (Name)	Size	Operands		Operation performed	CC flags affected			
		dst	src		S	Z	O	C
MOVZX (Zero extend byte into register)	B	reg reg	reg mem	reg ← zero extend [src]				
MUL (Unsigned multiplication)	B,D		reg mem	(double-length product) for B: AX ← [AL] × [src] for D: EDX,EAX ← [EAX] × [src]	?	?	x	x
NEG (Negate)	B,D	reg mem		dst ← 2's-complement [dst]	x	x	x	x
NOP (No operation)				alias for: XCHG EAX,EAX				
NOT (Logical complement)	B,D	reg mem		dst ← $\overline{[dst]}$				
OR (Logical OR)	B,D	reg reg mem reg mem	reg mem reg imm imm	dst ← [dst] ∨ [src]	x	x	0	0
OUT (Isolated output)	B,D	dst = imm8 or [DX] src = AL or EAX		dst ← [AL] or [EAX]				

Mnemonic (Name)	Size	Operands		Operation performed	CC flags affected			
		dst	src		S	Z	O	C
POP (Pop off stack)	D	reg mem		dst ← [[ESP]]; ESP ← [ESP] + 4				
POPAD (Pop off stack into all registers except ESP)	D			Pop eight doublewords off stack into EDI, ESI, EBP, discard, EBX, EDX, ECX, EAX; ESP ← [ESP] + 32				
PUSH (Push onto stack)	D		reg mem imm	ESP ← [ESP] − 4; [ESP] ← [src]				
PUSHAD (Push all registers onto stack)	D			Push contents of EAX, ECX, EDX, EBX, ESP, EBP, ESI, EDI onto stack; ESP ← [ESP] − 32				
RCL (Rotate left with C flag)	B,D	reg reg mem mem	imm8 CL imm8 CL	See Figure 2.32*b*; src operand is rotation count			?	x
RCR (Rotate right with C flag)	B,D	reg reg mem mem	imm8 CL imm8 CL	See Figure 2.32*d*; src operand is rotation count			?	x
RET (Return from subroutine)				EIP ← [[ESP]]; ESP ← [ESP] + 4				

(Continued)

Mnemonic (Name)	Size	Operands		Operation performed	CC flags affected			
		dst	src		S	Z	O	C
ROL (Rotate left)	B,D	reg reg mem mem	imm8 CL imm8 CL	See Figure 2.32a; src operand is rotation count			?	x
ROR (Rotate right)	B,D	reg reg mem mem	imm8 CL imm8 CL	See Figure 2.32c; src operand is rotation count			?	x
SAL (Shift arithmetic left) same as SHL	B,D	reg reg mem mem	imm8 CL imm8 CL	See Figure 2.30a; src operand is shift count	x	x	?	x
SAR (Shift arithmetic right)	B,D	reg reg mem mem	imm8 CL imm8 CL	See Figure 2.30c; src operand is shift count	x	x	?	x
SBB (Subtract with borrow)	B,D	reg reg mem reg mem	reg mem reg imm imm	dst ← [dst] − [src] − [CF]	x	x	x	x
SHL (Shift left) same as SAL	B,D	reg reg mem mem	imm8 CL imm8 CL	See Figure 2.30a; src operand is shift count	x	x	?	x

Mnemonic (Name)	Size	Operands		Operation performed	CC flags affected			
		dst	src		S	Z	O	C
SHR (Shift right)	B,D	reg reg mem mem	imm8 CL imm8 CL	See Figure 2.30*b*; src operand is shift count	x	x	?	x
STC (Set carry flag)				CF ← 1				1
STI (Set interrupt flag)				IF ← 1				
SUB (Subtract)	B,D	reg reg mem reg mem	reg mem reg imm imm	dst ← [dst] − [src]	x	x	x	x
TEST (Test)	B,D	reg mem reg mem	reg reg imm imm	[dst] ∧ [src]; set flags based on result	x	x	0	0
XCHG (Exchange)	B,D	reg reg	reg mem	[reg] ↔ [src]				
XOR (Exclusive OR)	B,D	reg reg mem reg mem	reg mem reg imm imm	dst ← [dst] ⊕ [src]	x	x	0	0

(*Concluded*)

first column. The second column indicates the operand size that can be used: B (byte) or D (32-bit doubleword). The third column lists possible locations for the source and destination operands, abbreviated as:

reg   —   one of the eight processor registers

mem   —   a memory location

imm   —   an 8- or 32-bit immediate operand

imm8   —   an 8-bit immediate operand

The operation performed by the instruction is described in the fourth column. The last column indicates how the condition code flags are affected by executing the instruction using the following symbols:

x   —   affected

0   —   set to 0

1   —   set to 1

"blank"   —   not affected

?   —   unpredictable

D.2.1   CONDITIONAL JUMP INSTRUCTIONS

The conditional jump instructions are listed in Table D.5. As discussed in Section 3.19.1, the target address is used directly in an assembly language program. The machine instruction actually contains a signed number (an offset) that specifies the distance in bytes to the target address relative to the updated contents of the Instruction Pointer register. Two sizes of offset are used: 1 byte and 4 bytes. The assembler computes the offset when converting an assembly language program to machine language.

D.2.2   UNCONDITIONAL JUMP INSTRUCTIONS

Section 3.19.2 describes the unconditional jump instruction JMP. As well as the relative addressing mode used in conditional jumps, the general addressing modes can be used to specify the target address. This provides more flexibility in implementing multiple-way branching that arises in CASE statements used in high-level languages.

D.3   PREFIX BYTES

Instruction prefix bytes, shown in Figure D.1a, are divided into four groups. More than one prefix byte can be used with an instruction. But, only one byte from each group can be used. The first group includes *repeat* byte codes for indicating that the instruction operation is to be repeated some number of times. Instructions that allow this option are called string instructions. They will be described in Section D.4. We saw an example of

Table D.5 IA-32 conditional jump instructions

Mnemonic	Condition name	Condition code test
JS	Sign (negative)	$SF = 1$
JNS	No sign (positive or zero)	$SF = 0$
JE/JZ	Equal/Zero	$ZF = 1$
JNE/JNZ	Not equal/Not zero	$ZF = 0$
JO	Overflow	$OF = 1$
JNO	No overflow	$OF = 0$
JC/JB	Carry/Unsigned below	$CF = 1$
JNC/JAE	No carry/Unsigned above or equal	$CF = 0$
JA	Unsigned above	$CF \vee ZF = 0$
JBE	Unsigned below or equal	$CF \vee ZF = 1$
JGE	Signed greater than or equal	$SF \oplus OF = 0$
JL	Signed less than	$SF \oplus OF = 1$
JG	Signed greater than	$ZF \vee (SF \oplus OF) = 0$
JLE	Signed less than or equal	$ZF \vee (SF \oplus OF) = 1$

repetition of string instruction operations in the block transfer of doublewords between an I/O device and memory in Section 3.21.3. The streaming SIMD extension (SSE) instructions, described in Sections 3.23.3, 11.3.6, and 11.3.7, are also indicated by a byte code in this group.

Two of the groups consist of only one byte code each. These codes are used to override the default operand size or the default address size, as described in Section D.5.

The fourth group of prefix bytes is used to override the default selection of the segment registers used in generating memory addresses. A general description of the use of segment registers was given in Section 11.3.1.

D.4 OTHER INSTRUCTIONS

The full IA-32 instruction set contains many more instructions than those listed in Table D.4. Four of the instruction types not included in the table are briefly described here.

D.4.1 STRING INSTRUCTIONS

Special instructions are provided to perform common repetitive operations efficiently on data items contained in consecutive memory locations. These data structures are called *strings* and the instructions are called string instructions. The individual items of a string can be bytes or 32-bit doublewords. String instructions can be used, for example, to move a string from one area of memory to another area or to compare two strings to determine if they are equal.

We will use the string move instruction to illustrate how string instructions are executed. The OP codes MOVSB and MOVSD are used for byte and doubleword moves. These instructions differ from the regular Move instruction in that they consist of only the OP code and do not have explicit operands. The address of the source operand is assumed to be in register ESI, and the destination operand address is assumed to be in EDI. The execution of MOVSB consists of moving a byte from the source location to the destination location and then incrementing the ESI and EDI pointer registers. This instruction can be placed inside a loop to move all bytes of the string. Alternatively, a repeat prefix can be used with the instruction to move the complete string. In this case, in addition to initializing the ESI and EDI registers, the ECX register must be initialized to the length of the string. It is decremented after each byte is transferred. Execution of the instruction

REP MOVSB

moves a complete string of bytes. The instruction is fetched once and its operation is repeated until the count contents of the ECX register have been decremented to zero.

String instructions with the repeat option are provided for performance reasons. The same task could be programmed by using the instruction

MOV   BYTE PTR [EDI],[ESI]

inside a loop in which the pointer registers are explicitly incremented and the count register ECX is decremented until it contains zero. But that method would take much longer to execute.

D.4.2 FLOATING-POINT, MMX, AND SSE INSTRUCTIONS

There is a full range of operations on floating-point data in the IEEE format (see Chapter 6) provided by IA-32 instructions. The eight floating-point registers shown in Figure 3.37 are used to hold these data. In addition to add, subtract, multiply, and divide operations, trigonometric functions are also provided.

The MMX (multimedia extension) instructions, described in Section 3.23.2, are used to perform simple arithmetic and logic operations in parallel on short integers packed into 64-bit quadwords located either in the floating-point registers or in memory. These operations are required in graphics and signal-processing applications.

The SSE (streaming SIMD extension) instructions, first introduced in the Pentium III processor and enhanced in the Pentium 4 (see Sections 11.3.6 and 11.3.7) perform parallel arithmetic operations on floating-point numbers packed into a set of eight 128-bit processor registers. These registers are separate from the general-purpose and floating-point registers. The individual data items can be 32-bit or 64-bit floating-point numbers. The SSE instructions are useful for vector and matrix calculations in scientific applications. In the Pentium 4 enhancements, the operands can also be 64-bit integers. These data types are used in encryption and decryption operations in secure data applications.

D.5 SIXTEEN-BIT OPERATION

In Sections 3.16.1 and 11.3.2, it was noted that an IA-32 processor can execute programs in a mode that uses 16-bit addresses and data operands, as used in earlier Intel processors, as well as in the mode that uses 32-bit addresses and data operands, which is the mode that we have described in this book. In either of these two modes, byte operands can also be manipulated. When operating in the 32-bit mode, a bit in the OP code determines whether an operand is a byte or a 32-bit doubleword; in the 16-bit mode, the same bit determines whether an operand is a byte or a 16-bit word. The default mode of operation is set by a bit in the segment descriptors. These descriptors were briefly described in Section 11.3.2.

In our discussions, we have tacitly assumed that the processor is operating in the 32-bit default mode. However, on an instruction-by-instruction basis, the default mode can be overridden for the duration of one instruction by using a prefix byte as the first byte of an instruction as shown in Figure D.1. The default operand size or the default address size, or both, can be overridden by different prefix bytes.

D.6 PROGRAMMING EXPERIMENTS

A convenient way to experiment with assembly language programming is to use the in-line assembly language facility provided with a high-level language. An example of this is given in Chapter 9 where I/O routines are programmed in assembly language inside a C program. Here, we outline how to use the in-line facility in C/C++. The Microsoft Corporation provides a compiler for this language that runs under their Windows operating systems on personal computers built with Intel IA-32 processors.

Figure D.2 shows how the addition loop program in Figure 3.40a can be incorporated into a C/C++ program. The assembly language instruction code is encapsulated in the construct

$$\_asm \{ \dots \}$$

The data declarations and initialization operations are done in C/C++ at the beginning of the program, and the result of executing the assembly language program, which is the value in memory location SUM, is printed by the printf statement at the end of the program.

The operations of naming and opening a file for the source program and entering, compiling, and executing it, are not given because they vary depending on the particular software environment used.

A hexadecimal listing of the machine instructions generated for an assembly language program, such as the one in Figure D.2, can be produced by the compiler. It is instructive to study the listing to see examples of the binary encoding of IA-32 instructions in the format shown in Figure D.1. The listing for the four-instruction loop is shown in Figure D.3. Hexadecimal representations of the bytes used to encode each instruction are shown to the left of the assembly instructions in Figure D.3a. Parts *b* and *c* of the figure show the binary encoding details for the ADD and JG instructions.

```
# include <stdio.h>

void main(void)

{
        long NUM1[5];
        long SUM;
        long N;

        NUM1[0] = 17;
        NUM1[1] = 3;
        NUM1[2] = -51;
        NUM1[3] = 242;
        NUM1[4] = 113;
        SUM = 0;
        N = 5;

        _asm {
                        LEA     EBX,NUM1
                        MOV     ECX,N
                        MOV     EAX,0
                        MOV     EDI,0
        STARTADD:       ADD     EAX,[EBX + EDI*4]
                        INC     EDI
                        DEC     ECX
                        JG      STARTADD
                        MOV     SUM,EAX
        }

        printf ("The sum of the list values is %ld \n", SUM );
}
```

Figure D.2   IA-32 Program in Figure 3.40a encapsulated in a
C/C++ program.

First, consider the ADD instruction. The two bits set to 1 at the right end of the OP code have the following meaning: The last 1 signifies that the operand size is 32 bits. The second last 1 signifies that the source operand is the operand located in the memory. Using Table D.2, we observe that the Mod field (00) and the R/M field (100) of the ModR/M byte specify the Base with index addressing mode for the memory operand, and the Reg/OPcode field (000) specifies the EAX register as the destination. The Base field (011) of the SIB byte specifies EBX as the base register and the Index field (111) specifies EDI as the index register. The Scale field (10) selects 4 as the scale factor.

Machine instructions (hexadecimal)	Assembly language instructions
03 04 BB	STARTADD: ADD EAX,[EBX + EDI*4]
47	INC EDI
49	DEC ECX
7F F9	JG STARTADD

(a) Loop body encoding

OP code	ModR/M byte	SIB byte
03	04	BB
00000011	00 000 100	10 111 011
ADD (doubleword)	(see Table D.2)	(see Figure D.1*c*)

(b) ADD instruction

OP code	Offset
7F	F9
01111111	111111001
JG (short offset)	−7

(c) JG instruction

Figure D.3   Encoding of the loop body in Figure D.2.

The JG instruction encoding in Figure D.3*c* is interpreted as follows. The first four bits of the OP code (0111) specify a conditional jump with a 1-byte offset, and the last four bits (1111) specify the "greater than" condition. The offset byte contains the 2's-complement representation for −7. This is the distance in bytes from the address of the instruction following the JG instruction back to the address of the ADD instruction at the beginning of the loop.

Use of the Processor Stack

The compiler uses registers ESP and EBP as the processor stack pointer and the frame pointer, respectively. Therefore, in-line assembly language programs cannot use these registers for other purposes. Also, the compiler allocates memory variables, such as NUM1, SUM, and N, declared inside the "main" procedure, as local variables on the stack. When they are referenced using the Direct addressing mode in assembly language, as in the first two instructions in the program in Figure D.2, the compiler generates the Base plus displacement mode to access them. The frame pointer EBP is used as the base register and the displacements are negative offsets into the stack, which grows toward lower addresses. If these variables are declared outside the "main" procedure, they are allocated as global variables and they are accessed by the Direct addressing mode.

CHARACTER CODES AND NUMBER CONVERSION

E.1 CHARACTER CODES

Information storage and processing in computers involves coding the individual items of information by using several binary variables. Positive and negative numbers are represented in some variation of the binary number system. The most usual formats are presented in Chapter 6, where both integer and floating-point numbers are discussed.

In computers used mainly for business data processing, it is useful to represent and process numbers in the base-10 (decimal) format. Table E.1 gives the most usual coding for individual digits, called the binary-coded decimal (BCD) code. This code is simply the first 10 values (0–9) of the 4-bit binary number system. Strings of these 4-bit code values can be used to represent any desired range of positive and negative integers, with an appropriate code used for the sign position.

Alphabetic characters (A–Z), operators, punctuation symbols, control characters (+ − / , : ; LF CR EOT), and numbers must be represented for text storage and editing and for high-level language input, processing, and output operations. Two standard codes for this purpose are the American Standards Committee on Information Interchange (ASCII) code and the Extended Binary Coded Decimal Interchange Code (EBCDIC). The standard ASCII code is a 7-bit code, and the EBCDIC code is an 8-bit code. Tables E.2 and E.3 show the standard ASCII and EBCDIC codes, respectively. The ASCII code is by far the most frequently used.

In many applications, it is preferable to use 8-bit quantities; thus, the basic ASCII code is often extended to 8-bits. A common way of doing this is to set the high-order bit position, bit 7, to zero. Another popular possibility is to use bit 7 as a parity bit for the encoded character.

Some comments about the structure of the ASCII and EBCDIC codes are helpful. Note that in both codes the low-order 4 bits of the decimal character codes (0–9) are the BCD codes of Table E.1. This facilitates two operations. First, two characters that represent decimal digits can be compared to determine which is larger. This can be done with the same type of logic circuits that are used to perform the standard arithmetic

Table E.1 BCD encoding of decimal digits

Decimal digit	BCD code
0	0000
1	0001
2	0010
3	0011
4	0100
5	0101
6	0110
7	0111
8	1000
9	1001

Table E.2 The 7-bit ASCII code

Bit positions	Bit positions 654							
3210	000	001	010	011	100	101	110	111
0000	NUL	DLE	SPACE	0	@	P	´	p
0001	SOH	DC1	!	1	A	Q	a	q
0010	STX	DC2	”	2	B	R	b	r
0011	ETX	DC3	#	3	C	S	c	s
0100	EOT	DC4	$	4	D	T	d	t
0101	ENQ	NAK	%	5	E	U	e	u
0110	ACK	SYN	&	6	F	V	f	v
0111	BEL	ETB	’	7	G	W	g	w
1000	BS	CAN	(	8	H	X	h	x
1001	HT	EM	)	9	I	Y	i	y
1010	LF	SUB	*	:	J	Z	j	z
1011	VT	ESC	+	;	K	[	k	{
1100	FF	FS	,	<	L	/	l		
1101	CR	GS	−	=	M	]	m	}
1110	SO	RS	.	>	N	^	n	~
1111	SI	US	/	?	O	—	o	DEL

NUL	Null/Idle	SI	Shift in
SOH	Start of header	DLE	Data link escape
STX	Start of text	DC1-DC4	Device control
ETX	End of text	NAK	Negative acknowledgment
EOT	End of transmission	SYN	Synchronous idle
ENQ	Enquiry	ETB	End of transmitted block
ACK	Acknowledgment	CAN	Cancel (error in data)
BEL	Audible signal	EM	End of medium
BS	Back space	SUB	Special sequence
HT	Horizontal tab	ESC	Escape
LF	Line feed	FS	File separator
VT	Vertical tab	GS	Group separator
FF	Form feed	RS	Record separator
CR	Carriage return	US	Unit separator
SO	Shift out	DEL	Delete/Idle

Bit positions of code format = | 6 | 5 | 4 | 3 | 2 | 1 | 0 |

Table E.3 The 8-bit EBCDIC code

| | | | | Bit positions 7654 | | | | | | | | | | | |
Bit positions 3210	0000	0001	0010	0011	0100	0101	0110	0111	1000	1001	1010	1011	1100	1101	1110	1111
0000	NULL				SP	&	–									0
0001		RES	BYP	PN			/		a	j			A	J		1
0010									b	k	s		B	K	S	2
0011									c	l	t		C	L	T	3
0100	PF	RES	BYP	PN					d	m	u		D	M	U	4
0101	HT	NL	LF	RS					e	n	v		E	N	V	5
0110	LC	BS	EOB	UC					f	o	w		F	O	W	6
0111	DEL	IL	PRE	EOT					g	p	x		G	P	X	7
1000									h	q	y		H	Q	Y	8
1001									i	r	z		I	R	Z	9
1010			SM		¢	!		:								
1011					.	$	,	#								
1100					<	*	%	@								
1101					(	)	_	'								
1110					+	;	>	=								
1111					¬		?	"								

NULL	Null/Idle	NL	New line	PRE	Prefix
PF	Punch off	BS	Backspace	SM	Set mode
HT	Horizontal tab	IL	Idle	PN	Punch on
LC	Lowercase	BYP	Bypass	RS	Reader stop
DEL	Delete	LF	Line feed	UC	Uppercase
RES	Restore	EOB	End of block	EOT	End of transmission
				SP	Space

Bit positions of code format = $\boxed{7}\boxed{6}\boxed{5}\boxed{4}\boxed{3}\boxed{2}\boxed{1}\boxed{0}$

operations on binary numbers. This is helpful when strings of decimal numbers must be sorted into numerical order. Second, when it is determined by context that consecutive 7- or 8-bit codes in some input string represent a decimal number that is to be stored and processed as a single entity, then it is sometimes practical to remove the leftmost 3 or 4 bits of each digit code and compress the number being represented into a string of 4-bit BCD digits. This compression or packing of data requires starting and ending delimiters, but it is justified in many situations in which storage space requirements are a concern. Similar comments apply to the codes for the alphabetic characters. The fact that their binary bit patterns are in numerical sequence facilitates alphabetic sorting.

E.2   DECIMAL-TO-BINARY CONVERSION

This section shows how to convert a fixed-point decimal number to its binary equivalent. The value, V, represented by the binary number

$$B = b_n b_{n-1} \cdots b_0 . b_{-1} b_{-2} \cdots b_{-m}$$

is given by

$$V(B) = b_n \times 2^n + b_{n-1} \times 2^{n-1} + \cdots + b_0 \times 2^0$$
$$+ b_{-1} \times 2^{-1} + b_{-2} \times 2^{-2} + \cdots + b_{-m} \times 2^{-m}$$

To convert a fixed-point decimal number into binary, the integer and fraction parts are handled separately. First, the integer part is converted as follows. It is divided by 2. The remainder is the least significant bit of the integer part of the binary representation. The quotient is again divided by 2, and the remainder is the next bit of the binary representation. The process is repeated up to and including the step in which the quotient becomes 0.

Second, the fraction part is converted by multiplying it by 2. The part of the product to the left of the decimal point, which is either 0 or 1, is a bit in the binary representation. The fractional part of the product is again multiplied by 2, generating the next bit of the binary representation. The first bit generated is the bit immediately to the right of the binary point. The next bit generated is the second bit to the right, and so on. The process is repeated until the required accuracy is attained.

Figure E.1 shows an example of conversion from $(927.45)_{10}$ to binary. Note that conversion of the integer part is always exact, but the binary fraction for an exact decimal fraction may not be exact. For example, the fraction $(0.45)_{10}$ used in Figure E.1 does not have an exact binary equivalent. This is obvious from the pattern developing in the figure. In such cases, the binary fraction is generated to some desired level of accuracy. In general, the maximum absolute error, e, in generating a k-bit fractional representation is bounded as $e \leq 2^{-k}$. Of course, some decimal fractions have an exact binary representation. For example, $(0.25)_{10}$ equals $(0.01)_2$.

Convert $(927.45)_{10}$

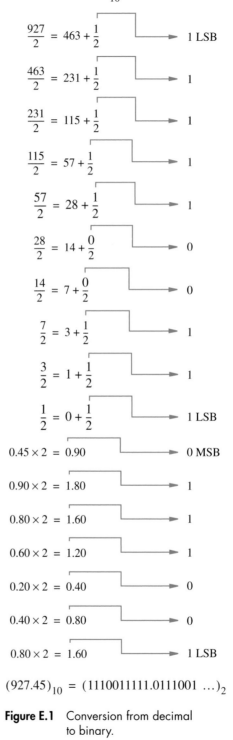

$$\frac{927}{2} = 463 + \frac{1}{2} \qquad \text{1 LSB}$$

$$\frac{463}{2} = 231 + \frac{1}{2} \qquad 1$$

$$\frac{231}{2} = 115 + \frac{1}{2} \qquad 1$$

$$\frac{115}{2} = 57 + \frac{1}{2} \qquad 1$$

$$\frac{57}{2} = 28 + \frac{1}{2} \qquad 1$$

$$\frac{28}{2} = 14 + \frac{0}{2} \qquad 0$$

$$\frac{14}{2} = 7 + \frac{0}{2} \qquad 0$$

$$\frac{7}{2} = 3 + \frac{1}{2} \qquad 1$$

$$\frac{3}{2} = 1 + \frac{1}{2} \qquad 1$$

$$\frac{1}{2} = 0 + \frac{1}{2} \qquad \text{1 LSB}$$

$$0.45 \times 2 = 0.90 \qquad \text{0 MSB}$$

$$0.90 \times 2 = 1.80 \qquad 1$$

$$0.80 \times 2 = 1.60 \qquad 1$$

$$0.60 \times 2 = 1.20 \qquad 1$$

$$0.20 \times 2 = 0.40 \qquad 0$$

$$0.40 \times 2 = 0.80 \qquad 0$$

$$0.80 \times 2 = 1.60 \qquad \text{1 LSB}$$

$$(927.45)_{10} = (1110011111.0111001 \dots)_2$$

Figure E.1   Conversion from decimal to binary.

INDEX